THE
WESTERN
EXPERIENCE

VOLUME I:
To the Eighteenth Century

PHYSIOGRAPHY OF EUROPE

0   200   400 Miles

Reykjavik ✪
ICELAND

NORWEGIAN SEA

FAEROE ISLANDS

Trondheim ●

KIØLEN MOUNTAINS

SCANDINAVIAN PENINSULA

SHETLAND ISLANDS

Gulf of Bothnia

Dal R.

HEBRIDES

ORKNEY ISLANDS

Oslo ✪

L. Vanern

Stockholm ✪

ÅLAND I.

Helsi

Gu

GRAMPIANS

Edinburgh ✪

SCOTTISH LOWLANDS

NORTH SEA

Skagerrak

Alborg ●

JUTLAND PENINSULA

Kattegat

L. Vattern

Gotland

Oland

BALTIC SEA

Niem

IRISH CENTRAL PLAIN

Dublin ✪

Cork ●

IRISH SEA

PENNINE CHAIN

St. George's Channel

The Wash

FRISIAN I.

Copenhagen ✪

Gdansk (Danzig) ●

Masuria Lakes

BRITISH ISLES

MIDLAND PLAIN

Amsterdam ✪

IJsselmeer

NORTH GERMAN PLAIN

Elbe R.

Warta R.

Vistula R.

Bristol Channel

Thames R. ✪
London

Berlin ✪

Oder R.

Wars

ATLANTIC OCEAN

Scilly I.

Land's End

English Channel

Strait of Dover

Maas R.

Rhine R.

Weser R.

HARZ MTS.

ERZ MTS.

SÜDETEN MTS.

Ushant I.

BRITTANY PENINSULA

Paris ✪

Marne R.

Meuse R.

Prague ●

BOHEMIAN PLAIN

BOHEMIAN FOREST

Seine R.

VOSGES MTS.

BLACK FOREST

Danube R.

Inn R.

Vienna ✪

Tisza R.

TRA

BAY OF BISCAY

Cape Finisterre

Bordeaux ●

PLAIN OF FRANCE

Loire R.

Saone R.

JURA MTS.

L. Constance

ALPS

L. Geneva

Budapest ✪
PLAIN OF HUNGARY

L. Balaton

Drave R.

Lyons ●

Rhône R.

△ Mt. Blanc

MASSIF CENTRAL

CEVENNES

PLAIN OF LOMBARDY

Venice ●

Trieste ●

Save R.

Belgrade ✪

IBERIAN PENINSULA

CANTABRIAN MTS.

PYRENEES

Po R.

DINARIC ALPS

DALMATIAN I.

Sarajevo ✪

Mora

Douro R.

SPANISH

GUADARRAMAS

Ebro R.

LIGURIAN SEA

Elbe

APENNINES

ADRIATIC SEA

BALKAN PENINSULA

PINDUS MTS.

Lisbon ●

Tagus R.

Madrid ✪

PLATEAU

Guadiana R.

SIERRA MORENA

CORSICA (France)

Rome ✪
ITALIAN PENINSULA

Corfu

BALEARIC I. (Spain)

Minorca

Majorca

SARDINIA (Italy)

△ Mt. Vesuvius

Guadalquivir R.

Iviza

Cape Trafalgar

SIERRA NEVADA

TYRRHENIAN SEA

Patras

IONIAN I.

Strait of Gibraltar

Gibraltar ●

Algiers ✪

Mt. Etna △

SICILY

Strait of Messina

IONIAN SEA

MOREA PENINSU

Casablanca ✪

LITTLE ATLAS MOUNTAINS

Tunis ✪

Pantelleria (Italy)

Malta

MEDITERRANEAN S

MIDDLE ATLAS MOUNTAINS

SAHARAN ATLAS MOUNTAINS

S A H A R A   D E S E R T

Tripoli ✪

Gulf of Sidra

THE WESTERN EXPERIENCE

VOLUME I:
To the Eighteenth Century

SIXTH EDITION

MORTIMER CHAMBERS
University of California, Los Angeles

RAYMOND GREW
University of Michigan

DAVID HERLIHY
Late Professor of History
Brown University

THEODORE K. RABB
Princeton University

ISSER WOLOCH
Columbia University

McGRAW-HILL, INC.
New York • St. Louis • San Francisco • Auckland • Bogotá • Caracas • Lisbon • London • Madrid
Mexico City • Milan • Montreal • New Delhi • San Juan • Singapore
Sydney • Tokyo • Toronto

THE WESTERN EXPERIENCE
VOLUME I:
To the Eighteenth Century

2 3 4 5 6 7 8 9 0 VNH   VNH 9 0 9 8 7 6 5

ISBN 0-07-011068-9

This book was set in Palatino by CRWaldman Graphic Communications.
The editors were Pamela Gordon and Ira C. Roberts;
the designers were Wanda Lubelska and Wanda Siedlecka;
the production supervisor was Kathryn Porzio.
The cartographer was David Lindroth.
Von Hoffmann Press, Inc., was printer and binder.

Cover art: Roman Mosaic from Palestrina (detail). Michael Holford.

PHOTO AND TEXT CREDITS

PHOTOS

Chapter 1: Opener: NASA; p. 6: Georg Gerster/Comstock ◆ p. 7: Giraudon/Art Resource ◆ p. 10: Hirmer Fotoarchiv ◆ p. 12: Fred J. Maroon/Photo Researchers ◆ p. 13: Elliot Erwitt/Magnum ◆ p. 14: The British Museum ◆ p. 15: The Metropolitan Museum of Art, Rogers Fund, 1931. (31.3.166) ◆ p. 16: Photo, M. Büsing/Bildarchiv Preussischer Kulturbesitz ◆ p. 17: C. M. Dixon ◆ p. 19: Gianni Tortoli/Photo Researchers ◆ p. 24: Princeton University Press/Art Resource ◆ p. 25: Hirmer Fotoarchiv ◆ p. 27: George Holton/Photo Researchers ◆ p. 28: Photograph by Dr. G. G. Cameron; The University Museum, University of Pennsylvania (Neg # ANEP Plate 462) **Chapter 2:** p. 30: Nimatallah/Art Resource ◆ p. 32: The British Museum ◆ p. 34: Top, Erich Lessing/Art Resource. Bottom, C. M. Dixon ◆ p. 35: C. M. Dixon ◆ p. 36: Top, C. M. Dixon. Bottom, Michael Holford ◆ p. 37: Top, C. M. Dixon. Bottom, Michael Holford ◆ p. 38: C. M. Dixon ◆ p. 47: Nimatallah/Art Resource ◆ p. 50: Michael Holford ◆ p. 51: American School of Classical Studies at Athens ◆ p. 55: American School of Classical Studies at Athens: Agora Excavations ◆ p. 56: Both, Hirmer Fotoarchiv ◆ p. 57: Scala/Art Resource **Chapter 3:** p. 62: Erich Lessing/Art Resource ◆ p. 66: Naples, Archeological Museum. Photo, © Luciano Pedicini/Index ◆ p. 67: Photo, Johannes Laurentius, 1992/Bildarchiv Preussischer Kulturbesitz ◆ p. 69: Scala/Art Resource ◆ p. 70: The British Museum ◆ p. 72: Michael Holford ◆ p. 73: Acropolis Museum, Athens ◆ p. 74: John W. Snyder/The Stock Market ◆ p. 75: Hirmer Fotoarchiv ◆ p. 77: Unknown, perhaps a pupil of Lysippos, "Statue of a Victorious Athlete" Last quarter of 4th century B.C. Bronze, H: 151.5 cm. Collection of the J. Paul Getty Museum, Malibu, California ◆ p. 78: Scala/Art Resource ◆ p. 80: C. M. Dixon ◆ p. 81: Courtesy the Museum of Fine Arts, Boston ◆ p. 83: C. M. Dixon ◆ p. 84: Scala/Art Resource **Chapter 4:** p. 88: Scala/Art Resource ◆ p. 90: Alinari/Art Resource ◆ p. 91: Scala/Art Resource ◆ p. 93: Trëe; p. 93: Alinari/Art Resource ◆ p. 101: Scala/Art Resource ◆ p. 102: Unknown, "Man of the Republic." Graeco-Roman. Contribution, Purchase of E. P. Warren. Courtesy of Museum of Fine Arts, Boston ◆ p. 105: Giraudon/Art Resource ◆ p. 107: Michael Holford ◆ p. 109: Brian Brake/Photo Researchers ◆ p. 112: C. M. Dixon **Chapter 5:** p. 116: Scala/Art Resource ◆ p. 120: Trëe ◆ p. 121: C. M. Dixon ◆ p. 123: Nimatallah/Art Resource ◆ p. 124: C. M. Dixon ◆ p. 126: Trëe ◆ p. 127: H. C. Kinne/Comstock ◆ p. 129: Michael Holford ◆ p. 134: Hirmer Fotoarchiv ◆ p. 136: C. M. Dixon ◆ p. 138: Erich Lessing/Art Resource ◆ p. 141: Both, Scala/Art Resource ◆ p. 143: Alinari/Art Resource ◆ p. 144: Scala/Art Resource ◆ p. 147: Alinari/Art Resource **Chapter 6:** p. 150: Scala/Art Resource ◆ p. 155: The Huntington Library, San Marino, CA ◆ p. 156: The Metropolitan Museum of Art, Gift of J. Pierpont Morgan ◆ p. 158: The British Museum ◆ p. 160: Biblioteca Medicea Laurenziana, Florence. Photo, D. Pineider ◆ p. 161: Walters Art Gallery, Baltimore ◆ p. 162: Art Resource ◆ p. 163: Florence, Bibliotheca Seminario Vescovile/Photo, P. Tosi/Index ◆ p. 164: Stiftsbibliothek, St. Gallen. Photo, Carsten Seltrecht ◆ p. 165: Left, The Pierpont Morgan Library, New York. M.429, f. 183. Right, Bibliothèque Nationale, Paris ◆ p. 166: The Board of Trinity College Library Dublin ◆ p. 176: Bibliothèque Nationale, Paris ◆ p. 177: Scala/Art Resource ◆ p. 178: Bibliothèque Nationale, Paris **Chapter 7:** p. 180: 32.62: Leaf from a Qur'an. Egypt, 9th–10th century. 20.5 × 29.1 cm. Courtesy of the Freer Gallery of Art, Smithsonian Institution, Washington, D.C. ◆ p. 182: Scala/Art Resource ◆ p. 183: The Metropolitan Museum of Art, Gift of J. Pierpont Morgan, 1917 ◆ p. 186: Bibliothèque Nationale, Paris ◆ p. 187: Moscow, Historical Museum; photo, Ecole des Hautes Etudes, Paris ◆ p. 190: Bibliothèque Nationale, Paris ◆ p. 191: Tibor Bognár/The Stock Market ◆ p. 193: Giraudon/Art Resource ◆ p. 196: General Research Division, New York Public Library. Astor, Lenox, Tilden Foundations ◆ p. 199: Courtesy of The Arthur M. Sackler Museum, The Edwin Binney, 3rd Collection of Turkish Art at the Harvard University Art Museums ◆ p. 203: Bibliothèque Nationale, Paris ◆ p. 204: J. Messerschmidt/Leo de Wys ◆ p. 206: The British Museum ◆ p. 207: The Bodleian Library, University of Oxford. Ms. Marsh 144, page 273 ◆ p. 208: Fridmar Damm/Leo de Wys **Chapter 8:** p. 210: By Permission of The British Library ◆ p. 215: Giraudon/Art Resource ◆ p. 221: Giraudon/Art Resource ◆ p. 223: Erich Lessing/Art Resource ◆ p. 227: André Held ◆ p. 229: Giraudon/Art Resource ◆ p. 230: Collection Viollet ◆ p. 232: Erich Lessing/Art Resource ◆ p. 236: Archiv für Kunst und Geschichte ◆ p. 238: University Library of Freiburg-im-Breisgau ◆ p. 239: Victoria and Albert Museum, London/Art Resource ◆ p. 242: Top, Bibliothèque Nationale, Paris. Giraudon/Art Resource ◆ p. 243: Casimir/Leo de Wys ◆ p. 244: Marburg/Art Resource ◆ p. 245: Giraudon/Art Resource **Chapter 9:** p. 248: Nationalbibliotek Austria ◆ p. 251: Collection Viollet ◆ p. 252: Scala/Art Resource ◆ p. 253: Bibliothèque Nationale, Paris ◆ p. 257: Bettmann ◆ p. 259: Master and Fellows of Corpus Christi College,

Giraudon/Art Resource ◆ p. 548: Tass/Sovfoto ◆ p. 551: Sir Joshua Reynolds, "Lady Smith (Charlotte Delaval) and her Children (George Henry, Louisa, and Charlotte)." Oil on canvas. 55⅜ × 44⅛". The Metropolitan Museum of Art, Bequest of Collis P. Huntington, 1900 (25.110.10) ◆ p. 553: By Courtesy of the Trustees of Sir John Soane's Museum, London ◆ p. 554: Samuel Scott, "The Building of Westminster Bridge." Oil on canvas. 24 × 44⅜". The Metropolitan Museum of Art, Purchase, Charles B. Curtis Fund and Joseph Pulitzer Bequest, 1944 (44.56) ◆ p. 561: Staatliche Schlösser und Garten, Schloss Charlottenburg, Potsdam ◆ p. 563: Scala/Art Resource ◆ p. 564: The British Museum ◆ p. 565: Radio times Hulton Picture Library ◆ p. 568: Giraudon/Art Resource.

TEXT

Chapter 2: p. 39: Bernal, Martin. Abridged excerpt from *Black Athena: The Afroasiatic Roots of Classical Civilization Volume 1*, 1987, pp. 17–23. Copyright © 1987 by Martin Bernal. Reprinted by permission of Rutgers University Press. ◆ p. 39: Lefkowitz, Mary. Excerpt from *The New Republic*, February 10, 1992. Reprinted by permission of Professor Mary Lefkowitz, Wellesley College, MA. ◆ p. 42: Sappho, untitled excerpts. In Guy Davenport, trans. *Archilochos, Sappho, Alkman.* 1984. Reprinted by permission of University of California Press, Berkeley. **Chapter 3:** p. 68: Thucydides. Abridged excerpt from *The Peloponnesian War, Book V*, pp. 89–105. Rex Warner, ed. Copyright © Rex Warner, 1954. Reproduced by permission of Penguin Books Ltd. ◆ p. 71: Plato. Excerpt from *The Last Days of Socrates.* Hugh Tredennick, trans. Copyright © Hugh Tredennick, 1954, 1959, 1969. Reproduced by permission of Penguin Books Ltd. **Chapter 5:** p. 146: Saint Augustine. *Confessions, VIII.* In Whitney Oates, ed. *Basic Writings of Saint Augustine.* J. Pilkington, trans. Copyright © 1948 by Random House, Inc. Reprinted by permission of Random House, Inc. **Chapter 6:** p. 158: Tacitus, Cornelius. Excerpt from *The Agricola and the Germania.* H. Mattingly, trans. Copyright © the Estate of H. Mattingly, 1948, 1970. Reproduced by permission of Penguin Books Ltd. **Chapter 7:** p. 194: Cross, S. H., ed. Excerpt from *Russian Primary Chronicle*, pp. 62–63. trans. O. P. Sherbowitz-Wetzor. The Medieval Academy of America. Publication No. 60, 1953. Reprinted by permission of the Medieval Academy of America, Cambridge, MA. ◆ p. 200: Muhammad. Excerpt from *The Koran.* Trans. N. J. Dawood. Copyright © N. J. Dawood, 1956, 1959, 1966, 1968, 1974, 1990. Reproduced by permission of Penguin Books Ltd. **Chapter 8:** p. 228: Suger, Abbot of St. Denis. Excerpt from *Vie de Louis VI Le Gros.* Waquet, ed. Trans. David S. Spear. Societé d'Edition "Les Belles Lettres," 1964, pp. 172–179. © Les Belles Lettres, Paris. Reprinted by permission. **Chapter 9:** p. 272: Pope Boniface VIII. *Unam Sanctam*, 1302. In Brian Tierney, ed. *The Crisis of Church and State 1050–1300.* Prentice-Hall, 1964, pp. 188–199, 191. © 1964, 1992. Used by permission of the publisher, Prentice-Hall/A Division of Simon & Schuster, Englewood Cliffs, NJ. **Chapter 10:** p. 297 and 300: Knolles, Richard. *A Generall Historie of the Turkes.* In John J. Saunders, ed. *The Muslim World on the Eve of Europe's Expansion.* Adapted by Theodore K. Rabb. Prentice-Hall, 1966, pp. 20–22, 25–26. Used by permission of the publisher, Prentice-Hall/A Division of Simon & Schuster, Englewood Cliffs, NJ. ◆ p. 304: Carroll, Harry J., Jr.; Embree, Ainslee T.; Mellon, Knox, Jr.; Schrier, Arnold; & Taylor, Alastair M.; eds. Excerpt from *The Development of Civilization: A Documentary of Politics, Society and Thought*, Vol. I. Scott, Foresman, 1961, pp. 217, 220. Reprinted by permission of HarperCollins College Publishers. **Chapter 11:** p. 316: Boccaccio, Giovanni. Excerpt from *The Decameron.* In Ferdinand Schevill, ed. *The First Century of Italian Humanism.* New York: Russell & Russell, 1967, pp. 32–34. Reprinted by permission of Simon & Schuster. ◆ p. 334: Excerpt from *The Trial of Jeanne d'Arc*, 1438. In Bernard, Leonard & Hodges, Theodore B.; eds. *Readings in European History*, 1958, pp. 181–182. Copyright © 1958 by Macmillan College Publishing Company. Reprinted with the permission of Macmillan College Publishing Company. **Chapter 12:** p. 369: d'Este, Isabella. Letters, 1502, 1505, 1504. In D. S. Chambers, ed. *Patrons and Artists in the Italian Renaissance.* London: Macmillan, 1970, pp. 123–130 and 147–148. Reprinted by permission of The Macmillan Press Ltd. ◆ p. 379: Hus, Jan. Letter, 1415. In Matthew Spinka, ed. *The Letters of John Hus*, pp. 195–197. 1972 © Columbia University Press, New York. Reprinted with permission of the publisher. **Chapter 13:** p. 389: Table adapted from Febvre, Lucien & Martin, Henri-Jean. *The Coming of the Book: The Impact of Printing 1450–1800.* Trans. David Gerard, 1976, pp. 178–179 and 184–185. Reprinted by permission of Verso/New Left Books, London. ◆ p. 397: Luther, Martin. Preface, 1545. Trans. from the Latin by Theodore K. Rabb from Otto Schell, ed. *Dokumente zu Luther's Entwicklung.* Tubingen: J. C. B. Mohr, 1929, pp. 191–192. Reprinted by permission ◆ p. 415: St. Theresa. Excerpt from her autobiography, begun 1562. In E. Ellison Peers, *The Life of Theresa of Jesus*, pp. 258–260, 273–274. Reprinted by permission of Sheed & Ward, Kansas City, MO. **Chapter 14:** p. 423: Elliott, John H. Table adapted from *Imperial Spain, 1469–1716.* London: Edward Arnold, publisher, 1964, p. 175. Reprinted by permission of Professor Sir John

ABOUT THE AUTHORS

Mortimer Chambers is Professor of History at the University of California at Los Angeles. He was a Rhodes scholar from 1949 to 1952 and received an M.A. from Wadham College, Oxford, in 1955 after obtaining his doctorate from Harvard University in 1954. He has taught at Harvard University (1954–1955) and the University of Chicago (1955–1958). He was Visiting Professor at the University of British Columbia in 1958, the State University of New York at Buffalo in 1971, the University of Freiburg (Germany) in 1974 and Vassar College in 1988. A specialist in Greek and Roman history, he is coauthor of *Aristotle's History of Athenian Democracy* (1962), editor of a series of essays entitled *The Fall of Rome* (1963), and author of *Georg Busolt: His Career in His Letters* (1990) and of *Staat der Athener*, a German translation and commentary to Aristotle's *Constitution of the Athenians* (1990). He has edited Greek texts of the latter work (1986) and of the *Hellenica Oxyrhynchia* (1993). He has contributed articles to the *American Historical Review and Classical Philology* as well as other journals, both in America and in Europe.

Raymond Grew is Professor of History at the University of Michigan. He earned both his M.A. (1952) and Ph.D. (1957) from Harvard University in the field of modern European history. He was a Fulbright Fellow to Italy (1954–1955), and Fulbright Travelling Fellow to France (1976, 1990), Guggenheim Fellow (1968–1969), Director of Studies at the Écoles des Hautes Études en Sciences Sociales in Paris (1976, 1987, 1990), and a Fellow of the National Endowment for the Humanities (1979). In 1962 he received the Chester Higby Prize from the American Historical Asso-

ciation, and in 1963 the Italian government awarded him the Unita d'Italia Prize; in 1992 he received the David Pinkney Prize of the Society for French Historical Studies. He is an active member of the A.H.A.; the Society for French Historical Studies; the Society for Italian Historical Studies, of which he has been president; and the Council for European Studies, of which he has twice served as national chair. His books include *A Sterner Plan for Italian Unity* (1963), edited *Crises of Development in Europe and the United States* (1978), and with Patrick J. Harrigan, *School, State, and Society: The Growth of Elementary Schooling in Nineteenth-Century France* (1991); he is also the editor of *Comparative Studies in Society and History* and its book series. He has also written on global history and is one of the directors of the Global History Group. His articles and reviews have appeared in a number of European and American journals.

David Herlihy was the Mary Critchfield and Barnaby Keeney Professor of History at Brown University and the author of numerous books and studies on the social history of the Middle Ages. His most recent publications were *Opera Muliebria: Woman and Work in Medieval Europe* (1990); *Medieval Households* (1985); and, in collaboration with Christiane Klapisch-Zuber, *Tuscans and Their Families: A Study of the Florentine Catasto of 1427* (1985). He received his M.A. from the Catholic University of America in 1952, his Ph.D. from Yale University in 1956, and an honorary Doctor of Humanities from the University of San Francisco in 1983. He was a former president of several historical associations, and in 1990 served as president of the American History Association, the largest historical society in America. He was a fellow of the Guggenheim Foundation (1961–1962), the American Council of Learned Societies (1966–1967), the Center for Advanced Study in the Behavioral Sciences (1972–1973), and the National Endowment for the Humanities (1976). He was a fellow of the American Academy of Arts and Sciences and the American Philosophical Society. His articles and reviews have appeared in numerous professional journals, both here and abroad.

Theodore K. Rabb is Professor of History at Princeton University. He received his Ph.D. from Princeton, and subsequently taught at Stanford, Northwestern, Harvard, and Johns Hopkins universities. He is the author of numerous articles and reviews, and has been editor of *The Journal of Interdisciplinary History* since its foundation. Among his books are *The Struggle for Stability in Early Modern Europe* and *Renaissance Lives*. Professor Rabb has held offices in various national organizations, including the American Historical Association and The National Council for Historical Education. He was the principal historian for the PBS series, *Renaissance*.

Isser Woloch is Professor of History at Columbia University. He received his Ph.D. (1965) from Princeton University in the field of eighteenth- and nineteenth-century European history. He has taught at Indiana University and at the University of California at Los Angeles where, in 1967, he received a Distinguished Teaching Citation. He has been a fellow of the A.C.L.S., the National Endowment for the Humanities, the Guggenheim Foundation, and the Institute for Advanced Study at Princeton. His publications include *Jacobin Legacy: The Democratic Movement under the Directory* (1970), *The Peasantry in the Old Regime: Conditions and Protests* (1970), *The French Veteran from the Revolution to the Restoration* (1979), and *Eighteenth-Century Europe: Tradition and Progress, 1715–1789* (1982), and *The New Regime: Transformations of the French Civic Order, 1789–1820s* (1994).

*This book is dedicated
to the memory of David Herlihy
whose erudition and judgment
were central to its creation
and whose friendship and example
continue to inspire
his co-authors*

CONTENTS

2

THE FORMING OF GREEK CIVILIZATION   31

3

CLASSICAL AND HELLENISTIC GREECE   63

4

THE ROMAN REPUBLIC 89

5

THE EMPIRE AND CHRISTIANITY 117

6

THE MAKING OF WESTERN EUROPE 151

7

THE EARLY MEDIEVAL EAST 181

8

TWO CENTURIES OF CREATIVITY 211

9

THE SUMMER OF THE MIDDLE AGES   249

10

THE CRUSADES AND EASTERN EUROPE   283

11

THE WEST IN TRANSITION: ECONOMY AND INSTITUTIONS 313

12

THE WEST IN TRANSITION: SOCIETY AND CULTURE 347

13

REFORMATIONS IN RELIGION   383

14

ECONOMIC EXPANSION AND A NEW POLITICS   421

15

WAR AND CRISIS   461

16

CULTURE AND SOCIETY IN THE AGE OF THE SCIENTIFIC REVOLUTION 497

17

THE EMERGENCE OF THE EUROPEAN STATE SYSTEM 533

LIST OF MAPS

INTRODUCTION

[*Publisher's Note:* In order to provide an alternative to the hardcover edition, THE WESTERN EXPERIENCE is being made available in two-volume and three-volume paperbound editions, as well as a paperbound edition that runs from the Renaissance to the Modern Era. Volume I includes Chapters 1–17; Volume II includes Chapters 15–30 and the Epilogue; Volume A includes Chapters 1–12; Volume B includes Chapters 11–21; Volume C includes Chapters 19–30 and the Epilogue; the volume From The Renaissance to the Modern Era includes Chapters 12–30 and the Epilogue. The page numbering and cross-references in these editions remain the same as in the hardcover text.]

Everyone uses history. We use it to define who we are, to connect our personal experience with the collective memory of the groups to which we belong and to attach ourselves to a particular region, nation, or culture. We invoke the past to explain our hopes and ambitions and to justify our fears and conflicts. The Charter of the United Nations, like the American Declaration of Independence, is based on a view of history. When workers strike or armies march, they cite the lessons of their history. Because history is so important to us psychologically and intellectually, historical understanding is always shifting and often controversial.

Some questions must be asked repeatedly; some issues arise again and again. But historical knowledge is cumulative, for while asking new questions, historians integrate the answers learned from previous studies. History is not merely a subjective exercise in which all opinions are equally valid. No matter what motivated a particular historical question, the answer to it stands until overturned by better evidence. We now know more about the past than ever before and understand it as the people we study could not. Unlike them, we know how their history came out; we can apply methods they did not have, and often we have evidence they never saw. This knowledge and the ways of interpreting it are the collective achievement of thousands of historians.

We also use history for pleasure—as a cultivated entertainment. The biographies of admirable or monstrous men and women, dramatic accounts of important events, and colorful tales of earlier times can be fascinating in themselves. Through these encounters with history, we experience the common human concerns of all people; and through the study of European history, we come to appreciate the ideals and conflicts, the failures and accidents, the social needs and human choices that formed the Western world in which we live. When understood in their historical context, the achievements of European civilization are all the more remarkable, hammered out among competing interests and burning controversies.

The Western Experience was designed to provide a reasonably comprehensive and analytic account of the various circumstances within which, and the processes by which, European society and civilization evolved. This is the book's sixth edition, evidence of a long life sustained with the help of prior revisions. Even so, this edition is more completely rewritten and recast than any of its predecessors—our response to changes in students and in historical study. Each cohort of students carries different experiences, interests, and training into the classroom. These changes are easily exaggerated, but they can be important; and the women and men we teach have taught us enough about what currently engages or confuses them, about the impression of European history they bring to college, and about what they can be expected to take from a survey course to make us want to reconsider the way the book presented its material. This led to a rewriting and reordering that we think has made the book clearer and more accessible without sacrificing our initial goals of writing a sophisticated, interpretive, and analytic history.

Adapting the latest developments in historical understanding to a general work presents a problem of a particular kind. From its first edition, this book incorporated more of the results of quantitative and social history than general European histories usually did, an obvious reflection of the several authors' own research. Each subsequent edition provided an occasion to incorporate current methods and new knowledge, an opportunity to reconsider paragraphs, sections, and whole chapters in the light of new approaches and new research, sometimes literally reconceiving part of the past. Recent work—in demographic, economic, diplomatic, and intellectual history as well as social history, and most of all in gender studies and cultural studies—increases those opportunities, and we have sought to convey something of the excitement of this new understanding. At the same time, we have wanted to preserve a special kind of balance. The professional scholar prefers new perspectives to familiar information, but other readers are less likely to make such distinctions. For them, the latest interpretations need to be integrated with a presentation of standard controversies, of the people and events that are part of our cultural lore, and of the basic information necessary to build a framework for the historical understanding that they are beginning to form.

Other kinds of balance are important, too. We believe that this history must be interpretive but also that its readers—instructors, students, and general readers—should be free to use it in many different ways and in conjunction with their own interpretive approaches, their own areas of special knowledge, and their own diverse interests

and curiosity. Of course, there is no simple standard by which to judge when such a work is comprehensive enough to offer that freedom yet selective enough to be comprehensible. For this edition, the authors once again jointly planned revision of the entire volume, read and criticized each other's drafts, and benefited from the criticisms and suggestions of more than a score of other scholars and teachers. The book carefully includes evidence from which alternative interpretations can be formulated and a platform that allows classroom teachers of any period to emphasize social, political, cultural, economic, or institutional history in lectures and selected readings.

The use of color throughout the book and a new design obviously make it more attractive, and the maps have been completely redrawn. They convey more information more clearly and allow the basic geography of Europe a visual presence throughout the book. The greater range of illustrations has made it possible for them to be more fully integrated into the text than ever before. We have also adopted the common device of including selections from primary sources, choosing samples that expand points made in the text, provide some flavor of the period under discussion, and grant to the reader some of that independence that comes from personal engagement with historical sources.

Throughout the book, from the earliest civilizations to the present, certain themes are pursued. They appear most distinctly in the early chapters, in discussions of how the land is settled, divided among its inhabitants, and put to use; how production and the division of labor are organized and whether there are slaves, classes that do not work at all, and recognized specialists in fighting or crafts or trade; how the family is structured, the gendered roles within and outside the family, and the relationship of that to the overall social structure; how religion and belief systems are sustained and connected to power; how the political system operates, who participates in it, and how it maintains order and makes war; how the institutions of society and the system of law work to permit or constrain social change; and how the forms of cultural expression relate to the social structure and important issues of an era. Attentive readers will note that these themes, introduced early, are then picked up in subsequent sections of the book as changes in these themes are important for understanding other eras of European history.

We think of that history as the history of Western civilization, but the very concept of a Western civilization is itself the result of history. The Greeks gave the names *east* and *west* to the points on the horizon where the sun rises and sets. Because the impressive Persian Empire and India lay to their east, the Greeks thought of themselves as living in the West, on the edge of the continent they called *Europe*. The distinction between Western civilization and others—ethnocentric, often arbitrary, and frequently exaggerated—continued even as that civilization changed and expanded with the Roman Empire, Christianity, and the European conquest of the New World. The view that this is one civilization, with America tied more closely to ancient Greece than Greece is to Egypt or Spain to Islam, can be easily challenged in every respect save cultural tradition.

The Western Experience gives primary attention to a small part of the world and in doing so honors that cultural tradition. The concentration on Europe includes important examples of city and of rural life; of empires and monarchies and republics; of life before and after industrialization; of societies in which labor was organized through markets, serfdom, and slavery; of cultures little concerned with science and of ones that used changing scientific knowledge; of non-Christian religions and of all the major forms of Christianity in action.

To discuss history in this way is to think comparatively and to employ categories of the social history that has greatly affected historical understanding in the last half of the twentieth century. The desire to broaden the scope of historical writing is not new. As early as the eighteenth century many historians (of whom Voltaire was one) called for a history that was more than chronology, more than an account of kings and battles. In the nineteenth century—even while historical studies paid dominant attention to past politics, diplomacy, and war (taking the evidence primarily from official documents found in state archives)—there were important and systematic efforts to encompass the history of intellectual and cultural trends, of law and constitutions, of religion, and of the economy. Social history, as a field of study, emerged as one of these efforts at broader coverage. For some, it was primarily the history of labor movements. For others, it was the history of daily life—in ancient Rome or Renaissance Florence or old New York as reflected in styles of dress, housing, diet, and so on. This "pots and pans history" was the sort of history featured in historical museums and popular magazines. Appealing in its concreteness, it tended (like the collections of interesting objects that it resembled) to lack a theoretical basis.

Modern social history is more systematic. In the theories and methods it employs, it borrows from the social sciences—especially anthropology, sociology, economics, and political science. It seeks to compensate for the fact that most historical writing has been about the tiny minority of the powerful, rich, and educated (who, after all, left behind the fullest and most accessible records of their activities); and it aims to be mindful of popular culture as well as formal or official culture, as interested in the family and living conditions as in the state and political theory.

The growth of social history facilitated a remarkable expansion in the history of women. Stimulated by contemporary feminism as well as by developments within social history, the history of women has in turn grown into gender studies, a set of approaches that has proved enormously revealing about society as a whole, showing how politics and culture together with leisure and work, are shaped by and reproduce assumptions about gender. This new work has affected the historical understanding of every era and nearly every subfield of history. Gender studies have also tended to draw attention to social symbols and to the values expressed in social behavior, drawing history closer to the literary and philosophical theories underlying what is currently called *cultural studies*. These approaches, as well as the renewed interest in intellectual history, emphasize the role of interpretation over objective science and the relativity of all writing on culture and society.

Such interests, theories, and techniques have greatly expanded the range of useful historical sources and the range of issues historians must consider. They also make those mainstays of historical organization—clear chronology and periodization—more complex. The periodization of history based on the rise and fall of dynasties, on the formation of states, and on the duration of wars and revolutions usually does not fit the periodization most appropriate for highlighting changes in culture and ideas, economic production, or science and technology. Historical surveys have therefore frequently been organized topically as well as chronologically, with special chapters on economic or intellectual developments, which can weaken awareness of interconnection.

In *The Western Experience* an effort has been made to combine the newer approaches with more established perspectives. The tradition of the introductory course in European history (and our cultural tradition as well) is recognized by keeping the book's chapters essentially chronological in sequence, sometimes using groups of chapters to cover a whole period. At the same time each chapter is presented as an interpretative essay, introducing a set of historical problems important to the understanding of the period treated. The information within a chapter serves as evidence to illustrate the interpretive argument, but it is also selected to meet the general requirements of a survey of European history, to provide the basis for constructing a coherent picture of the development of Europe, and to exemplify different kinds of historical interest.

Readers of this book may thus use it as an introduction to historical method, find within it a framework to which they can attach whatever else they know about Western society, and discover here some challenge to their preconceptions—about the past, about how societies are organized, and about how people behave. Historical study is an integrative enterprise in which long-term trends and specific moments, as well as social structure and individual actions, are brought together.

A college course is not the only way to build a personal culture. Nor is history the only path to integrated knowledge. Western history is not the only history one should know, nor is an introductory survey necessarily the best way to learn it. Still, as readers consider and then challenge interpretations offered in this text, they will exercise critical and analytical skills; and they will find that the world beyond (and before) our own lives is relevant to our current concerns. They can acknowledge the greatness of their Western heritage and its distinctiveness, which includes injustice, cruelty, and failure. In doing these things, they will experience the study of history as one of those vital intellectual activities by which we come to know who and where we are.

Acknowledgments

▼

We wish to thank the following reviewers, consultants, and users for their helpful suggestions for *The Western Experience:* Catherine Albanese, Wright State University; Thomas M. Bader, California State University–Northridge; B. D. Bargar, University of South Carolina; Edward E. Barry, Montana State University; S. Scott Bartchy, University of California–Los Angeles; Iris Berger, State University of New York–Albany; Alan E. Bernstein, University of Akron; Charles R. Berry, Wright State University; Thomas Blomquist, Northern Illinois University; Stephen Blum, Montgomery County Community College, PA; Jack Bournazian; Elspeth Brown, Hamilton College, NY; Paul Chardoul, Grand Rapids Junior College; Craig A. Czarnecki, Baltimore, MD; Ronnie M. Day, Eastern Tennessee State University; Michael De Michele, University of Scranton; Bradley H. Dowden, California State University–Sacramento; Veron Egger, Georgia Southern College; Nancy Ellenberger, United States Naval Academy; Elfriede Engel, Lansing Community College, MI; Steven Epstein, University of Colorado at Boulder; R. Finucane, Georgia Southern College; Willard C. Frank, Jr., Old Dominion University, VA; Ellen G. Friedman, Boston College; James Friguglietti, Eastern Michigan College; Laura Gellott, University of Wisconsin at Parkside; Robert Gottfried, Rutgers University; Carl Granquist, Jr., Keene State College; Katherine J. Gribble, Highline Community College, WA; Margot A. Haberhern, Florida Institute of Technology; Barbara Hanawalt, University of Minnesota; Drew Harrington, Western Kentucky University; Patricia Herlihy, Brown University; Neil M. Heyman, San Diego State University; Deborah L.

Jones, Lexington, KY; Thomas E. Kaiser, University of Arkansas–Little Rock; Nannerl O. Keohane, Wellesley College; Donald P. King, Whitman College, WA; William J. King, Wright State University; Ellen E. Kittell, University of Oregon; Steven P. Kramer, The University of New Mexico; Lisa Lane, Mira-Costa College; Gordon Lauren, University of Montana; Phoebe Lundy, Boise State University; Gilbert H. McArthur, College of William and Mary; Edward Malefakis, Columbia University; Vesta F. Manning, University of Arizona–Tucson; William Mathews, State University of New York at Potsdam; William Carl Mathews, Ohio State University; Edgar Melton, Wright State University; Carol Menning, University of Toledo; Julius Milmeister, Pittsburgh, PA; Frederick I. Murphy, Western Kentucky University; Sandra Norman, Florida Atlantic University; Peter Pierson, Santa Clara University; Linda J. Piper, The University of Georgia–Athens; Carl Pletsch, Miami University; Phillip Racine, Wofford College; Ronald A. Rebholz, Stanford University; John F. Robertson, Central Michigan University; Louisa Sarasohn, Oregon State College; Judy Sealander, Wright State University; Ezel Kural Shaw, California State University–Northridge; Eileen Soldwedel, Edmonds Community College; Alan Spetter, Wright State University; Richard E. Sullivan, Michigan State University; John Sweets, University of Kansas; George Taylor, University of North Carolina–Chapel Hill; Armstrong Starkey, Adelphi University, NY; Richard Wagner, Des Moines Area Community College; Richard Weigel, Western Kentucky University; Robert H. Welborn, Clayton State College; Michael J. Witt, FSC, Christian Brothers College, TN; and Richard M. Wunderli, University of Colorado.

Mortimer Chambers
Raymond Grew
Theodore K. Rabb
Isser Woloch

The earth, seen from space, showing the Tigris
(east) and Euphrates (west) rivers, which irrigated
the cradle of civilization in the Near East.

CHAPTER ONE

THE FIRST CIVILIZATIONS

HE subject of this book is the Western experience—that is, the history of European civilization and its origins in earlier civilizations located in Mesopotamia and around the Mediterranean Sea.

Human beings began to abandon a nomadic existence and live in settled agricultural villages about 8000 B.C. By about 3000 B.C. they had created settlements of some size along the banks of the Tigris, Euphrates, Nile, and Indus rivers. People's efforts to build a better life transformed the agricultural villages into something we can recognize as cities—having a scale and pattern crucial for the development of civilization. In these valleys types of behavior and institutions first appeared that have persisted, in varying forms, throughout all periods of Western civilization.

Powerful kingdoms and great empires, centered on sizable cities, gradually arose in Asia Minor and in Egypt. Their achievement of literacy and their many written records; their long-distance trade; their invention of increasingly ingenious tools, utensils, vehicles, and weapons; their development of monumental architecture and representative art; and their advances in medicine, astronomy, and mathematics marked the change from primitive life and constituted civilization.

I. *The Earliest Humans*
▼

Our first task as we try to grasp historical chronology is to gain a sense of the overwhelmingly long period that we call "prehistory." The astronomer Carl Sagan has reckoned that, if the entire history of the universe were plotted out over the span of one year, everything that we usually think of as European history—the subject of this book—would have taken place in the last two or three minutes of the year.

Human beings are members of the species Homo sapiens ("thinking human being"), which appeared, according to present evidence, about 350,000 years ago. The immediate predecessor was Homo erectus, which may have emerged as long ago as 1,500,000 years. Back in time beyond Homo erectus is an area of doubt and controversy. There is growing support for the theory that humanity originated in east Africa about 2 million years ago, but this is not yet fully proved.

HUMAN BEINGS AS FOOD GATHERERS

Human beings have always had to try to come to terms with their environment. For the greatest part of their time on earth, they have struggled simply to hunt and gather food. Only relatively recently have people been able to produce food and thus create a stable basis for life. And only within the last few decades have we recognized that we have the power to destroy the environment that nourishes us.

From the beginning of human society, people had to decide how to share labor. Historians have usually guessed that men did most of the hunting and gathering in earliest times, while women nourished the young, but recent research has cast doubt on this pattern. The division of labor was probably flexible, depending on circumstances; even today in some communities women hunt animals and babies are suckled by more than one woman. At times, men may have hunted food while women tended crops as well as bearing the young; in such societies women may have dominated the economic and social organization.

If the men in some community trapped and killed a large animal, this achievement may have enabled them to claim leadership, and physical strength may explain why men have led most societies that have left records. The records themselves have usually been shaped by males, but they still reveal indispensable roles for women as organizers and sustainers of human communities. To the extent that males have taken the lead, it has probably been the result of the need for physical strength to repel aggression. One hunting band, for example, might have had to turn aside the claims of another band to certain territory. In such clashes, we may guess that men assumed leadership through their strength and thus created a division of roles based on sex that gave them dominance of their communities. One result of this social division has been a comparative lack of information about the role of women in history; the reconstruction of this role, the restoring of women to history, has been a leading theme of historical research in the present generation.

The period when people gathered food is often called the Old Stone Age, or Paleolithic Age, and ranges from the beginning of human history to about 10,000 B.C. Even in this early period, some human beings developed a remarkably sophisticated kind of art. The most striking creations we have from food-gathering societies are a series of cave paintings that survive at their finest in Lascaux in France and Altamira in Spain. Most of them show wild animals, enemies of human beings and yet part of their essential support. The paintings may have a quasi-religious meaning as symbolic attempts to gain power over the quarry; scars on the walls suggest that people threw spears at the painted animals, as if to symbolize killing them. If so, the cave paintings provide our earliest evidence for one of the main themes of history: the attempt to communicate with forces outside human control through symbolic action, art, and thought—that is, through religion and ritual acts.

HUMAN BEINGS AS FOOD PRODUCERS

About 10,000 B.C. there occurred the most important event in all human history: People turned from hunting animals and gathering food to producing food from the earth. This event, the rise of agriculture, is called the Neolithic Revolution and introduced the Neolithic, or New Stone, Age.

The word *revolution* usually implies dramatic action over a short time, which was in no way true of this one: Yet revolution it was, for it made possible the feeding of larger populations. The rise of agriculture gave continuity to human existence and demanded long-term planning and the practice of new skills and specialties. Those people not needed in agriculture could engage in hunting (for this skill was still needed), weaving, pottery, metalwork, and trade.

But *why* did this revolution take place? What caused people to turn from the pattern of roaming the countryside that had lasted hundreds of thousands of years? There may be no one simple answer, but it is clear that the earth's glaciers, which had long been advancing from both polar regions toward inhabited areas, began to shrink back toward the poles. This allowed the animals that had been driven by the glaciers into the arms and weapons of human beings to wander away again. To hunt and trap animals now demanded longer journeys in search of less abundant prey: Therefore farming became a necessity.

It has also been suggested that agriculture developed in response to increasing population. Some historians have argued that larger populations in the later (or "upper") Paleolithic Age made it imperative to develop new sources of food. Other historians have denied this, suggesting that a large increase in population became possible only *after* the agricultural revolution had ensured a supply of the necessities that would sustain humanity—domesticated animals (sheep, pigs, cattle), vegetables, and grains. There is probably truth in both views: The need for a new supply of food may have been pressing even as people came to seek more settled homes, rather than face the constant upheavals of a nomadic existence.

Moreover, when people invested much labor in their settlements and knew that their sustenance depended on their land, the issue of protecting and even expanding their claims to territory became of immense importance. Therefore one effect of the agricultural revolution was the impetus to fight over territory—to make war. War is one of the constantly recurring themes of Western civilization. The reasons for making war will vary considerably through the centuries, and the tools of war will become ever more sophisti-

cated; but the willingness to seize a weapon and be willing to shed other people's blood and risk one's own life to protect territory descends from the earliest permanent human settlements.

EARLY NEAR EASTERN VILLAGES

The Neolithic Revolution first occurred among the hills of what is now southern Turkey and northern Iraq, especially in the Zagros hills east of the Tigris River. But, again, why was *this* region the cradle of agriculture? Historians have concluded that only here was there a sufficient supply of animals for domestication along with the needed vegetables and cereals. The earliest known settlements, dating from about 9000 B.C., were unwalled and unfortified, and their people lived in simple huts. About 8000 B.C. the first somewhat larger villages appeared. The oldest seem to have been Jericho and Jarmo, but even

AN OVERVIEW OF EVENTS
(ALL DATES B.C.*)

c. 7000	First permanent villages in Near East.
c. 3000	Formation of cities in Sumer; unification of Upper and Lower Egypt.
c. 1900	Hebrews begin immigration into Palestine.
1792–1750	Hammurabi unifies Babylonia and issues his law code.
c. 1595	Sack of Babylon by Hittites.
c. 1570–1085	Egyptian Empire (New Kingdom).
c. 1400–1200	High point of Hittite kingdom.
c. 1230	Exodus of Israelites from Egypt and their invasion of Canaan.
c. 900–612	Assyrian conquests.
559–530	Cyrus founds Persian Empire.
521–486	Rule of Darius in Persia.

*Some historians use an alternate system of dating: B.C.E. (Before the Common Era) and C.E. (Common Era).

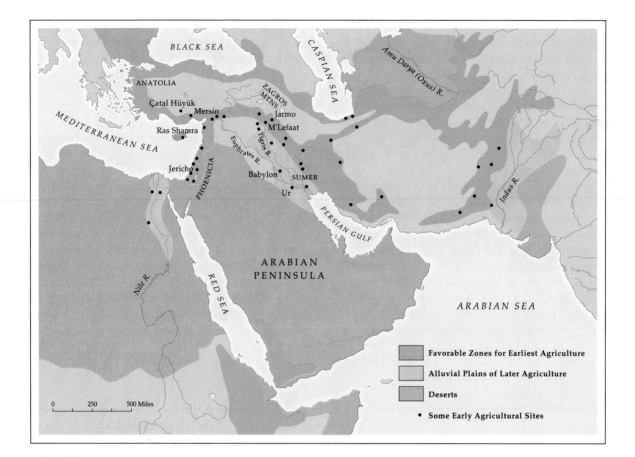

Map 1.1 THE EARLIEST CIVILIZATIONS
Note the famous "fertile crescent," running north from Jericho, then curving southeast toward Sumer; this area supported the first permanent agricultural villages.

these were still small settlements; Jarmo's population is estimated to have been about 150.

As such villages became more permanent, they also became more versatile in their inventions; our first evidence of pottery, for example, comes from what is now Iran and dates from about 6500 B.C. This invention allowed the storage of food and sustained the population in periods when hunting and gathering were more difficult. Another invention, the art of weaving, was practiced in Anatolia, now within modern Turkey, by about 6000 B.C. and provided both new occupations and new resources for a village. About this time, too, people began to travel in crude rafts and in carts with wheels. Potters gradually learned to fashion their wares on the sur-

face of a turning wheel, so that they could make in minutes what had previously taken hours; and the pot, the raft, and the wheel combined to provide the means to transport grain and other goods. Thus arose another institution of all later societies: the mutually profitable exchange of goods in trade, pursued by people skilled enough to make a living at it. Some archaeologists have suggested that a number of towns were formed not for the sake of local agriculture but to serve as trading centers. Trade needs safe routes and a guarantee of safety for traders, which in turn require some kind of political protection and control.

The early agriculturalists were naturally much concerned with breeding and fertility; in their cities we therefore find evidence of attempts at communication with goddesses, in the form of statuettes of unmistakable earth-mothers, with large buttocks and breasts, whose fertile bodies, it was hoped, would make the soil productive. Such figures probably also signify the importance of human mothers, for the villages flourished only if women produced and sustained each new generation. The emphasis on the importance of females and female deities has led some historians (though without clear evidence) to deduce that matriarchy, the political domination of a society by women, existed during the early period of agricultural towns, and that men had to overturn this system in order to gain or regain mastery.

So by stages there arose agrarian communities with communal gods, domesticated animals, simple technologies and economies, and some regulation of social behavior. Yet we must remember how painfully slow was the transition from nomadic hunters to food-producing villagers. And still another 6000 years were to separate such agricultural villages from the first civilizations.

II. *The First Civilizations in Mesopotamia*

THE EMERGENCE OF CIVILIZATION

From about 3000 B.C., the historian speaks of civilization, a social organization with more complex rules for behavior than those that guided dwellers in caves or the earliest farmers. In a civilization, there are more sophisticated divisions of authority and labor, including duties, powers, and skills that pass down within certain families. Such forms of social life first appear about 3000 B.C., though they were not the result of a sudden explosion but rather of long social development.

The establishment of firm authority requires the acceptance by both governors and the governed of their status; we shall see this balance throughout history, but we shall also observe its collapse when conflict leads to the replacement of one governing group by another. Rulers, however named, arise from among the heads of powerful families. Seeking social order, people give authority to a man or woman who seems to have some special power or ability.

An equally essential part of the social cement, in all periods of civilization, has been law, formally accepted codes of behavior, as distinct from the simple customs of a village. Law may develop slowly, but eventually it is recorded in detailed law codes, which tell us how societies controlled relations among their people. But there is tension, in any civilization, between control and freedom; law codes are thus also a way of restraining encroachment of one citizen on another. The constant discussion and refinement of law is another permanent theme of our history.

Cities are larger and therefore stronger than villages; they have the power to dominate the hinterland and even to enslave its population. Slavery, though deplorable in modern eyes, allowed the enslavers more varied occupations by freeing them from the mundane requirements of existence. As people began to use this new freedom to pursue special skills, some gained a reputation for religious knowledge and became the state's communicators with divine powers; and such is the strength of religious belief that these priests could form a class of advisers whom even kings could not ignore.

Other citizens used their new freedom to develop new arts and crafts. Along with improved techniques of pottery, weaving, and domestication of animals, a major step forward took place when workers discovered how to blend other metals with copper to fashion bronze, especially for weapons. As the first cities reached significant size, humanity thus entered the Bronze Age, which started about 3000 B.C. and ended between 1200 and 1000 B.C.

SUMER

Mesopotamia is a rich alluvial plain created by deposits from the Tigris and Euphrates rivers. At the southern end of this plain arose the first real cities and the first recognizable civilization, in the area known as Sumer. The people of Sumer and their language appear to be unrelated to any other known people or language. By about 3000 B.C. Sumer contained a dozen or more city-states—in other words, cities that were each independent of the others, each ruled by its own king and worshiping its own patron deity, a god that offered protection to the city. The citizens of each city were divided into three classes: nobles and priests, commoners, and slaves. This is the first example of what we shall often meet in history: a recognized, legal division of people into social orders. The king was not considered divine; he held power only so long as he could command support from the powerful priests and nobles.

At the center of a Sumerian city there usually stood a ziggurat, a terraced tower built of baked brick and culminating in a temple, probably for the patron god of the city. A ziggurat might be a stupendous structure: The wall surrounding one of them was some 36 feet thick. The Old Testament contains many echoes from Sumer, and it seems likely that the story in the Bible of the Tower of Babel was ultimately based on the memory of a ziggurat.

In Sumerian culture, the patron god theoretically owned the whole city; but, in fact, much of the land was private property, held mainly by princes and their families but also by private citizens. Most houses were of a single story and were jammed into narrow streets, but some richer houses had two stories and an open court. The people were monogamous, and women held property and took part in business but did not hold political office.

Trade was essential for the growth of Sumerian cities, for, despite the region's astonishing fertility, it lacked good timber and stone. Sumerians pioneered the art of building in baked brick, but to obtain other materials they had to export in exchange such goods as metalwork, in which they became outstanding craftsmen.

Perhaps to bolster their expertise in the essential art of trading, the Sumerians developed a precise system of mathematical notation. Their system was the sexagesimal, in which the number 60 (*sexaginta* in Latin) is one of the main elements; this system has the advantage of including 3, 10, and 12 as factors. One of the longest-lasting legacies of Mesopotamia to our world is this system:

▶ **A ziggurat from Ur. The stairway leads up to a room in which a god could rest and take his pleasure. The ziggurat formed the core of a temple compound, while around it were storehouses.**

The foot has 12 inches; the day, twice 12 or 24 hours; the minute and hour, 60 units each; and the circle, 360 degrees.

Sumerian Literature   The Sumerians' chief contribution to later civilizations was the art of writing. The most important intellectual tool ever discovered, writing enables people to keep records, codify laws, and transmit knowledge. All the record keeping, libraries, and literature of later times are made possible by this invention. We know of some earlier attempts at communication through written symbols, but the Sumerians developed the art in an efficient form. Their script was pictographic: Each sign was originally a simplified picture of the article that the scribe had in mind. In time, scribes reduced the complexity of the system by simplifying pictures and by combining several pictures into one. In this process of abstraction, the meaning of a sign might change. For example, a crude picture of a star was simplified into four wedge-shaped marks and given the meaning of "god" or "heaven."[1] In another kind of refinement, the Sumerian script became at least partly alphabetic and phonetic, rather than remaining purely a system of pictographic writing. Sumerian texts were written on clay tablets by pressing the end of a reed or bone stylus into the wet clay; the resulting wedge-shaped marks are called *cuneiform* (Latin *cuneus*, meaning "wedge"), a name used for all such scripts in whatever language they occur.

The Sumerians had a developed mythology and saw the world as having been created by a god. Moreover, the gods had established the standards by which people had to live. One of their main deities, Enlil, was primarily a storm god who lived in heaven. Normally kind and fatherly, Enlil made the rich soil of Mesopotamia fertile and was credited with designing the plow. At times, however, when Enlil had to carry out the harsh decrees of other gods, he became terrifying. This alternation may reflect the uncertainty bred in the Sumerians by the threat of floods that always hovered over them. When the rivers overflowed and destroyed the crops, the Sumerians thought the gods had withdrawn their

▷ A relief showing the Sumerian hero Gilgamesh holding a conquered lion, from the reign of Sargon II of Assyria, eighth century B.C. The relief shows the long continuation of the Sumerian legend.

---

[1]The Sumerian method of writing is described by S. N. Kramer in *The Sumerians*, 1963, pp. 302 ff.

favor, and they rationalized such treatment by assuming that they had somehow offended the gods or failed to observe their requirements.

In Sumerian mythology, humanity was almost completely dependent on the gods. Indeed, Sumerian myth taught that the gods had created people merely to provide slaves for themselves. In the Sumerian epic *The Creation of Mankind*, Marduk the creator says, "Let him be burdened with the toil of the gods, that they may freely breathe." Other Sumerian myths foreshadow the biblical accounts of eating from the tree of knowledge in Paradise and of the Flood that covered the earth.

Sargon and the Revival of Ur Wars among the cities of Sumer weakened them and prepared the way for the first great warlord of Western history: Sargon, of the region of Akkad, an area just north of Babylon. He ruled from 2371 to 2316 B.C.[2] and conquered all Mesopotamia; his kingdom even reached the Mediterranean Sea. From Akkad his language is named Akkadian; it is of the Semitic linguistic family. Thus through Sargon we first meet one of the most important of all groups of peoples in Western civilization, the Semites. They spoke a number of related languages including Akkadian, Hebrew, and Canaanite. Akkadian, also written in cuneiform, now replaced Sumerian as a spoken language, although Sumerian continued to be written until about the beginning of the Christian era.

Sargon and his successors ruled from Akkad until about 2230, when invasion, and perhaps internal dissension, dissolved the Akkadian kingdom. The Sumerians then regained control of southern Mesopotamia and established the so-called Third Dynasty of Ur. The chief ruler of this period was Ur-Nammu (2113–2096 B.C.). He created another practice that we will see again and again in history, when he issued the first comprehensive law code and spelled out regulations and penalties for a broad range of offenses. He also established standard weights and measures, a recognition of the importance of trade to the people of his state. His law code is preserved in only fragmentary form, but it is clear that he laid down fines in money rather than calling for physical retribution: "If a man has cut off the foot of another man . . . He shall pay ten shekels . . . If a man has severed with a weapon the bones of another man . . . He shall pay one mina of silver."

[2]Dates in early Near Eastern history are constantly being revised. For dates in this chapter we normally rely on the *Cambridge Ancient History*, 3rd ed., 1970 ff.

THE BABYLONIAN KINGDOM

The cities of southern Mesopotamia succumbed, toward the year 2000 B.C., to the rising power of a Semitic people called Amorites. These invaders destroyed Ur in 2006 and soon established their own capital at Babylon, within the region known as Babylonia. Hammurabi, the sixth king of the dynasty in Babylon itself, finally succeeded in unifying Mesopotamia under his rule.

Hammurabi (1792–1750 B.C.) is a towering figure whose greatest legacy is the most significant of all the documents written down to his time: a cuneiform stone column, now in the Louvre Museum in Paris, recording a long series of legal judgments published under his name. This so-called Code of Hammurabi, like the earlier one of Ur-Nammu, is not a complete constitution or system of law; rather, it is a compilation of those laws and decisions that he thought needed restating. The code includes some 270 sections, much more carefully organized than any earlier one that we know (*see box*, p. 9). Hammurabi has always been considered the primary example of the lawgiver, the man who grasped the organizing power of royal declarations of law; this example was to be followed by many other potentates, whether or not they consciously looked back to the Babylonian model.

We cannot, in a few lines, summarize Hammurabi's fascinating document, which regulates virtually every aspect of relations between citizens. The penalties for crime were severe, to say the least. If a son struck his father, his hand was cut off; if a man broke into a house, he was put to death; anyone who looted a burning home was thrown into the fire. Among the most forward-looking provisions in the code were those regarding the family. Hammurabi evidently recognized the vulnerable position of women and children in his society and took care to protect them. If a man's wife became ill, he could marry

Hammurabi's Law Code

Here are some excerpts from the "judgments" laid down by Hammurabi in his famous law code.

"When Marduk [the patron god of Babylon] sent me to rule the people and to bring help to the country, I established law and justice in the language of the land and promoted the welfare of the people. At that time I decreed:

"1. If a man accuses another man of murder but cannot prove it, the accuser shall be put to death.

"2. If a man bears false witness in a case, or cannot prove his testimony, if that case involves life or death, he shall be put to death.

"22. If a man commits robbery and is captured, he shall be put to death.

"23. If the robber is not captured, the man who has been robbed shall, in the presence of the god, make a list of what he has lost, and the city and the governor of the province where the robbery was committed shall compensate him for his loss.

"138. If a man wants to divorce his wife who has not borne him children, he shall give her money equal to her marriage price and shall repay to her the dowry she brought from her father; and then he may divorce her.

"142. If a woman hates her husband and says, "You may not possess me," the city council shall inquire into her case; and if she has been careful and without reproach and her husband has been going about and belittling her, she is not to blame. She may take her dowry and return to her father's house.

"195. If a son strikes his father, they shall cut off his hand.

"196. If a man destroys the eye of another man, they shall destroy his eye.

"197. If he breaks another man's bone, they shall break his bone.

"200. If a man knocks out a tooth of a man of his own rank, they shall knock out his tooth."

The Code of Hammurabi, Robert F. Harper (tr.), 1904, language modified.

another woman but had to continue to support the first wife; and she, if she wished, could move out and keep her dowry. Again, a widower could not seize his dead wife's dowry and spend it but had to save it for her sons; and a widow could keep her dowry, that is, the contribution from her family that she had brought into her marriage. Divorce was also allowed. A wife could divorce her husband for adultery, but only if she had been chaste; if not, she was thrown into the river along with her lover.

MESOPOTAMIAN CULTURE

Hammurabi's subjects used all manner of commercial records (bills, letters of credit, and the like), and their knowledge of mathematics was amazing. They built on foundations laid by the Sumerians, using the sexagesimal system, with 60 as the base. They had multiplication tables, exponents, tables for computing interest, and textbooks with problems for solution.

The Mesopotamians also developed complex systems of astrology and astronomy. It is not certain which science inspired the other, but we have both astrological predictions and astronomic observations from the second millennium. The Babylonian calendar had 12 lunar months and thus had only 354 days, but astronomers learned how to regularize the year by adding a month at certain intervals. When the Hebrews and Greeks wanted to order time through a calendar, they learned the method from the Babylonians. In fact, the calendars of both Jerusalem and Athens were also lunar, with 354 days and a month added from time to time.

III. Egypt

▼

The early cities of Mesopotamia had turbulent histories, falling now to one warlord, now to another. The kingdom of Egypt, by contrast, achieved a nearly incredible permanence; its people and monuments survive even today. The basic element in the long history of Egyptian civilization is the Nile River. The Nile overflows its banks each summer, reviving the land with fresh water and depositing a thick layer of alluvial soil for cultivation. Only this yearly flood protected the Egyptians from starvation.

THE OLD KINGDOM

Early Egypt was divided into two regions, Upper Egypt (the Nile Valley) and Lower Egypt (the river delta). A king, Menes (also known as Narmer), who lived about 3000 B.C., unified Upper and Lower Egypt and established a capital at Memphis. By the beginning of the Old Kingdom, the land had been consolidated under the strong central power of the king, who enjoyed a supremacy that we can hardly imagine today. The king (he was not called *pharaoh* until the New Kingdom) was the owner of all Egypt and considered a god as well. The whole economy was a royal monopoly; and serving the king was a hierarchy of officials, ranging from governors of provinces down through local mayors and tax collectors. Artisans, peasants, and slaves, all working for the king, nourished the whole system.

The supreme monuments of the Old Kingdom are the three immense pyramids, tombs for kings,

built at Giza (now within the city of Cairo) between 2600 and 2500 B.C. These staggering feats of engineering dwarf any other monuments from any age. Building such a pyramid may well have been the chief activity of the king during his rule.

▶ **Top: The ceremonial palette of King Narmer is a symbolic representation of the unification of Upper and Lower Egypt. This side of the palette shows the king, wearing the white crown of Upper Egypt, smashing the head of an enemy. The god Horus, in the form of a falcon, holds a rope attached to a captive of Lower Egypt, a region symbolized by six papyrus plants.**
Bottom: On this side of the palette King Narmer has completed his conquest of Lower Egypt and wears the red crown of that kingdom. He is reviewing the bodies of decapitated victims. The exotic beasts with necks intertwined may symbolize the unity of the two Egypts.

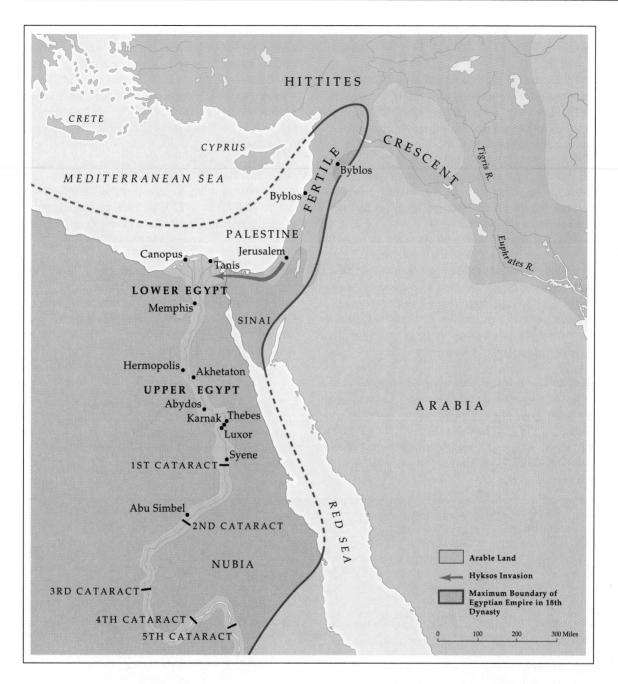

Map 1.2 ANCIENT EGYPT
The kingdom reached from the fourth cataract to the Mediterranean.

Religion The king, together with the gods whom Egyptian belief associated with him, stood at the pinnacle of Egyptian religion. Other gods, who occupied lesser positions in Egyptian the-ology, appeared in a variety of forms, often as animals, and in origin were probably deities of the villages up and down the Nile. The Egyptians believed in a pleasant life after death, in which people would perform their usual tasks but with more success. The king, already a god, would be-come a greater god; viziers, priests, and admin-istrators would hold more responsible positions.

For everyone who had lived a good life there would be pleasures such as boating and duck hunting.

In Egyptian mythology, the god who ruled over the dead was Osiris, originally a god of fertility. He had given Egypt its laws and taught the people how to prosper. But he was murdered by his treacherous brother, and his body was cut into fragments, which his loving wife Isis reassembled, thus resurrecting him. Osiris' son, Horus, was identified with the king, who was considered the incarnation of Horus on earth and the center of the world.

In harmony with their expectation of survival beyond death, the Egyptians made careful preparations for the physical needs of the afterlife, especially by placing favored possessions such as jewelry and wine cups into a tomb and embalming and making mummies of the dead. Statues sat in the tombs of kings as receptacles for their spirits in case their bodies should be destroyed.

Maat The Egyptians recognized an abstract ethical quality called *maat*, which Egyptologists translate roughly as "right order." *Maat* existed if everything was in the order that the gods had ordained. It was a kind of primeval and cosmic harmonizing force that arranged all created things in the right relationships. All ancient societies valued order and harmony—most of them had a monarchic system that naturally prized discipline—but the notion of *maat* seems to show a new way of advocating moral behavior. When a society can give a name to the abstract idea of right order without having to attach it to a god, a subtler kind of thinking is taking place. Right order would, indeed, help to hold Egyptian society together. Thus *maat* illustrates another frequent use of religion throughout history: as a carefully crafted tool of politics and a promoter of order, in addition to an expression of people's feeling toward divine powers.

Writing Egyptians developed a form of writing known as *hieroglyphics* ("sacred carvings"). The indispensable key to the Egyptian past has been the Rosetta stone, discovered when Napoleon occupied part of Egypt in A.D. 1798. This stone, now in the British Museum, contains a partly preserved hieroglyphic text along with translations

▷ **The step pyramid of Zoser (about 2800 B.C.), the center of a large religious complex, shown with part of the surrounding wall that gave into the courtyard. Note a small shrine in front of the pyramid.**

in the cursive Egyptian script that evolved from hieroglyphics and also in Greek, a known language that offered a way of deciphering the other two.

Like the cuneiform script of Mesopotamia, hieroglyphics began as pictorial signs. Experts believe that the Sumerians influenced the Egyptians in the early stages, around 3000 B.C.; but the pictures that the Egyptians developed were mostly original. Hieroglyphics sometimes use merely a picture of the object represented; for example, a small oval represents "mouth." But at some point the scribes decided to use the pictograms as phonetic signs; thus *ra* continued to mean "mouth" but was also used for the sound *r*. Fully developed hieroglyphics, like Sumerian cuneiform, are therefore a combination of pictograms and phonetic signs.

The Egyptians made writing material from the papyrus plants (from which comes our word *paper*) that grew in abundance along the Nile. The reeds of the plant were placed crosswise in layers, then soaked, pressed, and dried to produce sheets and rolls. Because of the dry climate, thousands of papyri have survived in legible condition; most of these come from a later period when the Romans administered Egypt.

▶ **The Pyramids of Giza. Left to right, the pyramid of Menkaure, Khefre, and Khufu (the "great" pyramid).**

Literature Egyptians developed a rich, lively literature. Their works often dealt, as did their art, with mythology and the afterlife; and their hymns to various deities, poems celebrating the king's victory over death, and stories about the gods reflect the serene Egyptian confidence in the beneficence of the gods. Various texts, collectively known as the Book of the Dead, provide charms and other methods of ensuring a successful transition to the other world.

Success in this world appears as the central concern of another literary genre, appropriately known as "instructions" or "instructions in wisdom." These books, in which a wise man gives advice about how to get ahead in the world, reveal much about Egyptian social attitudes, especially the supreme position of the king. The writers counsel discretion and loyalty: "If you are a man of note sitting in the council of your lord, fix your heart upon what is good. Be silent—this is better than flowers. Speak only if you can unravel the difficulty . . . to speak is harder than any other

▶ **An Egyptian papyrus showing an antelope and a lion in a game of chess; a playful scene from daily life.**

work. . . . Bend your back to him that is over you, your superior in the king's administration. So will your house endure with its substance, and your pay be duly awarded. To resist him that is set in authority is evil."[3]

We also have scraps of Egyptian love poetry: "It is pleasant to go to the pond in order to bathe in your presence, that I may let you see my beauty in my tunic of finest royal linen, when it is wet." And there are meditations, songs, ghost stories, and fables of all kinds. In fact, not until the Greeks did the ancient world have another literature with the variety and beauty equal to that of Egypt.

Mathematics and Medicine   The Egyptians were pioneers in applied science. The need for careful planting in the silt deposits of the Nile forced them to master arithmetic, geometry, and the art of surveying; for an unusually rich overflow

---

[3]Adolf Erman, *The Ancient Egyptians: A Sourcebook of Their Writings*, 1966, pp. 61–62 (language modified).

might wipe out the boundaries between plots of land, and when this happened the land had to be remeasured.

Medicine in Egypt depended largely on driving out demons from the body. The Egyptians believed that a separate god ruled over each organ and limb, and treatment consisted largely in finding the right chant to appease the appropriate deity and then delivering it in the right tone of voice. Sometimes a sorcerer simply threatened a demon by promising to invoke the aid of the gods if it did not depart at once.

But medicine was not based entirely on magic. One papyrus, a treatise on surgery, displays a more empirical approach to illness. It discusses some 48 medical problems, classified according to the various parts of the body. Whenever possible, the author gives a diagnosis and suggests a treatment. A verdict is often given in one of three forms—"An ailment that I will treat," "An ailment with which I will contend," or "An ailment not to be treated"—probably according to whether the prognosis was favorable, uncertain, or unfavorable. This text is a witness to the birth of a kind of inquiry that transcends haphazard folk medicine. Such maturing and broadening of knowledge independent of magic characterize the civilizing process throughout history.

The Invasion of the Hyksos A major disaster befell Egypt about 1720 B.C., the invasion of the Hyksos (the name means roughly "rulers of foreign lands"). Historians are still not certain who these invaders were, but they were probably a group of western Asiatic peoples from Syria and Palestine. They controlled mainly the region of the delta, but by about 1570 B.C. Egyptian warriors from Thebes had counterattacked and had driven the Hyksos from the delta and back into Asia Minor. The period following the expulsion is called the New Kingdom, or the Egyptian Empire.

THE NEW KINGDOM

During the Eighteenth Dynasty the rulers from Thebes, now called *pharaohs*, strengthened the power of the central government over the nobles and organized Egypt into a military state. They enlarged their domain by encroaching on Asia Minor, where they encountered another large kingdom, that of the Hittites. These two kingdoms, the Egyptian and the Hittite, were the most powerful ones down to their time, and also the last great kingdoms of the Bronze Age.

Hatshepsut Within the Eighteenth Dynasty there reigned the first, and greatest, female ruler of ancient times, Hatshepsut. This dynamic woman seized power and in 1503 B.C. had herself crowned king of Egypt, representing this act as the will of the god Amen. It was an act of breathtaking audacity in a social system where men had always held the absolute power of monarch. Perhaps to emphasize her right to rule as king, she had herself portrayed as a sphinx with a beard.

Hatshepsut wanted to be remembered above all as a builder, the restorer of Egypt. "I have repaired," she proclaimed on inscribed walls, "what was destroyed by the Hyksos; I have raised up what was in pieces ever since the Asiatics had been in the Delta, overthrowing what had been made." Her great temple tomb in the Valley of the Kings is the equal in majesty of any other building in Egypt.

Thutmose III, her successor, became Egypt's greatest military statesman. He made 17 expeditions into Asia Minor and expanded the empire as far as the Euphrates River. His successors, exploiting these conquests, grew rich on the tribute paid by subject peoples such as the Israelites, many of whom became slaves in Egypt. With this economic power the Egyptians expanded their trade, honored their gods with more temples, and continued working the rich copper mines in the Sinai peninsula.

Akhnaton's Religious Reform After the conquests of Thutmose III, a dramatic conflict of religions took place in the New Kingdom. This

▶ **Queen Hatshepsut of Egypt (1512–1482 B.C.), history's first female ruler, pictured as a sphinx, which was a divine animal. Surrounding her face are a lion's mane and a ceremonial false beard.**

struggle arose from a contest between the phar-aoh and certain priests and nobles, as each party strove to make its own god the supreme one. Thus the apparent religious battle—not for the last time in history—was, in reality, a political one. Although it was but one event during the centuries of the New Kingdom, the reforming aims of one side in this conflict have fascinated modern observers.

Early in his reign King Amenhotep IV (1379–1362 B.C.) began to oppose the worship of Amen-Re, for centuries the traditional god of the Thebes, and sponsored the worship of the *aton*, the physical disk, or circle, of the sun. Supported by his wife Nefertiti, Amenhotep appears to have been trying to overcome the influence of priests and bureaucrats in Thebes. To advertise the new faith among his people, he changed his own name to Akhnaton, which may be translated as "he who serves Aton." He moved his capital from Thebes to a completely new city called Akhetaton, "the horizon of Aton" (a village called El Amarna today), where he built a temple to Aton. He composed a soaring hymn in praise

of Aton, hailing him as the creator of the world—an account of creation comparable to those of the Sumerians and the Israelites.

There is evidence that Akhnaton fought the worship of other gods, and some historians have gone so far as to call him the first monotheist. Such a conception is anachronistic and overlooks how Aton was worshiped: The royal family alone worshiped the god; the Egyptian people were ex-pected to continue to worship the pharaoh him-self. Artistic scenes show priests and nobles in attitudes of reverence, but they are addressing their prayers to the pharaoh, not directly to Aton.

The more conservative priests, and probably most Egyptians, continued to worship Amen-Re, and Akhnaton's religious reform ended with his death. The next pharaoh changed his name from Tutankhaton to Tutankhamen, thus indicating

▶ **Akhnaton and Nefertiti in a familial scene hold three of their children, while the sun-disk blesses and cherishes them. The style of art (round bellies, slender bodies, elongated jaws) is typical of the Amarna period.**

that Amen-Re, the older chief deity, was again in favor. The royal court moved back to Thebes, and the city named for Aton, Akhetaton, was abandoned and destroyed. Akhnaton's name was savagely effaced from monuments and king lists, and he was now known as "the criminal of Akhetaton." The young king Tutankhamen reigned for only seven years and was buried with dazzling splendor. His tomb, discovered in A.D. 1922, intact with all its treasures, has remained the most stunning single find in the history of Egyptology.

The New Kingdom now emerged from the period of religious conflict with renewed strength and was led by ambitious pharaohs, the most famous of whom was Ramses II. He fought a major, though inconclusive, battle with the Hittites in 1300 B.C., at Kadesh in Palestine, and carried on the war until the two kingdoms signed a peace treaty in 1284. The temporary peace that Ramses achieved allowed him to spend time and money on remarkable building projects, which became notorious in the Old Testament as the hardest labor of the Israelite slaves. At Karnak, for example, he completed an enormous hall of columns sacred to Amen-Re, who had now fully regained his old position. Ramses' supreme achievement as a builder is the colossal temple that he had

▶ **Syrian subjects presenting tribute to the pharaoh of Egypt on a wall painting at Thebes in the period of the empire.**

carved out of the rocky cliffs along the Nile at Abu Simbel. The building of the Aswan Dam by the modern Egyptians would have drowned the temple and its statues beneath the water of an artificial lake; but an international group of engineers preserved Ramses' desire to be remembered for all time by cutting the outer monuments free and raising them above the level of the water.

A VIEW OF EGYPTIAN SOCIETY

In antiquity, communication by ship was greatly superior to overland transportation in animal-drawn carts. The Nile therefore imposed a natural administrative unity on Egypt. The kings secured their power through the help of ministers and advisers, especially the class of priests, while a complex bureaucracy carried out the routine work of government and saw to the royal monopoly over the economy.

Slaves existed, but the economic difference between free citizens and slaves was not always vast. Both classes worked the fields, labored on

---

Dates in Egyptian History

The basic source for Egyptian chronology is a list of the rulers compiled about 280 B.C. by Manetho, an Egyptian priest, who wrote in Greek. He grouped the kings into 30 dynasties (later chronicles added a thirty-first). Modern scholars accept Manetho's divisions and have established these approximate dates B.C.:

Archaic Period (Dynasties 1–2)	3100–2700
Old Kingdom (Dynasties 3–6)	2700–2200
First Intermediate Period (Dynasties 7–10)	2200–2050
Middle Kingdom (Dynasties 11–12)	2050–1800
Second Intermediate Period (Dynasties 13–17, invasion of Hyksos)	1800–1570
New Kingdom, or Empire (Dynasties 18–20)	1570–1085
Postempire (Dynasties 21–31)	1085–332
Conquest of Egypt by Persia	525
Conquest of Egypt by Alexander the Great	332

---

the pyramids, and were indeed the ultimate economic basis for the regime, although their own lives changed little from one generation to another.

It was possible to enter and rise in the Egyptian hierarchy through education. The kings and their gods needed all manner of scribes, treasurers, and functionaries, and Egyptian children might learn the art of writing in a school run by a temple or a palace or even from a private teacher in a village. They studied normally from age 4 to age 16 and could then enter the army or the royal service. Scribes were also needed for the arts of medicine and architecture and for the priesthoods; most priests were men, but some were women.

Egyptian society was liberal in the scope given to women—more so, in fact, than Judaic or Greco-Roman societies. Women could own and pass on property, could appear as witnesses in court, and could initiate action at law if anyone tried to take their land away. Officials were nearly always men, but women sometimes acted as scribes, even treasurers, something unknown in Greece and Rome. Among peasants, women toiled with men in agriculture and did most of the baking and spinning.

We must not overlook the turmoil within Egyptian history: the invasion of the Hyksos, wars in Asia, the collapse of the New Kingdom, and its conquest by Assyria and then by Persia (*see box*). Yet there remains the awesome *permanence* of Egypt: No other state, in the nations we call Western, has ever survived so long. On the whole, over the span of some 30 centuries, life flowed predictably, as did the Nile, making severe demands but bringing the material for a well-earned reward.

IV. The Early Indo-Europeans

Down to this point, our survey has looked at the great kingdoms of the ancient Near East. During the later centuries of these kingdoms, a new family of peoples began to appear, speaking the languages from which the languages of modern Europe were to descend. English, French, Greek, Latin, Russian, Spanish, and the languages of India, Pakistan, and Iran all belong to the family of languages known as Indo-European. These languages descend from a tongue that we call Indo-European, though we have no preserved writings in such a language. Perhaps about 6000 to 5000 B.C. the Indo-European peoples began a slow dispersion across Europe and parts of Asia. Some of them ultimately settled on the Indian subcontinent, while others moved westward into Italy, Greece, central Europe, and Asia Minor.

THE HITTITE KINGDOM

One of the Indo-European peoples was the Hittites. By about 1650 B.C. they established a capital at Hattusha (Boghazköy in modern Turkey). Excavations here have unearthed about 10,000 cuneiform tablets, the decipherment of which has made it possible to recover at least some of Hittite history.

▶ **Soldiers, carved in the living rock, shown guarding a shrine in a cleft at the Hittite site of Yazilikaya near Boghazköy.**

The greatest early warrior of this nation, Murshili I, in the sixteenth century B.C. led armies south as far as Babylon, which he sacked about 1595, thus ending the kingdom once ruled by Hammurabi. Between 1400 and 1200 B.C. the Hittite kingdom reached its zenith. During the reign of Akhnaton in Egypt the Hittites took advantage of the pharaoh's preoccupation with religious reform to tear away from Egypt the region of northern Syria. Under Ramses II, as we have seen, Egypt's attempt to regain this territory led, in 1284 B.C., to a treaty of nonaggression between the two nations. This modern-seeming document shows a growth in the techniques of diplomacy among ancient states.[4]

The Hittites shared various customs with other eastern states. They believed, for example, that the king became a god after death. But they had other features that historians consider characteristic of Indo-European peoples. The whole army formed a kind of assembly, called the *pankus*, which acted as a court of law to punish criminals. Some historians think the *pankus* once chose

the kings, but this power had passed away before our records begin, for it seems clear that kings had the right of inheritance. The queen retained her position even after the king's death, perhaps so that her religious duties should not be interrupted. The king was general, chief judge, and high priest, serving the many Hittite gods; the Hittites adopted most of these deities when they entered Asia Minor.

The Hittites had kings, but much of the political power was in the hands of a limited number of families, who received grants of land and were bound to the king by oaths. This system addressed a common problem of all rulers, how to win and maintain loyalty among potentially dangerous rivals.

Like other societies in this era, the Hittites published law codes, which reveal that their society was patriarchal. Fathers gave their daughters in marriage, and a widow was normally married off to her father's next of kin. But women did have some rights of their own; for example, a free woman who married a slave remained free.

---

[4]Both the Hittite and Egyptian texts of this document are translated in James B. Pritchard (ed.), *Ancient Near Eastern Texts Relating to the Old Testament*, 1969, pp. 199–203.

THE CLOSE OF THE BRONZE AGE

Between 1250 and 1200 B.C. new waves of invaders (probably including mysterious raiders generally called "sea peoples") poured into Asia Minor, breaking up the Hittite kingdom. These peoples had learned the secret of working iron and applied their knowledge to weaponry. As a result, they overcame the older civilizations that still relied on bronze weapons. Between 1200 and 1000 B.C. the Bronze Age disappeared, to be replaced by an Iron Age, in which we still live.

The introduction of iron had profound social and political consequences. Iron, more readily available than bronze, is not only harder but, most important for this discussion, cheaper as well. As a result, more people could own weapons, and states in the Iron Age grew more formidable in war. As more of the population obtained weapons, there followed a partial shrinking of the distance between some socioeconomic groups in the society. Those who now served the state in the army began to claim some role in determining its policies, and the ruling elites had to open their ranks to armed newcomers in order to maintain control over the masses. A noted historian, V. Gordon Childe, hit the mark when he called iron the "democratic metal."

V. Palestine

CANAANITES AND PHOENICIANS

The region of Palestine was originally inhabited by a group of Semitic tribes known as the Canaanites, among whose cities were Jericho and Jerusalem. By about 1200 B.C. the Canaanites had settled mainly in Phoenicia, a narrow region along the Mediterranean Sea. They drew part of their culture from the Mesopotamian and Egyptian states nearby, but they were also innovators. Their outstanding contribution was a simplified alphabet with only about 30 characters that was later adopted by the Greeks and became the ancestor of Western alphabets. It is impossible to overstate the political and social importance of this invention. It ended the long period during which people had to learn thousands of pictorial

symbols to be reasonably literate and writing was a mysterious art known to only a few. Especially in the hands of the Greeks, writing brought a knowledge of law codes and historical records within the intellectual reach of ordinary citizens and led to reevaluation of the past and skepticism about mythology.

The Phoenicians lacked the military power to create an empire, but they influenced other cultures, especially through trade on both land and sea. They established trading posts or colonies far from Palestine, the most famous of which was Carthage, a powerful city on the north coast of Africa that controlled parts of North Africa and Spain.

Among the Phoenician articles of trade was a reddish dye that the ancients called *purple*; cloth dyed in this color became a luxury and has remained a mark of royalty or eminence. The Phoenicians were also the first people to treat the art of war as a profession, and because of their sailing ability they provided the navy for the Persian Empire. They and other Canaanite peoples had thus developed a high urban civilization by the time the Israelites began their invasion of the Palestinian coast.

HEBREW SOCIETY

South of Phoenicia is the region of Palestine that today is known as Israel, also settled in antiquity by speakers of the Semitic Hebrew language. The Old Testament of the Bible provides a continuous record of how this people viewed its past, but before historians can use the narratives and chronicles of the Bible as a source, they must take a stand on the credibility of the documents. Scholars in the nineteenth century questioned whether the Old Testament contained unchallengeable, divinely revealed truth. Archaeology in recent years has often confirmed the Bible, at least in questions of geography and topography, but literal accuracy is not, after all, the central issue. Religious traditions of any society, whether or not they are strictly verifiable, can provide historical information, just as do law codes and lists of kings.

The Israelite chroniclers concentrated on a single god and on humanity's relationship to him. This great theme, varied in countless ways, fuses the Old Testament into a story about one god and the history of his chosen people. Unlike Mesopotamian epics, the Bible deals with real people and real times; it combines ethics, poetry, and history into the most influential book in the Western tradition.

The Early Hebrews   There is little reason to doubt the biblical tradition that, beginning around 1900 B.C., tribes of nomads began to wander into Palestine from the east. Each one was led by a patriarch, and they did not form a unified society. One such patriarch was Abraham, whose grandson, Jacob, is said to have organized the nomadic people into 12 tribes under the leadership of his 12 sons. Jacob himself also took the name Israel (meaning "God strove" or "God ruled"). The people were therefore a tribal society, unlike the urban society of Sumer or the unified monarchy of Egypt.

Some Israelite tribes settled in Canaan. Others migrated to Egypt, which they abandoned, probably about 1270 B.C., in the "exodus" (*see box*, below). At their head was a man with the Egyptian name of Moses, who led them across the Sinai peninsula during the period of general unrest in the Near East. Moses organized the tribes

of Israel and some neighboring Canaanites into a confederation bound by a covenant to the god he named YHWH (by convention, we write this word Yahweh; in English it later became Jehovah) and placed all the people in Yahweh's service. So far as we can tell, this was the first time that any consolidated group in Western civilization accepted one god. This tremendous moment is thus the birth of monotheism.

But *why* did Israel accept one god, in contrast to the rest of the ancient world, where families of deities were the rule? Was Moses perhaps influenced by the monotheism of Akhnaton? We do not know, but we may guess that Moses saw the need to unify his people so that they would be strong enough to regain their home in Palestine; and what could forge a stronger bond than having the whole people swear allegiance to a single god?

Moses proclaimed the new convenant between God and his people on Mount Sinai, in the wastes of the desert. According to the Old Testament Book of Exodus, he received his instructions directly from Yahweh. These instructions, a document of the greatest historical interest, include the Ten Commandments, in which Yahweh issues the terse order "Thou shalt have no other gods before me."

The Salvation of Israel

The Old Testament book of Exodus narrates the escape of the Israelites from Egypt and preserves the hymn of praise sung by Moses and his people after they reached the holy land. The poem celebrates the strength of God and his generosity in saving Israel. It also shows that Israel saw itself as having a special compact with God.

"I will sing to the Lord, for he has triumphed gloriously; the horse and his rider he has thrown into the sea. The Lord is my strength and my song, and he has become my salvation; this is my God, and I will praise him, my father's God, and I will exalt him. The Lord is a man of war; the Lord is his name. Pharaoh's chariots and his host he cast into the sea; and his picked officers are sunk in the Red Sea. The floods cover them; they went down into the depths like a stone. Thy right hand, O Lord, glorious in power, thy right hand, O Lord, shatters the enemy. [. . .] Thou hast led in thy steadfast love the people whom thou has redeemed, thou hast guided them by thy strength to thy holy abode [. . .], the sanctuary, O Lord, which thou hast made for thy abode, the sanctuary, O Lord, which thy hands have established. The Lord will reign for ever and ever."

Exodus 15, *Holy Bible*, Revised Standard Version, 1962.

Early Israelite society was clearly father-dominated through the patriarchs and God, whom they considered their supreme father. This structure shaped the legal status of women. The commandments imply that a woman is the legal possession of her husband: "Thou shalt not covet thy neighbor's house, nor his wife, nor his servant, nor his ox, nor his ass." Marriage occurs through purchase throughout the Old Testament, and a daughter might simply be given as a kind of salary: "Jacob loved Rachel and served seven years to gain her" (Gen. 29:20). The heroism of those women of the Bible who rose above this control—Ruth, Judith, and Deborah, for example—is all the greater.

Moses also laid down a code of laws, which, unlike earlier codes, is a series of laws prescribing ethically right conduct. This appears to be the first intervention of religion into the private behavior of human beings. The historical reality of Moses, the fact that his laws are connected with the experience of a people, and the power of the ethical concerns of that people have given the faith of Israel an immediacy to which Sumerian or Egyptian religion could hardly pretend.

The Israelite Monarchy By a series of attacks on Canaanite cities and by convenants made with other tribes, the Israelites established themselves in Palestine. About 1230 B.C. they invaded Canaanite territory in a campaign aimed at expansion. Biblical stories say that Joshua, the successor of Moses, led the tribes of Israel across the Jordan River and followed God's instructions to take the Canaanite city of Jericho by siege.

During the years of the conquest of Canaan, Israel still lacked a central government. A series of leaders (called "judges"), one of them a woman named Deborah, managed to reunite the people in periods of crisis, but the tribes then habitually drifted apart. According to the Bible, the people finally demanded a king, evidently wanting to imitate the practice of the Canaanites: "We will have a king over us; then we shall be like other nations, with a king to govern us, to lead us out to war and fight our battles" (1 Sam. 8:20). The first king, Saul (1020?–1010?), and his successor, David (1010?–960?), captured Jerusalem and made it Israel's capital. The entire nation now took the name Israel, and during his reign David extended the kingdom to its farthest boundaries.

Solomon, David's son and successor (960?–920?), was famed for his wisdom. Like all great kings of the period, Solomon was a builder. He left behind him the physical memorial that symbolized the faith of Israel through the centuries—the Temple in Jerusalem. But the temple could not compare in size with his magnificent palace and citadel, whose stables, according to tradition, housed 12,000 horses.

Solomon's autocratic rule and extravagance caused resentment among his people, who were heavily taxed to pay for his palace and army. After his death the kingdom split into two parts. The northern half, centered on the ancient town of Shechem, retained the name of Israel; the southern half, ruled from Jerusalem, was now called Judah. Weakened by internal quarrels, the northern kingdom of Israel was conquered in 722 B.C. by the Assyrians to the northeast, who deported much of the population. This scattered people became known in biblical lore as the 10 lost tribes of Israel.

Judah was now the only Israelite kingdom, and from this time on the remaining Israelites are known as Jews. Judah also fell in 586 B.C. to the Chaldean, or Neo-Babylonian, Kingdom. The captives were deported to Babylon, in the so-called Babylonian captivity, but later in the same century they were allowed by the king of Persia to trickle back into Palestine. There were occasional revivals of an independent Jewish kingdom at other times; but in general the Jews became pawns of the various forces that ruled Palestine until 1948, when a revived Jewish state—the republic of Israel—took its place among sovereign nations.

The Faith and the Prophets Judaism was also shaped by a few resolute critics, known as the prophets: men of the people, tradesmen, and preachers, such as Amos, Micah, Hosea, Jeremiah, and Isaiah. They were not kings and had no military power that could make the people listen to their message. The most authoritative prophet had been Moses, and all successors looked back to him for guidance. The later prophets spoke one general message: Israel was becoming corrupt and only a rigid moral reform could

Jeremiah Reproaches Israel

The people of Israel discovered monotheism, but to maintain it was not easy. The prophet Jeremiah warned his people that they were backsliding into worshiping false gods such as Baal, rather than retain allegiance to the one true God.

"The Lord said to me, 'There is revolt among the men of Judah and the inhabitants of Jerusalem. They have turned back to the iniquities of their forefathers, who refused to hear my words; they have gone after other gods to serve them; the house of Israel and the house of Judah have broken my covenant which I made with their fathers. Therefore, thus says the Lord, Behold, I am bringing evil upon them which they cannot escape; though they cry to me, I will not listen to them. [...] The Lord once called you, "A green olive tree, fair with goodly fruit"; but with the roar of a great tempest he will set fire to it, and its branches will be consumed. The Lord of hosts, who planted you, has pronounced evil against you, because of the evil which the house of Israel and the house of Judah have done, provoking me to anger by burning incense to Baal.' "

Jeremiah 11, *Holy Bible*, Revised Standard Version, 1962.

---

save it. Worship of Yahweh had sometimes been blended with that of the gods, or Baalim, of the Canaanites. Luxury, promiscuity, and extravagance were weakening the discipline of Israelite society (*see box*, above).

But even as they denounced the prevalent wickedness, the prophets promised that God would forgive Israel if the people repented, and he would further prove his love to Israel by sending a Messiah. The word *Messiah* (*mashiah* in Hebrew) means a person or even a thing possessing a divine power or purpose; referring to people, it came to mean one "anointed" by God to perform a special mission. From about 200 B.C. onward, Jewish thought held that a king would some day appear, a descendant of David, who would restore the power and glory of Israel on earth. The famous Dead Sea Scrolls (discussed in Chapter 5), ranging in date from the second century B.C. through the first century A.D., often speak of the awaited Messiah. Christians, too, developed their theory of a Messiah, who would return to rule on earth over all humanity: To them, the "anointed one" (*ho christós* in Greek) is Jesus, but to Jews, the hero is still unborn or unknown.

Another event that strengthened Judaism was the organization of the sacred writings. Ezra, who wrote about 445 B.C., is the prototype of a new kind of spiritual leader—the scribe and scholar. He collected and published the first five books of the Old Testament (the Pentateuch); later scholars collected the books of the prophets. The Temple in Jerusalem, destroyed during the Babylonian invasion, was rebuilt during the sixth century B.C. and, in the absence of a free Jewish state, assumed even greater importance as the nucleus of the faith. It fell once more, in A.D. 70, this time to the Romans, who destroyed it. But part of the western wall of the outer court survived, and at this site the Jews were permitted to gather and pray.

THE JEWISH LEGACY

The Jews are the only society originating in the ancient Near East whose traditions have remained vital in modern times. For reasons that no one can fully explain, adversity has never broken the Jewish spirit, and over many centuries the Jews have persisted as a society even without an independent state. Their faith provided the most persuasive answer to the problem that also troubled their neighbors—the nature of the relationship between humanity and God. To Israel, there was only one god; unlike the gods of the pagans, he was an exclusive and intolerant one.

He judged severely, but was also prepared to forgive those who sincerely regretted wrong behavior. He created the world and stood outside the world; he had no association with the world of nature and never appeared as an animal or in any other form. Above all, he was a god for everyone, not just for nobles, priests, and kings. Christianity, the religion of medieval and modern Europe, is a child of Judaism and has drawn upon the morality and ethics of the older faith.

VI. The Near Eastern Empires

▼

A series of general disruptions about 1250 to 1150 B.C. left no state dominant for the next few centuries until the Assyrians began their conquests. They became the first people to accomplish a political unification of large parts of the Near East (see Map 1.3). The Persians, the next great imperialists of this region, built on foundations laid by the Assyrians and ruled with an administrative skill that only the Roman Empire would

▷ **An extreme rarity, the only example of frescoes in a Jewish synagogue showing scenes from the Bible. From Dura Europus, circa A.D. 239; now in a museum at Damascus.**

equal in ancient times. The Persians also developed a widely accepted religion, Zoroastrianism, some of whose doctrines persisted long after the Persian Empire disappeared.

THE ASSYRIAN STATE

The Assyrians were descended from Semitic nomads who had entered northern Mesopotamia about 2500 B.C. and founded the city of Ashur, named after their chief god. From this name comes the designation *Assyrian* for the people. Their language was a Semitic dialect closely resembling that of the Babylonians, and they wrote in the cuneiform script that had originated in Sumer and had remained in general use.

About 900 B.C. the Assyrians began their most important period of conquest and expansion. They became masters of the upper reaches of Mesopotamia, and their territory included Babylonia to the south, the cities of Palestine to

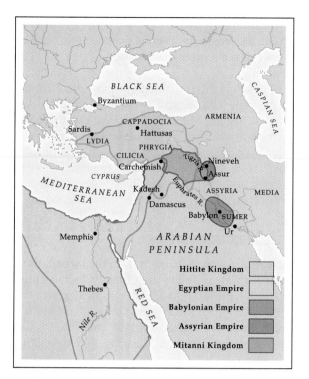

Map 1.3 THREE ANCIENT STATES
Sumer, Babylonia, and the Hittite kingdom, down to about 1200 B.C.

the west, and Egypt. By the late seventh century their empire embraced most of the Near East.

If any one concept could characterize Assyrian society it would be militarism. The army was especially dominant and efficient, and the Assyrians greatly extended the use of iron weapons. In administering their empire, the Assyrians faced a greater challenge than any earlier state in absorbing large kingdoms such as Egypt and Babylonia. They ruled with a degree of control unknown in any of the earlier conglomerates.

The Assyrian kings exacted heavy payments of tribute as the price of leaving the conquered territories in peace. Some peoples, such as the inhabitants of Judah, escaped further burdens, but other less independent peoples had to accept a vizier, or governor, serving the king. In some cases the imperial government deported subject peoples who might prove troublesome—for example, those inhabitants of Israel who were dispersed within the Assyrian domain. Assyrian armies stationed in the provinces were a further guarantee of stability.

Language became another means of unifying the empire; the Semitic language known as Aramaic was ultimately spoken everywhere in lands dominated by Assyria, and it became the common tongue of the Near East. In Palestine it was spoken by the Jews, including Jesus.

For all their harsh militarism and their brutal rule over their conquered subjects, the Assyrians created magnificent works of art. Much of the wealth extracted from the empire was spent on glorifications of the king and his conquests. Most notable are the reliefs cut on the palace walls at Nineveh, the capital, and elsewhere. The last powerful Assyrian king, Ashurbanipal (668–627), also created a library of cuneiform texts. The largest single group of these texts concerns omens, divination, or observations of the stars, for Assyrian kings relied heavily on omens and their interpretation by priests to guide their policy.

It is hardly surprising that the subjects of the Assyrians watched for any chance to rebel. Finally, in 612 B.C., a combination of forces, led by Babylonians, captured Nineveh, and the Assyrians lost control of their empire.

▶ **An Assyrian relief showing Ashurbanipal's soldiers attacking a city. Some soldiers swim to the attack; others scale the walls with ladders while defenders fall from the ramparts.**

THE CHALDEANS AND THE MEDES

The Assyrian Empire gave way to two successor states: the Chaldean, or Neo-Babylonian, Kingdom and the Kingdom of the Medes. The Chaldeans, the dominant tribe within a new kingdom based on Babylon, were the most learned astronomers of antiquity. They kept minute records of eclipses, charted a plan of the heavens, and calculated the length of the year mathematically. Their discoveries were passed on to the Greeks and Romans and influenced all medieval and modern astronomy.

Babylon, the capital of the Chaldean Kingdom, was notorious as a center of luxury and wealth. Nebuchadnezzar (604–562 B.C.), the most famous king of the Chaldean dynasty, built lavish temples to the gods and also constructed the terraced roof garden known as the Hanging Gardens, which was considered one of the Seven Wonders of the ancient world.

There now appears a new people, the Iranians, another branch of the Indo-European family of languages. Two Iranian societies especially concern us: the Medes and the Persians. The Medes, living in the area of Media to the east of Mesopotamia, formed a coherent kingdom about 625

B.C., and they took part in the capture of Nineveh in 612 B.C. We know little of their society, because no written documents from Media have yet been found.

Their neighbors, the Persians, lived in the same general area and eventually subdued the Medes. Yet the Medes had enough prestige to be named first in official documents in which both Medes and Persians are mentioned. The Greeks, too, used *Medes* as the term embracing both Medes and Persians, and they called their two wars with the Persian empire the *Medic* wars.

THE PERSIAN EMPIRE

The Persians proceeded to form the largest, most efficient state down to their time. In fact, because of its territorial extent and complexity and the skill with which the Persian kings ruled their domain, many historians would call the Persian state the first "empire," as opposed to a large kingdom.

Map 1.4 FIVE KINGDOMS OF THE NEAR EAST, DOWN TO ABOUT 500 B.C.

Cyrus The founder of the Persian Empire was King Cyrus (559–530 B.C.). His actions show him as a determined imperialist, and his first conquest was his victory over Media, to the north, in 550. A few years later Cyrus led his forces into western Asia Minor and conquered the kingdom of Lydia. This advance brought the Persian Empire westward as far as the Aegean Sea, which separates Asia Minor from Greece, and set the stage for a direct clash between the vast empire of the Near East and the new culture of the Greeks; but this clash was not to come for another two generations.

To secure the southern flank of his growing empire, Cyrus led his forces against the Chaldeans and captured Babylon. The inhabitants evidently welcomed him, for they offered little resistance. Their judgment was sound; Cyrus treated the city with moderation, not sacking it as an Assyrian conqueror might have done. In fact, his administration was marked by a notable toleration of the customs and religions of the people he brought under his control.

Cyrus' successor, Cambyses (530–522 B.C.), made the third conquest that completed the Persian Empire: He conquered Egypt in 525 B.C., and the rich valley of the Nile remained under Persian rule until Alexander the Great captured it in 332 B.C.

▷ **Two panels on a staircase of the great reception hall at the Persian capital, Persepolis. In each panel an official leads a messenger whose followers bear tribute for the king of Persia.**

The Persian kings ruled their immense empire from several capital cities, of which Susa and Persepolis were the most famous. The king was the absolute and supreme ruler. His word was law, and he was surrounded with pomp and ceremony; his isolation from his subjects contributed to his reputation for awesome power, which went far to establish the aura of magnificence that has colored monarchy in the Roman Empire and the subsequent kingdoms of Europe.

Darius The most skillful administrator of the Persian Empire was Darius (521–486 B.C.). He left behind a superb monument—a proud summary of his reign written, like the Rosetta Stone from Egypt, in three languages (Old Persian, Akkadian, Elamite). Carved under a relief showing Darius and some of his captives, this text survives high on the face of a rock at Bisitun in Iran. In a series of paragraphs, each beginning "Saith Darius the king," it records his conquests, including that of Babylon, and the defeat and mutilation of his enemies. He also clarifies that he is the only source of law: "As was said by me, thus it was done." The tone and physical setting of this grandiose monument confirm the lofty position of the king. A later inscription on his tomb also proclaimed his devotion to justice: "I am a friend to right, not to wrong. Whoever does harm, I punish him according to the damage he has done." This statement reminds us of the insistence on restitution built into Hammurabi's code and shows how some Near Eastern kings, for all their unchallengeable power, tried to earn a reputation for fairness.

Darius divided his empire into some 20 satrapies, or provinces, each ruled by a satrap ("protector of the realm"). The king, naturally, was the supreme glory of the state, but the satraps had a high degree of independence; they

▶ Part of the Bisitun inscription in Iran, showing King Darius of Persia (530–486 B.C.) receiving the submission of rebels. Carved in three languages, this inscription provided the key to the decipherment of cuneiform writing.

dispensed justice, designed foreign policy, and were in charge of finance. Each satrap, for example, was responsible for collecting an assigned amount of revenue from his province. This system of delegating authority became the model for the Roman Empire when it expanded Rome's domain outside Italy.

The Greek historian Herodotus, writing in the fifth century B.C., mentions with admiration the Persian system of roads begun by Cyrus and perfected by Darius. A great highway ran across the empire from the capital at Susa westward to Sardis in Lydia, a distance of more than 1000 miles. The first long highway built anywhere, this road served trade and commerce and also bound the far-flung empire together.

Zoroastrianism The Persian king was never considered divine, but he often served as a priest and claimed to have received his authority from the god of the Persians, Ahura Mazda. The prophet who formed the Persian faith was Zoroaster (also known as Zarathustra). The date of his life and work cannot yet be proved, but a number of historians think he lived about 600 B.C. or soon after. He, too, was not considered divine; rather, he taught that the supreme god, Ahura Mazda, had created the world and directed the heavens and seasons. Around Ahura Mazda gathered good deities such as "Truth," "Righteous Thought," "Devotion," and so on, whose ideals humanity should follow. But Ahura was opposed by Ahriman, a wholly evil spirit—a devil, in fact. Thus Zoroaster taught a dualist religion, although obviously only Ahura is the true god whose message we are to hear. Zoroaster further proclaimed that, after thousands of years, a day of judgment will see the final triumph of good, and those who have followed Ahura will gain paradise and the rest will suffer in the realm of endless night. Thus Zoroaster preached ethical demands on a high level.

Zoroaster also rejected such ancient practices as the sacrifice of animals. The faith he taught demanded recognition of the one good spirit and a life of devotion to Ahura's ideals. His noble thought far outlasted the Persian Empire and resembles doctrines of Christianity, which also has a bad spirit opposed to God, a final judgment, and the possibility of immortality.

The mighty legacy of the ancient Near Eastern societies—including the art of writing, monumental architecture, the development of pottery and weaponry—also influenced the development of their neighbors, the Greeks. They further learned from the older societies the use of coinage, the measurement of time, and forms of diplomacy. The Greeks added to this heritage a radical individualism and a passion for logical argument; their policies and institutions have influenced our own, even more directly and profoundly, as will be apparent when we turn to the Mediterranean and the peoples of Greece.

Recommended Reading

▼

Sources

Lichtheim, Miriam. *Ancient Egyptian Literature: A Book of Readings* (3 vols.). 1973–1980. Excellent gathering of original sources in modern translation.

Pritchard, James B. (ed.). *Ancient Near Eastern Texts Relating to the Old Testament.* 1969. A collection of translations from cuneiform and hieroglyphic texts, with brief commentaries, by eminent scholars.

Studies

Adams, Robert M. *The Evolution of Urban Society*, 1971. Contains chapters on both early Iraq and Mexico.

Albright, William Foxwell. *The Biblical Period from Abraham to Ezra.* 1963. A brief history of Israel by a giant in the field.

The Cambridge Ancient History (3rd ed.) (12 vols.). 1970– in progress. The standard history of the ancient world; chapters by numerous scholars, with wide-ranging bibliographies.

Childe, V. Gordon. *What Happened in History.* 1985. Compact but profound analysis of history by a great anthropologist.

Cook, J. M. *The Persian Empire.* 1983.

Dahlberg, Frances (ed.). *Woman, the Gatherer.* 1981. Studies of the economic and social roles of women in the earliest societies.

Eliade, M. (ed.). *Religions of Antiquity.* 1989. Essays on the various religions of this long epoch.

Emery, Walter B. *Archaic Egypt.* 1961.

Frankfort, Henri. *The Birth of Civilization in the Near East.* 1951. A comparison of early Mesopotamian and Egyptian history.

Frye, Richard N. *The Heritage of Persia.* 1963.

Gardiner, Sir Alan. *Egypt of the Pharaohs.* 1966. A detailed political narrative.

Gurney, O. R. *The Hittites.* 1954. Old but still reliable.

Hallo, William W., and William K. Simpson. *The Ancient Near East: A History.* 1971. American textbook survey of Mesopotamian-Egyptian history.

Kramer, Samuel Noah. *The Sumerians: Their History, Culture, and Character.* 1963. Full portrait of Sumerian society by a leading authority.

Laessøe, Jørgen. *People of Ancient Assyria: Their Inscriptions and Correspondence.* 1963.

Leakey, Richard. *The Making of Mankind.* 1981. By the son of Sir Louis Leakey, presenting a view different from that of the author's father.

Loewe, Raphael. *The Position of Women in Judaism.* 1966. Brief but exact discussion of the role of homemaker in Judaism.

Michalowski, Kazimierz. *Art of Ancient Egypt.* 1969.

Oates, Joan. *Babylon.* 1979. Survey for the nonspecialist.

Olmstead, A. T. *History of the Persian Empire.* 1948.

Price, T. D., and J. A. Brown. *Prehistoric Hunter-Gatherers.* 1985. Earliest techniques of survival and growth of villages.

Roux, Georges. *Ancient Iraq.* 1966. Detailed but readable survey of ancient Mesopotamia.

Saggs, W. F. *The Greatness That Was Babylon.* 1962. Mesopotamian history and society surveyed.

Sahlin, Marshall. *Stone Age Economics.* 1972. The life of earliest humanity.

Skaggs, H. W. F. *Everyday Life in Babylonia and Assyria* (rev. ed.). 1987.

Trigger, B. G. (ed.). *Ancient Egypt: A Social History.* 1983. Chapters by several historians giving modern treatment.

Wilson, John A. *The Culture of Ancient Egypt.* 1956. Subtle treatment of cultural history of Egypt; superb for the history of ideas. A classic.

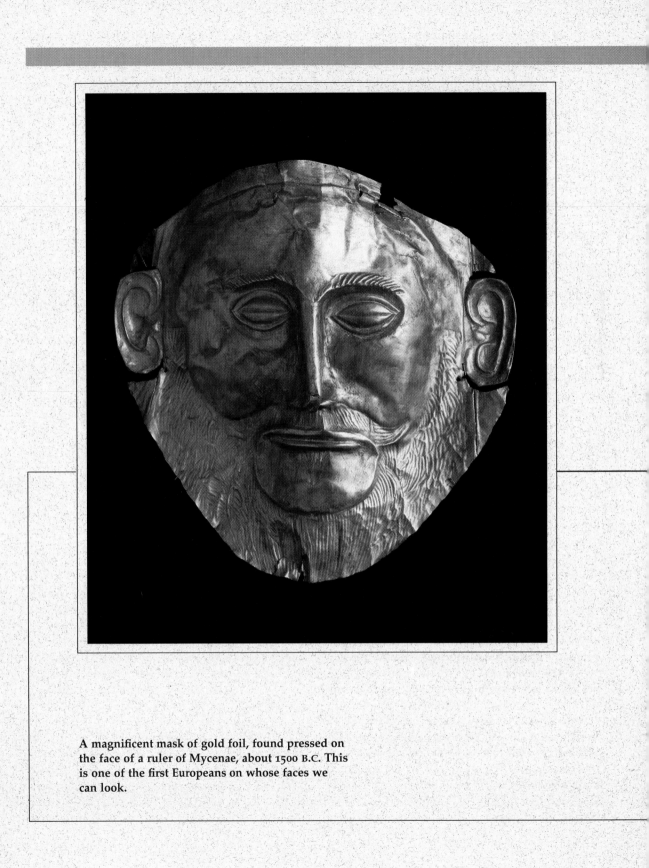

A magnificent mask of gold foil, found pressed on the face of a ruler of Mycenae, about 1500 B.C. This is one of the first Europeans on whose faces we can look.

CHAPTER TWO

THE FORMING OF GREEK CIVILIZATION

GREEK civilization has been praised by our own more than any other for its creativity, its artistic genius, its intellectual daring. It created forms of thought and expression that have been imitated ever since: philosophy, drama, epic poetry, and history. This civilization honored personal heroism and independence, and its literature is the oldest one with individually known writers.

The Greeks developed a civic culture that broke with the Near Eastern traditions of monarchy. They lived in independent communities, or city-states, in which the most common model seems to have been domination by an upper class of some kind, but even this structure extended power beyond the sole ruler of older civilizations. Citizens of Greek city-states took pride in their temples, their civic traditions, the individual qualities of their own state, their participation in its life. In Athens the government had many features that resembled those of modern democracy. Sparta, Athens' leading rival, chose by contrast a severe, authoritarian form of rule and was the only Greek state to retain a monarchy after it had vanished in all others.

These two states led Greece into its most brilliant victories in war, the defeat of forces twice sent from the vast Persian Empire. They also became the nuclei of alliances that followed this triumph with tragedy, as their rivalry escalated into the long, destructive Peloponnesian War.

I. Crete and Early Greece (Ca. 3000–1100 B.C.)

The first important society in the Greek world developed on the island of Crete, just south of the Aegean Sea. The people of Crete were not Greek: they probably came from western Asia Minor well before 3000 B.C. But their influence on Greek culture was so significant that the history of Greece must begin with Crete.

CRETAN CIVILIZATION

Our major source of knowledge of Cretan civilization is archaeological evidence found in a magnificent villa at Knossos known as the Palace of Minos; the civilization of Crete is thus often called *Minoan*. Greek legend told of the Minotaur (or "Minos-bull"), a monster that lived in a labyrinth (surely a memory of the complex palace) and devoured girls and boys sent to it as tribute. The myth suggests that Greeks had at least a dim recollection of a powerful ruler called Minos, and the historian Thucydides tells of Minos, the powerful king who "cleared the seas of piracy, captured islands, and placed his sons in control over them." Other palaces on Crete exist, but none is so elegant as that at Knossos.

The Palace of Minos was built over a period of about 700 years from 2200 to about 1500 B.C. It was an extensive structure, with a vast eastern courtyard, an impressive grand staircase leading to upper rooms, and many wings and storage chambers. A throne room for the king was added at a late stage of the building, and the throne still survives. The palace even had a plumbing system with water running through fitted clay pipes.

The walls of the palace at Knossos were decorated with frescoes showing the Cretans' delight in nature. Gardens, birds, and animals are vividly portrayed, and one spectacular painting shows young men vaulting over the horns of a bull. The absence of walls around the palace suggests that Minoan civilization was essentially peaceful.

Knossos was clearly the wealthiest of the Cretan cities, and the king was served by an efficient bureaucracy. So far as we can distinguish the roles of the sexes, the rulers were probably men;

▶ This marble statuette of a goddess is a product of the Cycladic culture (so named from its home in the Cyclades Islands of Greece), which preceded the coming of the Greeks. Carved circa 2800 to 2300 B.C., it represents the early emphasis on female rather than male gods. Neolithic art preferred abstraction to Paleolithic realism and points the way toward later abstract thought. In our own century artists like Brancusi and Mondrian have returned to this type of noble, elegant simplicity.

one wall painting shows a man, often identified as a priest or king, leading an animal to some kind of ceremony. Women had a significant place in this society, for not only were jeweled ladies in elegant gowns portrayed in Minoan wall paintings but they were clearly the object of worship as deities. Statuettes of women have been found, probably goddesses of nature holding snakes in their hands.

Much of the wealth of Crete came from trade, and Cretan pottery has been found far and wide

throughout the Mediterranean world. There are about a dozen sites in the Greek world, probably trading posts, called *Minoa*, obviously named after Minos. But we cannot speak of a true Cretan empire with political control of wide areas like the dominions of Assyria or Persia, for Crete lacked the population to conquer and permanently subdue overseas possessions.

CRETE AND THE GREEKS

Yet Minoan civilization influenced the Greek world as it reached its height between 1550 and 1400 B.C. Greek art of this period shows Minoan

Map 2.1 EARLY GREECE DURING THE BRONZE AGE, CA. 2000–1100 B.C.

▶ A wall painting from Knossos, showing athletes vaulting over the horns of a bull. The figure at the right will catch the leaper in the center. The location of this painting in the palace suggests that the sport was a kind of ceremony. The bull may represent raw nature being tamed in this agricultural society.

▶ A "marine style" vase by a Greek artist, about 1500 B.C., clearly imitating Cretan models. Sea creatures were often used in Minoan pottery in a free, naturalistic style.

influence, and at least two Greek goddesses, Athena and Artemis, were probably adopted from Crete. The Minoans also had interchange with the Greeks through writing. Clay tablets have been found at Knossos in two similar scripts, called Linear A and Linear B. Both scripts are syllabic: Each symbol represents a sound, such as *ko*, rather than a letter of an alphabet. The language written in Linear A, the older script (used circa 1700–1500 B.C.), has not yet been deciphered; but Linear B, the younger of the two scripts (used circa 1450–1400 B.C.), has been deciphered as an early form of Greek. The tablets contain inventories, rosters, and records of all kinds, listing foot stools, helmets, vessels, seeds, and the like.

That these Linear B tablets were written in a form of Greek is a startling discovery, for it shows that the Greeks, who at this time had not developed writing of their own, learned to write their

▶ **A large vase from Crete in the Late Minoan II style, circa 1450 to 1400 B.C., when Cretan art came under Greek influence and became more disciplined and geometric. Note the double ax motif, found in the palace at Knossos.**

language in a Cretan script. Their presence on Crete during this period suggests that Greeks had come to dominate Knossos, perhaps through outright military seizure. Probably the only Greek community that could have done this was that of Mycenae.

About 1380 B.C., a catastrophe, whose causes are uncertain, engulfed Knossos and other Cretan cities; several of the stately palaces were burned or destroyed. A massive earthquake shook the island at this time, but the disaster may also have been connected with a quarrel or rebellion against Greek rule.

MYCENAEAN CIVILIZATION
(Ca. 1600–1100 B.C.)

The Greeks, the people who spoke and imported the Greek language, began to settle in Greece about 2000 B.C., arriving from the Balkan areas to the north; they were members of the general family of Indo-Europeans who had started to migrate into Europe at an uncertain time, perhaps around 5000 B.C. (see Chapter 1, p. 18). They called themselves Hellenes and their country Hellas; the Greeks still use these names, and only in West European languages are they called *Greeks*, a name given them by the Romans.

The City of Mycenae Geography divides Greece into many small valleys and forced the Greeks to develop independent communities with kings,

Map 2.2 MYCENAE
The most impressive city in Bronze Age Greece, Mycenae, was first settled on its citadel. As the population expanded, a lower town developed, also surrounded by a wall. Outside the walls were terraced agricultural plots.

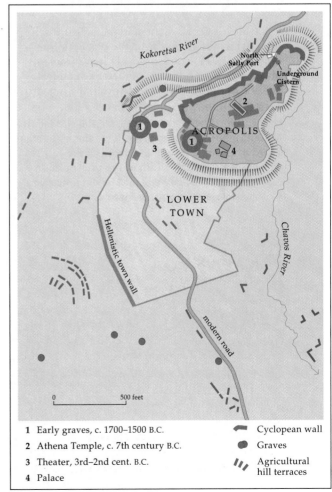

1 Early graves, c. 1700–1500 B.C.
2 Athena Temple, c. 7th century B.C.
3 Theater, 3rd–2nd cent. B.C.
4 Palace

Cyclopean wall
Graves
Agricultural hill terraces

▶ **A tablet in Greek, written in the Linear B script, from Pylos, about 1200 B.C. Note that each line contains a brief listing, probably items from an inventory, followed by a number. Such tablets reveal a complex bureaucracy within the monarchy at Pylos during the Mycenaean Age.**

▶ **The "Lion Gate," the entrance to the citadel at Mycenae, built about 1350 B.C. Two lionesses stand guard over the city; note the depth of the entranceway and the width of the threshold. In early civilizations, power could be demonstrated by the moving of enormous stones.**

but without the direction—or oppression—of a central ruler like a pharaoh. By about 1600 B.C., the Greeks had created wealthy, fortified cities, among which the most prominent was Mycenae, built on a huge citadel in the Peloponnese. The years from 1600 to 1100 B.C. are therefore often called the Mycenaean Age.

Two sets of graves found at Mycenae have given us a glimpse of the wealth and artistic accomplishments of this city. They contained such stunning luxuries as masks of gold foil that were pressed on the faces of the dead and a complete burial suit of gold foil wrapped around a child, as well as swords, knives, and hundreds of gold ornaments. Tablets written in Linear B, attesting a palace bureaucracy, have been found at Mycenae and other sites of the Mycenaean Age.

The Zenith of Mycenaean Power and the Trojan War Between 1400 and 1200 B.C., Mycenae reached the height of its prosperity and created the most imposing monuments in Bronze Age Greece. A mighty decorated gateway with a relief of lions carved over it, known as the Lion Gate, formed the entrance to the walled city. Some rulers were buried in immense vaulted tombs in beehive shape, of which the grandest and best preserved is the so-called Treasury of Atreus, named by modern archaeologists for the legendary father of King Agamemnon; but we do not really know which ruler or rulers were buried here.

Each city of the Mycenaean Age was probably independent under its own king. The only time these cities appear to have united was during the war against Troy, a rich city of obscure ethnic origin in Asia Minor near the Dardanelles. The evident wealth of the city must have offered a tempting prey to pirates and looters. Such was probably the real cause of the war against Troy, but Greek legend explained the war by the romantic story in Homer's *Iliad* about the seduction by a Trojan prince of Helen, the wife of a king of Sparta. Since Homer is the only source recording the Greek attack on Troy, we must proceed with caution if we are to believe that there really was such a war, for Homer was a poet, not a historian. Nevertheless, excavations at Troy have revealed several layers of building, among which one layer, called Troy VII A, was destroyed by some invaders about 1250 B.C., and this may well be the Troy that Homer says the Greeks attacked.

The Decline of Mycenae and the Dorian Invasion

The war against Troy was the last great feat of the Mycenaean Age. Between about 1300 and 1200 B.C., marauders called sea-peoples made trade by sea so dangerous that the export of Mycenaean pottery virtually ended. The identity of these warriors is still uncertain, but their homes

▶ A gold cup from Vaphio, near Mycenae, about 1400 B.C. The man in the center is taming an animal by tying its leg; the animals to the left are already tamed and nestle up against each other.

▶ The most spectacular tomb at Mycenae, the "Treasury of Atreus," built in beehive style about 1300 B.C. The long entrance alley and the tomb itself are almost perfectly preserved.

▶ **The "warrior vase" from Mycenae, showing armed warriors departing for battle; at the left, a woman waves her farewell.**

were probably somewhere in Asia Minor. Even more significant to the collapse of the Mycenaean Age was a series of attacks by land, lasting roughly from 1200 to 1100 B.C.; around 1100 B.C., Mycenae itself was overrun, though not obliterated.

This invasion by land was probably the work of a later wave of Greeks who spoke the Doric dialect of the Greek language. Between about 1200 and 1100 B.C. these Greeks made their way southward from central Greece and settled mainly in the Peloponnese, especially in Corinth and Sparta, which became the most important cities where Doric Greek was spoken.

The period 1100–800 B.C. is called the Dark Age of Greece, because throughout the area there was sharp cultural decline: less elegant pottery, simple burials, no massive buildings. Even the art of writing in Linear B vanished. But the decline was not a total collapse. Farming, weaving, making pottery, the Greek language in spoken form, and other skills survived.

The invasions of the twelfth century B.C., in which the Dorian Greeks played at least a part, ended forever the domination of the palace-centered kings. In a sense, the shattering of the monarchic pattern of the Mycenaean Age can be viewed as liberating. If these monarchies had survived, Greece might have developed as Egypt and Asia Minor did, with centralized rule and

priests who interpreted religion in ways that justified kingship. Self-government in Greece might have been delayed for centuries, if it appeared at all.

II. The Greek Renaissance (Ca. 800–600 B.C.)

With the passing of time, Greek culture revived after the Dark Age and entered a period of extraordinary artistic and intellectual vitality. Poetry and art broke new frontiers; the economy expanded, partly through overseas colonization; and the polis, or independent city-state, emerged. Historians borrow a term from a later period and call this movement the Greek Renaissance.

GREEK RELIGION

The Greeks brought with them, during their earliest immigration around 2000 B.C., the worship of some of their gods, above all Zeus, the sky god, whose name is Indo-European; his counterparts are Dyaus in early India, Jupiter in Rome, and Tiu in Norse myths. Other gods were adapted from other regions: Apollo, the sun god, from western Asia Minor; Aphrodite, goddess of love, from Cyprus; Athena, goddess of wisdom, and Artemis, the hunter goddess, from Crete. At a much later stage, Greeks adopted some Egyptian gods (Isis, for example), but there is no solid evidence for the belief, recently put forth, that they received all or even many of their gods from Egypt (*see box*, p. 39).[1]

Greek gods are not the remote, transcendent deities of Mesopotamian peoples. They intervene in human affairs, they assist their favorites, and they are anthropomorphic: That is, they are human-like super-beings, differing from people only in their physical perfection and immortality. Even Mount Olympus, their legendary home, is an actual mountain in northern Greece.

---

[1]Herodotus, the first historian, writing around 450 B.C., does say this, but he was perhaps so impressed with the antiquity of Egypt, and with the resemblance of gods in the two cultures, that he drew this false conclusion.

The Greeks never developed a code of behavior prescribed by religion, as Israel did. Some acts, such as killing a parent or leaving a relative unburied, were obviously wrong, as were offenses against generally accepted conduct, such as betraying a friend. If people became too arrogant, Nemesis, an avenging force, would sweep down on them and destroy them. But, on the whole, Greek religion had no spirit of evil and scarcely any demanding spirits of good.

The gods were viewed as generally benevolent, but they had to be appeased through offerings and suitable ceremonies. The most remarkable feature of Greek religion—especially in contrast to monarchies of Egypt and Asia Minor—was that the Greeks had priests and priestesses for their temples and smaller shrines, but no priestly class that intervened in politics. To put it simply, the Greeks had no church. Why the Greeks felt they could worship without succumb-

The Debate over Black Athena

Martin Bernal, in **Black Athena***, has set forth the challenging thesis that Greek civilization, and even much of the Greek language, rest on cultural borrowings from Egypt and the Levant from about 2100 to about 1100 B.C. Bernal also holds that anti-Semitic nineteenth-century scholars deliberately concealed the contribution of Egypt and the Phoenicians. This excerpt, in Bernal's words, summarizes his thesis.*

"The scheme I propose is that while there seems to have been more or less continuous Near Eastern influence on the Aegean over this millennium, its intensity varied considerably at different periods. The first "peak" of which we have any trace was the 21st century. It was then that Egypt recovered from the breakdown of the First Intermediate Period, and the so-called Middle Kingdom was established by the new 11th Dynasty. This not only reunited Egypt but attacked the Levant and is known from archaeological evidence to have had wide-ranging contacts further afield, certainly including Crete and possibly the mainland. [. . .] It is generally agreed that the Greek language was formed during the 17th and 16th centuries B.C. Its Indo-European structure and basic lexicon are combined with a non-Indo-European vocabulary of sophistication. I am convinced that much of the latter can be plausibly derived from Egyptian and West Semitic. This would fit very well with a long period of domination by Egypto-Semitic conquerors. [. . .] [I] discuss some of the equations made between specific Greek and Egyptian divinities and rituals, and the general belief that the Egyptian were the earlier forms and that Egyptian religion was the original one."

Martin Bernal, *Black Athena*, vol. 1, 1987, pp. 17–23 (abridged).

Mary Lefkowitz, a professor of classics at Wellesley College, commented thus on Bernal's work.

"Bernal relies too much on Herodotus's treatment of Egypt. [. . .] [He] cites Herodotus on the Egyptian origin of Greek religion and ritual, discussing the many rough but intriguing parallels that can be drawn between Egyptian and Greek myth and cult. Again, none of these seems in itself conclusive. Nor does Bernal show how the Greeks came to borrow their "philosophy" as well. He does not discuss the implications of Herodotus's very explicit statement that Egyptian habits and customs in his own time were totally different from those of the Greeks. [. . .] [W]ith the data that he has assembled, he may have sharpened the quality of the debate about the origins of Greek culture. But I do not think that he has brought about any dramatic change in the way that the evidence about Greek origins should be interpreted."

The New Republic, Feb. 10, 1992.

ing to the direction of a priestly hierarchy we do not know, but the reason must be connected to the independence of the 600 to 700 individual Greek city-states. There was no king, pharaoh, or emperor who had the power to install such a system. Religion and civic life were intertwined, and the beautiful temples all over Greece were built by decision of the governing power, but not at the orders of priests or viziers.

Most gods were common to all Greeks, and their worship is a sign of a Panhellenic culture that arose during the Greek Renaissance. Each locality, while recognizing the several gods generally, could have its own patron. For example, various gods had temples in Athens, but Athena was accepted as the protecting goddess of the city. Zeus, though worshiped everywhere as the chief god, was the main local deity at Olympia. Apollo was the chief god at Delphi and supposedly inspired the oracle, a woman who gave guidance to inquirers after payment of a fee. The Greek faith in this oracle is another sign of growing common identity among the Greeks. Though never more than a small village, Delphi was adorned with treasure houses built by the various cities to house the gifts they dedicated to Apollo when seeking his guidance.

PUBLIC GAMES

Another sign of a growing community among Greeks is the founding of Panhellenic athletic games in 776 B.C. (This date is commonly agreed to mark the beginning of the "historic" period of Greek civilization: broadly speaking, the period when writing began and we begin to have fairly solid dates for events.)

The first games were held at Olympia, in the Peloponnese, and were dedicated to Zeus; thus from the beginning the games were connected with religion and demonstrate that religious ceremonies in a community could embrace several different practices. But they were also a way of celebrating human perfection and heroism, an aspiration typical of Greek civilization. Originally, the Olympics featured only foot races and wrestling, but gradually they came to include horse and chariot races, boxing, javelin throwing, and other events. Only the winner gained a prize, an

olive wreath, but victory also brought rich awards from one's city and lifelong glory. In imitation of the Olympics, other cities founded games, and there was eventually one set of Panhellenic games each year, as well as games in many individual cities.

COLONIZATION (Ca. 750–550 B.C.)

The growth in population during the Dark Age finally forced the Greek cities into foreign colonization: In effect, the mainland Greeks of the eighth and seventh centuries exported their excess population. They colonized vigorously from about 750 to about 550 B.C., and by the end of this period there were Greeks spread throughout the Mediterranean. Wherever they went, they settled on the edge of the sea, never far inland. Colonies, when founded, were wholly independent cities, and among them are some of the great ports of modern Europe: Byzantium (today Istanbul in Turkey), Naples, and Syracuse.

This expansion overseas led to a revival of trade after the stagnation of the Dark Age. The Greeks now had access to a greater food supply, above all grain from southern Italy and the Black Sea. Trade brought prosperity to many Greek cities and, even more important, spread Greek civilization throughout the Mediterranean.

THE ALPHABET

The Greeks apparently lapsed into illiteracy when the Linear B script vanished, soon after 1200 B.C.; but by about 750 B.C. their trade had brought them to Palestine and into contact with the Phoenicians, who used a Semitic script called the alphabet. This alphabet had only some 30 characters, but many different sounds could be represented by these few symbols; and their precision and versatility made this script far easier to master than pictorial cuneiform scripts (see p. 7). Fortunately for the future of European literacy, the Greeks adopted the alphabet, changing some of the characters, which were all consonants, to vowels.

Two versions of the Greek alphabet developed. A Western version made its way to Cumae, a Greek town in Italy, and then to the Etruscans, the people in Italy who then controlled Rome. They passed it on to the Romans, who turned it into the alphabet used throughout the Western world. The Eastern version became the standard alphabet in Greece itself. Much later, many letters of the Greek alphabet were used in the Cyrillic script of Russian and other Slavic languages. Thus large parts of the world today use one or another derivative of the Phoenician alphabet in the form it received from the Greeks.

In Greece, the alphabet was first used in public for the proclamation of laws, which ordinary people could read and grasp; information could circulate more rapidly, with dynamic consequences for political life. Later, from about 500 b.c., especially in Athens, people began to publish every kind of public decision and record on prominently displayed stone inscriptions; these were not simply boastful monuments to a king's victories but were documents enabling citizens to understand and control the activities of the state.

ARCHAIC LITERATURE

The Homeric Epics The greatest literary creations of the Greek Renaissance are the epic poems about the glorious heroes who had supposedly led the war against Troy. The supreme achievements of this tradition are two epics ascribed to Homer, the *Iliad* and the *Odyssey*. The *Iliad* is a portrait—in rolling, majestic verse—of a warrior aristocracy in which greatness in combat is the highest virtue. Heroism is exemplified by the proud warrior Achilles, who withdraws from the siege of Troy when his concubine is taken from him; he then allows his friend Patroclus to wear his armor in combat and, after Patroclus is killed by the Trojan hero Hector, avenges his death by killing Hector in a scene of savage power. The gods take sides with their favorites, but the *Iliad* is essentially a poem about men and women in conflict.

The *Odyssey*, by contrast, celebrates cleverness rather than sheer military prowess. Its hero Odysseus makes his way home after the Trojan War through dozens of adventures that test his skill and tenacity and enable Homer to explore human character and behavior in widely different situations. Eventually Odysseus reaches his home, the island of Ithaca, and drives off a band of suitors who are wooing his noble wife Penelope.

These epics were probably first recited at feasts by traveling bards, but over the years they became known to all through presentation at festivals and finally through study in schools. We have no idea who wrote these great epics. Neither ancient Greeks nor modern scholars have been able to prove whether a person named Homer really lived, whether the epics are the work of one writer or several, and whether they were originally composed orally or in writing. The poems are usually dated to the period around 750 b.c., just when the Greeks were learning to write, and it would be surprising if anyone immediately used this new technique to compose such long sagas; the more probable view is that the poems were composed orally, recited for generations, and written down later. In any case, Homer remained the chief inspiration for Greek literature in all periods.

Hesiod Homer never speaks in the first person (except to invoke the Muses to inspire him), but his successors began to express their own thoughts and feelings and to create a literature of intensely frank self-expression. The first major post-Homeric poet was Hesiod of Boeotia (in central Greece), whose *Works and Days* dates from around 700 b.c. Hesiod was a farmer, and his poem is a farmer's almanac, celebrating agriculture and, in the "days" of the title, telling the reader when to plow and plant. The poem also contains a bitter attack on the injustice of aristocratic landlords ("gift-devouring rulers") toward their peasants.

In his other surviving poem, the *Theogony*, Hesiod recounts the genealogy of the various gods. He narrates frankly the bloody rise of Zeus to supreme divine power. The god Cronus had castrated his own father, Uranus, to gain rule over the world and had killed his own children except Zeus, who escaped. After a long struggle Zeus wins the final battle and becomes supreme. This conflict resembles similar sagas in Hittite literature, in which gods kill and mutilate one another. But the difference in the Greek conception is that the supremacy of Zeus is seen not just as another act of vengeance but as a fulfillment of the proper divine order.

Lyric Poets   About 650 B.C. Greek poets began to experiment with a variety of more personal themes. Archilochus of Paros has left us brief poems of brilliant vigor and audacity, written as bursts of self-revelation, a typically Greek kind of literature that has no predecessors in the ancient Eastern cultures. He was a traveler, a man of action, and a mercenary soldier who fell in battle. He criticizes traditional forms of chivalry and can be cynical about supposed aristocratic conduct. He boasts, for example, that he once threw away his shield to save his life and laughs off this unmilitary act: "Never mind, I'll buy another one just as good." His love poetry can be astonishingly frank. In one poem he tenderly yet passionately describes his seduction of a girl, including his own sexual fulfillment.

The most intense and subtle poet of the age was Sappho of the island of Lesbos (about 600 B.C.). We have only one complete poem from her pen and many short quotations (*see box*). She was evidently a widow who maintained a school on Lesbos where young girls learned music, dance, poetry, and elegant dress as preparation for marriage. Sappho sings of the beauty of the girls and the pleasures of love and apparently shared physical love with some of them. In its exact evocation of emotion, its inventive images, its individuality, her poetry reveals a writer of the highest originality and power.

Sappho's Love Poetry

The poetry of Sappho of Lesbos is amazingly sensitive and original. This short excerpt from a poem frankly acknowledges her need for love.

"You have come, and done,
And I was waiting for you
To temper the red desire
That burned my heart."

The following is addressed to a young woman.

"He seems to be a god, that man
Facing you, who leans to be close,
Smiles, and, alert and glad, listens
To your mellow voice.

"And quickens in love at your laughter
That stings my breasts, jolts my heart
If I dare the shock of a glance.
I cannot speak,

"My tongue sticks to my dry mouth,
Thin fire spreads beneath my skin,
My eyes cannot see and my aching ears
Roar in their labyrinths.

"Chill sweat slides down my body,
I shake, I turn greener than grass,
I am neither living nor dead and cry
From the narrow between.

"But endure, even this grief of love."

Translations by Guy Davenport, *Archilochus, Sappho, Alkman*, Berkeley-Los Angeles-London, 1980.

III. The Polis

ORGANIZATION AND GOVERNMENT

For the social and political history of Western civilization, the most important event in the Greek Renaissance was the emergence, soon after 800 B.C., of the independent city-state, the *polis* (plural, *poleis*). Physically, the polis had a central inhabited area (the *astu*), often surrounding a citadel called the *acropolis* ("high city"). Over time, the acropolis came to be reserved for temples, shrines, treasuries, and other official buildings. Within the astu, the nucleus of the city, the people dwelt in closely packed houses, each normally built on more than one level, without internal staircases but with the rooms opening to a courtyard. A wall normally surrounded the astu; outside it, but still part of the polis, were suburbs and fields.

Greek cities usually had a large open space, the *agora*, that served as a main public square and civic center. Although used as a public market, the agora was always a sacred place and, like the acropolis, it housed temples and official buildings. In Athens, the agora was the site of trials, of buildings containing laws and other documents, and of many free-standing inscriptions on marble recording further public business.

The polis was a community of both male and female citizens. Male citizens could vote, pass on their property through wills, and generally participate in civic life; women did not vote but, like men, were protected against seizure and violence. Outside this group, and without civic rights, were slaves and resident aliens. No citizen of a polis had rights in any other polis; thus poleis were both cities and small states. When Greeks referred to the size of the citizen body, they reckoned only adult males, and by this measure the poleis ranged from a few hundred citizens to tens of thousands. Athens, the largest, had from 35,000 to 45,000; if to this we add the estimated number of women, children, resident foreigners, and slaves, the total population of Athens and the outlying villages, which were also part of the polis, was between 200,000 and 300,000 (the whole region is known as Attica). Sparta, by contrast, probably had an adult male population of no more than 12,000.

Despite considerable diversity within the 600 to 700 poleis, one development seems to have been common to all those that we know anything about, namely, the growth of some kind of self-government by the male citizens. The major social problem that Greek poleis solved was how to harness the energies of all the citizens in support of a city, rather than allow the rivalries inherent in such crowded quarters to erupt into civil war. In many poleis (Corinth, for example), oligarchy (a system in which wealthier citizens governed) held sway, while other cities, especially Athens, developed control of affairs by the masses.

Evolution toward self-government is rare in history, and the various forms of self-government that arose in Greece may, like the Greeks' lack of a priestly class, be the result of topography and scale. In a small state, locked within a ring of hills, no monarch could long remain a remote, transcendent figure like those who ruled Eastern kingdoms. Homer attests that the Greeks of the Mycenaean era had kings, but by about 700 B.C. they had vanished—though we can seldom say precisely how—in nearly all poleis. Sparta, the most authoritarian Greek state, was an exception and retained a system with two kings, each descended from a royal family, ruling together. The Spartans apparently felt safer in a system where one king could act as a control over the other.

The wealthier classes—using the term loosely, we may call them aristocrats, but there was no hereditary nobility—must have governed, if Homer is to be believed, through assemblies that originated as the armed forces of the poleis. But as populations increased and armies came to include citizens outside the circle of the elite, the upper classes could no longer ignore the wishes of others. It is significant that the first Greek legal codes defining citizens' rights were published within the seventh century B.C.—evidence that the populace was no longer willing to accept direction from the wealthy.

Also in the seventh century we hear of the first popular leaders who united the masses and overturned the rule of the old aristocracy. These men installed themselves as "tyrants" (the Greek word *tyrannos* meant an autocrat who ruled without strict legal foundation, not necessarily a cruel oppressor). The tyrants, though certainly no sponsors of democracy, did help to undermine rule by the wealthy alone and in a way opened the path to self-government.

THE ECONOMY OF THE POLEIS
(Ca. 700–400 B.C.)

The poleis were sufficiently similar to allow a general picture of their economy. The basic activity was agriculture, but in many areas of Greece the soil is thin and rocky, not suited to raising grain or pasturing animals. A shortage of food was therefore a constant threat to economic stability. Some states, as we have seen, drained away part of their excess population through colonization and imported grain from areas on the fringe of the Greek world.

All Greek dwellings were modest, and sanitation was primitive, although the Athenians had a main drain under their central market. Grain, occasionally fish, were staples of the diet; meat was usually reserved for festival days. Breakfast, if taken at all, was a lump of bread dipped in olive oil, which also served as fuel for lamps and even as a kind of soap. Sugar was unknown; the only sweetening agent was honey. With few luxuries available, Greeks could subsist on small incomes. Fishing and farming were suspended in winter, so Greeks had considerable leisure time, which they spent mainly in public places, as is still true today.

The development of an economy based on coinage was slow. Greece did not begin to use coins until about 625 B.C., and even then they played little part in daily trade: The smallest coin was usually a drachma, said to have been at that time the price of a sheep. In the fifth century the use of coinage expanded rapidly. Taxation in poleis paid for the upkeep of walls, drains, roads, harbors, and the like, though Greeks had little grasp of the mechanics of public finance. There were no permanent military treasuries until the 300s B.C., a surprising fact since the cities were so often at war. Infantry soldiers had to arm themselves, but they were paid at the expense of the state. When large projects such as public buildings and maintenance of ships were planned, the expenses were assigned to citizens who were judged capable of bearing the cost.

The Roles of the Sexes In Greek society people found certain roles assigned to them according to their sex. Men were the rulers and leaders, and in no Greek state did women vote or hold offices with the exception of certain priesthoods. They were, however, citizens and could not be violated or sold into slavery.

Thus roughly half the citizens of Greek poleis must have been women, but to reconstruct their place in Greek society is not easy, mainly because nearly all our sources were written by men. Nor is there likely to have been a single view of women in Greek society, as we can see from our oldest source, the Homeric poems. In the *Iliad*, the story opens as Achilles and Agamemnon quarrel over a concubine who is nothing but a sexual slave, while the Trojan hero Hector honors and cherishes his wife Andromache; equally, in Homer's *Odyssey* Penelope, the wife of the absent Odysseus, is a model of wisdom and fidelity.

As we look from the idealized figures of Homer to the women of the polis, we see a much less benign attitude toward women. A woman was always under the control of her *kyrios*, or master—at first her father, then her husband, then her father again if she became divorced or widowed. Her father gave her in marriage with a dowry, normally at about age 15, to a man perhaps 10 to 20 years her senior. Xenophon describes the education of a young wife in obedience and household skills, and the picture is like the training of a young animal. Her main duty, apart from managing the household, was to provide a male heir in order to maintain the family's hold over its property. If the family had no male heir, the property came to a daughter, but she held it only temporarily. She must then be married to the nearest available male relative, thus preventing the property from passing from the family. Yet the duty of women to provide heirs did not cause Greeks to think of a woman as a mere breeding machine. On the contrary, the power, possessed only by women, to bear children seems to have made them objects not only to be cherished but also to be feared.

Since women could be transferred from one husband to another, Greeks were not sure about their fidelity, and adultery was a grave threat because it could bring outsiders into the family and threaten the preservation of property within the correct line. Such suspicions may partly account for some passages by Greek poets and philosophers where women are viewed as undisciplined, emotionally unstable, and sexually inexhaustible. To preserve a woman's fidelity, the door of the home was considered her proper frontier, but such restrictions were not possible for families without servants; yet even when women did go out, they were normally accompanied.

If we have rightly understood the threat that women could present to men, we may be near to understanding why women of Greek drama such as Clytemnestra, Antigone, and Medea are such powerful characters, far stronger and more dangerous than the men in their plays. Again, in myths the furies, who could drive people mad, were female, as was Ate, the spirit that brought punishing destruction; so too the three Fates who spun out the thread of life and cut it off at the end. Yet we must not expect perfect consistency where such emotions are at play. Many of the most revered deities are women: Athena, who was respected for her warlike nature and never had lovers in myth, was also the protecting goddess to the Athenians, who held her in affection.

Aphrodite, who could involve human beings in ruin through sexual passion, was treasured as the model of ideal beauty and was so portrayed in hundreds of statues.

Elegant single women might become paid companions at men's social affairs; the most famous of all, Aspasia, had a long affair with the statesman Pericles and bore him a son. Only these women could participate in the refined intellectual life of the city. Poorer women worked, for example, as seamstresses, nurses, sellers in the market, or prostitutes (these were normally slaves or foreigners).

Modern scholars warn that it is fruitless to wonder whether Greek men and women shared emotional love. The recommendation of Plutarch, that a man should sleep with his wife three times a month, suggests that love played only a modest part in marriage. On the other hand, gravestones from many poleis show the affection in which some women were held; typically, a woman is seated, members of her family stand nearby, and a son or her husband takes her hand in a quiet farewell.

Slavery   A great social-economic historian, M. I. Finley, once asked the challenging question: Was Greek civilization based on slave labor? It is undeniable that the presence of slaves gave Greeks freedom to pursue civic affairs. Many Greeks looked down on manual labor as beneath their dignity, and it was usually performed by poor citizens or slaves. The troubling institution of slavery was accepted by all ancient societies and was justified by philosophers like Aristotle, who asserted that nature had divided humanity into natural masters and natural slaves—the latter including all "barbarians," that is, non-Greeks. Nor did anyone in antiquity ever recommend abolishing slavery on the ground that it was morally wrong: The only criticism of it was the occasional warning to manage it efficiently. Greeks commonly obtained slaves through conquest of other territory, though kidnapping and even the sale of children added to recruitment. An ordinary slave might cost about 150 drachmas, roughly four months' pay for a laborer, but a highly skilled one could cost much more.

Industry was rarely more extensive than household craft, and Greece, unlike Rome, did not use gangs of slaves in agriculture; the only industries in which slaves worked in large numbers were mining and stone quarrying, where conditions were atrocious. These and domestic service were the only tasks always assigned to slaves. In a unique exception to this rule, Athens had a police force composed of slaves from Scythia. The Athenian writer Xenophon said, "A man buys a slave to have a companion at work." Potters, shoemakers, and stonecutters might have a slave or two, though a few larger workshops are known: One shield maker, for example, had 120 slaves.

The prejudice against manual labor, and the availability of slaves, may explain why slaves worked on the building of the Parthenon in Athens and were paid the same as free men—one drachma a day, about the same wage paid to soldiers and sailors—and it partly explains the lack of inventions among the Greeks that could have made industry more productive.

SPARTA AND ATHENS (Ca. 700–500 B.C.)

We know little about the internal workings of most poleis, and the two we know best, Sparta and Athens, were not typical; but their importance requires detailed discussion.

Sparta   Sparta, the most influential of the Dorian states in the Peloponnese, chose to solve its problem of overpopulation by conquering Messenia, the territory to its west, in a war usually dated 736 to 716 B.C. Only males of demonstrably pure Spartan descent could be full citizens, and they were each given an allotment of land to be worked for them by the Messenians, who were known as helots. They were public slaves, with no rights whatever, but differed from other slaves in Greece in that they could not be bought and sold. Spartan landowners spent their lives in constant military training in order to maintain control over the helots, who outnumbered them by about seven to one.

Around 650 B.C. the Messenians tried to rebel, but the uprising failed, and the Spartans responded by making their army more invincible and their state even more rigid. The new arrangements, attributed to a lawgiver named Lycurgus, date from about 600 B.C. The identity of

Map 2.3 ARCHAIC AND CLASSICAL GREECE, CA. 800–400 B.C.

Lycurgus was obscure even in antiquity, though such a man apparently lived around 800 B.C., and many historians believe that Spartan reformers of around 600 B.C. ascribed their system to him in order to give it the appearance of ancient authority.

In the Spartan regime, oligarchy, or the rule of a small number, was tempered with some measure of democracy. The public assembly included all males over 30, who elected a council of 28 elders over 60 to serve for life and to plan business

for the assembly. The assembly also chose five *ephors* ("overseers") each year; they received foreign delegates, summoned the assembly to meet, and in general acted as a check on the power of the kings. When proposals came before the assembly, it was limited to voting yes or no, without debate. As a further safeguard against too much popular control, the ephors and council could simply dismiss the assembly if, in their opinion, it made the wrong choice. Thus the limited democracy of Sparta yielded to its ultimate faith in oligarchy. To Greek political philosophers, Sparta was a superb example of a "mixed" constitution, in which the kings represented the element of monarchy, the council oligarchy, and the citizenry a kind of democracy.

For a time Sparta tried to dominate other Peloponnesian states by outright conquest. But by around 560 B.C. this policy had failed, and about 530 B.C. the Spartans sought strength through alliance rather than warfare by forming the Peloponnesian League with their neighbors. The league is one of the earliest examples of alliance in the Greek world and is a rare instance of the Greeks' transcending the normal exclusiveness of city-state politics. The Spartans led the league but did not wholly control it, and action required approval of the member states.

The Spartan male dedicated most of his life, from age 7 through 60, to soldiering. The warriors lived and trained together, and their discipline could be sadistic. As tests of their courage and resourcefulness, young men were taught to steal if necessary, to go without food and shelter, even at times to kill a helot.

Spartan women also had a life style that other Greeks found extraordinary. Again the military commitments of the state played a role in shaping social practices, for the girls trained in games in order to become physically strong mothers. Spartan men, living with one another, seldom visited their wives, and if a marriage was childless, a woman could bear a child by a man other than her husband. These customs were meant to ensure enough manpower for the army and to focus loyalty on the state, not on the individual family.

Spartans were cut off from the other Greeks by two mountain ranges, and they traded little with other people, even adopting an intrinsically worthless iron currency to maintain their isolation. They rarely traveled and were shielded from new ideas that might have inspired intellectual pursuits such as philosophy or historical writing. Though they did make fine pottery, at least until about 525 B.C., when the art declined, their military regime left little time for or interest in the arts. Thus the isolation of Sparta from other Greeks was both geographic and psychological, but it reflected the deliberate choice of the people.

Athens The city of Athens also had expansionist beginnings, extending its domain by about 700 B.C. to include the whole plain of Attica. It was a large polis with widespread trading interests,

▶ **An Attic kouros, or young man, in the "severe" style, about 510 B.C. The figure is one of ideal physical perfection, typical of the humanity-centered aesthetics of Greece.**

and its political currents were strong and turbulent. As the people experimented again and again with their constitution, their political history became the most varied of all the city-states of Greece.

Athens, like other states, once had kings; but the monarchy ended in 683 B.C. (we do not know exactly how), and the city was managed by three (later nine) archons, or administrators, elected annually by an assembly, in which all adult male citizens could vote. After their year in office, the nine archons moved permanently into a council called the Areopagus, which eventually numbered about 300 men. Since it comprised senior men with permanent membership, the Areopagus was probably more influential than the board of archons in setting public policy.

Our first information about a reform in Athens after the monarchy is dated around 621 B.C. when Draco, an otherwise unknown statesman, codified the law on homicide, apparently distinguishing between voluntary and involuntary homicide. This was a large step forward, for early societies often looked on any kind of homicide as defiling the community in the eyes of the gods. This was also another in the series of law codes that established a recognized basis for justice and did away with forcing citizens to rely on the dictates of tribal elders.

Solon and Political Reform   In the 500s B.C. Athens went through far-reaching social changes, the likes of which no Greek state had ever seen. As often happens in history, economic conditions demanded a social response. Down to about 600 B.C. the Athenian economy was trying to do the impossible, namely, feed the growing population of Attica from its own limited area; and this strategy caused a nearly desperate social and economic crisis. Some farmers had evidently borrowed food from others who were better off and had gone so deeply into debt in the form of grain that they had lost their own land and had even fallen into slavery by pledging their bodies as security for more food. Their frustration might have exploded into violent revolution had the Athenians not found a rational solution by giving (probably in the 570s) powers of arbitration to

Solon, who had been archon in 594 B.C.[2] He was a poet and statesman whose courageous, compassionate work has made him a towering figure in Greek history, indeed in the history of civilization.

Aware that the poor farmers could probably never repay their debts, Solon took the daring step of canceling all agricultural debts and forbade further borrowing against the body. At one stroke the enslaved men were free, but the land they had lost probably remained in the hands of its new owners, who were thus compensated for the cancellation of debt. This legislation left many families without land and made them seek work elsewhere, but the crucial thing was that Solon had prevented civil war. Such arbitration by a private citizen without an army to fight with is heretofore unknown in history.

Since an economic crisis had threatened the community and brought him to power, Solon determined to transform the economy of Athens. He decreed that no product from the soil could be exported except olive oil; by this means he forced the Athenians to cultivate olive trees, which they could grow more successfully than grain. He also changed the commercial weights used by the Athenians, making them the same as those more widely used in Greece, a reform that brought Athens into a wider circle of trade.

He now seized the opportunity to reform the Athenian state, with the aim of breaking the grip of the wealthy and those with eminent family backgrounds on public office. He therefore divided all Athenian citizens into four classes based on their income from farmland and allowed members of the two highest classes to hold office. The significance of this reform is that men could improve their status economically and thus achieve positions of leadership, regardless of their ancestry.

Solon also created a court of appeal, the Heliaea, somehow drawn from the people, but

---

[2] That Solon was archon in 594 B.C. is fairly certain, and most historians follow ancient sources in dating his reforms to this year as well. But the assumed linkage between his archonship and his reforms was probably only an inference drawn in antiquity, and there is good reason to think that the reforms took place in the 570s; see C. Hignett, *A History of the Athenian Constitution*, 1952, p. 316.

Map 2.4 CLASSICAL ATHENS, ABOUT 400 B.C.

our sources tell us little of how it worked. His chief contribution was to see the common people as a group with grievances and to take bold steps to help them. He thus pointed the state toward eventual democracy, but he did not want to go too far and by no means gave the masses supreme power; in his own poetry he declared, "I gave the people just enough privilege and no more." Nor did his legislation, humane though it was, wholly end the agricultural problem; freeing farmers from servitude was not the same as guaranteeing them enough to eat, and the agony of those peasants who had lost their land continued.

The Tyrant Pisistratus Pisistratus, a popular Athenian military leader supported by poorer farmers from the hill country in eastern Attica, saw his chance in this turmoil. In 561 B.C. he and his followers seized power; though twice driven out, he returned in 546 with a mercenary army to gain permanent control and ruled from that year until his death in 528.

Pisistratus fits well the pattern of the Greek tyrants sketched earlier. He rewarded his supporters with grants of land, surely taken from the estates of landowning aristocrats who had opposed him, thus completing the work of Solon, who lacked the power and probably the will to redistribute land. And like many another "big city boss," he saw to a splendid program of public works. He built temples to Athena and Zeus and established a yearly festival to the god Dionysus. By encouraging dramatic contests at this festival he opened the way for the development of Athenian tragedy in the next century.

He ruled by clothing his despotic power in legal form. The assembly still chose archons, but these were trusted men picked by the tyrant himself. The legal facade was actually one of his chief

▶ **A superb red-figure vase (the figures are left in the natural red of the clay), illustrating a scene from Homer's *Odyssey*, Book 12. Odysseus, bound to the mast of his ship, listens to the song of the Siren, who guides him into troubled waters; by the Siren Painter, about 490 to 480 B.C.**

contributions, for the Athenians now became familiar with democratic procedures, and this made them receptive to real democracy when it came into existence at the end of the sixth century.

Cleisthenes and **Demokratia** Pisistratus' son Hippias ruled securely until 514 B.C., when a conspiracy frightened him into using terror as a means to maintain his control. He forced many Athenians into exile, including Cleisthenes, the leader of the Alcmaeonids, a powerful family. While in exile in Delphi, Cleisthenes and his supporters enlisted the help of the Spartans in driving Hippias from Athens in 510. Cleisthenes returned to his native city and in 508—perhaps to secure his own supremacy—carried the social

revolution further by proposing a scheme whereby the masses would actually direct the state. The Greek word *demos* means "the people," but in Greek political language it also means "the masses," and the domination of the Athenian state by the whole mass of voters came to be called *demokratia*. Participation extended only to the adult male citizens of Athens, for women, aliens, and slaves did not vote; but this system was by far the closest to a democracy that had ever existed.

Cleisthenes anchored his system in popular support by a stroke of genius: He created a council of 500 members to prepare business for the assembly, allowing all male citizens above 30 to serve in it for a year. In later times (and perhaps from the beginning, though our sources do not say so) councillors were chosen by drawing lots, and no man could serve more than twice. There was a fair chance that every eligible Athenian would be chosen to serve during his lifetime, and this widespread participation in the council ensured that the people would want to maintain the new regime. Within about 50 years this new council came to surpass the old Areopagus council, which continued to exist, in political power.

Cleisthenes also determined to break up the possible influence of regional groups in Attica through a complex system of building blocks. Every man was now enrolled as a citizen within the single village in which he lived, and which kept registers of its citizens. These villages throughout Attica were then grouped into 10 tribes, so composed that each tribe contained citizens from all parts of Attica. The council's 500 men included 50 men from each tribe and were thus automatically a cross section of Athenian citizens. As a result, when the council met to prepare business for the assembly, no single region could dominate the discussion. Each of the 10 tribes fought as a unit in the army, and here, too, men from all over Attica, not from a single region, stood together in each tribal regiment.

The sovereign body was, as before, the assembly, including all adult male citizens, whether landowners or not. The assembly passed laws and resolutions brought before it by the council, elected magistrates, voted for or against war, and accepted alliances with other states.

After passing his reforms in 508 B.C., Cleisthenes vanishes from our sources, but the Athenians continued to refine his system, especially through the use of the lot. In 487 B.C. they began to choose their nine annual archons, the executive committee, by drawing lots from a slate of candidates. Later, in the fifth and fourth centuries, all manner of officials, such as public auditors and managers of public land and mines, were so chosen. The theory behind this practice held that there were many men equally honest and capable of serving in a democracy; and choosing officials by lot reduced corruption and angry competition in the process of selection. Also in 487 B.C., for the first time, a man was expelled from Athens for 10 years by the process of ostracism; Aristotle attributed the practice to Cleisthenes himself, but this remains controversial.

Choosing officials by lot greatly diminished the prestige of such positions and caused the most ambitious men not to bother to seek them. As a result, political power shifted to the 10 generals, who were elected annually and could be reelected. From this point onward we find the great Athenian politicians within the ranks of the generals.

▶ **The interesting procedure of ostracism was instituted in Athens about the time of Cleisthenes. Once a year the Athenians could vote for the man they considered most dangerous to the state by inscribing his name on** *ostraka,* **or scraps of pottery. Six thousand votes in all had to be cast, and the "winner" went at once into exile for 10 years.**

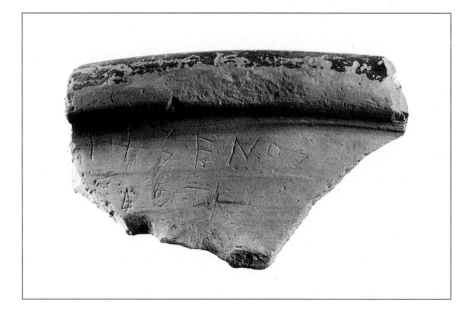

IV. The Challenge of Persia

By the beginning of the "classical" period of Greek history, lasting from about 500 to 323 B.C., the Greek states had reached the political form they would retain for more than two centuries. But almost at once they faced their supreme challenge, a clash with the great Persian Empire.

THE INVASION UNDER DARIUS AND MARATHON (490 B.C.)

King Darius of Persia (521–486 B.C.) had expanded his empire throughout Asia Minor, including the Greek cities on the west coast, the region called Ionia. Some of these Greeks sought their liberty from Persian control in 499 B.C. in the "Ionian revolt," but the revolt collapsed in 493. Darius now proposed to invade Greece itself, largely for the sake of revenge against Athens, which had shown solidarity with the Ionian rebels by sending a force to help them. After a brief campaign in 492, he sent a fleet across the Aegean in 490. The Persians first attacked Eretria,

Map 2.5 THE FIRST PERSIAN WAR, 490 B.C.

on the island of Euboea, and then landed in Attica on the beach at Marathon, a village north of Athens. The Athenian infantry routed them in a brilliant victory and even marched back to Athens in time to ward off a Persian naval attack. The Athenians never forgot this immortal feat of arms; they lost only 192 men, whose burial mound still stands at Marathon, and the Persians lost about 6400.

THE SECOND PERSIAN WAR
(480–479 B.C.)

To avenge this defeat, Darius' son Xerxes (486–465 B.C.) readied a huge force and swore

that this time there would be no mistake. Fortunately for Greece and Europe, the Athenians were guided by a shrewd strategist, Themistocles. In 483 B.C., seeing the Persian menace on the horizon, he had persuaded the Athenians to use some newly found veins of silver in their mines to increase greatly the size of their fleet. Early in 480 some 30 Greek states, also fearing annihilation, formed a military alliance and entrusted to the Spartans command on both land and sea.

Map 2.6 **THE SECOND PERSIAN WAR, 480–479 B.C.**
Note the canal cut through Mt. Athos in 492 B.C.

A few months later Xerxes began his march toward Greece with a force of perhaps 60,000 men and 600 ships, in a grandiose amphibious invasion of Europe. The first Greek force sent out in 480 against the Persians was defeated at the pass of Thermopylae in central Greece in a stand always remembered for its heroism. At the same time, a sea battle at nearby Artemisium was inconclusive.

As the Persian forces continued southward, the Athenians abandoned Athens and the Persians burnt the city down. In this nearly desperate situation, Themistocles devised a brilliant trick. He sent a slave to the Persian king with a false message: Themistocles wished him well and advised him that, if he attacked the Greek fleet with his own at once, he would win the decisive battle practically without a blow.

The Persians were taken in by the ruse and sent their ships into the narrows between Athens and the island of Salamis, where the Greek fleet, lying in wait, utterly defeated them. His navy shattered, Xerxes, who had watched the battle from a height, abandoned Greece and marched back toward the Dardanelles (*see box*, below).

Yet the Persians could still have won the war, for a large Persian army remained in central Greece. The reckoning with this force came in a battle in 479 B.C., at the village of Plataea. Once more a Greek army, under the Spartan general Pausanias, crushed the Persians; out of perhaps 50,000 Persians, only a few thousand survived.

The Greeks won a further battle at Mycale on the shore of Asia Minor in 479. The Ionian Greeks now proclaimed their freedom and thus completed the work of throwing off Persian control that they had begun 20 years earlier. The Greek victory over Persia was the most brilliant one in the history of Greek civilization. If the Greeks had lost the war and become another Persian province, it is by no means clear that Greek art, drama, philosophy, historical writing, and above all self-government would have survived—or how different Western civilization might have been.

"They Have a Master Called Law"

As King Xerxes leads his army into Greece in 480 B.C., he asks a former king of Sparta,
who is accompanying him, whether the Greeks will really fight against the Persians.

"Now, Demaratus, I will ask you what I want to know. You are a Greek and one from no minor or weak city. So now tell me, will the Greeks stand and fight me?" Demaratus replied, "Your Majesty, shall I tell you the truth, or say what you want to hear?" The king ordered him to tell the truth, saying that he would respect him no less for doing so.

"Your Majesty," he said, "I am not speaking about all of them, only about the Spartans. First, I say they will never accept conditions from you that would enslave Greece; second, that they will fight you in battle even if all the other Greeks join your side." Xerxes said, "Demaratus, let's look at it in all logic: why should a thousand, or ten thousand, or fifty thousand men, if they are all free and not ruled by a single master, stand up against such an army as mine? If they were ruled by one man, like my subjects, I suppose they might, out of fear, show more bravery than usual and, driven into battle by the lash, go up against a bigger force; but if allowed their freedom, they wouldn't do either one."

Demaratus said, "Your Majesty, I knew from the beginning that if I spoke the truth you wouldn't like my message, but, since you ordered me to do so, I told you about the Spartans. They are free men, but not wholly free: they have a master called Law, whom they fear far more than your soldiers fear you. And his orders are always the same—they must not run away from any army no matter how big, but must stand in their formation and either conquer or die. But, Your Majesty, may your wishes be fulfilled."

Herodotus, Book VII, chaps. 101–104 (abridged), M. H. Chambers (tr.).

THE ATHENIAN EMPIRE

The victorious Greeks continued the war against Persia in 479 and 478 B.C., liberating, for example, the Greek city of Byzantium on the Bosporus from Persian control. But in 478 Sparta returned to its perennial isolationism and withdrew from the alliance that had been formed to oppose Persia. In response, many of the newly liberated Greek states met on the island of Delos in 478 and formed an alliance, known as the Delian League, to continue the war and take further vengeance on Persia. Athens was recognized as head of the league and determined which members should supply ships to the common navy and which ones should contribute money. The military campaigns, often fought under the command of the Athenian general Cimon, were successful until the warfare between Greeks and Persians ended about 450. Meanwhile, Athenian control of the league had become stricter through the years. Sometimes Athens forcibly prevented members from withdrawing from the league; sometimes it stationed garrisons or governors in the supposedly independent member states. Athenian domination became unmistakable in 454, when the league transferred its treasury from Delos to

▶ Themistocles, the great Athenian strategist, was ostracized about 472 B.C. This ostrakon, cast against him, says, "Themistocles, son of Neocles, let him depart" (ITO).

CHRONOLOGY OF THE PERSIAN WARS

499, autumn	Greek cities of Ionia in Asia Minor revolt from Persian Empire.
498	Athens and Eretria (on island of Euboea) take part in burning of Sardis in Persian Empire.
496	Persians besiege Miletus, leading city in the revolt.
494	Fall of Miletus.
493	End of Ionian revolt.
492, spring	Persian expedition to northern Greece suffers heavy losses in storms.
490, mid-August	Battle of Marathon near Athens; Persians defeated.
486, November	Death of King Darius of Persia; accession of Xerxes.
484, spring–480, spring	Xerxes prepares for new invasion of Greece.
480, spring	Persian army sets out from Sardis.
480, late August	Battles of Thermopylae and Artemisium.
480, late September	Battle of Salamis.
479, early August	Battle of Plataea.
479, mid-August	Battle of Mycale on coast of Asia Minor (according to Herodotus, fought on the same day as Plataea).

V. The Wars of the Fifth Century (479–404 B.C.)

After a brief period of cooperation, the two leading Greek cities, Athens and Sparta, led their allies into the long, tragic war that fatally weakened the Greek poleis.

Athens. The cash contributions were now nothing but tribute to Athens, and the alliance of equals had become an Athenian empire.

THE AGE OF PERICLES

The leading statesman in the period of the Athenian empire was Pericles (490?–429 B.C.), an aristocrat from a wealthy family who had the support of the common people. Now that the archonship was no longer a position for an ambitious man, Pericles held only the post of general, to which he was reelected from 443 to 429. He was a powerful orator and a highly competent general, and was renowned for his personal honesty; moreover, his policies generally favored the common people. In 447 B.C., for example, he proposed that the Athenians should begin to rebuild the temples on the Acropolis that the Persians had destroyed in their invasion of 480. Between 447 and 432 B.C. they built for their goddess Athena the most nearly perfect of all Greek temples, the Parthenon, and a magnificent gateway to the Acropolis. These public works

▶ **A portion of the frieze from within the Athenian Parthenon, showing officials carrying the robe that will be presented to Athena. On the right, gods sit in conversation, awaiting the procession; note that they are portrayed as larger than the human beings.**

both beautified the city and provided work for the people.

Moreover, Pericles' lifetime coincided with the zenith of Athenian literature, when Athenian drama, especially, reached its highest development in the plays of Sophocles (a friend of Pericles) and Euripides. So brilliant was this era, and so strongly marked by his leadership, that historians often call the era from 450 to 429 the Age of Pericles. His political dominance drew praise from the historian Thucydides because "he controlled the masses, rather than let them control him. [. . .] Though the state was a democracy in name, in fact it was ruled by the most prominent man."[3]

The expansion of the empire must have been one of the causes for the development of the judicial system. Juries were chosen by lot and comprised 200, 500, or even more citizens drawn from all classes. There was no detailed body of civil or criminal law, and juries had wide powers of interpretation without the possibility of appeal from their decisions. They heard all manner of cases with exception of homicides, which were tried by the Areopagus. Critics of this system saw it as too democratic, but it expressed the spirit of the Greek state: that the average citizen could and should play a part in governing the city.

---

[3]Thucydides 2.65.

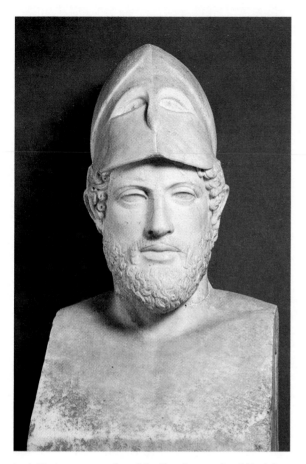

▶ **A Roman copy of an idealized portrait of Pericles, the leading Athenian statesman of his time. The helmet symbolizes his position as commander.**

THE PELOPONNESIAN WAR (431–404 B.C.)

"Historical laws" are difficult to establish and dangerous to use, but the observation of the British historian Lord Acton is hard to resist: "Power tends to corrupt." The Athenian empire, which had emerged out of the heroic victory in the Persian Wars, became more and more dominating over its subject states—its former allies. This movement, and the resentment that it caused, brought about the long war that sealed the doom of the Greek city-states. By far the longest and most dramatic of all collisions in Greek history, it also received an immortal analysis from the greatest of ancient historians, Thucydides of Athens (circa 455–circa 395 B.C.).

The Outbreak of War   In the 430s aggressive action by Athens convinced the allies of Sparta that they must declare a preventive war on Athens. First, in 435 Corinth, an ally of Sparta, went to war with one of its colonies, Corcyra (today the main city on the island of Corfu). The quarrel threatened to become a Panhellenic one when Corcyra appealed for help to Athens in 433. Despite the warning of ambassadors from Corinth that any assistance would make war inevitable, the Athenians signed an alliance with Corcyra and actually fought with their new allies in a naval battle against Corinth.

Second, also in 433, the Athenians ordered the town of Potidaea, in northern Greece, to demolish its walls, send hostages to Athens, and banish its magistrates. Though Potidaea was a member of the Athenian empire, these demands infuriated the allies of Sparta, especially Corinth. The allies demanded a meeting of the Peloponnesian League and voted to declare war on the Athenians and their allies. Thucydides gives his opinion that these events were only the immediate, incidental causes of the war: "The truest cause, though the least talked about openly, was that the growth of Athenian power frightened the Spartans and finally compelled them to go to war."[4] This judgment seems accurate, for neither the affair of Corcyra nor that of Potidaea threatened the Spartans directly; more menacing was the general disturbance of the balance of power caused by Athenian boldness.

This war, known as the Peloponnesian War, opposed two kinds of states. Sparta, though the head of the Peloponnesian League, controlled no empire and maintained itself through its own resources. Athens relied on its empire to provide grain for its people and tribute to pay for its navy. Sparta had the strongest army in Greece, and Athens was the chief naval power.

The Archidamian War (431–421 B.C.)   The first 10 years of the war are called the Archidamian War, so named for Archidamus, one of the kings of Sparta when the war began. Fighting opened in 431 B.C. but was inconclusive for several years. Sparta sought to break Athenian morale by

---

[4]Thucydides 1.23.

Map 2.7 GREECE IN 431 B.C., ON THE OUTBREAK OF THE PELOPONNESIAN WAR
Shows the members of the alliances headed by Athens and Sparta.

invading Attica annually, ravaging farms, and then departing for the Peloponnesian harvest. But the Athenians withdrew behind their "long walls" that reached down to their harbor until the enemy left, and Pericles refused to allow the Athenian infantry to challenge Sparta on the field. Instead, the Athenians launched raids by sea against coastal towns in the Peloponnese, but these raids left Sparta untouched. Far more dam-

aging to Athens than the Spartan invasions was a devastating plague (not yet identified with any known disease) that attacked the Athenians, packed inside their walls, in 430 and later years. The plague took thousands of lives within the crowded, unsanitary city; Thucydides survived it and has left us a horrifying description of its effects on the body.

Unfortunately for Athens' effectiveness in the war, Pericles died in 429 B.C. None of his successors could maintain his stable leadership, and some were unscrupulous demagogues playing only for their own temporary power. In the 420s both sides achieved certain successes, but the casualties that all parties suffered in the next few years made them ready to end, or at least suspend, the war. A peace treaty was signed in 421 B.C., called the Peace of Nicias from the Athenian general who led the negotiations.

The "Suspicious Truce" (421–415 B.C.)   At this point the Greeks could have turned their backs on war, for both Athens and Sparta had shown courage and neither had gained a decisive advantage. Thucydides called the next few years a time of suspicious truce, but during this period one event demands attention, the brutal subjugation of the small island of Melos by the Athenians in 416.

The Athenians sailed up to this neutral island and commanded the Melians to join the Athenian empire. Thucydides describes the negotiations in a brilliant passage, called the Melian Dialogue, in which envoys on each side argue their cases. It is by no means clear how he could have known what was said by either side, and this dialogue is probably based on his own conjectures. In any case, the Melians protest that they are so few in number that they cannot in any way threaten the Athenians, to which the Athenians reply that it is precisely their weakness that makes them dangerous: If the Athenians allow so small a state to remain neutral, this will show weakness in the Athenians themselves and may tempt their subjects to rebel.

The Athenians brush aside all arguments based on morality and justice and, in the end, seize the island, kill all the adult men (probably 2000 to 3000), and sell the women and children as slaves. Without explicitly stating any moral conclusion, Thucydides shows the Athenians giving way to the corrupting influence of war; as he says in another passage, "War teaches men to be violent."[5]

The Defeat of Athens   In 415 B.C. another occasion for war arose. The people of Segesta, a city in Sicily, appealed to Athens for help in a war they were fighting against Syracuse, the leading power on that island. In commenting on the

---

[5]Thucydides 3.82.

death of Pericles, Thucydides noted that his successors were often lesser men of poor judgment. It was so now, as Alcibiades, a talented young political leader of enormous ambition and—as it later turned out—few scruples, persuaded the Athenian assembly, against the advice of the Athenian general Nicias, to raise a large fleet and attack Syracuse, with himself as one of the generals. This campaign in effect reopened the Peloponnesian War despite the peace treaty of 421 B.C.

Thucydides makes it clear that a quick, resolute attack might well have succeeded, but the Athenians failed to strike when they had a clear advantage. One event that blunted the Athenian attack was the loss of Alcibiades. He was recalled to Athens to stand trial on charges of violating the state's religion, but fearing that his political enemies would be able to secure his conviction, he defected to Sparta and advised them how to fight the Athenians.

In Syracuse, the Athenians finally decided to break off the campaign, but they lost a critical battle in the harbor and could not sail away. Trying to retreat toward the interior of the island, they were cut off and decimated. Those who survived this calamity were imprisoned in terrible conditions in a quarry at Syracuse; as Thucydides grimly says, "Few out of many returned home."

The disaster in Sicily led to many defections among Athens' subjects, but Sparta still could not strike the final blow. The war dragged on for another eight years until, in 405 B.C., the Spartan admiral Lysander captured the Athenian fleet at a spot called Aegospotami, in the Dardanelles. Athens, now deprived of its food supply through the straits, had to surrender in desperate hunger in 404. It abandoned its empire and, as a guarantee for the future and a symbol of humiliation, had to pull down the "long walls" that had protected the population during the war. Sparta proclaimed this event, in language often used by winners of wars, as the "liberation of Greece" and imposed on the Athenians a cruel regime (known as the "30 tyrants"). This hated clique lasted only some eight months, and democracy was restored in 403 B.C.

Athens never regained its former power, although democracy survived for long years after the war. The quality of political leadership had declined after the death of Pericles, as Thucydides observed. Several times when the war could have ended, ambitious politicians raised support for rash ventures that ended in disaster, of which the Sicilian expedition was only the most notable.

Looking back at the fifth century B.C., we can see that the Greek poleis made little constructive use of their brilliant victory over the invaders from Persia. Freed of a foreign enemy, they divided themselves into two blocs that turned against one another and, like characters in a Greek tragedy, involved themselves in the catastrophe of the Peloponnesian War.

The Athenians lost their empire, which had made them the richest polis in Greek history. Sparta, persuaded by its allies to go to war in 431, had dissolved the Athenian empire, but this empire had been no threat whatever to Sparta's isolated life within the protecting mountains of the Peloponnese. The losses in manpower had been heavy on both sides, but Sparta could less easily sustain these losses because of its smaller population, and in the fourth century it could put fewer and fewer troops in the field.

Besides these losses, there now came a failure of will, a spirit of pessimism and disillusion among Athenian intellectuals. Many thought uncontrolled democracy had led to social decline and military disaster, and they contrasted the discipline of Sparta, the victor, with the frequent chaos of Athenian policy. Thucydides often speaks critically of "the masses" and "the rabble," and similar ideas run through the work of Plato and other philosophers, who asked what had gone wrong with democracy and what system should replace it.

Recommended Reading

Sources

Herodotus. *The Histories.* Aubrey de Sélincourt (tr.). 1954. The only translation to catch the witty personality of the first historian.

Homer. *The Iliad.* Robert Fagles (tr.). 1990. A stirring translation in verse.

———. *The Odyssey.* Richmond Lattimore (tr.). 1968.

Studies

Andrewes, Antony. *The Greeks.* 1973. Chapters on Greek social and political life, not a continuous history.

———. *The Greek Tyrants.* 1963. Brief but highly concentrated book on the tyrants in early Greece.

Boardman, John. *Greek Art.* 1973.

Burkert, Walter. *Greek Religion.* 1987. By the most original and trenchant expert of our times.

Burn, A. R. *The Lyric Age of Greece.* 1960. History and literature in the archaic period.

———. *Persia and the Greeks.* 1962. Accurate narrative of the Persian Wars.

Cartledge, Paul. *Sparta and Lakonia.* 1979. Detailed historical-geographical survey.

Chadwick, John. *The Decipherment of Linear B* (2nd ed.). 1970. A study of the Cretan scripts, with notes on the method of decipherment.

Drews, Robert. *The Coming of the Greeks.* 1988. On the arrival of the Greeks in the general context of migrations.

Ehrenberg, Victor. *From Solon to Socrates.* 1968. A political textbook on the central period of Greek history, with good references to primary sources.

Finley, M. I. *The World of Odysseus.* 1979. The values, customs, and life style of Homeric society, by the leading social-economic historian of his time.

Guthrie, W. K. C. *A History of Greek Philosophy* (6 vols.). 1962–1981. Encyclopedic history, brilliant and sensitive.

Hignett, C. *A History of the Athenian Constitution.* 1952. For advanced students; microscopic study of every problem, often critical of ancient sources.

———. *Xerxes' Invasion of Greece.* 1963. Most detailed narrative; accepts Herodotus over all other evidence.

Hooker, J. T. *The Ancient Spartans.* 1980.

Hopper, R. J. *The Early Greeks.* 1976. Highly readable survey of ancient Greece to the beginning of the Classical period.

Jeffery, L. H. *Archaic Greece: City-States c. 700–500 B.C.* 1976. Mainly a close political narrative.

Kagan, Donald. *The Archidamian War.* 1974. Detailed history of the first part of the Peloponnesian War (followed by two other volumes).

Kitto, H. D. F. *The Greeks.* 1950. Classic appreciation of Greek culture, written with sensitivity and wit.

McGregor, Malcolm F. *The Athenians and Their Empire.* 1987. A narrative, less technical than Meiggs.

Meiggs, Russell. *The Athenian Empire.* 1972. For advanced students; discussion of every historical problem, especially good at interpreting evidence from inscriptions.

Ostwald, Martin. *From Popular Sovereignty to the Sovereignty of Law.* 1986. Detailed study of development of the Athenian state.

Page, Denys L. *History and the Homeric Iliad* (ed. 2). 1966. Especially good on Near Eastern connections with the epic.

Sealey, Raphael. *A History of the Greek City States.* 1976. The best textbook history, concentrating on problems rather than mechanical narrative.

Snodgrass, Anthony. *Archaic Greece: The Age of Experiment.* 1981. Excellent use of archaeological evidence.

de Ste Croix, G. E. M. *The Origins of the Peloponnesian War.* 1972. Really a detailed history of the fifth century; many appendixes on special topics.

Staveley, E. S. *Greek and Roman Voting and Elections.* 1972. Illuminates many practices in the Athenian constitution.

Taylour, Lord William. *The Mycenaeans.* 1983. Solid and learned treatment of earliest Greek civilization.

Vermeule, Emily. *Greece in the Bronze Age.* 1972. Classic work of synthesis by a noted art historian.

Warren, Peter. *The Aegean Civilisations.* 1975. Fully illustrated study of Minoan-Mycenaean period.

Woodhead, A. G. *The Greeks in the West.* 1962. The Greek colonies in Sicily and South Italy.

Zimmern, A. E. *The Greek Commonwealth* (4th ed.). 1924. Despite its age, still a classic portrait of social-political life in Athens.

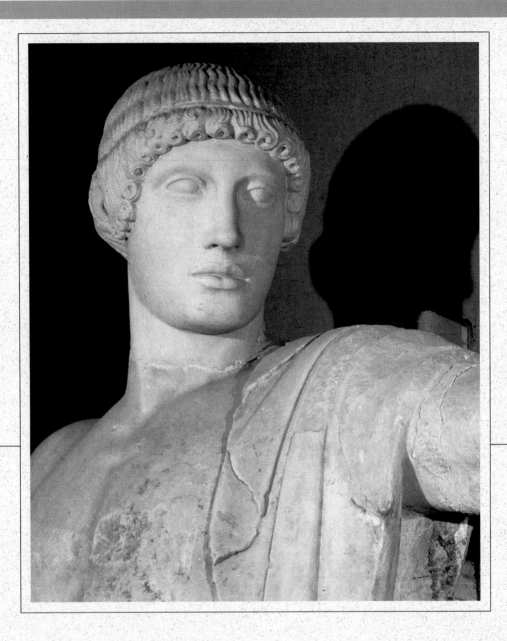

A superb statue of the god Apollo from the west pediment of the Temple of Zeus at Olympia. In a commanding gesture, the god controls a centaur and symbolically brings Hellenic rationality to bear over an undisciplined universe. The statue combines the power and dignity of a god with the ideal perfection of a human being.

CHAPTER THREE

CLASSICAL AND HELLENISTIC GREECE

THE Peloponnesian War left the two main Greek political alliances, those built around Athens and Sparta, weak and demoralized. The war thus prepared the way for the conquest of Greece in the next century by the Macedonian king Philip II and his son Alexander the Great, who went on to conquer Egypt, Persia, and vast stretches of Asia Minor.

Despite the tumultuous conditions of Greek politics—and perhaps because of the uncertainties and upheavals—the fifth and fourth centuries witnessed an extraordinary flowering of intellectual and artistic achievements. This sudden burst of creative energy was concentrated in time and space to a degree that was unprecedented in history and, some would argue, has never been duplicated. In these years were written the plays of the tragedians Aeschylus, Sophocles, and Euripides, and the comic poet Aristophanes; Herodotus and Thucydides invented the writing of history; and philosophers probed in new ways virtually every phase of human experience.

During the last decades of the fourth century the Greeks, having lost the world of the independent polis, embraced the larger world of Alexander's empire, which brought them into expanded contact with other peoples. There followed a series of intellectual encounters that were to affect dramatically the experience of the West.

I. Classical Greek Culture (Ca. 500–323 B.C.)

In less than two centuries Greek society went through an amazing transformation, nowhere more apparent than in the Greeks' written culture: their drama, their historical writing, and their philosophy. It was an era of Athenian preeminence, and thus the study of Greek civilization in this "golden age" inevitably focuses on Athens.

GREEK TRAGEDY

One of the most lasting achievements of the fifth century B.C. was the creation and perfection of a new literary and theatrical form, tragedy. Greek dramas were written in the most sublime poetry since Homer, and they first appeared in Athens, at religious festivals honoring the god Dionysus. At these celebrations, also marked by dancing and revelry, there were dramatic performances that addressed increasingly serious moral issues. The writers of tragedies derived most of their plots from tales of gods and heroes in Greek mythology, and their central themes are the questions fundamental to all religions: What is humanity's relationship to the gods? What is justice? And if the gods are just, why do they allow people to suffer? That tragic drama arose at this time and in this place may be the result of the new confidence of the Athenians following their victory over Persia and the founding of the Athenian empire. Their inspiration may also have derived from their awareness of how short-lived triumphs can be. Greek tragedy relentlessly pursued its main theme—that worldly success and arrogance can invite destruction.

The surviving plays explore subtle moral problems with shattering power. The stature of the main characters gives the tragedies additional force, for they deal with heroic, strong-willed men and women like Oedipus and Antigone, powerful personalities who are caught in fearful dilemmas. Thus Antigone, in Sophocles' play of that name, defies the ruler of Thebes, who has forbidden her brother a traditional burial because he died in war against the city; she chooses to follow divine, not human, law, and her courageous decision destroys her. Along with these characters there is a chorus of a dozen or so men, who comment on the action and the moral problems in odes set to music.

In the fifth century these dramas were performed before audiences of as many as 15,000 people of all classes; the plays not only moved and inspired but also provided an education in ethics for citizens, who were gripped by the complex debates over which persons were acting justly and which ones should suffer retribution for moral error and crime. Just as philosophy was to explore the subject of ethical responsibility and right conduct, so do the dramas—but with far greater emotional power. Greek tragedies are still performed and filmed, and they continue to inspire operas, plays, and ballets over 2000 years after their creation.

Playwrights presented dramas in sets of three, accompanied by a comic playlet known as a satyr play (probably meant to relieve the heavy emotion of the main drama). Only one such "trilogy" has survived: the *Oresteia*, the tragedy of Orestes, the son of Agamemnon, by Aeschylus, which was produced in 458 B.C. The central theme is the nature of justice, which Aeschylus explores in a tale of multiple murders and vengeance. Agamemnon, the leader of the war against Troy, found his fleet becalmed and had to sacrifice his daughter to revive the winds so that he could fulfill his oath to make war on Troy. On his return, his wife kills him and is in turn killed by her son Orestes, who is finally tried and acquitted in an Athenian court presided over by the goddess Athena. The cycle of retribution runs its course as the themes of fate and revenge focus on the family, all developed through majestic poetry and intense emotion.

In Sophocles, who wrote mainly during the Peloponnesian War, when the very definition of the polis was under challenge, social concerns became central, and the focus shifts to the community. The chorus plays a larger role, and Sophocles adds a third actor (in Aeschylus there are never more than two on the stage any time) in order to concentrate more on the interplay of characters and the larger issues of society that they explore. He also shows a greater interest in personality than Aeschylus. In *Oedipus the King* he created perhaps the most nearly perfect specimen of surviving Greek tragedy; its central concern is the relationship of the individual and the polis. The play is about Oedipus, king of Thebes, who, through mistaken identity, unknowingly commits the terrible crimes of killing his father and marrying his mother. As the play opens, a religious curse has brought a plague on his people. Oedipus orders a search to discover the offender who has brought this pollution on the city. As the search narrows with terrifying logic to Oedipus himself, he discovers that his crimes of patricide and incest, though unintentional, have disturbed the order of the universe and his polis in particular. The only remedy is for him to serve justice and atone for them. When the truth emerges, Oedipus' wife-mother hangs herself and Oedipus, in a frenzy of remorse and public humiliation, plunges her brooches into his eyes and begins a life of wandering as a blind outcast; once the powerful monarch, he is now a broken, homeless fugitive (*see box*, below).

The Athenian poet Euripides, a contemporary of Sophocles, emphasized above all the psychology of his characters. Reacting to the violence of his times, he throws his characters back on their own searing passions. They forge their own fates, alienated from their societies. As a result, we see in Euripides how the workings of the mind and emotions shape a person's destiny. His intense, even fanatical, characters determine the course of events by their own often savage deeds, though the themes of justice and retribution for crime are still central to the drama.

In Euripides' *Medea*, for example, Jason, Medea's husband, has deserted her for a princess of Corinth. Driven by overwhelming emotion to take revenge, Medea kills the Corinthian girl and then turns on her own children. As love and hatred battle within her, she weeps over her children but, despite a momentary weakening of will, completes her vengeance and kills them. The powerful woman has found her own way of dealing with the terrors of the world.

Oedipus' Self-Mutilation

In Sophocles' tragedy **King Oedipus**, *Jocasta, the mother of Oedipus, hangs herself after learning that she has married her own son. An attendant then narrates what follows. (Those he "should never have seen" are the daughters Oedipus fathered by his mother-wife.)*

"We saw a knotted pendulum, a noose,
A strangled woman swinging before our eyes.
  "The King saw too, and with heart-rending groans
Untied the rope, and laid her on the ground.
But worse was yet to see. Her dress was pinned
With golden brooches, which the King snatched out
And thrust, from full arm's length, into his eyes—
Eyes that should see no longer his shame, his guilt,
No longer see those they should never have seen,
Nor see, unseeing, those he had longed to see,
Henceforth seeing nothing but night . . . To this wild tune

He pierced his eyeballs time and time again,
Till bloody tears ran down his beard—not drops
But in full spate a whole cascade descending
In drenching cataracts of scarlet rain.
  "Thus two have sinned; and on two heads, not one—
On man and wife—falls mingled punishment.
Their old long happiness of former times
Was happiness earned with justice; but to-day
Calamity, death, ruin, tears, and shame,
All ills that there are names for—all are here."

Sophocles, *The Theban Plays*, Penguin, 1971, E. F. Watling (tr.), pp. 60–61.

▶ **Roman wall paintings often show scenes from Greek drama and mythology; this painting shows Medea, in Euripides' play, about to kill her children. "My friends, I am resolved to act, to slay my children quickly and depart from this land ..."**

COMEDY

Comedy abandoned these serious themes and satirized contemporary situations and people in the real world. Almost the only comedies that have come down to us are those written by the Athenian Aristophanes, a younger contemporary of Sophocles and Euripides. Again and again he emphasized the ridiculous in the situation of individuals as well as society at large. Aristophanes used fantasy and burlesque to satirize the Peloponnesian War, political leaders, intellectuals—including Socrates—and the failings of democracy. Whatever his political motives in writing his satires, they sometimes exposed the folly of human behavior more devastatingly than the tragedies. And they were particularly cutting in

their depiction of the absurdities of arrogant persons in Athenian society.

The earliest of Aristophanes' 11 surviving plays is the *Acharnians* (425 B.C.), an antiwar comedy from the early years of the Peloponnesian War. He continued his antiwar theme in other plays, notably *Lysistrata*, which he wrote after the disastrous Athenian expedition to Syracuse. In this comedy the women of Athens, despairing of any other means of ending the long war, go on a sex strike that humiliates their blustering menfolk, and they succeed in enlisting the other women of Greece in their cause.

Aristophanes reserved some of his sharpest attacks for the democratic leaders who succeeded Pericles. In *The Knights* (424 B.C.) a general tries to persuade an ignorant sausage-seller to unseat Cleon, one of those leaders:

Sausage-Seller: Tell me this, how can I, a sausage-seller, be a big man like that?

General: The easiest thing in the world. You've got all the qualifications: low birth, marketplace training, insolence.

Sausage-Seller: I don't think I deserve it.

General: Not deserve it? It looks to me as if you've got too good a conscience. Was your father a gentleman?

Sausage-Seller: By the gods, no! My folks were scoundrels.

General: Lucky man! What a good start you've got for public life!

Sausage-Seller: But I can hardly read.

General: The only trouble is that you know anything. To be a leader of the people isn't for learned men, or honest men, but for the ignorant and vile. Don't miss the golden opportunity.[1]

HISTORICAL WRITING

Drama is one way of examining the human condition; writing history is another. The constant wars in the fifth century B.C. prompted some

---

[1]From L. S. Stavrianos, *Epic of Man to 1500*, 1970.

men to seek to explain why war was their perpetual companion. They looked to the past to understand what causes war and how people behave during conflict. In so doing, they invented a new literary form: history.

Herodotus Herodotus, a Greek from Asia Minor and a contemporary of Sophocles, is rightly called the "Father of History," for he was the first to write a sustained narrative of political events, in his case the Greek victory over Persia. Yet this was no mere chronicle. Herodotus understood that an event like a major war could be seen as a clash between two differing cultures. He therefore began by trying to learn the history of the Persian Empire in order to explain its pressure on Europe.

The most impressive dimension of his work is his demonstration that all the cultures of the ancient world were interconnected. Using travelers' tales, interviews, and oral tradition, much as a modern anthropologist does, he described the character and outlook of the several peoples of the Near East. He also reduced centuries of Near Eastern history into order, chronicling the dynasties and successions from one monarch to an-

other. He did this without the help of any earlier narrative, and the structure he gave to the history of the Persian Empire has not been shaken. He explained the growth of the Persian Empire as the work of powerful, ambitious monarchs, constantly striving for a larger realm. In the end, Herodotus shows his Greek heritage with his verdict that the Greek victory in the Persian Wars was the inevitable triumph of a free society over a despotic one, but he also recognizes the strength and solidity of the Persian Empire and is generally free of racial prejudice. It was his methods for regaining the past, rather than any particular interpretations, that gave him his stature as the pioneer in the writing of history.

Thucydides Greek historians "published" their work by giving readings, perhaps also allowing copies to be made. Thucydides, a younger con-

▶ An Attic red-figure vase (about 470 B.C.), showing scenes from a school. At left, a master teaches a boy to play the lyre; at right, a boy learns to recite poetry from a scroll held by another master, while another supervises the class.

temporary of Herodotus, is said to have heard him read, and this may have inspired him when, as a participant in the Peloponnesian War, he decided to write its history. He did not live to finish his work, which breaks off within 411, seven years before the end of the war. Thucydides has a narrower theme than Herodotus, for he concentrates on a limited period and area. Yet he is the more profound inquirer into causation and the motives for the actions of statesmen and warriors. His entire first book, out of the eight that make up his history, explores the causes, both immediate and long-term, for the outbreak of the war. Thucydides brings to bear on events the kind of logical and unemotional analysis that philosophers developed in the late fifth century. Throughout his work he presents a series of speeches and debates about various issues and decisions to lay bare the motives of the participants. The speakers are usually contemptuous of moral principles, and arguments based on justice

and mercy, if brought up at all, are ruthlessly swept aside by whichever individual or force has the upper hand. It is by no means clear that Thucydides himself rejected compassion, but he presents the whole war as a cold pursuit of power. It was by such rigorous analysis that he brought order out of the cruelties and disruptions of his age.

In Thucydides' view, the Athenian state was in good order under Pericles because he could control the Athenian people. His political successors, by contrast, allowed the masses to influence decisions, with tragic consequences for Athens, including above all the expedition to Sicily in 415 B.C. Thucydides combines accuracy and concentration on detail with descriptive powers that rival those of the dramatists, particularly when he brings a scene of horror to life. No reader can avoid feeling a chill over the clinical description of the plague that attacked Athens in 430 B.C. or the shattering defeat of the proud armada that

---

Thucydides: The Melian Dialogue

In 416 B.C., the Athenians mercilessly inform the people of the small island of Melos that they must join the Athenian empire. Thucydides presents the cold logic of their demand.

"**Athenians:** We will use no fine phrases saying, for example, that we have a right to our empire because we defeated the Persians, or that we have come against you now because of the injuries you have done us. And we ask you not to imagine that you will influence us by saying that you have never done us any harm. You know as well as we do that the strong do what they have the power to do and the weak accept what they have to accept.

"**Melians:** So you would not agree to our being neutral, friends instead of enemies, but allies of neither side?

"**Athenians:** No, because it is not so much your hostility that injures us; rather, if we were on friendly terms with you, our subjects would regard that as a sign of weakness in us, whereas your hatred is evidence of our power.

"**Melians:** We trust that the gods will give us fortune as good as yours, because we are standing for what is right against what is wrong.

"**Athenians:** Our opinion of the gods and our knowledge of men lead us to conclude that it is a general and necessary law of nature to rule wherever one can. This is not a law that we made ourselves, nor were we the first to act upon it when it was made. We found it already in existence, and we shall leave it to exist forever. We are merely acting in accordance with it, and we know that you or anybody else with the same power as ours would be acting in precisely the same way."

Thucydides, *The Peloponnesian War*, Penguin, 1980, Rex Warner (tr.), Book V, chaps. 89–105 (abridged).

sailed against Syracuse. He is the undisputed master among ancient historians, and for gripping narrative power and philosophical breadth he remains unsurpassed (*see box*, p. 68).

PHILOSOPHY

The supreme intellectual invention of the Greeks is the special search for knowledge called philosophy—the attempt to use reason to discover why things are as they are. Philosophy is born when people are no longer satisfied with supernatural and mythical explanations of the world or of human behavior. It is hard to say just why Greeks gradually became skeptical about the accounts that they inherited in their own mythology, but around 600 B.C. they began to suspect that there was an order in the universe beyond manipulation by the gods—and that human beings could discover it. Life in Greek poleis was conducive to argument and debate, and such conditions encouraged rational inquiry and even dispute. And philosophy, like drama and history, became a means of understanding change and upheaval.

The Beginnings of Philosophy   The first Greek philosophers lived in the city of Miletus, a prominent trading center on the western shore of Asia Minor in the region of Ionia. Its citizens had direct contact with the ideas and achievements of the Near East, and these intellectual currents must have helped form the city as a center of thought. Soon after 600 B.C., certain Milesians were discovering a world of speculation in an apparently simple yet profoundly radical question: What exists? They sought their answer in some single primal element. One philosopher, Thales, for example, taught that everything in the whole universe was made of water, a notion that echoes Babylonian myths of a primeval flood.

A pupil and follower of Thales, Anaximander of Miletus, held (probably about 560 B.C.) that the origin of everything was an infinite body of matter, which he called "the boundless." A whirling motion within the boundless divided its substance into the hot, which rose to form the heavens, and the cold, which sank and assumed form in the earth and the air surrounding it. A further separation into wet and dry created the oceans and the land. This theory points toward a

▶ **Roman wall painting, showing Theseus having killed the Minotaur; he is surrounded by grateful Athenian children, whom he has saved from possible death by being devoured by the half-man, half-beast monster.**

common later classification of all matter into four elements (earth, air, fire, water). Anaximander also suggested what modern biology has confirmed: that people and other animals developed from fish-like beings.

Among the theories proposed to explain the order or substance of all things were those of Pythagoras of Samos (around 530 B.C.), who developed a strikingly different theory to explain the order of the world. He saw the key to all existence in mathematics and approached the universe through the study of numbers. He discovered the harmonic intervals within the musical scale and stated the Pythagorean theorem about the sum of the sides of a right triangle. Pythagoras went on to say that all objects are similar to numbers, by which he probably meant that within objects there is always a numerically balanced arrangement of parts. He thus anticipated the modern discoveries of mathematical relationships within all things, including even the genetic code in our bodies.

Yet another way of looking at the universe was proposed by one Leucippus and his contemporary, Democritus of Abdera, about 450 B.C. They saw the world as made up of invisibly small particles or atoms (*a-toma* in Greek, meaning "things that cannot be divided"), which simply come together and cohere at random. Death, according to this theory, leads simply to the redistribution of the atoms that make up our body and soul and thus need hold no terror for humanity. The scientific validity of the atomic theory was eventually to be recognized in the modern era; like the Pythagorean and other theories, it attests the ferment of ideas in ancient Greece—ideas that were to influence Western thought for millennia.

The Sophists and Socrates Around 450 B.C. philosophers turned away from speculations about the structure of the universe and toward the study of human beings and the ways they led their lives. The first Greeks to undertake this study were those commonly known as Sophists (*sophistés* in Greek, meaning "expert" or "learned man"). They came from various places to Athens about 450 B.C. and challenged nearly all accepted beliefs. One of the early Sophists, Protagoras, declared that "man is the measure" of everything; that is, human beings and their perceptions are the only measure of whether a thing exists at all. The very existence of the gods, whom people cannot really perceive, is only an undemonstrable assumption. From such a statement it is only a short step to the belief that it is almost impossible to know anything; in the absence of objective knowledge, the only recourse is to make your way through the world by coolly exploiting to your own advantage any situation you encounter.

The Sophists also drew an important distinction between human customs on the one hand and the law of nature on the other. Thus they argued that what was made or designed by people was arbitrary and inferior; what existed naturally was immutable and proper. This argument called into question all accepted canons of good behavior. Freed of moral constraints, the Sophists suggested that intellectual activity was valuable only in helping one succeed in life. They accepted pupils and said they could train them for success in any calling, since in every line of work there are problems to be solved through reasoning. They taught the art of rhetoric, persuasive speech making that could be used to sway an assembly or to defend oneself in court. Their pupils, they implied, could gain power by coolly analyzing the mechanics of politics and by using the skills the Sophists taught them.

The main critic of the Sophists was Socrates (469–399 B.C.), a contemporary of Sophocles and Euripides, who was active during the intellectually dynamic period before and during the Peloponnesian War. He faulted the Sophists for taking pay for teaching, yet failing to teach ethically right behavior. In the course of his critique, Socrates transformed philosophy into an inquiry

▷ **The olive was one of the basic crops in Greek agriculture. In this black-figure vase (the figures are painted black, while the background is the natural red of the clay), two men knock olives off a tree at harvest time, while another climbs the branches and a boy gathers the fruit.**

Socrates Is Sentenced to Death

Plato's version of Socrates' words to the jury that sentenced him to death:

"You too, gentlemen of the jury, must look forward to death with confidence, and fix your minds on this one belief, which is certain: that nothing can harm a good man either in life or after death, and his fortunes are not a matter of indifference to the gods. This present experience of mine has not come about mechanically; I am quite clear that the time had come when it was better for me to die and to be released from my distractions. [. . .] For my own part I bear no grudge at all against those who condemned me and accused me, although it was not with this kind intention that they did so, but because they thought they were hurting me. [. . .] However, I ask them to grant me one favor. When my sons grow up, gentlemen, if you think that they are putting money or anything else before goodness, take your revenge by plaguing them as I plagued you; and if they fancy themselves for no reason, you must scold them just as I scolded you, for neglecting the important things and thinking that they are good for something when they are good for nothing. If you do this, I shall have had justice at your hands, both I myself and my children.

"Now it is time that we were going, I to die and you to live; but which of us has the happier prospect is unknown to anyone but God."

Plato, *The Last Days of Socrates*, Penguin, 1980, Hugh Tredennick (tr.), p. 76.

about the moral responsibility of people. His basic questions were not, What is the world made of, and How does it operate? but rather, What is right action, and How can I know it is right? His mission was to persuade the young men of Athens to examine their lives in the pursuit of moral truth, for "the unexamined life is not worth living." His technique was to engage his pupils in a dialogue of questions and answers and to refute, correct, and guide them by this "Socratic" method to the right answers. He held that no man is wise who cannot give a logical account of his actions and that knowledge will point to the morally right choices; this belief led to his statement that "knowledge is virtue," one of several Socratic theses that seem paradoxical, for even ignorant men may be virtuous. Yet it was through ironic statements like these that he made people think critically and thus discover moral truths. The Roman orator and essayist Cicero said that Socrates brought philosophy down from the heavens and placed it in the cities of humanity.

Socrates' doctrines and his insistent questioning annoyed many Athenians. He also had political critics, for he was the tutor of several Athenians who had opposed democracy during the last years of the Peloponnesian War (Alcibiades was one of his followers). As a result, he was suspected of sympathy with the enemies of Athenian democracy, and in 399 B.C. he was brought to trial on charges of "worshiping strange gods and corrupting the youth"—a way of implying that Socrates had connections with enemies of the democratic state. One can understand why the Athenian jurors, who had just regained their democratic constitution from a short-lived oligarchy that fell in 403, would have wanted to punish anyone who had collaborated with the oligarchs. Convinced through misguided patriotism, the jury convicted him; when he proposed as his penalty a fine of 100 drachmas, while also ironically requesting an honorary dinner at the town hall, they reacted in anger by voting for the death penalty (*see box*, above). He accepted his fate, declined to seek exile outside his polis—for what would he do elsewhere at age 70?—and drank a cup of poison with simple courage.

Plato Our knowledge of Socrates' thought comes mainly from the writings of his most fa-truth. According to Plato, we see objects as real, but in fact, they are only poor reflections of ideal models, or "forms," which are eternal, perfect originals of any given object or notion.[2] In his *Republic*, Plato illustrates our lack of true perception with a famous metaphor. Imagine men sitting in a cave, facing a wall, with a fire behind them. As others carry objects through the cave, in front of the fire, the men see only vague shadows of the objects and therefore cannot make out the reality. Everything that we see is like these imprecise shadows; so what we see as justice, for example, is nothing but an approximation of the true "form" of justice. Only through long training in philosophy can we learn how to perceive and understand the true ideal forms, which exist outside our world.

Plato presents this thesis in several dialogues, of which the most widely read is *The Republic*. Like some other Athenian intellectuals, Plato opposed democracy as a political system dominated by emotion rather than thought. His repudiation of democracy intensified when a jury was persuaded to condemn Socrates to death, even though he had served the state as a soldier and had committed no crime. Socrates is the main speaker in the *Republic*, and in the work's long debate over the right form of state, he expresses severe criticisms of democracy as a volatile, unpredictable, and ineffective system. Yet it is by no means certain that these opinions were really those of the historical Socrates. It has been argued that Plato was the real antidemocrat and that he put these opinions into the mouth of Socrates. Whatever its source, Plato's denunciation of broad participation by the people in governing has remained a challenge to political theorists ever since.

Looking back at the death of his teacher at the hands of a popular court, Plato sought to dem-

▶ An Etruscan vase (about 520 B.C.) with a scene from Greek literature. Odysseus and his men escape from the Cyclops, Polyphemus, by putting out his only eye (Homer's *Odyssey*, Book 9). This scene is found on several other vases from Greece.

mous pupil, Plato (428–347 B.C.), for Socrates wrote nothing. Plato continued Socrates' investigation of moral conduct by writing a series of complex and profound philosophical books, mainly in the form of dialogues in which Socrates is the main speaker. In these works, Plato went far beyond the ironic paradoxes proposed by Socrates and sought truth through a subtle process of reasoning and inquiry that modern readers still endlessly discuss and probe.

Plato made his greatest impact on the future of philosophy with his theory of knowledge. Socrates' answer to the question, How can I know what is right? was simply that one must listen to one's conscience. Such reliance on the inner voice within each human being did not satisfy Plato, who believed that we must go beyond the evidence of our senses to find ultimate reality and

▶ *Facing page* An Attic relief, showing the goddess Athena leaning on her spear and gazing at a tablet, perhaps a list of men fallen in battle. If so, this would justify the name often given to this relief, the "Mourning Athena."

[2]Plato used the Greek word *idéa*, which means an image that one can see. Thus "form" is a better translation than the English "idea," even though the latter is widely used.

onstrate that people without a philosophical education should never exercise political power. Their chief disqualification was that they had no grasp of reality, since they were unable to perceive the forms. Government should therefore be in the hands of men who had received an education in philosophy. This ruling elite would see to it that "everyone will do his proper task." In Plato's preferred system, a second class, warriors, would defend the state; a third class, workers, would produce the needed material goods. Plato sums up his conception of good government in an epigram: "The state will be ruled well when philosophers become kings and kings become philosophers."[3]

Like other visions of a perfect state, Plato's *Republic* has had little effect on actual constitutions, but its analyses probe nearly every problem of philosophy, from statesmanship to the nature of perception, the power of language, and psychology. Through this rich book run many threads, but one above all: the question, What is justice? As we have seen, the issue of justice was central to Greek drama and also to the debates in the history of Thucydides: Indeed, it recurs throughout the whole fifth century. That the pupil of Socrates, who had seen his teacher condemned in what he considered a brutal distortion of justice, should have been obsessed by this question only emphasizes the degree to which Plato was a product of the Athenian society of his time.

[3]*Republic,* 473 c.

Aristotle Plato had a pupil of equal genius, Aristotle (384–322 B.C.), who was for a time the teacher of Alexander the Great of Macedonia. His investigations, in which he was assisted by his pupils in Athens between 336 and 322 B.C., embraced all fields of learning known to the ancients, including logic, metaphysics, astronomy, biology, physics, politics, and poetry.

Aristotle departed from Plato's theory that there is an ideal reality that cannot be perceived by the senses. For Aristotle each object has a purpose as part of a grand design of the universe. "Nature does nothing by accident," he said. The task of the philosopher is to study these individual objects to discover their purpose; then, from the conclusions he draws, he may ultimately be able to uncover a grand design.

Aristotle made that task his life's work. He and his pupils, meeting in a grove in Athens called the Lyceum, devoted themselves to collecting and systematizing knowledge in all fields. In one of his works, the *Politics*, he classified the types of political constitutions in the Greek world and distinguished three basic forms: monarchy, aristocracy, and moderate democracy. He warned that monarchy can turn into tyranny; aristocracy, into oligarchy; and moderate democracy, into

▶ **The so-called Temple of Concord from Agrigento, Sicily. Superb example of a fifth-century Doric temple. The stone was of inferior quality and was originally covered with stucco, still visible on some columns.**

radical democracy, or anarchy. Of the three un-corrupted forms, Aristotle expressed a preference for moderate democracy—one in which the masses do not exercise too much power. The chief end of government, in his view, is a good life, for both the individual and the community as a whole. This is an extension of the view expressed in his *Ethics* that happiness is the greatest good of the individual. To achieve this end, people must seek moderation, a mean between extremes of excessive pleasure and ascetic denial—a goal that reflected the Greek principle of harmony and balance in all things.

Aristotle's conception of the universe re-mained influential in scientific speculation for 2000 years. By about 350 B.C. philosophers gen-erally recognized four elements: earth, air, fire, and water. Aristotle gave them purpose and movement. Air and fire, he said, naturally move upward; and earth and water, downward. Move-ment he explained by saying that elements seek their natural place. Thus a stone falls because it seems to return to the earth. It also seeks to be at rest; all motion is therefore unnatural and has to be accounted for by an outside force.

To the four elements Aristotle added a fifth, ether, the material of which the stars are made. He explained that the stars move in a natural cir-cular motion, and outside the whole universe there exists an eternal "prime mover," which im-parts movement to all the other parts. This prime mover, or God, as Aristotle finally designates him, does not move or change; God is a kind of divine thought or mind which sets the whole uni-verse in motion.

Among the most interesting of all Aristotle's works are his writings on biology, which are based on extensive firsthand observation. In the *Generation of Animals*, he examines the birth and reproduction of animals, birds, fish, insects, and human beings. In the *Parts of Animals*, he dis-cusses the functions of the various parts of the body. Aristotle believed that nature, the creator of living things, designed every part with a spe-cific function. Thus, for example, the lion and wolf were given no vertebrae in the neck, because nature intended that they should have rigid necks for charging their prey. Such explanations are called *teleological* (from the Greek word *telos*, meaning "aim, goal"), and they remained influ-

▶ **An Attic kouros, or young man, leaning on one foot, showing a movement away from the severe toward a more natural style.**

ential for many centuries. Even more influential was Aristotle's effort to classify all that he ob-served in separate categories. His organizing principles remained the basis for investigations of nature until the scientific revolution of the sev-enteenth century.

II. *The Rise of Macedonia*

Plato and Aristotle theorized about the classical polis as it was entering a period of decline. The Peloponnesian War had exacted terrible losses in manpower; and instead of the needed healing period, there followed decades of interstate warfare that left the poleis weaker than ever.

THE WEAKNESSES OF THE POLEIS

Sparta, the victor in the Peloponnesian War, had established a puppet regime of obedient Athenians, known as the Thirty Tyrants, to govern Athens in 404 B.C.; but within a few months popular opposition swept this group away. As the Athenians sought to regain power, they revived their naval league in 394 B.C., though with many fewer members than it had had in the fifth century. But their arrogance had not subsided. Despite their promises to respect the independence of the league's members, the Athenians began to demand tribute from them as they had done under the Delian League. Rebellions followed, and this second league collapsed about 355 B.C.

Map 3.1 **Macedonia under Philip II,**
359–336 B.C.

By now there were no longer only two dominant cities in Greece. The polis of Thebes was becoming an important power, siding now with Athens, now with Sparta, in a series of never-ending quarrels. There was no clear trend in these struggles except that the constant intrigue and war, spanning several decades, drained the energies of all the antagonists. In 371 B.C. the brilliant Theban general Epaminondas won a victory over Sparta, which finally exploded the long-held belief in Greece that the Spartan infantry was invincible. The Thebans liberated Sparta's slaves, the helots, and helped them to found their own city, called Megalopolis, in the Peloponnese. The Spartans were thus deprived of much of their territory and of the slaves who had worked their land. A shortage of manpower accelerated the decline in Sparta's strength. Aristotle informs us about 335 B.C. that Spartan armies in the field had fewer than 1000 men, rather than the 4000 or 5000 who had gone into battle during the wars of the fifth century. Epaminondas himself died in another battle near Sparta in 362 B.C., and no comparable leader in any polis took his place. The era of independent city-states was all but over, doomed by the constant wars of the fourth century.

PHILIP II OF MACEDONIA

Macedonia, a kingdom in northern Greece, emerged as a leading power under an ambitious, resourceful king, Philip II, who reigned between 359 and 336 B.C. With shrewd political skill Philip developed his kingdom, built up a powerful army, and planned a program of conquest.

Using both aggression and diplomacy, Philip added poleis and large territories to his kingdom and extended his influence into central Greece. The great Athenian orator Demosthenes (384–322 B.C.), in a series of fiery speeches called "Philippics," beginning in 351, called on his countrymen to recognize the danger from Macedonia and prepare to make war against it. But by the time the Athenians responded, it was too late to halt the Macedonian advance. Philip won a decisive battle against Athens and several other poleis at Chaeronea in 338 B.C. All the city-states of southern Greece, except isolated Sparta, now lay at his mercy. He could have devastated many of them, including Athens, but his sense of tactics warned him not to do so. Instead, he gathered the more important poleis into an obedient alliance called the League of Corinth, which recognized Philip as its leader and agreed to follow him in his next project, an invasion of Persia.

But before Philip could open his Persian war, he was murdered in 336 B.C. by one of his officers who apparently had a personal quarrel with the king. Some historians have wondered whether Philip's wife or his son Alexander may have been involved in a plot to kill Philip and put Alexander on the throne; but tempting as such speculations may be, the sources do not give them clear support.

▶ The "Getty Bronze," a fourth-century statue in a soft, relaxed style. Surviving bronze statues from Greece are rare. Greek Sculpture Red tho Standard

Statue of victorious athlete. Artist unknown. Late 4th century B.C.

ALEXANDER THE GREAT

The empire built by Philip now passed to his son, Alexander III (reigned 336–323 B.C.), known as Alexander the Great, and never has a young warrior prince made more effective use of his opportunities. During his brief reign Alexander created the largest empire the ancient world had known and, more than any other man, became responsible for the eastward expansion of the Greek world.

In the next year, 335, a rumor of Alexander's death caused a democratic revolution in the city of Thebes. Alexander marched on Thebes and sacked it with the utmost brutality, destroying every building except temples and the house of the poet Pindar. Having thus warned the Greek cities against any further rebellions, Alexander began the invasion of the Persian Empire. The Persia that he attacked was a much weaker state than the one that had conquered Babylon or the one that Xerxes had led against the Greeks in 480 B.C. Intrigue and disloyalty had weakened the administration of the empire. Moreover, the king, Darius III, had to rely on Greek mercenary soldiers as the one disciplined element in his infantry, for native troops were mainly untrained. The weakness of Persia helps to explain Alexander's success, but in no way does it diminish his reputation as one of the supreme generals in history. His campaigns were astonishing combinations of physical courage, strategic insight, and superb leadership.

Alexander swept the Persians away from the coast of Asia Minor and in 332 B.C. drove them out of Egypt, a land they had held for two centuries. The Egyptians welcomed him as a liberator and recognized him as their pharaoh. While he was in Egypt (also in 332), Alexander founded the city of Alexandria. He intended this city to serve as a link between Macedonia and the valley of the Nile, and he had it laid out in the grid pattern typical of Greek city planning. Although he did not live to see it, Alexandria remained one of the conqueror's most enduring legacies: a great metropolis throughout history.

In the next season, 331 B.C., Alexander fought Darius III at Gaugamela, winning a complete victory there that guaranteed he would face little further opposition in Persia. Darius III was mur-

dered by disloyal officers in 330 B.C., and Alexander assumed the title of king of Persia. The expedition had now achieved its professed aim; yet Alexander, for whom conquest was self-expression, continued to make war. During the

▶ **The Venus of Cyrene (early third century B.C.), a most elegant, graceful depiction of ideal female beauty.**

Asia minor — India
11 thousand miles

Map 3.2 The Empire of Alexander the Great

next few years he campaigned as far east as India, where he crossed the Indus River (see Map 3.3), and finally, in 326 B.C., he began his march back. But at Babylon in 323 B.C., he caught a fever after a bout of heavy drinking, and within a few days he died, not yet 33. *He conquered the world & then died at age 33*

Alexander is a figure of such stature and power that he defies easy interpretation, and even today radically different biographies are written about this most famous man in Greek history. Part of our difficulty is that our best narrative source for his life, the Greek historian Arrian, lived four centuries after Alexander's death; and Arrian, for all his merits, was not the kind of probing historian who might have given us a rounded psychological portrait of the king. Yet it is clear that along with Alexander's courage and drive, perhaps as their necessary accompaniment, came a personality sometimes barely containing a raging animal. He executed a number of his friends for supposedly being aware of conspiracies against him; another one he murdered himself in a sudden fury. On the other hand, Arrian tells the moving story of Alexander's pouring a cup of water, offered him by his parched troops, into the desert because he refused to drink if his men could not.

sponsored the do new foundation of new cities. named after himself

Nor do we know just what Alexander was trying to accomplish. There is little reason to believe the popular myth that he hoped to conquer the world. His goal may have been a stable empire that would maintain his vast conquests, but if so he failed, for he had designated no successor and the empire disintegrated on his death. Some historians have believed that Alexander had a vision of the unity of the human race and was trying to establish an empire in which different peoples would live in harmony as within one family, but this view is widely, and rightly, rejected as sentimental and too idealistic. Others focus on his acts of cruelty and vindictiveness and see him as a paranoiac tyrant. In any case, no portrait of him should overlook his patronage of scholarship, which extended even to his bringing scientists and geographers with him as he invaded Persia. However we interpret him, he has remained the prototype of a world conqueror. Some of his successors put his portrait on their own coins, and even Roman emperors also issued medallions portraying him, as if to borrow his glory and power for their often threatened reigns.

III. The Hellenistic Age (323–30 B.C.)

We have said that the Classical Age of Greek civilization began about 500 B.C., just after the reform of the Athenian state under Cleisthenes. The next period, the Hellenistic Age, is usually dated from 323 B.C., when Alexander the Great died, to the death of Cleopatra of Egypt in 30 B.C. During this period the Greeks carried their culture throughout the Near East in the movement known as Hellenization.

THE DISSOLUTION OF ALEXANDER'S EMPIRE

Alexander's empire was shattered almost at once after his death, as his generals seized various parts for themselves. By about 275 B.C., after years of warfare and diplomatic intrigue, three large kingdoms emerged. A fourth kingdom was formed about 260 around the city of Pergamum in western Asia Minor. The kings of these states became absolute rulers, with complete authority over their realms. The subsequent history of these kingdoms is one of continual warfare until they were all eventually absorbed by the Roman Republic.

The king of Macedonia controlled northern Greece. The poleis in the south retained their autonomy, and some of them formed defensive leagues to protect their independence from the monarchy. The most influential were the Aetolian League in western Greece and the Achaean League on the northern coast of the Peloponnese. These leagues tried to strengthen themselves by awarding citizenship in the league to all citizens of their member cities; but this principle of confederation for mutual security arrived too late in Greek history to take firm root before Greece fell

▶ A scene from the magnificent "Alexander Sarcophagus" found at Sidon; fourth century B.C. Alexander is shown, left, hunting accompanied by a Persian. Although we have no reason to think Alexander was ever buried in this sarcophagus, the scene symbolizes Alexander's heroism and virility and calls attention to his conquest of the Persian Empire.

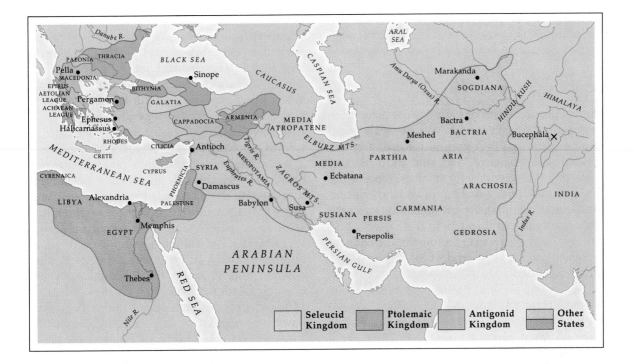

Map 3.3 HELLENISTIC KINGDOMS AFTER ALEXANDER, CA. 240 B.C.

to the expanding Roman Republic. As to the Egyptians and inhabitants of the Near East, they had long seen their rulers as divine or semidivine beings, and the Hellenistic kings in these areas exploited this tendency and established themselves as absolute monarchs who owned the kingdom.

Remarkably, considering the military roots of these kingdoms, the Hellenistic Age witnessed the reemergence of women as rulers. Their power first became evident in Macedonia, where Olympias, the mother of Alexander, was a more important political figure than any other woman in classical Greece. The most famous and skillful of all Hellenistic queens was Cleopatra of Egypt, who manipulated such Roman military leaders as Julius Caesar and Mark Antony to the advantage of her kingdom.

Hellenistic monarchs ruled through strong armies and large bureaucracies, and their systems of taxation were extremely efficient. Certain products, such as oil in Egypt, were royal monopolies and could be traded only at official prices. Greeks usually held the chief public of-

fices in the army and bureaucracy, and rulers did allow some democratic institutions, such as a town council, to function in Near Eastern cities; but the autonomy of these cities was limited to

▶ **The head of Alexander the Great in heroic profile; the obverse of a silver coin issued by Lysimachus, one of Alexander's bodyguards, who after his master's death became king of Thrace.**

local affairs. The king controlled all foreign policy, and he alone granted and could cancel such rights of self-government as the cities enjoyed.

ECONOMIC LIFE

One of the sharpest contrasts between the classical and Hellenistic worlds was the scale of economic activity. In classical Greece, farmers worked small plots of land, and industry and commerce were ventures of small entrepreneurs. In the Hellenistic states of Egypt and the Seleucid kingdom, vast estates predominated. Industry and trade operated throughout the Near East on a larger scale than ever before in the ancient world, requiring the services of bankers and other financial agents.

The Hellenistic world prospered as ambitious Greeks, emigrating from their homeland to make their fortunes, brought new vigor to the economies of Egypt and the Near East. They introduced new crops and new techniques in agriculture to make production more efficient. For example, Greeks had long cultivated vines, and they now enhanced the wines of Egypt. At the same time, they improved and extended the irrigation system and could thus devote more acreage to pasturing animals, which provided leather and cloth for the people and horses for the cavalry.

The growth of long-distance trade was even more remarkable. The Hellenistic rulers encouraged these efforts by establishing a sound money system, building roads and canals, and clearing the seas of pirates. Traders ventured eastward to India and, in the west, beyond the Mediterranean to the Atlantic coasts of Africa and Europe.

The resulting prosperity, however, was unevenly distributed. Rulers and members of the upper classes (usually Greek) amassed great fortunes, but little of this wealth filtered down to the small farmers and laborers. This great disparity between rich and poor led to increasing social conflict.

HELLENISTIC CITIES

The greater part of the vast lands of the new kingdoms was devoted to agricultural pursuits, but it was in the numerous Greek cities founded by Alexander and his successors that the civilization that we call Hellenistic was formed. Most of these new cities were in western Asia, in the Seleucid kingdom. Alexander had founded the brilliant city of Alexandria, in Egypt, but the Ptolemies who ruled Egypt did not follow his example by founding many cities. They considered a docile, rustic civilization far easier to control than citizens of a politically active urban society.

Some Hellenistic cities were magnificently ornate and spectacular. Besides their political institutions the Greeks brought from their homeland many of the amenities of polis life—temples, theaters, gymnasiums, and other public buildings. Pergamum, an outstanding example of city planning, contained a stupendous altar to Zeus, a renowned library, and a theater high above the main city with a superb view. It may have had as many as 100,000 inhabitants (under the Roman Empire its population was about 200,000), while Alexandria, the largest of all, had at least a half million.

Local families in the upper classes copied Greek ways and sent their children to Greek schools. Moreover, a version of Greek, *koiné* ("common") Greek, became an international tongue. Now, for the first time, people could travel to any city in the known civilized world and make themselves understood.

LITERATURE, ART, AND SCIENCE

The most significant literary achievements in the Hellenistic Age were in the field of scholarship. The kings of Egypt took pride in constructing a huge library in Alexandria that probably contained, by about 200 B.C., a half million papyrus rolls. Along with the library they built the Museum, a kind of research institute, where literary, historical, and scientific studies flourished, each employing its own experts. One of the main interests of literary scholars in Alexandria was the literature of the classical period, and among their achievements was the standardization of the Greek text of Homer. By comparing the many versions that had been handed down in manuscripts over the centuries, they were able to establish the text on which modern versions of Homer are based.

The specialization of scholars was characteristic of the growing professionalism of the age. Whereas the citizen of fifth-century Athens could be a farmer, a politician, and a soldier at the same time, now each of these roles was filled by a professional. The army consisted of professional soldiers, while professional bureaucrats ran the government.

▶ **Panels from the altar to Zeus at Pergamum, showing gods in combat with giants. Greek art preferred abstraction to reality, and such scenes probably represent the triumph of Greek civilization over non-Greek peoples. The violence and dramatizing are in the "baroque" tradition of Hellenistic art of the second century B.C.**

Hellenistic rulers also wanted to glorify their cities and provided generous subsidies for art and architecture. The architecture of the age tends to emphasize size and grandeur, as compared with the simplicity and human scale of classical architecture. Thus the Altar of Zeus from Pergamum, now in Berlin, included a great stairway, flanked by a frieze 400 feet long. The figures on the frieze, typical of Hellenistic sculpture, are carved in high relief, with an almost extravagant emotionalism that makes them seem to burst out of the background. Hellenistic sculpture also differed from that of the classical period through its devotion to realism. Instead of creating figures of ideal perfection, artists now showed individual-

▶ Bronze statue of a boxer from Rome, second century B.C. Greek sculptors had abandoned statues of ideal beauty and were now experimenting with scenes of frank realism. Note the boxer's battered face and bandaged hands.

ity in faces and bodies (see picture, above), even depicting physical imperfection or frank ugliness.

Advances in the field of science drew strength from the cross-fertilization of cultures in the Hellenistic Age. The Greeks had long speculated about the nature of the universe, and the Near East had an even longer scientific tradition, particularly in the fields of astronomy and mathematics. After Alexander's conquests joined the

two cultures, other conditions favored scientific advance: the increased professionalism of the age, the use of Greek as an international language, and the facilities of the Museum in Alexandria. The result was an age of scientific achievement that was not surpassed until the seventeenth century.

In mathematics, Euclid (about 300 B.C.) compiled a textbook that is still the basis for the study of plane geometry. Some of his theorems were already known, and others (for example, his demonstration that nonparallel lines must meet somewhere) may seem obvious. His remarkable accomplishment was to construct a succession of elegant proofs for these theorems, each based on earlier proofs, starting with the simple proposition that the shortest distance between two points is a straight line. The analytical method of his proofs is a characteristic of Greek thought, for Greek philosophers believed that knowing something entailed being able to prove it.

The greatest mathematician of antiquity—indeed, one of the greatest ever—was Archimedes of Syracuse, who also lived during the Hellenistic era (287?–212 B.C.). He calculated the value of *pi* (the ratio between the circumference and diameter of a circle); he developed a system for expressing immensely large numbers, by using 100,000,000 as the base (as we use 10); and he discovered the ratio between the volumes of a sphere and a cylinder circumscribing it (2:3, a proportion he had engraved on his tombstone). Archimedes was also a pioneer in physics; he demonstrated that a floating body will sink in a liquid only to the point at which it displaces its own weight. He understood the principle of using the lever for lifting massive weights and is said to have proclaimed, "Give me a place where I can stand and I will lift the earth" (that is, outside the earth entirely and with a long enough lever). He also invented the water screw still used for irrigation in Egypt. Tragically, he was murdered by a Roman soldier during the Roman attack on Syracuse in 212 B.C.—as he sat drawing a mathematical figure in the sand.

About 250 B.C., Aristarchus, an astronomer and mathematician, advanced a heliocentric theory of the movement of the planets. The view that the earth revolves around the sun was not new, but Aristarchus refined it by stating that the earth revolves on its own axis while it, together with the other planets, circles the sun. Not until the sixteenth century did astronomers prove the soundness of Aristarchus' system; meanwhile, the Greek astronomic tradition continued to follow an older geocentric theory, which held that the earth was the center of the solar system and that the sun revolved around it. The geocentric theory was the basis for the most important Hellenistic text on astronomy, the *Almagest* of Ptolemy of Alexandria (about A.D. 140). This book systematized Greek study of astronomy and remained the accepted text on the subject for more than 1000 years.

Hellenistic scientists also made important advances in the realm of measurements. Hipparchus calculated the length of the average lunar month to within one second of today's accepted figure. Eratosthenes about 225 B.C. computed the circumference of the earth to be about 28,000 miles, only 3000 miles more than the actual figure. Other scientists worked out the division of time into hours, minutes, and seconds, and of circles into degrees, minutes, and seconds.

PHILOSOPHY AND RELIGION

The change in life style from the relative security of the polis to the increasing uncertainties of a larger world shifted the direction of Greek philosophy. Plato and Aristotle had been philosophers of the polis in the sense that they were concerned with the individual's role in the intimate world of the city-state; the ideal state in their theories would have only a few thousand citizens. But when the city-state came to be governed by a large kingdom headed by a remote ruler, individual men and women could hardly influence its policies even though they were caught up in its wars and its many changes of fortune. Moreover, the large Hellenistic cities lacked the cohesiveness, the sense of belonging among citizens, that had made the classical poleis internally united. In such conditions, philosophers sought means of accommodation with the larger Hellenistic world that was shaping their lives. They tried to provide people with guidance in their personal lives and were less concerned about the nature of the political framework. Thus the two most important schools of Hellenistic philosophy, Epicureanism and Stoicism, were philosophies designed to provide comfort and reassurance for the individual human being.

Epicureans and Stoics Epicurus, who taught in Athens during the generation after Alexander, believed that people should strive above all for tranquillity, which he sought to provide through the atomic theory of Democritus. Our bodies and souls, Epicurus taught, are made up of atoms that cohere only for our lifetimes. When we die, the atoms will be redistributed into the universe again, and nothing of us will remain behind to suffer any desire for the life we have lost. Since death therefore holds no terrors, we should concern ourselves only with leading pleasurable lives, avoiding physical and mental pain. But emotional commitment and passionate love, in Epicurus' view, are equally unrewarding, since they may lead to disappointment and pain. Thus the wise person withdraws from the world to study philosophy and enjoy the companionship of a few friends. Some later Epicureans came close to advocating an almost heedless pursuit of pleasure, but in its early days this philosophy was intended as a powerful antidote to anxiety and suffering.

A different approach to this problem was that of a contemporary of Epicurus—namely, Zeno of Cyprus—who founded a philosophical school known as Stoicism, so named because he taught his pupils in a building in Athens called the Stoa. He believed that a single divine plan governs the universe and that to find happiness one must act in harmony with this plan. One should be patient in adversity, for adversity is a necessary part of the divine plan and one can do nothing to change it. By cultivating a sense of duty and self-discipline, people can learn to accept their fate; they will then become immune to earthly anxieties and will achieve inner freedom and tranquillity. The Stoics did not advocate withdrawal from the world, for they believed that all people, as rational beings, belong to one family. Moreover, to ensure justice for all, the rational person should discover his or her place in the world and consider it a duty to participate in public affairs.

The Stoics advanced ideas that were to have a profound influence on later Western history, especially as they were interpreted in the Roman and Christian visions of civilization: the concept that all humanity is part of a universal family; the virtues of tolerance; and the need for self-discipline, public service, and compassion for the less fortunate members of the human race. Furthermore, while most earlier Greeks had accepted the institution of slavery, the Stoics believed that the practice of exploiting others corrupted the owner (the slave could endure bondage by achieving inner freedom). Stoicism became the most influential philosophy among the educated of the Hellenistic Age and achieved great influence among the Romans, who adopted with conviction the ideals of discipline and fulfillment of public and private duty.

New Religions   The search for meaning in life preoccupied all levels of Hellenistic society, but none so painfully as the great masses of the poor. The answers of philosophy were addressed to an intellectual elite: wealthy scholars, as it were, meditating in the study. But the poor—lacking the education, leisure, and detachment for such a pursuit—looked elsewhere for spiritual and emotional sustenance in their daily encounters with the harshness of Hellenistic life. For many, religion answered their need for escape and consolation.

Among the new religious practices were the Near Eastern mystery cults that had some features in common as a result of the frequent intermingling of cultures in the cosmopolitan Near East. They are called mystery cults because they centered on the worship of a savior whose death and resurrection would redeem the sins of humanity; their rituals were secret, known only to the participants, and were elaborate, often wildly emotional; and they nourished hope by promising an afterlife that would compensate for the rigors of life on earth. One of the most popular mystery cults was the worship of the Egyptian deities Isis and Osiris. In this myth, Osiris had been dismembered but was reassembled and saved by Isis, his devoted wife; thus the myth suggested that its followers might also attain salvation and life after death.

All these political, scientific, and intellectual explorations were parts of the legacy of Alexander, the Macedonian who brought Greek civilization and the Greek language into another world. Greek was to be the language in which the New Testament was written, and therefore some historians have also seen his campaigns as preparing the way for Christianity and have even called Christianity his most important legacy. Be this as it may, the Greeks and Macedonians could not maintain permanent control over the remains of Alexander's empire. Not Greece but Rome became the uniting force that passed the legacy of classical civilization to medieval and then to modern Europe.

Recommended Reading

▼

Sources

Aristotle. *The Athenian Constitution.* P. J. Rhodes (tr.). 1984. The great philosopher's brief history and description of the Athenian state, with helpful commentary.

Arrian. *The Campaigns of Alexander the Great.* Aubrey de Sélincourt (tr.). 1958. Our main source for the life of the great conqueror.

Grene, David, and Richmond Lattimore (eds.). *The Complete Greek Tragedies.* 1959. The best collection of modern translations.

Plato. *The Republic.* Desmond Lee (tr.). 1974. The central work of Greek political philosophy.

Studies

Adkins, Arthur W. H. *Merit and Responsibility: A Study in Greek Values.* 1975. A summary of the ethical beliefs of the Greeks.

Cartledge, Paul. *Sparta and Lakonia: A Regional History, 1300–362 B.C.* 1979. Both a physical and a social-political history.

Cawkwell, George. *Philip of Macedon.* 1978. Macedonia before Philip II and the reorganization and expansion of the kingdom.

Dodds, E. R. *The Greeks and the Irrational.* 1951. Brilliant study of the Greek mind.

Dover, K. J. *Greek Homosexuality*. 1978. Dispassionate study of this feature of Greek life.

———. *Greek Popular Morality in the Time of Plato and Aristotle*. 1974. More limited in time than Adkins, by today's leading Hellenist.

Ellis, John R. *Philip II and Macedonian Imperialism*. 1976. Good modern study of the kingdom that was to dominate Greece.

Errington, R. Malcolm. *A History of Macedonia*. Catherine Errington (tr.). 1990. Compact one-volume treatment, carrying the story down through Alexander's successors.

Green, Peter. *Alexander to Actium. The Historical Evolution of the Hellenistic Age*. 1990. Now the most comprehensive historical and cultural survey; a colossal study.

Guthrie, W. K. C. *Socrates*. 1971. Excellent study of the man and his thought.

Hamilton, J. R. *Alexander the Great*. 1973. The best modern portrait of this controversial figure.

Hammond, N. G. L., G. T. Griffith, and F. W. Walbank. *A History of Macedonia* (3 vols.). 1972–1988. Monumental, detailed survey. For advanced students.

Hatzopoulos, Miltiades, and Louisa Lykopoulou. *Philip of Macedon*. 1981. Includes recent archaeological evidence about Macedonia.

Just, Roger. *Women in Athenian Law and Life*. 1988. Solid, often technical.

Kitto, H. D. F. *Greek Tragedy. A Literary Study*. 1969. Probably still the best general book on one of the supreme achievements of the Greeks.

Lacey, W. K. *The Family in Classical Greece*. 1968. Older treatment, still not wholly replaced as introduction.

Long, A. A. *Hellenistic Philosophy: Stoics, Epicureans, Sceptics*. 1974. The best introduction to the philosophies of these schools.

Pomeroy, Sarah B. *Goddesses, Whores, Wives and Slaves*. 1975. A groundbreaking study of the many roles of women in antiquity.

———. *Women in Hellenistic Egypt*. 1989. A study of women in the society offering the most evidence about their status.

Ross. W. D. *Aristotle*. 1956. Comprehensive study by a great master.

Vlastos, Gregory. *Socrates: Ironist and Moral Philosopher*. 1991. Most important recent study of style and significance of Socrates' philosophy.

Walbank, F. W. *The Hellenistic World*. 1982. The best one-volume introduction to the period.

"Noble" Romans, those whose ancestors had been consuls, had the right to have masks representing them carried in funeral processions. This republican noble of about 30 B.C. shows the masks of two of his ancestors.

CHAPTER FOUR

THE ROMAN REPUBLIC

THE contrast in the political and social systems of the two great ancient cultures that shaped Western civilization is unmistakable. The Greeks flourished in small, intensely competitive communities, but the Romans established a huge and long-lived empire. The character of the Roman people shines forth throughout their history. They valued discipline, obedience, and social cohesion. When the kings of early Rome disappeared, self-government emerged in a republic, but its practices were never so democratic as those of Athens. And from Rome's earliest days as a republic, the theme of its history was conquest and domination.

The result was the creation of a society that was primarily a military machine. Since an army is not a democracy, but a disciplined body governed by a few experienced men—an oligarchy—the effects were felt in every area of life.

The military machine formed in the Roman Republic united first the Italian peninsula and then the entire Mediterranean basin. In these conquests the state showed political skill, tenacity, and power of calculation easily superior to the volatile policies of Greek city-states. But in the process, a series of military dynasts became so powerful and ambitious that, over the course of a long revolution, they destroyed the republican constitution. This revolution also killed the elements of political freedom that had been put into place under the Republic. The response was the formation of a far more powerful autocracy, from which Europe was to descend—the Roman Empire.

I. The Unification of Italy (to 264 B.C.)

THE GEOGRAPHY OF ITALY

Italy is not, like Greece, divided into many small valleys or islands. The main geographic feature is the Apennine range, which runs diagonally across Italy in the north and then turns southward to bisect the peninsula. North of the Apennines, the Po River flows through a large, fertile valley that was for centuries the home of Celtic peoples known as Gauls. The hills of Italy, unlike those of Greece, are gentle enough for pasturing. The landscape is of unsurpassed beauty; some of the best Roman poetry—by Virgil, Horace, and Catullus—hymns the delights of the land and the pleasure of farming.

EARLY ROME

The legends about the founding of Rome by Aeneas or by Romulus and Remus are myths, so we must depend on archaeology to recover early Roman history. Pottery finds suggest that the site of Rome, along the Tiber River in the plain of Latium, was inhabited as early as 1400 B.C. Ancient scholars relied on myths to date the "founding" of Rome in 753 B.C. This date is not to be taken seriously as the moment when Rome came into existence, but there must have been considerable habitation in the area by that time, especially on the seven hills that surround the city. About 625 B.C. the settlers drained the marshes below the hills and built a central marketplace, the Forum. This was to be forever the center of Roman history.

Etruscans and Greeks Beside the Romans themselves, two other peoples are important in the early history of Rome. The first were the Etruscans, who actually dominated early Rome from about 625 to 509 B.C. The name *Roma* is Etruscan, and at least some of the kings of Rome were Etruscans. The origin of the Etruscans is obscure and has provoked a famous controversy. Some ancient sources say that they were a native European people, while the Greek historian Herodotus asserts that they arrived from Asia Minor. In any case, they appeared in Italy soon after

▷ **This sarcophagus is from a late sixth-century Etruscan tomb. The reclining couple on the lid reflects the influence of Greek art on the style of the Etruscans.**

▶ **The art of Etruscan tombs often showed dancing and banqueting in the afterlife. This fifth-century painting, from the Tomb of the Lionesses at Tarquinia, shows two dancers with jugs of wine.**

800 B.C., in the region north of the Tiber River known as Etruria (modern Tuscany). Their language is still undeciphered even though thousands of short Etruscan inscriptions exist.

The Etruscans had an urbane, technologically advanced culture and traded with Greeks and Phoenicians; Greek vases, especially, have been found in Etruscan tombs, and Etruscan art is strongly influenced by that of the Greeks. They also bequeathed to the Romans the technique of building temples, and they introduced the worship of a triad of gods (Juno, Minerva, Jupiter) and the custom of examining the innards of animals to foretell the future.

The second non-Roman people were the Greeks. Beginning about 750, they established about 50 poleis in southern Italy and on the is-

land of Sicily. So numerous were the Greek cities in southern Italy that the Romans called this region *Magna Graecia* ("Great Greece") and thus gave us the name *Greeks* for the people who called themselves Hellenes.[1]

Greek culture from these colonies influenced the Etruscans and, in turn, the Romans. For example, from the village of Cumae, the oldest Greek colony in Italy, the Etruscans learned the Western version of the Greek alphabet and passed it on to Rome; it became the basis for the alphabet used throughout the Western world.

About 500 B.C. (the Romans reckoned the date as 509) Rome somehow freed itself of its last Etruscan king and established a republican form of government. Thereafter, the Etruscans gradually declined as a power until they were finally absorbed by the Romans in the fourth century.

---

[1]The name *Graikoi* (Graeci, or Greeks) probably comes from one or more villages in central Greece called Graia; one such place is mentioned in Homer's *Iliad* (2.498).

The Early Constitution A large part of the history of the Roman Republic concerns the development of its constitution; this was never a written document but rather a set of carefully observed procedures and customs. The Roman system, like that of Sparta, had three major components, which tended to offset and balance one another. The executives were two officers called consuls, who were the supreme civil and military magistrates. On rare occasions the Romans appointed a man as "dictator," whose authority surpassed that of the consuls, but his office was limited to six months. There was also an advisory body of elder statesmen called the Senate. Finally, there were assemblies including all adult male citizens.

The consuls were elected annually by the Assembly of the Centuries, which was made up of the entire army; in this assembly the wealthier citizens voted first and could determine the result

▶ **This temple in central Rome, from the second century B.C., perhaps dedicated to Portunus, the god of harbors, is a typical Roman temple with a closed room for an image of the god. An altar stood in front. The columns are in the Greek Ionic order, and the temple has a deep basement, common in Etruscan building. Thus the temple unites the three cultures that went into the making of Rome.**

if they all voted the same way. This arrangement illustrates the hierarchical and conservative instincts of the Roman mind; so does the law providing that, in cases where the two consuls disagreed, one could block the action of the other, and the consul advocating no action had to prevail. Consuls possessed a right known as *imperium*, which gave them the power to command troops and to execute any other assignments they might receive from the Senate.

There were two other assemblies, the more important being the Assembly of Tribes, which was divided into 35 voting units (or tribes). Membership in a specific tribe was determined by a man's residence. This tribal assembly elected officers who did not command troops and therefore did not have imperium; and these magistrates, known as quaestors and aediles, looked after various financial matters and public works. The other body was the Assembly of Curiae, or wards of the city; this assembly met only to validate decisions taken elsewhere and gradually lost importance. Over the centuries, the Assembly of Tribes became the most active of the three assemblies and passed most of Rome's major laws.

The Senate was the nerve center of the whole state. It did not, in the Republic, pass laws, but it did appoint commanders, assign funds, and generally set the direction of the state. The Roman

Senate house, which still stands in the Forum, was thus the cradle of Roman power. The senators (usually about 300) were men who had held elected offices, and membership was for life. Their solid conservatism acted to restrain hotheaded politicians, and more than once they provided the moral leadership that saw the state through a military crisis. Rome had no political parties in the modern sense, but the Senate did have factions that were rivals in the struggle for power.

But the real basis of political power was the family: Indeed, modern historians have learned how to tell the story of the Republic through the study of the family. Alliances, divorces, marriages, and adoptions could all add to the political power of the family. A larger unit, the *gens* (or clan), included a group of related families consisting of, for example, all Romans whose second name was Cornelius or Aemilius. The great clans and their subdivisions contrived to maintain such firm control over high office that by about 100 b.c. it was rare for any man to attain the consulship who lacked ancestors who had

▶ **Many inscriptions, written by professional painters, in favor of this or that candidate in elections have been found on the walls of Pompeii, the city buried in the eruption of** A.D. **79.**

already been consuls. Such an outsider (for example, the orator Cicero) was referred to as a "new man."

THE STRUGGLE OF THE ORDERS (494–287 b.c.)

Within the citizen body, the Romans established a distinction that had no parallel in any Greek state. The patricians, a small number of clans (about 5 to 7 percent of the whole people), were recognized as being socially and legally superior to the vast majority, who were called plebeians. Ancient sources do not explain how the distinction arose; it was probably based on wealth gained from owning land and on the less easily defined criterion of social leadership. Membership in the patrician class was based on birth (or, occasionally, adoption), and originally only pa-

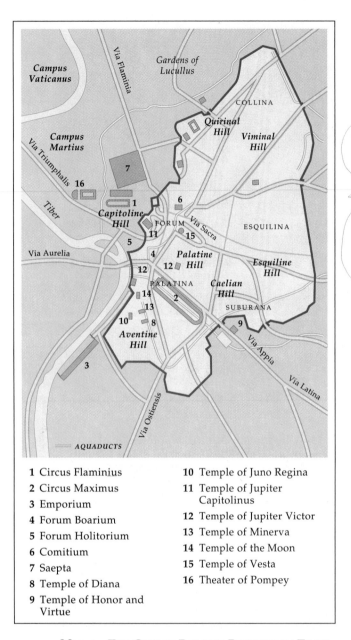

1 Circus Flaminius
2 Circus Maximus
3 Emporium
4 Forum Boarium
5 Forum Holitorium
6 Comitium
7 Saepta
8 Temple of Diana
9 Temple of Honor and Virtue
10 Temple of Juno Regina
11 Temple of Jupiter Capitolinus
12 Temple of Jupiter Victor
13 Temple of Minerva
14 Temple of the Moon
15 Temple of Vesta
16 Theater of Pompey

Map 4.1 THE CITY OF ROME IN REPUBLICAN TIMES

tricians could belong to the Senate and hold office.

The plebeians did gain a number of privileges in a long process called the struggle of the orders (or classes). When the struggle ended, the plebeians could point to significant gains, but the great families were still secure in their domination. Indeed, one effect of the struggle of the orders was to make the state an even more efficient machine for conquest, since the plebeians could now feel that they had a more favorable position within the system and were thus more willing to fight for their country.

Concessions to the Plebeians   The plebeians' first victory in the struggle came in 494 B.C., when they evidently threatened to secede from the state.[2] They now obtained the right to elect annually two men, called tribunes, to represent them; the number eventually rose to ten. The powers of the tribunes reveal the Roman genius for political compromise in the interests of a united state. The patricians evidently recognized that spokesmen for the people were a necessary evil, and they took an oath that made it a religious crime to violate or injure the body of a tribune. The "sacrosanctity" of the tribunes allowed them to interfere in any action, since no one could lay hands on them. Out of this protected status arose the famous veto power of the tribunes (sometimes called *intercession*); they could forbid any magistrate from acting and could even arrest consuls. Such power might have threatened to cause anarchy, but in fact, because it reassured the plebeians, it proved to be a stabilizing influence.

Other extensions of privilege to the plebeians included the publication of a code of laws, in 450 B.C. on the so-called 12 wooden tablets, and the right, in 445, to intermarry with patricians. Intermarriage created a patrician-plebeian aristocracy that replaced the original one restricted to patricians alone.

In 367 B.C. it was agreed that one consul each year should be a plebeian. Another office was now created—that of praetor, a kind of assistant consul who also held imperium. Eventually there were eight praetors elected every year, but there were never more than two consuls at a time. Therefore, as the road to the highest office narrowed, a praetor who wanted to become consul was well advised to observe the generally traditional ways of Roman politics.

[2]The sources give contradictory dates for, and accounts of, many events in Roman history down to about 280 B.C.; the order adopted here cannot always be proved right in every detail.

The state also restricted, in 367 B.C., the amount of public land that any citizen could occupy (the precise acreage allowed is disputed). This measure prevented the upper classes from acquiring an overwhelming share of farming land and made possible a dramatic growth of manpower among farmers who could, when necessary, serve in the army. It was, in fact, the huge reserve of fighting men that guaranteed Rome's expansion within Italy and its victories in the long Punic Wars.

The End of the Struggle of the Orders   The final concession to the plebeians came in 287 B.C., when a law (the Lex Hortensia)[3] made decisions of the Assembly of Tribes binding on the whole state without further action by any other body. Thus the common people now had the absolute legal right to pass laws; but in practice most legislation had the sponsorship of the Senate before it came before the Assembly of Tribes. The struggle of the orders was a real conflict, and it led to greater power for the plebeians; but the patrician-plebeian upper class managed to control the changes in the constitution before they could lead to the actual direction of affairs by the masses.

EARLY EXPANSION OF ROME

Rome's First Conquests   While the Romans were developing their form of government, they were also expanding their holdings on the Italian peninsula. Sometimes they could use peaceful diplomacy, for example, by making a treaty with other peoples living, like them, in the plain of Latium. More often they turned to outright military conquest in wars that were clearly long and arduous. One important victory was won over the last remaining Etruscan stronghold, the town of Veii, just across the Tiber River, which they took and destroyed in 396 B.C.

The period of conquest was not uniformly successful and was in fact punctuated by one major disaster. About 390 B.C. a large force of Gauls left their stronghold in the Po valley and captured part of Rome. They exacted a ransom as the

---

THE STRUGGLE OF THE ORDERS

The main stages by which the Roman plebeians attained a measure of equality with the patricians are as follows:

494 B.C.	First "secession" of plebeians; appointment of two tribunes (later rising to ten).
450	The Laws of the Twelve Tables, Rome's first written law code, published.
445	The Lex Canuleia permits marriage between plebeians and patricians.
367	Licinian-Sextian laws limiting amount of public land anyone could hold.
366	First plebeian consul.
287	Laws passed by plebeians are binding on the whole state; final victory of plebeians.

price of their withdrawal, but Rome then renewed its policy of expansion, showing the resilience that made it, in the words of the historian Edward Gibbon, "sometimes vanquished in battle, always victorious in war."[4] By the 290s Rome dominated the Italian peninsula as far south as the Greek city-states of Magna Graecia.

In the 280s some of the Greek cities summoned Pyrrhus, the king of Epirus (near modern Albania), to direct a campaign against Rome. Pyrrhus fought two successful battles in 280 B.C., but at a heavy cost in casualties to his own men (hence the phrase "a Pyrrhic victory"). The Romans again rebounded from defeat and Pyrrhus abandoned his allies in 275, leaving the Romans free to pursue their conquests. By 265 B.C. Rome controlled the entire Italian peninsula but had not yet mastered the Po valley.

The Roman Federation   Rome showed great administrative skill in organizing the conquered

---

[3]All Roman laws were named for their sponsors, in this case one Hortensius; since *lex* is a feminine noun in Latin, the adjective with it must end in *-a*.

[4]*Decline and Fall of the Roman Empire*, chap. 38.

communities by establishing different degrees of privilege and responsibility among them. Residents of a few favored communities were granted the most highly prized status, full Roman citizenship. This meant that they were on the same legal footing as the Romans; they enjoyed the protection of Roman law, they could make legal wills to pass on their property, and they could even hold office in Rome. Members of some other communities became citizens who could not vote but had the right of intermarriage with Romans. At a lower level of privilege were the allied states (*socii*). They received Rome's protection from other peoples and were also liable to provide troops. This carefully designed system of confederation enabled the Romans to solve an administrative problem that had frustrated the Greek poleis: how to control a large territory without having to demolish or transform the conqueror's own institutions. Even more important, the creation of this chain of alliances greatly expanded the manpower available to Rome in its progressive domination of the Mediterranean.

Map 4.2 ITALY IN 265 B.C., ON THE EVE OF THE PUNIC WARS

II. The Age of Mediterranean Conquest (264–133 B.C.)

THE PUNIC WARS

Rome—by which we now mean not only the ancient city but also the group of peoples in Italy allied with the city—at last had the strength in population to become a world power. The Romans achieved that goal in three wars with Carthage, a city that had been founded by Phoenicians about 700 B.C. and over the next century had established its own Mediterranean empire. By the time Rome had unified the Italian peninsula, Carthage controlled cities in northern Africa, parts of Spain, the islands of Corsica and Sardinia, and much of Sicily. It was beyond comparison the leading naval power in the western Mediterranean and could live off the tribute paid by its possessions. With good reason a German historian called Carthage "the London of antiquity."

The confrontation with Rome began in 264 B.C. as a minor conflict over the Sicilian city of Messana (modern Messina). The war soon became a contest for control of the island of Sicily itself and was the first of the three Punic Wars, so named from the Latin word *Poeni* for the Phoenicians who had founded Carthage. Roman tenacity finally won this war in 241, but with heavy casualties. Carthage abandoned Sicily entirely, large parts of the island passed to Rome, and it became the first Roman province (a territory outside Italy controlled by Rome). In 238 B.C. the Romans seized the islands of Corsica and Sardinia, formerly held by Carthage, and these islands, administered together, formed the second province.

The second Punic War (219–202 B.C.) was the most critical of the three. A quarrel arose over Saguntum, a town in Spain friendly to Rome. Hannibal, the brilliant Carthaginian general, seized Saguntum, thus in effect opening war with Rome, and determined to carry the war to the enemy. In autumn 218 he led his army from Spain across the Alps and down into Italy. Once there he hoped to arouse the Gallic tribes in the Po valley and break up the alliances of the various peoples with Rome, following which he would conquer Rome itself. In the end, Hannibal's twofold strategy failed. He won a stupendous victory over the Romans at Cannae, in southeastern Italy, in 216 B.C., which has remained a classic study for strategists ever since; but not even then could he arouse the allies to revolt. At least half of them chose to remain loyal to Rome, and without their help Hannibal's manpower was no match for that of the Roman federation.

While Hannibal was in Italy, the Roman commander Publius Cornelius Scipio carried the war into Spain. In 209 B.C. he captured the important city of New Carthage and by 206 he controlled most of Spain. In 204 he landed in Africa, near Carthage itself, where his victories brought about the recall of Hannibal from Italy and set the stage for a final clash between these two great generals and their forces. Scipio won the decisive battle in 202, at Zama in North Africa. In honor of the victory, Scipio received the name *Africanus* and proudly added it to his traditional Roman name. Besides paying Rome a huge indemnity, Carthage had to give up all its territory except its immediate surroundings in Africa and was forbidden to raise an army without Roman permission.

Thus the second war ended in a hard-earned victory for Roman perseverance and skill; but a large bill would later have to be paid. Hannibal had laid waste large tracts of farming land in southern Italy and had driven many farmers off their soil. In casualties, too, the cost to Rome had been severe: It is estimated that Roman military manpower fell from about 285,000 in 218 to about 235,000 in 203.

The third and final Punic War was a squalid affair, lasting from 149 to 146 B.C. There was in Rome a bitterly anti-Carthaginian group, led by a former consul, Marcus Cato, whose name has become symbolic of narrow intolerance. He succeeded in provoking this war and in making it a campaign of punishment against Carthage. Another Scipio, Aemilianus, captured and destroyed Carthage in 146. The city was utterly razed and cursed (the tale that the victors poured salt into the soil is, however, a modern fiction), and the territory became the Roman province called simply Africa. The conquest of the territory formerly held by Carthage in Europe was completed as Rome conquered almost all of Spain by 133 B.C.

EXPANSION IN THE EASTERN MEDITERRANEAN

In the following decades the Romans continued their conquests until they had mastered the whole Mediterranean basin. Historians have long debated whether this policy represented deliberate imperialism or was at least partly accidental. Certainly the first stage was forced on Rome by the king of Macedonia, Philip V (ruled 221–179 B.C.). He drew Rome into war by forming an alliance with Hannibal after the battle of Cannae and thus opened the gate through which, over centuries, Roman troops and administrators

---

THE ROMAN PROVINCES

The dates when some of the major Roman provinces were formed.

227 B.C.	Sicily and Sardinia.
197	Nearer and Farther Spain.
146	Macedonia; Africa (old territory of Carthage).
129	Asia (old territory of Pergamum).
c. 120	Transalpine Gaul.
62	Syria.
16–13	Three Gauls (northern France, conquered by Caesar).

poured as far east as Armenia and changed the course of European history.

During this era Rome also became involved in war with Antiochus III, the Macedonian ruler of Syria, the kingdom founded by Seleucus after the death of Alexander. Roman forces defeated his army at Magnesia in 190 B.C.—another significant moment in Rome's expansion, as Roman legions left Europe and fought in Asia for the first time.

After further quarrels, the Roman Senate realized that outright annexation of the Greek mainland was the only way to secure its interests. Therefore, in 146 B.C., Macedonia and southern Greece were combined into a province—Rome's first acquisition of territory in the Greek world. Thus the Romans brought to an end the independent political life of mainland Greece, and from this time on their dominance in the Mediterranean could not be denied or reversed.

Some experienced rulers in the region were shrewd enough to perceive what had happened and began a process of accommodation to Rome. For example, in 133 B.C., the last king of Pergamum died without leaving a successor and the Romans found that he had willed his kingdom to Rome—surely because he had seen that the kingdom of Pergamum could not long survive without Roman protection. Four years later Rome created the province of Asia, based on the territory of Pergamum (see Map 4.3). This province possessed great wealth and offered tempting opportunities for a governor of Asia to enrich himself through corruption; the post became highly desirable for ambitious politicians and also brought with it a posting to the pleasant climate of the beautifully built Greek cities.

Map 4.3 THE EXPANSION OF THE ROMAN REPUBLIC, 241—44 B.C.

THE NATURE OF ROMAN EXPANSION

Rome's success in its domination of the Mediterranean rested on certain unique historical conditions. Early in its history, events had forced the city to seek defensive alliances. After the expulsion of the Etruscan monarchs, for example, Rome had to unite militarily with its neighbors in the plain of Latium against a possible Etruscan counterattack. Constant wars in the fourth and third centuries, such as the invasion by the Gauls in 390, further emphasized the need for common security. The result was a commitment to, and mastery of, military force that proved to be unsurpassed, and this soon developed into a highly effective and (when necessary) utterly ruthless policy of conquest. Scipio Aemilianus, for example, forced the people of Numantia, in Spain, to surrender in 133 by reducing them to cannibalism and even cut off the hands of 400 young men in a neighboring city who had advocated aiding their Spanish brethren. The Senate at home considered Aemilianus' achievements worthy of a triumphal parade, the highest military honor that Romans could bestow on a successful commander.

Provincial Administration The Latin word *provincia* means "a duty assigned to a magistrate," and the Romans extended the meaning to denote the various regions that they acquired through conquest. The Senate chose the governors for the various provinces, often giving them the title *proconsul* ("in place of a consul"). These governors ruled their provinces with absolute power, though they could not violate Roman law or act illegally against Roman citizens. Some provinces were well ruled, but others were notorious for their corrupt governors. From the Roman view the advantage of the system was its efficiency: Rebellions were not common, and troops stationed in the provinces could maintain control without resorting to massacres.

The provinces furnished financial support for the Roman Republic. Some had to pay tribute in various forms, usually food, while others were assigned a fixed sum of money. In order to obtain these taxes, the state devised a convenient, but corruptible, system of tax collection. Companies of tax collectors bid for the contracts to collect the taxes of certain provinces, especially Asia. They paid the state a fixed sum in advance and then tried to make a profit by collecting taxes in excess of what they had paid. The natives of the provinces were nearly helpless against the raids of the *publicani*, as tax collectors were called. Their only protection was the governor of the province, who was supposed to see that the *publicani* did not collect more than a reasonable amount. Unfortunately, however, the collectors could use their funds as bribes to persuade the governor to overlook their rapacity.[5] These tax collectors came from a nonsenatorial class known as *equestrians* (their name, *equites*, originally meant "cavalry"). Besides collecting taxes, equestrians formed companies to build roads and aqueducts, owned land, and managed businesses of all kinds. Senators were forbidden to be in business, and some equestrians could far outstrip senators in wealth through their multiple enterprises, but they held no political office.

ROMAN SOCIETY IN THE REPUBLIC

The Roman Family The forceful part played by the family in Roman politics was reflected in the organization of the family itself. The Romans accepted direction from the top in most areas of their society, and this kind of structure was built into the family of patricians and plebeians alike. The father of the family, the *paterfamilias*, was the absolute owner of the whole family, which included children, land, other property, animals, and slaves. So long as he lived, his sons, even if married with their own households, remained in his power. On the death of the father, each of his sons became a *paterfamilias* in his own family. Such a severe system differs from anything known in Greece but has parallels in Israelite society.

In early Rome, wives were also legally within the power of their fathers or husbands (again as in ancient Israel), and their chief virtues were considered to be silence and obedience. The sources tell stories about women legally executed by their families for adultery or other offenses. A young woman was normally married at about 14,

---

[5]Cicero, a firm supporter of the *publicani*, called them "the flower of the Roman equestrians, the ornament of the state, and the foundation of the Republic."

as in Greece, and in early times she was transferred to her new family and lost her right to her native family's property. But this system could not last forever. As Rome became wealthier, the narrow framework of women's lives was loosened. Marriage less often involved the placing of a woman under the absolute power of her husband. The reason for this change was not necessarily a wish to respect women's rights: Rather, it was that wealthy families with well-off daughters did not wish to lose control over their property. Marriages now became less stable, and we find women of prominent families, especially in Rome itself, moving in society, and even from husband to husband, with a freedom impossible in Greece. In apparent alarm at the emancipation of women, the elder Cato supported an existing law forbidding women to possess jewelry and wear colored dresses, which tells us that they were doing so in the second century B.C. Despite Cato's dislike of such women's liberation, we do not find in Rome that undercurrent of fear of the mysterious powers of women that can be seen in Greek myth and literature.

As in Greece, Roman women could not hold office or vote, but they greatly surpassed Greek women as influences behind the scenes. One especially eminent woman was Cornelia, the daughter of Scipio Africanus, the victorious general in the second Punic War. On the death of her husband she refused all offers of marriage, including one from a king of Egypt, and devoted herself to the education of her 12 children, among whom were the tribunes Tiberius and Gaius Gracchus. She was a woman of high education who maintained a salon and whose letters were praised for their elegant style; indeed, she had a position and prominence unparalleled by any woman in classical Greece.

Other women in the Republic also became important as a link between prominent families in marriage alliances, which were arranged by fathers, often for the political advantages they would confer. One notable such marriage made Julius Caesar the father-in-law of Pompey and cemented the alliance of the two men during Caesar's rise to supreme power. Julia, the daughter of the first emperor, Augustus, was also married to men favored by this emperor, in order to continue his family line. The influence of women in politics continued to grow enormously during the Roman Empire, when the long periods of an emperor's reign allowed wives and mothers of rulers to learn and control the levers of power in the imperial court. Yet we must not exaggerate the degree to which Roman women were liberated. In all periods, as in Greece, sarcophagi and tomb reliefs portray men with their wives in conventional poses, and on some inscriptions, the women are praised for modest domestic virtues: "She was chaste, she was thrifty, she remained at home, she spun wool."

Religion Roman religion consisted largely of forms of worship that upheld Roman tradition. Within the household, the father acted as the priest and led the family in its worship of household gods—for example, Janus, the god protecting the doorway; Vesta, the spirit of the hearth; and household spirits known as Lares and Penates.

Public religion, on the other hand, was closely connected with the interest of the state. Priesthoods were mainly political offices, held only by men. Women were, however, responsible for one of the most important religious duties: It fell to six virgins to maintain the sacred fire of Vesta that guarded the hearth of the state. These Vestal Virgins were held in high honor and lived in a spacious, elegant villa in the Forum; by a remarkable exception, these women were freed of the power of their father. Roman rites seem to have been designed mainly to placate the gods—almost to keep them at arm's length through sacrifices. Eventually the rites hardened into patterns whose original meaning had sometimes been forgotten; but so long as the priests did not deviate from routine, the Romans assumed that the gods were satisfied and would not frustrate their enterprises.

As for mythology, nearly all of it was an adaptation of Greek legend, and Roman gods were often Greek deities with Roman names. The Greek father-god Zeus became Iuppiter, or Jupiter; his wife Hera became Juno; Athena became Minerva; Hermes became Mercury; and so on. These gods were officially worshiped in public and also in the home along with the household deities, these latter being minor gods with no connection to the Greek pantheon. Perhaps because Greek myths often show gods behaving spitefully or immorally, the Romans also created certain uplifting ideals—such as Virtus (manly conduct), Pax (peace), Fides (loyalty), and Pudor (modesty)—and transformed them into gods.

Early Roman Literature It may seem surprising that it took the Romans centuries to develop a literature. Homeric epic is older than the Greek city-states themselves, but Rome had been independent of the Etruscans for the better part of three centuries before a significant literature emerged. Evidently the Romans needed contact with Greek civilization, which came about during the age of conquest, to stimulate their own literary efforts. After the first Punic War, one Naevius wrote an epic poem (thus imitating Homer), but it has not survived.

The earliest preserved Latin literature is the comedies, influenced by the Greeks, that were written by Plautus (250?–184? B.C.) and Terence (190?–159? B.C.). These playwrights imitated Greek New Comedy, as it is called, in which the plays were entirely fiction. The Romans did not approve of Old Comedy, such as the plays of Aristophanes, which savagely lampooned active

▶ **A late Republican gravestone showing one Lucius Vibius and his wife and child. Roman realism is evident in the portraiture. The face of the man suggests the determined conservatism that shaped the Roman character during the Republican period.**

politicians. Plautus filled his comedies with stock situations and characters, such as mistaken identities, lecherous old men, and frustrated romances. One of his plays about mistaken identities, the *Menaechmi*, was used by Shakespeare as the model for his *Comedy of Errors*. Terence wrote comedy in a more refined and delicate style than Plautus. His characters are less earthy, and the humor emerges from more subtle situations or such human foibles as greed.

The Greek Polybius (200?–118? B.C.), though not a Latin writer, helped create a Roman literary tradition as a historian of the Roman Republic. He was deported as a hostage to Rome in the 160s, where he met many Roman statesmen and became an expert in Roman history. He wrote a general history of the Greco-Roman world from the first Punic War down to his own times, largely to demonstrate the inevitable domination of the Mediterranean by the Romans.

Polybius believed that much of Rome's success in government was due to its well-designed constitution—a commendable mixed form of state that would probably long maintain Rome's power. He traveled widely and insisted on the need to visit sites in order to grasp the importance of geography to history. His work is analytic and methodical and attempts to revive the high standards of historical writing that Herodotus and Thucydides had established. He is both the most important historian of the Hellenistic Age and the most reliable guide to earlier Roman history.

III. *The Roman Revolution (133–27 B.C.)*

SOCIAL CHANGE AND THE GRACCHI

The Changing World of Italy The breakdown of the Roman Republic has been called Hannibal's legacy, for the ravages of years of fighting up and down Italy had brought many farmers to the point of ruin. On the other hand, wealthy citizens had enriched themselves with booty and the spoils of war. The less fortunate had often lost their land or were willing to sell it to these newly wealthy men. There had also been a great increase in the slave population on Italian soil from prisoners of war, and these slaves depressed the wages paid to private workers. Often the displaced farmers had little choice but to join the ranks of the permanently unemployed. Their poverty threatened to impede the recruitment of soldiers into the Roman army, for Rome had nothing like a modern war treasury, and only men who had enough money to buy their own armor could be drafted into the legions. Without sufficient recruits, the gains from the conquests might be lost.

Tiberius Gracchus Two ambitious young Roman statesmen, Tiberius and Gaius Gracchus, moved to solve these problems. Their mother, Cornelia, was a well-known daughter of a great family; her father was the Publius Cornelius Scipio Africanus who had won the war against Hannibal. She had married a prominent plebeian

politician, Tiberius Gracchus, and thus her sons were plebeian, though descended from the loftiest aristocracy. Tiberius, the older brother (162–133 B.C.), became tribune for 133 and proposed a bill to the Assembly of Tribes that would allow the state to assign parcels of public land, reclaimed from the wealthy, to dispossessed farmers, with the aim of increasing the supply of potential recruits for the army. The bill was opposed by another tribune, who tried to veto it on behalf of vested interests. Tiberius persuaded the people to remove this tribune from office, a dangerous action barely within the constitution. Once such a step had been taken, what tribune would be safe in the future from a similar threat? But the people followed Tiberius, and the bill was passed.

▷ **An unknown Roman of the Republic. The realistic portrait shows the dignity and virility of a Roman *paterfamilias*.**

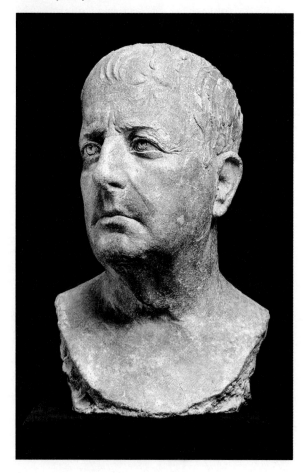

The distribution of land was in progress when Tiberius decided to run for reelection. This was a breach of custom, for tribunes held office for only one year. Some of his opponents feared that he might seize permanent leadership of the propertyless and lead them into social revolution. A group of senators, late in 133, took the law into their own hands and provoked a riot in which Tiberius was clubbed to death—an event that gave grim warning of a new intensity in Rome's political struggles. Above all, the taboo against assassination had been violated, and this first step, once taken, became easier to repeat. Despite Tiberius' death, the distribution of land continued, and his enemies even took credit for the success of the project.

Gaius Gracchus Tiberius' younger brother, Gaius, became tribune 10 years later, in 123. He proposed several measures that sought to limit the prerogatives of the Senate. One of the most important concerned the extortion court, which investigated cases of alleged extortion by provincial governors and tax collectors. The jurors, all senators, were usually not severe in judging governors, who were fellow members of the Senate. Gaius had a bill passed that assigned the seats on this jury to members of the equestrian class.

All tax collectors were equestrians, and it was now they who had the potential to favor members of their group who might be accused and brought to trial. Gaius' arrangements were later revised, but he was the first to make the extortion court the subject of a bitter political quarrel.

Gaius weakened his own standing with the people by proposing that Roman citizenship be offered to large numbers of Italians who were not yet Roman citizens. They had been asking for this status to protect themselves against having their land confiscated for distribution to those whom the Romans were resettling. But the voters of Rome, warned by Gaius' opponents that they would now have to share their privileges with outsiders, refused to extend their citizenship.

Like his brother, Gaius Gracchus came to a violent end. After he left office, his enemies asserted that he was planning a revolution. The Senate then instructed one of the consuls for the year 121 to "see to it that the state suffered no harm," thus inviting the consul to use force to

---

THE ROMAN REVOLUTION

The main landmarks in the Roman revolution were as follows:

133 B.C.	Tiberius Gracchus elected tribune and is killed in riot.
123–2	Gaius Gracchus tribune; equestrians gain control of extortion court; Gaius killed.
107	First consulship of Marius.
91–88	War with Italian allies.
81–79	Sulla's dictatorship.
70	First consulship of Pompey and Crassus.
66	Pompey given command against Mithridates in Asia.
59	Julius Caesar consul, receives command in Gaul.
58–50	Caesar's conquest of Gaul.
49	Caesar invades Italy, opening of civil war.
44	Caesar murdered.
31	Battle of Actium, defeat of Mark Antony.
27	Supremacy of Octavian, later called Augustus; beginning of Roman Empire.

---

suppress the younger Gracchus. When the consul raised a mob to hunt him down, Gaius had one of his own slaves kill him.

The Gracchi had unleashed a whirlwind when they invited the Assembly of Tribes to take a more activist role. It is true that the people had long possessed the right to legislate in this assembly, but they had not always had the will; nor had ambitious tribunes always dared to use such a weapon. But now demagogues began to turn more and more to this assembly to pass bills in favor of their military patrons. From this moment began the slow but sure Roman revolution.

THE YEARS OF THE WARLORDS

The Gracchi could not protect themselves from the violence of the Senate because they had no army. But as Roman conquests brought the state into further wars, powerful generals appeared who did have the support of their armies and used it to seize power. Their struggles against one another undermined the republican constitution and the state finally collapsed into dictatorship.

Marius   The first general to play this game was Gaius Marius (157?–86 B.C.), a "new man" from the country near Rome. He is a crucial figure because he changed, radically and forever, the membership of the Roman army and the direction of its loyalty. He gained high prestige by winning a war (111–106 B.C.) against Jugurtha, a king in North Africa. Marius' reputation grew even more after he drove back an attempted invasion (105–101 B.C.) by some Germanic tribes moving toward northern Italy. Such was his stature in this period that he was consul for five consecutive years and dominated politics from 107 to 100 B.C.

In order to raise large numbers of men for the German wars, Marius abolished the old requirement that a soldier had to own at least a modest amount of property, and he also accepted volunteers instead of just drafting men for service. As a result, the army came to be composed largely of poor men who served their commander, received booty from him, relied on him as their main patron, and expected him to obtain for them a grant of land that they could then farm after they were discharged. Thus Marius converted the army into an instrument for ambitious commanders during the remaining years of the Republic and even throughout the Roman Empire.

The War with the Italians   The Italian peoples who were Rome's allies had never been granted Roman citizenship, and in 91 B.C. some of them proclaimed themselves independent and opened a war that continued until 88. In the end the Romans negotiated with the Italians and allowed them to acquire citizenship. But the fact that it required a war to obtain this concession shows that both the upper classes—the senators and equestrians—and the common people were still jealous of their privileges.

Senatorial Reaction under Sulla   The Italian War made the reputation of another powerful general, Lucius Cornelius Sulla (138?–78 B.C.). In the 80s civil war broke out in Rome among various factions of senators. One group rallied behind Sulla and his legions, seeing in them the best vehicle for their own ambitions. In 88 Sulla invaded the city of Rome itself with his supporters—the first but not the last time that the ancient city was thus seized by Romans themselves. All that Sulla wanted for himself was command of a war against Mithridates, who ruled the kingdom of Pontus (extending along the south coast of the Black Sea) from 120 to 63 B.C. Sulla departed for this campaign in 87 B.C., and during his absence, other politicians, just as unscrupulous as he was, seized Rome in turn. But as soon as Sulla was free of his Eastern war he returned to Italy and once more occupied Rome (November 82). He had hundreds of his opponents executed and had himself named dictator without limit of time, thus breaking the customary six-month limit for holding that office.

Sulla used his supreme power to reshape the state on strictly authoritarian and conservative lines. Two forces, he thought, had menaced the rigid control over Rome that the Senate should enjoy: the tribunes of the people, who had made the Assembly of Tribes more conscious of its power, and the generals who had used the loyalty of their armies to gain political leverage. To deal with the first of these threats, Sulla forced through a law forbidding tribunes to offer legislation without prior approval from the Senate and denying them the right ever to hold any other office—a rule that would make the tribunate unattractive to young men with political ambitions.

Sulla handled the army commanders by restricting their service as governor of a province to a period of one year. This scheme neatly ensured that no commander could remain on the scene long enough to become a familiar hero to his troops and possibly the leader of a new march on Rome. He further established minimum ages

▶ **This idealized statue of the first century B.C. shows the ruthless tyrant Cornelius Sulla in the dignified pose of a classical orator.**

at which a man might hold the various offices in a political career (a consul, for example, had to be 42 or over). He also canceled the work of Gaius Gracchus on the jury system; as one might have expected from this strict traditionalist, he gave all the seats on the juries back to senators.

Sulla resigned the dictatorship in 79 B.C., a rare act in any supreme ruler, but he evidently thought he had put the Senate so firmly in control that he was no longer needed; he died in 78. To his enemies he was pitiless, and his executions of Roman citizens were horrifying, but he was also a clever political strategist. He had done his part for the conservative cause by putting the Senate in charge, but this body proved unable to manage the next generation of warlords.

The Rise of Pompey Sulla had used the tool forged by Marius—an army loyal to a commander—and another warlord soon followed his example, namely Gnaeus Pompeius (106–48 B.C.), usually called Pompey. He first gained a reputation in 77 B.C., when he was sent to Spain to end a revolt there. After completing this task, and while his army was still intact, he helped suppress a rebellion of slaves in Italy led by a Thracian slave named Spartacus. This campaign was already being waged by another ambitious Roman, Marcus Licinius Crassus, the richest man of his time. No sooner was the slave revolt crushed in 71 B.C. than the joint commanders, Pompey and Crassus, marched their armies to the gates of Rome and demanded both consulships for the year 70. Pompey was legally unqualified for this office, for he was only 36 and had held no previous magistracy. The Senate, however, lacked the will to enforce the constitution and resist the two men, and they were elected consuls.

During their consulship Pompey and Crassus canceled several of Sulla's arrangements. They restored to the tribunes their right to propose legislation, and they mixed senators and equestrians in the always controversial juries. At the end of their year in office, both consuls retired without demanding any further appointment—an action that, though at first surprising, was really consistent with Pompey's ambitions. He wanted to be the first man in the state, but he disliked committing himself to open revolution. A modern historian has compared him to Shakespeare's Macbeth: He would not play false and yet would wrongly win.

In 67 B.C. Pompey was next given an extraordinary command to deal with pirates operating in the Mediterranean who were interfering with the grain supply for Rome—a critical matter, since the city had to live on grain shipped to its harbor. Pompey fulfilled his orders and cleared the seas in a swift campaign. Then in 66 B.C. he received through the Tribal Assembly an even more important command in Asia Minor, where Rome was involved in war with Mithridates, Sulla's old enemy, who was still on his throne. Pompey successfully fought the difficult war in Asia Minor and set up a system of client kings, rulers of smaller states whose loyalty to Rome was ensured by the familiar device of "friendship."

Cicero During Pompey's absence overseas, Marcus Tullius Cicero (106–43 B.C.) became the chief nonmilitary statesman in Rome. Like Marius, he was a "new man" from the countryside, but unlike him, he chose a career in law and administration. His administrative skill won for him each successive political office at the earliest possible legal age. He was genuinely dedicated to compromise and political negotiation and thought that such procedures would establish the combined rule of the two upper classes, the senatorial and equestrian.

Cicero was also the most versatile Latin writer of his time, and his polished prose style became the model in Latin for clarity and elegance. His philosophical treatises do not follow the doctrines of any particular school; he was equally interested in Stoicism, the thought of Plato, and several other schools, and he chose whatever seemed persuasive from Greek writings for his own theories. In *On the Republic,* for example, he accepted the Platonic view that wise leaders ought to govern the state, but he disregarded the more technical aspects of Plato's philosophy.

Cicero's political speeches are a continuous record of his career and his frustrated ambitions. He enjoyed his political success as a "new man" and sought a place for himself among the upper classes, believing that they should guide the state along established constitutional lines. Unfortu-nately, most politicians in the later Republic could be tempted away from any allegiance to the constitution and selfishly followed their own personal advantage. Cicero never became a magnetic leader around whom others gathered. His letters are a frank and often painful record of the compromises that he was forced to make in the treacherous world of Roman politics.

When Pompey returned to Rome in 62 B.C. from his Eastern victories, he had two political aims. He wanted the Senate to ratify the arrangements he had made in Asia Minor; and he requested a grant of land for his men. This latter request, as we have seen, was nothing unusual. It reflected the relationship between a general and his troops, which was that of patron and client—one of the oldest traditions in Rome. But some senators, either jealous or fearful of his prestige, combined to frustrate his wishes. This short-term victory practically doomed the Senate and the Republic, for it drove Pompey into a political alliance with Julius Caesar, who proved to have the revolutionary will that Pompey lacked.

THE FIRST TRIUMVIRATE

Gaius Julius Caesar (100–44 B.C.), a descendant of an old patrician family, returned to Rome in 60 B.C. from his post as governor of Spain. Politically, he is an example of the aristocrat who bases his power on the common people. He, too, had enemies within the Senate, where many looked on him as a brash upstart. They refused his request to be allowed to run for the consulship of 59 in absence and then lead a triumphal parade through the city. Faced with this direct affront to his dignity, Caesar made a political bargain with Pompey and with Crassus, who was also at odds with some powerful senators over a financial matter. The three formed a coalition known to historians as the First Triumvirate, and their united influence at the polls elected Caesar as one of the consuls for 59. To confirm the bargain in a manner customary in Roman politics, Pompey married Caesar's daughter.

Caesar's Consulship and the Gallic War Caesar's influence secured allotments of land for Pompey's army and the approval of his arrangements in the East. Crassus' financial quarrel was also settled to his satisfaction. Caesar then secured for himself the command over Cisalpine Gaul (the Po valley) and the coast of Illyria for a guaranteed period of five years beginning on March 1, 59 B.C. About this time the governor of Transalpine Gaul (Provence, in the south of France) died, and this province was also added to Caesar's command.

Caesar intervened in the politics of the Gallic tribes and opened a series of campaigns that finally brought the whole area of modern France and Belgium under Roman rule. The Romans implanted in Gaul the Latin language, the origin of modern French, Roman technology, and Roman ways in general. Caesar narrated and defended

▶ Perhaps the most spectacular classical monument in Europe, the Pont du Gard was built in the first century A.D. to carry water to Nîmes (ancient Nemausus) in France. The water ran through a trough above the top layer of arches. The aqueduct is an example of the Romans' mastery of hydraulic technology and construction in arches.

Map 4.4 GAUL IN THE TIME OF CAESAR

his actions in his *Commentaries on the Gallic War*, which to this day remains a superb textbook in political-military decision making.

The Gallic War lasted from 58 to 50 B.C. Caesar's two partners in the triumvirate, Pompey and Crassus, were always suspicious of each other, but they maintained fairly good relations and even held a second consulship together in 55. They also had Caesar's command in Gaul renewed for another five years, so that it would not expire until March 1, 49, and they obtained commands for themselves. Crassus lost his life in a war in Syria in 53, while Pompey was given command over the two provinces of Spain, which he governed through assistants, preferring to remain at the center of power near Rome.

THE SUPREMACY OF JULIUS CAESAR

The Break between Caesar and the Senate Caesar's conquest of Gaul greatly enriched the state, but to his enemies it was a cause of dismay. They feared that he might use his victories, and his popularity among the people, to become another, and perhaps a permanent, Sulla. As protection against Caesar, his enemies in the Senate began to draw Pompey into their camp. Some of them had quarreled with him in the past, but they were willing to gamble that they could eliminate him when they no longer needed him.

As 49 B.C. opened, the Senate met in a state near hysteria. A small band of implacable senators forced through a motion ordering Caesar to lay down his command, even though he was then taking no action beyond remaining in his province of Cisalpine Gaul. The Senate passed a decree establishing martial law and ordering Pompey to command the armies of Rome against Caesar. The ill-advised Pompey accepted the command; but in doing so he signed his own death warrant and condemned the Republic to extinction in yet another civil war. Finally, the Senate defied the oldest of Roman traditions by threatening the lives of any tribunes who opposed these extreme measures. They thus handed Caesar a superb theme for his own propaganda: He could proclaim that he was defending the rights of the tribunes, the common people of Rome who had elected them, and the men in his army who had loyally served in the Gallic wars.

Caesar's Invasion of Italy Caesar saw that his enemies were in effect challenging him to war and decided that he had no course but to fight for his dignity and, as he could now assert, for the people and their sacred tribunes. On about January 11, 49 B.C., he crossed the boundary of his province, the small Rubicon River north of Ravenna, thus invading his own country at the head of Roman legions.

Caesar advanced swiftly, and Pompey and his followers had to retreat to Greece; Caesar pursued them and won a decisive battle in 48 B.C. at the town of Pharsalus, in Thessaly. Pompey sought refuge in Egypt, but as he stepped on shore he was murdered by advisers to the pharaoh. After other victories Caesar returned to Rome in 46.

Caesar's Rule to 44 B.C. Caesar now decided to make his rule impregnable and assumed the positions of both dictator and consul. On the model of Sulla he extended his dictatorship beyond the legal six-month limit; then, in 44, he had himself named dictator for life. He swept aside all restraints on his power that Roman tradition might have imposed and took complete authority to pass laws, declare war, and appoint men to office.

As dictator, Caesar saw to a series of rapid reforms in many areas of Roman life. He raised the membership of the Senate to about 900, packing it with many of his veteran officers. From this time onward the Senate lost its former authority as the bulwark of the state. Caesar also divided all Italy into municipal areas, giving each town administrative control over the surrounding countryside. He scaled down his large army by settling many of his soldiers in newly founded colonies and extended Roman citizenship into some of the provinces. His most lasting reform was one by which we still regulate our lives—the establishment of a calendar based on the old Egyptian reckoning of 365 days, with one day added every fourth year. This "Julian" calendar lasted until 1582, when it was revised by Pope Gregory XIII to our present Gregorian calendar.

The Death of Caesar The full effect of Caesar's plans was not to be realized, for on March 15, 44, after four years of supremacy, he fell to the dag-

▶ **An arena in El-Djem, Tunisia, imitating the Colosseum in Rome. Built in the second/third century A.D., this arena could seat 50,000 spectators. Wild animals were housed in the long rectangular pit in the center. Roman buildings were widely copied throughout the Empire as other cities sought to identify themselves with the great capital.**

march, 15 44 B.C.

gers of conspirators led by two of his lieutenants, Marcus Brutus and Gaius Cassius. His autocracy had been a grave affront to the upper class; because their dignity as members of the governing class had been undermined, they united against Caesar and carried out the most famous political murder in all history. It is said that Caesar was warned that morning of an imminent conspiracy and that he brushed the warning aside. As the Senate met near a theater built by Pompey, the killers plunged on him; when he recognized his protégé Marcus Brutus in the group, he said in Greek, "You, too, my boy?" and covered his head with his toga as he fell. His body was carried to the Forum and burned on a rock that still stands in a small temple built to his memory after his death (*see box*, p. 110).

Assessments of Caesar are baffling and controversial, even as they were to his contemporaries. He was pitiless toward Gauls and Germans, and he enriched himself by selling prisoners of war as slaves; but indifference toward captured foreigners was common in the ancient world. In Rome he showed too little respect for republican forms once he became dictator, and for this mistake he paid with his life. On the other hand, in the civil war he was generous enough to dismiss opposing generals whom he had captured, and

The Murder of Julius Caesar

The biographer Plutarch, who wrote about A.D. *120, looked back to describe the scene when Caesar was killed, 44* B.C.

"The place chosen for this murder, where the Senate met on that day, contained a statue of Pompey, one of the adornments for the theater he had built; this made it clear to all that some divine power had guided the deed and summoned it to just that spot. As Caesar entered, the Senate rose as a sign of respect, while those in Brutus' faction came down and stood around his chair. Tillius Cimber seized Caesar's toga with both hands and pulled it down from his neck, which was the signal for the assassination. Casca was the first to strike him in the neck with his sword, but the wound was neither deep nor fatal, and Caesar turned around, grasping and holding the weapon. Those who knew nothing of the plot were terrified and did not dare run away or help Caesar or even utter a sound. But those who came prepared for the murder whipped out their daggers, and Caesar was encircled, so that wherever he turned he met with blows and was surrounded by daggers leveled at his face and eyes and he was grappling with all their hands at once. Everyone was supposed to strike him and have a taste of the murder; even Brutus stabbed him once in the groin. Some say that, as he fought off all the rest, turning his body this way and that and shouting for help, he saw Brutus draw his dagger and pulled his toga down over his head and let himself fall at the base of Pompey's statue, whether by chance or because he was pushed by the assassins. There was blood all around the statue, so that it seemed that Pompey was presiding over the vengeance taken against his enemy, who now lay at his feet and breathed out his life through his wounds. They say he was struck 23 times, and many of the assassins were wounded by one another as they all directed their blows at his body."

Plutarch, *Life of Caesar*, chap. 66 (abridged), M. H. Chambers (tr.).

they lived to fight him another day. Such actions may have rested on cool calculation of their value as propaganda, but they may also show genuine gallantry. No one can question Caesar's fiery leadership. His troops followed him into Italy with enthusiasm and fought with amazing discipline.

Caesar clearly thought that the old institutions of the Senate and the assemblies were obsolete. "The Republic," he is said to have remarked, "is only a name without body or face, and Sulla did not know the ABCs of politics in resigning his dictatorship."[6] The political weakness of the late Republic largely confirms this harsh evaluation. But in the end his authoritarian behavior proved unacceptable to the experienced politicians whom he needed for his administration. Caesar's career thus blends triumph and tragedy. He rose to the absolute summit of Roman politics, but in doing so he destroyed both the Roman Republic and himself.

IV. The End of the Roman Republic

THE SECOND TRIUMVIRATE

Antony and Octavian   Brutus, Cassius, and the other assassins imagined that republican government could be restored with Caesar out of the way. Yet partisans of Caesar commanded armies throughout the Roman world, and they were not

---

[6]Suetonius, *Life of Caesar*, chap. 77.

men who would meekly surrender their powers to the Senate. One survivor was Marcus Antonius, or Mark Antony, a follower of Caesar and consul for the year 44 B.C. Antony tried to seize for himself the provincial command in Cisalpine Gaul, even though the Senate had already assigned it to another governor for the year 43. The Senate turned on him with Cicero, now a senior statesman, leading the attack. The state sent an army out to bring Antony to justice, and it must have seemed to many that the old institutions of the Republic had indeed come back to life.

Among the commanders whom the Senate put in action against Antony was a young man of 19—Caesar's grandnephew and adopted son. His name, originally Gaius Octavius, became Gaius Julius Caesar Octavianus upon his adoption; modern historians call him Octavian, but he called himself Caesar. He used his name skillfully to win a following among Caesar's former soldiers, but he also played the part of a discreet young supporter of the Senate in its battle against Antony. Cicero, the chief supporter of the old constitution, naively wrote of Octavian after their first meeting, "The young man is completely devoted to me."[7]

Octavian and Antony realized that the Senate was committed to the destruction of the Caesarian faction from which they derived their political support. Therefore, in 43, they allied together, and Octavian turned his back on the duty laid on him by the state, to attack Antony. They brought into their partnership a lesser commander, Lepidus; then, following the example of Sulla and others, they invaded Rome and made themselves the military rulers of the ancient capital. Faced with their armies, the Senate had to acknowledge their leadership, and a tribune proposed a law that turned the state over to their control for a period of five years; their official duties were "to provide order for the state"—a charge broad enough to supply a legal basis for nearly any action they might wish to take. Thus was formed the Second Triumvirate. In due course their collective power was renewed for another five years.

[7]*Letters to Atticus*, 14.11 (April 25, 44 B.C.).

Brutus and Cassius, seeing that they did not have popular support, fled to the East and managed to gain control of the provinces of Syria and Macedonia. But in 42 B.C. the triumvirs eliminated these enemies at the Battle of Philippi in northern Greece. To reward their troops with land, the rulers had already marked out the territory of no fewer than 18 prosperous towns in Italy. The rule of the Second Triumvirate (43–33 B.C.) was thus made secure by the seizure and redistribution of property. Further security was provided by a series of "trials" mounted against those who had had the bad luck to be on the losing side. As in the time of Sulla, the autocrats brushed aside the traditional guarantees of Roman law as they coldly purged their enemies. One of those killed without trial was Cicero.

OCTAVIAN TRIUMPHANT

Suspicion now began to grow between the two major partners, Antony and Octavian (Lepidus had been forced into retirement when he tried to take control of Sicily away from Octavian). The basic cause of their enmity was the lust for supreme power, and Antony did his own cause grave harm by remaining in the East for long periods, fighting the Parthian kingdom, which had taken certain Roman territories after the death of Crassus in 53. Octavian stayed in Rome and skillfully exploited the rumors that surrounded Antony's romance with Cleopatra VII of Egypt. In particular, Octavian falsely asserted that Antony was planning to place this Eastern queen in command of the state.

The final break between the two men came in 32 B.C. Octavian raised a large force from Italy and the western provinces; led by his skillful general Marcus Agrippa, this force defeated Antony in 31 B.C. at Actium, a promontory on the western coast of Greece. Antony withdrew to Egypt and took refuge with Cleopatra, and his army surrendered to Octavian.

The next year Octavian unhurriedly advanced on Alexandria for the reckoning with Antony and Cleopatra. Antony took his own life, and Cleopatra soon followed him. With Cleopatra's death ended the last Macedonian kingdom and, therefore, the Hellenistic Age, which had begun with the death of Alexander the Great in 323.

V. The Founding of the Roman Empire

AUGUSTUS AND THE PRINCIPATE

When Octavian returned to Rome in 29 B.C. from his conquest of Egypt, his supremacy was beyond challenge. The issue now was whether he would solve the problem that had defeated Caesar: how to rule without seeming to be an autocrat. He achieved this by restoring the appearance—but no more—of republican government. His designated candidates ran for office, and a willing Senate executed only the policies that he favored. Republican structures remained intact, but they were managed by his loyal men. At no time did he announce that he was converting the Republic into an empire. As a result, there is no official beginning for the Roman Empire; the best date is probably 27 B.C., for in that year Octavian laid the foundations of his system.

In 27 Octavian assumed control of an enormous provincial command, including Spain, Gaul, and Syria. Most of the legions were concentrated in these provinces; thus Octavian was the legal commander of most of the Roman army.

Egypt was handled in a special manner; it was treated as a private possession of Octavian's and managed by his own appointee.

Along with this command (also in 27) the Senate conferred on Octavian the name Augustus, meaning "blessed" or "fortunate." This title brought with it no powers, but its semidivine overtones were useful to Augustus (as we shall now call him) in establishing his supremacy. In 23 he resigned the consulship but received two additional powers from the Senate. His imperium was extended to cover not only his provinces but the whole Roman world. He also obtained the authority of a tribune. As a patrician (by his adoption into Caesar's family), Augustus could not actually be a tribune. Yet his having the "power" of a tribune suggested that he was the patron and defender of the common people of Rome. This power also gave him the legal right to veto any actions and to offer legislation. He was usually called the *princeps*, an old republican

▶ The Ara Pacis (Altar of Peace) was built in Rome in 13 B.C. to celebrate the establishment of peace by Augustus. Relatives of the imperial family are portrayed in idealizations of their stations in life rather than in strict Roman realism.

Map 4.5 THE ROMAN PROVINCES, 44 B.C.–A.D. 14

title denoting the senior ex-consul in the Senate. Modern writers often refer to the system Augustus established as the Principate.

AUGUSTUS, THE FIRST ROMAN EMPEROR

The Administration The long reign of Augustus from 27 B.C. to A.D. 14 established many abiding features of the Roman Empire. He provided a cash payment from the public treasury to soldiers who had served for 20 years, thus securing the loyalty of the legions to the state, not to their generals. He also made the Empire more secure by extending and solidifying the northern frontier (see Map 4.5). The provinces north of Italy now reached as far as the Rhine and Danube rivers. His control was nearly absolute, yet he did not install a reign of terror, and most people were relieved at the ending of the long period of civil war.

Augustus also created a force of soldiers stationed in Rome, known as the Praetorian Guard. This group of some 9000 men served as the city's police force and as Augustus' personal bodyguard, but after a few decades it came to play a decisive, and violent, role in the designation of new emperors.

Social Policy of Augustus Augustus also assumed the office of Pontifex Maximus, or high priest, and made attempts to revive the old Roman religion, probably as a device to promote political stability. He also grasped the possibilities of a ruler-cult. First he assigned Julius Caesar a place among the Roman gods and built a Temple to the Deified Julius. He also called himself

Divi Filius, or son of the divine Julius, though he was only the adopted son of Caesar. This verbal trick invited people to imagine that Augustus, though not divine, might some day become so. The poets Virgil and Horace, who wrote at his court, discreetly referred to Augustus as a future deity; and, in fact, Augustus was deified on his death, a political action that was imitated on the deaths of several later emperors who were considered to have ruled well. He also sponsored the building of temples to "Rome and Augustus"— a further suggestion, though not an offensive demand, that the emperor should be worshiped. It also became customary to make an offering to the Genius (protecting spirit) of the emperor.

Part of the religious revival was the rebuilding of scores of temples, but temples were by no means the only Augustan buildings; a famous saying was that "he found Rome made of brick and left it made of marble." The prosperity of the later years of Augustus' rule reflects the general peace that he brought to the Roman world. Freed of the expense of wars, Rome enjoyed a confidence that expressed itself in artistic and literary creativity.

Augustus also legislated in favor of the Roman family. To encourage the repopulation of Italy after the losses in the civil wars, he awarded special privileges to fathers of three or more children, and he issued a strong law against adultery.

Augustus died in A.D. 14. Through his careful control of the army and magistrates, he had given Rome three decades of healing after the civil wars, and the success of his work is shown by the fact that the state did not relapse into civil war after his death. He was Caesar's adopted son and also his final successor, the last of the warlords of the Republic. His personality seems to lack the panache of Caesar, who was invincible in the field and a talented man of letters, but his claim to greatness is that he ended the civil wars and formed the structure from which modern Europe has descended—the Roman Empire.

Recommended Reading

▼

Sources

Julius Caesar. *War Commentaries*. Rex Warner (tr.). 1960. An unsurpassed textbook in political-military decision making.

Cicero. *Selected Political Speeches*. Michael Grant (tr.). 1977.

———. *Selected Works*. Michael Grant (tr.). 1960.

Livy. All surviving parts of his history of Rome are in four volumes published by Penguin (various translators). 1965–1982.

Plutarch. *Fall of the Roman Republic*. Rex Warner (tr.). 1972. Biographies of Caesar, Pompey, Cicero, and other leading politicians of the Republic.

Polybius. *The Rise of the Roman Empire*. Ian Scott-Kilvert (tr.). 1979.

Sallust. *Jugurthine War and War with Catiline*. S. A. Handford (tr.). 1963.

Studies

Badian, E. *Foreign Clientelae*. 1958. Classic study of the patron-client relationship at work in Roman foreign policy.

———. *Publicans and Sinners*. 1983. Together, this and the following book survey the reasons for Rome's acquisition of an empire and the financial administration that managed the regime.

———. *Roman Imperialism in the Late Republic*. 1971.

Dixon, S. *The Roman Mother*. 1988. On the role of women within the Roman family.

Errington, R. M. *The Dawn of Empire: Rome's Rise to World Power*. 1973.

Gelzer, Matthias. *Caesar: Politician and Statesman*. 1968. For more advanced students; contains precise references to ancient sources.

Gruen, Erich S. *The Hellenistic World and the Coming of Rome*. 1984. Full historical narrative, arguing against the view that Rome tried to make Eastern possessions adopt Roman ways.

———. *The Last Generation of the Roman Republic*. 1973. On the collapse of the Sullan system and the final struggle between Caesar and Pompey.

Habicht, C. *Cicero the Politician*. 1990. Concise treatment, placing Cicero within Roman politics; especially good for students.

Heurgon, Jacques. *The Rise of Rome to 264 B.C.* 1973. Good on the rise of the city and its earliest history.

Lintott, A. W. *Violence in the Roman Republic*. 1968.

Ogilvie, Robert M. *Early Rome and the Etruscans*. 1976. The interaction of the two cultures.

———. *The Romans and Their Gods in the Age of Augustus*. 1970. A brief, approachable discussion.

Richardson, Emeline. *The Etruscans: Their Art and Civilization*. 1964. Well illustrated.

Rose, H. J. *A Handbook of Latin Literature*. 1954. The best brief history, better for reference than for continuous reading.

Scullard, H. H. *From the Gracchi to Nero* (5th ed.). 1982. The best textbook for the central period of Roman history, with good references to sources.

Stockton, D. *The Gracchi*. 1979. The best modern study of the two who discovered and used popular support.

Syme, Ronald. *The Roman Revolution*. Originally 1939. Brilliant analysis of the passing of the Republic and the founding of the Empire by Augustus. For advanced students.

Taylor, L. R. *Party Politics in the Age of Caesar*. 1949. Analysis of the factions within the late Republic.

Ward, A. *Marcus Crassus and the Late Roman Republic*. 1977. The best study of the partner of Caesar and Pompey.

Warmington, B. H. *Carthage*. 1960. History and society of Rome's main rival.

Gaius Octavius, given the title "Augustus" by the
Roman Senate, is portrayed as ruler and military
commander in this idealized statue.

CHAPTER FIVE

THE EMPIRE AND CHRISTIANITY

THE history of the Roman Empire is one of remarkable continuity. The system of government devised by Augustus and maintained by his successors gave the Empire two centuries of solid prosperity. Historians call this the period of the *Pax Romana*, "the Roman Peace," and the Empire as a system of government remained an ideal in Europe for centuries. Its remains—stadiums, public baths, marketplaces, temples, official buildings—have inspired imitations down into our own times.

At the beginning of the third century, the Empire entered a period of crisis. Control of the army became the key to power, and emperors and would-be emperors followed one another in rapid succession. When order finally returned during the fourth century, the old Roman Empire was no more. In the East, the Byzantine Empire was formed; in the West, the Empire steadily declined, finally ceasing to be governed by Roman emperors in 476.

But even as antiquity was passing, ancient peoples were laying the basis for a new form of civilization. Their most important innovation was the development of a new set of religious beliefs—Christianity, which was destined to transform the life and culture of the Western heirs of the Roman Empire.

I. The Empire at Its Height

Three unifying elements preserved the Roman Empire that Augustus founded. First was the figure of the emperor, whom all subjects identified as the head of the regime. With some exceptions, the emperors maintained an active, personal ruling style until about A.D. 200. Second were the civil servants and city councils, who collected taxes and maintained urban life. Third was the army, both the ultimate security of the emperor himself and the protector of the frontiers. The three elements supported one another, and the failure of any one of them threatened the others and thus the fabric of the state (*see box*, below).

THE SUCCESSORS OF AUGUSTUS

The Julio-Claudian Dynasty   The first emperor, Augustus, had no male heir. His last wife, Livia, was from an old patrician family and evidently persuaded him to adopt her son, Tiberius, and to designate him as his successor. She thus played a leading role in the shaping of the imperial dynasty.

After the death of Augustus in A.D. 14, the Senate recognized Tiberius as ruler and thus confirmed the principle of dynastic succession, establishing the fact that an empire, not a republic, now existed. The dynasty founded by Augustus, called the Julio-Claudians, reigned until A.D. 68. Much can be said against the rule of the Julio-Claudians. Tiberius was morbid, suspicious, and vengeful. His successor, Gaius (or Caligula), suffered from insanity. Claudius was gullible and was manipulated by his wives and assistants. Nero was one of the worst emperors, whose tyranny led to a rebellion in Gaul. When the revolt spread to Rome, he saw that he was doomed and killed himself.

Yet these emperors did maintain, and even expand, the heritage left by Augustus. Claudius, for example, saw to the conquest of southern Britain, which became a Roman province in 47. Moreover, the Empire remained at peace internally, and the provincial administration that Augustus had established continued to function effectively.

Imperial Administration   The process of centralization of power in the person of the emperor and away from the Senate continued. From

---

Tacitus on the Powers of Augustus

The first emperor of Rome, Augustus, maintained that he had restored the Republic after years of civil war. The historian Tacitus, writing about A.D. 120, gave a different evaluation of his work.

"After Brutus and Cassius were killed, the state had no military force. [...] Even the party of Julius Caesar had no leader left but Augustus, who laid aside the title of Triumvir and called himself a consul. For controlling the people he contented himself with the rights of a tribune. When he had seduced the army with gifts, the people with distributions of food, and everyone with the pleasure of general calm, he began little by little to increase his authority and to gather to himself the powers of the senate, the magistrates, and the laws. No one opposed him, since the strongest men had fallen either in battle or through legalized executions, and the rest of the nobles, according to who was more ready to accept servitude, were awarded gifts and public offices; since they profited from the new arrangements, they preferred their present security to the previous uncertainties. The provinces, too, accepted this state of affairs, since the former government by the senate and people was suspect owing to the struggles among the powerful and the greed of local governors; the protection of the laws had been worthless, because the laws were constantly overturned by violence, intrigue, and finally outright bribery."

Tacitus, *Annals*, book 1, chap. 2, M. H. Chambers (tr.).

Map 5.1 THE ROMAN EMPIRE, A.D. 14–284

Tiberius onward, the emperor appointed magistrates directly, without the charade of having a single list of candidates "elected" by the people. Claudius turned many affairs of state over to his trusted assistants, usually Greeks who had been freed from slavery (thus called *freedmen*), who helped to found the bureaucracy that more and more ran the Empire.

Another factor that weakened senatorial power was the frequent interference in affairs of state by the Praetorian Guard, the emperor's bodyguard. The Guard first intervened in politics in 41, when it forced the Senate to recognize Claudius as emperor. It did the same for Nero in 54. This repeated invasion of civil authority by the Praetorian Guard was a step on the road toward militarization; within little more than a century the emperors were to become totally dependent for power on their ability to buy the good will of the soldiery. The army, which had kept the emperors secure, sometimes became a force beyond control.

The military played a significant role in the struggle over the succession after Nero's death in 68, as troops in various quarters of the Empire backed their own candidates for emperor. The year 69 is often called "the year of the four emperors" because in the course of the year four men claimed to be emperor. Vespasian finally stabilized the situation and emerged as sole ruler late in 69. He founded the Flavian dynasty (so called from his middle name, Flavius), which lasted through the reigns of his two sons.

THE FIVE GOOD EMPERORS

The Flavian dynasty ended in violence in 96, when a group of senators instigated the murder of the emperor Domitian, Vespasian's despotic son. The Senate then picked a quiet older senator, Nerva (96–98), to be the new emperor. Nerva, in turn, adopted an experienced military officer,

Trajan, and designated him as his successor. This system remained in use for nearly a century: An emperor would choose a qualified successor and adopt him as his son, thus ensuring a peaceful transfer of power. The men thus chosen were so capable that historians have called Nerva and the next four rulers the "five good emperors."

On the whole, in the period of the five good emperors the Empire remained stable and even expanded. In 116 it reached its farthest extension to the East as Trajan, in a war of conquest, temporarily marched down the Tigris-Euphrates valley to the head of the Persian Gulf; but he died while trying to return to Rome. Hadrian, his successor, decided to withdraw from this extreme eastern position.

▶ **In A.D. 113 the emperor Trajan erected a monumental column to celebrate his war against peoples living across the Danube River. These panels show preparations for the war. Note the figure of the river god at the bottom, under a bridge built for the army.**

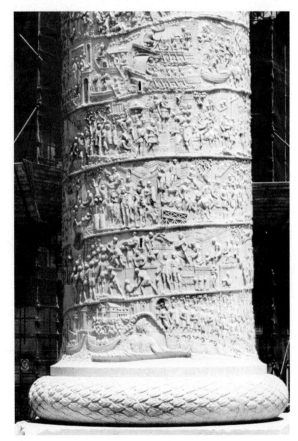

Hadrian continued the development of a frank autocracy. The Roman assemblies no longer met in order to pass laws. Instead, Hadrian himself issued laws—known as "decisions" (*constitutiones*)—often without bothering to obtain the approval of the Senate. He was advised by an informal council known as the "friends" (*amici*) of the emperor, which included the leading experts in Roman law. One of these, Salvius Julianus, collected the edicts that Roman praetors had issued over the centuries, in an attempt to standardize the procedures of civil law; this action pointed the way toward the great codification of law in the sixth century under the emperor Justinian. Hadrian's laws, though issued without any pretense of democratic process, were generally fair and humane. They tried to improve the condition of soldiers and slaves and gave women the same rights in court as men.

Trajan and Hadrian undertook a vast building program. Trajan erected many structures throughout the Empire and added an impressive column to the newly built Forum of Trajan, on which is carved a series of scenes recording episodes in wars against tribes across the Danube. He also expanded his new Forum by adding a group of buildings—shops, offices, a library—to the east of his column. Hadrian undertook various building projects in the provinces. Most famous is Hadrian's wall (much of it still stands) built across Britain to protect the frontier between the Roman province of Britain and the areas controlled by Celtic tribes to the north.

Hadrian arranged the succession of the next two emperors, Antoninus Pius (138–161) and Marcus Aurelius (161–180), who are the last of the "five good emperors." The rule of Antoninus was peaceful, and under the reign of Marcus Aurelius the Empire enjoyed its last years of prosperity. But in his final years a gathering storm broke in all its fury, and Marcus had to fight invasions by tribes on the Danube River and in the East. One campaign was especially disastrous, for the army returning from Asia Minor in the 160s brought with it a devastating plague that spread through much of Europe. This plague must have been one cause of the later weakening of Rome, but the nearly total lack of records prevents our knowing how many died.

Marcus abandoned the principle of adoption

and passed the throne to his worthless son, Commodus (180–192), whose extravagance and cruelty were reminiscent of Nero and Domitian. His murder on the last day of 192 opened a period of terrible instability, to which we shall return (p. 127).

ROMAN IMPERIAL CIVILIZATION

Economy   In the first two centuries of the Empire, Italy and the provinces reached a level of prosperity and of flourishing population that Europe would not see again for a thousand years. The results of Roman censuses, which have partially survived, indicate that Italy at the death of Augustus contained about 7.5 million inhabitants. (In about 1500, the earliest date at which we can make a comparable estimate, the same area contained about 10 million people.)

Cities were a distinctive feature of settlement throughout the Empire. In the Western provinces, cities were, for the most part, small; to judge from the area enclosed by Roman walls, most towns contained only a few thousand resi-

▶ **The emperor Hadrian had this famous wall built across Britain to mark off the Roman Empire and keep foreign peoples out.**

dents. Yet they usually imitated Rome with temples, markets, arenas, courthouses, and other public buildings, and thus displayed an authentic urban character. In the East, cities were often much larger. Alexandria in Egypt is estimated to have had about 400,000 inhabitants; Ephesus in Asia Minor, 200,000; Antioch in Syria, 150,000. The size of the cities in the East is surely one reason why the economy in the Eastern part of the Empire was stronger than that in the Western part.

Largest of all the imperial cities, and a true wonder of the ancient world, was Rome. Estimates of its size generally suggest about 1 million inhabitants. Not until the eighteenth century would European cities again contain such a concentration of people; in the 1780s, for example, Paris held about 600,000 people. Roman civil engineering maintained, even under crowded conditions, acceptable standards of public hygiene

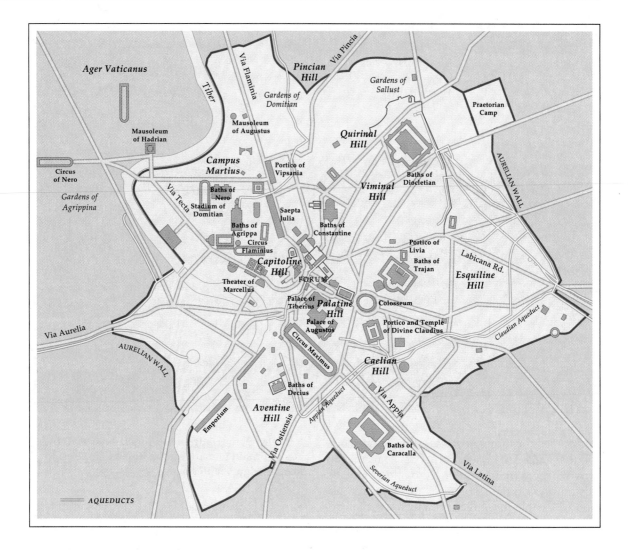

Map 5.2 The City of Rome in the Empire

and supplied enormous quantities of pure water and food.

Agriculture still remained the basic support of the economy, supplying, according to rough estimates, more than 75 percent of the total product of the Empire. One important change in Italian agriculture in the last century of the Republic had been the triumph of the great slave-run estates, called *latifundia*, at the expense of small peasant farms. The owners of the big *latifundia* were wealthy senators and equestrians, even entrepreneurs from outside the traditional governing classes. Trimalchio, a freed slave who appears as a character in Petronius' novel, the *Satyricon*,

boasted that he could ride from Rome to the area near Naples without leaving his own land.

The managers of these vast plantations favored varied forms of agriculture—the cultivation of vines, olives, and fruit, and the raising of large numbers of cattle, sheep, and goats. Only enough grain was cultivated to feed the resident staff of workers, most of them slaves. The great estates also supplied the cities with building stone, lumber, and firewood; huge quantities of wood were required, for example, to keep the Roman baths at comfortable temperatures. In the view of many historians, extensive deforestation and overgrazing led inevitably to erosion of the land and the loss of fertile topsoil—principal reasons for the economic decline of Roman Italy.

Even ancient peoples had the power to injure their environments.

In the provinces, the "Roman peace" favored the development of what had once been backward areas to the point where they threatened Italy's economic leadership. The wine market, for example, passed into the hands of Spanish cultivators in the second century, for Spanish wine was better than Italian and was cheaper to produce, thanks to lower labor costs. In some areas of industry, too, the provinces began to outrun Italian production. One of the main Italian industries was pottery, but by about A.D. 50 pottery made in Gaul had replaced Italian pottery even in Italy and had also taken over the market in the provinces and military camps. Thus Rome's success in establishing a commercial network created markets for products from the provinces and eventually contributed to Italy's own economic decline.

Social Conditions   The upper class in Rome lived on a far higher scale, and was more widely separated from the common people, than the rich of Greece. The wealthy had running water tapped into their homes, slaves to tend them hand and foot, and elegant country villas for recreation. Hadrian's villa, or country retreat, near Rome was the size of a small city. These villas approached economic self-sufficiency, for slaves manufactured articles of light industry (clothing, leather goods, domestic utensils) on the farms.

▶ **An arch built by the emperor Trajan at Beneventum. Some panels show sacrifices to the gods, and the whole was intended to commemorate Trajan's generosity to his people. Triumphal and commemorative arches were among the proudest monuments in Rome and have been imitated in many modern cities.**

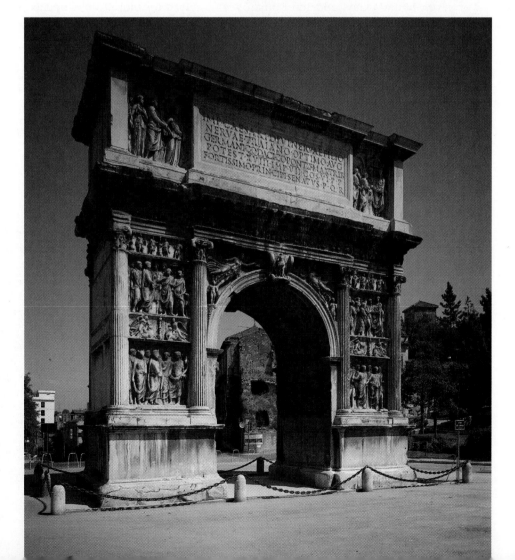

A modern feature of Roman cities was the existence of suburbs and resorts. Pompeii was a commercial town, but its neighbor Herculaneum was a residential suburb. Both towns, buried and thus preserved by the volcanic eruption of Mt. Vesuvius in 79, contain examples of the airy Roman house, built around a central open court, or atrium, and decorated with graceful wall paintings.

The workers of Rome had no such elegant housing, living rather in flimsy and inflammable apartments. They lacked running water, but a complex system of aqueducts gave easy access to water outside the home, and Rome always took pride in its enormous, cheap public baths. There were trade groupings in Rome for every kind of worker: fishermen, engineers, cobblers, silk workers, and so on. These city laborers had working conditions that were beyond the dreams of a Near Eastern peasant. They worked only about six or seven hours a day, and the Roman year contained about 160 holidays, to which the state added from time to time special days of celebration.

The major amusements for the people during days of leisure were public games, especially chariot races, which brought honor and wealth to the skilled charioteers, in arenas such as the huge Circus Maximus. Besides races, the Romans gave themselves over to brutal contests, which sometimes went on to death, between professional gladiators or between men and animals. The main arena for these spectacles was the grandiose Colosseum, begun by the emperor Vespasian in the 70s. It held about 50,000 spectators, and much of it still stands in central Rome, probably the one monument that most vividly recalls the classical city.

Rome was wealthy enough to support roughly half its population at public expense through free allotments of food, especially grain, which was the most common item in the diet. In the less prosperous years after 200 the cost of these subsidies was to place a heavy strain on the Empire's economy.

Social mobility became easier under the Empire. For example, some Greeks who had been freed from slavery enjoyed enviable careers as secretaries to emperors or as businessmen. The need for more troops opened new opportunities

▶ **A well preserved apartment house (second to third century A.D.) in the city of Ostia, which served Rome as a port. The dwelling space is located over shops on the ground floor. The tradition of snack bars everywhere in Rome and Italy is an old one.**

for provincials, who entered the Roman legions, especially during the second century and later; and even the Senate began to include men born in the provinces. In time the Empire became less "Roman," for in both manpower and economic strength the primacy of Italy was of the past.

Law   A complex system of law and procedure was one of the chief cultural contributions of Roman civilization. Roman law had already developed under the Republic, but its growth under the Empire made it even more comprehensive. The assemblies, both that of the Centuries and that of the Tribes (see Chapter 4), issued laws mainly on large public issues, such as distributions of land or assignments of military commands overseas. The reshaping of laws that affected relations among citizens, private rights, and the like, was largely the work of individual magistrates.

Normally, cases came before a judge, who was a private citizen relying on the advice of other private citizens who were reputed to understand the law. These advisers were called jurists (*iurisprudentes* or *iurisconsulti*), and their opinions constantly influenced the growth of the law. Another impact on the law came from magistrates, especially praetors, who issued edicts that explained the principles by which they would interpret the law during their year in office; these edicts acquired the authority of tradition and ultimately passed into permanent law.

The Romans distinguished their own citizens from the other members of the Empire. Roman citizens were subject to the "civil law" (*ius civile*), or law applying to citizens; others were allowed to maintain many of their own customs, which came to form the *ius gentium*, or law of other nations. These two kinds of law were assigned, logically enough, to two magistrates for administration, the "urban praetor" (*praetor urbanus*) and the "traveling praetor" (*praetor peregrinus*). As the Empire grew and embraced more peoples, the *ius gentium* gradually displaced the *ius civile*.

The Romans' respect for their law is consistent with the remarkable cohesiveness that one sees throughout their society. In war they were often brutal, but then so were many others in all periods of history. Rome's achievement in designing and preserving a system of laws govern-

ing the behavior of citizens toward one another has served as a model for much of the law of Western Europe. Codes of law, as we have also observed, are a feature of several other ancient societies, but in richness and complexity the codifications of the late Roman Empire easily surpass all the rest.

Engineering and Architecture   The Romans showed brilliance in the fields of engineering and construction. The most enduring monument to Roman civilization is the impressive network of roads found everywhere from Britain to Africa. Originally designed as highways for the rapid movement of legions, these roads became trade routes in more peaceful times and eliminated all barriers to travel. From the earliest times the Romans also built aqueducts that converged toward the cities, sloping down and carrying fresh water from the mountains; Rome's imposing system of sewers was constantly flushed by water from the aqueducts. The Romans placed more emphasis on personal cleanliness than any other civilization until modern times. Several emperors commissioned the building of immense public baths, of which the grandest of all were the Baths of Caracalla, built in the third century. The English city of Bath is named for the facilities that the Romans built there.

Roman temples, imitating those of the Greeks, were supported by columns, usually in the Corinthian style, crowned with a bell-like acanthus flower. Their temples had large interiors and were often completely walled at the rear, because Romans performed their ceremonies indoors. They were the first to grasp the possibilities of using arches and vaults on a large scale, thus giving their buildings a vastness that the Greeks could not achieve. They also invented concrete, which is inexpensive and can be laid by relatively unskilled labor. It can also be shaped into forms impossible in marble, and it is lighter in weight and can easily be supported in vaulted buildings. One of its most successful applications is the spacious Pantheon—built in the time of Augustus and then rebuilt under Hadrian—covered by a dome with a striking opening in the center. Sculpture and architecture coincided in triumphal arches, which often bear reliefs depicting the historical event that the arch commemorates.

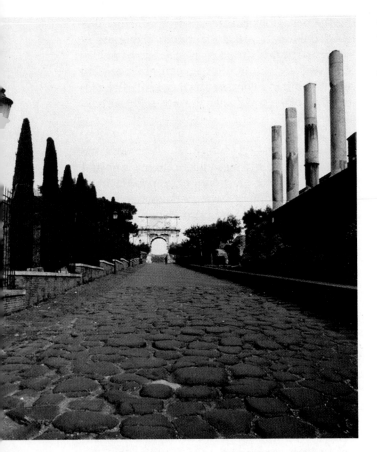

▶ **The Sacred Way leads into the Roman Forum through the Arch of Titus, which was erected to celebrate the end of the great Jewish rebellion in A.D. 70. A triumphal procession would enter the Forum through this elegantly placed arch and parade up to the Temple of Jupiter on the Capitoline Hill.**

Literature in the Empire   The leisure provided by Rome's prosperity encouraged the patronage of literature. In Rome, literature was far more the enjoyment of the upper classes than in Greece, where, for example, dramas were presented before 12,000 or more spectators. The most famous Latin poet, Virgil (70–19 B.C.), borrowed from Greek models, as Roman poets often did. His early poems, the *Bucolics* and *Georgics*, are polished hymns of praise to the Italian landscape, which reflect the style of Theocritus and Hesiod; but the gentle, human spirit of Virgil himself is always present. The best qualities of Virgil appear when he treats civilized emotions—mercy,

compassion, and sadness; then his work echoes with a graceful melancholy.

These qualities appear in his patriotic epic, the *Aeneid*, which borrows and transforms materials from Homer. In this work Virgil narrates the wanderings of Aeneas, the Trojan whose descendants were the legendary founders of Rome. Leaving his native city after the fall of Troy, Aeneas reached Carthage and had a romance with its queen, Dido; but his sense of duty compelled him to abandon her in order to reach Italy and fulfill his destiny. Virgil's aim was to sing the glory of Rome and its salvation by Augustus after the civil wars of the late Republic.

A contemporary of Virgil's was Horace, whose *Odes, Epodes,* and *Satires* examine love, amusement, annoyance, contentment—in short, the feelings of everyday life. Now and then Horace makes an attempt at serious patriotic verse, but these poems are self-conscious and moralizing and do not speak with the real Horatian voice of gentle, amusing irony.

Juvenal, a more pungent satirist than Horace, wrote shortly after 100. He took as his motto "Indignation inspires my poetry" (*facit indignatio versum*). His poems denounce the excess of pride and elegance in Roman society. His language is colorful, often bitter and obscene. One of his richest and wisest satires concerns the vanity of human wishes. After reviewing the foolishness of human beings, Juvenal gives his advice in a famous epigram: One should pray for "a sound mind in a sound body" (*mens sana in corpore sano*).

Historians   The histories of Rome written during the Republic were usually the work of men directly involved in politics. Under the Empire this changed, for political contest had almost vanished. It therefore seemed appropriate to look back on the Republic and write a final history of its politics and imperialism. Titus Livius, or Livy, undertook this task during the reign of Augustus, when the decisive political transformation occurred. Livy narrated Roman history from its legendary beginnings until 9 B.C. Because he usually drew on the work of earlier historians, he was sometimes unable to escape the influence of the myths that had clouded the history of the early Republic; thus he is at his best when he uses a good source such as Polybius.

Livy's *Roman History* is a kind of prose epic, filled with patriotism and admiration for the great men who had led Rome when the Republic was conquering the Mediterranean. Just as Virgil became the last Roman epic poet, so Livy was the last writer in Latin to attempt a full history of Rome. His work inspired many later writers who looked back at the Republic as the Golden Age of Rome; it was accepted as authoritative until soon after 1800, when historians began to be more skeptical about Roman tradition.

The leading Roman historian in accuracy and seriousness is Cornelius Tacitus (55?–120?). His first major work is the *Histories*, in which he treats Roman history from 69, the year of the four emperors, through the death of Domitian in 96, with emphasis on the analysis of character. Deeply influenced by satire, the dominant literary form of his age, Tacitus loved to fashion stinging epigrams aimed at members of the governing class, and he treated nearly all his main characters as selfish or corrupt. His disillusioned attitude was partly the result of his being an outsider, probably from southern Gaul; he saw Roman society through the cool eyes of a provincial who became a senator and even rose to the office of consul.

His other major work is the *Annals*, which covers the reign of the Julio-Claudian emperors from Tiberius through Nero. Tacitus looked back at the early Empire from the vantage point of a later period; and though he said he wrote "without anger or partisanship" (*sine ira et studio*),[1] he found little good to say about the first emperors and few modern critics would call him impartial.

II. *Changes in Ancient Society*

THE PERIOD OF CRISIS (192–284)

The Crisis of Leadership The centuries of the "Roman peace" ended with the death of the emperor Commodus in 192, and in the following years the political balance shifted to the military.

During the third century dozens of emperors claimed the throne, but many of these men were really no more than political gamblers or warlords who for a short time purchased the loyalty of their soldiers. Thus two of the stabilizing elements of the Empire—the strong, effective emperor and the disciplined army—began to fall apart.

The Roman Senate, which had once been the inspiration and bulwark of the state, now had neither interest nor ability to intervene in affairs of state as the emperors assumed more and more dictatorial powers and governed through court favorites. The economy of the Empire, too, nearly collapsed during this period, largely because defense costs had risen as raiders plundered the wealth of the Empire on several frontiers. Moreover, the emperors had been supplying the inhabitants of Rome with free food and public games, or "bread and circuses," in the usual phrase—a fairly effective means of political domination, but a heavy drain on the economy. Adding to these financial problems was a shortage of silver, on which the imperial currency was based. The emperors resorted to depreciating the currency, but this forced people to hoard what silver

▶ The ancient Greek city Ephesus, on the coast of Turkey, remained prosperous in the Empire. T. Julius Celsus, consul in A.D. 92, endowed this magnificent library, which his son completed about 135.

---

[1] *Annals*, 1.1.

they had and actually drove more of the metal out of circulation.

A further problem was the increasing reluctance of people of independent means to hold civic offices, which paid no salary. Finally, the government was forced to compel people to take office, a step that pointed to the practice, which was to become common in the fourth century, of binding people to their occupations. This in turn led to the collapse of the third crucial element of stability in the state, the efficient administrators and civil servants. Many of the emperors during the century of crisis were men of little leadership; but some of them must have been among the most able rulers in the history of Rome, for otherwise the Empire would have totally disintegrated.

Slavery and its Dilemmas Like most other ancient states, Rome used slaves widely, but no earlier society had organized the institution of slavery to such a degree or used slaves in such large numbers. Ancient slavery, unlike slavery in the United States, was never restricted to members of a single ethnic group. Anyone might have the bad luck to be rounded up and forced into slavery. During the late Republic, the number of available slaves increased dramatically, as Rome overran Greece, Asia Minor, Spain, and Gaul. Julius Caesar reports in his *Gallic War* that he once sold 53,000 Gauls into slavery in a single day. One owner of a large estate mentioned in his will that he owned no fewer than 4116 slaves. Of the 7.5 million inhabitants of Italy at the death of Augustus, an estimated 3 million were slaves.

The mounting flood of cheap slaves allowed the expansion of the great plantations during the last century of the Roman Republic. In most places slaves lived in modest quarters and were more or less properly fed. On the other hand, in Sicily they were often turned loose without shelter to feed off the land.

Slaves were better treated in the cities, where they served as artisans, hairdressers, secretaries, and, of course, personal servants. Slaves from the East, Greeks in particular, commonly tutored the children of the free classes. Slaves supplied much of the entertainment in ancient society. Girls and boys who could sing, dance, or recite were highly valued; there was also active traffic in beautiful young slaves of both sexes, often for sexual purposes. Gladiators were slaves, and reputedly fought harder because of it. If they prevailed over an opponent, they might win their freedom; if they lost, they forfeited nothing more than a miserable existence.

Judged solely as an economic system, ancient slavery offered the Empire certain advantages. It permitted a calculated use of labor in relation to land and capital. But in the long run, the slave system of antiquity also had serious weaknesses, which we must include in the causes for the decline of the Empire in the West.

Rome declined in part because its economy could no longer support the army needed to defend the frontiers against invaders. Why was the economy not equal to the task? One principal reason was that the slave system could not resolve two problems that every economy must face: the creation of incentives, to ensure that workers will labor hard and well; and the recruitment of replacements for the aging and the dead.

Especially in the countryside, the principal incentive that bent slaves to their tasks was the dread of punishment. For this reason, they were best employed in work that required little skill, diligence, or effort. The association of slavery with physical labor drained work of its dignity and dampened interest in technological innovation. And, in the view of most historians, demoralized slaves were poor producers of children, even when they were allowed to marry. Why pass misery down the generations? And conquests ceased from the time of Hadrian, a fact that threatened the continued supply of slaves.

The Plight of the Poor Within the free population, the spread of the great estates in the last century of the Republic had driven many small cultivators off the land. Many drifted to the Roman metropolis, where free bread and circuses purchased their docility. In many provinces, too, rural depopulation and the abandonment of cultivated fields had become a major problem in the centuries after Augustus.

Faced with shrinking numbers of cultivators and taxpayers, the Roman government sought desperately to reclaim and resettle the abandoned fields. For example, Marcus Aurelius initiated a policy of settling foreigners on deserted lands within the Empire. The state also sought to attract free Roman cultivators back to the countryside. The free cultivator who settled on another's land was called a *colonus*, and the institution was called the *colonate*.

Roman policy toward the *coloni* and other free cultivators was ambivalent and shifting. In many cases the *colonus* was treated well, with a light and fixed rent that he paid to the landlord, or *dominus*. He could sell the land he improved or pass it on to his heirs, and he could depart from it at will. But by the fourth century the picture was much worse: The *colonus* was bound to the soil, as were his children after him, and he was subject to the personal jurisdiction of his lord.

The long-term interests of society dictated that resettlement within family-owned farms should be encouraged. On the other hand, the hard-pressed government could not overlook any source of revenue, and it often resorted to outrageous fiscal practices. It ruthlessly requisitioned food; it forced settlers to pay the taxes of their absent neighbors; and it subjugated settlers to the authority of their landlords, who could be held responsible for collecting from them services and taxes. By the fourth and fifth centuries, under conditions of devastating fiscal oppression, some peasants preferred to flee the Empire rather than face ruin at home.

CULTURAL DISINTEGRATION

The cultural system of classical antiquity, in spite of its intellectual appeal, had some crucial weaknesses. It spoke primarily to the privileged and the gifted, the elites of ancient society. Even as they failed to develop a technology that might have eased the labors of slaves and the poor, so also the intellectual leaders of the age could point to little meaning in the lives of the unfree, the unhealthy, the disadvantaged, those without property, those without talents.

Moreover, after the Augustan Age Roman civilization produced fewer original thinkers. A certain morose resignation pervades their writings. The emperor Marcus Aurelius, in his *Meditations*, expressed the Stoic virtue of resignation: "When necessity is there, why strain against it?" The earth was in decline, and history was approaching its term.

III. *The Late Roman Empire*

RESTORATION AND REFORM

The political crisis of the third century finally ended in 284 when Diocletian, a high army officer, seized the imperial throne. He was from the peasantry of Illyria and was a strong, ruthless man, who ruled through an authoritarian bureaucracy. Recognizing that the Empire was too large and too unstable to be directed by one man, Diocletian enlisted three corulers, forming the Tetrarchy (rule of four). Each of the four rulers was placed wherever he was needed.

In order to solve the financial crisis, Diocletian had every plot of land taxed at a certain amount, to be paid to the emperor's agents. Trades and professions were also taxed so that the burden would not fall solely on landowners. The cities in the Empire each had a local city council, or *curia*; the officials, called *curiales*, were personally responsible for the required tax and had to pay it

▶ **The Tetrarchs (Diocletian and his co-rulers), shown supporting each other: Diocletian and Maximian are on the right; Galerius and Constantius on the left. The heads on the swords are Germanic.**

themselves if they could not collect it from others. Diocletian tried to hold back inflation with a famous Edict on Prices, which fixed a maximum price for nearly all goods. But natural economic forces led to further inflation, and he had to let the edict lapse after a few years.

Diocletian's severe rule stabilized the Empire, though it is hard to find in it much to praise. Many of his practices continued throughout the fourth century, especially his establishment of a despotism that resembled the ancient kingdoms of the Near East in its absolute monarchic rule.

Diocletian retired in 305, and soon afterward his system of shared rule broke down. Years of complex intrigue and civil war followed, as several leaders fought for the throne. One of the ruling circle was Constantius, the father of Constantine. When Constantius died in 306, Constantine began to fight for supreme power; in 324 he overcame the last opposition and was recognized as sole emperor of Rome. Thus 40 years after the accession of Diocletian, the Empire once again had a single ruler. In 330 Constantine renamed the old Greek city of Byzantium as New Rome and established it as his capital; popular usage gave it the name Constantinople.

CONSTANTINE AND THE BUREAUCRACY

By the end of his reign in 337 Constantine had set the pattern that remained throughout the fourth and later centuries. The whole state was now one rigid structure, almost one massive corporation that brutally discouraged individual initiative.

The economy was in virtual stagnation. Members of all trades and professions were grouped into *corpora*, or corporations, and to change professions was difficult. To make certain that the various day-to-day services would be performed,

Map 5.3 THE EASTERN AND WESTERN EMPIRES IN 395

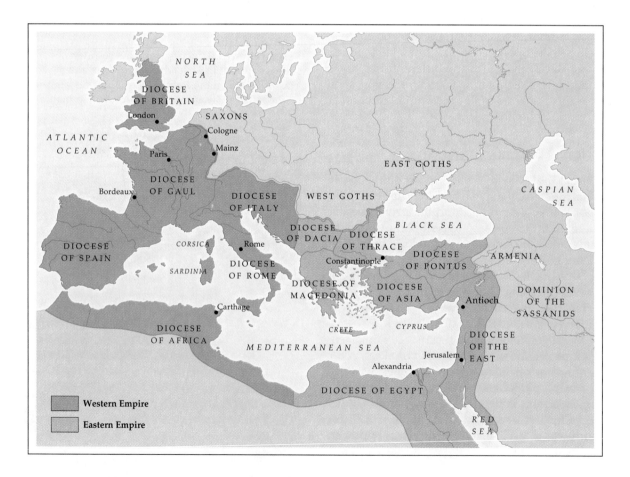

the state made professions hereditary. A small class of independent farmers clung to their existence, but the general trend was toward converting agricultural workers into near slaves. There was a deep gulf between the monarch's court and the common people. Even within the court the emperor stood apart from the rest, surrounded by ceremony. Fourth-century rulers wore expensive cloaks dyed in purple, and courtiers had to kiss a corner of the emperor's robe when approaching the throne. Diadems, the custom of kneeling before the emperor, and other marks of royalty became traditional and have remained so in European monarchies.

THE DECLINE OF THE WESTERN EMPIRE

After Constantine's death in 337, the chief administrative question for more than a century was whether one man could be strong enough to rule as sole monarch. For most of the time this proved impossible, and some kind of shared rule became common. On the death of Theodosius, in 395, the Empire was divided into an Eastern half and a Western half, with the dividing line just east of Italy.

In the last centuries of the Empire, society became more and more rigid; it did not, and perhaps could not, allow people to move freely from one class to another. As the central government weakened, local estates, usually called *villas*, became self-sufficient units resembling the later manors of the Middle Ages, with hunting lands and workshops that supplied the goods that the local population needed; they therefore became the main economic and political units of the Western Empire. At the same time, trade was declining because of a shortage of new markets and the constant threat of invasions along the frontiers. Moreover, a shortage of labor caused fertile lands to lie fallow and mines to remain unexploited.

The "Fall" of Rome? Such was the background for the dramatic turning point in history that is the end of the Western Empire. The formal end of the Western Empire is traditionally dated to 476, when a Germanic warlord deposed the youth whom we call the last Western emperor, Romulus Augustulus, and the Senate resolved

not to try to name any further Western emperors. Modern readers inevitably think of this event in the terminology imposed by the historical masterpiece of Edward Gibbon—that is, as the "decline and fall" of the Empire. But, of course, no political structure as large as the Roman Empire really falls like a tree in a forest without further influence or legacy. Moreover, some emperors in Constantinople, notably Justinian in the sixth century, saw themselves as the head of the whole traditional Empire, West and East, and tried to reunite the two geographic parts.

Yet even though historians take care to speak of the transformation of the Empire rather than of its disappearance, there is no doubt that the

CHRONOLOGY OF THE "FALL" OF ROME

476 is known to all readers of history as the year of the fall of Rome, but the true chronology is more complex.

393	Theodosius I, ruling in Constantinople, installs his son Honorius as emperor in the West.
395	Death of Theodosius; the division of the Empire into Eastern and Western parts is maintained.
423	Death of Honorius in West; other Western emperors continue to be appointed.
474, June 24	Leo I, emperor in East, appoints Julius Nepos as emperor in West.
475	Nepos appoints Orestes, a former lieutenant of Attila the Hun, as Master of the Soldiers. Orestes insists that his young son, Romulus Augustus (or Augustulus), be recognized as Western emperor. Nepos flees to Salona in Dalmatia. Romulus is proclaimed emperor in Ravenna, October 31, but the act is without legal force, and Nepos continues to be recognized as official Western emperor.

476	The German warlord Odovacar (sometimes Odoacer) leads a rebellion against Orestes and kills him, August 28. He deposes Romulus in Ravenna (September 4) and exiles him with a pension to Campania. The Roman Senate sends an embassy to Zeno, the Eastern emperor (474–491), proclaiming that there is no further need for a Western emperor; but Zeno continues to recognize Nepos until his death.
480, April or May	Nepos is murdered in his villa at Salona.
about 520	Marcellinus, in his Latin *Chronicle* written in Constantinople, states that the Western Empire (Hesperium imperium) "perished" with the deposition of Romulus Augustulus in 476, thus establishing this date for the "fall" of Rome.

Empire in the West did pass away while the Eastern part, called the Byzantine Empire, survived for nearly another thousand years. The problem is to explain why the Western regions could not maintain themselves under a continuous government while no similar dissolution threatened the Eastern portion of the Empire.

Some historians have been enticed into trying to state the one great cause for the fall of Rome—and this may be an impossible quest. Gibbon, for example, blamed the destructive work of barbarism and religion. But to say that Rome declined because of invasions by Germans, Franks, and Goths only pushes the inquiry back one step: Why were these peoples able to defeat an Empire that had ruled the civilized world for centuries? And why did the Eastern part of the Empire not decline along with the Western?

Causes for the Fall Some historians suggest that the emperors unintentionally paved the way for the fall of Rome by exterminating possible political rivals in the upper class, thus weakening the group that could have supplied leadership for the state. Others have advanced an economic argument, saying that the Empire was bound to decline because it never really emerged from a domestic economy. But this second theory is hardly convincing, for some societies—admittedly much less complex than the Empire—have existed for many centuries with no more than a domestic economy. If there had been no convulsions and strains in the Empire, the production of goods and food could have continued more or less unchanged. Exhaustion of the soil and fluctuating cycles of rainfall and drought have also been proposed in order to explain Rome's economic depression, but there is little exact knowledge about the cycles of crops and weather conditions that would indubitably account for the fall of the Empire.

Others have suggested that the weakness of the Western Empire was due to a shortage of manpower. This explanation does have some merit, because the Eastern cities appear to have been more populous than the Western ones, and thus they had more strength and resilience. The numerical inferiority of the West became even more serious when the villas became self-sufficient units and there was no longer a centralized military system. It was much easier for outsiders to invade the Empire when they met haphazard resistance from local forces. The relocation of the capital to Constantinople moved the administrative center even farther from the Western provinces and probably accelerated the dissolution of the regions of Italy and Gaul.

But the shortage of manpower was not the only factor in the weakening of the Western Empire. Its physical geography doomed it to be more vulnerable to invasion than the Eastern Empire. Warlike peoples streamed along the Danube valley and through the terrain of Central Europe into the Western provinces, a less hazardous route than the journey south through the difficult mountains of the Balkans, Greece, and Asia Minor into the Eastern Empire.

Social Conditions and Decline Other conditions made the Western Empire less able to resist destructive invasions. In the late second and third centuries the emperors had deliberately increased the prestige of the army and depressed the Senate and the civil service. The creature that they fashioned soon began to rule them, for the armies and their leaders made and unmade emperors at will. The only way to preserve civilian control over the military machine would have been to entrust more responsibility to the Senate and maintain strong civil servants. But the emperors simply continued along the path of absolute coercion, stifling initiative and making the lower classes apathetic and resentful. These conditions gave citizens only slight motivation to defend their oppressive government; domination by invaders may have seemed not much worse than being in the grip of the Roman state.

One must also consider the large number of holidays and many forms of amusement within the city of Rome: To what degree did such luxuries contribute to the transformation of the Western Empire? There is evidence here and there that the masses in the city gradually lost their feelings of responsibility. For example, in

Map 5.4 THE RHINE FRONTIER OF THE ROMAN EMPIRE

▶ **The emperor Constantine tried to increase his glory by commissioning colossal portraits of himself, such as the one shown here. The original full-length statue was some 40 feet tall.**

69, as Tacitus reports, the crowd cheered with pleasure as rival troops fought in the streets for the throne.[2] When the masses no longer had to exert more than minimal effort to survive, they abandoned the discipline and civic cooperation that had created the Empire. Public office was shunned, non-Italians supplied the troops, and appeals for traditional Roman firmness in danger found little response.

Finally, historians must take into account the great upheaval in ideas and faith. We cannot express this view in the language of science or statistics, but the new religion, Christianity, may also have weakened the defenses of the Empire. This thesis was first espoused by Edward Gibbon, who had rejected Catholicism in his own life and scorned Christianity. But even as we recognize Gibbon's prejudices, we must allow that he may have hit a part of the truth. In the Roman scheme the emperors, governors, and administrators stood far above the people, and Roman religion provided little spiritual compensation for a low rank in the world. The Christian faith offered something better: the message that all persons are potentially equal in the eyes of God and may hope for a better afterlife through salvation. As the Western Empire came under constant attack, the increasing number of Christians may have been less than eager to fight to preserve the old system. This spiritual rejection, as we might call it, worked along with the mighty pressures of invasion to cause the "fall" of Rome.

IV. Christianity and Its Early Rivals

The triumph of Christianity within the Roman Empire was one of the most remarkable cultural revolutions in history—all the more extraordinary since its values were opposed to those of classical thought, which sought the good life in

---

[2]*Histories*, 3.83.

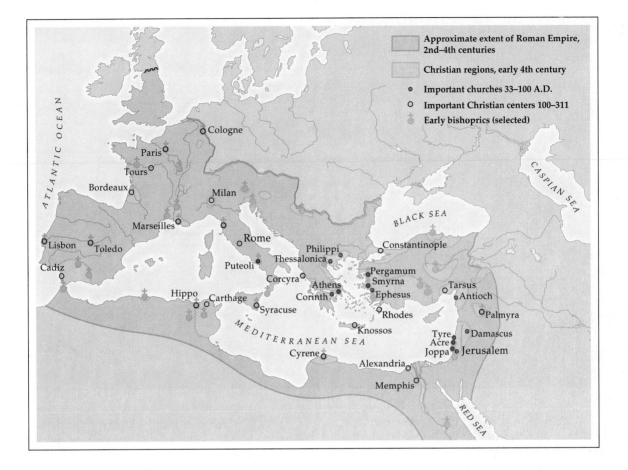

Map 5.5 THE SPREAD OF CHRISTIANITY

the present world. *Carpe diem,* "Seize the day," said Horace; there is no certainty about tomorrow. But classical values were failing to reach the disadvantaged, the subjugated, the losers. Small wonder that people sought a meaning for their existence in new religious movements.

THE MYSTERY RELIGIONS

One element of a spreading religious ferment under the Empire was the growing popularity of the so-called mysteries, which promised a blessed life after death to those who were initiated into secret (therefore "mysterious") rites. Through these rites, the believer attained a mystical identification with the renewing cycles of nature.

The oldest and most famous rites were held each fall at Eleusis, a day's walk from Athens. A drama-filled night culminated in the initiate's conviction that he or she would be given a lovely

life after death by Demeter, the goddess of grain, just as she caused beautiful new grain to come forth from the apparently dead seed.

This hope for survival after death did not bring with it any expectation of a changed moral life, nor did initiation lead to membership in any kind of community of believers or "church," with one notable exception: the religion known as Mithraism. Mithras was originally a Persian god of light and truth and an ally of the good god, Ahura Mazda; he symbolized the daily triumph of life over death by bringing back the sun to the dark heavens. Initiation was open only to men, and Mithraism—with its emphasis on courage, loyalty, self-discipline, and victory—became especially popular in the Roman army.

When Christians began, around A.D. 30, to proclaim the good news (or "gospel") of the recent

► A Mithraeum, or shrine to the savior god Mithras, with benches for worshipers. It was built in the second or third century within a large first-century apartment. On the altar, Mithras is shown sacrificing a bull to Apollo. Above this level was built the church of San Clemente in Rome.

death and resurrection of their leader Jesus of Nazareth[3] throughout the Empire, many who responded thought they were hearing about the best "mystery" of all: A historical person had conquered death and promised a blessed afterlife to all who believed in him. Yet much early Christian literature was written to teach believers that Christianity was far more than a "mystery." The new faith demanded that every believer practice love and justice in new communities made up of Jew and Greek, slave and free, male and female, rich and poor, educated and ignorant.

---

[3]"Jesus" was his name; after his death he was called *ho Christos*, "the anointed one" or the Messiah, by his followers; thus the names "Christ" and "Jesus Christ," though universally used, are not historically accurate; and "Jesus, called the Christ" is cumbersome.

This new religion hardly looked "religious." Christians had no temples or other holy places, no priests, no ordinary sacrifices, no oracles, no visible gods, no initiations; they made no pilgrimages, did not practice divination, would not venerate the emperor, and challenged the final authority of the father (or oldest male) in family life. No wonder Christians were accused of being atheists who undermined traditional society. The roots of these radical beliefs and practices are found in the long Judaic tradition and its sacred writings. Christians maintained that prophecies in the Hebrew Bible, which in the light of new revelation they began to call the *Old* Testament, had foretold the coming of Jesus as the Messiah, the deliverer of the Jewish people, and as the future lord of the world. Like the Jews, Christians emphasized their god's wish to create a community of men and women who practiced justice and mercy. All the first Christians were Jews, but they parted company with Jewish tradition by insisting that Jesus' life, his sacrificial death, and his resurrection all meant that God's community had become open to everyone from every background.

IV. CHRISTIANITY AND ITS EARLY RIVALS ◀ *137*

THE JEWS IN THE ROMAN EMPIRE

The Jews had been favored subjects of the Persian Empire until Alexander's invasion of the East (334–323 B.C.) swept away Persian rule. In the Hellenistic Age they were governed, during the third century B.C., by the Ptolemies of Egypt and then by the Seleucid kings of Syria, who began to force Greek culture on them and finally outlawed the Jewish religion altogether. Pious Jewish nationalists responded under the leadership of Judas Maccabaeus with guerrilla warfare. This successful Maccabean Revolt (167–164 B.C.) is celebrated today with Hanukkah, the Festival of Lights. After a century of virtual independence, the Jews in Judea (the province created out of the Jewish kingdom of Judah) were brought under Rome's control by the arrival in Jerusalem of the Roman general Pompey in 63 B.C.

When Julius Caesar was at war with Pompey in 47 B.C., he was assisted by a Jewish force, and he rewarded the Jews with reduced taxes and exemption from military service. The Romans also agreed that Jews could not be called to court on the Sabbath and that they could continue to worship in their synagogues, even in Rome itself. Thus, despite the loss of their century-long freedom, the Jews enjoyed at least some measure of toleration.

Rome permitted client kings, local rulers who pledged loyalty to Rome, to rule Judea. The most notorious was Herod the Great (ruled 40–4 B.C.), hated by most Jews, whom he sought to win over by remodeling the Temple in Jerusalem into one of the wonders of the ancient world. Political weakness in the son who followed Herod forced Rome to begin direct rule in Judea through civil servants from Rome, usually called procurators, the most famous of whom was Pontius Pilate.

Constant quarrels between the Roman officers and the Jews reached a climax in A.D. 66, when Jerusalem burst into rebellion. This great Jewish War, as the Romans called it, lasted until 70, when the Romans demolished the Temple, except the Western Wall, at which Jews were allowed to pray once a year. Hoping to retain the favor of the Jews by respecting their god, the Romans did not at first try to suppress the Jewish faith itself; but they finally did attempt this after another Jewish rebellion (131–135). Nonetheless, Judaism retained its coherence and strength, assuring its people that God would one day send them their redeemer.

Jewish Factions The attractiveness of Hellenistic culture, combined with the insult of Roman occupation, led to a continuing crisis of identity among the Jews. After the Maccabean Revolt, three principal factions arose, each stressing the part of Jewish tradition that it considered most essential for the survival of the Jews as God's people.

First, the landed aristocracy and high priests formed the Sadducees, religious conservatives who rejected belief in an afterlife and in angels because they did not find such teaching in the Books of Moses (the Pentateuch, called the *Torah* by Jews). A second faction, the Pharisees, were pious middle-class lay people who taught the resurrection of the dead, believed in angels, and accepted gentile converts.[4] During the century following the Roman expulsion of the Jews from Jerusalem in 135, the spiritual heirs of the Pharisees, the great rabbis, organized their oral legal traditions, which updated the practice of the Torah, into a book called the Mishnah. This compendium became fundamental for all subsequent Jewish thought and was augmented in the East by an authoritative commentary (the Gemara) to form the Babylonian Talmud, or general body of Jewish tradition. A similar process in the West created the less elaborate Persian Talmud.

The third faction was the Essenes, who have drawn the most attention in recent years because of the astonishing discovery of the Dead Sea Scrolls, documents found from 1947 onward in 11 caves near the Dead Sea. Although scholarly debate continues, the consensus is that the writers were ascetic priests who settled at Qumran, 15 miles into the desert east of Jerusalem, after the Maccabean Revolt; they were evidently protesting against the leadership of the Temple by high priests whom they considered corrupt and unworthy.

---

[4]The Latin word *gentiles* (akin to *gens*: see p. 93) means "foreigners," those born to non-Jewish mothers.

These rolls and many fragments of leather have given historians an extraordinary view of the apocalyptic beliefs and strict practices of this protesting faction, which was active from about 150 B.C. to A.D. 70. The Essenes were convinced that evil in the world had become so powerful—even prevailing in the Temple—that only a cataclysmic intervention by God, which would soon arrive, could cleanse the world and open the way for righteousness to prevail.

A certain "Teacher of Righteousness," the priestly champion of the forces of light, is thought to be the anonymous author of many of the scrolls; his opponent in Jerusalem, who he says serves the powers of darkness, is called the Wicked Priest. At least two God-anointed leaders are foreseen in the scrolls: the Messiah of David (a military commander) and the Messiah of Aaron (a high priest). The return of the "Teacher" is also predicted.

The relations of the Essenes at Qumran to Jesus and the first Christians remain much debated. The Essenes are never mentioned in the New Testament, the books of the Bible that record the life of Jesus. To be sure, in the spectrum of Jewish factions, these two groups could hardly have differed more widely. The Essenes were exclusive, hierarchic, priestly, and withdrawn from society. Jesus and his followers welcomed everyone; they were egalitarian, uninterested in sacrifices in the Temple, and wholly "in the world."

ORIGINS OF CHRISTIANITY

The modern historical investigation of Jesus of Nazareth has challenged scholars for two centuries. He seems to have been a charismatic Jewish teacher, yet he wrote nothing that we know of. His existence and his execution by the Romans are confirmed by such first- and second-century historians as Josephus, Tacitus, and Suetonius.

For details we must sift the writings of early converts, such as Saul of Tarsus (who did not know Jesus) or the authors of the Gospels (the first four books of the New Testament), which focus on Jesus' power over evil forces, his message of hope and moral demands, his healing miracles, and his radical inclusiveness (even lepers were welcomed into the faith). But ancient writers had little interest in presenting his biography in chronological order or in probing his inner life. We know almost nothing about his career as a youth and young adult apart from his being raised a Jew in Galilee; thus, despite the efforts of many, it is impossible to write a biography of Jesus.

▶ The church of Santa Costanza in Rome, built in the early fourth century as a mausoleum for Constantia and Helena, daughters of the emperor Constantine, contains some of the oldest Christian mosaics. This scene from daily life shows workers bringing in the grape harvest.

As his followers recalled his career, Jesus was born of a virgin named Mary, betrothed but not yet married to a man named Joseph, in the last years of Herod the Great, at a date that modern scholarship sets about 4 B.C. At around age 30 he went to John the Baptist, an outspoken prophet, to be baptized—that is, to become purified through a ritual washing—and join his apocalyptic movement, which foresaw the coming end of the world. Soon afterward John was imprisoned, and Jesus began a program of itinerant teaching and healing, apparently rejecting John's apocalyptic message by proclaiming instead the "good news" that God's rule had already begun *before* the final judgment. Jesus affirmed the Pharisees' belief in resurrection, yet he urged his disciples to pray that God's will be done here on earth as it is in heaven, that God's kingdom should come to people here.

In the Sermon on the Mount, the summary of Jesus' basic principles recorded in the Gospel of Matthew, Jesus declared that when God rules, the poor, the meek, the pure in heart, the peacemakers, and the justice seekers will be honored. He said too that prayer and piety were matters of personal commitment, not public gestures to win society's acclaim.

With all other Jews he believed that God was a gracious, welcoming God. The related questions were: To *whom* is God gracious? and, therefore, Whom must I treat as my neighbor? As Jesus demonstrated by his fellowship at open meals, every person was potentially such a neighbor, especially a person in need.

Jesus' fellowship at meals reached its climax at his last supper at the time of Passover, a Jewish religious holiday. At this meal he urged his disciples to continue a ritual practice in memory of him, using bread and wine to symbolize the gift of his body and the sacrifice of his blood. The early Christians regularly did so, calling this meal the eucharist, or thanksgiving.

Christian sources state that Jesus was accused by the high priests in Jerusalem of blasphemy (he had challenged their authority in the Temple), of pretending to be God's Messiah and a king, and of opposing paying taxes to the Roman emperor. Apparently convinced that Jesus presented a serious threat to public order at the Passover, the Roman governor, Pontius Pilate, ordered his cru-

cifixion, a horribly painful form of execution (about A.D. 30).

Jesus' followers became convinced that God raised him from the dead after three days and that this resurrection confirmed the truth of his deeds and words despite his rejection and persecution. The Christians further believed that he ascended bodily into heaven but would return to save his followers and establish his kingdom. Armed with this conviction, they began to convert other Jews to their faith; some converts, such as Stephen, the first Christian martyr, took the lead in extending the all-inclusive new movement to gentiles.

Paul and His Mission A Pharisee, Saul of Tarsus, known to us as Paul, became a leader in persecuting Jews who had become Christians. Then, about A.D. 33, on his way to Damascus to organize further persecutions, he saw on the road an apparition of the risen Jesus, who asked him to explain his hatred. Paul realized he had been given a special mission to the gentiles and became Christianity's tireless advocate, traversing the Roman world, organizing Christian communities of both Jews and gentiles, and advising their members through his letters. He was executed in Rome about A.D. 62 while planning a mission to Spain (see Map 5.6).

Paul became the best known of all the early Christian teachers. His letters, or epistles, written to give specific guidance to the congregations he founded, were widely circulated and then collected as part of the Christians' authoritative Scriptures. Luke devotes nearly half of the Acts of the Apostles to Paul's career as a courageous witness who fought with burning missionary fervor for his new lord.

Above all, Paul rejected the policy of some early Jewish Christians who wanted to restrict membership in the new faith to Jews or to gentiles who had become Jews through circumcision. In one of his tautly argued letters in the Bible's Book of Romans he asked: "Is God the God of the Jews only? Is he not also the God of the Gentiles? Yes, of the Gentiles also." By rejecting circumcision as a condition of membership, Paul helped firmly establish the Christian church on the basis of personal faith, not limited by ethnic identity, bloodlines, or observation of the Mosaic law.

Map 5.6 The Journeys of St. Paul

He and later Christian teachers saw themselves as the direct heirs of the Jewish tradition, from which they drew their concept of one God and their notions of creation and the early history of humanity. The first human beings, Adam and Eve, had disobeyed God, thus introducing sin and death into the world. By nature Adam was the founder of the human race; by grace—that gift by which God redeems sinners and gives them life after death—Jesus was its second founder, restorer, and redeemer.

Paul taught Christians to regard themselves as citizens of heaven and to begin living with one another in humility and love, in joyous expectation of their final destiny. The Christians were sure that God would soon consign their world's system of honor and shame based on violence, pride, and class discrimination to the trash heap of history. Paul also redefined the notion of the

Messiah. For Jews, this leader would some day arrive and create another kingdom on earth. For Paul, the messianic age had begun with Jesus, interrupting the age of violence and death as the sign and promise of what the future would bring. Paul's vision of human freedom and a renewed human community characterized by mutual service is one of the most compelling social images in Western culture. Taking this message throughout the lands of the eastern Mediterranean, Paul and his successors brought converts by the thousands into the new church.

Persecutions Toward the many religious sects of the Empire, the Roman government adopted a general policy of toleration, seeking the blessings of all divine powers on the Empire. The Romans even paid for sacrifices to be performed on behalf of the Empire in the temple in Jerusalem. They asked only that veneration be shown on official occasions to the traditional gods and to the

▶ The fourth-century sarcophagus of Junius Bassus, in classicizing style, showing Adam and Eve in Eden, with the threatening serpent.

deceased and deified emperors—little more than public patriotism. But the Christians, like the Jews before them, refused even this apparently small compromise with polytheism. As a result, many despised them as enemies of the human race.

Sporadic persecutions and long periods of peace marked the history of the Church—that is, the Christian community—into the fourth century. Then, in the period 303–313, came the Great Persecution under Diocletian and his successors, as the rulers sought to stamp out what they saw as a potential menace to the state. Their unsuccessful efforts testify to the widespread strength of Christianity. Moreover, the persecutions created a list of venerated Christian martyrs, which led to the cult of saints, thereafter an integral part of Christian piety.

An Emperor Becomes the Church's Patron   One of the most surprising events in Roman history is the radical shift in the policy of the government

toward the Christians initiated in 313 by the emperor Constantine. In the traditional story, first appearing around the period 318–320, Constantine had a dream on the evening before he was to fight a rival for supremacy over Italy in 312, at the Milvian Bridge near Rome. In the dream he was told to decorate the shields of his soldiers with the monogram of Christ: "In this sign you shall conquer." Constantine won the battle and thereafter recognized divine power in the name of Christ.

At what point Constantine personally converted to Christianity is debated. In any case, in

▶ The fourth-century emperor Valentinian I shown as Christian ruler in a colossal statue from Barletta in southeast Italy. In one hand, he holds a (restored) orb to signify his imperial power; in the other, the cross to show his devotion to the Church. The portrait thus unites the two forces that sustained the later Empire.

313, at a conference held at Milan, Constantine ended the age of persecutions by extending complete freedom of worship to the Christians and ordering the return of their confiscated goods. Other favors followed: Churches could own property and enjoyed exemptions from certain taxes, and bishops were allowed to judge the legal disputes of the members of their congregations. Thus the Church acquired a privileged juridicial status that it would retain, in many Western lands, until the eighteenth and nineteenth centuries.

Just before his death in 337 Constantine received baptism from the bishop Eusebius of Nicomedia, but Christianity was not yet the official religion of the Empire. The emperor Julian, known as the Apostate, tried in the period 361–363 to restore the position of the traditional gods, but by then the wave of Christianity could not be turned back. In 392 Theodosius the Great forbade the practice of all religions except the form of Christianity recognized by the government, thus transforming in one move the character of both the Empire and Christianity. He reversed Rome's long-standing policy of religious toleration and changed the Church from a brave alternative society sharply critical of "this world" into a friend of worldly power; it thus began attracting some "converts" who sought personal gain rather than spiritual renewal.

BATTLES WITHIN CHRISTIANITY

Dogma and Heresies   Usually, the Christian community did not bother to define matters of dogma or discipline until disputes threatened its internal unity. The losers in these disputes, if they did not amend their beliefs, were regarded as heretics (from the Greek word *hairesis*, meaning "choice"—that is, a wrong choice).

A heresy that threatened the character of the Christian revelation was that of Marcion of Sinope in Asia Minor (circa 150). He sought to reform Christianity by restricting it to the message of St. Paul alone. He therefore edited his version of the New Testament, which included and recognized as divine only the Gospel of Luke and the Epistles of Paul.

Another heresy was that of a bishop from Asia Minor, Montanus (about 170 to 200), who maintained that certain living believers were prophets who were continuously receiving direct inspiration from the Holy Spirit. Women were prominent among these prophets, and Montanus' ideas eventually won the allegiance of the great North African writer Tertullian. The movement forced Christians to ask: Who should rule the Christian congregations—teachers, who could only interpret texts from the past, or prophets, who might expect continuing new revelations.

Christians who accepted the standard doctrines of the Church branded the ideas of Marcion and Montanus as heresy. Since such heresies have vanished over the centuries, one might well ask: What is their historical importance? The answer is that they stimulated the early Church to redefine its positions. Out of the turmoil and disagreement, the Church emerged stronger, even though the price was sometimes the blunt suppression of sincerely held opinions.

Orthodox theologians of the second century answered Marcion by defining the canon of sacred writings to include, in effect, the modern Bible—the entire Old and New Testaments. And the Church answered Montanus by declaring that the age of divine inspiration had come to an end. All the truths needed for salvation, the Church now said, were complete with the work of St. John, the last inspired author (about 100), and no new revelations were needed. In the fourth century, too, the Church refused to accept as inspired certain other writings, calling them the Apocrypha (obscure or unclear writings).

The Government of the Church   Evidence from the first century indicates that James, a brother of Jesus, was the recognized head of the Christians in Jerusalem. During this period, too, we meet the terms *deacon* (*diakonos*), *bishop* (*episkopos*, or "overseer"), and *elder* (*presbuteros*), which at first were nearly synonymous. Then, in the second century, the bishop became the elected leader of a group of elders (later called priests) and deacons (both men and women), who became responsible for collecting donations, distributing charities, and managing the Church's material affairs.

In the early generations of the Church women were often valued as leaders, as for example one Junia, mentioned in the Book of Romans by Paul as "outstanding among the apostles." Other

▶ **The finest mosaics in Europe are in Ravenna. This sixth-century group (below) depicts a line of saints and martyrs under some prophets. The top row shows scenes from the life of Jesus.**

gifted women served as teachers and coworkers with Paul, but as the Church came under patriarchal social pressures, women were limited to working as deaconesses and serving in orders of widows and virgins.

The bishops gained the right to appoint priests, define doctrine, maintain discipline, and oversee morals. This political structure gave Christianity a stable administration that no ancient mystery religion enjoyed. In the West, the number of bishops remained small; they thus obtained power over fairly large areas. Bishops in cities with the largest Christian communities—Rome, Alexandria, Antioch—became the most influential. Finally the bishop of Rome became the head of the Church in the West. The general name for a bishop was *papa*, or father, but eventually the bishop of Rome was the only one who could so call himself (in English, *pope*).

Donatists and Arians In 303, in proclaiming the last persecution of the Christians, Diocletian had ordered priests to surrender their sacred books. Those who did so were called *traditores* ("those who handed over" the Scriptures—thus our word *traitor*) and were hated by the more steadfast Christians. When the persecutions ended in 313, a party of North African Christians led by a bishop named Donatus declared that the traitors, even if repentant, had forever lost membership in the Church; all the sacraments they had ever administered—all baptisms, marriages, ordinations, and the like—were declared worthless.

Since the traitors were many, acceptance of the Donatist program would have brought chaos to the North African church.

The result was violent schism, which mounted on occasion to civil war. Refusing to accept the rule of traitors, the Donatists established their own bishops and hierarchy. In response, the more forgiving orthodox Church declared that the sacraments conferred grace on the recipients *ex opere operato*, simply "from the work having been performed," and that the spiritual state of the priests at the time did not matter. This remained the official Christian position until challenged during the Protestant Reformation of the Middle Ages.

Another major dispute arose about 320 when Arius, an Alexandrian priest, began to teach that Jesus was not coequal with God the Father but had been created by him at a moment in time: "There was a time when he [Jesus] was not." Arius' teachings raised a furor in Egypt and soon throughout the Empire. To restore peace, Constantine summoned the first "ecumenical" council (that is, one representing the entire inhabited world) of the Church, which met at Nicaea in Asia Minor in May 325. The council condemned Arius in the "Nicene Creed," which declared that Jesus was coeternal with the Father and of one substance with God. But not until the Council of Chalcedon of 451 was Jesus clearly defined as one person with two natures. As a human being, he was the son of Mary; as God, he was coequal with the Father and had reigned and would reign with him eternally. This definition has since remained the belief of orthodox Christians.

▶ **An early mosaic (circa 400) showing Christ holding a book and surrounded by apostles in Roman dress. Two women, perhaps saints, crown St. Peter and St. Paul, with the holy city of Jerusalem in the background. The commanding figure of Jesus resembles that of Jupiter in Roman art.**

The Church and Classical Culture Christian writers, although they were proclaimed enemies of pagan culture, had no choice but to be indebted to classical traditions. The basic grammars and texts, the authoritative models of argument and style, were all pagan. To defend the faith, Christian apologists had to master the art of rhetoric and use the arsenal of pagan learning. This Christian accommodation with pagan learning had decisive repercussions. Nearly all the texts of the great classical authors have reached us in copies made by Christians, who believed they were useful in education. Paradoxically, these outspoken enemies of pagan values actually preserved a rich cultural heritage that they sought to undermine.

THE FATHERS OF THE CHURCH

Christianity became the chief religion of Europe partly because it reached the people through the languages and thought of Greco-Roman civilization. Even before the birth of Jesus, Greek-speaking Jews in Alexandria had translated the Old Testament into Greek; this version, said to have been made by 72 scholars, is called the *Septuagint* (from the Latin *septuaginta*, meaning 70), and the authors of the New Testament referred to it and wrote in the common Greek of the day. On the basis of these sacred texts there came an ocean of commentary and persuasion by the so-called Fathers of the Church, the leading theologians of the second to fifth centuries.

Origen and Eusebius The most learned father writing in Greek was Origen (185?–253?), a priest in Alexandria. Both the volume and the profound scholarship of his writings were a wonder of late antiquity. He worked especially on the text of the Scriptures by comparing the original Hebrew and the Septuagint; he also wrote extensive commentaries on books of the Bible and a tract, *Against Celsus*, in which he answers the arguments of an elitist Aristotelian critic of the Christians.

Another highly influential Greek father was Eusebius of Caesarea (260?–340?). His most original work was a history of the Church, which became the model for later such histories. The most learned man of his time, he also wrote a *Chronicle*

of universal history, which is one of our most important sources for ancient history in general.

The Latin Fathers Among the fathers who wrote in Latin was Ambrose, bishop of Milan from 374 to 397. His most important doctine was that the Church must be independent of the emperor and that bishops should have the right to chastise rulers. In 390 he excommunicated the emperor Theodosius after he had massacred the rebellious citizens of Thessalonica, forbidding him to receive the eucharist and thus placing him outside the body of the Church. Theodosius admitted his guilt and repented, and the popes of later centuries who struggled with secular officials owed much of their power to the resolute example of Ambrose.

Jerome (340?–420) succeeded Eusebius as the most learned Church father of his time. His translation of both the Old and the New Testaments into Latin, usually called the Vulgate version of the Bible, is probably the most influential book ever written in the Latin language. It became the medium through which the Judeo-Christian writings permeated the Latin-speaking nations of Europe and was the biblical text most often used during the Middle Ages.

Augustine Augustine (354–430), the best known of the fathers, was born in North Africa of a pagan father and a Christian mother and accepted Christianity under the influence of Ambrose in 387 (*see box*, p. 146). He became bishop of Hippo in North Africa in 395 and spent the remaining years of his long life writing, preaching, and administering his see.

In his voluminous writings Augustine had something to say about almost every question of Christian theology. He profoundly influenced, for example, Christian teachings on sexual morality and marriage. Like some of his pagan contemporaries, he believed that the world was already filled with people. "The coming of Christ," he wrote, "is not served by the begetting of children." He therefore urged all Christians to a life of celibacy, even though this would mean their own declining numbers: "Marriage is not expedient, except for those who do not have self-control." He banned all sexual activity for the unmarried. Within marriage, husband and wife

Augustine Is Brought to His Faith

St. Augustine describes how, after many struggles to overcome his lustful nature, he was inspired at age 31 to pick up and read in the New Testament; this was the critical moment in his conversion.

"And, not indeed in these words, but to this effect I spoke often to you: 'But you, O Lord, how long? Will you be angry forever? Do not remember against us the guilt of past generations.' I sent up these sorrowful cries—'How long, how long? Tomorrow, and tomorrow? Why not now? Why is there now no end to my uncleanness?'

"I was saying these things and weeping in the most bitter contrition of my heart, when I heard the voice of a boy or girl, I do not know which, coming from a neighboring house, chanting, and often repeating, 'Take up and read; take up and read.' Immediately my face changed, and I began to consider whether it was usual for children in any kind of game to sing such words; nor could I remember ever hearing anything like this. So, restraining the torrent of my tears, I rose up, interpreting it as nothing but a command from heaven to open the Bible, and to read the first chapter I saw. So I returned to where I had put down the apostles. I grasped it, opened it, and in silence read the first paragraph I saw—'Not in rioting and drunkenness, not in debauchery and lust, not in strife and envy; but let Jesus Christ be your armor, and give no more thought to satisfying bodily appetites' [Romans 13–14]. I read no further, I did not need to; for instantly, as the sentence ended—by a light of security that poured into my heart—all the gloom of doubt vanished."

St. Augustine, *Confessions*, VIII, 12, J. G. Pilkington (tr.), in *Basic Writings of Saint Augustine*, vol. 1, Random House (1948), p. 126, language modified.

should unite sexually only for procreation, and the pleasure they took even in this act, representing a triumph of passion over reason, was a small, though pardonable, sin.

In theological matters, Augustine was passionately interested in the operations of grace (see p. 140). He sought the work of grace in his own life, and the result was his *Confessions*, an intensely personal autobiography; it is both a record of his early life, when he was consumed by material and sexual passions, and a celebration of the providence that had guided him in his struggle toward God. This masterpiece of introspective analysis is a type of literature virtually unknown in the classical tradition.

Augustine distinguished between God the creator (the author of nature) and God the redeemer (the source of grace), and insisted that these two figures not be confused. God as creator had given humanity certain powers, such as intelligence superior to that of beasts, but those powers, injured by the original fall of Adam and Eve, are insufficient to earn salvation. Only through grace, which Jesus' sacrifice had earned, could humanity hope to be saved. Moreover, God had already decided on whom he would bestow grace; hence, even before we are born, we are all predestined either to heaven or to hell.

Augustine was consumed by the problem of sin—the breaking of God's law—and quarreled with Pelagius, a British monk, who argued that sin was only the result of a wrong choice and that people could achieve perfection, do good works, and thus attain salvation. For Augustine, sin descended from Adam into every human being, and doing any good works offered only a temporary reprieve: Humanity's salvation must await a glorious transformation at the end of time.

Augustine further believed that the whole course of human history might be redeemed by the power of grace. In his greatest work, *The City*

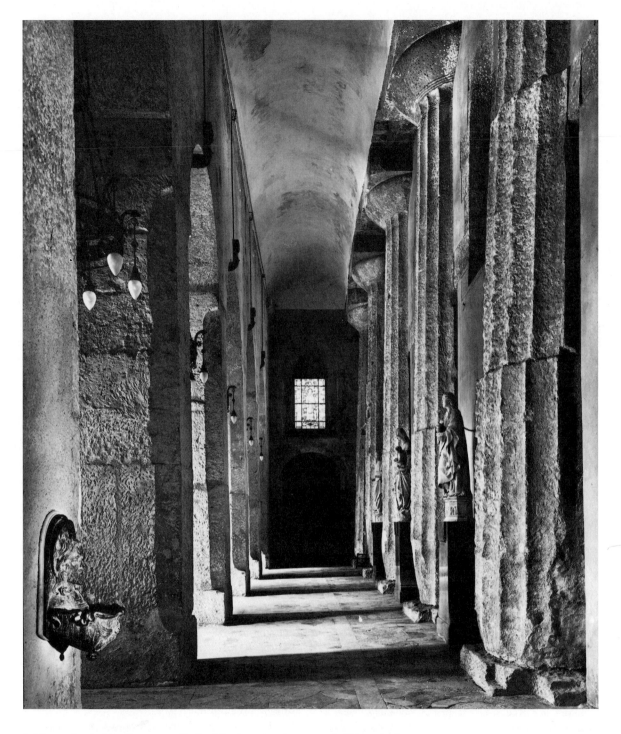

▶ The cathedral in Syracuse, Sicily. The interior, in powerful historical symbolism, shows a Doric temple to Athena (fifth century B.C.) with its original columns, now supporting the walls and roof of a Christian church built in the seventh century.

of God, he set out to show that there was order in history: Behind the manifold events of the past there was evident the hand of God, directing people through his grace to their destiny. Into this immense panorama, Augustine brought the sacred history of the Jewish Testament, the history of his own times, and the Christian expectation of resurrection. He held that the grace of God united the chosen in a form of community or city, which was set against the community of those joined by the love of earthly things. The city of God, in which live those chosen for salvation, was as yet invisible, and the elect who were its members should recognize that this present earth was not their true home. To Christians of his own troubled age and to those of later ages, Augustine held out the beckoning vision of a heavenly city, a celestial Jerusalem, where at last they would be at home with God.

Christians therefore felt able to ignore or transcend the "fall" of Rome—an event that the modern world sees as a possible model of its own fate. The transformation of the Empire, as it is better called, is a challenge and a warning to all who read history; it is also the recognized end of the ancient world and the beginning of a long period in which new nations would use the legacy of antiquity in their own development.

Recommended Reading

▼

Sources

Ayer, Joseph Cullen. *A Source Book for Ancient Church History.* 1913.

Early Christian Writings: The Apostolic Fathers. M. Staniforth (tr.). 1968.

Suetonius. *Lives of the Caesars.* Robert Graves (tr.). 1972.

Tacitus. *Annals of Imperial Rome.* M. Grant (tr.). 1978.

———. *The Histories.* K. Wellesley (tr.). 1964. The two works give the history of the Empire in the first century A.D. by the leading Roman historian.

Studies

Barnes, T. D. *The New Empire of Diocletian and Constantine.* 1982. On the two most important late emperors.

Bradley, K. R. *Slaves and Masters in the Roman Empire.* 1988. On the relations between slaves and their owners.

Brown, Peter. *Augustine of Hippo: A Biography.* 1967.

———. *The World of Late Antiquity, A.D. 150–750.* 1971. Together, superb historical and cultural discussions.

Cross, Frank M. *The Ancient Library of Qumrân and Modern Biblical Studies.* 1976. A balanced introduction to the study of the Dead Sea Scrolls.

Daniélou, Jean, and Henri Marrou. *The First Six Hundred Years.* Vol. I of *The Christian Centuries,* L. J. Rogier and others (eds.). 1964. The most comprehensive study of the early Catholic Church.

Dodds, E. R. *Pagan and Christian in an Age of Anxiety: Some Aspects of Religious Experience from Marcus Aurelius to Constantine.* 1970. On the inner reasons for the great change of gods in the Roman Empire.

Frend, W. H. C. *The Rise of Christianity.* 1984. Now the most extensive single discussion.

Garzetti, Albino. *From Tiberius to the Antonines: A History of the Roman Empire, A.D. 14–192.* 1974. The best political narrative of this important period.

Gibbon, Edward. *The History of the Decline and Fall of the Roman Empire.* 6 vols. 1776–1788. Many modern editions, the best by J. B. Bury, 7 vols., 1896–1900.

Grant, Michael. *The Army of the Caesars.* 1974. Comprehensive discussion of the development of the Roman army in the Empire.

———. *The Fall of the Roman Empire: A Reappraisal.* 1976.

Hopkins, K. *Conquerors and Slaves.* 1978. Essays on the social and economic consequences of Roman imperialism.

Jones, A. H. M. *The Later Roman Empire, 284–602*. 1964. Encyclopedic narrative, with detailed citation of primary sources; for advanced students.

———. *The Decline of the Ancient World*. 1975. Essentially a shortened version of the foregoing.

Luttwak, *The Grand Strategy of the Roman Empire*. 1976. An original analysis by a professional strategist.

MacMullen, Ramsay. *Corruption and the Decline of Rome*. 1988. On the transformation of ideas and conduct in the Empire.

———. *Enemies of the Roman Order*. 1966. On the internal causes for the weakening of Rome.

———. *Paganism in the Roman Empire*. 1981.

Millar, Fergus (ed.). *The Roman Empire and Its Neighbors*. 1981. With chapters by various experts on the nations bordering on the Empire.

Millar, Fergus. *The Emperor in the Roman World*. 1977. Study of the emperor and the imperial bureaucracy.

Nock, Arthur Darby. *Conversion*. 1961. The best book on the reasons for the transition from paganism to Christianity, by a great scholar.

Raaflaub, K. A., and M. Toher (eds.). *Between Republic and Empire*. 1990. Essays on Augustus and the politics and culture of the Empire.

de Ste Croix, G. E. M. *The Class Struggle in the Ancient World*. 1981. A Marxist survey of Greco-Roman culture, concentrating largely on the Empire.

Syme, Ronald. *Tacitus*. 1958. Not only a study of the historian but also a microscopic analysis of the politics of the Empire. For advanced students.

Watson, G. R. *The Roman Soldier*. 1969.

Wells, C. *The Roman Empire*. 1984. A good modern account.

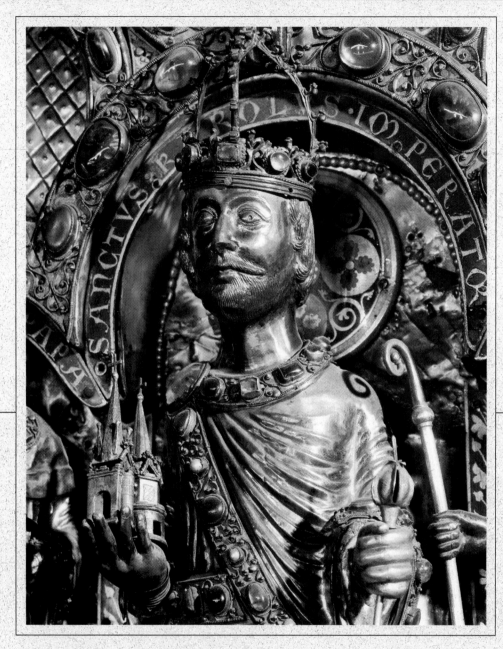

This twelfth-century silver reliquary from Aachen represents Charlemagne as emperor, saint, and protector of the Church. After his death, through all the subsequent medieval centuries, Charlemagne was remembered and viewed as the ideal Christian emperor.

CHAPTER SIX

THE MAKING OF WESTERN EUROPE

THREE new civilizations fell heir to the Classical tradition after the fall of Rome. A separate religion marked each of them: Roman, or Catholic, Christianity in western Europe; Eastern, or Orthodox, Christianity in Asia Minor and eastern Europe; and Islam in the Middle East and North Africa. The new societies were predominantly peasant; although slavery remained important, it was no longer the principal basis for their economies.

The new cultures were dominated by the Christian and Muslim visions of an afterlife, visions that offered to even the humblest members of society a sense of individual dignity and destiny. All men and women could learn from Christianity and Islam that their lives, however hard and cruel, were not meaningless. God, they believed, had created them, and obedience to his will might earn them eternal life.

The age also witnessed a vast movement of peoples. Celts, Germans, Slavs, Arabs, and others shifted or enlarged the areas of their former settlements. The migrations permanently affected the composition of peoples in Europe and the Middle East. They also caused violent upheavals, but economies were slowly rebuilt, largely through innovations in agriculture that enabled peasants to cultivate areas that had not been efficiently farmed before. Medieval societies also built new economic institutions such as the large estate or manor, based in Europe on semifree or serf labor.

I. The New Community of Peoples

The civilization that took root in the west and north of Europe after the decline of the Roman Empire was unmistakably the direct ancestor of the modern Western world. Historians call the millennium between the fall of the Roman Empire and approximately 1500 *the Middle Ages*, or medieval period, of European history and have further divided this era into three distinct periods:

Early Middle Ages	500–1000
Central Middle Ages	1000–1350
Late Middle Ages	1350–1500

The Early Middle Ages witnessed the emergence of the first recognizably Western civilization from the shambles of the Roman Empire; this new civilization embraced both the former subjects of the Empire and peoples from beyond its borders. The Greeks and Romans called all these peoples *barbarians*[1] because of their unintelligible languages and strange customs. There was no single barbarian nation: These peoples were many and differed considerably in language and culture.

THE GREAT MIGRATIONS

Among the barbarian peoples were the Celtic tribes in northern Scotland (the Picts, the "painted ones," so called by the Romans from their habit of tattooing themselves) and in Ireland. (The common name for the Celtic Irish was, confusingly, Scots.) The Picts and Scots escaped the Roman domination that had befallen their cousins, the Britons and Gauls.

More numerous and more formidable than the Celts were the Germans, who were settled in a great arc that stretched from Scandinavia to the Black Sea. The Germans had long been exposed to Mediterranean influences and were culturally among the most advanced of the barbarian peoples. From about 350, Christianity spread among

---

[1]The Greeks invented the word *barbaros* to imitate the strange sounds of unintelligible languages.

the Germans north of the Danube, but in its Arian form (see p. 144). Beyond this Germanic cordon lived the still pagan Slavic tribes, probably the most numerous of the barbarians.

Huns and Germanic Peoples Germanic tribes had for centuries challenged the Roman frontiers because their primitive, unproductive economies forced them to search constantly for new lands to plunder or settle. The Germans were attracted by the wealth and splendor of the Roman world, and the Romans admitted them into the Empire, even while resisting their armies. The barbarians came initially as slaves or prisoners of war, then as free peasants to settle on deserted lands, and finally as mercenary soldiers and officers. In the fourth century the barbarian penetration of the Empire was made more violent because the barbarians themselves were being invaded and forced southwestward by nomadic hordes from central Asia.

The nomads who sowed tumult in the barbarian world were the Huns, a people probably of Mongolian or Tatar origin. Perhaps in reaction to climatic changes and the desiccation of their pastures, the Huns swept out of their Asiatic homeland and terrorized western Europe. Their great chief Attila (433?–453), the "scourge of God" according to Christian writers, established his horde on the plain of the middle Danube and from there led them on raids into both Gaul and Italy. With Attila's death in 453, the Hunnic empire disintegrated, but the Huns had already given impetus to the great movement of peoples that marks the beginning of the Middle Ages.

The Visigoths (or West Goths) were the first of the Germanic tribes to be dislodged by the Huns. In 376 the emperor Valens admitted them into the Empire, but the starving barbarians soon rebelled at the high prices that Roman officials demanded for food. To put down the uprising, Valens led an expedition against them but was defeated by the Visigothic cavalry in the battle of Adrianople in 378. This battle ended the Romans' military advantage over the barbarians and showed the superiority of the mounted warrior (the prototype of the medieval knight) over the foot soldier. Continuing their westward movement, the Visigoths sacked Rome in 410 and crossed the Alps into Gaul, where in 418 they established the first

Map 6.1 Invasions, Fourth through Sixth Centuries

autonomous kingdom on Roman soil. At its height in the mid-fifth century the kingdom of the Visigoths extended from Gibraltar to the Loire River. Another Germanic people, the Franks, conquered the Visigothic kingdom in Gaul in the sixth century; and the Saracens[2] overpowered the surviving Visigothic kingdom in Spain in the eighth century.

Another Germanic people pushed by pressure from the Huns were the Vandals. The Vandals

came from what is now eastern Germany and broke across the Rhine River into Gaul in 406. Perhaps 80,000 in number, they continued south through Spain and crossed to North Africa, where they established a permanent kingdom in 429. They were Arians and persecuted orthodox Christians. They became so powerful on the Mediterranean Sea that in 455 they were able to plunder Rome. This act, the cruelty involved in their religious persecutions, and their piracy in the Mediterranean earned the Vandals a reputation

---

[2]The name *Saracens* originally referred to Arabs living in the Sinai peninsula; in the Middle Ages the name was used to refer to Muslims in general.

for senseless violence, which the modern word *vandal* still reflects. The Vandal kingdom survived until the Byzantine emperor Justinian saw to its destruction in the sixth century.

The Burgundians, another Germanic tribe from eastern Europe, followed the Vandals into Gaul, probably in 411. These Germans established an independent kingdom in the valleys of the upper Rhône and Saône rivers in 443, which gave the region its permanent name, Burgundy.

The ease with which all these Germanic peoples invaded the Roman frontiers shows that the Empire had lost virtually all authority by the middle of the fifth century. The emperor Valentinian III was the last Roman to exercise any real power in the West and was followed by a series of feeble emperors. They were raised to the throne and then deposed or murdered by German officials, who were the effective rulers. One of these, Odovacar, deposed the last emperor in 476 (see p. 131). Although no more than a palace mutiny, this coup marks the final passage of power from Roman to German hands. Odovacar remained in control until he was overthrown in 493 by Theodoric, the leader of the Ostrogoths (eastern Goths). A shrewd ruler, Theodoric founded a kingdom in Italy that provided more than 30 years of peace and even some prosperity as Romans and Germans learned to live together. Although his kingdom was not destined for long survival, it may justly be regarded as the first medieval state.

Germanic Tribes in Gaul   In the third and fourth centuries the Germanic tribes living just beyond the Roman frontier in the Rhine valley coalesced into two large federations, the Alemanni in the upper valley and the Franks in the lower valley. The Alemanni pushed beyond the Rhine into the middle of Gaul and founded a kingdom in 420. They give to both modern French and Spanish their names for Germany (*Allemagne, Alemania*). The Franks slowly penetrated into northern Gaul, moving across the valley of the Seine up to the Loire River. By the fifth century they had separated into two peoples: the Salian, or "salty," Franks, who occupied the lands from the shores of the British Channel to the Loire valley (excluding only Brittany); and the Ripuarian, or "river bank," Franks, whose history is wrapped in ob-

scurity, but who seem to have settled between the Rhine and Meuse rivers. The first-mentioned king of the Salians, a figure who stands on the dark margin between legend and history, was called Merovech, and he gave his name to the first dynasty of Frankish kings, the Merovingians. The true founder of the kingdom of the Franks, however, was his putative grandson Clovis (481–511).[3]

Clovis' great accomplishment was the political unification of nearly the whole of Gaul, corresponding roughly to most of modern France. Already king of the Salians, he had himself elected king of the Ripuarians and thus ruled a united Frankish people. His sons added both Burgundy and Provence to the kingdom, nearly completing the conquest of Gaul.

No less important for unification than military force was Clovis' conversion, probably about 496, to Roman, rather than Arian, Christianity. This step facilitated his conquests and made possible the peaceful assimilation of the diverse peoples he ruled. As the first barbarians to accept Roman Christianity, the Franks became the "eldest daughter" of the Western Church and soon its acknowledged sword and champion.

Germans in Britain   The Germanic invasions of Britain differed from the conquests on the continent. The Germans—Angles, Saxons, Jutes, even some Franks and Frisians—came in small bands under the authority of chiefs. These Germans did not settle and assimilate with the native peoples (the Britons) as they did in most other Roman provinces; they either exterminated the Britons or pushed them westward into Cornwall and Wales. In a search for safer homes, some Britons crossed the Channel to settle in the Roman province of Armorica, which therefore came to be called *Brittany*, or "little" Britain, as distinct from Great Britain, their former homeland. For a few decades in the early sixth century the Britons in Britain unsuccessfully rallied against the Germans under a king whom later sources call Arthur, but after 550 the Germans were triumphant

---

[3]His name is really a cognate of Louis; thus, by this historical oddity, all the long line of French kings named Louis are misnumbered.

▶ **BAPTISM OF CLOVIS I**
Although this depiction of Clovis comes from a fourteenth-century manuscript, it suggests the continuing power of his image, and particularly the importance of his conversion and baptism, which is here commemorated some 800 years after the event. Even as the bishop performs the baptism, he is helped by an angel from above. Apart from its content, this miniature is a splendid example of the way the initial letters of chapters were decorated by medieval monks.

and imposed their language on the region. So sharp was the linguistic change thus enforced that modern English, apart from place names, shows little trace of the speech of the original Britons.

The Early Slavs   The Slavic tribes living to the east of the Germans embarked on their own extensive migrations. In the fifth and sixth centuries some Slavic tribes pushed their settlements as far west as the Elbe River and as far north as the Baltic Sea; they are the ancestors of the modern West Slavs—the Poles, Czechs, and Slovaks. During the same years other Slavic tribes penetrated into the Balkan peninsula and Greece; their descendants are the modern South Slavs—the Serbs, Croats, Bulgarians, and Macedonians. Still other tribes moved east beyond the Dnieper River and north into the forest regions of Russia; they are the ancestors of the modern East Slavs— the Russians, Ukrainians, and Belarussians (or White Russians). No other Indo-European peoples came to occupy so extensive a geographic area as the Slavs, although distance inevitably weakened their ethnic and cultural unity.

GERMANS AND ROMANS

Historians have estimated, although on flimsy evidence, that the Germans who settled within the Roman Empire constituted no more than 5 percent of the total population. In the course of time, the Germanic chiefs and armies obtained perhaps a third of the territory of the former Empire. Most of the humble freemen (those who were not slaves) apparently settled as cultivators, obligated to pay rents and perform services to the owners of the property; but unlike the *coloni* in the Late Roman Empire, these freemen retained their liberty of movement. The Germans did not exterminate the Roman middle classes; rather, through intermarriage with Romans, the Germans adopted lives that made them almost indistinguishable from their Roman counterparts.

Historians no longer speak confidently, as they once did, of specifically Germanic contributions to medieval and Western civilization. Even before entering the Empire, many Germans, particularly those settled near the frontiers, had achieved a cultural level that resembled that of the Romans. Nonetheless, they arrived as invaders, and the destruction they wrought and their apparent reluctance to settle in cities accelerated the decline of urban life in the West. The centers of economic, social, and cultural life shifted to the countryside. This was a critical change, for cities had dominated the economy and culture of the Classical Mediterranean world.

GERMANIC SOCIETY

The Role of Women A sensitive indicator of social values in the study of any society is the status of women. The Roman historian Tacitus praises the Germans for their chastity and fidelity, but he notes that men "of high position" took several wives. German women, Tacitus also tells us, were mature at first marriage, and their husbands were their equals in age. To his surprise, the family of the groom paid a dowry to the bride, which was hers to keep and pass on to her heirs.

Women made essential contributions to the Germanic household at every social level. The

▶ This small (8⅝ inches) ivory depiction of the Virgin was probably executed at Aachen, one of the capitals of Charlemagne, in the ninth century. Note that the Virgin holds spindles in her left hand; spinning was typically woman's work. But surprisingly, she also wears armor—gauntlets on her wrists and what look to be shoulder pieces. Though a woman doing woman's work, she is a militant, imperious figure, strikingly different from the motherly madonnas of later medieval art.

The Metropolitan Museum of Art.

free German male aspired to be a warrior; a wife who would tend his fields and watch over his flocks and herds during his absences enabled him to fight. The chief or king similarly looked for a wife who could collect his dues, pay his retainers, and manage his lands. Germanic women did these things, which slaves or freedmen had done in Classical society. The social importance of Germanic women was not, however, an unmixed benefit. According to Tacitus, they worked harder than the men. In a violent society they were often the prized booty for raiding expeditions and constant targets of abduction. Their life expectancy seems to have been shorter than that of males, and their resulting smaller number added to their social value.

Children The Germanic attitude toward children was also distinctive. The cultures of the Mediterranean world, based on literacy and learning, invested heavily in the education of the young. The illiterate Germans, by contrast, reared many children but invested little in their upbringing. Tacitus notes that the Germans, unlike the Romans, did not practice infanticide, though children of rich and poor were reared with equal indifference. This contrast in cultures helped ensure that the Germanic peoples would eventually overwhelm the Roman world through sheer numbers.

Social Structure The Germanic freemen owned land, and individual ownership existed as far back in their history as our knowledge goes. And individual ownership allowed some families to become richer than others. Germanic society was not egalitarian. Families with a common ancestry were linked together into kindreds (groups of near relatives; the common name for the Germanic kindred was the *Sippe*). The kindred fought, migrated, settled, and held certain forms of property (forests and wastelands) in common.

The kindred also adjudicated disputes among its members and avenged injuries done to them. Compensation was defined in money for loss of a person's life (his or her *Wergeld*, meaning basically "man money"), arm, eye, or nose. Since the circle of kin was frequently unable to protect its members, Germanic society often formed associations of self-help. Such an association was called by Tacitus a *comitatus* ("following"), in which young warriors would join the retinue of an established chief, follow him to battle, and fight under his leadership in return for his protection and a share of his booty. Another kind of self-help was provided by the guild, an association of equals, originally having no relation to economic life. Guild brothers sacrificed to the gods, feasted and drank together, and aided one another in danger.

Kindreds grouped together to form a tribe, a people, or a nation; members of a tribe always looked upon themselves, rightly or wrongly, as descendants from a common ancestor. Before the Germanic invasions of the Roman Empire, the tribes or peoples did not usually have kings; only the invasions, which required a continuing military command, made the king (who also served as chief priest) usual within Germanic society.

Law and Procedures Germanic laws were not written down until the sixth century, and reliance on oral tradition explains several peculiarities of Germanic institutions. To recall the ancient laws, the Germans consulted old, respected men of the community, who could remember what was done in the misty past. One of the most distinctive features of tribal government was its reliance on large councils or assemblies. The chief or king had only limited power and never made decisions alone; he always acted in an assembly or council of freemen who could help him recall the customs and aid him in making his judgments.

To confirm the making of contracts within the community, Germans (and the medieval world after them) relied heavily on symbolic gestures publicly performed. In conveying property, for example, the former owner would hand over a twig or a clod of earth to the new owner in the presence of witnesses. But since the memory of witnesses was often unreliable as a record of such agreements, the Germans also determined truth or falsehood, guilt or innocence, in disputes by investigating the character of the litigants or by appealing to magic. In a practice known as *compurgation*, 12 good men who typically knew nothing about the facts at issue would swear to the honest reputation and presumed innocence of the accused. Or the accused would undergo an *ordeal* (the word originally meant "judgment"), such as

stepping barefoot over hot irons or immersing a hand in boiling water; if the feet or hand showed no severe burns, the accused was declared innocent. Sometimes two litigants would simply fight before the court on the assumption that God would not allow the innocent to be vanquished.

All these practices influenced the development of medieval law and government. The use of juries in trials, a common practice of Europe in the Middle Ages, was based on the assumption that the entire community, represented by sworn men, should determine when a law was violated. The medieval king, like his early Germanic predecessor, was also expected to make his major decisions with the advice of senior men, assembled in councils or parliaments (*see box*, p. 158).

Germanic Culture Since the Germans made little use of writing, their literature was preserved by oral transmission. Poetry, more easily memorized than prose, was the favored form of literary expression. The earliest surviving examples of Germanic poetry were not written down until the ninth century, but they still provide an authentic reflection of barbarian culture, testifying to a violent age. In the Anglo-Saxon epic *Beowulf*, the king of the Danes, Hrothgar, is powerless against the terrible monster Grendel; his plight illustrates the weakness of tribal kingship. Hrothgar must appeal for help to the hero Beowulf, a great warrior who offers the community its one hope of salvation.

Religion displayed an abiding sense of pessimism. The Germans saw nature as a hostile force controlled by two sets of gods. Minor deities, both good and bad, dwelt in groves, streams, fields, and seas, and directly affected human beings. Through incantations, spells, or charms, people tried to influence the actions of these spirits. Such magical practices strongly influenced popular religion and mixed with it a large element of superstition, which lasted through the Middle Ages and long beyond.

The higher gods lived in the sky and took a remote interest in human affairs. Chief among them was Woden or Odin, god of magic and victory, whom Tacitus equates with the Roman Mercury. Woden, his wife Friia or Frig, Thor the thunderer, Ti or Tyr the god of war—all give their names to days of the week in all Germanic

Tacitus on the Early Germans

The short book by Cornelius Tacitus, Germania, published in 98, is virtually the only surviving portrait of early Germanic society. In this passage Tacitus describes the customs of the Germans in government.

"On matters of minor importance only the chiefs deliberate, on major affairs the whole community; but, even where the people have the power to decide, the case is carefully considered in advance by the chiefs. Except in case of accident or emergency they assemble on fixed days. [. . .] When the mass so decide, they take their seats fully armed. Silence is then demanded by the priests, who on that occasion have also power to enforce obedience. [. . .] If a proposal displeases them, the people roar out their dissent; if they approve, they clash their spears.

"One can launch an accusation before the Council or bring a capital charge. The punishment varies to suit the crime. The traitor and deserter are hanged on trees, the coward, the shirker and the unnaturally vicious are drowned in miry swamps under a cover of wattled hurdles. The distinction in the punishment implies that deeds of violence should be paid for in the full glare of publicity, but that deeds of shame should be suppressed. Even for lighter offences the punishment varies. The man who is found guilty is fined so and so many horses or cattle. Part of the fine is paid to the King or State, part to the injured man or his relatives."

From Cornelius Tacitus, *Germania*, H. Mattingly (tr.), pp. 11–12.

► **SUTTON HOO DRAGON**
There were many metallic buckles and pins found at Sutton Hoo, the ship burial site of the East Anglian king Anna, who died in 654. Shown here is a dragon, made of gilt bronze and garnet. The body, extending from the head—with its jaws, teeth, and garnet eye—to the tail, is embellished in a style common at the time, with intricate beasts intertwined in long ribbon-like patterns.

languages, including English. According to late Scandinavian myth, warriors who died in battle joined the following of Odin in a great banquet hall, Valhalla. But the entire company of gods and heroes was doomed to destruction by fire during a cosmic twilight when the ravaged earth would sink entirely into the sea. It is not known whether the early Germans shared this elaborate myth. They certainly shared in the exaltation of heroes and in a deep pessimism about humanity's ultimate fate.

Because they changed their homes so frequently, the Germans developed no monumental art—no temples, palaces, or large statues—before settling within the Empire. Their finest art was jewelry made from precious metals, often embodying forms of animals. This animal style, probably originating in the steppe region of eastern Europe and Asia, strongly influenced early medieval art; even the lettering and illuminations in the manuscripts of that epoch reflect some of its motifs.

The age after the Germanic invasions saw a near triumph of a nonliterate culture over the literate culture of the Roman aristocracy. The invaders were not alone responsible for the victory of this nonliterate culture, for the great, unlettered masses of the Empire surely shared many of the Germanic attitudes and practices; but the invasions did lend this vulgar culture a new strength and stability.

II. The New Economy, 500–900

The great achievement of the Early Middle Ages was the emergence of the single-family peasant farm as the basic unit of agricultural production. There were three reasons for this development. First, the declining supply of slaves induced many owners of villas to settle their slaves on these family farms. Second, changes in warfare, specifically the new supremacy of the mounted warrior, made fighting an expensive profession and converted many freemen into full-time cultivators. Finally, a series of technological innovations in agriculture aided the peasant in supporting himself, his family, and the new society.

AGRICULTURE

The most fertile agricultural region of Europe is the great alluvial plain that stretches from southeast England and France to the Urals. The peoples of the ancient world had not been able to farm it efficiently. The light plow of antiquity only scratched the heavy soils of the north, though it was suitable enough for the thin soil and dry climate in the Mediterranean, where only the surface needed to be pulverized to retain moisture. On the northern plain, however, the earth had to be cut deeply and turned to form the furrows needed to carry away excess water from the abundant rains. Thus a heavier, more powerful plow was needed. Most historians date the emergence of such a plow, simultaneously among the Germans and the Slavs, to the sixth century.

The development of the heavy plow was accompanied by other changes in farming techniques. The Mediterranean plow was dragged by two oxen, while the northern plow required as many as eight. Thus peasants in the north often kept oxen collectively and therefore needed to live in communities rather than in isolated individual settlements.

At the same time, new techniques allowed peasants to substitute the horse for the ox as a draft animal. The Romans had harnessed the horse with almost incredible inefficiency. The animal was bound to its load by pliant straps around the throat and belly that rewarded its best efforts with strangulation. Moreover, the load was bound so high on the horse's withers that the animal could not throw its full weight against the harness. In the ninth century northern Europeans developed a collar and harness that made efficient use of the horse as a draft animal. At about the same time there appeared the tandem harness, which permitted teams of horses to be hitched one behind the other, and the horseshoe, which gave the animal better traction and protected his sensitive hooves. By virtue of these devices the Early Middle Ages, in the words of one historian, "discovered horsepower."[4]

Northern Europeans also developed a new method of crop rotation: the three-field system, based on a triennial cycle and first documented in 763. The field was planted in winter wheat, then in a spring crop—oats, barley, peas, or beans—then permitted to lie fallow for a year. The older two-field system, based on the yearly alternation of winter wheat and fallow, continued to be used in Mediterranean lands, where spring crops were difficult to raise because rain was scarce in the spring and summer; but they grew well in the north because of the abundant year-round rainfall.

The three-field system kept a larger portion (two-thirds) of the soil under crops. It raised the productive efficiency of the peasant's labor by an even higher degree; the fallow, although it returned no crop, still had to be worked, and with a smaller fallow (one-third rather than one-half the land), the peasant had more time for productive labors. The spring crop restored fertility to the soil, provided a more varied diet for the people, and lessened the risk of total failure because

---

[4]Lynn T. White, Jr., *Medieval Technology and Social Change*, 1966, pp. 57–69.

▶ BAD AND GOOD REGIMENT, CA. 1125
**This manuscript illustration shows a typical
medieval plow team of oxen. The heavy plow used
on the plain of northern Europe included three
indispensable parts: a colter or knife to cut the soil,
a share or wedge to widen the breech and break up
the clods, and a moldboard to lift the earth and turn
the furrow.**

two crops were planted in one year. The spring
crop was often used for fodder and thus helped
support a larger number of animals, which in
turn provided manure for more abundant crops.
For the first time the agricultural resources of the
northern plain were used with some measure of
efficiency.

These technological innovations were not victorious overnight; they spread through Europe at
a glacial pace, but their eventual adoption profoundly affected the new Western civilization.
They allowed northern Europe to support a
denser population and established a tradition of
technical innovation that has remained alive and
unbroken to the present.

The Manor   In the opening centuries of the Middle Ages, Europeans developed a new form of
agricultural organization: the *manor*, or large estate. It differed from the Roman colonate above
all in the status of the laborers. The owner of the
Roman villa depended primarily on slaves or
hired labor to work his lands, whereas the lord
of the manor relied upon his *serfs*, as laborers dependent on the owner are called.

The manor was characteristic of southeast
England, northern France, western Germany,
and certain areas of the south, such as the Rhône
and Po valleys. These were regions of fertile soil
where grains were cultivated intensively. The
manor, a tightly disciplined community of peasants organized under the authority of a lord, was
therefore a fundamental unit of economic, political, and social organization.

The lands of most manors were divided into
two roughly equal parts: the small farms that belonged to the peasants and the large demesne, or
land owned by the lord that the peasants worked
for him. All manors had extensive meadows, forests, and wastelands, where the lord hunted and
the peasant grazed his animals or collected firewood. Forests and wastelands were usually part
of the lord's demesne; the peasants would often
have their own commons, a collectively owned
meadow in which each resident had the right to
graze a fixed number of animals. Many manors
also had workshops that produced garments,

tools, and other products needed by the community. Self-sufficiency, in other words, remained an ideal in manorial organization, although it was never completely realized.

The lord was the chief police officer and judge. He or his steward ran the court, which was an important source of revenues. The lord held the rights to operate the bakery, brewery, mill, and winepress on the manor and to sell the peasants salt or iron. He was also the chief military officer, recruiting soldiers from among the free peasants and leading them to war. For many peasants the manorial lord was the only government they ever directly confronted.

Most of the peasants inhabiting the manor were serfs; they, and their children after them, could not leave the land without the lord's permission. The defining element of serfdom was enforced labor. Men were usually obliged to work three days a week on the lord's land and to provide additional service at special times of the year, particularly at harvest. Women had to spend some time in the workshops producing cloth and clothing. The serfs paid, usually in goods, a yearly rental on their land and sometimes a small head tax to the lord. They also honored him with yearly gifts, such as eggs in the spring or a capon in the fall. When a serf died and his farm passed to a son, the family usually paid an inheritance tax, either the best animal or piece of furniture, to the lord. If a serf wished to marry someone outside the manor, he had to seek, and usually purchase, the lord's permission.

Although serfs lived harsh lives, their condition was still superior to that of the Roman slaves. Serfs had a moral right to their land, and they and their children could profit from the improvements they made on it. Moreover, the serfs' obligations were traditional and fixed and could not be raised.

THE EXCHANGE OF WEALTH

A new set of economic relations began to bind medieval society, relations largely defined by the flow of treasure—brooches, rings, plates, armor, and coins. The exquisite jewelry of the Early Middle Ages pleased the eye but also rewarded accomplishment, advertised status, and cemented the social structure. Kings gained treasure through pillage, gift, or tribute, and distributed the precious objects to their warriors and retainers.

The gift thus established a social bond between donor and recipient. Gifts made to churches that housed the bodies of saints placed these holy potentates under the obligation to bless and favor the donor. Finally, the flow of treasure defined social status. Even in death, the treasure buried with the king proclaimed his royalty to another world. The humble folk shared in this gift economy only by providing food to their rulers.

The gift economy all but replaced the market economy of the Classical Roman world. The Mediterranean above all had been a great commercial artery for the exchange of goods from the West for the spices and fine cloths of the Levant and for papyrus and grain from Egypt. By the seventh century the peasants and warriors of Western society no longer had the skill, or perhaps the desire, to maintain an economy based on commercial exports.

▶ **VISIGOTHIC FIBULAE**
Fibulae were decorative pins used to fasten clothes. These sixth-century Spanish examples are typical of the sophisticated metalwork practiced by medieval artisans. Gems set in gold and bronze reveal the outline of an eagle form, as well as a delight in pattern that was characteristic of the age.

III. *The Leadership of the Church*

The Church exercised an unrivaled leadership in the Early Middle Ages. This institution retained the Roman tradition of effective social organization and also kept alive the Classical tradition of literacy, rhetoric, and logic. One of history's great paradoxes is that the Church, so hostile to many values of the Classical tradition, was more effective than any other institution in ensuring their survival.

ORIGINS OF THE PAPACY

The papacy, the office through which one man governs the Roman Catholic Church, is the oldest living institution in the Western world; it is the only office that can trace its history back without interruption to the age of the Caesars. According to the traditional Catholic (and medieval) view, Jesus himself endowed the apostle Peter with supreme responsibility for his church.

> And I say unto thee, thou art Peter and upon this rock I will build my church, and the gates of hell shall not prevail against it.
>
> [MATT. 16:18]

In the Aramaic language that Jesus spoke, as well as in Greek and Latin, *Peter* and *rock* are the same words, implying that the Church was to be founded upon Peter. This play on words has been called the most momentous pun in history. Medieval tradition further held that Peter became the first bishop of Rome and was martyred there about the year 60.

The pronouncements of the Roman bishops were often accepted by the bishops of other churches with extraordinary reverence. In the second century Ignatius, bishop of Lyons, taught that beliefs accepted by the Roman bishops as orthodox should be considered orthodox by the entire Church. But in the third century Cyprian, bishop of Carthage, maintained that all bishops were equal in authority; there could be within the Church no "bishop of bishops."

It is hardly surprising that the church at Rome should have acquired preeminence. Rome was, after all, the city of the Caesars, the capital of the world, and the center of Latin culture; people were accustomed to seeking guidance from Rome. The Christian community there dated from apostolic times, and it had no Western rival in age, size, wealth, and talent.

Growth of Papal Primacy The idea of the absolute primacy of the pope, or bishop of Rome, gained support in the fourth and fifth centuries. The emperors, eager to use the Church as an ad-

▷ **Pope Gregory the Great was one of the key figures in the transition from the ancient world to the Middle Ages. He is regarded—along with Jerome, Ambrose, and Augustine—as one (and the last) of the four fathers of the Latin Church. His efforts to defend Rome against the Lombards and to advance missionary work gave added prestige to the papal see.**

junct to their own imperial administration, favored the concentration of religious authority in Roman hands. The most effective promoter of the conception of Roman primacy was Pope Leo I (440–461). In numerous letters and sermons Leo identified the person of the living pope with the person of Peter, who was divinely commissioned to rule the Church. At the Council of Chalcedon in 451 (see p. 144) the bishops received the declaration of the papal legates with the words "Peter speaks through Leo." Although the popes were not exercising an autocracy over the Church, their prestige in the Western world was unrivaled.

Gregory the Great The popes increasingly assumed responsibility for the security of Italy and the defense of the Church. They negotiated with a sequence of invaders—Huns, Vandals, Ostrogoths, and Lombards—and repeatedly sought help from the distant and distracted Eastern emperors. The pope who best exemplifies the problems and accomplishments of the early medieval papacy is Gregory I (590–604).

When Gregory became pope, the Lombards (Germans who had entered Italy in 568) were plundering the Roman countryside and threatening Rome with destruction and starvation. Under these difficult conditions he maintained the productive capacity of the Church's estates, kept food coming to Rome, ransomed captives, aided widows and orphans, and organized the defense of the city. Gregory finally negotiated a truce with the Lombards in 598, although they continued to pose a threat to the security of Rome for more than a century.

Gregory was no less solicitous for the welfare of the entire Church. During his pontificate Gregory gave new momentum to missionary efforts and achieved some remarkable successes. He sent a monk named Augustine and 30 companions to bring Christianity to England, and these missionaries ultimately converted the Anglo-Saxons to Christianity. The Spanish Visigoths were also converted from Arian to Roman Christianity during Gregory's reign. By establishing a tradition of active involvement in the affairs of the world, to which most of his medieval successors would faithfully adhere, Gregory widened enormously the influence of the Roman see.

MONASTICISM

Even more effective than the papacy in shaping medieval civilization were the monks. The ascetic ideal of fleeing the world in order to devote oneself to worship is common to many religions. Beginning in the third century, monks—highly devout Christians who sought refuge in permanent prayer and isolation—began to live apart from humanity. The first to do so was St. Anthony, who lived a life of rigid asceticism in the desert of Egypt. But soon monks began to live and work together in cenobitic ("living in common") monasticism.

The monk who brought order into the movement, St. Benedict of Italy, founded a community at Monte Cassino in 529 and drew up a rule, or manual of conduct, for its members. The Benedictine rule referred to all the main problems of monastic life and was a constitution meant to be applicable to many individual communities; it is an example of the survival of Roman governmental genius in the service of the Church. The abbot was to be elected for life with full authority over the community, but he was to consult the

▶ **St. Benedict Presenting His Rule**
This fourteenth-century image depicts Saint Benedict presenting his rule to a group of nuns. His connection with female spirituality went back to his own lifetime, because his sister, Scholastica, was also devout and lived at a convent near Benedict's at Monte Cassino.

elder and even the younger monks. One of the most famous regulations required some manual labor, lending to it a dignity that both the Greeks and Romans had denied. "Idleness," said the regulation, "is the enemy of the soul."

The Role of the Monk The monks exerted an extraordinary influence on every level of medieval civilization. They were the most successful agriculturists of the age, first as farmers in their own right and then, gradually, as managers of ever larger estates; thus they set an example of good farming practices from which laypeople could benefit.

Monasteries came to play a major role in early medieval society and government. Powerful families often established monasteries on their lands. The abbots and abbesses were often closely related to these prominent laypeople, and they administered the monastery's lands and resources in the interest of their lay relatives. Monasteries, in other words, became integrated into the structures of local power.

Kings, too, relied heavily on monastic farms to supply food for their administrations and armies and often appropriated part of the monks' income to finance their own needs. Culturally, monks were almost the only people who were literate and learned. The Benedictine rule assumed that the monk could read; and the monasteries, although not expressly obliged to do so, maintained both libraries and schools for the training of young monks and, sometimes, lay children. The monks also organized *scriptoria*, or writing offices, in which manuscripts that were

► **PLAN OF AN IDEAL MONASTERY, ST. GALL, SWITZERLAND, CA. 820**
According to the rule of St. Benedict, a well-regulated monastic life centered around the liturgical hours, but also included a full range of physical activity. This plan for an ideal monastery from about 820 depicts the church and cloister at the center of a sprawling complex that also includes workshops for artisans, a school, and a hospital, as well as extensive agricultural lands.

and officials from the monasteries, and nearly all the administrative records that have survived were written by monastic scribes. Finally, the monks, as holy men, were thought to ensure God's blessings for the world, and this helped

▶ **CENTULA ABBEY, AFTER ELEVENTH-CENTURY MANUSCRIPT**
Centula Abbey, in northwestern France, was founded in 790 by Angilbert, a poet-scholar in Charlemagne's circle. This seventeenth-century engraving after a lost eleventh-century manuscript depicts the heart of a vast complex that included three churches (all known) and seven villages, and housed more than 300 monks.

▶ **This Spanish manuscript illumination of daily life in the monastery shows that the writing of manuscripts was one of the monks' principal occupations. In addition, one of the monks is ringing the bells that marked the different services of the day and would have served to remind the surrounding countryside of the activities of the monastery.**

needed for liturgy or education were copied. The great bulk of the surviving Latin literary works of both pagan and Christian antiquity were preserved in copies made in monasteries. Sometimes monks decorated, or illuminated, the manuscript pages; manuscript illuminations are among the loveliest art forms that have come from the age. Because they maintained the schools and libraries, the monks were virtually the only intellectuals in society. Rulers recruited their counselors support the morale of the troubled peoples of the Early Middle Ages.

Part of the monks' importance to society came from their communal organization, which enabled them to cope relatively effectively with the problems of a turbulent age. They could divide essential tasks among their members, assigning some monks to work the earth, others to arrange for the defense of the community, and still others to read and study. The community was also, in a real sense, immortal and could maintain continuity of effort over generations.

A second reason for the influence of monks on their society is that the ascetic temperament equipped monks to be powerful instruments of both economic and cultural change. Early medieval society was desperately poor. Like the people of every poor society, those of the Middle Ages hoped to shape a better future by saving and investing some part of the current, meager production. Grain uneaten and cattle not slaughtered meant more abundant harvests and larger herds the next year; whether the motivation that saved the grain or cattle was religious or economic hardly matters. Monks were the great savers and investors of the age, and their saving and investing may have influenced others to do the same.

Asceticism seems also peculiarly suited to an age of transition. The ascetic by his life calls into question the accepted attitudes of his age. The monks rejected both the Classical and barbarian systems of values and thus helped uproot or weaken such attitudes as the Classical aversion to physical labor and the barbarian love of violence. In so doing, they prepared the way for the elaboration of the new values and the new culture of the Central Middle Ages.

IV. *The New Political Structures*

THE FRANKISH EMPIRE

Clovis had established a strong Frankish kingdom in Gaul, but his Merovingian successors, known traditionally as the "do-nothing kings,"

showed the weaknesses of tribal monarchy. Unable to conceive of the kingdom as anything but a private estate, they divided and redivided their lands among their heirs. They showed no sense of political responsibility and relied primarily on violence to define their powers. The history of their reigns is largely a dismal story of intrigue and destructive feuds.

Yet amid the wars and rivalries the character of Frankish society was changing; the decisive shift was in the technique of making war. The

▶ CHI-RHO, *BOOK OF KELLS*
The Greek letters chi and rho, the first two letters of Christ's name, were frequently used as symbols of Christianity by early believers. This page, from the late eighth-century Irish manuscript *The Book of Kells*, is an example of the complex interlacing characteristic of Anglo-Saxon manuscript illumination in this period.

introduction of the stirrup, probably in the early eighth century, gave a final advantage to the mounted warrior over the foot soldier: He could now strike a hard blow without falling from his horse. This improvement confirmed the superiority, which had been evident for several centuries, of cavalry over infantry. Since horses were expensive, war became a preeminently aristocratic occupation; therefore a new functional and social division appeared in Frankish society. In the past most freemen had been both peasants and warriors. Now freemen who could not afford horses and arms—a majority of the population—became full-time peasants and serfs; those freemen who could afford the new implements of battle became full-time fighters and formed the new military aristocracy.

Because of the negligence of the Merovingian kings, their chief household official, known as the mayor of the palace, gradually took over the real powers of government. The mayor's functions were to manage the palaces and supervise the royal lands; he was also able to distribute the lands largely as he saw fit. Using this privilege, some of the mayors began to supply the aristocracy with the estates they needed to maintain expensive animals and arms. The mayors thus built a following among the new military aristocracy. One mayor, Pepin of Heristal, who already administered the eastern lands of the kingdom, gained control over the western lands in 687, thus unifying nearly the whole kingdom of Gaul under his rule.

Pepin's son and successor, Charles Martel, cultivated the support of the warrior aristocracy and gave substantial support to Christian missionaries. With the aid of these two groups, Charles began to extend Christianity and Frankish domination over the Germanic tribes settled beyond the Rhine River.

Charles's son, Pepin the Short, courted the allegiance of the other aristocracy of Frankish society, the great churchmen, by making a lasting alliance with the pope. The continuing support of the military aristocracy and the new sympathy of the ecclesiastical aristocracy enabled Pepin to effect a major constitutional change. In 751 an assembly of Frankish notables declared that the last Merovingian king, the feeble Childeric III, was not truly a king and recognized Pepin as their legitimate sovereign. In 754 Pope Stephen II visited Pepin's court, confirmed his coronation, and anointed him king. In return for these expressions of support Pepin defeated the Lombards, a Germanic people who had been harassing papal lands in Italy, and confirmed papal possession of the Patrimony of St. Peter (Rome and its environs). Later popes would repeatedly point to this Donation of Pepin as establishing the Papal States. By building strong Christian and Roman influences within his kingship, Pepin strengthened and transformed his reign. He bequeathed to his successors a monarchy founded on the support of great warriors and priests and dignified by association with the Christian and Roman past.

Charlemagne Pepin's son, Charles the Great, or Charlemagne (768–814), pursued the policies of his predecessors with unprecedented energy. His biographer, the court scholar Einhard, says that he was a large man, "seven times the length of his own foot," and that he delighted in physical exercise, particularly hunting, riding, bathing, and swimming. His taste for food and women seems to have been no less exuberant. Perhaps more remarkable in this man were his intellectual curiosity and alertness. He was probably illiterate; Einhard says that he kept tablets by his bed to practice forming letters at night though with "ill success." But Einhard also says that he spoke and understood Latin, comprehended Greek, and enjoyed the company of learned men (*see box*, p. 168). The vast empire Charlemagne built (called the "Carolingian" Empire from Carolus, his Latin name) was in large measure a personal accomplishment, a tribute to his abounding physical energy and intelligence.

Charlemagne's success as king depended on his success in waging long wars on every frontier. His chief concern was to spread Christianity and thus subservience to Frankish authority among pagan peoples. Where permanent conquest and conversion were not possible, the expeditions would still weaken neighboring enemies and prevent them from striking into the Frankish domains. At the pope's request he campaigned four times in Italy against the Lombards and against factions at Rome opposed to the pope. He suppressed the independent Bavarians and over-

Einhard on Charlemagne

The most important ruler of the Early Middle Ages was Charles the Great,
or Charlemagne. A member of his court, Einhard, wrote his life
and describes him as follows.

"Charles was large and strong, and of lofty stature; his height was seven times the length of his foot. In accordance with the national custom, he took frequent exercise on horseback and in hunting. He often practiced swimming, in which he was so skilled that none could surpass him. He was temperate in eating, and particularly so in drinking, for he hated drunkenness in anybody, much more in himself and in members of his household. While dining, he listened to reading or music. The subjects of the readings were the stories and deeds of older times; he was fond, too, of St. Augustine's books, and especially of 'The City of God.'

"Charles had the gift of ready and fluent speech, and could express himself with the utmost clearness. He was not satisfied with a command of only his native language, but studied foreign ones, and was such a master of Latin that he could speak it as well as his native tongue; but he could understand Greek better than he could speak it. He zealously cultivated the liberal arts, held those who taught them in great esteem, and conferred high honors on them. He also tried to write, and used to keep tablets under his pillow, so that in leisure hours he might train his hand to form the letters; but as he began his efforts late in life, he had poor success."

From Einhard, *Life of Charlemagne*, S. E. Turner (tr.) (shortened and modified).

came the Saxons after 33 years of fighting and thus brought them fully and finally into the community of Western peoples (*see box*, p. 169). These victorious wars added new territories to his empire (see Map 6.2).

On Charlemagne's fourth visit to Italy in 800, when he was praying before St. Peter's altar on Christmas night, Pope Leo III crowned him emperor of the Romans. The coronation of 800 added nothing to his possessions but still was of great symbolic importance. It confirmed the alliance of the papacy and the Frankish monarchy, and at a stroke created the alliance of Catholic states, Gaul and Italy, that defined the political axis of subsequent Western history and gave it its pronounced north-south orientation. It was a public declaration of the independence of the West, a final rejection of even a theoretical submission to the Eastern Empire that had become the heir of the Roman Empire. The coronation of 800 therefore marks the birth of Europe, for it proclaimed the complete political and cultural autonomy of the Western community of peoples.

Government The coronation added much to Charlemagne's dignity, and a grandiose imperial ideology developed around his person. The cult of the emperor played a vital role in preserving the unity of the empire because the government did not have the material force to hold it together. Charlemagne was presented to the people as the new David (the ideal king of the Old Testament), the new Augustus (the greatest of the pagan emperors), and the new Constantine (the champion of the Church). By presenting the emperor as a figure of such sanctity and brilliance, the government hoped to make rebellion against him unthinkable. Ideas might thus accomplish what armies could not do alone.

The emperor was, of course, the head of the government; and he was aided by several officials. The head of the palace clergy, the chief ecclesiastic of the realm, was the chaplain, who advised the emperor and the entire court in matters of conscience. The chaplain also supervised the chancery, or secretariat, where the official documents were written. The chief lay official was the count of the palace, who supervised the administration, judged cases that the emperor did not personally handle, and acted as regent during the emperor's frequent absences. Other officials included the chamberlain, who looked after the royal bedroom and treasury; the seneschal, who kept the palace in food and servants; and the constable, who cared for the horses.

At the local level the fundamental administrative unit was the county, which resembled in its extent the Roman provinces. The count was the administrator, judge, and military leader of the county. The county was further divided into small judicial units under a *vicarius*, who heard minor cases.

Charlemagne's chief administrative problem was to maintain an effective supervision and control over the local officials. He used three devices to resolve this problem. First, Charlemagne himself traveled widely to ascertain how the land was being administered and to hear appeals from the decisions of the counts. Second, he appointed special traveling inspectors, called *missi dominici*, to inspect a particular county every year. These men scrutinized the behavior of both the lay and the ecclesiastical officials, heard complaints, published imperial directives, and reported their findings to the emperor. Third, Charlemagne required that the important men of his realm, both laymen and ecclesiastics, attend a general assembly almost every year. There they reported on conditions in their local areas, advised the emperor on important matters, and heard his directives. Many of the imperial directives have survived. Divided into chapters (*capitula*), these informative records are known as *capitularies*.

To promote unity, Charlemagne also standardized weights, measures, and money throughout his empire. The monetary system came to be based on a single minted coin, the silver *denarius*, or penny. Twelve of these made a solidus, or shilling (although such a coin was not actually

Charlemagne Imposes Christianity on the Saxons

Charlemagne fought against the Saxons, a Germanic people, for about 30 years. After subduing them in 804 he made them Christians and imposed a kind of martial law, from which the following are some regulations.

"3. If anyone enters a church by violence and carries off anything in it by force or theft, or has burned the church itself, let him be punished by death.

"4. If anyone, out of contempt for Christianity, has despised the holy fast of Lent and has eaten flesh, let him be punished by death. But let the matter be considered by a priest, in case anyone has eaten flesh from necessity.

"5. If anyone has killed a bishop or priest or deacon, let him be punished by death.

"6. If anyone deceived by the devil has believed, in the manner of the pagans, that any man or woman is a witch and eats men, and on this account has burned the person, or has given the person's flesh to others to eat, or has eaten it himself, let him be punished by death.

"8. If any one of the race of the Saxons concealed among them has wished to hide himself unbaptized, and has scorned to come to baptism and has wished to remain a pagan, let him be punished by death.

"18. On the Lord's day no meetings and public judicial assemblies shall be held, unless in a case of great necessity or when war compels it, but all shall go to the church to hear the word of God, and shall be free for prayers or good works."

From *Capitulary for Saxony*, from *University of Pennsylvania Transactions and Reprints*, vol. VI, no. 5, 1900 (language modified).

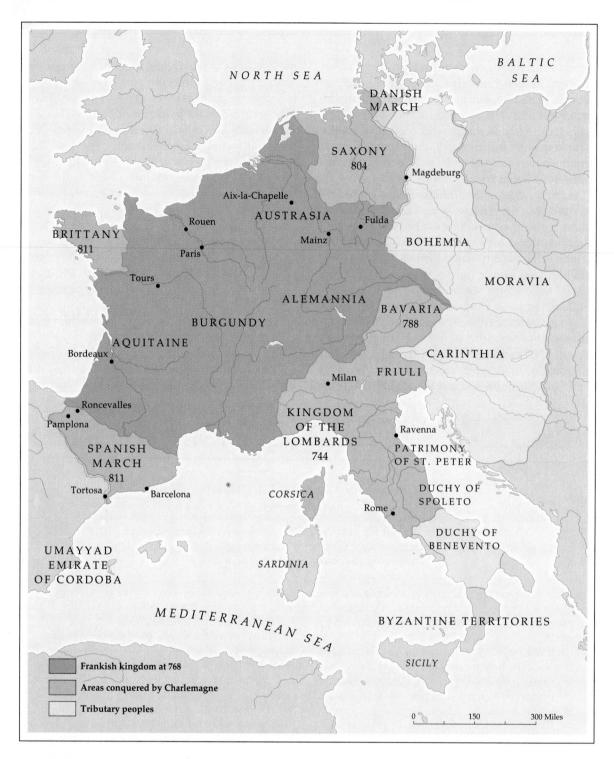

Map 6.2 FRANKISH EMPIRE UNDER CHARLEMAGNE

The dates indicate the years when the regions were added to the empire. Marches were the frontier provinces (except Brittany, which was a maritime province) specially organized for the military defense of the empire. Magdeburg was the episcopal see that took the leadership in the conversion of the Danes and Slavs to Christianity. Aix-la-Chapelle, also called Aachen, was the capital of the empire. The tributary peoples were those beyond the frontiers of the empire over whom the emperor exercised a loose authority. They owed allegiance to him but were never integrated administratively into the empire.

minted), and twenty shillings made a pound. The Englishman who reckons prices in pounds, or the Italian in *lire*, still today uses terms of Carolingian origin.

Decline of the Empire   Charlemagne passed on at his death to his single surviving son, Louis the Pious, a united and apparently strong empire. Louis, a weak and indecisive man, soon lost control over his own family, and his sons rebelled against him. After his death the three surviving sons partitioned the empire at the Treaty of Verdun in 843 and established their own kingdoms (see Map 6.3).

As the family of Carolingian rulers divided amid civil wars and partitions, the loyalty of the military aristocracy also waned. The new rulers conquered no new lands; so they had no new offices or properties with which to buy the loyalties of the aristocracy. The office of count, appointive under Charlemagne, became hereditary under his successors. The Carolingian rulers no longer summoned the great men of the realm to the yearly assemblies and no longer dispatched the *missi dominici* on their circuits. The institutional and moral bonds tying their central governments to the peripheral territories were thus broken or abandoned.

Map 6.3 PARTITION OF THE FRANKISH EMPIRE

RENEWED INVASIONS

Under Charlemagne's weak successors invasions of the Frankish empire resumed, and centrifugal forces tore at the empire as well. To the south, Saracens from North Africa invaded Sicily and southern Italy in 827, attacked the valley of the Rhône in 842, and raided Rome in 846. Concurrently, from the East a new nomadic people, the Magyars, established themselves by about 895 in the valley of the Danube; and from this base for the next 50 years, they struck repeatedly into the areas that are now France, Germany, and Italy (see Maps 6.4 and 6.5).

The most wide-ranging of the new invasions were those mounted by the Northmen, or Vikings, who were Germanic tribes settled in Scandinavia. Their movements may be considered the last phase of the Germanic invasions begun in the fourth century. Several facts explain their invasions. The Vikings could not support a large population in the harsh northern climate, and they were familiar with the attractive wealth of the neighboring areas. The tribes were constantly at war with one another because there was no stable kingdom; a defeated chief, rather than become a vassal under his conqueror, often preferred to seek out new land overseas. The Vikings were skilled and versatile seamen whose explorations took them as far as a western territory they called Vinland, undoubtedly part of the North American continent. Iceland, settled as a result of these explorations, became a major center of medieval Scandinavian culture.

In England and on the continent the Vikings appeared first as merchants and pirates, then as conquerors and colonists. Vikings, chiefly Danes, began raiding England in 787; then in 866 a Danish army landed in eastern England and established a permanent settlement. The Vikings followed the same pattern on the continent. They attacked cities along the western coast of Europe, penetrated into the Mediterranean Sea, and invaded the valley of the Rhône. They sailed along the Russian river system to reach the Black Sea and raided Constantinople. In 911 the Viking Rollo secured from Charles the Simple, the king of France, the territory near the mouth of the Seine River, which became known as Normandy (from the name *Northmen*).

This new wave of invasion, though less dis-

Map 6.4 INVASIONS OF NORTHERN EUROPE, EIGHTH THROUGH NINTH CENTURIES

ruptive than the great movements of peoples in the fourth and fifth centuries, opened for Western Europe a new dark age. Amid the violence, however, the work of Christianizing the pagan peoples continued. Missionaries in the tenth and eleventh centuries successfully converted the Magyars, Vikings, and Western Slavs (Poles and Czechs).

With their conversion to Christianity and simultaneous establishment of a stable kingdom, the Magyars, alone among the nomadic tribes that had invaded Europe, retained their linguistic and ethnic identity until the present as the modern Hungarians. From about the year 1000 neither Magyars nor Vikings nor Western Slavs represented a foreign or heathen threat to Christian Europe; rather, they had all become full partners in the community of Western peoples.

ANGLO-SAXON ENGLAND

The Germanic invasions in the fourth through sixth centuries divided England into more than 20 petty dynasties and kingdoms. They became fused into a single kingdom, but true political unity was not reached until after the Norman Conquest in 1066.

Map 6.5 INVASIONS OF SOUTHERN EUROPE, NINTH THROUGH TENTH CENTURIES

England achieved religious unity before political unity. Augustine and his fellow missionaries dispatched by Pope Gregory arrived in Kent in 597; but other Christian missionaries, especially the Irish, were already converting the island to a Christianity that differed from the Roman version.[5] Not until the late seventh century did Theodore of Tarsus, a monk from the Middle East who served as archbishop of Canterbury, complete the work of ecclesiastical unification. He reformed monastic education, held numerous councils, made the authority of Canterbury felt through the land, and helped give England one of the most vigorous and learned churches of the age.

Political unity came more slowly. The numerous petty dynasties coalesced into seven fairly stable kingdoms, traditionally known as the heptarchy: Northumbria, Mercia, East Anglia, Essex, Sussex, Kent, and Wessex (see Map 6.6). The first

---

[5]Irish Christians set the date of Easter later than the Romans (reflecting later springs in the north), applied the tonsure (the haircut symbolizing clerical status) in their own way, and conceived differently the role and powers of the bishop.

kings to exert a stable hegemony over England were the rulers of Northumbria in the seventh and eighth centuries. This was the golden age of Northumbrian culture; the monastery at Wearmouth-Jarrow then counted among its members Bede the Venerable, the greatest scholar of his day. But Northumbrian rule was short-lived, and by the late ninth century leadership passed to Egbert of Wessex and his successors.

Alfred the Great   To the kings of Wessex fell the task of defending England against the Danes. The greatest of these kings was Alfred (871–899), the first king effectively to rule over the entire English people. After experiencing military defeats by the Danes in the early years of his reign, Alfred reorganized the defense of the kingdom. He reformed the militia to keep a larger and more mobile army in the field and built fortresses to defend the land and ships to defend the coast. His reforms proved successful. Before 880 several Danish chiefs received baptism as part of a treaty with Alfred, and in 886 the Danes agreed to confine themselves to a region in the north and east of England. This region, which the Danes continued to dominate for several generations, was later to be known as the *Danelaw*, in recognition of the fact that the Danish laws in force there dif-

Map 6.6 ANGLO-SAXON ENGLAND

fered from the English laws of other parts of the country.

Alfred also renewed intellectual activity; for example, he gathered a group of scholars and began a program of translating into Anglo-Saxon the works of several historians and theologians. During his reign an unknown author compiled a history of England known as the *Anglo-Saxon Chronicle*. Continued thereafter by various authors and now extant in several versions, the *Chronicle* is an indispensable source for the later Anglo-Saxon period in English history.

The English resurgence initiated under Alfred continued under his successors for almost a century. However, by 991 King Ethelred was unable to overcome renewed Danish advances and agreed to pay tribute to the Danes. The tax he imposed to meet the tribute was called the Danegeld. Its payment was a mark of weakness, but the Danegeld was still a national tax and shows that the kingdom remained united. In 1013 the Danish King Swein invaded and conquered England, which became a province in a great northern empire. His son Canute ruled Denmark, Norway, and England; but at his death in 1035 the empire disintegrated and Edward, a descendant of Alfred, became the king of England.

V. Letters and Learning

The great movement of peoples in the fourth and fifth centuries nearly destroyed the great Classical heritage of literature and learning. But the tradition of Classical learning did not entirely succumb. It survived in a peculiar context and for a peculiar purpose: to serve the Christian Church and to promote the interests of the Christian religion.

THE CHURCH AND CLASSICAL LEARNING

Because Christianity rebelled against Classical values, it is understandable that many prominent Christian writers condemned Classical literature as foolishness and an incitement to sin. Yet almost from the beginning Christianity had to make some accommodation to secular learning.

Christianity was a religion founded on a book, the Bible. God had spoken to his people through the written word, and Christian theologians had to have the skill to read and interpret the sacred texts. The only way they could obtain this skill was to study at secular schools, because the Church had not yet established its own schools. The leaders of the Christian community, therefore, had to study under the same teachers, read the same authors, and master the same techniques of philosophical argument and rhetorical expression as their pagan neighbors.

Christian scholars preserved a tradition of literacy in the fifth and sixth centuries, but their output accurately reflects the difficult conditions of their times and the biases of their own mental outlook. An important part of their literary effort was devoted to the preparation of textbooks that would preserve a modicum of ancient learning and the ability to read the ancient authors. One of the most influential of these textbooks was the *Introductions to Divine and Human Readings* by a sixth-century Italian official and monk, Cassiodorus. In it he listed the religious and secular books that he thought a monk should copy and read. This book is about as appealing to modern readers as a library catalog, but it was carefully studied and helped to determine the holdings of medieval libraries.

Another sixth-century Italian Christian scholar, Boethius, translated several of Aristotle's treatises on logic from Greek into Latin; these translations were the main source of early medieval writers' limited but significant familiarity with Aristotelian logic. Boethius wrote on many other subjects as well and was most famed for his *Consolation of Philosophy*, a meditation on death that does not mention the Christian religion. The *Consolation* helped preserve the dignity of learning by showing the role that reason and philosophy play in solving human problems. Less elegant than the *Consolation*, but equally popular, were the *Etymologies* by Isidore, bishop of Seville, which were a vast encyclopedia of ancient learning, covering in 20 books subjects from theology to furniture and providing a rich source of Classical lore and learning for medieval writers.

Christian Writings Scholars also helped through original works to shape the character and interest of the age, especially by writing *exegeses*, or comments and interpretation, on the Bible. In this field the most important writer after St. Augustine was Pope Gregory. In his *Moralia in Job*, a commentary on the Book of Job, Gregory made extravagant use of allegory in explaining the biblical text and set the style for biblical exegesis in the medieval world.

Pope Gregory also taught readers about the lives of the saints and the miracles God wrought through them, notably through his *Dialogues*, a record of the lives and miracles of the holy men of Italy. Since Christians viewed history as a vast panorama illustrating and proclaiming God's miraculous providence, the study of history also evoked great interest among scholars. One of the most influential accounts was the *History of the Franks* by Gregory, bishop of Tours. Like many of the early medieval historians, Gregory began with Creation; he then recounted the history of the human race up to 591.

Modern readers are often surprised by the endless parade of miracles reported in medieval sources and slightly stunned by the apparent gullibility of the scholars who wrote such accounts, but we must view the miracles as did those who recorded them. For these writers the miraculous interventions of God leading his people to salvation gave purpose to human life and order to an otherwise chaotic world. In a universe shaped by the operations of grace, the miraculous was the natural and the expected.

Learning and Scholarship   Scholarship on the continent sank to its lowest level in the seventh and early eighth centuries, but it flourished in Ireland in the seventh and England in the early eighth century. Scholars there enjoyed the relative shelter of an insular home. They had the zeal of new converts and a strong monastic system that supported the schools. Since they did not speak a language derived from Latin, they could learn a correct Latin in schools without being confused by related vernacular forms.

The finest English scholar was undoubtedly Bede the Venerable (673?–735), whose *Ecclesiastical History of the English People*, an account of the conversion of the English and the growth of their Church, established his fame even until today. His high sense of scholarship is evident in the careful way he collected and used documents and interviewed witnesses. As a faithful Christian, Bede accepted miracles, and the story of salvation is the principal theme of his history. But his belief that history was the unfolding of God's plan did not lead him to distort the material in his sources. He is a man whom any age would recognize as a scholar.

THE CAROLINGIAN RENAISSANCE

The Frankish rulers—Pepin, Charlemagne, and their successors—promoted learning within their domains in the movement known as the Carolingian Renaissance. These rulers were interested in learning for several reasons. In the sixth and seventh centuries, when the continent was divided among many small kingdoms, different styles of writing, known as *national hands* (Visigothic, Merovingian, Lombard, Beneventan, and so on), had developed; and numerous variant readings had slipped into such basic texts as the Bible and the Benedictine rule. The Latin grammar used by scholars had also absorbed many regional pecularities.

Literate persons in one part of Europe thus had great difficulty recognizing or reading a text written in another. The widespread decline in education had left few persons who could read at all. Furthermore, poorly educated priests could not properly perform the liturgy, on which God's blessings on the community were thought to depend; and variations in religious rituals were also growing. Both situations weakened the unity of the Church as well as the state.

Pepin and Charlemagne attempted to develop a standard curriculum, based on the same versions of the same texts and written in the same form of handwriting. They invited to court scholars from all over Europe for this purpose. To increase the supply of locally trained scholars, both Pepin and Charlemagne ordered all bishops and monasteries to establish schools to educate boys. Charlemagne himself set the example by founding a palace school for the sons of his own courtiers, but the school seems to have had little permanent impact on the intellectual life of the age.

One great achievement of this educational revival was a reform in handwriting. About the year 800, monks at the monasteries of Corbie and

Tours devised a new type of formal literary writing, a "book-hand," using lower-case letters and known as the Carolingian minuscule. Previously, the book-hands used for important texts had been based on various styles of capital letters only. But a book page written entirely in capitals is difficult to read rapidly; the eye is not aided in distinguishing letters by protrusions above and below the line. The Carolingian minuscule, the first book-hand based on lower-case letters, made rapid reading easier. In addition, more letters could be written on a page with this new script; thus more books were produced at less expense.

▶ **The ninth-century manuscript illumination from the first Bible of Charles the Bald displays the Carolingian minuscule, which is the model for the lower-case letters used today in what printers call Roman type.**

Use of this graceful new script eventually spread across Europe.

Another achievement of this educational revival was the development of a common scholarly language. Carolingian scholars perfected a distinctive language now known as Medieval Latin, which largely retained the grammatical rules of Classical Latin but was more flexible and open in its vocabulary, freely coining new words to express the new realities of the age. Medieval Latin was also clearly different from the vulgar, or Romance, Latin spoken by the people. The establishment of Medieval Latin as a distinct language of learning thus freed the Romance vernaculars to develop on their own. One of these vernacular languages is Old French, whose oldest surviving text dates from 842.[6]

The Latin created by the Carolingian scholars enabled travelers, administrators, and scholars to make themselves understood in all parts of Europe; and it continued to serve this function until the modern era. Even when it disappeared as an international language, it helped promote European unity. All the modern vernacular tongues of Europe developed under the strong influence of these scholars' Latin. One of the reasons why it is possible to translate quickly from one European language to another is that their learned vocabularies are in large measure based on common Latin models.

A further achievement of the educational revival was the standardization of important texts. Pepin "decorated all the churches of the Gauls with the songs of the Roman church"; that is, he sought to standardize the liturgy on the basis of Roman practice. Charlemagne continued this policy of standardization. He had the English scholar Alcuin of York, who served as a sort of minister of cultural affairs from about 783 until 794, prepare a new edition of Jerome's Vulgate translation of the Bible. This edition became the common biblical text for the entire Western Church. Charlemagne procured from Monte Cassino a copy of the Benedictine rule and had it

---

[6]At Strasbourg in 842, Charles the Bald and Louis the German, two of the sons of Louis the Pious, took an oath that was recorded in Latin, Old French, and German. The oath at Strasbourg not only preserves the oldest surviving text in Old French but also marks the first use of German in a formal legal document.

copied and distributed, so that monks everywhere would follow a standard code. He also initiated standardization into the school curriculum, based on the seven liberal arts. Alcuin divided the curriculum into the *trivium*, or verbal arts (grammar, rhetoric, and logic), and the *quadrivium*, or mathematical arts (arithmetic, astronomy, geometry, and music).

Carolingian scholars wrote lengthy educational tracts and huge quantities of didactic poetry, but little of their work can be considered

▶ **EZRA RESTORING THE BIBLE**
The image of Ezra restoring the Bible, in this eighth-century English manuscript, gives the work of the medieval monk an exalted self-justification. Here we see a biblical figure doing exactly what monks did—namely, writing and copying. In this case, Ezra was purifying the text of the Bible, and the implication was that monks were engaged in the same task. The vivid depiction of the bookshelves, with their open doors, and the table and stool are clearly an attempt to bring to life a scene from a monastery of the time.

notable for original thought or rhetorical grace. This is understandable. Most of the scholars were grammarians and educators, engaged in producing teachers' manuals, textbooks, and school exercises; they went back to the Latin classics to find models of correct grammar, usage, and vocabulary, but not for aesthetic satisfaction or philosophical insights. Their work was nonetheless of the greatest importance for the intellectual growth of Europe. The revived mastery of correct Latin equipped scholars of later generations to return to the Classical heritage and to recover from it philosophic and aesthetic values.

▶ **PHILOSOPHY CONSOLING BOETHIUS, EARLY ELEVENTH CENTURY**
In his *Consolation of Philosophy*, Boethius described the embodiment of philosophy as a mature woman who had grown as tall as the heavens, carrying a scepter and books. This image, from an eleventh-century manuscript, depicts philosophy as equal in height to the building whose solid facade and row of small windows may be the prison where Boethius wrote his famous work.

The Carolingian Renaissance made possible all subsequent renaissances in the history of Western thought. The establishment of Latin as a universal language permitted easy communication within Europe and made possible that vigorous and creative dialogue across linguistic frontiers on which the growth of Western scholarship has since depended. Even if the Early Middle Ages left no brilliant cultural monuments, it did lay the foundations on which the achievements of all subsequent periods of Western history have rested.

Recommended Reading

Sources

Colgrave, B. (ed.). *The Life of Bishop Wilfrid . . . , Two Lives of Saint Cuthbert . . . , Felix's Life of Saint Guthlac, and The Earliest Life of Gregory the Great.* 1985. An anthology of seventh- and eighth-century saints' lives, prime sources for social as well as Church history.
*Einhard. *The Life of Charlemagne.* 1962.
*Herlihy, David (ed.). *Medieval Culture and Society.* 1968.

*Available in paperback.

Hillgarth, J. N. (ed.). *The Conversion of Western Europe, 350–750.* 1969.
*Mattingly, H. (tr.). *Tacitus on Britain and Germany. A Translation of the ''Agricola'' and the ''Germania.''* 1967.

Studies

*Baker, Derek (ed.). *Medieval Women.* 1981. Essays on both individual women and social movements concerning women.
Boussard, Jacques. *The Civilization of Charlemagne.* 1968.
Brown, Peter. *The Cult of the Saints. Its Rise and Function*

in Latin Christianity. 1980. Locates its rise not in popular religion but in the power structures of late ancient society.

Burns, Thomas S. *A History of the Ostrogoths.* 1984. Based on archaeological as well as literary evidence.

Byock, Jesse. *Medieval Iceland.* 1988. The history of a society without a state.

The Cambridge Economic History of Europe. 1941–. Four volumes to date; the standard reference for all economic questions. A revised edition of Volume I (on agriculture) was published in 1966 and of Volume II (on trade) in 1987.

The Cambridge Medieval History, 1911–1936. Partially outdated but still a useful work of reference.

Campbell, James (ed.). *The Anglo-Saxons.* 1982. Essays presenting the latest archaeological and other research.

*Duby, Georges. *The Early Growth of the European Economy: Warriors and Peasants from the Seventh to the Twelfth Century.* Howard B. Clark (tr.). 1974. The early medieval economy viewed in terms of "gift and pillage."

*Dunbabin, Jean. *France in the Making: 843–1180.* 1985. On the formation of the political structure of France and the growth of a strong monarchy.

*Fell, Christine (and others). *Women in Anglo-Saxon England and the Impact of 1066.* 1984. Anglo-Saxon social history with women at its center.

*Fichtenau, Heinrich. *The Carolingian Empire.* P. Munz (tr.). 1963. An unsympathetic view of Charlemagne and his policies.

Fleckenstein, Josef. *Early Medieval Germany.* Bernard F. Smith (tr.). 1978. Germanic institutions from the migrations to the eleventh century.

Fossier, Robert (ed.). *The Cambridge Illustrated History of the Middle Ages, I: 350–950.* Janet Sondheimer (tr.). 1989. Essays by French scholars, including four on Eastern Europe. Full bibliographies; lavishly illustrated.

*Geary, Patrick. *Before France and Germany: The Creation and Transformation of the Merovingian World.* 1988. A comprehensive summary of recent research, stressing the importance of the Roman heritage for the growth of Frankish institutions.

Goffart, Walter. *Barbarians and Romans, A.D. 418–584: The Techniques of Accommodation.* 1980. A careful inquiry into the obscurities of barbarian settlement within the Empire.

———. *The Narrators of Barbarian History (A.D. 550–800): Iordanes, Gregory of Tours, Bede and Paul the Deacon.* 1988.

*Herrin, Judith. *The Formation of Christendom.* 1987. A survey of the development of the Christian world, from Constantine to the mid-ninth century, with particular emphasis on the Western debt to Byzantium.

Herwig, Wolfram. *History of the Goths.* Thomas J. Dunlap (tr.). 1988. Stresses the instability of Gothic tribal formations.

Horn, Walter W., and Ernest Born. *The Plan of St. Gall.* 1979. Reconstruction of the architecture and the life of a major Carolingian monastery.

James, Edward. *The Franks.* 1988.

———. *The Origins of France, 500–1000.* 1982. Community and authority in the Merovingian-Carolingian world.

Laistner, Max. *Thought and Letters in Western Europe: A.D. 500 to 900.* 1955. Basic guide to early medieval authors.

*Lawrence, C. H. *Medieval Monasticism: Forms of Religious Life in Western Europe in the Middle Ages* (2d ed.). 1989. On the Rule of Benedict, the rise of Cluny, and other topics.

*Moss, H. St. L. B. *The Birth of the Middle Ages: 395–814.* 1977. An older historical survey; solid, detailed narrative.

Musset, Lucien. *The Germanic Invasions: The Making of Europe, A.D. 400–600.* Edward and Columba James (trs.). 1975. Excellent survey.

*Reuther, Timothy (ed.). *The Medieval Nobility.* 1978.

Riché, Pierre. *Daily Life in the World of Charlemagne.* Jo Ann McNamara (tr.). 1975.

Sawyer, P. H. *Kings and Vikings: Scandinavia and Europe A.D. 700–1100.* 1984. Excellent summary of recent research on the Vikings.

Stenton, Frank. *Anglo-Saxon England.* 1971. Basic introductory text.

*Thrupp, Sylvia L. (ed.). *Early Medieval Society.* 1967. Essays emphasizing social development, the family, and commerce; modern sociological approaches.

*Wallace-Hadrill, J. M. *The Barbarian West.* 1962. Brief and readable essays.

Wemple, Suzanne Fonay. *Women in Frankish Society: Marriage and the Cloister, 500 to 800.* 1981. An important study of a neglected topic.

Wickham, Chris. *Early Medieval Italy: Central Power and Local Society 400–1100.* 1981. Mainly social history of the decline of unity within Italy after the fall of the Roman Empire.

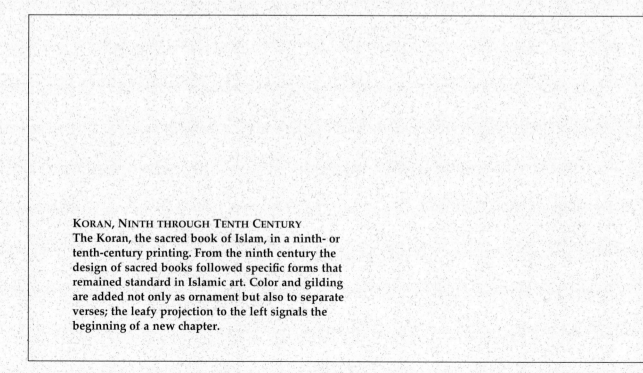

KORAN, NINTH THROUGH TENTH CENTURY
The Koran, the sacred book of Islam, in a ninth- or
tenth-century printing. From the ninth century the
design of sacred books followed specific forms that
remained standard in Islamic art. Color and gilding
are added not only as ornament but also to separate
verses; the leafy projection to the left signals the
beginning of a new chapter.

CHAPTER SEVEN

THE EARLY
MEDIEVAL EAST

HE Early Middle Ages were a period of profound social and spiritual change in the East as well as in the West, as a new peasant economy replaced the slave systems that had principally supported ancient civilizations. The three leading civilizations of the East—Byzantine, Kievan, and Islamic—nonetheless differed greatly from the less developed societies of the West. The Roman Empire did not fall in the East, and Roman institutions lived on, as did the Hellenistic cultural heritage, based on the Greek language. The new religion of Islam grew up among a people, the Arabs, who (like the Germans in the West) had lived on the fringes of the Classical Mediterranean world. The expansion of Islam brought it into lands—Egypt, Palestine, Syria, Persia—that had ancient and rich traditions of literate culture. Islamic civilization, in turn, was deeply affected by the Hellenistic, Semitic, and Persian cultures that flourished in the areas it overran.

The East also surpassed the West in the number of cities that survived in the Byzantine and Islamic worlds. Even the Principality of Kiev, founded by a people now first appearing in history—the East Slavs—rapidly developed an urban culture. The cities in the East helped maintain commerce, governmental institutions, and high levels of learning. All these accomplishments gave the Eastern civilizations a marked superiority over contemporary Western societies in the Early Middle Ages.

I. The Byzantine Empire

The name *Byzantine* is, strictly speaking, a historical misnomer. The inhabitants of the Eastern Empire recognized no break between their civilization and that of Classical Rome. Throughout their history they called themselves *Romans*, even after Rome had slipped from their power and they had adopted Greek as their official language. Indeed, modern Western historians sometimes forget that the Roman Empire did not fall in the East until 1453.

Historians differ in the way they divide Byzantine history, but the following periodization probably enjoys the widest acceptance:

Early Byzantine Period	324–632
Middle Byzantine Period	632–1071
Late Byzantine Period	1071–1453

THE EARLY BYZANTINE PERIOD

Byzantine history begins when the emperor Constantine transferred the capital of the Roman Empire from the West to the East in 324. The emperor's motives were primarily military, for many powerful enemies were menacing the wealthy and populous Eastern provinces of the Empire.

Constantine chose as his new capital the site of the ancient Greek colony of Byzantium. The colony had been founded about 660 B.C.E. on a narrow peninsula that juts into the Sea of Marmara like a hand extended from Europe toward Asia. The official name of the rebuilt city was New Rome; however, it soon came to be called the City of Constantine, or Constantinople, after its founder.

The location of this capital influenced the character of Byzantium and the course of its history. The city stood at the intersection of two heavily

▶ **EMPEROR JUSTINIAN, RAVENNA**
The mosaics—patterns made from small chips of tinted glass backed with gold leaf—that cover the wall of the church of San Vitale in Ravenna are one of the greatest achievements of the Byzantine era. Here, the emperor Justinian is surrounded by both priests and warriors, emphasizing his power over the religious as well as the secular domain.

traveled trade routes: the overland highway from the Balkans to Asia Minor and the maritime route between the Black and Mediterranean seas. Moreover, the city at once acquired the aura of a Christian city, the capital of the Christian empire. Because of his close association with the emperor, the bishop of New Rome enjoyed the high status of patriarch, and in the entire Church only the bishop of Rome ranked above him.

The successors of Constantine had no intention of abandoning the powers of the old Roman Empire in either the West or the East. Thus they struggled continuously, if in vain, to restore the Empire to its former size, power, and glory. The emperor whose actions best illustrate this aim was Justinian (527–565).

Justinian the Great   Historians have much information, or at least many allegations, about Justinian from the court historian Procopius. While the emperor lived, Procopius praised him in two histories: *On the Wars* recounts Justinian's victorious campaigns, and *On Buildings* describes his architectural achievements. But after Justinian's death, Procopius also wrote one of the most vicious efforts at character assassination in history. The *Secret History* paints Justinian, the empress Theodora, and several high officials of the court as monsters of public and private vice. Historians still have not satisfactorily reconciled the contradictory portraits left to us by the two-tongued Procopius.

Justinian's will was made strong by his ambitious wife Theodora and made effective by capable men in his service. Born about 500, Theodora became a famous actress and a celebrated courtesan before she was 20. She traveled through the cities of the empire, earning her way, according to Procopius, by skilled prostitution. In her early twenties she returned to Constantinople, mended her morals but lost none of her charm, and married Justinian. She was, in sum, an outsider, with no roots in the social establishment of the capital and no inclinations to respect its conventions.

Theodora's influence on her husband was decisive from the start. In 532, for reasons not entirely known, the popular factions of Constantinople rose in rebellion. Justinian panicked and planned to flee. But in a moving speech, as re-

Photo: Metropolitan Museum of Art, gift of J. Pierpont Morgan, 1917.

▶ **This Byzantine gold cup, dating from the sixth or seventh century, was found at Durazzo in modern Albania. Four female figures in gold repoussé symbolize the cities of Rome, Cyprus, Alexandria, and Constantinople. The detail shows the figure of Constantinople. The representation of cities in allegorical form shows the prominence of urban centers in Byzantine thought and society.**

corded by Procopius, Theodora urged her husband to choose death rather than exile. Justinian remained and crushed the uprising. The domestic peace that followed his victory freed him to pursue the three principal goals of his reign: the restoration of the Western provinces to the empire, the reformation of laws and institutions, and an ambitious program of splendid public works.

To restore imperial rule over the lost Western provinces, Justinian attacked the kingdoms of the Vandals, Ostrogoths, and Visigoths, and sought a precarious peace with the Persians beyond his eastern frontier. By 554 his troops had destroyed the Vandal kingdom in North Africa and established Byzantine rule there; had triumphed, at least for a while, over the Ostrogothic kingdom in Italy; and had forced the Visigoths in Spain to

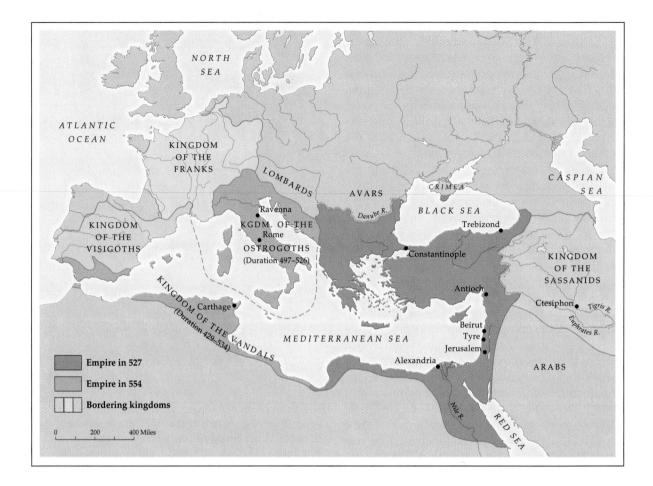

Map 7.1 EUROPE IN THE AGE OF JUSTINIAN

cede the southern tip of the peninsula (see Map 7.1). Justinian also sought to reconcile the Eastern and Western branches of the Church, which were bitterly divided over a theological question concerning the nature of Christ.[1] He had the pope abducted from Rome and taken to Constantinople, where he bullied him into accepting an unwelcome compromise. His coercive tactics did not bring union and peace to the Church and were bitterly resented by all the conflicting parties.

In 528 Justinian appointed a commission to prepare a systematic codification of Roman law.

The result was the *Corpus Iuris Civilis* ("Body of Civil Law"). It consisted of four compilations: the *Codex Justinianus* (or "Law of Justinian"), an arrangement of the imperial edicts according to topics in an easily consulted order; the *Digest*, or *Pandects*, a summary of legal opinions; the *Institutes*, a textbook to introduce students to the reformed legal system (*see box*, p. 185); and the *Novellae*, a collection of new imperial edicts issued after 534.

It would be hard to exaggerate the importance of the *Corpus Iuris Civilis*. It has remained for all subsequent generations the largest and richest source of information concerning the legal institutions and thought of Roman antiquity. It profoundly influenced the canon law of the medieval and modern Church. The modern legal systems

---

[1]The Monophysite theory holds that Jesus has one nature, partly divine and partly human; he was not, in other words, simply true man. Condemned as heretical at the Council of Chalcedon (451), the belief remained strong in the East. The orthodox view is that Jesus has two natures, one human and one divine, and is both true God and true man.

of most Western countries are based on the principles of Roman law as preserved in the *Corpus*.[2]

The destruction caused by the rebellion in Constantinople gave Justinian the chance to start a rebuilding program, with the aim of making Byzantium reflect the physical splendor of Rome. The most spectacular of his many new churches, palaces, and public works was the great church of Hagia Sophia, or Holy Wisdom.

Justinian was remarkably successful in all his ambitious policies until the last years of his reign. Beginning in 542, terrible plagues repeatedly struck the imperial lands, while he waged a two-front war against the Persians to the east and the resurgent Ostrogoths on the western frontier. The strains on manpower left the empire everywhere on the defensive at his death.

Historians have tended to view Justinian's policies as unrealistic, excessively ambitious, and ultimately disastrous. Memories of ancient Roman greatness blinded him to the inadequacy of his own resources. Yet Hagia Sophia and the *Corpus Iuris Civilis* assure him a permanent and brilliant reputation in both the East and the West.

In the years following Justinian's death new invaders overwhelmed the frontiers and wrested from his successors most of the territorial acquisitions of his reign. These emperors could not recover the Western provinces of the old Roman Empire, and the Byzantine Empire, unable to remain a universal state, had to find its way as an Eastern, and exclusively Hellenic, empire.

THE MIDDLE BYZANTINE PERIOD

The reign of the emperor Heraclius (610–641) was pivotal in giving Byzantine policy and civilization their new Eastern orientation. His reign began amid repeated military disasters. The

---

[2]The British Commonwealth and the United States (except Louisiana) follow common law, based on cases decided in medieval England; but common law too was strongly influenced by Roman legal concepts.

From the Institutes *of Justinian*

The Institutes, *published at the order of the emperor Justinian as part of his general restatement of Roman law, form a kind of introductory textbook to the whole study. Near the beginning of the work the compilers give this succinct definition of justice and of the differences among the "civil" law that applies to Roman citizens, "natural" law, and the "law of all nations." Note that the second and third classes are treated as partly identical. It was one of the great strengths of Roman law and administration to recognize and protect traditions of peoples whom the Romans brought into their Empire.*

"Justice is the set and constant purpose which gives to every man his due. Jurisprudence is the knowledge of things divine and human, the science of the just and the unjust. [. . .] The law of nature is that which she has taught all animals; a law not peculiar to the human race, but shared by all living creatures, whether denizens of the air, the dry land, or the sea. Hence comes the union of male and female, which we call marriage; hence the procreation of children, for this is a law that we see even in the lower animals.

"The civil law of Rome, and the law of all nations, differ from each other thus. The laws of every people governed by statutes and customs are partly peculiar to itself, partly common to all mankind. Those rules which a state enacts for its own members are peculiar to itself, and are called civil law: those rules prescribed by natural reason for all men are observed by all people alike, and are called the law of nations. Thus the laws of the Roman people are partly peculiar to itself, partly common to all nations."

From *The Institutes of Justinian*, J. B. Moyle (tr.), 1896.

aggressive Persians took Antioch, Jerusalem, and Alexandria. By raising money through treasures donated by the churches, Heraclius strengthened the army and then boldly opened a successful war against the Persians in 622. In campaigns waged over six years Heraclius fought his way to the Persian capital of Ctesiphon, where the Persians agreed to a humiliating peace. Then a new menace arose. After the death of Muhammad, the founder of Islam, in 632, his Muslim followers from the Arabic world embarked on a tidal wave of conquests, overrunning most of the empire in scarcely more than 10 years.

At the same time that Heraclius was defending the empire against invaders, he was also reforming its administration. One of his predecessors had begun to give land to soldiers in exchange for military service. The military units and the provinces where they were settled were called *themes*. Heraclius and his successors extended this system to the navy and the entire empire. Soldiers and sailors, settled on their own farms and fighting in their own provincial army or navy, proved far more effective as both workers and warriors than the slaves, conscripts, and mercenaries on whom the empire had earlier relied. But a cen-

▶ **AGRICULTURE**
Cultivating their own plots was the principal work of Byzantine peasants. This manuscript illustration shows the various labors of digging, harvesting, and watering taking place in a fanciful landscape.

tury elapsed before the Byzantines were able to take the offensive against the Muslims. The emperor Leo III (717–741) beat back a Muslim attack on Constantinople in 717 and 718 and then began a reconquest of Asia Minor.

Leo introduced iconoclasm (image-breaking, from the Greek *eikón*, or "image") in the empire in 726 when he forbade the veneration of images within churches. Historians still do not agree about his motives. Iconoclasm may have been a legal pretext for obtaining land to support the army, by seizing the holdings of the monasteries, which strongly advocated the worship of images. Or it may have been an attempt to make Christianity more appealing to the Muslims whom he was seeking to conquer, by emulating the Islamic condemnation of the worship of images. Whatever the reasons, Leo's iconoclastic policy had a disastrous effect on relations with the West; it antagonized the popes and was a major factor in their decision to seek out a Frankish champion in the person of Pepin the Short (see p. 167). The veneration of images was restored in the Byzantine Empire between 784 and 813 and permanently after 843. But the iconoclastic policy helped to widen the cleavage between the Western and Eastern churches.

The military revival reached its height under the great warrior emperors of the ninth through eleventh centuries. They pushed the Muslims back into Syria and waged successful wars in southern Italy, the Balkan Peninsula, and the Caucasus. Their principal military accomplishment was in the Balkan Peninsula, where they defeated the nomadic people known as the Bulgars. The modern Bulgarians, who are entirely Slavic in language and culture, retain only the name of the original nomads.

BYZANTINE CIVILIZATION

The Byzantines adopted the assumptions of the Hellenistic world, especially of the Epicureans and Stoics, who had maintained that all people were one in nature and should be included in a single state. As there was one God, one true faith, and one universal Church, so there should be only one empire to rule all Christian peoples. The empire was thus given the sacred duty of aiding the salvation of the human race. The Byzantines

▶ **ICONOCLAST WHITEWASHING AN IMAGE OF CHRIST, CA. 900**
Byzantine iconoclasts, protesting the worship of images and the leadership of a Latin pope, destroyed the decorations of numerous churches. This page from a Psalter illuminated around 900 depicts the obliteration through whitewashing of an icon of Christ.

believed that if the empire served this function, God would never permit its destruction. This idea gave the Byzantines the spirit they needed to resist for centuries a nearly continuous onslaught of invaders.

The Byzantines also believed that the emperor was a holy figure as the head of a state with a sacred function. Of course, a Christian emperor could not claim divinity; but the emperor lived surrounded by ceremony that imparted an aura of sanctity to his person; and the term *sacred*, used much as we use the word *public*, was liberally applied to his person, palace, and office.

Historians have traditionally used the term *caesaropapism* to describe the emperor's position in the Church. This term suggests that the emperor was both Caesar and pope, the true head of both Church and state. Recently, objections have been raised against the use of this term because the emperor's powers over the Church were restricted. He could not repeal the Nicene Creed or personally flout laws of Christian morality. He was not a priest and therefore could not say Mass or administer the sacraments.

Yet the emperor exercised a wide authority over ecclesiastical matters. He supervised the discipline of the Church, set the qualifications for ordinations, created bishoprics and changed their boundaries, investigated the monasteries and reformed them when necessary, and appointed patriarchs and at times forced their resignation. Even dogma was not beyond his influence. The emperor summoned councils, supervised their proceedings, and enforced their decisions. The clergy was largely limited in its functions to the performance of the sacred liturgy and the administration of the sacraments.

The Two Churches The Eastern Church developed and functioned under the supervision of the emperor. In the West, on the other hand, the collapse of central authority in the Roman Empire gave the clergy a position of leadership in secular affairs. These contrasting experiences in the Early Middle Ages deeply affected the character and spirit of the two major branches of Christianity. The differences between the two Churches clarify other contrasts in the history of the Eastern and Western peoples.

Both the Eastern Church and the Western Church considered themselves catholic (that is, universal) and orthodox (that is, holding true beliefs); the terms *Roman Catholic* and *Greek Orthodox* used to identify the Churches today are exclusively modern usages. The two Churches maintained nearly identical beliefs. Perhaps the principal, or at least the most famous, disagreement was, and still is, the *filioque* dispute (meaning "and from the son"), which concerns the relationship between members of the Trinity: the Father, Son, and Holy Spirit. The Eastern Church held, and still holds, that the Holy Spirit proceeds only from the Father, while the Western Church maintained that the Holy Spirit proceeds from the Father "and from the Son." The Eastern Church permitted, as the Western Church did not, divorce for reasons of adultery and the ordination of married men to the priesthood, although bishops had to be celibate.

The most significant difference between the two churches in liturgy was that the Eastern Church allowed the use of vernacular languages—Greek, Coptic, Ethiopian, Syriac, Armenian, Georgian, Slavonic, and others—in the liturgy. Liturgical usage added great dignity to these Eastern languages and stimulated their development. The East Slavs, for example, possessed a rich literature in Slavonic within a century after their conversion to Christianity. Western vernacular literature was much slower in developing. On the other hand, the toleration of many vernacular languages weakened the unity of the Eastern Church. An Eastern cleric using his own vernacular language could not easily communicate with clerics from other regions, whereas a Western cleric who used Latin could make himself understood anywhere in the West. Because of linguistic differences from their neighbors, Eastern churches tended to develop in isolation from one another. Moreover, the toleration of many vernacular languages made difficult the

revival of Classical learning. In learning Latin, a Western cleric also acquired the ability to read the great Latin classics, while an Eastern cleric who did not know Greek was blocked from the Greek classics. Eastern cultures were thus deprived of one avenue of enrichment.

The Western and Eastern Churches also differed in their organization and relations with secular authority. In the Early Middle Ages the Western Church began to develop a centralized government under the papacy, a government often strong enough to defy secular rulers. By the late twelfth century the pope had become the absolute ruler of the Western Church, which he governed with the aid of an elaborate bureaucracy and a system of canon law common to the whole Western Church. The Eastern Church, however, remained thoroughly decentralized. It developed into a loose confederation of independent national churches that relied on secular authority to defend their temporal interests.

The close ties between Church and state in the East conferred advantages on both. The Church devoted itself to its essential functions of liturgical service and the administration of the sacraments; the state made full use of the great wealth and spiritual power of the Church. This was a critical advantage for rulers and peoples struggling to survive on the eastern frontier of Europe, where all resources had to be enlisted in the battle for existence. The East was largely spared and could have ill afforded the prolonged disputes between Church and state which marked Western history.

Yet the disputes between Church and state in the West, while often damaging and unseemly, served as a powerful stimulus to fruitful and original analyses of the nature of society and favored the emergence of a balance in which neither the king nor the Church exercised a monopoly of power. In the Byzantine Empire the withdrawal of the Church from temporal concerns established a pattern of Church-state relations that has lived on until the present. Even in our times, the divided Orthodox churches of eastern Europe have played a lesser role in secular political movements, such as the rejection of Communist rule, than the Catholic churches of Hungary, Poland, the Czech Republic, and Slovakia.

Byzantine Society   The outstanding feature of Byzantine civilization, compared with that of Western Europe, was the continuing vitality of cities. At one time the Byzantine Empire included such great urban centers as Alexandria, Antioch, Beirut, Constantinople, Trebizond, and Tyre. At its peak under Justinian, Constantinople probably contained more than 300,000 inhabitants. The city had paved and illuminated streets and many splendid churches and palaces. Urban society was, however, marked by a wide division between rich and poor. The rich lived among magnificent surroundings in huge palaces; the poor, in sprawling slums. Crimes committed in broad daylight were commonplace.

Rural society consisted largely of peasants. Those who owned property assembled together, made decisions concerning the use of uncultivated or common lands, assumed (or were required to assume) collective responsibility for the payment of taxes, and elected judges and other officials to supervise the village government.

The Byzantine Empire was wealthy compared with other states of the age. One great source of wealth came from the commerce that passed through the ports and gates of Constantinople. The Rus and other Slavs from the north carried amber, fur, honey, slaves, wax, and wheat; Armenians and Syrians from the east brought clothing, fruit, glass, steel, and spices; merchants from the west contributed arms, iron, slaves, and wood. The vigorous commerce attracted large colonies of foreign merchants. The commercial importance of Byzantium is revealed in the prestige of its gold coin, the bezant. Its weight and purity were kept constant from the reign of Constantine to the late eleventh century; no other major system of coinage can match its record of stability.

Another source of wealth was the numerous active guilds. The *Book of the Prefect*, written about 950 and describing the duties of a city's chief administrative officer, mentions 21 professional and craft guilds; most of these made luxury products, especially silk cloth. Byzantine artisans were also famed for goldwork, cups, ivories, jewelry, and reliquaries, all of which were shipped everywhere in the known world. The government closely regulated prices and movement of goods and maintained state monopolies, particularly over silk products. The best silk, rich purple cloths, could not be exported.

The emperor, like his predecessors in the old Roman Empire, enjoyed absolute authority and governed with the aid of an elaborate civil service. Military affairs were entirely separated from civil administration and entrusted to masters of the soldiers directly responsible to the emperor. All these offices relied on a large professional bureaucracy. The offices were decentralized and simplified when Heraclius reformed the government in the seventh century and combined civil and military administrations on the local level under the generals who governed the themes (the military units and the provinces where they were settled). All justice flowed from the emperor, and he or his chief official could hear appeals from any local court in the empire.

There were great contrasts between the Byzantine government and Western governments of the same era. Even after Heraclius reformed the government, it continued to be served by a well-organized local administration and an elaborate bureaucracy. Western kingdoms, on the other hand, functioned with a rudimentary administration and without a professional civil service. The Byzantine government supported such refinements as an effective fiscal system, a state postal service, and even a secret police, ominously called the *agentes in rebus* ("those doing things"). Western governments had none of these. At a time when Western governments operated almost without a budget, the Byzantine government collected large revenues from the 10 percent tariff it imposed on trade and from the profit it received from the state monopolies. The government also employed skilled diplomats, who were celebrated by contemporary observers for their ability to keep enemies divided and their liberal use of bribes, tributes, and subsidies.

The bureaucracy was largely staffed by literate and trained laymen. Eunuchs were preferred for important positions in the government because it was believed that they would not be tempted by sexual intrigue and would have no wife or children to compete with the emperor for their loyalties. Eunuchs also performed managerial functions that in the West were assumed by queens and women of the court. The services of eunuchs thus had the social effect of restricting the influ-

ΠΙ ιϲ δ' ὁ διοικῶν αξ ἐπὶ ὁ φαομα τ σοφίαν ἡ ποιλιάζι κλι᾽ ἐ πι ρη κλυ:—

► **WOMEN WEAVING AND SPINNING**
Textile production was an important industry in Byzantine culture. This manuscript illustration depicts a woman weaving on a simple rectangular frame and another who is spinning.

ence of women and led to the progressive seclusion of women within the inner reaches of the household, a tendency that set a model for the heirs of the Byzantine Empire.

Byzantine Culture Byzantine wealth supported a tradition of learning that benefited not only the clergy but also many laymen. There were three types of institutions of higher learning: A palace school trained civil servants in language, law, and rhetoric; a patriarchal school instructed priests in rhetoric and theology; and monastic schools taught young monks the mystical writings of the past. The poor people were dependent on their guild for what education they received.

Scholars used the Greek language almost exclusively after the sixth century. They composed school manuals, histories, saints' lives, biblical commentaries, and encyclopedias of ancient science and lore. Their greatest accomplishment, however, was the preservation of Classical Greek literature. With the exception of some few works preserved on papyri, virtually all the Western

world possesses of Classical Greek authors has come down through Byzantine copies, most of which date from the tenth to the twelfth centuries.

The first flowering of artistic achievement occurred in the sixth century, when Justinian literally rebuilt Constantinople. Among his many buildings is the church Hagia Sophia, begun in 532 and completed in 537. As Procopius described it, its great dome seemed to float in the air, as if suspended by a chain from heaven. Hagia Sophia is one of the acknowledged architectural masterpieces of the world. Like other Byzantine churches, it was decorated with brilliant mosaics, but most of these were destroyed by the iconoclasts in the eighth and ninth centuries. Because of the iconoclastic movement, the richest examples of the early mosaics are not to be found in Constantinople and Asia Minor but rather in areas that were no longer under Byzantine rule in those centuries. San Vitale and Sant' Apollinare in Ravenna, Italy, are particularly noted for early Byzantine mosaics.

With the final rejection of iconoclasm in the middle of the ninth century, there was a resurgence of artistic endeavor. Byzantine artisans designed and decorated many churches throughout the empire. Their work is found in such places as Messina and Palermo in Sicily and Venice in

Italy. Artists were summoned to such distant places as Kiev to aid in the design, construction, and decoration of churches.

The mosaics make vividly concrete the Byzantine concepts of empire, emperor, and church. The emperor is always presented as the august figure that Byzantine ideology made of him (see plate on p. 182). Christ is never shown as suffering; he is, in other words, always God and never man. The reason for this seems to have been the close association that the figure of Christ bore to the living emperor. To show Christ as suffering would suggest that the emperor too might be a weak and vulnerable man. The mosaics have no sense of movement, admission of human frailty, or recognition of the reality of change. Operating within this picture of the world, the artists nevertheless portrayed their solemn figures with a rich variety of forms, garments, and colors. Byzantine mosaics may be static, but they are neither drab nor monotonous.

DECLINE OF THE EMPIRE

The military power of the empire in its middle period was largely based on the system of themes, which created an army and navy of free peasant-warriors. But from the early tenth century these free peasant-warriors, apparently to escape mounting fiscal and military burdens, began to abandon their farms to more powerful

▶ **Interior of Hagia Sophia**
Hagia Sophia, the monumental project of the emperor Justinian, is a lasting reminder of the power of the Byzantine Empire. The saucer-like dome, which rises 180 feet, is carried on four pendentives (the wedge-shaped supports that allow a circular dome to rest on a square structure) and is a notable achievement of Byzantine engineering.

neighbors. In the eleventh century many of them became serfs. The disintegration of the theme system reduced the military manpower and led to a rural aristocracy of landlords, which in turn weakened the strength of the central government.

The emperors tried to limit the size and number of great estates, but by the late eleventh century, their weaker successors rather sought to purchase the loyalty of the rural aristocracy by distributing imperial estates to them. The aristocracy was also gaining control over ecclesiastical lands, as the Church granted them entire monasteries to administer in the best interest of the monks and the Church. But, in fact, these concessions represented virtual gifts of monastic properties.

Socially, Byzantium was being transformed from a disciplined society of peasant-warriors under a strong central government to a society with a dependent peasantry, strong local landlords, and a weak central government. Thus in time of war the emperors had to seek outside help to compensate for the shrinking forces among their own subjects. To maintain control of the sea, essential to the security of Constantinople, they sought the support of the growing naval power of Venice. In 998 and 1082 they gave generous trading concessions to the Venetians, which were major steps in the growth of Italian (and Western) naval strength in the waters of the eastern Mediterranean. The problem of land defense was even more pressing. A new people, the Seljuk Turks, had recently emerged from the steppes to threaten the eastern frontiers.

The Seljuks   The Byzantines gave the name *Turk* to a number of nomadic tribes that lived in the region east and north of the Caspian Sea (modern Turkestan) and had long threatened the settled Christian populations. In the eleventh century, members of one tribe, the Seljuks, penetrated beyond the eastern borders of the empire into Asia Minor. They shattered the largely mercenary army of the Byzantines and took the emperor Romanus himself captive at Manzikert in 1071.

As the Byzantine defenses broke down, Asia Minor lay open to the Seljuk forces. One Turkish chieftain, Suleiman, established himself and his warriors at Nicaea, only a few miles from Constantinople. He founded what eventually became the most powerful Turkish principality in Asia Minor: the Sultanate of Rum. The virtual loss of Asia Minor forced the Byzantine emperor to appeal to the West for help. This signaled the end of the Byzantine Empire as a great power in the East.

Schism with the West   The second disaster of the eleventh century was the formal schism between the Eastern and Western branches of the Church. The schism was provoked not by major dogmatic differences but by rivalry, disputes, and snobbery. For years the popes at Rome and the patriarchs at Constantinople had been rivals in converting the Slavs and had been bitterly disputing jurisdiction over churches in southern Italy and Illyria (modern Albania and Croatia). Furthermore, the Byzantines resented the papal claim to primacy within the Church. Rome by this time appeared to them as a provincial town without an empire and subject territory, whereas they considered Constantinople, the seat of wealth and power, the more appropriate capital for the Church.[3]

Perhaps even more fundamentally, the rupture of relations reflected the breakdown in communications between the East and the West, which had begun when Justinian failed in the sixth century to reconcile the two branches of the Church within the old Roman Empire. After his reign the two halves of the Roman Empire ceased entirely to speak or understand a common language; misunderstandings came easily and were overcome with difficulty, and commercial and diplomatic contact between East and West became sporadic.

Personalities played a major role in the actual schism of 1054. A dedicated but rigid reformer, Cardinal Humbert of Silva Candida, led a papal delegation to Constantinople. Failing to secure satisfactory concessions from the Byzantine Patriarch Michael Cerularius, the papal legates deposited a bull of excommunication on the high altar of Hagia Sophia and left the city in anger. Cerularius, a haughty and ambitious prelate who

---

[3]In the tenth century the Byzantines told Liutprand, bishop of Cremona, that they, and not the residents of Rome, were the true Romans and that Rome was a town inhabited exclusively by "vile slaves, fishermen, confectioners, poulterers, bastards, plebeians, underlings."

welcomed a break with the Western Church and had labored to provoke it, publicly declared to the other Eastern patriarchs that the supporters of the pope were steeped in heresy and had taken themselves out of the true Church.

The schism of 1054 destroyed the hope for a united Christian Church, although only later centuries showed the full extent of the damage. Even today, more than 900 years after the event, ad-herents of the Western and Eastern traditions are trying to overcome the rift. Only in 1965 did the pope and the Greek patriarch formally remove the excommunications of 1054.

THE WESTERN DEBT TO BYZANTINE CIVILIZATION

The East Slavs were the direct heirs of Byzantine civilization, but Western peoples also owe a vast debt to this civilization. Above all, we owe our knowledge of Classical Greek writings to Byzantine scholars who preserved this literature and thus allowed Western scholars to study the most original thinkers of the ancient world. Neither the Western Renaissance nor modern European culture would have been the same without their contribution.

The very existence of the Byzantine Empire, guarding the eastern approaches to Europe, gave Western peoples a measure of immunity from the destructive incursions of Arabs, Persians, Turks, and others. The sophisticated Byzantine economy and government served as a kind of school of civilized practices from which less advanced Western peoples could learn new techniques and grasp the possibilities and rewards of civilized life.

▶ **SILK TEXTILE**
A splendid example of the quality of silk manufacture in Constantinople around the year 1000, this textile shows the eagle, an ancient symbol of power and victory, holding in its beak a ring while resting its claws on a row of pearls. This particular work of craftsmanship is said to have been used to transport the remains of St. Germain, who died in Ravenna in 448, back to Auxerre in France.

II. *The Principality of Kiev*

During the Early Middle Ages the East Slavs, groups of people living in Eastern Europe, were converted to Eastern Christianity and gradually began forming societies based largely on the legacy of the Byzantine Empire and Eastern Christianity. Three modern Slavic peoples—the Russians, Ukrainians, and Belarussians—trace their ancestry directly to these East Slavs, and all regard the foundation of the first East Slavic state as the origin of their history. For this reason, it is inappropriate to call the East Slavic state *Russian*, since the Russians are not its exclusive heirs. In referring to these East Slavs we shall rather use a contemporary term, the *Rus*, a name of obscure origins that first referred to a dominant Viking tribe or group and then came to signify the entire people.

THE FOUNDATIONS OF KIEVAN RUS

Between the sixth and ninth centuries the East Slavs greatly expanded their area of settlement, and some tribes pushed to the east as far as the Volga River. There they met on the lower course of the river a Turkish-speaking people called the Khazars. The Khazars (or at least their upper classes) practiced Judaism; their obscure history has its own special fascination. Other Slavic tribes moved to the north nearly to the Baltic Sea. Two of their most important settlements were Kiev on the Dnieper River and Novgorod on Lake Ilmen, within easy access of the Baltic Sea.

In about 830, Vikings from Scandinavia penetrated into the lands of the East Slavs in quest of booty and profit. They also established trade routes that ran from the Baltic Sea over the rivers of eastern Europe to the Black Sea and thence to Constantinople, thus linking Scandinavia with Byzantium. Out of this encounter between Vikings and East Slavs emerged the first East Slavic state.

The most detailed and important source for the birth of the Rus state is the *Primary Chronicle* (*see box*, below). Many hands contributed to this work, which was not written down by East Slavs in its present form until 1117 or 1118, some 250 years after the events it describes. According to the *Primary Chronicle*, the Varangians, as the East Slavs called the Vikings, ruled Novgorod until the Slavic population rebelled against them and drove them back beyond the sea. Soon, however, the people of Novgorod began fighting among themselves. Unable to overcome their discord, they invited the Varangians to rule them once again. In response, a Varangian prince named Rurik, his two brothers, and "all the Rus," as the Varangians were called, came to govern Novgorod in 862. "On account of these Varangians," the *Primary Chronicle* explains, "the district of Novgorod became known as Russian land."

The *Primary Chronicle* goes on to say that Rurik soon left Novgorod and that his follower Oleg assumed authority in Novgorod and then Kiev. Oleg (873?–913) is thus considered the true

---

Literacy Comes to Rus

The **Russian Primary Chronicle,** *narrating events of the ninth century, gives one version of how the Slavs became literate and developed texts of the Scriptures.*

"When the Moravian Slavs and their princes were living in baptism, the Princes Rostislav, Svyatopolk, and Kotsel sent messengers to the Emperor Michael [Michael III of Byzantium], saying, 'Our nation is baptized, and yet we have no teacher to direct and instruct us and interpret the sacred scriptures. We understand neither Greek nor Latin. Furthermore, we do not understand written characters or their meaning. Therefore send us teachers who can make known to us the words of the scriptures and their sense.'

"The scholars suggested that there was a man in Salonika, by name Leo, who had two sons [Methodius and Constantine, the latter usually called Cyril], familiar with the Slavic tongue. The Emperor sent them into the Slavic country. When they arrived, they undertook to compose a Slavic alphabet, and translated the *Acts* and the Gospel. The Slavs rejoiced to hear the greatness of God extolled in their native tongue.

"Now some zealots began to condemn the Slavic books, contending that it was not right for any other nation to have its own alphabet apart from the Hebrews, the Greeks, and the Latins. When the Pope heard of this situation, he rebuked those who murmured against the Slavic books, saying, 'Let the word of the Scripture be fulfilled that "all nations shall praise God" (*Psalms* 71.17) and likewise that "all nations shall declare the majesty of God according as the Holy spirit shall grant them to speak" (cf. *Acts* 2.4).' "

From *Russian Primary Chronicle*, S. H. Cross (ed.), pp. 62–63 (condensed).

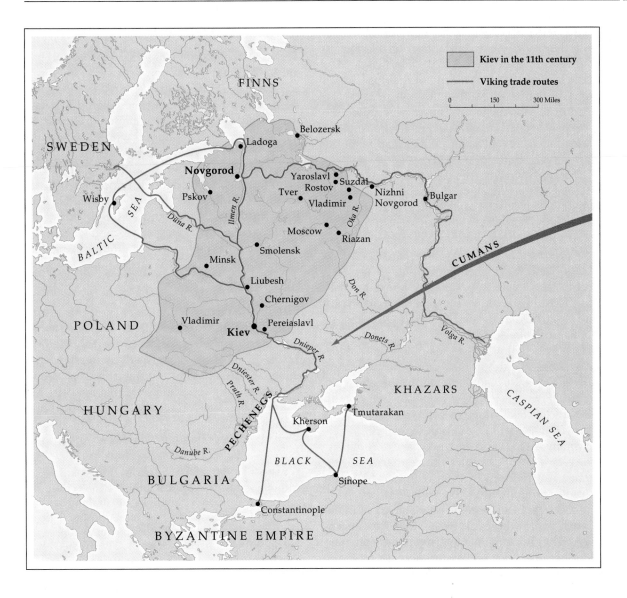

Map 7.2 PRINCIPALITY OF KIEV

founder of the Rus state because he united under his rule the two chief cities of Kiev and Novgorod. In 907 he led a fleet, allegedly containing 2000 ships, on a raid against Constantinople. The Byzantine emperor granted both tribute and trading concessions in order to purchase peace with the Rus. Oleg's successors completed the unification of the East Slavic tribes. This brought under their rule an area that stretched from the Baltic to the Black Sea and from the Danube to the Volga rivers. They also made war against the nomadic peoples of the steppes and strengthened commercial, diplomatic, and cultural ties with the Byzantine Empire. In 988 the ruler Vladimir converted to the Eastern form of Christianity and imposed baptism on his subjects. The East Slavs, the most numerous of all the Slavs, were thus brought within the Eastern cultural world.

Yaroslav the Wise The Principality of Kiev, as the federation of states based on Kiev is called (see Map 7.2), reached its height of power under Vladimir's son Yaroslav (1015–1054), who might well be termed the Slavic Justinian. Like Justinian, Yaroslav was a successful warrior, administrator, and builder. He defeated the Pechenegs, a nomadic people who roamed the grasslands south and east of Kiev and hampered contact with the Black Sea, and extended his territory to the north at the expense of the Finns (see Map 7.2). He won self-government for the Rus Church from the patriarch of Constantinople in 1037. The head of the independent Church was called the *metropolitan* and lived in Kiev, which became the ecclesiastical as well as the political capital of the East Slavs.

During his reign Yaroslav had prepared the first written codification of East Slavic law, the *Russkaia Pravda*. He built many churches and brought in skilled Byzantine artisans to decorate them. His masterpiece was the cathedral at Kiev. The *Primary Chronicle* says that Yaroslav loved books "and read them continually day and night," and that he wrote many books himself. He tried to promote learning in his principality and assembled many scribes to translate religious books from Greek into Slavic.

The Principality of Kiev maintained closer ties with Western Europe than any other Rus state for centuries. Rus is mentioned in the eleventh-century French epic the *Song of Roland*. The family of Yaroslav had marriage connections with the ruling dynasties of Byzantium, England, France, Germany, Norway, Poland, and Hungary. Yaroslav's own daughter Anna married King Henry I of France. Charters with her signature survive, carefully inscribed with Cyrillic letters; she seems to have been the only layperson in the French court who could write. She was instrumental in giving the name *Philip* to her son, who thus became the first French king to bear the name of an ancient Christian saint and apostle.

KIEVAN CIVILIZATION

The Kievan economy was both vigorous and balanced. Agriculture was productive on the fertile steppes. The *Primary Chronicle* describes peasants plowing with horses at a time when the less efficient oxen were the more common draft animals in the West. The Rus traded with the Scandinavians, the steppe peoples, the Muslims at Baghdad, and especially the Byzantines. Every year a great fleet of boats, led by the princes themselves, assembled at Kiev and floated down the Dnieper River to the Black Sea and across to Constantinople. Amber, fur, honey, slaves, and wheat were exchanged for silks, spices, and other luxuries of the East. In recent years Russian archaeologists excavating at Novgorod have uncovered numerous commercial documents written on birch bark that illuminate this lively trade. These documents indicate that the Rus merchants were less sophisticated in their business practices than the Byzantines, but they established the variety and quality of the products the Rus offered for trade.

Most of the population were free peasants, but there were slaves and some enserfed peasants. Although its foundations were agricultural, Kievan society had an important urban life.

▶ **YAROSLAV PRESENTING MODEL OF CHURCH** Although now destroyed, a group of eleventh-century frescoes in St. Sophia Cathedral in Kiev once depicted the family of Prince Yaroslav. This re-creation of the frescoes in a drawing by the seventeenth-century Dutch artist A. V. Westervelt shows Yaroslav presenting a model of a church to Prince Vladimir.

Within the many towns a wealthy aristocracy of princes, warriors, and great merchants rubbed shoulders with artisans, workers, and large numbers of destitute persons. The princes had to concern themselves with such social problems as the oppression of the poor, usury, and enslavement for debt.

Kiev in the eleventh century was one of the great cities of the age. The German chronicler Adam of Bremen considered Kiev a rival in size to Constantinople; the Metropolitan Hilarion described it as "glittering with grandeur"; another German chronicler, Thietmar of Merseburg, said it had 400 churches, 8 marketplaces, and unnumbered inhabitants. In 1124 a fire allegedly destroyed 600 churches. Kiev must have included 20,000 to 30,000 people—more people than any contemporary Western city.

The head of the Kievan government was the prince, who selected nobles, called *boyars*, to aid him in governing. In all important matters the prince sought advice from his boyars. The towns had large citizen assemblies, called *veches*, that the prince also consulted for advice. The government was thus based on a balance of monarchic, aristocratic, and popular elements. The prince, unlike the Byzantine emperor, was not the fountain of justice. Most cases were settled in popular courts from which there was no organized system of appeal, features that brought Kievan justice closer to the Germanic system than to the Byzantine. The limitations on princely autocracy imposed by the boyars and the *veches* make the Kievan period distinctive in Russian constitutional history.

The Influence of Christianity

The central event in Kievan cultural development was the acceptance of Eastern Christianity in 988. The arrival of some Byzantine clergy in Kiev changed the character of its culture. They established a formal educational system primarily to train the clergy; but their schools were open to the sons of ruling families, and a number of women, too, were educated in convents. Monks, as the first scholars in Kiev, used a modification of the Greek alphabet that missionaries had devised years before to convert the Slavs. They employed this alphabet in the translations of parts of the Bible and other ecclesiastical writings. These works constituted the dominant body of contemporary literature, and their religious themes served as models for the native writers.

The literary masterpiece of the age is the *Primary Chronicle*. Its principal theme is the conversion of the Rus to Christianity and their battles against the pagan peoples who surrounded them. This work illustrates the East Slavs' sense of national identity and acceptance of the Christian scheme of history. Although the account is of questionable accuracy in its earliest passages, it remains a classic of medieval literature. Few Western chronicles of comparable age can equal it in the wealth of information and liveliness of narration.

The monks, of whom the Metropolitan Hilarion was perhaps the most gifted, also produced many sermons, doctrinal and devotional tracts, and lives of the saints. These histories and the *Primary Chronicle* provide the best picture of the society and culture of medieval Rus. The poetry of medieval Rus is represented by the short heroic epic the *Song of Igor's Campaign*.[4] The poem records an unsuccessful campaign that the Rus princes conducted against the pagan Polovtsi in 1185 and depicts with considerable feeling the tragic but necessary costs of battle against the people of the steppes.

Christianity also had an immense influence on architectural and artistic development. After the conversion the East Slavs built many churches based on Byzantine models. The familiar "onion" domes of Russian churches, for example, were a late effort to imitate in wood the domes on ecclesiastical structures at Constantinople. The East Slavs loved magnificence and splendor in their churches and liturgical services. They learned the art of painting from the Byzantines and decorated their churches with icons—painted or enameled representations of sacred personages, such as Christ, a saint, or an angel.

Christianity imparted to the East Slavs a sense of world history and of their own place in it. They came to view their country as Holy Rus, the de-

---

[4]The original manuscript was discovered about 1790 by Count Aleksey Musin-Pushkin but was destroyed during the Napoleonic invasion in 1812, when Moscow was burned. Those who accept its authenticity usually date its composition to 1187. The *Song* is available in a fine English translation by the distinguished novelist Vladimir Nabokov.

fender of the true faith, facing and fighting a sea of pagan barbarians. Even though many accomplishments of the Kievan era were not maintained in the succeeding periods of East Slavic history, the Russians, Ukrainians, and Belarussians themselves did not lapse into barbarism.

DECLINE OF THE PRINCIPALITY

Both internal and external troubles destroyed the peace of the land after Yaroslav's death. To select his successor Yaroslav had introduced an extraordinarily complex procedure known as the rota system. The entire land was considered to be the property of the ruling family, and the towns were ranked in order of their importance and allotted to the princes, or sons of the ruler, according to their position within the family. When the senior prince of Kiev died, each of the junior princes became ruler of the next greatest town; brothers were given preference over sons. This cumbersome system of succession led to a constant movement of princes, to frequent bickerings, and often to civil wars. The political history after the reign of Yaroslav becomes an involved and dismal story of unending princely quarrels.

These struggles left the people unable to resist the renewed menace of the steppe nomads. In 1061 the Cumans, a nomadic Turkish people, began harassing the frontier, and they eventually cut off Kiev from contact with the Black Sea. This sundering of the trade route to Constantinople was a disaster for commerce and culture because it deprived Kiev of contact with the Byzantine Empire and the Western world.

Pressure from the nomads pushed the area of East Slavic settlement to the north and west, where extensive forests offered protection from nomadic forays. This dispersal prepared the way for the eventual separation of the East Slavs into three culturally distinct peoples. The Rus of the north—soon to be called Russians—were forced into a kind of isolation, removed and remote from the major centers of civilization. A new city, Moscow (not mentioned in the sources until 1147), assumed the arduous task of forming a united Russian state. In 1169 the soldiers of a northern prince, Andrew Bogoliubsky of Suzdal, sacked Kiev. With the ruin of Kiev, perpetrated by the steppe nomads and by the Rus themselves, the first major chapter of East Slavic history closes.

III. Islam

Sometime about 610 in the Arabian town of Mecca, a merchant's son named Muhammad began to preach to the people, summoning them to repentance and reform. Gradually, he brought his teachings together to form a new system of religious belief that he called Islam. The explosive impact of his preaching must be reckoned as one of the most extraordinary events of world history. Within a century after Muhammad's death his followers had conquered and partially converted territories larger than the old Roman Empire. Even today Islam remains the faith of perhaps 600 million people, more than an eighth of the world's population.

THE ARABS

The Arabian peninsula, the homeland of the Arabs, profoundly influenced their culture and history. Its vast interior and northern regions are dominated by steppes, wastelands, and some of the hottest and driest deserts of the world. The Arabs, however, adapted to this harsh environment. They supported themselves by raising sheep and camels, animals that provided nearly all their necessities: meat, milk, wool, skins for clothes and tents, and fuel from dried camel dung. The Arabs were extremely proud of their family, race, language, skill, and way of life. The harsh environment and their fierce pride made them spirited, tenacious, and formidable warriors.

The Arabian peninsula was in a state of intense political and social ferment on the eve of Muhammad's appearance. The stronger political powers—the Persians, Byzantines, and Abyssinians across the Red Sea—tried repeatedly to subdue the Arabs but could not dominate them in their desert home. Religious ferment was no less explosive. Several prophets, preaching new religious beliefs, had gained followers in Arabia before Muhammad; and this indicates a growing dissatisfaction among the Arabs with their traditional paganism, which gave no promise of an afterlife and offered no image of human destiny and the role of the Arabs in it. Both Christianity and Judaism had won numerous converts, but neither one was able to gain the adherence of most Arabs. The Arabs awaited a man who by the force of his vision could fuse all these contending ideas—pagan, Christian, and Jewish—into a single, commanding, and authentically Arabian religion.

MUHAMMAD

Historians have little information that is certain about the founder of Islam. Muhammad was born at Mecca about 570 or 571. His father died before his birth, and his mother died when he was 6. After being raised by his uncle, Muhammad worked as a camel driver in caravans. He may have been illiterate and may have had no direct knowledge of the Jewish and Christian Scriptures; but he did acquire a wide, if sometimes inaccurate, knowledge of the history and teaching of those two religions. About the age of 25 Muhammad married the widow of a rich merchant; thus freed from economic concerns, he gave himself to religious meditations in the desert outside Mecca.

In 610 Muhammad heard the voice of the angel Gabriel speaking to him, and he continued to receive such revelations in increasing frequency and length for the remainder of his life. After his first revelation from Gabriel, Muhammad began to preach publicly about personal moral reform, but only his wife and a small group of relatives initially accepted his teachings. The people of Mecca feared him because his strictures against paganism seemed to threaten the position of Mecca as a center of pilgrimages. Mecca possessed a renowned shrine containing the Kaaba, a sacred black stone that was the object of pagan worship. Rejected in his native city, Muhammad accepted an invitation to expound his ideas in Yathrib, a trading town 270 miles to the north, which he later renamed Medina.

Muhammad's emigration from Mecca to Yathrib is called the *hijra* and occurred in 622, which later became the year 1 of the Islamic calendar. The *hijra* was a turning point in Muhammad's career for two reasons: He became the political leader and governor of an important town, which gave him a base for the military expansion of the Islamic community; and his responsibilities as head of an independent town affected the character of his religious message. More and more, his message was concerned with public

▶ **PILGRIMAGE GUIDE**
A sixteenth-century illustration of a pilgrimage guide written around 900, this picture shows the Kaaba at Mecca. The Kaaba, said to have been built by the Prophet Abraham, is the black rectangular building, surrounded by domed arcades.

law, administration, and the practical problems of government.

Muhammad was more successful at Yathrib than he had been at Mecca in making converts. He told them that God ordered them to convert or conquer their neighbors; through enthusiastic proselytizing and war, the community of believers grew rapidly. With this support Muhammad marched against the Meccans, defeating them at

Badr in 624 and taking Mecca in 630. By his death in 632, Muhammad had given his religion a firm foundation on Arabian soil.

THE RELIGION OF ISLAM

Instructed by the angel Gabriel, Muhammad passed on to his followers the words or prophecies of Allah (from *al ilāh*, meaning "the God"). The collection of prophecies is known as the Koran; and Allah, in Islamic theology, is its true author. The Koran was written down in its present, official version in 651 and 652. The Koran imparts to the sympathetic reader a powerful mood, one of uncompromising monotheism, of repeated and impassioned emphasis upon the unity, power, and presence of Allah. The mood is sustained by constant reiterations of set formulas praising Allah, his power, knowledge, mercy, justice, and concern for his people (*see box*, below).

The chief obligation that Muhammad imposed upon his followers was submission (the literal meaning of *Islam*) to the will of Allah. Those who submit are Muslims. (*Muhammadan*, which suggests that Muhammad claimed divinity, is an inappropriate usage.) Muhammad was little concerned with the subtleties of theology; he was interested in defining for Muslims the ethical and legal requirements for an upright life. Unlike Christianity, Islam retained this practical emphasis; jurisprudence, even more than speculative theology, remained the great intellectual interest of Muslim scholarship. Also in contrast to Christianity, Islam did not recognize a separate clergy and church, for there was no need for specialized intermediaries between Allah and his people. Allah was the direct ruler of the faithful on earth; he legislated for them in the Koran and administered through Muhammad, the Prophet, and his successors, the caliphs. Church and state were not separate entities, at least in theory. There was only the single, sacred community of Allah.

The Koran on Christians and Jews

In the Koran, Muhammad proclaims that the faith of Islam also welcomes "the people of the Book"—that is, Christians and Jews who have the Bible as their sacred book—and that Islam is the fulfillment of these earlier faiths.

"Believers, Jews, Christians, and Sabaeans [of the kingdom of Saba in southwest Arabia]—whoever believes in Allah and the Last Day and does what is right—shall be rewarded by their Lord; they have nothing to fear or regret. To Moses We [that is, Allah] gave the Scriptures and after him We sent other apostles. We gave Jesus the son of Mary veritable signs and strengthened him with the Holy Spirit. And now that a Book [the Koran] confirming their Scriptures has been revealed to them by Allah, they deny it, although they know it to be the truth and have long prayed for help against the unbelievers.

"May Allah's curse be upon the infidels! Evil is that for which they have bartered away their souls. To deny Allah's own revelation, grudging that He should reveal His bounty to whom He chooses from His servants! They have incurred Allah's most inexorable wrath. An ignominious punishment awaits the unbelievers. The unbelievers among the People of the Book, and the pagans, resent that any blessings should have been sent down to you from your Lord. But Allah chooses whom He will for His mercy. His grace is infinite.

"Abraham enjoined the faith on his children, and so did Jacob, saying: 'My children, Allah has chosen for you the true faith. Do not depart this life except as men who have submitted to Him.' Say: 'We believe in Allah and that which is revealed to us; we believe in what was revealed to Abraham, Ishmael, Isaac, Jacob, and the tribes; to Moses and Jesus and the other prophets. We make no distinction between any of them, and to Allah we have surrendered ourselves. Your God is one God. There is no god but Him.' "

From *The Koran*, N. J. Dawood (tr.), 1968 (condensed).

Expansion of Islam The message of Islam exerted a powerful appeal to the Arabs. Compared with Christianity and Judaism, Islam was a starkly simple belief, easily explained and easily grasped. It was an effective fusion of religious ideas from Arabic paganism, Christianity, Judaism, and perhaps Zoroastrianism. Judaism influenced the legal code regulating diet and behavior. Judaism and Christianity provided the notion of prophecy, for Muhammad considered himself the last of a line of prophets that began with Abraham and included Jesus. More than that, the Bible tells that Abraham fathered Ishmael by Hagar, an Egyptian slave girl (Gen. 16–17), and Muslims believe that Ishmael was their ancestor and lies buried with Hagar in the Kaaba at Mecca. Christianity gave the concepts of Last Judgment, personal salvation, heaven and hell, charity to the poor and weak, and a universal religion. Christianity or perhaps Zoroastrianism suggested the figures of Satan and evil demons. Paganism contributed the veneration of the Kaaba and the requirement of pilgrimage to the sacred city.

Islam was therefore the fulfillment of religious ideas already familiar to the Arabs. Perhaps most important, Islam appealed strongly to the intense racial and cultural pride of the Arabs. The Koran was written in their native language, Arabic, and only in Arabic could Allah be addressed. Islam was seen as the final revelation, completing the message that God had partially conveyed through the Hebrew prophets and Jesus. The Arabs, a people who had hitherto played a negligible role in history, were given an important mission in life: to carry to the world the ultimate saving message. Even as Muhammad claimed to have supplanted Jesus as the supreme prophet, so the Arabs saw themselves as replacing the Jews as God's chosen people, with a sacred right to his holy places, including Jerusalem.

Allah instructed his followers to convert or conquer nonbelievers. Several factors aided the extraordinary expansion of Islam in the first century of its existence. Islam fused the once contending Arab clans and tribes into a unified and dedicated force. The Arabs, long familiar with camels, were masters of desert warfare. Their enemies, relying on horses, could not challenge them on desert terrain. Using the desert much as English imperialists later used the sea, the Arabs moved armies and supplies with facility across vast arid stretches, struck the enemy at places and times of their own choosing, and retreated to the safety of the desert when the odds turned against them. Moreover, the Arabs' immediate neighbors, the Byzantines and Persians, were mutually exhausted by their recurrent wars. Both empires included large Semitic populations that were linguistically and culturally related to the Arabs and, therefore, could comprehend the message of Islam.

The Arabs were able to make and hold their conquests through a unique combination of fanaticism and toleration. They were inspired to battle by the Prophet's promise of vast rewards to those who died in the Holy War against the nonbelievers and by the very real prospect of considerable booty if victory accompanied their efforts. The Prophet, however, also enjoined a policy of partial toleration toward Christians and Jews, who were both known as the "people of the Book." They were permitted to live under their own laws, but they paid a special tax for the privilege. Finally, because the Arabs did not have the numbers and the skills to govern all the territories they conquered, they opened the ranks of government to men from the newly conquered and converted peoples. This added stability to Islamic rule. The period of most rapid expansion of Islam followed Muhammad's death in 632 and coincided with the rule of the first four caliphs, as Muhammad's successors were called. Arabian forces seized the Byzantine provinces of Palestine and Syria, overran Persia, and conquered Egypt. By 661 Islam was firmly established as a world power. Islamic conquests continued under the caliphs of the Umayyad family, who were the first line of hereditary rulers. The Umayyads moved the capital from Mecca to Damascus. Under their rule the Muslims conquered North Africa and overran the kingdom of the Visigoths in Spain. After crossing the Pyrenees into the kingdom of the Franks, Muslim raiders were finally defeated by Charles Martel at Tours in 732. This battle, 100 years after Muhammad's death, marked the extent of the western advance and stabilized the frontier of Islam for the next several centuries (see Map 7.3).

The Schism As the territory under Islamic control grew to enormous size, powerful movements threatened and finally shattered Islamic unity.

Map 7.3 EXPANSION OF ISLAM

Jealousies and frictions disturbed the relations among the various peoples who had accepted Islam, and religious divisions also appeared. Islam had been an open and fluid religion at the death of Muhammad, but scholars and teachers gradually elaborated a theology that a majority of the believers accepted as orthodox. The scholars based the new orthodoxy not only on the Koran but also on the Sunnas, or traditions, which were writings that purported to describe how the first companions of Muhammad or Muhammad himself dealt with various problems. Some Muslims, however, rejected the new orthodoxy of the *Sunnites*, as they came to be called. Those who opposed the Sunnites were called the *Shiites*, or schismatics.

This earliest schism was more a political than a religious protest. The Shiites maintained that only the descendants of Muhammad's son-in-law, Ali, who was the fourth caliph, could lawfully rule the Islamic community; therefore, beginning in the seventh century, they rejected the Umayyads (and later the Abbasids) as usurpers. Shiism soon became a cloak for all sorts of antagonisms, protests, and revolts. It struck deep roots among the mixed populations, reflecting the dissatisfactions of non-Arabs with Arab preponderance and channeling the antagonism between the poorer classes and their masters.

The growing social and religious dissensions finally broke the Umayyad caliphate. A descendant of one Abbas, the uncle of Muhammad, revolted against the Umayyads, captured Damascus, and ruthlessly massacred the caliph's family in 750. He thus founded the Abbasid dynasty. Only one member of the Umayyads escaped, Abdurrahman. He fled to Spain, where he set up an independent caliphate at Córdoba in 755. Other independent regimes soon arose: Morocco in 788, Tunisia in 800, eastern Persia in 820, and Egypt in 868. All became virtually independent under their local dynasties. The new Abbasid caliph moved the capital from Damascus to a new city, Baghdad. The power of Islam reached its highest point under the Abbasid dynasty, which endured until 1258. But the community of Islam was never again to be united.

ISLAMIC CIVILIZATION

Despite disunity, medieval Islamic civilization reached its peak of prosperity, refinement, and

▶ **ABU-ZAYD VISITING A MUSLIM VILLAGE**
This thirteenth-century illustration is a leaf from the *al-Hariri Magamat* **(Assemblies of Entertaining Dialogues), a collection of tales set in various parts of the Muslim world. Here, the main character Abu-Zayd visits a lively village whose inhabitants carry on their daily tasks of spinning, agriculture, and worship.**

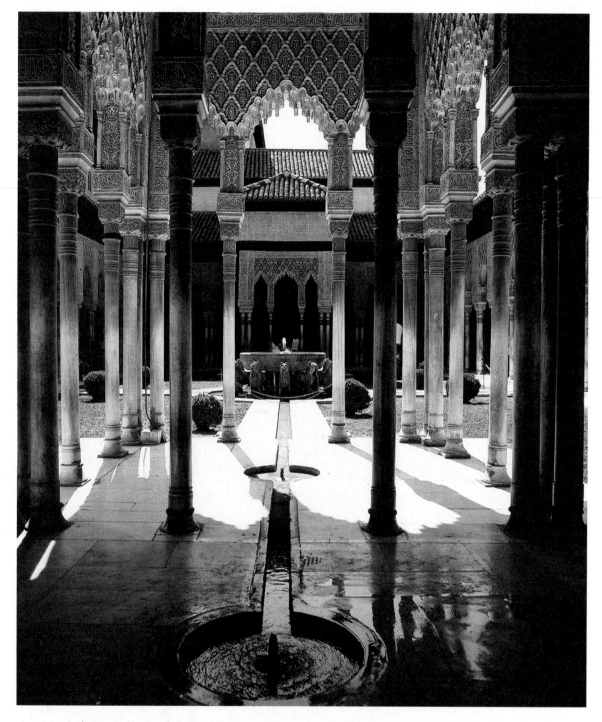

▶ The remarkable series of rooms and courtyards that make up the Alhambra Palace in Granada are one of the supreme achievements of Islamic art. The delicate tracery, the elegant details, and the constant presence of running water create a mood of luxury and refinement that can still be experienced by the visitor today.

learning in the ninth and tenth centuries. This period inspired the tales of the *Arabian Nights*, through which the name of Caliph Harun al-Rashid became known throughout the world. These exotic stories, put into their present form in the fourteenth century, convey a glamorous and idealized, but not a false, picture of the luxurious life at Baghdad during its most splendid age. Harun's son Al-Mamun reigned even more splendidly than his father. He was also a patron of learning. Al-Mamun founded an observatory for the study of the heavens and established a "House of Wisdom" (sometimes referred to as the first Islamic institution of higher education), where translations were made and a library collected for the use of scholars.

Spain was a notable center of medieval Islamic civilization. The brilliance of Islamic-Spanish civilization is best reflected in three great architectural monuments: the mosque (now a cathedral) at Córdoba, the Alhambra Palace in Granada, and the Alcazar at Seville. Jewish communities in Spain, the most creative of Jewish communities in the West, contributed to the high quality of intellectual life. It was also in Spain that Western Christians came into intimate contact with Islamic learning and drew from it the greatest benefits.

As Islam expanded, it embraced numerous economic systems. The Bedouins in the Arabian peninsula, the Berbers in North Africa, and the Turkish people of Eurasia continued to have a pastoral economy. The majority of those living in Egypt, Persia, Sicily, and Spain lived from settled agriculture. The inhabitants of cities, especially those along the caravan routes that tied the Middle East to India and central Asia, relied on commerce.

Islam greatly improved communications through the imposition of a universal language, Arabic, and the obligation of at least one pilgrimage to Mecca ensured frequent travel. And Muhammad had been a merchant; Islamic law favored commerce, and Islam esteemed the merchant. Maritime commerce in the Mediterranean provided until the sixteenth century the chief commercial link among India, Egypt, and the West. A large collection of letters from Jewish merchants living in Cairo in the eleventh and twelfth centuries has survived and marvelously

illuminates trade and many other aspects of social life in the medieval East.[5]

Commercial exchange stimulated agriculture within the world of Islam. Cultivators in Sicily and Spain adopted new plants from Asia, such as rice, and new techniques of cultivation, such as the irrigation of fields. Muslims from Persia to Spain practiced an agriculture remarkably advanced for the age. Trade also stimulated urban artisans to improve the quality of their products. The steel of Damascus, the leather of Córdoba, and the fine cotton, linen, and silk of many Eastern towns were desired and imitated in the West. These same products were shipped to India and Indonesia, where they were traded for spices and other products.

Medieval Islamic society was also distinguished by a vigorous urban life, concentrated in the cities of Damascus, Baghdad, Cairo, and Córdoba. According to travelers' reports, Damascus had 113,000 homes and 70 libraries. Baghdad surpassed all other cities in the number of palaces, libraries, and public baths. In all the major cities products from almost all parts of the known world could be purchased at the markets, or bazaars. The streets teemed with slaves, servants, artisans, merchants, administrators, and beggars. The aura of the Islamic cities was preeminently cosmopolitan.

A common religion ensured similarities in Islamic societies everywhere in the world. Religious law allowed the male Muslim to have as many as four legal wives and an unlimited number of concubines. In fact, only the rich could afford to have several wives. More important than polygyny in determining the position of women were the relative ease of divorce and the life of seclusion imposed on all women after puberty. Religious laws permitted the husband to dismiss

---

[5]They are called the *Geniza documents*. The geniza was a storeroom attached to a synagogue; records mentioning God's name (including merchants' letters) could not be destroyed and were stored in the geniza. The geniza of the Cairo synagogue was sealed up and not rediscovered until the nineteenth century. Its contents were then sold to collectors of Jewish documents and to libraries and thus dispersed throughout the world. For examples of these extraordinary records, see S. D. Goitein, *Letters of Medieval Jewish Traders*, 1973.

his wife almost at will and prohibited a woman from revealing her face except to her husband. These laws were not enforced everywhere with equal rigor and weighed primarily on women of the upper classes. Moreover, within the cities, at least in certain periods, women enjoyed relative freedom.

Because Islam recognized no distinction between church and state, the caliph was the supreme religious and civil head of the Muslim world. But he was not free to change the laws at will, since Allah had already provided all the laws his people needed; therefore, he was primarily a military chief and a judge. Among the Muslims the chief administrator on the local level was the *kadi*. He was primarily a judge, and his task was to see that the faithful lived according to the law of the Koran.

The Islamic conquests brought the Arabs into intimate contact with older and more accomplished civilizations than their own, particularly with the intellectual achievements of the Greeks, which they were eager to preserve. During the eighth and ninth centuries scholars translated into Arabic many Greek authors: Aristotle, Euclid, Archimedes, Hippocrates, and Galen. These works provided the foundations for Islamic learning and preserved the thought of these writers through a period when Greek texts were not being widely copied in the West.

Scholars were especially interested in astronomy, astrology, mathematics, medicine, and optics; and in these areas their writings exerted a great influence on the Western world. Al-Razi (known as Rhazes in the West) of Baghdad wrote some 140 medical treatises, including an admirable description of smallpox. Arabic mathematicians adopted their impressive numbering system from the Hindus but made the critical addition of the zero, which is itself an Arabic word. Italian merchants became familiar with the Arabic numbers shortly before the year 1200 and carried them back to the West. Arabic mathematicians also developed algebra. Astronomers and astrologers invented an improved astrolabe (which measures the angular declination of heavenly bodies above the horizon) and were able to improve the astronomical tables of antiquity.

Scholars also wrote philosophical and theological treatises. The most important Islamic philos-

opher was the Spaniard ibn-Rushd, or Averroës (1126?–1198), who wrote commentaries on Aristotle and exerted a profound influence on Christian as well as Islamic philosophy in the subsequent Middle Ages. Islamic philosophical speculations nourished intellectual life in the West in two ways: Western philosophers gained a much broader familiarity with the scientific and philosophical heritage of Classical Greece through translations made from the Arabic, chiefly in Spain; and Islamic philosophers explored issues central to religious philosophy much earlier than did Christian thinkers. What is the relation between faith and reason, between an all-powerful God and the freedom, dignity, and individuality of the human person? In posing these problems and in suggesting answers, the Muslims stimulated and enriched thought in the West.

▶ **This thirteenth-century Arab commentary on the** *Geometry* **of Euclid illustrates the proof of the Pythagorean theorem. Mathematics was one science in which the Arabs surpassed the Classical achievements.**

Photo: British Museum.

ٮوكبه الراٮ على ٮاٮوں ڡ السا

CHALLENGES TO MEDIEVAL ISLAMIC CIVILIZATION

The earliest indication of decline was the growing military weakness of the various Islamic states in the face of new invasions in the middle of the eleventh century. In the West, Christian armies embarked on the reconquest of the Iberian peninsula, and Christian fleets broke the Islamic domination of the western Mediterranean islands. The Christian offensive blends imperceptibly with the First Crusade, which wrested Jerusalem from Islamic control in 1099. At the same time in the East, Turkish nomads infiltrated the Abbasid caliphate in considerable numbers, and the Seljuks seized Baghdad in 1055. Turkish rulers gained supremacy in all the Eastern Islamic states over the next few centuries.

The Arabic economic base was also changing. By the thirteenth century, maritime and commercial supremacy on the Mediterranean Sea passed to Italians and other Westerners. Arabian coins largely disappeared from circulation in the West,

▶ FORMS OF THE FIXED STARS, CA. 1009–1010
One of the earliest examples of Islamic book illustration, this manuscript, written around 1009–1010, contains 75 drawings noting the forms of the fixed stars. Sagittarius, shown as an armed rider, is traced from the pattern of the constellation and indicates the sophistication of Muslim astronomy.

documenting a headlong retreat from commerce. Simultaneously, the Islamic states were no longer supporting their warriors by salaries but by grants of land, which weakened central authority. The growing importance of an aristocracy of rural warriors seems to have brought a new militarism and rigidity into society.

To be sure, Islamic civilization continued to support some great cultural centers and to inspire some great artists and thinkers; but after the eleventh century it began to lose the qualities of openness, flexibility, and intellectual daring that had so distinguished it in the ninth and tenth centuries.

THE WESTERN DEBT TO ISLAMIC CIVILIZATION

Almost every aspect of medieval Western life was influenced by Islamic civilization. Western farmers imitated Muslim techniques of irrigation and learned to grow many new plants, such as rice, citrus fruits, and peaches. Western merchants adopted the Arabic numbers, universally used in the West, and probably some Islamic forms of business partnerships. Muslim mathematicians made enormous contributions to the development of algebra. Western physicians, philosophers, and theologians were influenced

▶ MOSQUE AT CÓRDOBA, 784–990
Begun around 784, the Mosque at Córdoba was enlarged throughout the ninth and tenth centuries. The flexible plan of parallel aisles creates a complex visual forest of double-tiered arches that originally supported a wooden roof. This immense structure, with 850 columns and 19 aisles, was one of the largest buildings in the Islamic world.

by Islamic scholars. The stunning artistic monuments of Islam, such as the Alhambra Palace and the mosque at Córdoba, are still the wonder of travelers.

Yet the more remarkable aspect of the meeting of the two medieval civilizations, East and West, is really how little they affected one another in their basic cultural attitudes, apart from specific techniques and institutions. The medieval West was not much influenced by, and in fact poorly understood, the fundamental theology or the spirit of Islam. But it still enlisted many Islamic accomplishments in the service of its own civilization, a civilization that was to burst forth in spectacular form after the year 1000.

Recommended Reading

▼

Sources

Cross, Samuel Hazard (ed.). *Russian Primary Chronicle: Laurentian Text.* O. P. Sherbowitz-Wetzor (tr.). 1968.

*Dmytryshyn, Basil. *Medieval Russia: A Source Book, 850–1700* (3rd ed.). 1991.

*Ibn, Khaldun. *The Mugaddimah: An Introduction to World History.* Franz Rosenthal (tr.). 1969. Reflections on societies and empires by a North African Muslim; written in the fourteenth century.

The Meaning of the Glorious Koran. M. Marmaduke Pickthall (tr.). 1948.

Procopius. *Secret History.* Richard Atwater (tr.). 1964. A scandal-filled history of Justinian's reign.

*Vernadsky, George (ed.). *Medieval Russian Laws.* 1964.

Zenkovsky, Serge A. (ed.). *Medieval Russia's Epics, Chronicles and Tales.* 1974. Includes sermons and saints' lives.

Studies

*Baynes, Norman H., and Henry Moss (eds.). *Byzantium: An Introduction to East Roman Civilization.* 1948. Elegant essays by leading scholars.

Fine, John V. A. *The Early Medieval Balkans. A Critical Survey from the Sixth to the Late Twelfth Century.* 1983. The only work of its kind in English.

*Geanakoplos, Deno J. *Byzantine East and Latin West: Two Worlds of Christendom in the Middle Ages and Renaissance.* 1966. The Western debt to Byzantium.

Goitein, S. D. *A Mediterranean Society: The Jewish Communities of the Arab World as Portrayed in the Documents of the Cairo Geniza.* 1967–. Portrayal of Jewish social life on the basis of the remarkable Geniza documents.

Grekov, B. D. *Kiev Rus.* Dennis Ogden (ed.). 1959. A Soviet interpretation.

Hodgson, Marshall G. *The Venture of Islam: Conscience and History in a World Civilization.* 1974. A lengthy examination of the traditional beliefs and values of Islam.

Hussey, J. M. *The Orthodox Church in the Byzantine Empire.* 1986.

*Lewis, Bernard. (ed.). *Islam from the Prophet Muhammad to the Capture of Constantinople.* Vol. 1: *Politics and War.* Vol. 2: *Religion and Society.* 1987. Collected essays.

Mango, Cyril. *Byzantium: The Empire of New Rome.* 1980. An introduction to the civilization of the Eastern Empire, with effective use of archaeological data.

Obolensky, Dimitri. *The Byzantine Commonwealth. Eastern Europe 500–1453.* 1971. Excellent general survey, dealing with politics, religion, art, and culture in general.

Ostrogorski, George. *History of the Byzantine State.* Joan Hussey (tr.). 1969. The basic reference for all matters of political history.

*Vasiliev, A. A. *History of the Byzantine Empire: 324–1453.* 1953–1959. Stronger on cultural matters than Ostrogorski; by a great Russian scholar.

Vernadsky, George. *A History of Russia.* 1946–1963. In five parts and six volumes, the most comprehensive history of early Russia by a single historian in any language.

*Von Grunebaum, Gustave E. (ed.). *Medieval Islam: A Study in Cultural Orientation.* 1966. By one of the great figures in Islamic studies.

---

*Available in paperback.

A medieval knight in armor.

CHAPTER EIGHT

TWO CENTURIES OF CREATIVITY

THE present historical view of the Middle Ages recognizes the year 1000 as a watershed between two contrasting periods. Before 1000 Western civilization changed slowly, nearly imperceptibly. Europe's population remained small, and the economy overwhelmingly agricultural. Trade was sporadic, and the few towns that survived the repeated invasions played only a minor role in economic life. Governments tended to be weak and unstable. In art and literature, very few of the works produced would be regarded today as masterpieces.

After 1000 change came rapidly on virtually every level. Population, stagnant or declining since the last years of the Roman Empire, increased. People cleared and settled new lands and extended Europe's land frontiers in every direction. Commerce grew, and the resulting expansion of wealth restored vitality to the cities. Rulers reorganized their governments in an effort to adapt the institutions of feudalism to a more stable political environment. Western philosophers embarked on a reexamination of Christian theology, and the Church itself generated a major reform. Artists were once again productive, primarily in service to the Church.

As historians have come to appreciate the dimensions of these changes, they have reassessed the contribution of the Middle Ages to Western development. Many historians now speak of a medieval renaissance during the eleventh and twelfth centuries, which laid the foundations for the civilization we label "traditional Europe." In many respects this civilization lasted until the revolutionary upheavals of the eighteenth and nineteenth centuries, the beginning of the authentically modern world.

I. Economic and Social Changes

From the year 1000, European society showed many signs of growth in its human numbers and in its geographic area of settlement. Moreover, some of these people were earning their livings in novel ways, which sparked a revival of trade and a rebirth of urban life. Simultaneously, Europeans were creating new forms of social and political organization and of cultural expression.

THE BEGINNINGS OF EXPANSION

Europe's population in the Early Middle Ages, to about the year 1000, was small in absolute numbers and was not distributed evenly across the countryside. Rather, the people tended to cluster into crowded communities separated from one another by vast stretches of wilderness. Within these islands of population there is much evidence of overcrowding, even though there was little or no absolute growth. Peasant farms (the *mansi*), each intended for the support of a single family, often contained several by the ninth century.

Why did the population not spread out from these impacted settlements and clear new farms in the extensive surrounding wilderness? Many factors obstructed such an exodus; among them were the bonds of serfdom, the safety provided by close settlement in a period of invasions, the bonds of kinship, and a fear of the wilderness.

This pattern of settlement changes from about the year 1000. Peasants poured out of their older centers of settlement to newly opened frontiers, both within Europe and beyond its former borders. What had happened? There is some evidence that the climate became milder, perhaps encouraging the colonization of new lands. In addition, by the middle and late tenth century, the incursions of Vikings, Hungarians, and Saracens were waning, and the new security made the wilderness less intimidating. Beginning in the late tenth century many lords and princes began to encourage the settlement of the wilderness areas they controlled; others assumed leadership in the expansion of the external frontier. They offered land to new settlers under favorable terms and assured them protection in the work of colonization. Their interest in increased rents perhaps indicates that the warrior aristocracy of Europe could no longer live, as it had in the past, predominantly from royal gifts and pillage taken in the frequent wars. The Church, too, Europe's largest landlord, by the late tenth century actively sought to increase its own revenues from the land in the interest of supporting a celibate and reformed clergy.

The opening of new lands encouraged reproduction. Children became an asset to families engaged in the hard work of clearing land. More land in cultivation meant more food. For the first time since the fall of the Western Roman Empire, Europe's population gives evidence of sustained and substantial growth.

Frontiers In England, France, and Germany, the peasants leveled forests and drained marshes; in England and the Low Countries, they also won land from the sea by building dikes and draining marshes. German peasants and knights, looking for new lands to settle, pushed eastward beyond the former borders of the Frankish Empire (see Map 8.1) into territories that were thinly inhabited by Slavs, Prussians, Letts, and Lithuanians. Some Germans settled just beyond the Elbe River and established the Principality of Brandenburg. Other Germans advanced along the shores of the Baltic Sea at the same time that Swedes began to move across Finland. The Russian prince of Novgorod, Alexander Nevsky, defeated the Swedes on the Neva River close to the Baltic Sea in 1240 and repulsed the Germans at Lake Peipus in 1242. Although these defeats halted further advances in northeastern Europe, the Germans and Swedes retained control of the shores of the Baltic Sea. The Germans had by then pushed through the middle Danube valley and founded another principality: Austria. By the mid-thirteenth century the "drive to the east" had clearly spent its strength, but it had tripled the area of German settlement over what it had been in Carolingian times (see Map 8.1).

Settlers also moved into the Iberian peninsula (present day Spain and Portugal). In the mid-eleventh century the Christian kings, whose kingdoms were confined to the extreme north of

Map 8.1 German Migration Eastward

the peninsula, began an offensive against the Muslims, who ruled most of Iberia. The Christians pushed south over two centuries, until they held most of the peninsula. The battle of Las Navas de Tolosa (in 1212), between an allied Christian army and an invading Muslim army from North Africa, confirmed this domination. By 1275 only the emirate of Granada remained under Muslim rule. The Christian kings actively recruited Christian settlers for the territories they reconquered and gave them land under favorable terms. The reconquest and resettlement of the peninsula, known as the *Reconquista*, proved lasting achievements; the Iberian frontier remained almost unchanged for the next 280 years, during which time Castile, Aragon, Portugal, and other states developed and flourished (see Chapter 9).

In Italy, too, pioneers pushed the Christian frontier to the south. From about 1015, knights from Normandy, initially serving as mercenaries, began fighting in southern Italy against Muslims, Byzantines, and local lords who had long been disputing dominion there. In 1124, now acting in their own name, they finally drove the Muslims and Byzantines from southern Italy and Sicily and united the two regions into the Kingdom of Naples and Sicily. European power swept over the sea as well as the land. The leaders were the maritime cities of Pisa and Genoa. In 1015 and 1016 fleets from Pisa and Genoa freed Sardinia from Islamic rule.

SOCIAL CHANGES

In many regions of Europe the expansion in settlement shifted the balance between the free and unfree classes. To attract settlers onto previously uncultivated lands, lords had to offer generous terms, frequently guaranteed in a written charter. Many landlords established free villages on their properties. The peasant who settled in a free village usually paid only a small fixed rent for the lands he cleared and was not required to labor for the landlord. He could leave the village at will, selling his lands and the house he had built at their market value. A runaway serf who resided in a free village for one year and one day without being claimed by his owner was thenceforth free.

The social conditions of the serfs also improved. Emancipation was considered a religiously meritorious act, and the period was one of marked religious enthusiasm. The increase in population eliminated the need for landlords to keep the entire labor force tied to the soil. Moreover, since the new frontiers attracted the serfs, only better terms, not brute force, could hold the laborers on the lord's land. Revived trade enabled some serfs to sell their produce at market; they could thus earn money with which to buy their freedom. Finally, serfdom bound landlords as well as serfs. Enterprising lords who wished to raise their rents or even change routines of cultivation were blocked by the custom, making servile obligations fixed and immutable. To reorganize their estates, to free their lands, to free themselves, the landlords had also to free their serfs.

By the early thirteenth century serfdom had almost disappeared in France, Spain, Italy, and western Germany, although some vestiges of it were to remain until the eighteenth century. In England serfdom also declined until the thirteenth century; but the growing cities of the continent created a large, profitable market for cereals, and English landlords were eager to produce for it. Rather than leasing out their estates, they continued to cultivate them directly. To find the necessary laborers, English lords maintained, or reimposed, conditions of serfdom over their peasants. But this Indian summer of English serfdom did not last much beyond the fourteenth century.

The changes in agriculture altered the character of noble life. Most landlords now rented their lands to peasants to cultivate; they were no longer direct cultivators but rent collectors. Since this new function did not require the constant supervision of their lands, the lords were free to live away from home for extended periods, perhaps traveling as pilgrims or crusaders to distant lands or mingling with their peers at the courts of great nobles. The new agricultural system, and the physical freedom it allowed the lords, permitted the growth of a courtly society, which in turn brought with it a rich lay culture.

Peasant Life   Life continued to be very hard, of course, for the peasants of Western Europe, but there were some improvements. To judge from skeletons found in medieval churchyards and from other slight evidence, the incidence of violent death declined, and life expectancy was growing; by the thirteenth century the average newborn might expect to live as long as 40 years. But rural conditions continued to be taxing for women. In the typical peasant village, men continued to outnumber, and presumably to outlive, women.

Although most peasants no longer lived in packed settlements, they still saw a good deal of their fellows. Markets and market days became a characteristic feature of rural life in Europe. Peasants slowly grew accustomed to selling or exchanging their surplus produce, purchasing their needs, borrowing money, or simply sharing information with their neighbors at the markets. The influence of markets further stimulated the growth of cottage industries, especially in the vicinity of towns. Within their homes, after their agricultural tasks were accomplished, the peasants and their families spun yarn, wove cloth, brewed ale, cured leather, made wood products, and produced other commodities that they could exchange at the urban markets.

The rural Church acquired new importance, and it is to this period that the rural parishes of Europe (and the Christianization of the countryside) must be dated. Churches were built at an extraordinary pace. The parish priest was usually of peasant origin and was often assisted by a young cleric or clerics in training for the priesthood (there were no seminaries). Because the priest was frequently the only member of the community who could read, he aided the peasants in their contacts with merchants, tax collectors, and other representatives of the literate culture of the city. Sundays and feast days brought the people together for divine services and for boisterous celebrations too. Church councils repeatedly condemned dancing and singing in the churchyard, especially since the songs on such occasions tended to be bawdy, but the denunciations had scant effect.

The Rise of the Nobility   The appearance of a hereditary nobility in the eleventh and twelfth centuries reflected a fundamental change in the structure of the elite family. In early medieval society the kindred—or set of relatives, even of important persons—traced their relationships through both males and females. Kindreds were formed, in other words, around a horizontal axis and did not extend far back in time. The kindred structure of the newly emerging nobility was much different. It placed exclusive emphasis on descent from, and relation through, males. And it pushed the line of descent through males far into the past, to the ancestor or founder of the line. It had, in other words, a vertical orientation. This set of male relatives descending through males from a common ancestor is called a *patrilineage*. (If, as was almost invariably the case until very recently, you bear your father's name, the same that his father bore, and so on up through the generations, then your surname recalls your own patrilineage. This custom reflects a tradition of family organization that has its origins among the nobility in the Central Middle Ages.)

Several factors contributed to the appearance of the noble patrilineage. The division of ancestral lands when there were many claimants threatened to destroy the economic base upon which the claimants' status depended, and to shore up their social position, the elite families sought to limit the number of heirs. The great families accordingly provided their daughters with dowries, but otherwise excluded them from a full share in the inheritance. They excluded

▶ **This enameled plate shows Count Geoffrey of Anjou, who died in 1151, holding a shield that depicts his family's new coat of arms.**

younger sons as well. Often these sons were denied the chance to marry, unless they could win prizes in war or the hand of an affluent heiress. The family wealth was principally reserved for the support of the eldest son, and with him went the chief hope for the preservation of the lineage. To proclaim their identity and distinctiveness from the rest of society, the nobles adopted family names, which usually recalled the name of the revered founder or of the ancestral castle. They

adopted other symbols of solidarity, such as coats of arms, mottoes, and sometimes fanciful genealogies.

To attract a suitable husband for a daughter, noble fathers had to offer ever larger dowries. Fathers were anxious to settle the future of their daughters as early as possible, even as they were requiring sons to marry late, if they were allowed to marry at all. Noble society, in which the patrilineage was the central institution, thus acquired certain peculiar features. Unattached young males abounded. They drifted from court to court as knights errant and were eager participants in tournaments, mock wars in which they hoped to win a prize that would make their fortunes. Or they wandered off on crusade to Europe's distant frontiers (see Chapter 10). The young women their own age would likely be married or deposited in convents. The interests of the firstborn male were not often the same as the good of all descendants, and the claims of the latter played upon parental consciences. Conflicts involving parents and siblings were commonplace in noble families.

THE REVIVAL OF COMMERCE

The European economy remained predominantly agricultural, although new forms of economic endeavor were emerging. Trade, which had dwindled to small importance in the Carolingian Age, became more vigorous. Most of the trade was local, between rural areas or between city and countryside, but there was also a dramatic rebirth of trade with regions beyond the European frontiers. Three trading zones developed based on the Mediterranean Sea in the south, the Baltic Sea in the north, and the overland routes that linked the two seas (see Map 8.2).

Venice, Pisa, and Genoa led this commercial expansion. In 998 and again in 1082 the Venetians received from the Byzantine emperors charters that gave them complete freedom of Byzantine waters. In the twelfth century Pisans and Genoese negotiated formal treaties with Islamic rulers that allowed them to establish commercial colonies in the Middle East and North Africa. Marseilles and Barcelona soon began to participate in the profitable Eastern trade.

In this Mediterranean exchange, the East

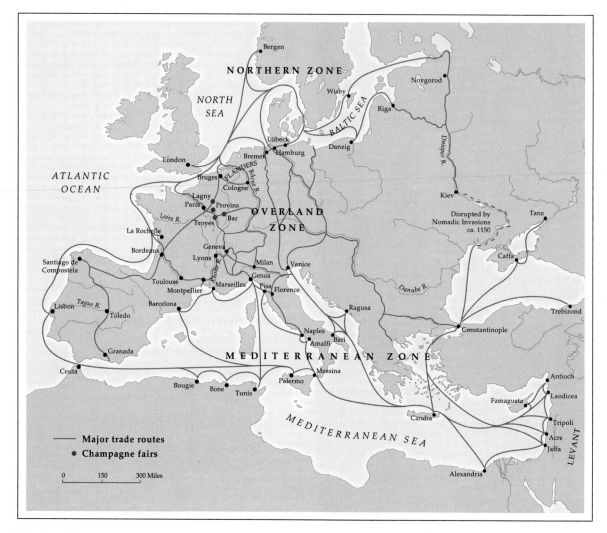

Map 8.2 MEDIEVAL TRADE ROUTES

shipped condiments, medicines, perfumes, dyes, paper, ivories, porcelain, pearls, precious stones, and rare metals such as mercury—all of which were known in the West under the generic name of *spices*. Eastern traders also sent a variety of fine linens and cottons (damask, muslin, organdy) as well as brocades and other silks. Western North Africa supplied animal skins, leather, cheese, ivory, and gold. Europe shipped wood and iron and products made from them (including entire ships), and grain, wine, and other agricultural commodities. By 1200 manufactured goods, especially woolen cloth woven in Flanders and finished in Italy, began to play an increasingly im-

portant role in the Mediterranean exchange. This cloth gave European merchants a product valued in the Eastern markets; with it they were able not only to pay for Eastern imports but also to generate a flow of precious metals into Europe.

Trade in northern Europe among the lands bordering the Baltic Sea linked the great ports of London, Bruges, Bergen, Cologne, Lübeck, and Novgorod with the many smaller maritime towns. The eastern Baltic regions sold grain, lumber and forest products, amber, and furs. Scandinavia supplied wood and fish. England provided raw wool and grains. Flanders was the great industrial area of the north, taking food and raw material for its excellent cloth.

The northern and Mediterranean trading

zones were joined by numerous overland routes. After 1100 the most active exchange between north and south was concentrated at six great fairs, held at various times of the year in the province of Champagne in France. Merchants could find at least one fair open no matter what time of year they came. They were guaranteed personal security at the fairs, low tariffs, and quick and fair justice. For two centuries the fairs remained the greatest markets in Europe.

THE REBIRTH OF URBAN LIFE

Although the towns in Western Europe were increasing in size and social complexity, their growth was very slow even in this age of economic expansion. Before 1200 probably no town in Western Europe included more than 30,000 inhabitants. These small towns, however, were assuming new functions.

In the Early Middle Ages the towns had been chiefly administrative centers, serving as the residence of bishops—or, much more rarely, of counts—and as fortified enclosures to which the surrounding rural population fled when under attack. (The original sense of the English word *borough* and of the German *Burg* is "fortress.") As the revival of trade made many of them centers of local or international exchange, permanent colonies of merchants grew up around the older fortresses. These merchant quarters were sometimes called a *faubourg* ("outside the fortress"). Many European towns, especially in the north, still show these two phases of their early history in their central fortress and surrounding settlements (see Map 8.3). By the thirteenth century some towns added to their administrative and commercial services a third function: They became centers of industrial production, especially of woolen cloth.

While growing in size, town populations, or at least their richest merchants, began demanding a greater measure of liberty from the bishop or lords who ruled them. They resented the cumbersome, expensive, and uninformed justice of the lord, who probably knew little about commercial needs, and they feared his powers to tax and to demand military service. The instrument by which the medieval townsmen sought to gov-

ern themselves was the *commune*, a permanent association created by the oath of its members and under the authority of several elected officials. Communes first appeared late in the eleventh century in northern Italy and Flanders, the two most heavily urbanized areas of Europe. Through force, persuasion, or purchase, many communes acquired from their lords charters

Map 8.3 THE GROWTH OF MEDIEVAL BRUGES Bruges (in modern Belgium) presents a fine example of the topographical dualism of many commercial towns of northern Europe. The town grew from two centers: the central fortress (A) and the merchants' settlement (B), gradually absorbing surrounding parishes and villages. The size of the late medieval walls conveys an accurate impression of the dimensions of medieval urban growth.

A	Burgus (9th century, probably on older site)		Suburb with "Vicus of Knights"
B	Faubourg, with "Wool Street" & "Clothier Street" (Merchants' Quarter, 9th century at latest)		First walled city (before 1089)
	Settlement around Church of St. Salvator		S. Gillisdorp (obtained by the city in 1280)
	Sysseele (village, 9th century, later included in first walled city)		Late medieval city with walls of 1297/1300

that set out their privileges and recognized their right to judge and tax themselves (*see box*, below).

Urban society also began to show considerable complexity. At the top of the social scale was a small aristocracy, usually referred to as *patricians*. In Italy this aristocracy included many nobles and great landlords from the countryside, who lived for part or all of the year in the towns. In contrast, in Flanders nobles and great landlords tended to keep to their rural estates, whence they viewed with disdain and fear the growing wealth of the towns. The powerful urban families in the north came chiefly from common origins, and most of them founded their fortunes upon commerce or the management of urban property. Social and cultural contrasts between town and countryside, then, were much sharper in the north than in Italy.

Below the patricians were the small merchants and shopkeepers, who were at first unspecialized in their economic interests. Most towns in the twelfth century still had only a single guild, or association of merchants. Soon after 1200, however, the guilds multiplied, showing an ever greater diversification in the commercial enterprises of the mercantile classes. At the same time the small merchants and shopkeepers were disputing, often with violence and soon with some success, the political domination of the patricians. Before the coming of industries the cities did not support a large class of artisans and workers. But here, too, the city presents a dynamic picture, and the commercial growth in the twelfth century was laying the basis for industrial expansion in the thirteenth.

Perhaps the most distinctive feature of urban society, even in the twelfth century, was the fluid division of the classes. Vertical social mobility was easier in the city than in any other part of the medieval world, the only possible exception

The Charter of Lorris

This charter was granted to the town of Lorris by King Louis VII in 1155 and was subsequently used as a model for other towns in northern France.

"1. Every one who has a house in the parish of Lorris shall pay as *cens* sixpence only for his house, and for each acre of land that he possesses in the parish.

"2. No inhabitant of the parish of Lorris shall be required to pay a toll or any other tax on his provisions; and let him not be made to pay measurage fee on the grain which he has raised by his own labor.

"4. No burgher shall pay toll on the road to Etampes, to Orléans, to Milly, or to Melun.

"5. No one who has property in the parish of Lorris shall forfeit it for any offense whatsoever, unless the offense shall have been committed against us or any of our *hôtes*.

"6. No person while on his way to the fairs and markets of Lorris, or returning, shall be arrested or disturbed, unless he shall have committed an offense on the same day.

"9. No one, neither we nor any other, shall exact from the burghers of Lorris any tallage, tax, or subsidy.

"16. No one shall be detained in prison if he can furnish surety that he will present himself for judgement.

"17. Any burgher who wishes to sell his property shall have the privilege of doing so; and, having received the price of the sale, he shall have the right to go from the town freely and without molestation, if he so desires, unless he has committed some offense in it.

"18. Any one who shall dwell a year and a day in the parish of Lorris, without any claim having pursued him there, and without having refused to lay his case before us or our provost, shall abide there freely and without molestation."

From B. Tierney, *The Middle Ages, I: Sources of Medieval History* (1992), pp. 191–192.

being the Church. The patrician class was always admitting new members, chiefly, wealthy recent immigrants from the countryside. The towns of the Middle Ages were much more efficient than rural society in recognizing, utilizing, and rewarding talent.

The dynamic towns of the Middle Ages, like the cities of the ancient world, shaped culture more than size alone might indicate. Urban commercial life required skill in calculations and a high level of literacy. The towns provided adept administrators who soon figured prominently in the governments of both Church and state. The urban milieu fostered new cultural attitudes, an approach to life based on exact observations and reasoned decisions.

II. *Feudalism and the Search for Political Order*

Europe in the eleventh and twelfth centuries enjoyed a higher degree of security and political order than it had in the chaotic tenth century; this security was in part responsible for the growth in population, expansion in trade, and changes in society that occurred during this era, while these developments in turn encouraged political stability. Stability was achieved above all through the set of institutions that is traditionally called the *feudal system.* However much they differed, the governments of England, France, the Holy Roman Empire, and other European states in this era may all be called *feudal.*

FEUDAL INSTITUTIONS

Feudalism and *feudal system* must be reckoned among the most abused and confusing terms in the historical vocabulary. These terms were unknown in the Middle Ages. Lawyers in the seventeenth century first devised them to denote the combination of laws and customs governing the kind of land tenure known as the *fief,* whose characteristics will be described shortly. Among reformers in the eighteenth century feudalism meant the unjustified privileges enjoyed by the nobles and the Church. Nineteenth-century so-

cialists, especially Karl Marx, used the term *feudalism* to mean an economic system based upon serfdom; they considered it a stage in economic development that followed slavery and preceded capitalism. To Marxists today the essential feature of feudalism is that it exploits peasants by binding them to the soil and forcing them to pay rent or labor service to the landlords. On the other hand, many books treat feudalism as if it meant no more than decentralized and weak government, or simple chaos. In popular usage, *feudal* is often indistinguishable from *backward.*

Most non-Marxist scholars currently use *feudalism* in reference to systems of political and social, *not* economic, institutions. Large estates and serfdom were not central to the feudal system and are better referred to as the *manorial system.* Still, feudalism remains an elastic term and is used in both a narrow and a broad sense. In its restricted meaning, feudalism refers to a set of distinct social and political institutions, defined by contract, that established the relationship between two freemen of differing social station, a lord and his vassal of lower rank. In practice, both lord and vassal came from the upper echelons of society. Feudal institutions did not include the serfs, who could not enter into a contract, and they touched only remotely and rarely the poorer freemen. In its broad sense, *feudalism* refers to the society and government in which social and political institutions created by contract played a major role in defining relationships within the upper classes. Perhaps the most distinctive feature of feudal government is that the powerful men in society defined their political rights and obligations through individual contracts. In contrast, in the ancient Roman Empire the public law of the state defined the rights and obligations of all citizens, with only minor exceptions.

Following the guidance of the great French historian Marc Bloch, many scholars now divide the era of Western feudalism into two periods. The first feudal age, which lasted from the disappearance of Roman government in the West until about 1050 or 1100, witnessed among the free classes of Europe the spontaneous development of feudal practices out of the early medieval and post-Carolingian chaos. In the second feudal age, which spans the period from about 1050 to

1300, princes began self-consciously to use and manipulate these institutions to buttress their own authority.

The Feudal Milieu

To understand the growth of feudalism, we must first recall the chaotic conditions prevailing in the Early Middle Ages, especially in the ninth and tenth centuries. In a milieu in which governmental authority counted for little, individuals had to seek their security through their own efforts. The freeman in search of protection had little recourse but to appeal to a neighbor stronger than himself. If the neighbor accepted, the two men entered by implied contract into a close, quasi-familial relationship. Like the bonds between father and son, the feudal relationship between the strong "lord" and the weak freeman was initially more ethical and emotional than legally binding. It remained so until the thirteenth century, when lawyers systematically began to clarify and define its legal implications.

In Celtic areas of Europe (Ireland, Scotland, Wales, Brittany) traditionally powerful clans could extend such protection; a true feudalism never developed in those lands. Similarly, among the South Slavs, the persistence of a social organization based on the clan made superfluous the creation of authentically feudal relationships. Northern Italy was also an exceptional area in the history of feudalism. Perhaps because of the early importance of towns there, the quest for security primarily favored the development of communal associations, in which social equals rather than lords and vassals were linked in what might be considered artificial families or clans. The power of the urban communes in northern Italy stunted, although it did not entirely suppress, the extension of feudal ties even in the countryside.

The true homeland of Western feudalism was the region between the Loire and the Rhine rivers. The institutions that developed there were subsequently exported to England in the Norman Conquest and to southern Italy, and they greatly influenced government and society in southern France, Spain, and Germany beyond the Rhine. In this region the family seems to have been too scattered or too weak to guarantee security for its members.

Vassalage

The honorable personal bond between the lord and his man is called *vassalage*, a term that derives from a Celtic word meaning "boy" or "servant." Vassalage was created by an act of homage, the prospective vassal placing his hands within those of his lord (sometimes, too, a kiss was exchanged) and perhaps swearing an oath of fidelity. The "joining of hands" was the central act in the ceremony of homage.

Vassalage imposed obligations on both the vassal and his lord. The vassal owed his lord primarily loyalty (or, in its feudal term, *fealty*), which meant that he had to render aid and counsel, or material and moral help, to his lord. He had to perform military service in the lord's army and usually had to bring additional men in numbers proportionate to his wealth. As the duty of service became more precisely defined, military service became more a matter of law than of the heart. The vassal might be expected to serve, for example, 40 days a year in a local war and less time if the lord intended to fight in foreign lands. The vassal could not refuse this service, but if asked by the lord for more time than custom allowed, he could demand compensation or simply return home. The lord could also demand financial aid, and there were four occasions which required that the vassals provide money without question: the ransoming of the lord, the knighting of the lord's eldest son, the marriage of the lord's eldest daughter, and the lord's own departure on crusade. At other times the vassal still had to consider requests for financial aid but could grumble and, if the lord was weak enough, refuse.

The obligation of counsel required the vassal to give good advice, to keep the lord's secrets, and to help him reach true judgments in legal cases that came before his court. The ordinary work of the court was the adjudication of disputes among the vassals and the hearing of complaints brought by the lord against his men. Feudal custom held that a vassal could be judged only by his own peers, that is, his fellow vassals. By the thirteenth century many great feudal courts were claiming the right to hear appeals from the courts of the individual vassals. The acceptance of such appeals was one of the principal ways by which royal governments were able to

▶ Investiture Scene, Fresco, Ferrande Tower, Pernes-les-Fontaines, France, ca. 1270
Kneeling before his overlord the king, a vassal offers homage and receives in return investiture in a fief—the roll of paper, which would have recorded the transaction in detail. As this thirteenth-century fresco from Pernes-les-Fontaines in France indicates, the ceremony takes place before witnesses.

strengthen their authority in the second feudal age.

The vassal's duties toward his lord were further complicated in the second feudal age by the development of multiple vassalage—acts of homage by the same man to several lords. In case of conflict among his different lords, whom should he serve? To escape this dilemma, feudal custom required that the vassal select one of his lords as his *liege*, that is, the one whom he would serve against all others. The growth of multiple vassalage and liege homage was itself a sign of the waning emotional content of the feudal relationship.

The lord, in turn, owed his vassal protection and maintenance, or military and material support. He had to come to his vassal's aid when requested, repel invaders from his possessions, and even help him if he was sued in another's court. In the formative period of feudalism the lord's obligation of material support was often carried out at his own table, but as vassals became more numerous and more distantly located and as great princes came to be included among them, sheer logistics prevented the lord from feeding all his men. Since a lord often had no cash revenues for making monetary compensations, he would distribute land as a form of payment for the vassal's allegiance. This concession of land was the fief. The granting of a fief superimposed upon the personal relationship of vassalage a second relationship, involving property, between the lord and his man. The close union of personal and property ties was, in fact, the most characteristic feature of the Western feudal relationship.

The Fief The lord granted the fief in a special ceremony called *investiture* (it usually immediately followed the act of homage), in which he extended to his vassal a clod of earth or sprig of leaves, symbol of the land he was receiving. In a strict juridical sense the fief was a conditional, temporary, and nonhereditary grant of land or other income-producing property, such as an office, toll, or rent. At the vassal's death, disability, or refusal to serve his lord, the fief at once returned to the lord who granted it. The juridical origins of the fief seem to go back to forms of ecclesiastical land tenure that grew up in the Early Middle Ages. Churches were canonically forbidden to sell or give away their property, but they could grant its "use" while retaining ownership over it. In Carolingian times the emperors took to ordering churches and monasteries to make such concessions to favored laymen. The true fief, however, involving only laymen and linked with vassalage, does not appear until after the Carolingian Age.

Although technically not inheritable, the fief became gradually assimilated to the allodium (property held in absolute ownership), which was unconditional, permanent, and hereditary. From the start lords had found it convenient to grant a fief to the adult son of a deceased vassal, since he could at once serve in his father's stead. The son had only to make a special payment (the "relief") to the lord to acquire the fief. Feudal custom also came to recognize the right of a minor son to inherit, but the lord retained the privilege—the right of wardship—of serving as the son's guardian or of appointing someone to fulfill that function. Feudal practice only reluctantly admitted daughters to the inheritance of a fief since they could not perform military service. Nevertheless, in most areas of Europe women did acquire a right of inheritance. Their lord, however, could select their husbands for them, inasmuch as their spouses had to assume the obligations of service. Initially, vassals were forbidden to sell the fief, grant it to a church, or otherwise transfer

it in whole or in part. By the thirteenth century, however, fiefs were commonly sold or granted—but only with the lord's permission, which almost always had to be purchased.

The fief was the dominant form of land tenure in northern France and western Germany from the late ninth and tenth centuries. The Norman Conquest carried it to England in the eleventh. In the same period it became common in southern France, but it never entirely supplanted the allodium. It was still later in arriving in Spain, and in Italy its importance always remained restricted. The diffusion of the fief, even if slow and incomplete, had important social effects nonetheless. Because vassals could not dispose of their lands without the lord's consent, property relationships (and society, indirectly) remained fixed and stable for long periods. Moreover, the economic pressure superimposed upon the moral force of vassalage gave the princes of the age an effective means of retaining the loyalty of their dependents: The disloyal vassal not only violated the ethics of his times but also risked losing the lands that supported him.

Stages of Feudal Development Although there were significant local variations in the character and chronology of medieval feudal institutions, it remains possible to speak of certain broad stages of feudal development. In the ninth and tenth centuries Carolingian administration on the local level disintegrated. The power of the count waned, and the *vicarii* (who judged minor cases) disappeared. Authority in the countryside largely passed into the hands of petty lords, most especially the castellans, or holders of castles. The eleventh and twelfth centuries saw a remarkable upsurge in the construction of castles in Europe. To cite one example, in the Diocese of Florence in Italy only 2 castles are mentioned in the sources before 900, 11 before 1000, 52 before 1050, 130 before 1100, and 205 before 1200. The proliferation of these fortresses reflects both the violence of European life and the growing effort to find protection from it.

The castellans initially had no official status in the shadowy structure of the post-Carolingian state, but they dominated the communities that lived in or near their fortresses. The castellan was the judge, tax collector, and military leader, and he usually controlled the local church as well. Within the confines of these small societies the institutions of feudalism developed spontaneously. The castles with their lands constituted fairly stable units.

From about the year 1050, counts, dukes, and some few kings were attempting to integrate these castles into fairly centralized principalities, insisting that the petty nobles assume toward them the obligations of vassals and fief holders. The use of these feudal concepts and institutions to serve the interests of princely authority initiates the second feudal age—the age of the feudal principality.

In granting a fief, the lord gave his vassal all possible sources of revenue the land could produce, including, usually, the right to hold a court and to profit from its fines and confiscations. This contributed to another characteristic of feudal society, private justice (that is, the exercise of public powers by private individuals as a right associated with their tenure of land). Lords and vassals, in other words, at every level of the feudal pyramid, could tax, judge, and punish their dependents.

By the second feudal age lawyers were arguing that the king, as the font of all justice, had the right of hearing appeals from the courts of his chief vassals (as well as those "rear vassals" who stood lower on the feudal ladder) and could also accept cases directly, which his vassals had traditionally heard. The exertion of these royal prerogatives brought about the gradual but unmistakable decline of private justice.

NORMAN AND ANGEVIN ENGLAND

We could use the history of any one of several principalities—the Duchy of Normandy, the County of Flanders, the Kingdom of Naples and Sicily, among others—to illustrate the political reorganization characteristic of the second feudal age. But England offers the best example of feudal concepts in the service of princes. The growth of feudalism in England was, in turn, intimately connected with the Norman Conquest of 1066, the central event of English medieval history.

The Norman Conquest Duke William of Normandy (1026–1087), the architect of the Con-

▶ The *Bayeux Tapestry*, reputedly woven by the wife of William the Conqueror, is a strip of linen 231 feet long and 20 inches wide depicting the Norman Conquest of England in 1066. In the portion shown here, William arrives at Pevensey (top); King Harold fights in the Battle of Hastings (bottom). The tapestry was completed toward the end of the eleventh century.

quest, is the epitome of the ambitious, energetic, and resourceful prince of the Central Middle Ages. A bastard who had to fight 12 years to make good his claim over his own Norman duchy, William early set his ambitions on the English crown. His claims were respectable, but not compelling. He was the first cousin of the last Saxon king, the childless Edward the Confessor, who allegedly had promised to make William heir to the throne. However, before his death, Edward selected the Saxon Harold Godwinson to succeed him, and his choice was supported by the Witan, the English royal council.

Edward died in 1066. William immediately recruited an army of vassals and adventurers to support his claim to the throne and gained a papal blessing for his enterprise, but unfavorable winds kept his fleet bottled up in the Norman ports for six weeks. Meanwhile Harold Hardrada, king of Norway, who also disputed Harold Godwinson's claim, invaded England with a Viking army but was shattered by the Saxons near York on September 28, 1066. That same day, the channel winds shifted and William landed in England. Harold Godwinson foolishly rushed south to confront him. Although his army was not, as was once thought, technically inferior to the Norman army, it was tired and badly in need of rest and reinforcements after the victory over the Vikings. At the Battle of Hastings on October 14, fatigue seems eventually to have tipped the scales of an otherwise even struggle. The Normans carried the day and left Harold Godwinson dead upon the field. Duke William of Normandy had won his claim to be king of England.

Although the exact importance of the Norman Conquest in English history is still disputed, most historians today believe that while the Norman Conquest did not radically alter the course of English development, it did add a new speed and decisiveness to changes already in evidence. For example, the Conquest oriented England away from Scandinavia and toward the continent and established a French-speaking aristocracy. Norman and continental influences, however, were growing well before 1066; Edward had been raised in Normandy, and Normans were familiar figures in the English court and Church. Nor did William radically change the political and social institutions of Anglo-Saxon England; rather, he built upon them.

The basic unit of local administration remained the shire under the supervision of the sheriff, who had primary responsibility for looking after the king's interests. The sheriff administered the royal estates, collected the taxes, summoned and led contingents to the national militia, and presided over the shire court. William left all these institutions of local government intact.

The real impact of the Conquest was felt at the upper levels of Anglo-Saxon society. The Saxon earls, as the great nobles were called, and most of the lesser nobles, or thanes, lost their estates, which William redistributed among his followers from the continent—his barons (a title of uncertain origin, now used to connote the immediate vassals of the king). William allotted land liberally but cautiously. He made up each fief from several blocks of land in different parts of the countryside, thus giving his followers adequate support to serve him but limiting their autonomy and opportunity to rebel. William redefined the relations between the king and the great men of the realm on the basis of essentially feudal concepts. He now insisted that all English land be considered a fief held directly or indirectly from the king. The barons had to serve the king, and the knights had to serve the barons or risk losing their estates.

In 1086 William conducted a comprehensive survey of the lands of England, the report of which was the *Domesday Book*, probably so called because its judgments in their finality resembled those to be made on the Last Day. It showed a population in England of about 1.1 million people. This survey, unique for its age among the European kingdoms, served two main purposes: It gave the king a clear record of his own holdings and those of his barons, and it enabled him to know how much service the land could support. In the Salisbury oath of 1086 every vassal had to swear loyalty to the king as the liege lord of all. Feudal concepts thus brought a greater precision to the obligations of English freemen toward their king and placed a new ethical and material force behind royal prerogatives.

To maintain close contact with his barons and vassals, William also took from the continent the institution of the great council, or Curia Regis. Essentially, it was an assembly of bishops, abbots, barons—in fact, anyone whom the king summoned. The great council fulfilled the feudal functions of giving the king advice and serving as his principal court in reaching judgments. It was a much larger assembly than the Saxon

Witan. However, as the great council could not be kept permanently in session, a small council, consisting of those persons in permanent attendance at the court whom the king wished to invite, carried on the functions of the great council between its sessions. The development of the great and small councils had major importance for English constitutional history. The great council was the direct ancestor of Parliament, while the small council was the source of the administrative bureaus of the royal government.

Angevin Kingship William was succeeded by his second son, William Rufus. One of England's worst kings, he terrorized his subjects and antagonized the Church. At his death in 1100 (probably from assassination), his younger brother, Henry I, became king. Henry began a series of administrative reforms, but a dispute over the succession at his death and a protracted civil war undermined his accomplishment. By 1154, however, a unified and pacified England passed to the rule of Henry II of Anjou (in France), grandson of Henry I and the first of the "Angevin" kings of England.

Through combined inheritances and his marriage to Eleanor of Aquitaine in 1152, Henry II ruled over a sprawling assemblage of territories that included, besides England, nearly the entire west of France from the English Channel to the Pyrenees Mountains (see Map 8.4). A man of great energy who carried to completion many of the reforms of Henry I, he ranks among the most gifted statesmen of the twelfth century and among the greatest kings of England.

It was in the sphere of English government and law that Henry II left a permanent mark. He made royal justice the common justice of the kingdom through the use of itinerant officials, or "justices in eyre" (that is, on journey), who were endowed with all the authority of the king himself. The itinerant justice traveled regularly to the courts of the shires, investigating and punishing crimes. Upon his arrival the justice would impound 12 "good men" and inquire of them under oath what crimes they had heard about since his last visit and whom they suspected of guilt. (This sworn inquest is the direct ancestor of the modern grand jury.) Those indicted by the 12 "good men" were still tried by the ancient ordeals of fire

and water, which were retained until the Church condemned these procedures in 1215. Thereafter, the small, or petty, jury was used, as it is today, to judge guilt or innocence.

The itinerant justice did not forcibly interfere in civil disputes, but he did offer the services of the royal court in settling them. Barons receiving fiefs from the king had also been given the right to hold a court and judge the disputes of their own knights and dependents. Normally, therefore, litigants in a civil dispute appeared before a baronial court. But as a result of Henry's reforms, a litigant could purchase one of many royal writs, which ordered the sheriff to bring the case under the scrutiny of the royal court presided over by the justice in eyre. The great superiority of royal justice in civil matters was that it relied not on ordeals or duels but on sworn inquests or juries. These juries in civil cases were composed of "good men" from the neighborhood who were likely to know the facts at issue and were able to judge the truth or falsity of claims. Henry made no effort to suppress baronial courts, but the better justice offered by the royal courts left them with a progressively shrinking role in the juridical life of England.

In time the justices built up a considerable body of decisions, which then served as precedents in similar cases. The result was the gradual legal unification of the realm, the development, in other words, of a "common law" of England—common in that it applied to the entire kingdom and was thus distinct from the local customs by which cases were formerly decided. It differed from Roman law in that it represented not the will of the king or legislator but the principles, formed by custom, that were followed in deciding cases. This marks the beginnings of the tradition of common law, under which most of the English-speaking world continues to live.

Thomas Becket The judicial reforms of Henry II led him into a bitter conflict with the English Church, which maintained its own courts, called canonical courts. In Henry's opinion the penalties these courts meted out to the guilty were too mild to deter them from future crime, and in 1164 he claimed the right to retry before his royal courts clerics accused of crime. The archbishop of Canterbury, Thomas Becket, rejected this claim. He

Map 8.4 MEDIEVAL ENGLAND, FRANCE, AND GERMANY

argued that both the Bible and canon law forbade what we now call "double jeopardy"—that is, a second trial and punishment for one crime.

Becket had been a warm personal friend of Henry's and had served him ably and faithfully as his chancellor, the chief official of the realm. Royal friendship and favor had brought him his election as archbishop of Canterbury in 1162. In the course of the six-year struggle between these former friends, Becket first submitted, then broke with Henry and fled to France, and then was reconciled once more in 1170. Yet a few months later he suspended the bishops that had supported the king. Henry, then in France, demanded in fateful rhetoric whether no man would free him of this pestilential priest. Four of the king's knights took the words to heart, journeyed to England, found Becket in his cathedral, and cut him down before the high altar on December 29, 1170. His death accomplished what his life could not. Henry revoked the objectionable reforms and performed an arduous personal penance for his unwise words.

Although Henry II was unable to dominate the Church, the English monarchy at his death in 1189 was the strongest in Europe. It remained for the thirteenth century to discover how the great power of the king might be managed and controlled.

CAPETIAN FRANCE

In France the pattern of feudal development was much different from that of England. Central government all but disappeared in the turmoil following the age of Charlemagne. What governmental functions could still be performed amid the chaos were carried out by counts, castellans,

▶ This depiction of the murder of Thomas Becket in Canterbury in 1170 was completed within a few years of the event. That it should have appeared as a wall painting in the church of Sts. Giovanni and Paolo in Spoleto, Italy, hundreds of miles away from Canterbury, suggests the intensity of the European-wide reaction to the assassination.

and other lords of small territorial units. These factors alone would have made the rebuilding of an effective national monarchy considerably more difficult in France than in England; but, in addition, France was a much larger country, and its regions preserved considerable cultural diversity.

Nonetheless, the second feudal age did witness considerable changes in France. First, we can discern the emergence of several compact and effectively governed principalities, especially in the north—the Duchy of Normandy, the counties of Flanders and Champagne, the royal lands of the Île-de-France, and others. Second, the French kings sought with some success to establish a lord-vassal relation with the great dukes and counts who governed these principalities. The kings did not envision, and could not have achieved, the unification of the entire realm under their own direct authority. The goal of monarchical policy was rather a kind of federation of principalities bound together by a common fealty to the king on the part of distant dukes and counts.

Louis VI Subdues a Violent Baron

This selection describes the attempt of Louis VI (1108–37), a strong and honorable monarch, to keep the peace in his realm. It comes from **The Life of Louix VI,** *a chronicle by Suger, the head of a French monastery and a great admirer of the king. It is a good example of the chronicles that form one of the historian's basic sources for studying medieval history.*

"A king is obliged by virtue of his office to crush with his strong right hand the impudence of tyrants. For such men freely provoke wars, take pleasure in plunder, oppress the poor, destroy the churches, and give themselves free reign to do whatsoever they wish. . . .

"One such wicked man was Thomas of Marle. For while King Louis was busy fighting in the wars which we mentioned earlier, Thomas ravaged the regions around Laon, Reims, and Amiens. . . . Thomas devastated the region with the fury of a wolf. No fear of ecclesiastical penalty persuaded him to spare the clergy; no feeling of humility convinced him to spare the people. Everyone was slaughtered, everything destroyed. He snatched two prize estates from the nuns of Saint-John of Laon. And treating the two castles of Crécy-sur-Serre and Nouvion-Catillon as his own, he transformed them into a dragon's lair and a den of thieves, exposing the nearby inhabitants to the miseries of fire and plunder.

"Fed up with the intolerable afflictions of this man, the churchmen of France met together (on December 6, 1114) at a great council at Beauvais. There they passed a sentence of condemnation against the enemies of Jesus Christ. The venerable papal legate Cuno, bishop of Praeneste, was particularly moved by the numerous pleas of the church and the cries of the orphans and the poor. He drew the sword of Saint Peter against Thomas of Marle, and with the unanimous assent of the council, declared him excommunicated, ripped from him *in absentia* the titles and honors of knighthood, branded him a criminal, and declared him unworthy of being called a Christian.

"Heeding the wishes of so great a council, King Louis moved quickly against Thomas. Accompanied by his army and the clergy, he turned at once against the heavily defended castle of Crécy. There, thanks to his men at arms, or should we say on account of divine aid, Louis achieved swift victory. He seized the new towers as if they were no more than the huts of peasants; he drove out the criminals; he piously slaughtered the impious; and as for those who had showed no pity, he in turn showed no pity towards them. . . . Flushed by the success of his decisive victory, the king moved quickly against the other illegally held castle, Nouvion. . . ."

From C. W. Hollister et al., *Medieval Europe: A Short Source Book* (1992), pp. 207–208.

The Capetians In 987 the great nobles of France elected as their king Hugh Capet, whose descendants held the throne until 1792. Hugh was chosen primarily because his small possessions in the Île-de-France, which included Paris and the surrounding region, made him no threat to the independence of the nobles. He and his successors for the next century made no dramatic efforts to enlarge their royal authority, but they carefully nursed what advantages they had: the central location of their lands; the title of king, which commanded a vague prestige; and a close association with the Church, which gave them an avenue of influence extending beyond their own territory. They also pursued a remarkably prudent policy of consolidating control over their own lands, and they had the good luck to produce sons. For 200 years the kings crowned their sons during their own lifetime and thus built the tradition that the crown was theirs, not by election but by hereditary right.

The Capetian policy first bore fruit under Louis VI, the Fat (1108–1137). His aim was to be master of his own possessions, and he successfully reduced to obedience the petty nobles and castellans who had been disturbing his lands and harassing travelers seeking to cross them (*see box*, p. 228). By the end of his reign he had established effective control over the lands between the cities of Paris and Orléans. This gave him a compact block of territory in the geographic heart of France. Louis VI promoted the colonization of forests and wastelands by establishing free villages, and he courted the support of the town communes. The economic growth encouraged by the king added to his own fiscal resources. He staffed his administration with new men from the middle ranges of society at the expense of the older, entrenched, and unreliable nobility.

His son Louis VII married Eleanor of Aquitaine, heiress to the extensive lands of the Duchy of Aquitaine. This marriage promised to more than double the lands under direct royal control. But manifest incompatibility of character and Eleanor's failure to produce a male heir set the spouses feuding, and the marriage was annulled in 1152. Eleanor, or at least her possessions, proved irresistible to Henry II of England, who married her two months later, although he was her junior by some 10 years. The loss of her vast

▶ **ELEANOR OF AQUITAINE EFFIGY**
Eleanor of Aquitaine bears comparison with other forceful female rulers of European history, such as Elizabeth I of England. She was a worthy consort for Henry II, one of the most powerful and innovative rulers of the Middle Ages, and is buried next to him. The site, a splendid French abbey, lies within the territories that Eleanor had inherited and added to the English kingdom. The crown and book in the effigy on her tomb are perfect symbols of the intelligence and power that characterized her life.

► **One of the castles that Richard I constructed to defend his Angevin holdings against attacks was the formidable Château Gaillard, upstream from Rouen.**

inheritance to the English monarchy was a major blow to the Capetian fortunes.

Louis VII's son by a later marriage, Philip II Augustus (1180–1226), set out to reclaim from the English the provinces of Aquitaine and Normandy. While King John of England dallied at home, French troops invaded Normandy and after an eight-month siege took the fortress of Château Gaillard, which Richard the Lion-Hearted had erected to defend the province. Normandy thus became part of the French royal domain (see Map 8.4). Finally, John bestirred himself to action. He organized a coalition of Philip's enemies, including Emperor Otto IV of Germany and the count of Flanders who, though Philip's vassal, viewed with considerable apprehension the growth of royal authority. Philip beat back the invading army at Bouvines in 1214, a victory that confirmed England's loss of Normandy and brought new prestige to the Capetian throne. It was convincing proof of the power the king now could wield.

Under Philip royal influence began to penetrate to the south of France. In 1208 Pope Innocent III declared a crusade against the Albigensian heretics of the south (see Chapter 9), who enjoyed the protection of many powerful nobles. Philip's vassals flocked to the pope's call, overwhelmed the counts of Toulouse and other prominent nobles, and seized much of their lands. The defeat of the southern nobility left a vacuum of power, which the king's authority soon filled.

Administration In addition to increasing his lands, Philip strengthened the administration of his own properties, the royal demesne, although he still made no effort to interfere directly in the governments of the kingdom's fiefs. On the local level the representative of the king—the French counterpart of the English sheriff—was the *prévôt*. About 1190, apparently in imitation of the English itinerant justices, Philip began to appoint a new official, the *bailli*, to oversee the work of the *prévôt*. The *bailli* supervised the collection of rents and taxes, the administration of justice, and all the king's interests within a certain prescribed circuit or area, but he never assumed the full range of functions and powers that the English justice in eyre had acquired. The central administration was also developing specialized bureaus, although less advanced than the English; the *Chambre de Comptes*, a special financial office, equivalent to the English Treasury, gradually assumed responsibility for the royal finances.

Louis VI and Philip Augustus made the French monarchy the unquestioned master in the Île-de-France, greatly enlarged the royal demesne, and insisted with considerable success that the great dukes and counts of the realm serve the king loyally. In France, as in England and widely in Europe, feudal practices did not necessarily mean weak government; on the contrary, the able and energetic princes of the age used these concepts and institutions to redefine the relationship between ruler and ruled in the interest of achieving a stronger central authority. The feudal system, as it was constructed in these principalities, was thus a major step toward a more ordered political life and toward the sovereign state of the early modern period.

THE GERMAN EMPIRE

In the tenth and eleventh centuries the German lands east of the Rhine show a pattern of political development very different from that of France or England. Whereas in France, after the collapse of the Carolingian Empire, power became fragmented among many petty lords and castellans, in Germany it came to be concentrated in certain relatively large territorial blocks. Saxony, Franconia, Swabia, and Bavaria—known as "Stem" duchies (from the German *Stämme*, meaning a distinct people, tribe, or ethnic group)—were originally districts of the Carolingian Empire that became independent political entities under powerful dukes. Because these duchies were close to the hostile eastern frontier, their inhabitants learned to appreciate the advantages of a unified leadership.

Moreover, in Germany the old idea of a Christian empire, which we have seen both in Byzantium and in the West under Charlemagne, retained considerable appeal. Perhaps because they were so close to the frontiers of Christendom, the German dukes considered themselves to be in a special way the champions of the Christian faith,

and they mounted a missionary effort among the unconverted peoples. The dukes desired a leader who, like Charlemagne, would aid the Church against its foreign enemies while promoting its interests at home.

Otto I, The Great The last direct descendant of Charlemagne in Germany, a feeble ruler known as Louis the Child, died in 911. Recognizing the need for a common leader, the German dukes in 919 elected as king one of their number, Henry of Saxony. His descendants held the German monarchy until 1024. The most powerful of this line of Saxon kings, and the true restorer of the German Empire, was Otto I, the Great (936–973). Otto was primarily a warrior, and conquest was a principal foundation of his power. He routed the pagan Magyars near Augsburg in 955 and ended their menace to Christian Europe; he organized military provinces, or marches, along the eastern frontier and actively promoted the work of German missionaries and settlers beyond the Elbe River; and in 951 he marched into Italy.

Historians are not certain what exactly drew Otto to the south. Perhaps, like Charlemagne, he hoped to rescue the papacy from the clutches of the tumultuous Roman nobility, to which it had once again fallen victim. It does appear, at any rate, that Otto conceived of himself not just as a German king but as the leader of all Western Christians. He could not allow Italy, especially Rome, to remain in chaos or permit another prince to achieve a strong position there. In 962, during Otto's second campaign in Italy, Pope John XII gave formal recognition to Otto by crowning him Roman Emperor. The title gave him no new powers, but it did provide him high prestige.

The coronation of 962 not only marked the restoration of a "Roman" empire in the West (in fact, it was German) but also confirmed the close relations between Germany and Italy that lasted through the Middle Ages. Although the German emperors claimed to be the successors of the Caesars and of Charlemagne, and thus the titular leaders of all Western Christendom, their effective power never extended beyond Germany and Italy and the small provinces contiguous to them—Provence, Burgundy, and Bohemia. Government of his far-flung territories presented

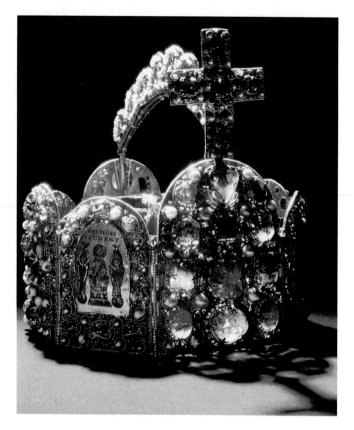

▶ CROWN OF THE HOLY ROMAN EMPIRE, TENTH
AND ELEVENTH CENTURIES
The crown of the Holy Roman Empire may
originally have been given to Otto I by Pope John,
but throughout the tenth and eleventh centuries
various pieces were added by different emperors. It
eventually consisted of eight panels, decorated with
cloisonné enamels, which are hinged together with
gold filigree and surrounded with jewels and
pearls.

When Otto died in 973, his state was the
strongest in Europe, but it was troubled by several difficulties. Foremost among them was the
growing discontent of the Church with the imperial domination of ecclesiastical life. (This will
be examined in the following section.) Reformers
sought to liberate the Church from the emperor's
tutelage, and they did succeed in undermining
this source of imperial authority. But the reform
did not end the efforts of the German kings to
build a strong empire that would unite Germany
and Italy and allow them to exercise a moral leadership over the whole of Western Europe.

Frederick I, Barbarossa   The ruler who came
closest to building a lasting foundation for the
German Empire was Frederick I (1152–1190) of
the House of Hohenstaufen. He was called *Barbarossa*, meaning "red beard." Large, handsome,
gallant, and courageous, Frederick, like Charlemagne before him, gained a permanent place in
the memories and myths of his people. He much
resembles in his policies, if not quite in his
achievements, the other great statesmen of the
twelfth century—Henry II of England and Philip
II of France. Frederick showed a broad eclecti-
cism in his political philosophy. He claimed to be
the special protector of the Church and therefore
a holy figure. He called his empire the Holy
Empire: This emphasis on the religious was retained in the later title, *Holy Roman Empire*, used
after 1254 and until Napoleon abolished this
German Empire in 1806. Frederick also introduced the new institutions and concepts of political feudalism to his government and effectively
exploited ideas concerning the emperor's powers
that the revived study of Roman law was providing.

Frederick pursued three principal goals. He
hoped to consolidate a strong imperial domain
consisting of Swabia, which he inherited; Burgundy, which he acquired by marriage; and Lombardy, which he hoped to subdue. These three
contiguous territories would serve him much as
the Île-de-France served the French king by giving him a central base of power from which he
could dominate those more distant areas that he
could not rule directly. In Germany he sought to
force the great princes in the north and east to
become his vassals. In Italy he claimed, as successor of the Caesars, to enjoy the sovereignty

Otto with problems even more formidable than
those that confronted the English and French
kings. He distributed the Stem duchies among his
relatives, in the poorly founded hope that they
would be loyal to him, and placed great reliance
upon the Church in both Germany and Italy, using its lands and officials as adjuncts to his own.
He therefore insisted upon the right to nominate
or approve the nominations of the great prelates
of his empire—bishops, abbots, and popes. Control of Church offices and Church lands gave the
emperor enclaves of power in the Stem duchies
and in Italy, which no potential rival could
match.

that Roman law attributed to the emperors.

Frederick's Italian ambitions disturbed the popes and the town communes, which from about 1100 had become the chief powers in the northern half of the peninsula. Both feared that a strong central government could be established only at the cost of their own independence. With active papal support the northern Italian towns, led by Milan, formed a coalition known as the Lombard League and defeated the imperial forces at Legnano in 1176. The Battle of Legnano not only marked the failure of Frederick's efforts to establish full sovereignty over the Lombard cities but also was the first time in European history that an army of townsmen had bested the forces of the established army under noble leadership. At the Peace of Constance in 1183 Frederick conceded to the towns almost full authority within their walls; the towns, in turn, recognized that their powers came from him, and they conceded to him sovereignty in the countryside. Frederick did not gain all that he had wished in Italy, but his position remained a strong one.

In Germany he was able to achieve a more resounding victory, this time over the powerful duke of Saxony, Henry the Lion, who had refused to aid him in his Italian war. Making effective use of feudal custom, Frederick summoned him in 1180 to face trial as a disloyal vassal. The court condemned Henry and confiscated his Saxon fief. With Henry humiliated and deprived of his lands, Frederick seemed to be the unchallenged master in Germany (see Map 8.4).

Frederick now wanted to advance the empire's prestige in Europe and sought out a position of leadership in the Third Crusade, as it is traditionally numbered. But the aged emperor drowned while trying to ford a small stream in Asia Minor, bringing to a pathetic end a crowded and brilliant career.

His successors proved unable to build upon, or even maintain, his accomplishments. The very extent of the lands they sought to dominate, and their great cultural diversity, worked against them. The chief powers in Italy, the pope and the towns, maintained their opposition to the establishment of a strong imperial government under German auspices. The heritage of the medieval empire was to be a divided Germany and Italy—divisions that would not be overcome until the nineteenth century.

III. The Reform of the Western Church

The Church, like lay government, experienced fundamental transformations in the eleventh and twelfth centuries, as it acquired characteristics it was to retain in large measure to the present day. The reform of the Church was the direct result of revolt against the traditional system of lay domination over ecclesiastical offices and lands.

MORAL CRISIS

After the disintegration of the Frankish Empire, a kind of moral chaos invaded the lives of the clergy. Since the fourth century the Church had demanded that its clergy remain celibate, but this injunction was almost completely ignored in the post-Carolingian period. Also rampant in the Church was the sin of simony—the buying or selling of offices or sacraments. Many bishops and even some popes purchased their high positions, and parish priests frequently sold their sacramental services (baptisms, Masses, absolutions of sins, marital blessings) to the people.

The constitution of the Western Church seems to have contributed to this moral breakdown. On the highest level the tradition of lay domination made the king or emperor effective head of the Church in all its temporal affairs. At the local level ecclesiastical offices and lands were largely under lay control. Landlords were considered to own churches built upon their property. They therefore could name the priests who served in them and profit from donations made to them, freely sell the offices they controlled, or distribute Church lands to their relatives and friends. The results were disastrous. The Church was flooded with unworthy men who were little concerned with their spiritual duties, and the pillaging of Church lands and revenues left many clerics without adequate livings. For these, simony was often an essential means of support.

EARLY ATTEMPTS AT REFORM

According to canon law, the bishops bore the chief responsibility for the moral conduct of the clergy. A few reforming bishops in the tenth and eleven centuries tried to suppress clerical marriage and the simony of their priests, but they could make little headway. The powers of a single bishop were perforce limited to his own diocese and to his own lifetime, since he could not name his successor.

Monastic discipline was the focus of a more effective attempt at reform, the center of which was the monastery of Cluny in Burgundy, founded in 910. First, the monastery was placed directly under the pope (neither lay lords nor bishops could interfere in its affairs). While monasteries had formerly been autonomous communities, electing their own abbots and supervising their own affairs, the administration was now centralized under the abbot of Cluny. He retained authority over the many daughter houses his monks had founded or reformed and could visit them at will, freely correcting any abuses. The congregation of Cluny grew with extraordinary rapidity in the eleventh and twelfth centuries until it included no fewer than 1184 houses, which were spread from the British Isles to Palestine.

The restoration of the German Empire in 962 opened another avenue of ecclesiastical reform. Otto I and his successors repeatedly condemned clerical marriage, simony, and the unauthorized usurpation of Church lands. However, in the interests of their own authority, the emperor's actions were limited, as they were not willing to abandon their own traditional control over ecclesiastical offices and lands. Thus, their efforts did not satisfy a growing number of radical reformers who believed that complete freedom of the Church from lay domination was the only means to effect change. To win and defend this liberty, they looked for leadership to the long-degraded office of pope.

PAPAL REFORM

The first of the reforming popes—selected, ironically, by the emperor—was Leo IX (1049–1054). He traveled widely and presided at numerous councils, where he promulgated decrees ordering reforms, summoned suspect bishops, and deposed many of them. He was the first pope to make wide and regular use of papal legates or emissaries, who, like Charlemagne's *missi domin*ici, traveled through Europe, inspecting, reprimanding, and reforming. For the first time lands distant from Rome were subject to the close supervision of the papacy.

Under Pope Nicholas II the movement toward ecclesiastical liberty took several forward strides. By allying himself with the Normans of southern Italy, Nicholas freed the papacy from military dependence on the German Empire. He was the first pope who expressly, if vainly, condemned the practice of "lay investiture"—that is, receiving churches and Church offices from laymen. In 1059 a Roman council reformed papal elections and defined the principles by which popes to this day have been elected.

Tradition required that the pope, like all bishops, be elected by the clergy and people of his diocese. In practice, however, the emperor named him, or in his absence the powerful noble families and factions of Rome did. However, the election procedures set up by the council of 1059 conferred this prerogative upon the cardinals, the chief clergymen associated with the Church at Rome, thereby ensuring that the College of Cardinals, and the reformers who controlled it, could maintain continuity of papal policy. (Even today all cardinals, no matter where they live in the world, hold a titular appointment to a church within the archdiocese of Rome.) Both the emperor and the Roman nobility were simultaneously deprived of one of their strongest powers.

GREGORY VII

The climax of papal reform came with the pontificate of Pope Gregory VII (1073–1085), who brought to his office a high regard for its powers and responsibilities and a burning desire for reform. With regard to Church matters Gregory asserted that the pope wielded absolute authority—that he could at will overrule any local bishop in the exercise of his ordinary or usual jurisdiction. His ideas on the relations of Church and state, however, are less than clear. According to some historians, he believed that all power on earth, including the imperial power, came from the papacy. According to others, Gregory held merely that the normal function of kings was far lower than the sacred authority of popes. This much at least is beyond dispute: Gregory believed that all Christian princes must answer to the pope in spiritually significant matters and that the pope himself had a weighty responsibility to guide them (*see box*, below).

The Investiture Controversy The major collision between the papacy and the Holy Roman Empire that occurred during the pontificate of Gregory VII is traditionally called the *Investiture Controversy*. The name suggests that the principal issue was the practice of great laymen, most notably the emperor, of "investing" bishops with ring and staff, the symbols of their spiritual office. More fundamentally, the struggle revolved around the claims of laymen to dispose of ecclesiastical offices and revenues by their own authority and in their own interests.

At a Roman council in 1075, Gregory, convinced that Emperor Henry IV had no sincere interest in reform, condemned lay investiture and excommunicated some of Henry's advisers. Henry reacted with unexpected fury; he summoned a meeting of imperial bishops and declared Gregory not the true pope but a false monk. Not one to pause in what he thought to be the work of God, Gregory, in turn, excommunicated Henry, deposed him, and freed his subjects from allegiance to him. These acts struck at the fundamental theory of the Christian empire, according to which the emperor was supreme head of the Christian people, responsible only to God.

Gregory's forceful appeal to spiritual power gained remarkable success in Germany. Henry's enemies leagued against him and demanded that

Gregory VII's "Dictates of the Pope"

This papal manifesto, drawn up under Pope Gregory VII's direction in 1075, was intended to guide papal officials in disputes with rulers or with bishops. It represents an extreme claim for papal supremacy both within the Church and within the world, and formed the basis for the papacy's position in the Investiture Controversy.

"1. That the Roman church was established by God alone.

"2. That the Roman pontiff alone is rightly called universal.

"3. That he alone has the power to depose and reinstate bishops.

"4. That his legate, even if he be of lower ecclesiastical rank, presides over bishops in council, and has the power to give sentence of deposition against them.

"7. That he alone has the right, according to the necessity of the occasion, to make new laws, to create new bishoprics, to make a monastery of a chapter of canons and vice versa, and either to divide a rich bishopric or to unite several poor ones.

"9. That all princes shall kiss the foot of the pope alone.

"12. That he has the power to depose emperors.

"13. That he has the right to transfer bishops from one see to another when it becomes necessary.

"14. That he has the right to ordain as a cleric anyone from any part of the church whatsoever.

"16. That no general synod may be called without his order.

"17. That no action of a synod and no book shall be regarded as canonical without his authority.

"18. That his decree can be annulled by no one, and that he can annul the decrees of anyone.

"19. That he can be judged by no one.

"22. That the Roman Church has never erred and will never err to all eternity, according to the testimony of the holy scriptures.

"24. That by his command or permission subjects may accuse their rulers.

"26. That no one can be regarded as catholic who does not agree with the Roman Church.

"27. That he has the power to absolve subjects from their oath of fidelity to wicked rulers."

From Hollister, *Medieval Europe: A Short Source Book* (1992), pp. 183–184.

the emperor be judged before an assembly of lords and prelates to be held at Augsburg in February 1077. They invited Gregory to preside, and he readily accepted. Henry resolved to fight spiritual weapons with spiritual weapons. He slipped across the Alps and intercepted Gregory, then on his way to Germany, at the Apennine castle of Canossa near Modena. He came in the sackcloth of a penitent, radiating contrition, pleading for absolution. Gregory, who doubted the sincerity of the emperor's repentance, refused for three days to receive him, while Henry waited in the snow. Finally, in the face of such persistence, Gregory the suspicious pope had to give way to Gregory the priest, who, like all priests, was obligated to absolve a sinner professing sorrow.

The incident at Canossa is one of the most dramatic events of medieval history. Through the centuries since, the picture of the supreme lay magistrate of Christendom begging forgiveness from the pope has symbolized a victory of spiritual over material power, a triumph of Church over state. The reality was more complex. Henry was the immediate victor. He had divided his opponents and stripped his German enemies of their excuse for rebelling. They named a rival emperor anyway, Rudolf of Swabia, but he was killed in battle in what seemed a divine judgment in Henry's favor. Gregory appears to have become unsure of himself after Canossa. He finally excommunicated Henry a second time in 1080 but was forced to flee Rome at the approach of an imperial army. Gregory died at Salerno in 1085 in apparent bitterness, avowing that his love of justice had brought him only death in exile.

After years of confused struggle pope and emperor settled the Investiture Controversy through the Concordat of Worms in 1122. They agreed that the emperor would no longer invest prelates with the symbols of their spiritual office, and the pope would allow the elections of imperial bishops and abbots to be held in the presence of the emperor or his representative. This clearly permitted the emperor to influence the outcome of elections. In addition, the emperor retained the right of investing prelates with their temporalities—that is, their imperial fiefs. In essence, the great bishops and abbots of the realm would have to be acceptable to both parties—worthy

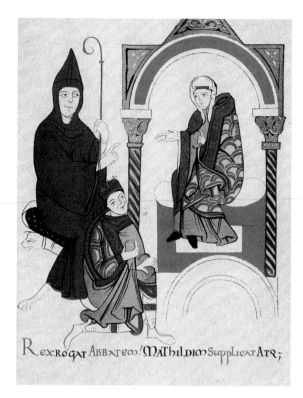

Rexrogat Abbatem / Mathildim Supplicat Atq;

▶ Holy Roman Emperor Henry IV is shown at Canossa on his knees, begging Pope Gregory for readmission to the church. Countess Matilda of Tuscany, a powerful supporter of the pope, appears on the right.

and religious men to please the Church and loyal and capable servants to please the emperor. This agreement at Worms established that major appointments in the Church ought to be made through consultation and compromise.

The Consolidation of Reform   In the twelfth century the popes continued to pursue Gregorian ideals—reform, liberty, and centralization—and to consolidate past advances. In their struggle to be free of lay authority the reformers had insisted that certain persons—such as clerics, widows, orphans, crusaders, and other wards of the Church—should be judged only in ecclesiastical courts and that cases touching on sacrilege, heresy, marriage, testaments, contracts, and the like should also, because of their religious nature, be under ecclesiastical jurisdiction, no matter who the parties might be. A complex system of ecclesiastical courts thus developed according to this premise, and these paralleled and at times rivaled the courts of the kings. Judicial decisions from these ecclesiastical courts could be appealed to Rome.

Legal scholars at this time were compiling and clarifying the canons of the Church—the authoritative statements from the Bible, Church councils, Church fathers, and popes, which constituted the law of the Church. The compilation ultimately recognized as official and binding was the *Decretum*, put together by the Italian jurist Gratian about 1142. With systematic compilations came trained canon lawyers to comment upon, interpret, and apply the law.

Centralization gained in other ways. The popes came to exert a progressively tighter control over the canonization of saints, hitherto a local, informal matter. They also gained a stronger voice in the election of bishops, until finally papal approval was accepted as essential to a valid choice. In papal tithes imposed upon the clergy and in the administration of yearly payments made by many churches to Rome, the outlines of a centralized financial administration appear, though the structures remained rudimentary in the twelfth century.

The reform of the Church in the eleventh and twelfth centuries left an indelible mark on both religious and secular life in the West. The successful establishment of sacerdotal celibacy set the clergy apart from the laity to a degree unknown in the ancient or Eastern Church. At the same time the disputes between Church and state over their respective authority greatly stimulated fruitful speculations on the nature of Christian society. The Gregorian reform was based on the assumption that good men facing an evil world need not timidly flee it; rather, they can and should seek to correct its abuses and bring it closer to what God intended it to be. The reform thus helps mark the emergence of a new faith in human power and in the possible improvement of this present world.

IV. *The Cultural Revival*

The reorganization of European life in the eleventh and twelfth centuries affected institutions of learning and even the direction and methodology

of Western thought. Its impact was notable in vernacular literature and even in art. The Western peoples entered upon a period of high creativity, which marked most forms of cultural expression.

THE RISE OF UNIVERSITIES

During the Central Middle Ages a new institution, the university, came to assume a role in the intellectual life of Europe, a role it has not since relinquished. The university ranks as one of the most influential creations of the medieval world.

Up to about 1050, monastic schools had dominated intellectual development in the West (see Map 8.5). But the monastic devotion to prayer, self-denial, and mystical meditation was not especially favorable to original thought, while the isolation of monasteries restricted the experiences of the monastic scholar and made difficult the exchange of ideas that intellectual progress requires.

Map 8.5 **GREAT MONASTIC CENTERS OF LEARNING**

From about 1050 to 1200, the cathedral, or bishop's, school assumed the intellectual leadership in Europe. Traditionally, bishops had been obliged to provide for the education of their

clergy. From the late eleventh century the growth of cities, the Gregorian emphasis on a trained clergy, the shock of the Investiture Controversy, and the stimulus of a more intimate contact with non-Christian areas all served to revitalize the long-moribund cathedral schools.

The cathedral schools were at first very fluid in their structure. The bishop's secretary, the chancellor, was usually in charge of the school and had the responsibility of inviting learned men, or "masters," to lecture to the students. Both masters and students roamed from town to town, seeking either the best teachers or the brightest (or best-paying) students and the most congenial atmosphere for their work. The twelfth century was the age of the wandering scholars, who have left us charming traces of their spirit or at least that of their more frivolous members in the form of "Goliardic" verses,[1] largely concerned with such unclerical subjects as the joys of wine, women, and song.

Townspeople frequently registered protests with the bishops or with the king against the students, whom they resented because of their boisterous ways and because their clerical status gave them immunity from the local police and courts. Riots involving town and gown were commonplace events. To impose some order on this flux, and to protect young students from incompetent or unorthodox teachers, the twelfth-century cathedral schools gradually insisted that masters possess a certification of their learning. The chan-

▷ **The university as a community of scholars, teachers, and learners was a medieval innovation. Its structure was such that students exercised a degree of control that they rarely possess today. Since there were no salaries, professors relied upon tuition fees for their daily bread, and students could starve out unpopular teachers merely by refusing to attend their classes. However, in other aspects, student life then was much the same as it is today. These scenes from a fifteenth-century manuscript show students gambling, opposing each other in disputations (class debates), and engaging in other activities of dormitory life.**

[1]The exact etymology of the word *Goliardic* remains unknown. It possibly derives from Goliath the Philistine, who was honored as a kind of antisaint by the boisterous students.

cellor awarded this "license to teach," the ancestor of all modern academic degrees.

The throngs of masters and students, many of them strangers to the city where they lectured and studied, eventually grouped themselves into guilds to protect their common interests. It was out of these spontaneously formed guilds of masters and students that the medieval university grew (*universitas* was a widely used Latin word for "guild"). The guild formed by the masters in Paris, for example, received a royal charter about 1200 and sanction from a papal bull in 1231. These documents confirmed the guild's autonomy and powers to license teachers. The University of Paris may thus claim to be the oldest of the northern European universities. From about 1200 we may also date the beginnings of the age of the university in European intellectual life.

The university in Italy sprang from slightly different origins. Even in the Early Middle Ages professional schools for the training of notaries, lawyers, and doctors survived in some Italian cities. The Italian schools, too, seem to have enjoyed rapid growth from the late eleventh century, and growth, in turn, led to the formation of guilds. Here, however, the students rather than the professors constituted the dominant "university." At the oldest of these schools, the University of Bologna, the students regulated discipline, established the fees to be paid to the professors, and determined the hours and even the content of the lectures.

Like all guilds, the university sought to protect and advance its "art" of thought and teaching and to preserve that art over generations through the appropriate training of the young. The ancient world, although it possessed several famous schools, had never developed a university system, in the sense of numerous institutions of higher learning, specifically organized for the pursuit and preservation of learning. The rise of the universities also marks the appearance in Western society of a social class professionally committed to the life of thought and to its transmission to future generations.

SCHOLASTICISM

In its broadest sense, Scholasticism refers to the teaching characteristic of the medieval schools,

▶ **Casket Depicting Grammar, Rhetoric, and Music, ca. 1170**
This chest, made around 1170, is decorated with enamel medallions representing the various courses of study that made up a medieval education: arithmetic, astronomy, dialectic, rhetoric, music, grammar, and natural philosophy.

that is, all the subjects taught in the four major branches of learning or faculties: the arts, canonical and Roman law, medicine, and theology. But in a narrower and perhaps more accurate sense, Scholasticism refers to theology, the medieval "queen of the sciences," in which the character and originality of Scholastic reasoning appear most clearly.

Theology had similarly dominated the monastic thought of the Early Middle Ages, but the monks had largely limited their interests to biblical interpretation, or exegesis. They sought in the sacred Scriptures four traditional levels of meaning (literal, moral, allegorical, and mystical) and wrote voluminous commentaries without constructing a rigorously logical system of theology.

The novelty of Scholasticism was its application of dialectic to Christian theology. Dialectic is the art of analyzing the logical relationships among propositions in a dialogue or discourse. The monastic theologian, through exegesis, wished to discover biblical truth; the Scholastic sought to learn how propositions of faith joined one another within a larger, consistent, and logically forceful theological system.

The first thinker to explore, although still not in rigorous fashion, the theological applications of dialectic was St. Anselm of Canterbury (1033–1109). Anselm defined his own intellectual interests as "faith seeking to understand"—in actuality, faith seeking to find logical consistency among its beliefs. In a work known as the *Proslogium* he tried to show that there is a necessary, logical connection between the traditional Judeo-Christian dogma that God is a perfect being and the dogma that he really exists. A perfect being must possess the perfection of existence. Otherwise, our concept of him would be absurd and unthinkable.

The Scholastic interest in dialectical relationships much resembles Classical Greek thought, with its eagerness to know the "whys" of things, to find order and consistency among statements accepted as true—with the important difference

that the Scholastics initially sought order among propositions presented by faith. (Later they would take further propositions from the ancient pagan philosophers and even, to a limited degree, from their own observations.) From the time of Anselm, Scholastic thought assumed that the human intellect was powerful enough to probe the logical and metaphysical patterns within which even God had to operate.

Abelard Peter Abelard (1079–1142), a second father of Scholasticism, brought a new rigor and popularity to dialectical theology. Abelard came to Paris in the early years of its intellectual growth, and his brilliant teaching helped give that city its reputation as Europe's leading center of philosophical and theological studies.

Abelard's major contribution to the growth of Scholasticism was his book *Sic et Non* ("Yes and No"), the first version of which probably appeared in 1122. Using what became the Classical

Abelard's "Sic et Non"

Completed in 1138, Peter Abelard's Sic et Non *("Yes and No") explained the techniques for reconciling divergent opinions in theology and law. His approach reflects the ambition of Scholasticism to bolster faith through reason.*

"Among the many words of the holy fathers some seem not only to differ from one another but even to contradict one another. . . . Why should it seem surprising if we, lacking the guidance of the holy spirit, fail to understand them?

"Our achievement of understanding is impeded especially by unusual modes of expression and by the different significances that can be attached to one and the same word. We must also take special care that we are not deceived by corruptions of the text or by false attributions when sayings of the [Church] fathers are quoted that seem to differ from the truth or to be contrary to it; for many apocryphal writings are set down under names of saints to enhance their authority, and even the texts of the divine scripture are corrupted by the errors of scribes. If, in scripture, anything

seems absurd, you are not permitted to say, 'The author of this book did not hold the truth,' but rather that the book is defective or that the interpreter erred or that you do not understand. But if anything seems contrary to truth in the works of later authors, the reader or auditor is free to judge, so that he may approve what is pleasing and reject what gives offense, unless the matter is established by certain reason or canonical authority.

"In view of these considerations we have undertaken to collect various sayings of the fathers that give rise to questioning because of their apparent contradictions. Assiduous and frequent questioning is indeed the first key to wisdom. For by doubting we come to inquiry; and through inquiring we perceive the truth."

From Tierney, *Sources of Medieval History*, pp. 172–175.

method of Scholastic argumentation, the posing of formal questions and the citation of authorities on both sides, Abelard assembled 150 theological questions. For each question he marshaled authorities from the Bible, Church councils, and Church fathers. In every case there was conflict. He made no effort to reconcile the discrepancies but left the authorities standing in embarrassing juxtaposition. His method was an ingenious retort to those who maintained that dialectic could make no contribution to Christian theology and that it was enough to hold fast to the ancient writings. *Sic et Non* implied that one must either enlist dialectic to reconcile the conflicts or concede that the faith was a tissue of contradictions (*see box*, p. 240).

In the early phases of the medieval intellectual revival, dialectic had to contend for supremacy with humanistic studies, which emphasized familiarity with the Classical authors and the ability to appreciate and write good Latin. Chartres, a small cathedral town near Paris, was the center of this twelfth-century humanism. But by the end of the century dialectic, as cultivated at Paris, predominated partly because it seemed to offer to the inquisitive men of the twelfth century a certain avenue to truth and a sound means for organizing the truths they had inherited. Another reason Scholastic dialectic could become dominant was that after the middle of the twelfth century, translators working chiefly in Spain and Sicily introduced European scholars to hitherto unknown works of Aristotle, as well as to the great commentary that the Muslim Averroës had written on them. Christian thinkers now had at their disposal the full Aristotelian corpus, and it confronted them with a thoroughly naturalistic and rationalistic philosophical system. Aristotle's philosophy was built on reason alone, and his assumptions drove Western scholars to examine his works and their own faith through dialectic. The difficult task of reconciling Aristotelian reason and nature with Christian revelation and divine grace remained the central philosophical problem of the thirteenth century.

VERNACULAR LITERATURE

Scholasticism reflected the cultural interests of only a small group of intellectuals in medieval society. What the broader masses of the people valued can be found in vernacular literature. Here, too, the themes treated and characters described largely reflect the life of the nobility, not that of the common people. But there is much reason to believe that this literature, or some oral version of it, was appreciated well beyond aristocratic circles. Townsmen and even peasants seem to have delighted in hearing of the doings of the great.

Of the vernacular literatures of Europe only Anglo-Saxon possesses a substantial number of surviving writings that antedate the year 1000. For most of the major languages of Europe an abundant tradition of literary work dates only from the eleventh and twelfth centuries. In forming the literary tastes of Europe, the Romance tongues (the vernacular languages descended from Latin) achieved a particular importance, especially the two great dialects of France, the langue d'oïl spoken north of the Loire River and the langue d'oc, or Provençal, used in the south. Castilian was slightly later in producing an important literature in Spain, and Italian, perhaps because of its similarity to Latin, did not emerge as a major literary language until the late thirteenth century.

There were three principal genres of vernacular literature: the heroic epic, troubadour lyric poetry, and the courtly romance. Heroic epics have survived in great abundance. The oldest and probably the best of them is the *Song of Roland*, which was composed in the langue d'oïl probably in the last quarter of the eleventh century. The subject of the poem is the ambush of the rear guard of Charlemagne's army under the command of Roland by the Basques at Roncesvalles in 778, but poetic imagination (or perhaps older legend) transformed this minor Frankish setback into a major event in the war against Islam.

With fine psychological discernment the poem examines the character of Roland. The qualities that make him a hero, his dauntless courage and uncompromising pride, are at war with the qualities required of a good vassal—obedience, loyalty, cooperation, and common sense. Roland is in serious danger but refuses for reasons of personal dignity to sound his horn in time for Charlemagne to return and save him and his men. By the time his pride relents and he does blow the horn, their deaths are ensured. The sensitive examination of the conflict between Roland's thoughtless if heroic individualism and the demands of the new feudal order gives this poem its stature as the first masterpiece of French letters.

The Troubadours   Very different from the heroic epic is troubadour lyric poetry, initially written in the langue d'oc of the south. The novelty of this complex poetry is its celebration of women and of love. The heroic epic was written for the thoroughly masculine society of the battle camp. The troubadours sang at courts, in which women exerted a powerful influence. In a mobile age, when knights and nobles would be away for long periods on crusades and wars, their mothers, wives, and daughters administered their house-

▶ HÉLOÏSE AND ABELARD, FROM *ROMAN DE LA ROSE*

Already a famous professor in Paris, Abelard began a secret relationship with Héloïse, and in revenge her relatives had him castrated. The two were then separated for decades, and their correspondence remains one of the most powerful human documents of medieval times. Despite the conventions of the day, Héloïse was clearly an equal partner in the relationship, as is indicated in this fifteenth-century depiction of the pair engaged in intense discussion.

▶ ARTHUR IN BATTLE

Legend had it that anyone who found the Holy Grail, a cup from which Christ was reputed to have drunk, would achieve eternal happiness. In medieval romances this story became a metaphor for a chivalrous search for perfection. In this miniature from Robert de Boron's thirteenth-century *History of the Grail*, King Arthur—the only figure whose face we can see—battles 10 rebel kings during his quest.

holds and estates and achieved considerable social prominence. The women became the arbiters of what constituted "courtly manners"—proper behavior—in their households, and they surely influenced the literature that was heard within their walls.

The troubadour usually addressed a lady of superior social station, almost always someone else's wife, whom he had little chance of winning. Although she was not a likely means of sensual gratification, love for her did offer a hope for inward consolation; it could, if returned, elevate the poet's spirits and transform his world to eternal spring. Courtly love (at least as the troubadours present it) was not a dalliance but quite literally a way of salvation, a means of rescuing the lover from despondency and introducing him into an earthly paradise. This discovery and intensive exploration of the emotion of love represents one of the most influential creations of the medieval mind.

The courtly romance, which entered its great age after 1150, combines traits of both heroic epic and troubadour lyric poetry. It is narrative in form like the epic; but, like Provençal poetry, it allots a major role to women and love. Chrétien de Troyes, whose works probably date from shortly before 1182, is the author of the oldest surviving romances, those about King Arthur of Britain and his coterie of knights. Many of these tales are concerned with an analysis of the tensions that love, the rebellious emotion, creates in society. Western letters have since endlessly explored this theme.

ROMANESQUE ART

The conventional term used to describe the architectural and artistic style of this period is *Romanesque*. It means "of Roman origins" but is, like many terms applied to the Middle Ages, misleading. Artists in the Central Middle Ages did imitate Classical models, but not exclusively; they also drew on nearly every other artistic tradition to which they had access—barbarian, Byzantine, and Arab.

The proliferation of castles across the face of Europe stimulated the development of new techniques of construction. These fortresses were built on a progressively larger scale, in contrast to the castles of the Carolingian Age, and by the thirteenth century, builders were working entirely in stone. Crusaders returning from the East brought with them new concepts of fortress design and perhaps also a desire to render castle life more gracious. The crafting of tapestries, furniture, and glass benefited from the new importance of cities, the strength of markets, and the growing number of artisans. Although life about 1200 was still remarkably crude even for the rich, it was clearly becoming less so.

Art, however, remained in most of its forms the servant of the Church. The religious reform in the eleventh century brought with it a liturgical revival. The monks of the Cluniac monasteries were especially devoted to (and occasionally criticized for) sumptuous religious services. Liturgical needs stimulated the art of metalwork (which produced chalices and other sacred vessels), glassmaking, and the weaving of fine fabrics for the priests' vestments. Music, too, advanced. The Gregorian chant (named for Pope

▶ **PISA CATHEDRAL, CA. 1063–1272**
One of the finest architectural ensembles in the new Romanesque styles of the eleventh and twelfth centuries is the cathedral and its surrounding buildings in Pisa, Italy. Although the famous leaning tower, which is now slowly being restored to the vertical, is the best known of these buildings, the huge marble-clad cathedral was in fact regarded as the supreme achievement of the Pisans and was widely influential in church building throughout Italy.

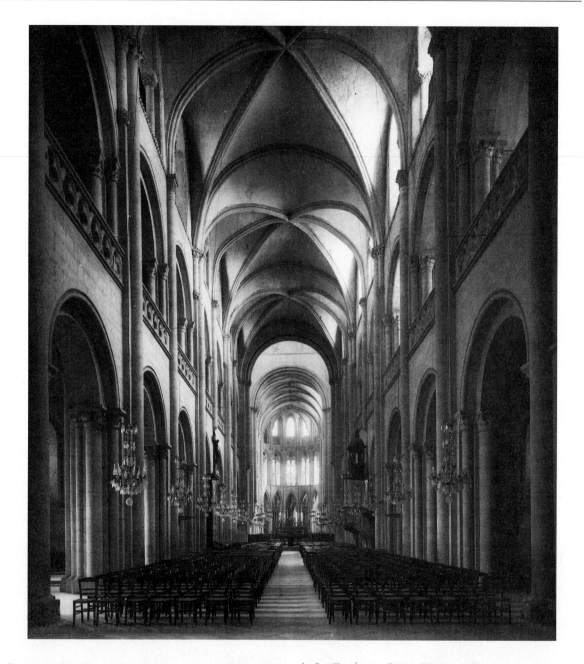

Gregory the Great, but in fact representing the traditional plainsong of the Church of Rome) had become established as the common music of the Western Church in the Carolingian epoch. The eleventh and twelfth centuries witnessed the development of polyphonic music (part-singing). The coordination of the vocal parts in choral music also required systems of musical notation. A monk named Guido d'Arezzo is credited with giving names to the notes.

▶ St. Etienne, Caen, Vaults, ca. 1115–1120
St. Etienne, Caen, was begun by William the Conqueror in 1067 and is considered a superb example of Norman Romanesque architecture. It was originally supposed to have a wooden roof, but it was vaulted in stone between 1115 and 1120. Each section of the roof was held up by six ribs that met at the center and two arches, all of which rested on pillars at the side of the nave. The resultant pattern added to the sense of height and drew the eye ever upward toward heaven.

The most impressive artistic monuments left to us from the Romanesque period are the churches themselves. In engineering, the great achievement of the Central Middle Ages was the roofing of churches in stone. From about the year 1000, small stone-roofed churches began to appear, especially in southern Europe. At first the builders used the simple barrel, or tunnel, vault, but this design did not allow for windows because the roof would collapse if holes were put into the supporting sides of the tunnel. Engineers then developed and mastered the use of the groin vault, which is formed by the intersection of two barrel vaults. The area of intersection is called the bay, and the roof over the bay is supported at four points, not by the entire length of the lateral walls. Bays could be built next to bays, an entire church could be roofed with stone, windows could be easily cut, and the monotony of tunnel vaulting would be avoided.

Romanesque churches were decorated on the exterior with stone sculpture. Monumental sculpture had been a dead technique in the West since the end of the Roman Empire. Romanesque statues, which exist by the thousands, show a marked quality of antirealism, a refusal to allow visual accuracy to dominate portrayals. The artists were striving to present a world as seen by faith. Christ, for example, had to be shown larger than others, in keeping with his dignity. Demons and monsters, many drawn from the popular imagination, abound in Romanesque sculpture. While similar to Byzantine portrayals in its antirealism, Romanesque style, unlike the Byzantine, overflows with movement, tension, excitement, and the spirit of mystical exhilaration. Romanesque statuary documents the exuberant spirit of this age of reform and crusades, when people seemed convinced that God was actively at work among them, setting right the world.

▶ **TYMPANUM OF SOUTH PORTAL OF ST. PIERRE, MOISSAC, CA. 1115–1135**
The revival of sculpture is one of the noteworthy achievements of Romanesque art. Integrating architecture and sculpture, this tympanum (the semicircular space above a church portal) shows the Second Coming of Christ, attended by symbols of the evangelists and the kings of the world seated in rows divided by stylized clouds.

The eleventh and twelfth centuries were vigorously creative at every level of European life. By 1200 Europe was very different from the old, or "first," Europe of Charlemagne. Its economy was more diversified and productive, its society more complex, its government more effective, its religion more sensitive, and its thought and art more original and daring. But the very innovations of the age posed severe problems for European society. How could the new forms of economic endeavor be reconciled with the older hostility and suspicion toward a life of buying and selling? How could the rising power of monarchs be reconciled with the self-consciousness and self-interest of the nobility, reformed Church, and privileged towns? How could the new confidence in human reason and in nature, reinforced by familiarity with Aristotle, be synthesized with the older notions that nature was corrupt, human beings weak, and the afterlife the only hope? From about 1200 the West was trying to consolidate its recent advances and bring them into harmony with its older heritage. This effort at consolidation, reconciliation, and synthesis is the theme of Western history in the thirteenth century.

Recommended Reading

▼

Sources

Anselm of Canterbury. *Basic Writings: Proslogium, Monologium, Gaunilon's On Behalf of the Fool, Cur Deus Homo.* S. W. Deane (tr.). 1962.

Chrétien de Troyes. *Yvain, The Knight of the Lion.* Burton Raffel (tr.). 1987. Recent translation of a great French romance.

Douglas, David C. (ed.). *English Historical Documents.* 1955. The largest available collection of translated sources bearing on English history.

Duby, Georges (ed.). *The Legend of Bouvines. War, Religion, and Culture in the Middle Ages.* Catherine Tihanyi (tr.). 1989. An anthology of contemporary and recent depictions of the great battle, with a commentary that sets the event and the legends in their cultural context.

Fitzneale, Richard. *The Course of the Exchequer.* Charles Johnson (tr.). 1950.

*Herlihy, David (ed.). *The History of Feudalism.* 1971.

John of Salisbury. *The Statesmen's Book.* John Dickinson (tr.). 1963.

Matthew Paris. *Chronicles. Monastic Life in the Thirteenth Century.* Richard Vaughan (ed.). 1984. Excerpts from an English chronicler with a worldview; a superb perspective on medieval monastic mentalities.

Oderic Vitalis. *The Ecclesiastical History.* Marjorie Chibnall (tr.). 1969–1980. Latin and English texts of a prolific Anglo-Norman monastic chronicler.

Studies

Baldwin, John W. *The Government of Philip Augustus. Foundations of French Royal Power in the Middle Ages.* 1986. A mature look at the great French king.

Barlow, Frank. *Thomas Becket.* 1986. Balanced biography of the martyred archbishop.

Boswell, John. *Christianity, Social Tolerance and Homosexuality in Western Europe from the Beginning of the Christian Era to the Fourteenth Century.* 1980. A long and learned survey of the treatment of homosexuals in medieval Europe.

Brundage, James. *Law, Sex, and Christian Society in Medieval Europe.* 1987. Encyclopedic survey of the sexual and marital legislation of the Western Church.

*Bynum, Caroline Walker. *Holy Feast and Holy Fast: The Religious Significance of Food to Medieval Women.* 1987. The mystical meanings of women's food consumption in the Middle Ages.

Chenu, M. D. *Nature, Man, and Society in the Twelfth Century.* Jerome Taylor and Lester K. Little (trs.). 1968. Seminal essays on twelfth-century thought by a French Dominican.

Chibnall, Marjorie. *Anglo-Norman England, 1066–1166.* 1987.

———. *The World of Oderic Vitalis.* 1984. The cultural world of the Anglo-Norman historian.

Chrimes, Stanley B. *An Introduction to the Administrative History of Medieval England.* 1966. Clear and authoritative.

Cowdrey, H. E. J. *Popes, Monks and Crusaders.* 1984. Collected essays.

*Available in paperback.

Dillard, Heath. *Women of the Reconquest. Women in Castilian Town Society, 1100–1300.* 1984. The status of women on the Spanish frontier, chiefly based on legal materials.

*Douglas, David C. *William the Conqueror: The Norman Impact upon England.* 1966. Outstanding among many biographies.

Duby, Georges. *The Chivalrous Society.* Cynthia Postan (tr.). 1977. Essays on feudal society by a prominent French medievalist.

———. *The Knight, the Lady and the Priest. The Making of Modern Marriage in Medieval France.* 1983.

*Dunbabin, Jean. *France in the Making, 843–1100.* 1987. From Carolingian to Capetian France.

Ennen, Edith. *The Medieval Town.* Natalie Fryde (tr.). 1979. By a German historian, now the best introductory survey available in English.

*Fawtier, Robert. *The Capetian Kings of France: Monarchy and Nation, 987–1328.* Lionel Butler and R. J. Adams (trs.). 1962.

Ferruolo, Stephen C. *The Origins of the University: The School of Paris and Their Critics, 1100–1215.* 1985. The universities as embodiments of a new educational ideal.

*Ganshof, François. *Feudalism.* P. Grierson (tr.). 1961. Standard introduction to feudal institutions.

Gold, Penny Schine. *The Lady and the Virgin: Image, Attitude and Experience in Twelfth Century France.* 1985. Women in image and reality.

Hallam, Elizabeth M. *Domesday Book through Nine Centuries.* 1986. The making, the uses, and the subsequent history of the great survey.

*Haskins, Charles H. *The Renaissance of the Twelfth Century.* 1927. A classic study.

*———. *The Rise of Universities.* 1957.

*Herlihy, David. *Medieval Households.* 1985.

*Kirshner, Jules, and Suzanne Wemple (eds.). *Women of the Medieval World.* 1986. Collected essays.

Poly, Jean-Pierre, and Eric Bournazel. *The Feudal Transformation, 900–1200.* 1990.

Reilly, Bernard F. *The Kingdom of Léon-Castilla under Alfonso VI, 1065–1109.* 1988.

*Southern, Richard W. *The Making of the Middle Ages.* 1955. Classic essay on twelfth-century culture.

*Tellenbach, Gerd. *Church, State and Christian Society at the Time of the Investiture Contest.* R. F. Bennett (tr.). 1970. Fine analysis of the issues involved in the Investiture Controversy.

GOD AS ARCHITECT OF THE UNIVERSE
The notion of God creating the universe as an architect was common during the Middle Ages. In this manuscript illumination, God is depicted holding a compass and literally measuring the structure of the physical world.

CHAPTER NINE

THE SUMMER
OF THE MIDDLE AGES

T

HE thirteenth century (or, more precisely, the period between about 1200 and the Black Death of 1348 and 1349) has been traditionally considered the summer of the Middle Ages. It can claim many impressive achievements: a largely prosperous economy, which supported more people than Europe possessed at any other time during the Middle Ages; reasonably effective systems of government in the feudal monarchies; parliamentary institutions; Gothic cathedrals; the great works of Scholastic philosophy and theology; and the *Divine Comedy* of Dante Alighieri, one of the great masterpieces of Western literature. Moreover, these products of medieval genius seem to share a certain spirit: a sense of logic and order and a serene confidence, not only in divine grace and faith but also in human reason and effort. Thirteenth-century men and women believed that God had created a harmonious world and that they could describe its ordered structure in their philosophy, imitate it in their art, and use this knowledge to guide their earthly lives.

Today, as research probes ever deeper, we know that these favorable impressions of the era are not entirely accurate. Thirteenth-century society was less placid than the smiles of Gothic angels urge their admirers to believe. The population may have grown too large to be supported by available resources, and this may have been an important factor in provoking the plagues and famines that occurred beginning in the mid-fourteenth century. The prosperity of the rich often rested on the rampant misery of the poor; the aspirations toward a united and peaceful Europe did not dispel the specter of war; the status of Jews in the West deteriorated; and Scholastic theology did not quench the flames of intellectual and religious revolt. In sum, medieval society in the thirteenth century could not achieve permanent solutions to the many problems it confronted. But this ultimate failure should not prevent us from recognizing the accomplishments of the people of this era. They strove to build both an ordered society and ordered systems of thought, in which conflicts, social or intellectual, would be reconciled.

I. Economic Expansion

▼

Population growth, land reclamations, and the expansion of external frontiers continued in the thirteenth century, though at a slackening pace after about 1250. Regional specialization in agricultural production also grew more pronounced. Southwest France (Gascony), for example, exported wine in large quantities to England and northern Europe. England itself, and soon Spain, supplied raw wool to the busy textile towns of Flanders and Italy. Peripheral areas—the Baltic lands beyond the Elbe River, Catalonia, Sicily, even parts of the Eastern Empire—delivered wheat to the more crowded central zones. Owners of agricultural land surrounding the towns usually devoted their fields to market farming. By raising what the natural endowment of their regions most favored, cultivators thus worked more productively. As peasants competed for land and workers for jobs, however, rents increased and wages fell while the profits of landowners and employers rose. In increasing measure, the prosperity of the propertied and business classes was coming to rest upon the deprivation and misery of the humble.

THE CITIES

Dramatic economic changes were also occurring in the cities.[1] Large-scale production, extensive trade, complex commercial and banking institutions, and the amassing of great fortunes became the commonplace features of urban economic and social life. Florence in 1252 began issuing gold florins—the first successful gold coinage in the West since ancient times. These urban centers pioneered many of the methods and show much of the spirit of modern business enterprises.

Medieval towns developed a new system of producing goods. With the exception of mines,

---

[1] We must, of course, recognize that the populations of towns everywhere in Europe remained small in comparison with the rural population. The largest medieval city seems to have been Paris, with a population of perhaps 210,000 in 1328. Few towns surpassed 40,000. In England in the fourteenth century only about 10 percent of the population lived in cities. In Flanders and certain regions of Italy, that figure may have reached 25 percent, but these areas were exceptions.

construction sites, and such enterprises as the arsenal in Venice, most work was performed in the home or in small shops; little use was made of power, and there were no factories. Increased efficiency was achieved through finely dividing the process of production and through developing highly specialized skills. A merchant or manufacturer acquired the raw material, gave (or "put") it out in sequence to specialized artisans, and then sold the finished products. Usually called the *putting-out system*, this method of production remained characteristic of the Western economy until the Industrial Revolution of the late eighteenth century.

Wool Cloth Production The making of woolen cloth, the largest industry of the medieval town, well illustrates the complex character of thirteenth-century manufacturing. The raw wool—often coming from England, Spain, or North Africa—was first prepared by sorters, beaters, and washers. Then the cleaned and graded wool was carded, or combed. The next task, the spinning, was usually done by women who worked in their own homes with a distaff, a small stick to hold the wool, and a spindle, a weight to spin and twist the strands into thread. The spinning wheel, apparently first invented in Italy in the late thirteenth century, added speed and better quality to thread making.

Weavers, almost always men, wove the thread into broadcloths that were 30 yards in length and might contain 2000 to 3000 warp (lengthwise) threads. The cloth was then fulled—that is, washed and worked with special earths that caused the wool to mat. This was arduous work and was often done at a water-driven fulling mill. The giant cloth was then stretched on a frame, so that it would dry properly and shrink evenly. Next, the dry cloth was rubbed with teasels to raise the nap, and the nap was then carefully cut. Several times repeated, this last operation gave the cloth a smooth, almost silky finish, but it was extremely delicate work; one slip of the scissors could ruin the cloth and the large investment it represented. At various stages in this process the wool could be dyed—whether as unspun wool, thread, or woven cloth. Medieval people loved bright colors, and dyers used a great variety of animal, vegetable, and mineral dyes and special earths, such as alum, to fix the colors.

The medieval woolen industry thus came to employ a large, diversified labor force, which worked materials brought from all corners of the known world. Capital and labor were sharply divided; a few great entrepreneurs controlled huge masses of capital. In Florence in about 1300, the number of wool shops ranged between 200 and 300; they produced between 80,000 and 100,000 big broadcloths with a value surpassing 1.2 million gold florins. Over 30,000 persons earned their living from this industry.

THE GUILDS

To defend and promote their interests in a world still ruled by warriors and priests, the merchants and master artisans took to forming associations of self-help known as *guilds*. The first guilds were organized by merchants and appear about 1000. By the twelfth century both master artisans and

▶ YPRES GUILD HALL, CA. 1260–1380
The Flemish towns were renowned for their textiles, and the economic importance of this manufacture is reflected by the size of the thirteenth-century cloth hall at Ypres (destroyed in World War I). Rows of arched windows and a central tower puncture the massive square edifice that functioned as the headquarters of the guild, as well as the place where goods were marketed.

merchants in special trades—for example, dealers in wool, spices, or silk—had organized their own independent guilds. A large industrial town such as Florence had more than 50 professional guilds.

Once a year the guild members met in their church or hall to elect permanent officials, or *consuls*. The consuls enforced the statutes, adjudicated disputes among the members, administered the properties of the guild, and supervised its expenditures. Equally important, the consuls regulated the methods of production in their trade in order to maintain the quality of the product and to protect the members from unfair competition. To this end they restricted the number of working hours and the number of employees that could be hired by any single master. Guilds might also aid those members who lost goods through fire or flood, and they supported the widows and educated the orphaned children of their deceased members. Banquets, public processions, and religious ceremonies enriched the social life of the membership. Many guilds assumed a further responsibility for the beauty and welfare of their town. They were among the principal donors to hospitals and charities, and they usually built and maintained their own church, or at least a chapel in the city cathedral.

One of the chief features of the guilds was the

apprenticeship system. The guilds stipulated what the apprentice had to be taught and what proof of skill he had to present to be admitted into the brotherhood of the trade, how long he had to work and learn in the shop of the master, and what the master had to give him by way of

▶ ITALIAN GRAIN MERCHANTS
This manuscript illustration shows Florentine grain merchants engaged in their trade and keeping their records in their shops. The manuscript itself noted the prices for grain between 1320 and 1335 that were set in the Or San Michele, the grain warehouse and market hall in Florence.

lodging, food, and pocket money. If, after finishing his training, the apprentice was too inexperienced or poor to open his own shop, he could work as a paid laborer, or journeyman, in the shop of an established master. By carefully saving his wages, the apprentice might eventually become a master in his own right and a member of the guild, but most medieval artisans continued to work as salaried laborers for their entire lives.

Only rarely did girls serve as apprentices, but Paris had five guilds composed exclusively or predominantly of women. Most wives and daughters helped their husbands and fathers in their labors. Many widows continued in their own name the trade of their deceased husbands. Women's contribution to the town economy was less visible than men's, but no less essential.

In protecting commercial skills under difficult conditions, offering a measure of insurance and social security to their members, and promoting education, the guilds played a crucial role in forming an environment favorable to commerce and manufacture.

BUSINESS INSTITUTIONS

The growth of trade and manufacturing stimulated the development of sophisticated commercial institutions. Christian ethics traditionally condemned the taking of usury (which then meant any interest or profit on a loan, however tiny); therefore, the medieval business community developed alternative instruments of credit.

Most important for properly commercial purposes was the bill of exchange, in essence a loan, but one that required repayment at a specified time in another place and currency. Thus a Florentine might borrow 100 pounds in Florence and agree to repay three months later in local money at a Champagne fair. He then bought goods in Florence, sold them in Champagne, and repaid the money. The rate of exchange between the currencies almost always concealed a substantial profit for the investor, but technically, he earned it for changing money, not for making the loan.

Partnerships and business associations were another important means of recruiting capital. At Venice, Genoa, and Pisa, overseas ventures were most often financed through special temporary partnerships. In its simplest form, an investor, leave their inheritance undivided and to trade together as a single company. By the thirteenth century such companies commonly included as partners persons who were not blood relatives but who could contribute capital and services, and they also accepted deposits from nonpartners in return for fixed yearly payments of interest that were called "gifts," lest they be considered usurious.

These companies performed a wide variety of functions and grew in size. They traded in any product that promised a profit, wrote bills of exchange, and fulfilled other banking services. From the late twelfth century they served the Roman Curia as papal bankers and were largely responsible for building and maintaining the financial system of the medieval papacy. They were also drawn into the risky business of extending loans to prelates and princes.

The most famous of such loans were those that the Bardi and Peruzzi Companies extended to King Edward III of England to fund the Hundred Years' War. The companies loaned approximately 900,000 and 600,000 florins, respectively, in 1338, to their eventual regret, as the English crown defaulted in 1342, leaving both companies bankrupt.

MEDIEVAL VIEWS OF ECONOMIC LIFE

The thinkers of the thirteenth century were coming to new and more favorable, if not exactly enthusiastic, views concerning wealth. Until then, the Church fathers had taught that difference in wealth in human society was a necessary evil arising out of sin. Sin had aroused concupiscence or greed and threatened to make social life a "war of all against all." Private property, defended by the power of the state, restrained greed and promoted peace. In contrast, Thomas Aquinas, the great thirteenth-century theologian, based his principal argument for private property on the practical advantages it supplied. Private property, he argued, provided incentive, ensured good care of belongings, and promoted peace and order. He thus gave property and wealth more dignity than the thinkers of an earlier age had accorded them.

Even commercial wealth was losing some of its ancient taint. As late as about 1150, canon lawyers had quoted with approval the aphorism that

▶ WOMAN SELLING POULTRY
Women worked at many trades during the Middle Ages. They contributed significantly to luxury crafts such as silk spinning and weaving, but they were also a major presence in the marketplace selling such items as bread, beer, and poultry.

who remained at home, gave a sum of money to a merchant traveling abroad in return for a share of the eventual profits (usually three-quarters); the investor bore the entire loss if the ship sank or the venture failed. The partnership lasted only for the length of the specified voyage.

In the inland Italian towns a more permanent kind of partnership developed known as the *compagnia* (literally, "bread together," a sharing of bread). These earliest companies seem to have been partnerships among brothers. The sons of a deceased merchant, for example, might decide to "rarely or never can a merchant be saved." By the thirteenth century, preachers in commercial cities were eloquently comparing merchants to Christ. After all, they, like Christ, lived by peaceful enterprise and not by violence. Nevertheless, the rich man could not use his wealth as his personal inclinations might dictate. Property could be private in possession, but it had to be used to promote the common good. The individual, in other words, was morally obligated to use his wealth to benefit the entire community, not just himself.

II. The States of Europe

Through its practices and institutions the thirteenth-century European economy acquired a more stable structure. Governments, too, were moving toward a new level of stability. Great laws helped define and fix governmental and legal procedures. They thus served to implant in the West a strong tradition of constitutionalism, a lasting belief that people should be governed by fixed and known procedures. The thirteenth century made one other lasting contribution to Western political development: the representative assembly. European princes extended to the great estates, or classes, of society—namely, the clergy, nobility, and eventually even the townsmen—the opportunity to hear and approve the major decisions of government. To make this participation possible, parliaments or assemblies of estates came to assume a recognized if still humble place among the institutions of government.

ENGLAND

At the death of Henry II in 1189, the English monarchy wielded exceptional authority, but neither in practice nor in theory was it clearly established within what limits, if any, royal powers should operate, or how, if at all, the great men of the realm might participate in government.

Henry's son and successor was Richard I, the Lion-Hearted. Although Richard had all the virtues of a model knight—boldness, military skill, stately bearing, even a flair for composing troubadour lyrics—he had none of the attributes of a good king. He loved battles and shunned conferences. In 1191 and 1192 he was off fighting in the Holy Land on the Third Crusade (see Chapter 10). Chivalry, which gave him his reputation, also took his life. He died in 1199 from a neglected wound received while besieging a castle in a minor war in southern France. Richard's presence in England was restricted to two visits, lasting less than 10 months, but the English government continued to function efficiently even in the absence of its chief—testimony to its fundamental strength.

Richard was succeeded by his younger brother John, who, rightly or wrongly, is considered a wicked king (significantly, no other English monarch has borne the name). While the towns and the common people supported him, he gratuitously antagonized his powerful subjects by his insolence and capricious cruelty. His reign is largely a record of humiliations suffered at the hands of the pope, Philip II of France, and his own barons.

In 1206 John brazenly tried to make a worthless favorite archbishop of Canterbury. The clergy of Canterbury appealed to Pope Innocent III, who selected for the office the learned, pious, and popular Stephen Langton. To force John to acquiesce, Innocent laid England under interdict in 1208. The interdict was a command to the English Church to go on strike. Priests were not to baptize babies, marry couples, or bury the dead in public ceremony. Parish bells were silenced, and the rhythm of life must have changed across England. But the Church's strike did not sway John at all. Only when he wanted papal support in his war against the French over the loss of Normandy did he finally submit in 1213. After his defeat by the French at Bouvines in 1214, John had to reap the bitter harvest that his long years of misrule at home and failures abroad had sown.

Magna Carta To meet the extraordinary expenses of war, the English kings had traditionally requested, and almost always received, special aids or contributions from their barons. But after Bouvines, when John's policies proved to be disastrous, the enraged barons refused further help. Encouraged by the Church, they took to arms. Their resistance was successful, and in June 1215

Excerpts from "Magna Carta"

"John, by the grace of God, king of England, lord of Ireland, duke of Normandy and Aquitaine, and count of Anjou, to the archbishops, bishops, abbots, earls, barons, justiciars, foresters, sheriffs, stewards, servants, and to all his bailiffs and faithful subjects, greetings. Know that we, out of reverence for God and for the salvation of our soul and those of all our ancestors and heirs, for the honour of God and the exaltation of the holy church, and for the reform of our realm . . . :

"[12] No scutage or aid shall be imposed in our kingdom unless by common counsel of our kingdom, except for ransoming our person, for making our eldest son a knight, and for once marrying our eldest daughter; and for these only a reasonable aid shall be levied. Be it done in like manner concerning aids from the city of London.

"[13] And the city of London shall have all its ancient liberties and free customs as well by land as by water. Furthermore, we will and grant that all other cities, boroughs, towns, and ports shall have all their liberties and free customs.

"[20] A free man shall not be amerced [subjected to a discretionary punishment] for a trivial offense except in accordance with the degree of the offense, and for a grave offense he shall be amerced in accordance with its gravity, yet saving his way of living; and a merchant in the same way, saving his stock-in-trade; and a villein shall be amerced in the same way, saving his means of livelihood—and none of the aforesaid amercements shall be imposed except by the oath of good men of the neighborhood.

"[21] Earls and barons shall not be amerced except by their peers, and only in accordance with the degree of the offense. . . .

"[30] No sheriff, or bailiff of ours, or anyone else shall take the horses or carts of any freeman for transport work save with the agreement of that freeman.

"[31] Neither we nor our bailiffs will take, for castles or other works of ours, timber which is not ours, except with the agreement of him whose timber it is.

"[38] No bailiff shall in future put anyone to trial upon his own bare word, without reliable witnesses produced for this purpose.

"[39] No free man shall be arrested or imprisoned or disseised or outlawed or exiled or in any way victimized, neither will we attack him or send anyone to attack him, except by the lawful judgment of his peers or by the law of the land.

"[54] No one shall be arrested or imprisoned upon the appeal of a woman for the death of anyone except her husband.

"[40] To no one will we sell, to no one will we refuse or delay right or justice.

"[52] If anyone has been disseised of or kept out of his lands, castles, franchises or his right by us without the legal judgment of his peers, we will immediately restore them to him: and if a dispute arises over this, then let it be decided by the judgment of the twenty-five barons who are mentioned below in the clause for securing the peace. . . .

"[61] . . . the barons shall choose any twenty-five barons of the kingdom they wish, who must with all their might observe, hold and cause to be observed, the peace and liberties which we have granted and confirmed to them by this present charter of ours, so that if we, or our justiciar, or our bailiffs or any one of our servants offend in any way against anyone or transgress any of the articles of the peace or the security, and the offense be notified to four of the aforesaid twenty-five barons, those four barons shall come to us, or to our justiciar if we are out of the kingdom, and, laying the transgression before us, shall petition us to have that transgression corrected without delay. And if we do not correct the transgression . . . within forty days . . . , the aforesaid four barons shall refer that case to the rest of the twenty-five barons. And those twenty-five barons together with the community of the whole land shall distrain and distress us in every way they can . . . until, in their opinion, amends have been made; and when amends have been made, they shall obey us as they did before."

at Runnymede the barons forced John to grant them the "Great Charter" (Magna Carta) of liberties, which was probably inspired, if not largely composed, by Archbishop Langton. The Magna Carta resembled oaths that English kings since Henry I had taken upon their coronation; it obligated the king to respect certain rights of his subjects. But no previous royal charter of liberties equaled it in length, explicitness, and influence (*see box*, p. 255).

The Magna Carta disappoints most modern readers. Unlike the American Declaration of Independence it offers no grand generalizations about human dignity and rights. Its 63 clauses, arranged without apparent order, are largely concerned with technical problems of feudal law—rights of inheritance, feudal relief, wardship, and the like. But it did establish, more clearly than any previous document, that the king ought not to disturb the estates of the realm—Church, barons, and all free subjects—in the peaceful exercise of their customary liberties. It thus guaranteed to the clergy the freedom to elect bishops and to make appeals to Rome, protected the barons against arbitrary exactions of traditional feudal dues, and confirmed for the men of London and other towns "all their liberties and free customs." To all freemen it promised access to justice and judgment by known procedures. Finally, the king could impose new taxes only with the common consent of the realm. While these concessions were certainly significant, the Magna Carta addressed the concerns of only the elite. The rights of the unfree classes, the serfs and villeins who constituted 80 percent of the population, are hardly mentioned.

The Magna Carta marked a major step toward constitutionalism, that is, toward government by recognized procedures that could be changed only with the consent of the realm. Of course, the barons and the bishops never anticipated that subjects other than themselves might be called upon to give consent, but this limitation in no way compromises the importance of the principle established. Future generations of Englishmen were to interpret the provisions of the Magna Carta in a much broader sense than its authors had intended. The document is of importance not only for what it said but also for what it allowed future generations to believe about the traditional relationship in England between authority and liberty.

Legal Reforms   The powers and procedures of the royal government received a still clearer definition under Edward I (1272–1307). Pious without being weak, committed to crusading but also concerned with the welfare of his realm, Edward ranks as one of the most influential of medieval English kings. In 1284 he seized Wales and later gave it as an appanage (a province intended to provide "bread," or support) to his eldest son. (Since 1301 the heir presumptive to the English throne has borne the title Prince of Wales.) In a misguided effort to promote the unity of the realm, he expelled England's Jews in 1290. However, Edward left his strongest mark on English law and institutions.

Edward produced no systematic codification of English law, which remained based principally on custom and court decisions of the past, but he did seek to correct and enlarge the common law in certain critical areas and to give the system a new flexibility. He issued the first Statutes of the Realm, initiating a series in which all the public laws of England have since been entered. Edward's statutes required the barons to show by what warrant (*quo warranto*), or royal license, they exercised jurisdiction in their own courts; this marked an important step in the decline of baronial justice. His laws also limited the growth of mortmain, that is, land held by the Church. The statutes were especially important in determining the land law of England, regulating inheritance and defining the rights of lords, vassals, and the king when land changed hands through inheritance or purchase. Edward laid the foundations upon which the English (and eventually American) law of real estate rested for centuries. In enacting these statutes and in governing the kingdom, Edward also placed a new emphasis on securing the consent of his subjects through Parliament.

Parliamentary Origins   Since the time of William the Conqueror the plenary meetings of the great council, or Curia Regis, had included the great barons, bishops, abbots, royal household officials—anyone whom the king wished to invite. During the reign of Henry III (1216–1272)

▶ **MAGNA CARTA**

Originally agreed to in 1215 by King John, the Magna Carta (or Great Charter) was intended to settle disputes over the rights and privileges of England's nobility. The document itself was issued in sealed copies and sent throughout England, but it was successively modified during the thirteenth century. This example, which is one of only four that have survived, dates from 1297, when the charter was confirmed in final form.

these plenary sessions of the royal court grew more frequent and clearly more important, and came to be called *parliaments*. (The word means only "conversation" and, derivatively, an assembly where discussion occurs.) It also became customary, but by no means mandatory, to invite knights from the shires to these sessions. In 1265, during an abortive baronial rebellion against King Henry, the rebel leader Simon de Montfort summoned a parliament that included two knights elected from every shire and two townsmen or burgesses from every town. Edward followed him in this precedent.

Historians cannot assign an exact date for the division of Parliament into separate houses of Lords and Commons. The knights and burgesses seem to have met informally together since the time of Edward I, and these meetings gained official recognition at least from the reign of Edward III. Two unique features of the English Parliament helped enhance the influence of Commons. First, the lower aristocracy (that is, those knights who were not the tenants in chief or immediate vassals of the king) sat with the burgesses and learned to act together in their mutual interests. (On the continent the lower aristocracy and the townsmen sat as separate groups and rarely developed or supported common causes.) Second, though the bishops continued to sit in the House of Lords, they gradually became less interested in using Parliament as a vehicle for political representation. The bishops discussed Church affairs and approved grants of money to the king in their own convocations. The functions of the House of Lords were thus reduced, a fact that benefited the House of Commons.

Representation   We now think of Parliament as a limitation on royal power, but it was not this at all in its earliest development. Parliament, as the assembly of the king's vassals, had the obligation merely of giving the king advice. In addition, the king found Parliament a valuable adjunct to his own administration, for it promulgated and enlisted support for his decisions, strengthened royal justice, and facilitated the collection of taxes. It was therefore in the king's interest to make the assembly broadly representative of the free classes. In summoning the Parliament of 1295 (this session would later be called the "model Parliament"), Edward cited a dictum taken from the Justinian Code: "What touches all, by all should be approved."

Parliament's role in the collection of taxes led to the development of a true system of representation. Feudal custom, the Magna Carta, and prudence had required that the king seek the consent of his subjects for new taxes. He could not ask all freeholders of the realm individually. He might seek the consent of the separate shires and the towns, but this was a slow and awkward process. Edward ingeniously simplified the procedure of consent. Through special writs, he ordered the shires and the towns to elect representatives and to grant them "full power" to grant him money. These representatives, gathered in Parliament, thus had authority to consent to taxes and to bind their electors back home. Paradoxically, the unique powers of the English king laid the basis for the eventual, unique powers of Parliament.

As the supreme feudal council, Parliament was also England's highest court (an honor the House of Lords retains today). The members attending its sessions would carry petitions or appeals from decisions made in lower courts; whereas a sheriff or shire court might have been subject to intimidation, Parliament would not be. By welcoming petitions, the king thus made his justice better known and respected throughout the realm. As with the U.S. Supreme Court, the decisions of Parliament determined the future policies of all English courts. The decisions were thus nearly the equivalent of legislation, and from them there was no appeal.

At Edward's death in 1307 the English constitution had acquired certain distinctive features. The constitution was not contained in a single written document but was defined by both custom and statute law. The king was the chief of the state, but it was recognized that the important men of the kingdom should have some participation in the decision-making processes, especially regarding taxes. Parliament gave this policy its practical implementation. The extraordinary continuity of these arrangements over centuries to come is testimony to the sound construction that the medieval English kings, lords, and commoners gave to their government.

FRANCE

In France, as in England, the thirteenth century was an age of constitutional consolidation. The successor of Philip Augustus, Louis VIII, ruled for only three years (1223–1226), but his reign was notable for several reasons. He was the first Capetian king not to be crowned in his father's lifetime; the Capetians had finally established that their claim to the monarchy was based on inheritance and not upon election. Louis VIII campaigned personally against the Albigensian heretics in southern France, and his victories prepared the way for the eventual inclusion of Toulouse and Languedoc in the royal domain (these were the last major additions to the royal lands until the late fifteenth century). He adopted the policy of supporting younger sons and brothers by granting them territories, the so-called appanages. This policy, continued by his successors, ultimately created powerful and troublesome princely lines in France.

St. Louis At Louis' death in 1226 the throne passed to Louis IX, St. Louis (1226–1270), one of the great figures of the thirteenth century. Louis was recognized as a saint even during his lifetime. He attended at least two Masses a day, was sternly abstemious in food and drink, often washed the feet of the poor and the wounds of lepers, and was scrupulously faithful to his wife, Margaret of Provence, who, like her husband, bore an aura of sanctity. However, his personal asceticism did not preclude a grand conception of royal authority. He added new pomp to court ceremonies and freely acted against the pope's wishes whenever the interests of the monarchy or his people seemed to require it. Three great ideals informed his policies as king: more effective justice within his kingdom, peace with its neighbors, and war against the Muslims, who still held Jerusalem (see Chapter 10).

Louis actively sought peace with his Christian neighbors. French monarchs had traditionally claimed some land south of the Pyrenees Mountains, and the Spanish kings of Aragon in turn claimed large areas of Languedoc in southern France (see Map 8.4). Rather than settling this dispute through war, Louis negotiated the Treaty of

▶ **DEATH OF LOUIS IX**
Louis IX of France died of the plague in Tunis during his Second Crusade. Attending his death bed in this manuscript illustration are his wife, Margaret of Provence, an unidentified bishop, and a mourner.

Corbeil (1258) with the Aragonese king, with each side renouncing its claims. This settlement defined the French-Spanish border for the next 200 years (see Map 9.1).

Peace with England was harder to attain. The English still held Aquitaine and Gascony and were not reconciled to the loss under King John of their extensive fiefs north of the Loire River. In the Treaty of Paris in 1259 Louis relinquished several territories that his troops had occupied along the borders of Gascony, and in return, King Henry III of England abandoned his claims to the lands that John had lost and agreed to perform liege homage to Louis for his fief of Gascony. The Treaty of Paris was unpopular in France; many believed that in ceding the Gascon borderlands Louis had given away more than the military situation warranted. Louis replied that these liberal terms might enable Henry's sons and his own to live thereafter in peace, as was proper for vassals and lords.

Legal Reforms   In his own realm Louis made no attempt to extend the royal domain at the expense of his nobles or to deprive them of their traditional powers and jurisdictions, but he did expect them to be good vassals. He forbade wars among them, arbitrated their disputes, and insisted that his ordinances be respected; he was the first king to legislate for the whole of France. Although Louis did not suppress the courts of the great nobles, he and his judges listened to appeals from their decisions, so that royal justice would be available to all his subjects. The king liked to sit in the open under a great oak at Vincennes near Paris to receive personally the petitions of the humble. The prestige that the piety and fairness of his decisions lent to royal justice was his great contribution to its growth.

Map 9.1 EUROPE, CA. 1250

▶ In this fourteenth-century manuscript
illumination, St. Louis hears the pleas of his
humble and defenseless subjects, chiefly women
and a monk. Note the hanged felons in the left
panel. The picture illustrates the abiding reputation
for justice that St. Louis earned for the French
monarchy.

During Louis' reign jurists began to clarify and codify the laws and customs of France. The most important of these compilations was the Establishments of St. Louis, drawn up before 1273. It contained, besides royal ordinances, the civil and feudal customs of several northern provinces and seems to have been intended for the guidance of judges and lawyers. It was not an authoritative code, but it and other compilations helped bring a new clarity and system to French law. Also during his reign the Parlement of Paris—a tribunal rather than a representative assembly like the English Parliament—was confirmed by Louis as the highest court in France, a position it retained until 1789.

Philip IV Louis' successors were able to preserve the strength, but not the serenity, of his reign. His grandson Philip IV, the Fair (1285–1314), is perhaps the most enigmatic of the medieval French kings; neither contemporaries nor later historians have agreed on his abilities. To some, Philip has seemed capable and cunning; to others, phlegmatic and uninterested, content to leave the business of government almost entirely to his ministers. If Philip lacked the personal ability to rule, he at least had the capacity to select strong ministers as his principal advisers. They were usually laymen trained in Roman law and possessing a high opinion of royal authority. They considered the king to be not merely a feudal monarch who ruled in agreement with the magnates of his realm but rather an "emperor in his own land" whose authority was free from all restrictions (the root sense of *legibus solutus*, "absolute") and subject to no higher power on earth.

The greatest obstacle to the advance of Philip's power was Edward I of England, master of the extensive fief of Gascony. Philip's resolve to drive England from the continent resulted in intermittent wars from 1294 to 1302. To punish the English economically, Philip tried to block the importation of English wool into Flanders. The Flemish towns revolted. Philip marched against them but was overwhelmed at Courtrai in 1302 by the towns' militias. This defeat deprived Philip of all hope of expelling the English from the continent.

These costly wars had placed a heavy burden on the royal finances. To replenish the treasury, Philip confiscated all the property of the Jews and expelled them temporarily in 1306; he also imprisoned foreign merchants to extort money from them and from a military-religious order called the Knights Templars (see Chapter 10), which

▶ BATTLE OF THE GOLDEN SPURS
In 1302, Flemish peasants, who had rebelled because Philip IV of France attempted to block the importation of wool from England, defeated the king at the battle of Courtrai. It was said that after the battle 700 pairs of spurs were collected and displayed in the local cathedral, and some sense of the brutality of the fighting is conveyed by this illustration, with King Philip brandishing his sword at the center and the pile of bodies at the lower right.

he pressured the pope to suppress. Finally, Philip insisted on his right to demand from the Church "free gifts," which were actually taxes. The issue led to a protracted dispute with Pope Boniface VIII. In seeking to dominate these international powers—the Knights Templars and the Church itself—Philip showed his determination to become truly sovereign in his own lands.

In trying to achieve an absolute monarchy, Philip upset the delicate feudal equilibrium of the France of St. Louis. He left at his death a deeply disturbed France. The Flemish towns remained defiant, and the strained relation of the monarchy with its principal vassal, the king of England, threatened to produce a major war. Under Philip's successors, with the outbreak of the Hundred Years' War, France entered one of the darkest periods of its history.

THE IBERIAN KINGDOMS

The Christian *Reconquista* had achieved all but final victory by 1236 with only Granada still in Muslim hands. The principal challenge now was the consolidation of the earlier conquests under Christian rule and the achievement of a stable governing order.

The three major Christian kingdoms that emerged from the Christian offensive were Portugal, Castile (including León), and Aragon (including Catalonia and Valencia), but they were not really united within their own territories. The Christian kings had purchased the support of both old and new subjects through generous concessions during the course of the *Reconquista*. Large communities of Jews and Muslims gained the right to live under their own laws and elect their own officials, and favored towns were granted special royal charters, known as *fueros*, that permitted them to maintain their own forum, or court. Barcelona and Valencia in the kingdom of Aragon and Burgos, Toledo, Valladolid, and Seville in the kingdom of Castile were virtually self-governing republics in the thirteenth century. Among other groups, the military aristocracy was highly privileged. The magnates, particularly in Castile, the largest of the Iberian kingdoms, held much of their lands not as fiefs but as alods (properties in full title), which reinforced their independent spirit. The clergy, of course, formed still another powerful and privileged group. Moreover, the Iberian kings had to reckon with three wealthy religious orders of knights, which had been founded about 1200 to aid in the struggle against the infidel and that were now able to wield independent financial and military power.

To hold all these elements together under a common government was a formidable task, but the kings also retained real advantages. The tradition of war against the infidel gave kings a special prestige. And their rivals were too diverse and too eager to fight one another to be able to present a united challenge.

Sooner than other Western monarchs, the Iberian kings recognized the practical value of securing the consent of their powerful subjects to major governmental decisions, particularly regarding taxes. By the end of the twelfth century they were frequently calling representative assemblies, called *Cortes*. Although they never achieved the constitutional position of the English Parliament because there were too many of them, the Cortes were the most powerful representative assemblies in Europe during the thirteenth century.

In order to impose a stronger, essentially feudal sovereignty over their subjects, the Iberian kings set about systematizing the laws and customs of their realms, thus clarifying both their own prerogatives and their subjects' obligations. Alfonso X of Castile issued an encyclopedia of legal institutions, meant to instruct lawyers and guide judges. This code, known as the *Siete Partidas* ("Seven Divisions"), was thoroughly imbued with the spirit of Roman law and presented the king as the source of all justice. Alfonso was in no position to achieve a true absolutism in his government, but the code did serve to educate the people to the high dignity of kingship. Even more than in England and France, feudal government in the Iberian kingdoms rested on a delicate compromise between royal authority and private privilege, and this apparently fragile system worked tolerably well.

With the achievement of fairly stable governments the Iberian kingdoms were able to play a larger role in the affairs of Europe. Aragon in particular, with an opening on the Mediterranean Sea, made its power felt and seized Sardinia from the Genoese and Pisans in 1326. A seemingly invincible company of Catalan mercenaries besieged Constantinople (1302–1307) and then captured Athens and subjugated it to Catalan domination until 1388. The expansion of the Iberian kingdoms was to be a major theme in European history for the next several hundred years.

THE HOLY ROMAN EMPIRE

While the English, French, and Iberian kingdoms were moving toward greater unity under more centralized governments, the German and Italian territories of the Holy Roman Empire were disintegrating into a large number of small and virtually autonomous principalities. Frederick Barbarossa had negotiated an uneasy peace with the pope and the Italian towns in the last years of his reign, but the struggle was renewed soon after his death in 1190. Barbarossa's son Henry VI had married Constance, heiress to the Norman Kingdom of the Two Sicilies. Their son would thus have a legal claim to southern Italy as Constance's heir and a moral claim to the German throne. The prospect of Italian unification under German auspices disturbed both the papacy and the free cities of Lombardy. The towns feared the direct domination of the emperor, while the papacy believed that its liberty would not survive were it to be encircled by German lands. In his brief reign of seven years, however, Henry VI had little chance to effect "the union of the Kingdom with the Empire," as contemporaries called this fateful policy. It was a dream that was to elude his son, Frederick II, as well.

Frederick II Hohenstaufen   Frederick II (1212–1250) is one of the most fascinating personalities

▶ **FREDERICK II'S TREATISE ON FALCONRY**
Frederick II was not only the dominant political leader of his age but also one of its most learned minds. He was an avid reader of Classical texts and apparently used Aristotle's *Historia Animalium* as a guide in one of his favorite pursuits, a study of birds. Illustrated here are a number of pages from his own copy of the treatise that he wrote on falconry.

of the Middle Ages. A contemporary called him *stupor mundi* ("wonder of the world"). Later historians have hailed him as the first modern ruler, the prototype of the cold and calculating statesman. Frederick spoke six languages, loved learning, patronized poets and translators, founded a university, and, after a fashion, conducted scientific experiments. He also corrected Aristotle by writing on the margins of his works in several places "It isn't so."

Several princes had contended for the German throne upon Henry VI's death, but the pope eventually crowned Frederick emperor in 1219 on the double promise that he would renounce his mother's inheritance of southern Italy and lead a crusade to Palestine. Frederick procrastinated on both agreements, creating lasting difficulties with the Church.

Emperor Frederick influenced German development in several fundamental ways. He established on the empire's eastern frontier a military-religious order, the Teutonic Knights, who eventually created the Prussian state; recognized Bohemia as a hereditary kingdom and Lübeck as a free imperial city; and issued the earliest charter of liberties to the Swiss cantons.

(Later in the century, in 1291, the cantons entered into a "Perpetual Compact," or alliance, which marks the formal beginnings of the Swiss Confederation.) His most important policy, however, was to confer upon the German ecclesiastical princes and the lay nobles virtual sovereignty within their own territories. The emperor retained only the right to set the foreign policy of the empire, make war and peace, and adjudicate disputes between princes or subjects of different principalities. All other powers of government passed to the princes, and no later emperor could regain what Frederick gave away.

In Italy Frederick pursued a much different policy. For the government of the Kingdom of the Two Sicilies he relied upon a trained lay bureaucracy. He rigorously centralized his administra-

▶ Emperor Frederick II, in the ship showing the imperial eagles, watches his soldiers assaulting prelates on their way to a council summoned by Pope Gregory IX in 1241. This contemporary illustration of the emperor's sacrilegious behavior, taken from a manuscript, is a good example of the war of propaganda by which both pope and emperor sought to win public sympathy.

tion, suppressed local privileges, imposed a universal tax in money upon his subjects, recruited his army from all classes and from Muslims as well as Christians, and issued a constitution which, in the spirit of Roman law, interpreted all jurisdiction as stemming from the emperor.

While seeking to build a strong and centralized government in Italy, Frederick had to face the increasingly bitter opposition of the popes and the free cities of the north. Pope Gregory IX excommunicated him in 1227 because of his failure to lead an Eastern crusade. Frederick then departed on the crusade, but he preferred to negotiate rather than fight and made a treaty with the Muslims that guaranteed unarmed Christian pilgrims access to Jerusalem. The more militant among the Western Christians believed that this treaty was dishonorable. Frederick returned to Italy in 1229 and came to terms with Pope Gregory a year later.

The Lombard towns remained fearful of his designs and finally leagued against him. He defeated them in 1237, but his success once more awakened in Gregory fears of encirclement, and Frederick was again excommunicated. Both sides struggled to win the public sympathy of Europe, but the tide of history began to turn against Frederick. To break the power of the Lombard towns, he unsuccessfully besieged Parma in 1248. In 1250 death cut short his efforts to unify Italy under imperial auspices.

There are some historical figures whose careers seem to summarize a given epoch and to predict the one to come. Frederick is such a figure. In Germany he reinforced a political fragmentation that had become ever more pronounced since the eleventh century. In southern Italy he completed the constitutional reorganization that the Norman kings, his forebears, had begun. Above all he was perhaps the last emperor to take seriously the grand vision of a Christian empire.

III. The Church

Since the time of the Gregorian reform of the eleventh century, the papacy had sought to build in Europe a unified Christian commonwealth, one based on faith and on obedience to the pope, in which European princes and peoples might work out their salvation in fraternal peace. In the thirteenth century the Church came close to achieving this grand design, but it still had to face powerful challenges to both Christian unity and its own leadership.

THE GROWTH OF HERESY

From the fifth until nearly the eleventh century no major heresies had troubled the Western Church, a sure indication of intellectual and spiritual torpor. From about the year 1000, however, chroniclers begin to note with growing frequency the appearance of heretics and sporadic attempts to suppress them.

The spread of heresy in the eleventh and twelfth centuries was partially a reaction to abuses within the established Church. Angered by the wealth and moral laxity of the clergy, heretics rejected the claimed privileges of the official priesthood. But heresy also had social roots. The continuing increase of population brought many social dislocations in its wake. The young were too numerous for the positions and jobs left to them by the aged. Society was filled with young men, frustrated in their hopes for a career, and unmarriageable young women. The movement into new territories, the growth of towns, the appearance of new trades and industries—all created strong psychological tensions, which often found an outlet in heretical movements. Within the towns, for example, heresy offered a form of social protest to the urban poor. It held potential for rich townsmen, too, inasmuch as traditional Christianity had been highly suspicious of wealth, particularly when earned in the marketplace, and gave the rich merchant little assurance of reaching heaven. Nobles envied the property and power of the Church; to them, heresy offered a justification for seizing the wealth of a corrupt Church for themselves.

Heresy further had a particular appeal to women. Many could not marry because of the large dowry demanded and for the same reason could not enter a religious order, as this also required a monetary contribution. Without a firm and stable social niche, many women had cause for intense dissatisfaction with both Church and society. Many heretics made a special effort to recruit women, conducting schools for them and teaching them how to read the Scriptures at a time when the established Church largely ignored their needs.

This was also an age of spiritual tension. Many laypeople wanted a more mystical and emotional reward from religion but were denied such satisfaction because they were given no opportunity to study the Bible, to hear it read in the vernacular, or to be moved by sermons. These were the exclusive activities of monks. A principal effort of both the new heresies and the new movements within the Church was to break this monastic monopoly of the religious experience.

THE WALDENSIANS AND THE ALBIGENSIANS

Around 1170 a rich merchant of Lyons, Peter Waldo, adopted a life of absolute poverty and gave himself to preaching. He soon attracted followers, who came to be known as "the poor men of Lyons" or Waldensians. The Waldensians attacked the moral laxness of the clergy and denounced the sacraments they administered. This group was declared heretical by the Lateran Council of 1215, but the Church never succeeded in suppressing the movement.

Far more powerful in their own day, though not destined to survive the Middle Ages, were the Cathari, or Albigensians, named for the town of Albi in Languedoc. The Albigensians' religious attitudes were greatly influenced by Manicheanism, a belief that antedated Christianity. It continued to survive among various small sects in Asia Minor and the Balkans. The Albigensians, like the Manicheans, believed that two principles, or deities, a god of light and a god of darkness, were fighting for supremacy in the universe. The good person must help the god of light vanquish the evil god of darkness, who had created and ruled the material world. The true Albigensians led a life of rigorous asceticism. They abstained from sexual intercourse, since procreation replenished the earth, the domain of the god of darkness. Marriage they regarded as hypocrisy, and intercourse within it worse than any other sexual sin. They abstained from meat, since it was sexually reproduced. Because a sect that preached

against marriage and procreation risked bringing about its own extinction, the Albigensians reached a practical compromise: Those who abided by these stringent regulations were the *Perfecti* (they formed the priesthood); those who did not live by this stern code were the believers.

The Albigensians, like the Waldensians, denied all value to the sacraments and priesthood of the established Church. They, of course, denied that Christ had ever taken on human flesh and saw no coming resurrection of the body. Their appeal came principally from their use of a vernacular Testament, from their willingness to preach in the vernacular to laypersons, and from their moral fervor. Eventually they developed a strong organization with councils and a hierarchy of *Perfecti* under a chief resembling a pope.

THE SUPPRESSION OF HERESY

The Church initially responded to the heretics by attempting to reconvert them. One of the first and greatest leaders supporting the policy of reconversion was a priest from Castile named Dominic, who began to preach among the Albigensians of Languedoc in about 1205. Dominic insisted that his followers—whose mission was to preach—live in poverty and support themselves by begging; they thus constituted a mendicant, or begging, order. This new Order of Preachers grew with amazing rapidity and was approved by the bishop of Toulouse in 1215 and shortly afterward by the pope. To prepare its members for their work, the Dominican Order stressed education and thus eventually became the intellectual arm of the medieval Church. It counted among its members Albertus Magnus, Thomas Aquinas, and many other important religious thinkers of the thirteenth century.

Reconversion through preaching, persuasion, and example remained, however, a slow and uncertain process. Moreover, canon law failed to provide an effective remedy against the powerful, organized heresies of the twelfth century. The law did give the bishop the right to try a suspected heretic before his own court, but a heretic protected by important men in the community was virtually immune to prosecution, inasmuch as the bishop often feared offending the lay powers of his diocese. The lack of any effective legal way of dealing with heretics led to frequent riots against them—the medieval equivalent of lynching—similar to the occasional massacres of Jews by anti-Semitic mobs.

By the early thirteenth century the Church began to suppress heresy systematically by force. Pope Innocent III, of whom more will be said later, favored peaceful solutions to heresy until his legate Peter of Castelnau, who had excommunicated the count of Toulouse for tolerating heresy, was murdered by one of the count's men. Innocent concluded that as long as the nobility of Languedoc abetted heresy, nothing short of force would be effective against it. He therefore proclaimed a crusade (1208–1229) against the Albigensians and the nobles who supported them. Knights from the north of France responded with zeal, but more out of greed for plunder than concern for orthodoxy. They defeated the nobles of Languedoc, but the problem of suppressing heresy remained.

The Inquisition In 1231 Pope Gregory IX instituted a special papal court to investigate and punish heresy. This was the famous papal Inquisition, which was to play a large and unhappy role in European history for the next several centuries. Through the Inquisition the popes sought to impose ordered and effective procedures upon the hunt for heretics. Like the English justices in eyre, the inquisitors were itinerant justices who visited the towns within their circuit at regular intervals. Strangers to the locale, they were not subject to pressures from the important men of the region. While the Inquisition was doubtless an improvement over riots and massacres, the procedures it adopted led to gross abuses. It accepted secret denunciations and, to protect the accusers, would not reveal their names to those denounced; at times it used evidence that was not even revealed to the accused. It denied the right of counsel and tortured stubborn heretics. The suspected heretics were, in fact, considered guilty before even being summoned to the Inquisition. They could confess and repent, with the likely consequence of a heavy penance and usually the confiscation of their property. But they had little chance to prove their innocence. As an ecclesiastical court, the Inquisition was forbidden to shed blood, but here too its procedures were

novel: It delivered relapsed or unrepentant heretics to the secular authority with full knowledge that they would be put to death (*see box*, p. 268).

The weaknesses of this system soon became apparent. Secret procedures protected incompetent and even demented judges, who shocked and disgusted even their contemporaries with their savage zeal. In addition, the Inquisition could function only where it had the close cooperation of the secular authority. It was never established in areas (for example, England) where strong kings considered themselves fully competent to control heresy. (Kings characteristically equated religious and civil rebellion and considered heresy to be identical with treason; even Frederick II, in spite of his bitter dispute with the papacy, imposed the death penalty upon heretics.)

The number of heretics who were executed is not known exactly, but they were probably not more than several hundred. Fines, confiscations of property, and imprisonment were the usual punishments for all but the most obstinate heretics. There is no denying the unfortunate effect of the Inquisition upon the medieval papacy and Church, chiefly the association of the papacy with persecution and bloodshed.

THE FRANCISCANS

Crusades and the Inquisition could not alone preserve the unity of the medieval Church. A spiritual regeneration was needed; the Church had to reach laypeople, especially those living in towns, and provide them with a spiritual message they could comprehend. The Dominicans were the first religious order to undertake this task as their primary mission. A major role was also played by a contemporary of St. Dominic's, St. Francis of Assisi.

Francis (1182?–1226) is probably the greatest saint of the Middle Ages and possibly the most sensitive poet of religious emotion. He succeeded in developing a style of piety that was both faithful to orthodoxy and abounding in new mystical insights. Since most of Francis' life is screened by legend, it is nearly impossible to reconstruct the exact course of his spiritual development. He seems to have devoted his young manhood to a self-conscious search for happiness or, in the

The Techniques of the Inquisition

To combat heresy the Inquisition tried above all to get suspects to confess, repent, and thus save their souls. Bernard Gui, inquisitor at Toulouse in southern France between 1307 and 1323, left a vivid account of the psychological techniques used in interrogations.

"When a heretic is first brought up for examination, he assumes a confident air, as though secure in his innocence. I ask him why he has been brought before me. He replies, smiling and courteous, 'Sir, I would be glad to learn the cause from you.'

"I [Inquisitor]. You are accused as a heretic, and that you believe and teach otherwise than Holy Church believes.

"A [Answer]. (Raising his eyes to heaven, with an air of the greatest faith) Lord, thou knowest that I am innocent of this, and that I have never held any faith other than that of true Christianity. . . .

"I. I know your tricks. What the members of your sect believe you hold to be that which a Christian should believe. But we waste time in this fencing. Say simply, Do you believe in one God the Father, and the Son, and the Holy Ghost?

"A. I believe.

"I. Do you believe in Christ born of the Virgin, suffered, risen, and ascended to heaven?

"A. (Briskly) I believe.

"I. Do you believe the bread and wine in the mass performed by the priests to be changed into the body and blood of Christ by divine virtue?

"A. Ought I not to believe this?

"I. I don't ask if you ought to believe, but if you do believe.

"A. I believe whatever you and other good doctors order me to believe. . . .

"I. Will you then swear that you have never learned anything contrary to the faith which we hold to be true?

"A. (Growing pale) If I ought to swear, I will willingly swear.

"I. I don't ask you whether you ought, but whether you will swear.

"A. If you order me to swear, I will swear.

"I. I don't force you to swear, because as you believe oaths to be unlawful, you will transfer the sin to me who forced you; but if you will swear, I will hear it.

"A. Why should I swear if you do not order me to?

"I. So that you may remove the suspicion of being a heretic.

"A. Sir, I do not know how unless you teach me.

"I. If I had to swear, I would raise my hand and spread my fingers and say, 'So help me God, I have never learned heresy or believed what is contrary to the true faith.'

"Then trembling as if he cannot repeat the form, he will stumble along as though speaking for himself or for another, so that there is not an absolute form of oath, and yet he may be thought to have sworn. . . . Or he converts the oath into a form of prayer. . . . [And when further hard pressed he will appeal, saying] 'Sir, if have done amiss in aught, I will willingly bear the penance, only help me to avoid the infamy of which I am accused.' But a vigorous inquisitor might not allow himself to be worked upon in this way, but proceed firmly until he makes these people confess their error, or at least publicly abjure heresy, so that if they are subsequently found to have sworn falsely, he can, without further hearing, abandon them to the secular arm."

From H. C. Lea, *A History of the Inquisition of the Middle Ages*, vol. I: (1887), pp. 411–414.

troubadour terminology he favored, for perfect joy. He first tried the rowdy amusements of the city. But dissatisfaction lingered; a biographer, Thomas of Celano, relates that after a severe illness Francis wandered on a May morning out to the blossoming fields but did not feel his accustomed joy. He then became a knight, but contentment still eluded him. Finally, he turned to

▶ This fresco from the basilica of St. Francis at Assisi, traditionally attributed to the Florentine painter Giotto, shows the saint preaching to the birds. He congratulates them on their bright plumage and bids them sing in praise of God. The implication is that if people too recognize God's providence over them, they will respond with gratitude and joy.

the religious life—instructed to do so, according to legend, by Christ himself—and adopted a life of poverty. Still, he believed that the test of true living, and indeed of true religion, ought to be joy: If all creatures, including human beings, recognized God's good providence over them, they would respond with joy. Joy would, in turn, ensure universal harmony in the world and bring a kind of golden age.

Disciples began to gather almost at once around the "little poor man" of Assisi. In 1208

Francis obtained papal approval for the formation of a new religious order. This Order of Friars Minor (Lesser Brothers) grew with extraordinary rapidity; within 10 years it included some 5000 members and spread from Germany to Palestine; before the end of the century it was the largest order in the Church. Although the problems of administering a huge order did not command Francis' deepest interests, he did write a brief rule for the Friars and shortly before his death gave them some further recommendations in a document known as his Testament, in which he stressed the importance of poverty and simplicity.

The success of the Friars Minor was an authentic triumph for the Church. Like the Dominicans, they carried their message primarily to laypeople in the growing towns, to the social classes where the heretics had hitherto won their greatest successes. Giving themselves to poverty and preaching, the Friars Minor came to include not only a second order of nuns but a third order of laypeople. Francis and his followers thus opened orthodox religion to delight in the natural world, to mystical and emotional experience, and to joy, which all people, they believed, including the ascetic and the pious, should be seeking.

PAPAL GOVERNMENT

In this period of social change and religious crisis the papacy faced serious obstacles in achieving its ideal of a unified, peaceful, and obedient European community. The pope of the thirteenth century whose reign best illustrates the aspirations and the problems of the medieval Church is Innocent III (1198–1216).

Innocent was somewhat ambiguous in defining his own powers. He once stated that God had given him "not only the universal Church, but the whole world to govern," yet he also declared to Philip II of France that he had no wish to "lessen or disturb the jurisdiction and power of the king." Although he seems to have been willing enough to leave the princes undisturbed in the routine exercise of government, he did insist that they obey him in matters concerning the rights of the Church, the peace and common interests of Christendom, and their own personal morality. He sought with vigor and with remarkable, if always partial, success to achieve three major goals: the unity of Christendom, the hegemony of the papacy over Europe, and the clarification of Christian discipline and belief.

Within Europe heresy was the greatest threat to Christian unity, and though he ordered the crusade against the Albigensians, Innocent primarily looked to the new mendicant orders to counter the appeal of the heretics. Beyond Europe he sought reunion with the Eastern Church. At first condemning the Fourth Crusade, which was directed against fellow Christians, Innocent came to consider the fall of Constantinople to the crusaders a providential act, meant to achieve unification of the Western and Eastern churches. From 1204 to 1261 an imposed union did hold the members of the Eastern Church, or at least some of them, in obedience to Rome, but the violence of the Western Europeans during the crusade sowed among the conquered a lasting hatred that frustrated later efforts at permanent union.

The pope also sought to exert his leadership over the princes of Europe in all spiritually significant affairs. Some of his efforts to bend kings to his will have already been mentioned, such as his struggle with King John to install Stephen Langton as archbishop of Canterbury. He also excommunicated Philip II of France for discarding his queen in order to cohabit with another woman. Innocent had occasion to reprimand the kings of Aragon, Portugal, Poland, and Norway. Indeed, no prior pope had scrutinized princely behavior with so keen an eye. Nevertheless, his interventions had uneven results, especially with regard to his dearest goal, the establishment of permanent peace among the European princes.

THE PAPACY IN THE THIRTEENTH CENTURY

Trained in canon law, Innocent wanted to bring a new order to Christian belief and government. In 1215 he summoned some 1500 prelates to attend the Fourth Lateran Council. The Lateran Council identified the sacraments as exactly seven and reaffirmed that they are essential to salvation; imposed an obligation of yearly confession and communion on the faithful; and defined the dogma of transubstantiation, according to which the priest, in uttering the words of con-

secration at Mass, annihilates the substance of bread and wine and substitutes for them the substance of Christ. Transubstantiation unambiguously affirmed the Mass as miracle and thus conferred a unique power on the Catholic priesthood. The council also pronounced on a wide variety of disciplinary matters: the qualifications for the priesthood, the nature of priestly education, the character of monastic life, the veneration of relics, and other devotional exercises.

Innocent's successors continued the work of codifying Church law. In 1234 Gregory IX published an authoritative collection of decretals (papal letters) to which additions were made in 1298 and 1314. Together with the *Decretum* of Gratian, these collections formed the Body of Canon Law, which in turn made up the finished constitution of the medieval Church.

Papal administration, and especially papal finances, continued to expand during the thirteenth century. Often desperate for funds to carry on their ambitious policies, the popes extracted substantial payments for appointments to office, imposed tithes (a tenth of income) upon the clergy, and sold exemptions and dispensations from the regulations of canon law. By the late thirteenth century the popes were clearly exploiting their spiritual powers for financial profit, and this was to prove a disastrous precedent.

Boniface VIII   By the late thirteenth century the papacy was facing a rising challenge from the princes of Europe, who sought to dominate the churches within their own territories. Both Philip IV of France and Edward I of England had been taxing the clergy through the fiction of asking for, and always receiving, gifts, or subventions. In 1296, in the bull *Clericis laicos* (all solemn papal letters were called *bulls* because they were closed with a seal, or *bulla*, and they are usually identified by their first two words), Pope Boniface VIII forbade all clergy to make grants without papal permission. Such a restriction would have given the pope a powerful, if not controlling, voice in royal finances, which no king could tolerate. The English simply ignored the order, but Philip retaliated by forbidding all exports of coin from his realm to Rome. Boniface, surprised by the forceful reaction, dropped his demands a year later.

In 1301 Philip arrested for treason a French

▶ **Gregory IX Decretals**

One of the principal accomplishments of Pope Gregory IX was his sponsorship of an effort to bring together and update the basic decisions and rulings of the Church. The resulting collection is known as the decretals of Gregory IX, and it became the main source of canon law. In this miniature from a fourteenth-century manuscript of the decretals, Gregory sits at the center holding the book and surrounded by monks.

bishop who also happened to be a papal legate, thus striking directly at the sovereignty of the pope and the immunities of his representatives. Boniface reprimanded Philip for his behavior, but the king responded by circulating defamatory accusations against the pope. Naturally, Boniface felt that both his personal character and the papal authority were being threatened. He therefore issued the bull *Unam Sanctam*, which declared that Philip must submit to his authority or risk the loss of his immortal soul (*see box*, below). In no mood to accept a rebuff, Philip sent one of his principal advisers to Italy, who with the aid of a Roman faction opposed to Boniface broke into the papal palace at Anagni and arrested the pope. The citizens of Anagni rescued Boniface shortly afterward, but he died in Rome only a few months later. The vulnerability of the papacy had been clearly demonstrated.

The succeeding popes capitulated to the French king and even revoked *Unam Sanctam*. Philip's victory was complete when a Frenchman was elected pope in 1305. Clement V never reached Rome, settling instead in the French-speaking, though imperial, city of Avignon in 1309. For the next 68 years the popes lived within the shadow of the French monarchy.

The medieval papacy hoped to serve as the

Unam Sanctam

This statement of papal monarchy was issued by Pope Boniface VIII in 1302 to combat assertions of royal power by the kings of England and France against the authority of the universal Church. It did little, however, to deter the claims of such rulers to a growing sphere of authority.

"That there is one holy, Catholic and apostolic Church we are bound to believe and to hold, our faith urging us, and this we do firmly believe and simply confess; and that outside this Church there is no salvation or remission of sins. . . .

"We are taught by the words of the Gospel that in this Church and in her power there are two swords, a spiritual one and a temporal one. For when the apostles said 'Here are two swords' (Luke 22:38), meaning in the Church since it was the apostles who spoke, the Lord did not reply that it was too many but enough. Certainly anyone who denies that the temporal sword is in the power of Peter has not paid heed to the words of the Lord when he said, 'Put up thy sword into its sheath' (Matthew 26:52). Both then are in the power of the Church, the material sword and the spiritual. But the one is exercised for the Church, the other by the Church, the one by the hand of the priest, the other by the hand of kings and soldiers, though at the will and sufferance of the priest. One sword ought to be under the other and the temporal authority subject to the spiritual

power. For, while the apostle says, 'There is no power but from God and those that are ordained of God' (Romans 13:1), they would not be ordained unless one sword was under the other and, being inferior, was led by the other to the highest things. . . . But that the spiritual power excels any earthly one in dignity and nobility we ought the more openly to confess in proportion as spiritual things excel temporal ones. Moreover we clearly perceive this from the giving of tithes, from benediction and sanctification, from the acceptance of this power and from the very government of things. For the truth bearing witness, the spiritual power has to institute the earthly power and to judge if it has not been good. . . .

"Therefore, if the earthly power errs, it shall be judged by the spiritual power, if a lesser spiritual power errs it shall be judged by its superior, but if the supreme spiritual power errs it can be judged only by God not by man. . . . Therefore we declare, state, define and pronounce that it is altogether necessary to salvation for every human creature to be subject to the Roman Pontiff."

From Hollister, *Medieval Europe: A Short Sourcebook* (1992), pp. 215–216.

vocal conscience of Europe. It was aided in this ambition by compelling theological and legal systems and by a huge administrative apparatus. But the growth of papal power weakened the bishop's ability to maintain the moral discipline of his clergy, and that permitted abuses to grow unchecked. Even the new intellectual rigor of Christian belief carried with it a certain risk for the spiritual life. Cold intellectualism or a narrow legalism might well threaten and dilute authentic piety—a problem the Church would encounter time and again.

IV. *The Summer of Medieval Culture*

▼

Whereas the twelfth century was the period of discovery and creation in the cultural growth of the medieval world, the thirteenth century was an age of intellectual synthesis. As the statesmen of Europe tried to unite law and custom in ordered constitutional systems, the cultural leaders tried to bring earlier intellectual traditions into harmony.

THE MEDIEVAL SYNTHESIS

An appreciation of thirteenth-century culture requires an understanding of the ideas and values the period was seeking to combine. The Scholastics were trying to reconcile the fundamental assumptions of Aristotelian philosophy with the fundamental attitudes of Christianity: The former asserting that human reason could probe the structure of the universe unaided; the latter insisting on the necessity of divine revelation and grace.

In their attempt to reconcile these views, medieval intellectuals aimed at nothing less than uniting two historical and cultural experiences, for medieval civilization was itself the product of two quite different epochs. The violence and desperation of the late Roman and early medieval periods had implanted in the medieval mind a deep conviction that the natural powers of human beings were inadequate to control their destiny, that they needed help through grace. The

experiences of society after 1000 had, on the other hand, bred a new confidence in human capabilities. Aristotelian philosophy lent intellectual force to what experience seemed to be teaching: that human beings could attain, through their own efforts, some measure of truth and fulfillment in this present world.

In seeking to reconcile faith and reason, medieval people were trying to extract the common denominator of truth from the vastly different experiences through which they had passed. They wanted to construct an open intellectual system that would give a place to all true values, wherever found, however they had been learned. The general nature of this effort at synthesis can be seen in three of the major achievements of the period: the Scholasticism of Thomas Aquinas, the Gothic cathedral, and the *Comedy* of Dante Alighieri.

THOMAS AQUINAS

The most gifted representative of Scholastic philosophy, and the greatest Christian theologian since Augustine, was St. Thomas Aquinas (1225?–1274), whose career well illustrates the character of thirteenth-century intellectual life. At 17 Thomas entered the new Dominican Order, perhaps attracted by its commitment to scholarship; he studied at Monte Cassino and Naples, and later, as a Dominican, at Cologne and Paris (see Map 9.2). His most influential teacher was another Dominican, Albertus Magnus, a German who wrote extensively on theological matters and questions of natural science, especially biology. Thomas was no intellectual recluse; he lectured at Paris and traveled widely across Europe, particularly on the business of his order and the Church.

In his short and active life Thomas produced a prodigious amount of writing: commentaries on biblical books and Aristotelian works, short essays on philosophical problems, and a lengthy compendium of Christian apologetics, the *Summa contra Gentiles*, which was probably intended for Dominican missionaries working to convert heretics and infidels. However, his most important work was one he did not live to finish. Divided into three parts on God, Man, and Christ, the *Summa Theologica* was meant to provide a com-

Map 9.2 MEDIEVAL UNIVERSITIES

prehensive introduction to Christian theology and to present a systematic view of the universe that would do justice to all truth, natural and revealed, pagan and Christian.

Thomas brought to his task a subtle and perceptive intellect, and his system (not unlike the feudal constitutions) rests upon several fundamental, delicate compromises. In regard to faith and reason, he taught that both are roads to a single truth. Reason is based ultimately on sense experience. It is a powerful instrument, but insufficient to teach people all that God wishes them to know. Nature is good, and humans can achieve some partial, temporary happiness in this life. But nature alone cannot carry them to ultimate fulfillment. Grace is still needed to bring nature to perfection and human beings to eternal salvation.

With respect to the fundamental structure of the universe, Thomas sought the common ground between two interpretations of reality, inherited from the ancient philosophers and called in the medieval schools *realism* and *nominalism*.

Though technically a moderate realist, Thomas argued that both interpretations were correct. Each object in the universe is autonomous and unique (the nominalist position), but it is also representative of general species or classes, which exist independently of the mind and which form a hierarchy or chain of being leading up to God (the realist position). To possess this double dimension of meaning, each object must be metaphysically a composite of two principles, one of which explains its unity with other objects and the other its individuality. In broadest terms, the principle of unity is "act," meaning the act of being, as it is ultimately in their being that objects resemble one another. The principle of individuation is "potency," which limits act and renders an object unique. Motion or change in the universe is essentially a transition from potency to act. Only God is unlimited, unindividuated Being—"pure act" in Thomas' definition. Only God cannot change, but He ultimately supports all change. In his proofs of God's existence, Thomas argued that instability, imperfection, and change, which we see all around us, point to the existence of an "unmoved mover," a principle of absolute perfection, stability, and power.

The *Summa* shows certain characteristic weaknesses of Scholasticism. Thomas affirmed that natural truth is ultimately grounded in observation, but, in fact, he observed very little. His critical distinction between act and potency, which he borrowed from Aristotle, was not founded on observation or experimentation. Many later thinkers found his system too speculative, too elaborate. Nonetheless, the *Summa* remains an unquestioned masterpiece of Western theology. It offers comment on an enormous range of theological, philosophical, and ethical problems, and consistently demonstrates openness, insight, and wisdom.

To be sure, Thomas' system fell under critical scrutiny even in the generation following his death. Among his early critics the most influential was a Scottish Franciscan, John Duns Scotus (1265?–1308). Drawing inspiration from St. Augustine, Duns Scotus affirmed that faith was logically prior to reason; that is, unless faith had first suggested to reason that spiritual beings—God and angels—could exist, reason would never have arrived at a concept of them. Once the mind accepted the idea of God from faith, it could then prove the necessity for God's existence. To Duns Scotus the proof of God's existence was not based, as with Aquinas, on the perception of change in the universe, for he did not trust the accuracy of sense observation; rather, it derived from an exclusively intellectual analysis of the concept of God as a necessary being.

THE GOTHIC CATHEDRAL

Artists as well as theologians were attempting to present a systematic view of the universe reflective of all truth. The artistic counterpart to the Scholastic *Summas* was the Gothic cathedral.

The word *Gothic* was coined in the sixteenth century as an expression of contempt for these supposedly barbarous medieval buildings. In fact, the Goths had disappeared some 500 years before any Gothic churches were built. As used today, *Gothic* refers to the style of architecture and art that initially developed in the royal lands in France, including Paris and its surroundings, from about 1150. The abbey church of Saint-Denis near Paris, built by the Abbot Suger in 1144, is usually taken as the first authentic example of the Gothic style. The early Gothic churches were almost all urban cathedrals and were characteristically dedicated to the Virgin Mary. In the thirteenth century the Gothic style spread widely through Europe and found special application in the large churches built by the Franciscan and Dominican orders.

Technically, three engineering devices helped stamp the Gothic style: the broken rather than rounded arch; ribbed vaulting, which concentrated support around the lines of thrust and gave the buildings a visibly delineated skeleton; and the flying buttress, an external support that allowed the walls to be made higher and lighter. The flying buttress also freed sections of the walls from the function of supporting the roof and therefore permitted the use of large areas for windows. Romanesque architects had pioneered all three devices, but the Gothic engineers combined them and used them with unprecedented vigor and boldness.

Innovations were also made in the statues that

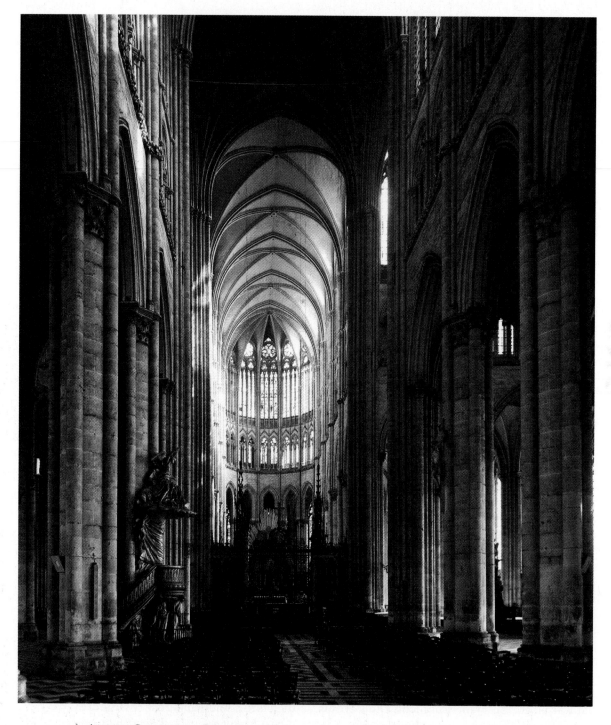

▶ AMIENS CATHEDRAL, CA. 1220–1236
Built between 1220 and 1236, Amiens Cathedral exemplifies the structure of a Gothic cathedral. The weight of the walls is supported by a system of buttresses and ribbed vaults, which allowed medieval builders to break up the walls with luminous areas of stained glass. The colored light that poured into these massive structures gave them an otherworldly majesty never before achieved.

a strong sense of order. The naked ribs and buttresses and the intricate vaulting constitute a spectacular geometry that instills in the viewer a vivid impression of intelligence and logical relationships. The churches, reflecting the structure of the universe, taught that God, the master builder, created and still governs the natural world with similar logic.

▶ SAINTE-CHAPELLE, PARIS, INTERIOR, 1243–1248
Sainte-Chapelle, the private chapel attached to the French royal palace in Paris, was built between 1243 and 1248 to house relics brought back from the crusades by Louis IX. The building was deliberately intended to resemble a reliquary, and the enormous jewel-colored stained-glass windows make up three-quarters of its wall surface.

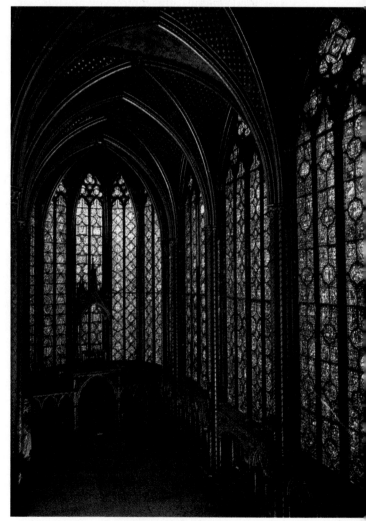

▶ In contrast to Romanesque sculpture, which overflows with great displays of emotion, Gothic sculpture evokes a sense of calm and orderly reality, as can be seen in the jamb figures on the central portal of Chartres Cathedral.

adorned the buildings. Romanesque sculpture often conveyed great emotion and power but did not reflect the visible world. Sculptors now wanted their works to emulate reality, or at least its handsomest parts (decorative foliage, for example, was carved with such accuracy that the botanical models can be identified). Their statues portray real and usually cheerful people, who subtly exert their own personalities without destroying the harmony of the whole.

The Gothic Spirit These magnificent churches with their hundreds of statues took decades to construct and decorate, and many were never completed. The builders intended that the churches provide a comprehensive view of the universe and instruction in its sacred history. One principal element of the Gothic aesthetic is

The most distinctive aspect of the Gothic style is its use of light in a manner unique in the history of architecture. Once within the church, the visitor has entered a realm defined and infused by a warm, colored glow. In Christian worship light is one of the most ancient, common, and versatile symbols. It suggests to the worshiper mystical illumination, spiritual beauty, grace, and divinity itself.

The impressions rendered by the architecture and the stained glass were further developed by the performance of the sacred liturgy. Here music was also enlisted to convey the sense of an intricate and sublime harmony in God's care of the world. Paris in the thirteenth century witnessed a marked development of polyphonic music; the choirmasters seem to have sought a musical style that would parallel the complexity and the harmony of the surrounding cathedral. Through architecture, sculpture, and music, the believer was encouraged to feel a universe permeated with the presence of God.

DANTE

Literary output in most vernacular languages grew continuously more abundant during the thirteenth century, except in English, which was retarded in its development by the continued dominance of a French-speaking aristocracy. Of several masterpieces the one that best summarizes the culture of the age is the *Comedy* of Dante Alighieri.

Dante was born in Florence in 1265. Little is known of his education, but he seems to have been immersed in scholarship. The *Comedy* is one of the most learned, and hence most difficult, poems of world literature.

Two experiences in Dante's life profoundly influenced his attitudes and are reflected in his works. In 1274, when (as he himself affirms) he was only nine years old, he fell deeply in love with a young girl named Beatrice. Much mystery surrounds her, but she seems to have been Beatrice Portinari, who later married into a prominent family and died in 1290. Dante could have seen her only rarely; we do not know if she ever returned his love. Still, in his youthful adoration of Beatrice he seems to have attained that sense of harmony and joy that the troubadours consid-

ered to be the great reward of lovers. In 1302 an experience of a much different sort shattered his life. For political reasons he was exiled from Florence. He spent the remaining years of his life wandering from city to city, a disillusioned, even bitter man. He died in 1321 and was buried at Ravenna.

The Comedy   Dante composed his masterpiece from 1313 to 1321. He called it a *commedia* in conformity with the Classical notion that a happy ending made any story, no matter how serious, a comedy; the adjective *divine* was added to its title only after his death. The poem is divided into three parts, which describe the poet's journey through hell, purgatory, and heaven.

The poem opens with Dante "in the middle of the way of this our life." An aging man, he has grown confused and disillusioned; he is lost in a "dark forest" of doubt, harassed by wild animals, symbols of his own untamed passions. The theme of the poem is essentially Dante's rediscovery of a former sense of harmony and joy. Leading him back to his lost peace are two guides. The first, Virgil, who represents human reason, conducts Dante through hell and then up the seven-storied mountain of purgatory to the earthly paradise, the vanished Eden, at its summit. In hell Dante encounters people who have chosen as their supreme goal in life something other than the love of God—riches, pleasure, fame, or power. Virgil shows Dante that the good life cannot be built upon such selfish choices. Reason, in other words, can enable humans to avoid the pitfalls of egoistic, material existence. In fact reason can accomplish even more than that; for, as embodied by Virgil, it guides Dante through purgatory and shows him how to acquire the natural virtues that are the foundations of the earthly paradise—a full and peaceful earthly existence.

In the dignity and power given to Virgil, Dante shares the high regard for human reason characteristic of the thirteenth century. However, reason can take humans only so far. To enter heaven, Dante needs a new guide—Beatrice herself, representative of supernatural revelation and grace. She takes the poet through the heavenly spheres into the presence of God, "in Whom is our peace." The peace and joy of the heavenly court set the dominant mood at the poem's con-

Nel uano tutti sua coda guizaua.
torcendo in su la uenenosa forcha.
cha guisa di scorpion la punta armaua
Lo duca disse oz conuien che si torcha.
la nostra uia un poco in fina quella.
bestia maluagia che colla si torcha.
Pero scendemmo a la destra mamella.
e diece passi femmo in su lo stremo.
per ben cessar la rena e la fiamella.

▶ **A detail from a fourteenth-century manuscript copy of Dante's *Divine Comedy* illustrates the section of hell reserved for usurers. The Church regarded usury as one of man's many earthly sins that condemn him in the eyes of God. Dante appears four times in this scene, on three occasions accompanied by his bearded guide, Virgil.**

clusion, in contrast to the confusion and violence of the dark forest with which it had opened.

Like many other literary masterpieces, the *Comedy* has several dimensions of meaning. On a personal level, it summarizes the experiences of Dante's own life; it affirms that the youthful idealism and joy he had once so easily found were not proved false by age and bitter exile. The poem further reflects the great cultural issues that challenged his contemporaries—the relations between reason and faith, nature and grace, human power and the divine will. Dante, like Aquinas, was trying to combine two opposed views of human nature and its abilities to shape its own destiny. One, rooted in the very optimism of the twelfth and thirteenth centuries and in the more distant Classical heritage, affirmed that human beings were masters of themselves and the world. The other, grounded in the Judeo-Christian tradition, saw them, fundamentally, as lost children in a vale of tears. Both views had helped support human life and were therefore worth preserving. Dante's majestic panorama summarizes not only the medieval vision of the universe but also his estimation of what it meant to live a truly wise, truly happy, truly human life.

In the thirteenth century medieval civilization attained a new stability. Large-scale manufacture, long-range commercial exchanges, and sophisticated business practices gave the economy a dynamic aura. In political life, feudal governments consolidated and clarified their constitutional procedures, and parliaments and representative assemblies came to play a recognized role in the processes of government. Confronted with heresies that threatened its unity and dominance, the Church responded in part with crusades and the Inquisition, ultimately to its own detriment. At the same time, orthodox religion enjoyed an authentic spiritual renewal, of which Francis of Assisi was the chief inspiration. The papacy energetically sought to lead the Western princes as their guide and conscience, but secular entanglements and fiscal problems threatened and gradually diluted its moral authority.

In cultural life this was a period of magnificent synthesis. The masterpieces of the age aimed at bringing together all parts of the medieval heritage into an ordered whole that would offer people a comprehensive understanding of the universe and a wise formula for living.

Medieval society in the thirteenth century seemed close to resolving its principal problems, whether economic, political, or cultural. In fact, however, the relative prosperity and peace, along with the institutional stability and intellectual synthesis, were not to survive much beyond the year 1300. In the fourteenth century a new era of turmoil dawned for the medieval world. The close of the Middle Ages was a period of spectacular disasters and profound changes, which greatly altered the character of the civilizations in both Eastern and Western Europe.

Recommended Reading

▼

Sources

*Alighieri, Dante. *The Divine Comedy*. Mark Musa (tr.).

Aquinas, Thomas. *Basic Writings*. Anton C. Pegis (ed.). 1945.

*Brown, Raphael (ed. and tr.). *The Little Flowers of St. Francis*. 1971. Legends collected in the early fourteenth century exemplifying the style of Franciscan piety.

Studies

*Abulafia, David. *Frederick II: A Medieval Emperor*. 1988.

Barraclough, Geoffrey. *The Origins of Modern Germany*. 1963. Classic interpretation of medieval German history.

*Bennett, Judith M. *Women in the Medieval English Countryside*. 1987. An assessment of women's changing status.

Bisson, Thomas. *Medieval Representative Institutions*. 1973. Introductory essays.

Boase, T. S. R. *Boniface VIII*. 1933. Standard biography of the controversial pope.

*Copleston, Frederick. *Aquinas*. 1955.

d'Avery, D. L. *The Preaching of the Friars: Sermons Diffused from Paris before 1300*. 1985.

Duby, Georges. *William Marshal: The Flower of Chivalry*. 1985. Sensitive biography of an Anglo-Norman lord.

———, and Philippe Aries (eds.). *A History of Private Life* (Vol. 2). 1988.

Epstein, Steven. *Wage Labor and Guilds in Medieval Europe*. 1991.

*Frisch, Teresa G. *Gothic Art, 1140–1450: Sources and Documents*. 1987.

*Hanawalt, Barbara. *The Ties That Bound: Peasant Families in Medieval England*. 1986. Peasant life sympathetically viewed.

*Heer, Friedrich. *The Medieval World: Europe, 1100–1350*. 1964. From an open to a closed medieval society.

*Herlihy, David. *Opera Muliebria: Women and Work in Medieval Europe*. 1990.

Hillgarth, J. M. *The Spanish Kingdoms, 1250–1516* (2 vols.). 1978. Spanish history across the Late Middle Ages.

Holt, J. C. *Magna Carta*. 1965. Gives useful guidance to an extensive literature.

Le Goff, Jacques. *Time, Work and Culture in the Middle Ages*. Arthur Goldhammer (tr.). 1980. Medieval culture studied through anthropological methods.

Little, Lester. *Religious Poverty and the Profit Economy in Medieval Europe*. 1978. Examines changes in economic attitudes in the thirteenth century.

Lyon, Bryce. *A Constitutional and Legal History of Medieval England* (2nd ed.). 1980.

*Available in paperback.

Mundy, John H. *Europe in the High Middle Ages.* 1973. A useful general survey.

Peters, Edward M. *Inquisition.* 1988. The Inquisition in fact and imagination.

Powicke, F. M. *The Thirteenth Century, 1216–1307.* 1953. Basic survey of English political history.

Reynolds, Susan. *Kingdoms and Communities in Western Europe 900–1300.* 1984. Medieval associations and their bondings.

*Strayer, Joseph R. *On the Medieval Origins of the Modern State.* 1973.

Von Simson, Otto. *The Gothic Cathedral: Origins of Gothic Architecture and the Medieval Concept of Order.* 1962. Interprets Gothic style primarily in terms of its use of light.

*Weinstein, Donald, and Rudolph M. Bell. *Saints and Society.* 1982. Statistical study of medieval saints.

WOMEN ASSISTING KNIGHTS
This manuscript illustration makes it clear that
women took part in battles alongside the male
crusaders. Here they wield picks and axes, and
throw stones in a siege. Moreover, it is clear that
the woman in the foreground, just behind the
ladder, who does not cower behind a shield like the
man on the ladder, is about to be killed by an
arrow.

CHAPTER TEN

THE CRUSADES AND EASTERN EUROPE

THE peoples of Western Europe had remained fairly cut off from the East during the Early Middle Ages, an isolation that added to their economic and cultural stagnation. After the year 1000, however, the isolation began to break down. Western pilgrims and crusaders in large numbers visited the Christian holy places in the East and for some two centuries maintained the Latin Kingdom of Jerusalem, a colony in Palestine. Western merchants established contact with the principal ports of the eastern Mediterranean and Black seas. A vigorous trade developed across the Mediterranean, and Westerners once more came to enjoy the spices and other products of the East. In the thirteenth century some missionaries and merchants penetrated into central Asia, and a few traveled as far as China. These greatly enlarged geographic horizons made Europeans aware that rich and brilliant civilizations existed beyond their borders, and Westerners entered into intense military competition, close trade relations, and fruitful cultural exchanges with their Eastern neighbors. The East in these centuries was itself in a state of flux, as the three states that dominated the region in the Early Middle Ages—the Byzantine Empire, the Arab Caliphate, and Kievan Rus—gave way to new regimes. By the 1400s a new force, the Ottoman Empire, dominated the land bridge between Europe and Asia and presented the West with a formidable military challenge. As the Ottomans rose, the spiritual and cultural heritage of both Byzantium and Kievan Rus passed to a new Russian state that had its capital at Moscow. The contacts, the rivalries, and the economic and cultural exchanges that resulted from these changes have shaped the history of the peoples in these areas ever since.

I. The Crusades

In the eleventh century the Western peoples launched a series of armed expeditions to the East in an effort to free the Holy Land from Islamic rule. Known as crusades (because the armies' banner was a cross), these expeditions stimulated trade, encouraged the growth of towns, and contributed to the establishment of a stable political order in the West. But they could also be seen as costly failures, draining resources for what proved to be a temporary foothold in Palestine; they worsened relations not only with the Muslims but also with Eastern Christians; and they set in motion one of Europe's grimmest traditions when crusading zeal stimulated dreadful riots and pogroms against those most accessible infidels, the Jews.

Above all, the crusades reveal more dramatically than any other event the spirit of Western society in the eleventh and twelfth centuries: its energy, brash self-confidence, compelling faith, and frequent bigotry. At the same time as the expeditions helped acquaint the Western peoples with ideas and techniques of civilizations more sophisticated than their own, they also proved to be the initial phase in the expansion of the West—the massive exportation of European people and skills beyond the confines of their narrow continent.

ORIGINS

The origins of the crusades must be sought in a double set of circumstances: social and religious movements in the West and the political situation in the East. In the Christian West a favorite form of religious exercise was the pilgrimage, a personal visit to a place made holy through the life of Christ or one of his saints or the presence of a sacred relic. Common in the West since the fourth century, pilgrimages gained in popularity during the eleventh century as Europe experienced religious revival and reform. Bands of pilgrims, sometimes numbering in the thousands, set forth to visit the places sacred to their religion, and of these destinations, Palestine was the most holy.

The Turks   This pilgrim traffic was threatened when the Seljuk Turks, Muslim nomads, overran much of the Middle East in the eleventh century. It does not appear that the Seljuks consciously sought to prevent the pilgrims from reaching Palestine, but they did impose numerous taxes and tolls on them, and many Christians became angry at the domination of the holy places of Palestine by a strong, aggressive Islamic power.

Even more daunting to the West was the possibility that the Christian empire of Byzantium would also be overrun. The Seljuks had crushed a Byzantine army at the Battle of Manzikert in 1071, and the road to Constantinople seemed wide open. The fall of Byzantium would remove the traditional barrier to Islamic advance toward the West and would be a major disaster for the Christian world. When, therefore, a delegation from the emperor of Byzantium requested the help of Pope Urban II in 1095, he resolved to appeal to the Western knights and princes to go to the aid of their fellow Christians in the East. Social and religious conditions in Europe helped ensure that Urban's summons would evoke a powerful response.

▶ **CHRIST LEADING CRUSADERS**
This fourteenth-century illustration from a manuscript on the Apocalypse captures an assumption that was common to all the crusaders—that their expedition was being led by Christ himself. On his magnificent charger, he leads into battle the troops carrying his symbol, the cross.

THE MOTIVES OF THE CRUSADERS

Religion The crusades were viewed by those who participated in them primarily as acts of religious devotion. Even before Urban made his appeal, the idea had gained currency in the West that God would reward those who fought in a good cause, that is, that wars could be holy. The crusaders also shared the beliefs expressed in the movement for Church reform that the good ought not simply to endure the evils of the world but should attempt to correct them. This active, confident spirit contrasted strongly with the resignation to evil and the withdrawal from the world recommended by most Christian writers of the Early Middle Ages.

Expansion Social and economic motivations also contributed to the expeditions. The age of mass pilgrimages and crusades, from about 1050 to 1250, corresponds to the period in medieval history when the European population was growing most rapidly. The crusades may be considered one further example of the expanding Western frontier, similar in motivation and character to the Spanish *Reconquista* or the German push to the East. Of course, the crusades differed in at least one significant way from these other ventures. They were almost exclusively military expeditions of Europe's warrior classes; peasants did not settle in Palestine in significant numbers, as they did in the lands of Eastern Europe and in the Iberian peninsula.

Knighthood The younger sons of European knights were particularly sensitive to the pressures being created by an expanding population. Parental lands were often not large enough to provide support for younger sons. Pope Urban apparently believed that this land shortage created social problems, for he is reported to have told the knights of France in 1095: "This land which you inhabit is too narrow for your large population; nor does it abound in wealth; and it provides hardly enough food for those who farm it. This is the reason that you murder and consume one another." An additional problem was that knights were educated to do little but fight, and it was natural for them to place their chief hopes for wealth, honor, and social advance in

▶ **MAKING COATS OF CHAIN MAIL**
This depiction of a craftsman making chain mail suggests the high skills and hard labor that were needed to bend the metal into elaborate shapes. Armor made of chain mail allowed the knight far greater freedom of movement, but it could be penetrated by the sharp thrust of a sword or arrow.

war. The growth of the feudal principalities, the efforts of the Church to restrict fighting among Christians, and the resultant slow pacification of European society threatened to leave the knights poor, unhonored, and unemployed. "You should shudder, brethren," Urban is also reported to have told the knights, "you should shudder at perpetrating violence against Christians; it is less wicked to turn your sword against Muslims. . . . The possessions of the enemy will also fall to you, since you will claim their treasures as plunder."

War against the infidel thus offered constructive employment for Europe's surplus and often violent population of knights. In the following century St. Bernard of Clairvaux, whose preaching inspired thousands to join the Second Crusade, frankly affirmed that all but a few of the knights on the crusades were "criminals and sinners, ravishers and the sacrilegious, murderers, perjurers, and adulterers." To have them crusading in the East therefore brought a double benefit. As Bernard remarked, "Their departure makes their own people happy, and their arrival cheers those whom they are hastening to help. They aid both groups, not only by protecting the one but also by not oppressing the other." The crusades were thus, in one respect, a violent means of draining the violence from medieval life.

Rhineland influential preachers were soon rousing the people and organizing movements that historians now call the Popular Crusade. Bands of peasants and the poor (together with a few knights) set out for the East, miserably equipped and lacking competent leaders. They marched down the Rhine valley, attacking Jews as they went, and on through Hungary and Bulgaria to Constantinople. Emperor Alexius of Byzantium, who could only have been shocked at the sight

THE FIRST CRUSADE

In 1095, before a Church council assembled at Clermont in southern France, Pope Urban II urged the knights at the meeting to go to the East to aid their endangered Christian brothers and to free the Holy Land from its blasphemous masters. His sermon was intended for the upper classes, but its plea had sensational results at all levels of Western society. In northern France and the

Map 10.1 THE EASTERN MEDITERRANEAN DURING THE EARLY CRUSADES
The effects of the first crusades on the Middle East can be seen in the territory the crusader kingdoms conquered and the expansion of the Byzantine Empire at the expense of the Seljuk Turks. Both of these newly Christian areas, won in the early 1100s, were to be regained by Muslims in the late 1100s and 1200s.

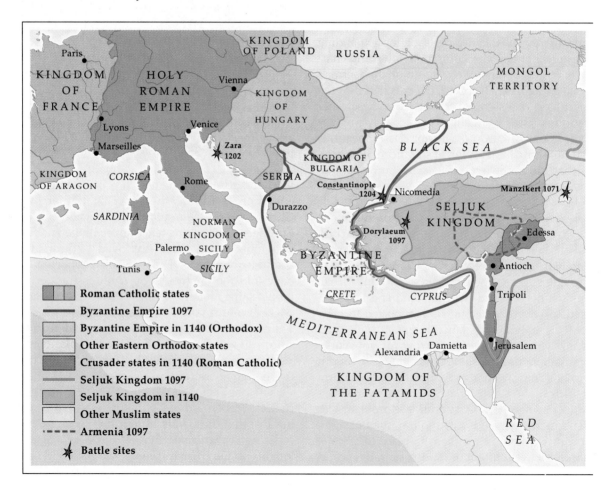

Roman Catholic states
Byzantine Empire 1097
Byzantine Empire in 1140 (Orthodox)
Other Eastern Orthodox states
Crusader states in 1140 (Roman Catholic)
Seljuk Kingdom 1097
Seljuk Kingdom in 1140
Other Muslim states
Armenia 1097
Battle sites

▶ **GODFREY APPROACHING THE GATE
AT CONSTANTINOPLE**
This miniature illustration of a history of the
expedition by one of its participants, William of
Tyre, shows Godfrey of Bouillon, the leader of the
First Crusade, entering Constantinople on his way
to Jerusalem. In the lower half of the picture he
approaches the city, and in the upper half he climbs
a ladder over the walls.

of this hapless army, gave them transport across
the Bosporus. The Turks at once cut them to
pieces.

Far better organized was the official First Crusade, which was led by nobles. Robert of Normandy, son of William the Conqueror, headed a
northern French army; Godfrey of Bouillon, his
brother Baldwin, and Robert of Flanders commanded an army of Lotharingians and Flemings;
Raymond of Toulouse led the men of Languedoc;
and Bohemond of Taranto and his nephew Tan-
cred marshaled the Normans of southern Italy.
These four armies moved by various overland
and sea routes to Constantinople (see Map 10.1)
and arrived there in 1096 and 1097.

The Byzantines Although the leaders of the
First Crusade had intended to conquer lands in
the East in their own name, Emperor Alexius demanded from them an oath of fealty in exchange
for provisioning the armies as they marched to
Palestine. Grudgingly, they agreed, promising to
regard the emperor as the overlord of any lands
they might reconquer from the Turks. Subsequently, both the emperor and the Western leaders accused each other of violating the terms of
the oath. The failure of the crusaders and the Byz-

antines to find a firm basis for cooperating ultimately weakened, although it did not defeat, the
enterprise.

Victories In 1097 the crusaders entered the Seljuk Sultanate of Rum, achieving their first major
victory at Dorylaeum. Baldwin then separated
his troops from the main body and conquered
Edessa, where he established the first crusader
state in the East. The decisive victory of the First
Crusade came in the battle for the port city of
Antioch. After that, the road to Jerusalem was
open. On July 15, 1099, the crusaders stormed the
Holy City and slaughtered its population of Muslims, Jews, and eastern Christians.

Besides a high level of organizational skill and
their own daring, the Westerners had a critical
advantage because of the tumultuous political
situation in the East. For all the brilliance of Islamic civilization, its leadership was in disarray.
The rulers of the Holy Land, the Seljuk Turks,
had only recently risen to power. They had not
yet consolidated their rule and were still fighting

▶ **THE PILLAGE OF JERUSALEM BY ANTIOCHUS**
Although the crusades were conducted in the name
of Christ, the behavior of their armies was no
different than that of soldiers throughout the ages.
In this scene in front of Jerusalem from a fifteenth-
century manuscript, the commander Antiochus
watches as his troops pile up the spoils they have
looted from the Holy City.

the Fatimids, the ruling dynasty of Egypt, over the possession of Palestine. In addition, the ancient schisms among Islamic religious sects continued to divide and weaken the community. The inability of Muslims to present a united front against the crusaders was probably the decisive reason for the final success of the First Crusade.

THE KINGDOM OF JERUSALEM

The crusaders now had the problem of organizing a government for their conquered territory and its population of Muslims and Eastern and Western Christians. They chose as ruler Godfrey of Bouillon, but he died in 1100, and his younger brother Baldwin, the conqueror of Edessa, succeeded him.

Baldwin set out to strengthen his realm through the application of feudal concepts and institutions. He kept direct dominion over Jerusalem and its surroundings, including a stretch of coast extending from Gaza to Beirut. To the north, three fiefs—the County of Tripoli, the Prin-cipality of Antioch, and the County of Edessa— were made subject to his suzerainty (see Map 10.2). Although King Baldwin and his successors were able to exert a respectable measure of authority over all these lands, profound weaknesses undermined their power. For one thing, the kings were never able to push their frontiers to an easily defensible, strategic border, such as the Lebanese Mountains. Furthermore, their administration remained critically dependent on a constant influx of men and money from the European homeland. Many knights and pilgrims came, but relatively few stayed as permanent settlers. The Westerners constituted a foreign aristocracy, small in number and set over a people of largely

▶ **CITIZENS OF EDESSA IN HOMAGE TO BALDWIN I** To emphasize the crusaders' triumph, this manuscript illustration shows Baldwin I, who captured Edessa in 1099, asserting his authority over the conquered Muslims. He sits on the left, with his knights next to him, and receives the homage and tribute of his new subjects.

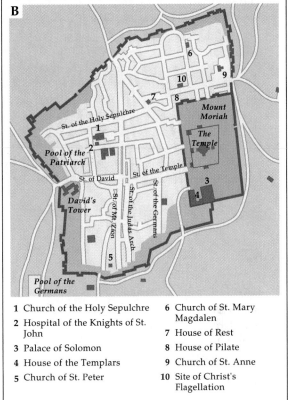

1 Church of the Holy Sepulchre
2 Hospital of the Knights of St. John
3 Palace of Solomon
4 House of the Templars
5 Church of St. Peter
6 Church of St. Mary Magdalen
7 House of Rest
8 House of Pilate
9 Church of St. Anne
10 Site of Christ's Flagellation

Map 10.2 THE CRUSADER STATES AT THEIR HEIGHT
For all the territory they covered, the crusader states proved vulnerable to reconquest from the East (A). Edessa was lost in less than 50 years, and even the fortified city of Jerusalem (B), captured in 1099, remained in Christian hands only until 1187.

different faith, culture, and sympathies. The wonder is not that the crusader states ultimately fell but that some of their outposts survived on the mainland of Asia Minor for nearly 200 years.

THE LATER CRUSADES

The Second Crusade   Although historians have traditionally assigned numbers to the later crusades, these expeditions were merely momentary swells in the steady current of Western people and treasures to and from the Middle East. The recapture of the city of Edessa by the Muslims in 1144 gave rise to the Second Crusade (1147–1149). Two armies, led by King Louis VII of France and Emperor Conrad III of Germany, set

out to capture Damascus to give the Kingdom of Jerusalem a more defensible frontier. However, they were soon forced to retreat ignominiously before superior Muslim forces.

The Third Crusade   The capture of Jerusalem by the Muslim chief Saladin prompted the Third Crusade (1189–1192), which was the climax of the crusading movement and its greatest disappointment. Emperor Frederick Barbarossa and kings Philip II of France and Richard I, the Lion-Hearted, of England all marched to the East. (Frederick drowned while crossing through Asia Minor, and most of his forces turned back.) Although the crusaders captured Acre, the Third Crusade ended in a stalemate. The Kingdom of Jerusalem remained limited to a narrow strip of the coast from Acre to Jaffa, but unarmed Christian pilgrims were given the right to visit Jerusalem. These were paltry gains from so grand an effort.

In the thirteenth century the crusades lost their appeal to Western knights, though Louis IX of

▷ **KNIGHTS IN COMBAT**
This contemporaneous manuscript illustration is a splendid depiction, full of motion and action, of two knights jousting. The figure on the left is thought to be Richard the Lion-Hearted, battling with Saladin himself.

France did lead two futile expeditions to North Africa. The population expansion in Europe, which had helped lend strength to the earlier crusades, was already leveling off. Moreover, many Europeans were shocked when the popes tried to direct crusades against the Albigensian heretics in southern France and against political enemies such as Frederick II of Hohenstaufen. With dwindling support from the West, the Christians in 1291 lost Acre, their last outpost in Palestine. Repeatedly during the Late Middle Ages the popes attempted to organize crusades; many knights and princes vowed to participate, and some traveled east, but none gained a major victory.

RESULTS OF THE CRUSADES

In terms of their main professed goal, the crusaders gained a partial success but not a permanent one: They had Jerusalem for nearly a century and maintained outposts on the Palestinian coast for nearly two centuries. Meanwhile, Christian pilgrims in large numbers were able to visit the holy places in Palestine in moderate safety. Even after the loss of Acre the Westerners continued to hold Cyprus and Greece, conquered during the early crusades. When the Ottoman Turks, successors to the Seljuks, finally seized these last crusader territories, the Western peoples had already found new routes to the Far East and were in the midst of a far broader overseas expansion. The crusades thus strengthened the security of the West by slowing the Turkish advance across the Mediterranean Sea and into Europe.

Warfare The crusades exerted a powerful influence on military techniques. After their initial invasions the crusaders waged a largely defensive war, and they became particularly skilled in the art of constructing castles. The numerous remains of crusader castles in nearly all the Eastern lands reflect these advances in such features as the overhanging tower parapets, from which oil or missiles could be rained down on attackers, and in the angular castle entranceways that prevented the enemy from shooting directly at the gates. Islamic castles show a similar evolution toward a more advanced military design.

The foes continually copied each other, and the Ottoman Turks in particular adopted many Western technical skills. By the fifteenth century the Ottomans, originally landlocked nomads, had begun to build a fleet and challenge Western maritime supremacy in the eastern Mediterranean Sea. They also learned from Western technicians the new arts of firearms, specifically cannons, without which they probably could not have conquered their vast empire.

Finance The crusades presented enormous, unprecedented problems of financing and logistical support, and therefore they exerted a major stimulus on the growth of financial and governmental institutions in the West. In the early crusades each knight or soldier had usually provided his own support. He brought money with him (often acquired by selling or mortgaging his estates) and purchased supplies from the natives of the lands through which he marched. He replenished his funds through booty or gifts from his lord and eventually through estates granted him in Palestine. But as the crusader wars became largely defensive in character, the opportunity for booty declined and the armies could no longer live off the land; support had to come primarily from Europe, thus requiring permanent institutional arrangements by which a constant flow of money (and men) could be directed from Europe into Palestine.

Traditional sources of revenue were inadequate, so both the popes and the princes began to impose direct taxes on their lands and subjects. In 1188, for example, the pope authorized, and the princes collected, the so-called Saladin tithe, a direct tax of 10 percent imposed on all clerical and lay revenues so as to finance the Third Crusade. (Previously, European governments had made little use of direct taxes because they were

difficult to assess and collect.) The imposition of the Saladin tithe and subsequent direct taxes required new institutional methods for assessment, collecting the moneys, and transferring the funds to where they were most needed. The crusades, in other words, helped the fiscal institutions of the governments of the West come of age.

One other financial course adopted by the papacy had great importance for the future. The popes allowed those Europeans who were too old or too weak to participate in the crusades to gain the spiritual benefits of crusading through monetary contributions, in return for which they were promised an *indulgence*—that is, a remission of punishment due for their sins. This practice was subsequently to become a major target of Church reformers and remained a central issue until the Reformation of the 1500s.

MILITARY-RELIGIOUS ORDERS

Templars Soon after the First Crusade a new kind of institution, the military-religious order, was founded to offer armed escorts and safe lodgings to pilgrims on their way to Palestine. Eventually it assumed a major role in supplying the settlers in the East with services, goods, defense, and means of communication. The military-religious orders combined the dedication, discipline, and organizational experience of monasticism with the military purposes of the crusade. The first of three great orders to emerge from the crusades was the Knights of the Temple, or Templars, founded some time before 1120 by a group of French knights. The knights took the three monastic vows of poverty, chastity, and obedience and, like monks, lived together in their own convents or communities. The Templars assumed a major role in the maintenance of safe routes between Europe and the crusader states and in the defense of the Kingdom of Jerusalem. The order also transported and guarded moneys in support of the Eastern war, and thus became the most important banking institution of the age until its suppression by the pope in 1312.

Hospitalers The Knights of the Hospital of St. John of Jerusalem, or Hospitalers, founded about 1130, enjoyed an even longer history. Never as numerous or as wealthy as the Templars, they

▶ **HOSPITALERS IN RHODES**
This fifteenth-century manuscript depiction of the capture of the island of Rhodes commemorates an event in 1306, when the Hospitaler knights attacked this fortress from the neighboring island of Cyprus. Wearing their distinctive tunic with its white cross, the Hospitalers swarmed through Rhodes, which they were to control until it was conquered by the Ottomans in 1522.

still made a major contribution to the defense of the Kingdom of Jerusalem. With the fall of Acre the knights moved their headquarters to Cyprus, then to Rhodes, and finally to Malta. As the Knights of Malta, they ruled the island until 1798. This "sovereign order" of the Knights of Malta survives today as an exclusively philanthropic

confraternity and is an important arm of papal charities throughout the world.

Teutonic Knights   About 1190, German pilgrims organized the Teutonic Knights to defend the roads to Palestine. These knights later transferred their headquarters to Venice, then to Transylvania (in modern Romania), and finally, in 1229, to Prussia, where they became the armed vanguard of the German eastward expansion and conquered for themselves an extensive domain along the shores of the Baltic Sea. In 1525 the last grand master, Albert of Hohenzollern, adopted Lutheranism and secularized the order and its territories. The German state of Brandenburg-Prussia eventually absorbed the lands, and also something of the militant spirit, of these crusading knights. The long history of these orders illustrates how organizational and military skills first acquired in the crusading movement continued to affect European life over the subsequent centuries.

ECONOMY

Historians still cannot draw up an exact balance sheet that registers accurately the economic gains and losses of these holy expeditions. Certainly the crusades were costly in blood and treasure. To support its armies, Europe exported large quantities of precious metals; the spoils of war and commercial profits undoubtedly brought some moneys back, but probably not enough to recoup the losses. Nevertheless, the crusades seem to have had a powerful and beneficial impact on the European economy, mainly by forcing into circulation moneys and treasures that hitherto had been hoarded in the West. Although there are no exact figures, both the volume of money and the speed of its circulation in Europe seem to have increased dramatically during this period. The new abundance of money stimulated commercial exchange and business investments and helped revive the Western economy, though the crusades were less significant in this respect than such influences as population growth and the settlement of new lands in Europe.

Trade   The crusades also enlivened trade with the East. After the First Crusade most of the large

Western armies went to Palestine by water, creating a lucrative business for the maritime cities of the Mediterranean Sea, especially in Italy. The Italians poured much of their profit from transporting and provisioning crusaders into commercial enterprises, and they established merchant colonies in many Eastern ports. Moreover, the crusades greatly strengthened the market for Eastern condiments in Europe. Knights and other pilgrims—who had become familiar with sugar, spices, and similar products in the East—continued to want them when they returned home, and they introduced them to their neighbors.

The Western demand for spices promoted commerce not only on the Mediterranean Sea but also between the Middle East and East Asia. Furthermore, it had an impact that went beyond the narrowly commercial. In the Late Middle Ages political disruptions in central Asia and the high taxes imposed by the Turks and Egyptians hampered trade with the East, but the call for Eastern products continued to be strong within Europe. This situation ensured rich rewards to the navigators and nations who discovered surer, cheaper ways to import spices and other Eastern commodities, and thus provided a direct incentive for the geographic explorations and discoveries of the 1400s and 1500s.

In familiarizing Europeans with many new products, the crusades helped raise the standard of living in the West, and this, in turn, intensified the pace of economic activity. From the eleventh century on, Europeans seem to have worked harder, partly perhaps to gain for themselves some of the products and the amenities of life they had observed in the East. New commodities altered the popular appreciation of what was essential for a good life and prompted Europeans to work more energetically to satisfy their newly raised expectations.

RELIGION AND LEARNING

The Church As acts of piety the crusades inevitably affected the organization and practice of religion, although it is all but impossible to distinguish their impact from that of many other forces at work in the West. Their initial success added to the prestige of the popes who sponsored them,

just as their subsequent failures undermined faith in papal leadership. Ecclesiastical finances and even canon law were influenced, as the Church sought to extend economic support and legal protection to both the crusaders and the families they left behind.

Scholarship It is difficult to assess exactly the importance of the crusades to the intellectual life of Europe. In one area of knowledge, geography, they did make important contributions. Starting from the crusader principalities in the East, first missionaries and then merchants penetrated deep into central Asia, and by the early thirteenth century they had reached China. Their reports, especially the memoirs of the Venetian Marco Polo at the close of the thirteenth century, gave Europe abundant information about East Asia and helped inspire Western navigators to seek new ways to penetrate beyond Islamic lands.

In other fields of knowledge the crusades seem to have brought little enlightenment. Most crusaders were rough warriors who had little interest in the subtleties of Islamic learning (*see box*, p. 295). However, the failure of these warriors to absorb new ideas from foreign cultures does not fully measure the cultural debt that the medieval West owes to Islam. Particularly through contacts in Spain and Sicily, Westerners learned new skills (the making of paper, perhaps the use of the compass) and new ideas that influenced the development of courtly love and scientific, philosophical, and religious thought in Europe. But it may also be true that by fomenting hatred against the infidel the crusades made Europeans less receptive to foreign ideas.

In the intellectual field as in all others, then, the crusades did not radically alter the course of medieval history, either in Christian or in Islamic societies; but they did powerfully reinforce existing tendencies and accelerate the pace of change on almost every level of life. Through the crusades Europeans learned about the geography of distant lands, became highly motivated to establish permanent and profitable contact with them, and acquired some experience in the conquest and administration of overseas territories. Appropriately, the crusades may be regarded as the initial chapter in the expansion of Europe.

▶ AN EARLY MAP OF THE WESTERN
MEDITERRANEAN
Cartography benefited as sea voyages multiplied, as
Europeans gained increased knowledge of the
world, and as they improved their skill in
illustration. This map by the Italian cartographer
Giovanni Benincasa describes in great detail the
coasts of Portugal, Spain, and North Africa.

II. Byzantium and the Ascendancy of the Ottoman Empire

Although the Byzantine Empire survived its defeat by the Turks at Manzikert in 1071, from then until its demise in the mid-fifteenth century the empire's control was effective only in Greece, the Aegean, and the area around Constantinople. The Ottoman Turks eventually fell heir to Byzantium's former power and influence, and by the early sixteenth century they were the unquestioned masters of southeast Europe and the Middle East.

THE DECLINE OF BYZANTIUM

The beginning of the thirteenth century saw the launching of the Fourth Crusade and, unexpectedly, the subsequent fragmenting of the Byzantine Empire. The expedition was first planned as a campaign against Egypt, but the Venetian Doge Enrico Dandolo bargained the short-funded crusaders into capturing, in return for passage east, the Christian city of Zara in Dalmatia, which was opposing Venice in the Adriatic Sea. Then Alexius IV, a pretender to the Byzantine throne, hired the crusaders to seize Constantinople in return for money, military help in the Egyptian campaign, and the reunion of the Eastern and Western churches. The crusaders restored Alexius to the throne, but he could not honor his promises. In retaliation, the crusaders stormed and looted

Constantinople in 1204. They then divided the Byzantine Empire among themselves.

A Flemish nobleman assumed the office of emperor, although he ruled directly only a small parcel of territory surrounding Constantinople. The Venetians, by contrast, gained nearly half of all Byzantine possessions: This acquisition marked the foundation of a Venetian colonial empire that was to survive for centuries. Byzantine refugees from Constantinople set up an empire-in-exile, with its capital at Nicaea in Asia Minor. In 1261 the emperor of Nicaea, Michael III Paleologus, recaptured Constantinople, but neither he nor his successors could restore the shattered unity of the old Byzantine Empire.

The decline of the Byzantine Empire allowed the hitherto subject Balkan peoples to build independent kingdoms under Frankish princes and to aspire to dominate the area. First the Bulgarians in the thirteenth century, and then the Serbs in the fourteenth, created large Balkan empires. At the height of their powers these empires seemed destined to absorb the remnants of the Byzantine Empire, but by the fourteenth century it was the Ottoman Turks who presented the greatest menace to Byzantium.

Arabic and Frankish Medicine

Western accounts usually portray the Muslims whom the crusaders encountered in the Holy Land as barbarians. It is therefore instructive to read a view from the other side. Ousama Ibn Mounkidh, a twelfth-century Arab, here quotes the report of a doctor who had visited the crusader Franks; he sharply contrasts the medical expertise (and general humanity) of the two sides.

"They brought before me a knight with an abscess in his leg and a woman who was wasting away with a consumptive fever. I applied a little plaster to the knight; his abscess opened and took a turn for the better. The woman I forbade certain food and improved her condition.

"It was at this point that a Frankish doctor came up and said: 'This man is incapable of curing them.' Then, turning to the knight, he asked, 'Which do you prefer, to live with one leg or die with two?' 'I would rather live with one leg,' the knight answered. 'Bring a stalwart knight,' said the Frankish doctor, 'and a sharp hatchet.' Knight and hatchet soon appeared. I was present at the scene. The doctor stretched the patient's leg on the block of wood and then said to the knight, 'Strike off his leg with the hatchet; take it off at one blow.' Under my eyes the knight aimed a violent blow at it without cutting through the leg. He aimed another blow at the unfortunate man, as a result of which the marrow came from his leg and the knight died instantly.

"As for the woman, the doctor examined her and said, 'She is a woman in whose head there is a devil who has taken possession of her. Shave off her hair!' His prescription was carried out, and like her fellows, she began once again to eat garlic and mustard. Her consumption became worse. The doctor then said, 'It is because the devil has entered her head.' Taking a razor, the doctor cut open her head in the shape of a cross and scraped away the skin in the center so deeply that her very bones were showing. He then rubbed the head with salt. In her turn, the woman died instantly.

"After having asked them whether my services were still required, and receiving an answer in the negative, I came back, having learned from their medicine matters of which I had previously been ignorant."

Adapted from Brian Tierney, *The Middle Ages*, Vol. I: *The Sources of Medieval History*, 5th ed. (McGraw-Hill, 1992), p. 164.

▶ **VIEW OF VENICE**
This elaborate depiction of Venice in a fourteenth-century manuscript shows the buying and selling that was characteristic of the citizens of this commercial and maritime center. Particularly notable at the upper left are the four bronze horses that the Venetians brought back to the city after the capture and looting of Constantinople in 1204 during the Fourth Crusade. The horses were placed on the facade of the cathedral of St. Mark's, and they have remained there ever since.

THE FALL OF CONSTANTINOPLE

The Rising Threat Turkish communities and peoples had been assuming a large military and political role in the Middle East since the late tenth century. The Seljuk Turks had established the Sultanate of Rum in the late 1000s, and they dominated western Asia Minor for the next century and a half. This sultanate survived the attacks of the Western crusaders but was defeated by the far more formidable invasion of an Asiatic people, the Mongols, in the thirteenth century. The Ottoman Turks followed the Mongol invasions and took over the area of the Sultanate of Rum. They then established themselves at Gallipoli on the European side of the Straits in 1354, and soon their possessions completely surrounded Byzantine territory.

The Byzantine emperors, fearing the worst for their small and isolated realm, tried desperately but unsuccessfully to persuade the West that they needed military help against this threat. At the council of Florence in 1439 Emperor John VII even accepted reunion with Rome, largely on Roman terms, in return for aid, but he had no power to impose the reunion of the churches on his people; in fact, many Eastern Christians preferred Turkish rule to submission to the hated Westerners.

The Capture of the City The Ottomans were unable to mount a major campaign against Constantinople until 1453, when Sultan Mehmet II, the Conqueror, finally attacked by land and water. The city fell after a heroic resistance, and Emperor Constantine XI Paleologus himself, whose imperial lineage stretched back more than 1400 years to Augustus Caesar, died in this final agony of the Byzantine Empire.

The fall of Constantinople had very little military or economic effect on Europe and the Middle East. The Byzantine Empire had not been an effective barrier to Ottoman expansion for years, and Constantinople had dwindled commercially as well as politically. The shift to Turkish dominion did not, as historians once believed, substantially affect the flow of trade between the East and West. Nor did the Turkish conquest of the city provoke an exodus of Byzantine scholars and manuscripts to Italy. Scholars from the East, recognizing the decline and seemingly inevitable fall of the Byzantine Empire, had been emigrating to Italy since the late fourteenth century; the revival of Greek letters was well under way in the West by 1453.

Effects The impact of the fall was largely psychological; although hardly unexpected, it shocked the Christian world. The pope sought to launch a new crusade and received from the Western princes the usual promises but no armies. Venice waged a protracted and inconclusive war against the Turks (1463–1479). These military responses were less important in the long run, however, than the responses of Western merchants. The fall of Byzantium added to their incentives to find trade routes to East Asia that would bypass the Islamic waters of the Mediterranean.

Above all, the end of the Byzantine Empire had great symbolic importance for contemporaries and, perhaps even more, for later historians. In selecting Byzantium as his capital in 324, Constantine had founded a Christian Roman empire that could be considered the first authentically medieval state. For more than 1000 years this Christian Roman empire played a major political and cultural role in the history of both Eastern and Western peoples. In some respects, the years of its existence mark the span of the Middle Ages, and its passing symbolizes the end of an era.

EXPANSION OF THE OTTOMAN EMPIRE

The Ottomans took their name from Osman, or Othman (1290–1326), who founded a dynasty of sultans that survived for six centuries. Under Mehmet II (1451–1481), who from the start of his reign committed his government to a policy of conquest, the Ottomans began a century of expansion (*see box*, below). After the fall of Constantinople, which became his capital under the name of Istanbul (though the name was not

▶ *Gentile Bellini*
Mehmet II
Mehmet II, here shown in a painting attributed to the Venetian artist Gentile Bellini, was the Conqueror of Constantinople in 1453.

The Sultan Mehmet II

One of the first histories of the Ottomans by a westerner was written by an English schoolmaster named Richard Knolles and published in 1603. It is obvious that a great deal of research went into his work, which is marked by vivid portraits, such as this one of the Sultan Mehmet II, known as the Conqueror because of his capture of Constantinople, who had lived a century before Knolles wrote.

"He was of stature but low, square set, and strongly limbed; his complexion sallow and melancholy; his look and countenance stern, with his eyes piercing, and his nose so high and crooked that it almost touched his upper lip. He was of a very sharp and apprehending wit, learned especially in astronomy, and could speak the Greek, Latin, Arabic, Chaldee, and Persian tongues. He delighted much in reading of histories, and the lives of worthy men, especially the lives of Alexander the Great and Julius Caesar, whom he proposed to himself as examples to follow. He was of an exceeding courage, and a severe punisher of injustice. Men that excelled in any quality, he greatly favored and honorably entertained, as he did Gentile Bellini, a painter of Venice, whom he purposely caused to come from thence to Constantinople, to draw the lively counterfeit of himself (see plate above), for which he most bountifully rewarded him. He so severely punished theft, as that in his time all the ways were safe. He was altogether irreligious, and most perfidious, ambitious above measure, and in nothing more delighted than in blood: insomuch that he was responsible for the death of 800,000 men; craft, covetousness and dissimulation were in him accounted tolerable, in comparison of his greater vices. In his love was no assurance, and his least displeasure was death; so that he lived feared of all men, and died lamented of none."

Adapted by T. K. Rabb from Richard Knolles, *A Generall Historie of the Turkes*, as printed in John J. Saunders, (ed.), *The Muslim World on the Eve of Europe's Expansion* (Prentice-Hall, 1966), pp. 25–26.

officially adopted until 1930), Mehmet subjugated the Morea, Serbia, Bosnia, and parts of Herzegovina. He drove the Genoese from their Black Sea colonies, forced the khan of the Crimea to become his vassal, and fought a lengthy naval war with the Venetians. At his death the Ottomans were a power on land and sea, and the Black Sea had become a Turkish lake.

Early in the following century Turkish domination was extended over the heart of the Arab lands through the conquest of Syria, Egypt, and the western coast of the Arabian peninsula. (The Arabs did not again enjoy autonomy until the twentieth century.) With the conquest of the sacred cities of Mecca and Medina the sultan assumed the title of caliph, "successor of the Prophet," claiming to be Islam's supreme religious head as well as its mightiest sword.

Suleiman II The Ottoman Empire was brought to its height of power by Suleiman II, the Magnificent (1520–1566), who extended the empire in both the West and the East. In 1521 he took the citadel of Belgrade, which had hitherto blocked Turkish advance up the Balkan Peninsula toward Hungary, and the next year he forced the Hospitalers, after a six-month siege, to surrender the island of Rhodes, a loss that was a crippling blow to Western naval strength in the eastern Mediterranean.

Suleiman achieved his greatest victory by destroying the army of the king of Hungary at Mohacs in 1526 and taking over his kingdom. He then launched his most ambitious campaign, directed against Austria, the Christian state that now assumed chief responsibility for defending Europe's eastern frontiers. However, this effort, the high-water mark of Ottoman expansion into Europe, failed when Suleiman was unable to capture Vienna in 1529, and the frustrated sultan returned home, turning his attention toward the East. His armies overran Mesopotamia and completed the conquest of southern Arabia, and for the next two centuries the Ottoman Empire included all of southeastern Europe as well as the Middle East, Egypt, and Arabia (see Map 10.3).

Suleiman brought his empire fully into the diplomatic as well as the military struggles of Europe, taking shrewd advantage of the Europeans' rivalries. He hated Charles V who, as Holy Roman Emperor, similarly pretended to rule the world; and in 1525 he joined Francis I of France in an alliance directed against Charles, later negotiating a commercial treaty that further cemented cooperation between France and the Ottoman Empire. Through his alliance with France, Suleiman confronted Charles V with the possibility of a war on two fronts and prevented the formation of a common Christian crusade against himself, which the popes ceaselessly but vainly advocated.

OTTOMAN INSTITUTIONS

The Ottomans had expanded a small, landlocked community in western Asia Minor into a great empire. Several advantages account for this achievement, one of them being their geographic position. Set on the frontier between the Islamic and Christian worlds, the Ottomans could claim to be the chief warriors for the faith, and the resultant prestige won recruits and moral support from the more distant Islamic communities. Moreover, the Ottomans soon became a power in the political struggles of both Europe and the Middle East and were able to take advantage of favorable opportunities in both regions, even enlisting allies in one area to wage war in the other.

The intense rivalries among the Christian faiths also facilitated Ottoman expansion. Some Balkan Christians accepted papal supremacy, others adhered to the Eastern Orthodox traditions, and still others were regarded as heretics by both the Roman Catholics and the Orthodox. Often a Christian sect preferred the rule of the tolerant Ottomans to that of a rival Christian sect. In preserving peace among these dissident Christians, the Ottomans could serve as impartial referees, while Christians obviously could not.

Military and Administrative Skills A major advantage of the Ottomans in their remarkable ascendancy was their cultural heritage and treatment of the conquered. From their nomadic origins and their long experience as frontier fighters, they had preserved a strong military tradition. Their devout adherence to Islam, which

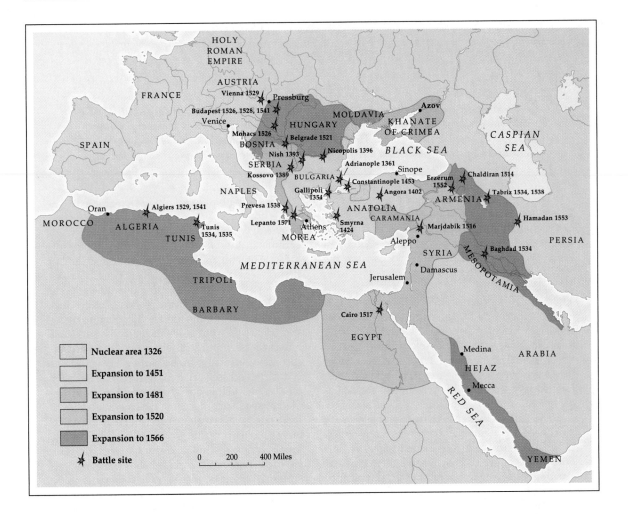

advocated holy wars against unbelievers, reinforced their aggressive tendencies; but they also showed a remarkable ability to organize conquered territories and gain the support, and to some degree even the loyalty, of the people they held in subjugation.

The Ottomans allowed the subject communities to live by their own laws under their own officials, requiring them only to pay taxes and supply men for the Ottoman army and administration. The conquests thus did not greatly disturb the society, economy, or culture of these communities, which were also able to play a role of considerable importance in the social and economic life of the Ottoman Empire. Trade, for example, which remained vigorous in the Black Sea and the eastern Mediterranean Sea, was still

Map 10.3 THE OTTOMAN EMPIRE, 1300–1566
The stunning speed of Ottoman expansion, especially during the 1400s, raised the specter of a powerful enemy to the east that kept many Europeans fearful for centuries.

largely in the hands of Greeks, Armenians, and Jews. The Ottomans themselves remained aloof from commercial undertakings and confined their careers to government service and the army.

The Divan In the course of their enormous expansion the Ottoman sultans faced the formidable problem of developing military and administrative institutions strong enough to hold together their vast empire. Like all other medieval rulers, the sultan originally governed with the

The Janissaries

Most observers of the rise of the Ottomans emphasized their military skill, and particularly the discipline and effectiveness of their Janissaries, when explaining their successes. Typical was the Habsburg ambassador Ogier Ghiselin de Busbecq, who served in Constantinople from 1555 to 1562 and here describes passing through the city of Buda, now Budapest.

"At Buda, I made my first acquaintance with the Janissaries; this is the name by which the Turks call the infantry of the royal guard. The Turkish state has 12,000 of these troops, scattered through every part of the empire, either to garrison the forts or to protect the Christians and Jews from outrage and wrong.

"A garrison of Janissaries is always stationed in the citadel of Buda. The dress of the men consists of a robe reaching down to the ankles, while to cover their heads they employ a cowl, part of which contains the head, while the remainder hangs down and flaps against the neck. On their forehead is placed a silver-gilt cone of considerable height, studded with stones of great value.

"The Turkish monarch going to war takes with him over 20,000 camels and nearly as many mules, of which a great part are loaded with rice and other kinds of grain. They reserve their stores as much as possible, and a ration just sufficient to sustain life is daily weighed out to the Janissaries and other troops of the royal household. They take out a few spoonfuls of flour and put them into water, adding butter, salt and spices; these ingredients are boiled, and a large bowl of gruel is thus obtained. Of this they eat once or twice a day, according to the quantity they have, without any bread. Sometimes they have recourse to horse-flesh.

"From this you will see that it is the patience, self-denial and thrift of the Turkish soldier that enable him to face the most trying circumstances and come safely out of the dangers that surround him. What a contrast to our men! Christian soldiers on a campaign refuse to put up with their ordinary food, and call for dainty dishes! It makes me shudder to think of what the results of a struggle between such different systems must be. On their side is vast wealth, experience in arms, a veteran soldiery, readiness to endure hardships, union, order, discipline, thrift and watchfulness. On ours are found luxurious habits, exhausted resources, broken spirits, a raw soldiery, greedy quarrels, no regard for discipline, drunkenness and debauchery. Can we doubt what the result must be?"

Adapted from John J. Saunders (ed.), *The Muslim World on the Eve of Europe's Expansion* (Prentice-Hall, 1966), pp. 20–22.

aid of a council of chosen advisers, which was called the *divan*. From the time of Mehmet the Conqueror, however, the sultan came to be considered too august to participate personally in the divan's deliberations. The function of presiding over the meetings of the divan fell to the grand vizier, who became the chief administrative official of the Ottoman state. The administration was divided into three major categories: civil, ecclesiastical, and military. The divan retained supreme responsibility over both the civil and the military branches; it supervised the collection of taxes and tribute, the conscription of soldiers, and the conduct of foreign affairs; it made recommendations to the sultan concerning peace, war, and other major decisions of state; and it also functioned as a court in disputes that were not religious in character.

Religion and the Army Religious affairs were administered by a class of judges trained in Islamic law, who constituted a special corps called the *ulema*. At their head, the sheikh-ul-Islam served as the supreme judge, after the sultan himself, in all matters of sacred law.

The army had two principal divisions: unpaid holders of fiefs granted by the sultan in exchange for military service; and paid soldiers, technically considered slaves, who remained permanently in the sultan's service. The holder of a fief was required to provide the military with armed men, the number being set in strict proportion to the revenue deriving from his estates. Among the paid soldiers the most important were those belonging to the highly trained, thoroughly professional, but legally unfree corps of the *Janissaries*, meaning "new troops." Slave armies had been common in Islamic states, but the Ottomans did not adopt the practice until the fifteenth century. According to the accounts of the earliest chronicles, Sultan Murad learned from a theologian in about 1430 that the Koran assigned him one-fifth of the booty captured by his army, including prisoners. Murad decided to convert his prisoners to Islam, teach them Turkish, and enlist them in a tough, well-disciplined military contingent, the Janissaries. Most medieval monarchs relied on mercenaries or poorly trained and poorly equipped feudal levies, composed of vassals with little enthusiasm for fighting, and feudal levies continued to make up the larger part of the Turkish army. But the Janissaries soon became an elite corps of professional fighters, dedicated to the sultan and to Islam, and were in large part responsible for Ottoman victories (*see box*, p. 300).

Local Government On the local level, the government of the empire was content to leave many administrative responsibilities to the self-governing communities of Christians and Jews and to the holders of fiefs, who collected taxes and mustered soldiers from those settled on their lands. Apart from the fiefs, the unit of local administration was the canton, or *kaza*, which was administered by a judge, or *qaid*. The cantons were grouped into departments and provinces, usually under the authority of a pasha, who was both a civil and a military official, since he bore the responsibility of leading the feudal levies of his provinces in time of war.

The Devshirme Some time in the fifteenth century a new system of recruiting slaves for the civil administration and the military was introduced—the *devshirme*, or levy of boys. In the *devshirme's* developed form, special commissioners every five years selected young boys from among the Christian population to be given special instruction in Turkish and converted to Islam. After their training they were examined and assigned either to the corps of Janissaries or to the palace administration. In the latter case they were given still more intensive training, and the most talented of them could aspire to the highest administrative offices of the empire. Even the grand vizier was usually a slave. Remarkably, in each generation the most powerful administrators were new to high position, with no family ties to the Turkish aristocracy and no reason to ally with them against the sultan's interests. This practice of recruiting slaves for the sultan's service is sometimes called the *fundamental institution of the empire*, for the sultan's power depended on its functioning properly.

THE SULTAN

The sultan united in his own person supreme civil, military, and religious authority. The way his power was defined was influenced by Byzantine views of imperial authority, which seem to have contributed to the pomp of court ceremony and the aura of sanctity surrounding the person of the sultan. Still more influential were Islamic traditions concerning governmental power, particularly the notion that the sultan was the successor of Muhammad, the legitimate ruler of all true believers. In a strict sense the sultan could not be an absolute ruler, for he was, like every member of the Islamic community, subject to the sacred law. But he was also the supreme judge of that law, and there was no way apart from revolution to challenge his decisions.

The early sultans devised a striking solution to a problem common to most medieval states: the peaceful transference of power from a ruler to his successor. From the fifteenth to the seventeenth century the Ottomans followed what has come to be called the law of fratricide. The sultan cohabited with numerous slave girls of the harem, who

ناكن وتخت اله سلطان سليمان   قلوردى ديوخصمى بله رومان

► SULEIMAN

This portrait of Suleiman the Magnificent from a sixteenth-century Turkish manuscript suggests the ornate splendor that was associated with the awesome figure of the sultan. His court was famous for its lavish festivities and splendid costumes and decorations.

shedding of their imperial blood.) The religious judges allowed such massacres, because an uncontested succession was essential to the welfare of the empire.

THE LIMITS OF OTTOMAN POWER

In the sixteenth century Suleiman the Magnificent brought the Ottoman Empire to unprecedented heights of power, but already certain pressures were imposing limits on its expansion. One was geographical. The Ottomans had operated effectively in areas close to their homeland in Asia Minor, but the efficiency of their army and administration inevitably diminished with distance. The unsuccessful campaign against Austria proved that that region was already beyond their reach, and the Ottomans encountered similar walls to further advance in the Iranian plateau and the waters of the central Mediterranean. With the opening of trade routes around Africa and across the Atlantic, the Ottomans were no longer at the center of the civilized world and no longer the masters of movements east and west. Although they left the commerce of their empire largely in the hands of subject communities, they were well aware of the importance of trade, and Suleiman therefore sent a force to destroy Portuguese ships and trading stations in the Indian Ocean. The failure of this attack was an ominous sign for the empire, because the geographic discoveries of the 1400s and 1500s caused dislocations in east-west trade—a shift in trade routes, an increase in the stock of precious metal in Europe, rising inflation—and brought the Ottomans few benefits.

Within the empire there was also a deterioration in the quality of leadership. For reasons hard to explain, the sultans after Suleiman showed little of the energy and ability that had marked the earlier rulers of the House of Osman. Technical advance was continuing in the West, and it was critical for the empire to keep abreast of these changes. The great sultans had welcomed Western technicians and made use of their skills, especially in armament, but their successors after Suleiman seemed distinctly less interested in learning from the West. Declining efficiency was also evident in Ottoman government. The chan-

were selected much as were the male household slaves, and usually he fathered numerous progeny. He then picked one of the boys to be his successor. At the sultan's death, the designated heir had the right and obligation to put his brothers and half-brothers to death. (They were strangled with a silken bowstring in order to avoid the ceries and secretariats kept precise and informative records in the 1400s, but they no longer did so in the late 1500s and seem to have been beset by mounting disorder. At the death of Suleiman in 1566, it is still much too early to speak of Ottoman decadence, but the fortunes of the Ottoman Empire were already past their height.

III. The Birth of Modern Russia

▼

A great Russian historian, V. O. Kliuchevsky, once identified the principal theme in the history of the Russian people as colonization—the long, arduous, and ultimately successful struggle to settle and subdue the huge Eurasian plain that was their home.[1] The history of that struggle records defeats as well as victories. From the ninth to twelfth centuries, the center of Rus civilization had been Kiev, on the fringes of the southern steppe. Although the Rus of Kiev were able to maintain contacts across the steppes to the Black Sea and the Mediterranean world beyond, they could not resist forever the successive waves of invading steppe nomads. From the 1100s, Pechenegs and Cumans, followed by the still more terrible Mongols, mounted ever more destructive raids against the Rus settlements and cut off their contact with the Black Sea. Eventually the vulnerability of the steppe settlements forced many of the Rus to seek out safer homes in the forested regions to the north and west, where they formed new institutions and built a new civilization, the direct ancestor of the modern Russian state (*see box*, p. 304).

THE MONGOLS

The resurgence of the steppe nomads was the decisive reason for the decline of Kievan Rus, especially when the Mongols appeared on Europe's

---

[1]*A History of Russia*, 1911, vol. 1, p. 2. This theory has interesting parallels to Frederick Jackson Turner's "frontier thesis" interpretation of American history.

borders in the early 1200s. The Mongol chief Genghis Khan was amassing in Asia the largest empire the world has even known. In 1223 a Mongol army penetrated Eastern Europe in what seems to have been a reconnoitering expedition. The Mongols defeated the allied princes of Rus in a battle on the Kalka River (a tributary of the Don) but almost at once returned to the East, only to invade once again, in greater force, a few years later. From 1237 to 1241 a Mongol army conducted raids throughout Eastern Europe and established at Sarai, on the lower Volga River, the capital of a division of the Mongol Empire that came to be called the *Golden Horde*.

▶ **COURT OF A MONGOL KING**
The courts of the Mongol kings, as this illustration from a Persian manuscript suggests, were dazzlingly opulent. When Louis IX of France sent presents of liturgical objects (chalices and books), the Mongol king rejected the gift and suggested that a tribute of gold and silver would be more appropriate.

The Birth of Christianity in Russia

*Essential to the self-image of the Russian state was the belief that it was the heir of Byzantium and that its religion distinguished it from other Christian kingdoms. To emphasize this distinctiveness the monks of Kiev, writing **The Russian Primary Chronicle** around 1200, stressed the choice among alternative faiths when a Kievan prince, Vladimir (who was to become the first Russian saint) made the crucial decision to join the Greek church.*

"Vladimir was overcome by lust for women. But Vladimir, though at first deluded, eventually found salvation. For at this time the Russes were ignorant pagans. The devil rejoiced. He knew not that the Prophet had said 'I will call those my people who are not my people.' (*Hosea*)

"Vladimir was visited by Bulgars of Mohammedan faith, who said, 'Though you are a wise and prudent prince, you have no religion. Adopt our faith, and revere Mahomet.' Vladimir inquired what was the nature of their religion. They replied that they believed in God, and that Mahomet instructed them to practice circumcision, to eat no pork, to drink no wine, and after death promised them complete fulfillment of carnal desires. Vladimir listened to them, for he was fond of women and indulgence. But circumcision and abstinence from pork and wine were disagreeable to him. 'Drinking,' said he, 'is the joy of the Russes. We cannot exist without that pleasure.'

"Then came the Germans as emissaries of the Pope. 'Our faith is the light. We worship God, who has made heaven and earth, the stars, the moon, and every creature, while your gods are only wood.' Vladimir inquired what their teaching was. They replied, 'Fasting according to one's strength. But whatever one eats or drinks is all to the glory of God.' Then Vladimir answered, 'Depart hence; our fathers accepted no such principle.'

"Then the Greeks sent a scholar, who exhibited to Vladimir a canvas on which was depicted the Judgement Day of the Lord, and showed him, on the right, the righteous going to their bliss in Paradise, and on the left, the sinners on their way to torment. Then Vladimir sighed and said, 'Happy are they upon the right, but woe to those upon the left!' The scholar replied, 'If you desire to take your place upon the right with the just, then accept baptism!' Vladimir took this counsel to heart, saying, 'I shall wait yet a little longer,' for he wished to inquire about all the faiths.

"[Vladimir then sought in marriage the sister of the Byzantine emperor, Anna, who was persuaded to go by the promise:] 'Through your agency God turns the land of Rus to repentance.' The Princess embarked on a ship, and set forth across the sea. By divine agency, Vladimir was suffering at that moment from a disease of the eyes, and could see nothing. The Princess declared that if he desired to be relieved of this disease, he should be baptized. When Vladimir heard her message, he said, 'If this proves true, then surely the God of the Christians is great,' and gave order that he should be baptized. The Bishop of Kherson, together with the Princess's priests, baptized Vladimir, and as the Bishop laid his hand upon him, he straightway received his sight. Upon experiencing the miraculous cure, Vladimir glorified God, saying, 'I have now perceived the one true God.' When his followers beheld this miracle, many of them were also baptized. After his baptism, Vladimir took the Princess in marriage."

Adapted from Harry J. Carroll, Jr., Ainslee T. Embree, Knox Mellon, Jr., Arnold Schrier, and Alastair M. Taylor (eds.), *The Development of Civilization: A Documentary History of Politics, Society, and Thought,* vol. I (Scott, Foresman, 1961), pp. 217–220.

The khans, or rulers, of the Golden Horde maintained suzerainty over the lands of what is now Ukraine and Belarus until the mid-1300s and over eastern Russia until the mid-1400s. The princes subject to the Golden Horde had to pay tribute to the khans and secure from them a charter, called *yarlik*, that confirmed them in office, but otherwise they could rule their own people.

As a result, despite the power they exercised over the East Slavs for centuries, the Mongols' influence on Slavic languages and cultures remained relatively slight.

Slavic Resettlement The nomad invasions and the formation of the Golden Horde had a devastating effect on the settlements in the southern steppes. A chronicler lamented that Kiev, once proudly known as the "mother of Rus cities," had only 200 houses left standing in the 1200s. Most of the Rus population sought more protected lands, and in the 1100s and 1200s three new areas of East Slavic settlement rose to prominence.

Some colonists moved west into the provinces of Galicia and Volynia along the upper Dniester River and became the ancestors of the modern Ukrainians and the Belorussians, or White Russians. After a short period of submission to the Mongols, these colonies fell under the political domination first of the grand dukes of Lithuania and then of the Polish kings. They developed their own literary languages and cultural traditions, and they were not politically reunited with their fellow East Slavs for centuries. (The province of Galicia, with a large Ukrainian population, remained under Polish or Austrian rule until 1944.)

Other colonists moved north into the vast and empty area ruled by the city of Novgorod, the region of Russia where Mongol rule lasted the shortest time. But the poor soil could not support a dense population. More important than these two areas was the third new center of settlement: the Russian "Mesopotamia," the lands between the upper Volga and Oka rivers, where dense forests offered both relative security from the nomads and a productive soil. Those who moved north to Novgorod and to the Russian Mesopotamia were the ancestors of the modern Great Russians, still the largest of the East Slavic peoples, and they formed the nucleus of a new Russian state.

Feudal Russia Historians call the period between the twelfth and fifteenth centuries the age of feudal Russia—the time when Russia was divided into many princely domains. Nearly all the small towns within Russian Mesopotamia had their own princes, their own citadels, or kremlins, and their own territories. All the princes were subject to the khan of the Golden Horde, but Mongol government remained limited to extracting tribute and granting *yarliks*. Russia lacked a central government.

In this feudal period, Russian economy, society, and culture acquired distinctive characteristics. With the exception of Novgorod, the towns of the north could not develop an active commerce with distant areas, as Kiev had, nor did they have much contact with Constantinople or other centers of learning. The Russian towns in the main were not commercial or industrial centers but rather served as fortresses to which the surrounding population could flee in times of danger. The economy was overwhelmingly agricultural, and the energy of the people was directed primarily to clearing the great forests. In social terms, most peasants remained free and their freedom was protected by their closeness to an expanding frontier, which offered them places of refuge if conditions at home deteriorated.

Art, which remained within the conventions of icon painting created by the Byzantines, was produced primarily for the Church. Architects as well as artists achieved remarkable delicacy, and Russia's supreme religious painter, Andrei Rublev (1370?–1430?), deserves to be recognized as one of the world's great artistic geniuses, even though few of his works survive.

THE RISE OF MOSCOW

In spite of the political differences that divided them, the Russians' religion and their submission to the Mongols preserved a sense of identity and unity among them, though it was long uncertain which of the many petty princes would take the leadership in building a politically united nation. One of the towns that seemed unlikely to achieve this hegemony was the new settlement of Moscow, which is mentioned in a chronicle for the first time in 1147. But its early obscurity proved an advantage because this small town was passed over by raiding nomads in search of richer plunder. Located on the Moskva River, Moscow also had other advantages. It was in the center of Russian Mesopotamia, close to the tributary rivers feeding the Volga River to the north and the Oka River to the south. The princes of Moscow could

▶ *Andrei Rublev*
OLD TESTAMENT TRINITY, 1410–1420
Andrei Rublev, one of the most influential
Russian artists of the fifteenth century,
worked within a Byzantine tradition of wall
painting. His *Old Testament Trinity*,
originally from a monastery, shows a
reinterpretation of the standard Christian
iconography: the three angels positioned
around a dish represent God the Father, the
Son, and the Holy Ghost.

pursue a "river policy" in their expansion, following the courses of streams in all directions
and depending on this network of water routes
to bind their state together. The region between
the Volga and the Oka rivers also formed the geographic heart of European Russia and allowed
the prince who ruled it to exploit opportunities
in almost any part of Russia.

Moscow gained preeminence primarily
through the talents of its early princes. Like other

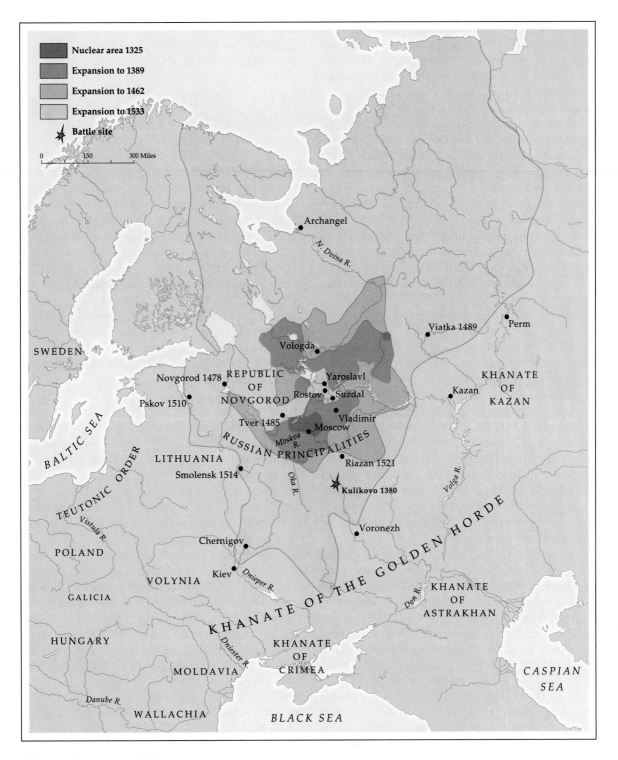

Map 10.4 THE RISE OF MOSCOW, 1325–1533
Despite its seeming backwoods location, Moscow was able to expand its power
dramatically, especially in the reign of Ivan III (1462–1505), and to establish itself as the
dominant force in Russia by the mid-1500s.

rulers in the area, they abandoned the disastrous Kievan system of splitting an inheritance and adopted primogeniture (inheritance by the eldest son) instead. A prince's acquisitions were thus kept intact rather than divided among many heirs, and each prince was able to build on the accomplishments of his predecessor. The princes set about "gathering the Russian land," as historians describe the process of uniting all of Russia, by pursuing simultaneously two distinct goals: They acquired new territories at every opportunity, through wars, marriages, and purchases; and they sought to make Moscow, together with the Church, the symbol and embodiment of Russian national unity—a distinct identity that contrasted with both the Mongols and the Western Christians. The prestige Moscow gained in this way helped persuade the princes of other cities to submit to its rule.

Ivan I The first Muscovite prince to raise this obscure little town to prominence was Ivan I (1328–1341). Chiefly through purchases from other princes but occasionally through conquest, he extended his possessions along the entire course of the Moskva River and won enclaves of territory to the north beyond the Volga River. Ivan courted the favor of the still powerful Mongol khan of the Golden Horde and often visited the khan in his capital on the lower Volga River. In return for his loyalty and gifts, the khan gave Ivan a special *yarlik* in 1328 that made him the chief representative of Mongol authority in Russia with the right to collect the Mongol tribute from all Russian lands. Thereafter Ivan and his successors permanently held the title *velikii kniaz* ("great prince," or "grand duke"). In collecting tribute for the Mongols, Ivan also increased his own treasury, thereby earning the nickname by which he is best known to history—Kalita ("moneybags").

Ivan no less determinedly sought the favor of the Russian Church, and he developed a strong friendship with Peter, the primate (or chief bishop) of the Church. Like his predecessor, a metropolitan of Kiev who had abandoned that decaying city, Peter had no fixed see but traveled throughout the new centers of Russian settlement. He visited Moscow frequently and by chance died there in 1326. His tomb became a national shrine, and his successors therefore chose Moscow as their permanent see, thus making Moscow the capital of the Russian Church even before it was the capital of the Russian people.

Decline of the Mongols By the late 1300s the power of the Mongols was declining, largely because of dissensions within the Golden Horde. The princes of Moscow now abandoned their traditional role as chief servants of the khan and began to present themselves as leaders of the growing national opposition to Mongol rule. Though far from ending the power of the Mongols, Prince Dmitri won the first Russian victory over a Mongol army in 1380, at Kulikovo on the Don River. In addition to this victory, which earned him the proud title *Donskoi* ("of the Don"), he also beat back a Lithuanian invasion. Dmitri thus made Moscow the special defender of Orthodoxy against both the infidel Mongols and the Western Christians, whom the Russians regarded as heretics, and he gave the city a prestige no other Russian city possessed.

Ivan III The ruler who completed the gathering of the Russian land and laid the constitutional foundations for modern Russia was Ivan III (1462–1505). His most important acquisition was Novgorod, a trading city that had strong ties with the West and controlled a huge if thinly populated area to the north. Through its vigorous trade with the Hanseatic League (see Chapter 11), Novgorod enjoyed considerable prosperity in the fourteenth and fifteenth centuries, but the consolidation of strong states along its borders—Lithuania and Poland as well as Muscovite Russia—threatened its independence. The merchant oligarchy that ruled the town wanted to accept the leadership of the Catholic Lithuanians, while the populace, which was Orthodox in religion, looked rather to the prince of Moscow. Ivan could not allow a territory so large and so close to his own to fall under the control of a powerful foreign prince. In 1471 he demanded and received the submission of the city; when it rebelled in 1478, he not only subdued the uprising but, as punishment, incorporated Novgorod and its territories into the Muscovite state. Ivan also took over the principalities of Yaroslavl, Perm, Rostov, and Tver. He ended the threat of Mongol rule over Russia by confronting an invading army at

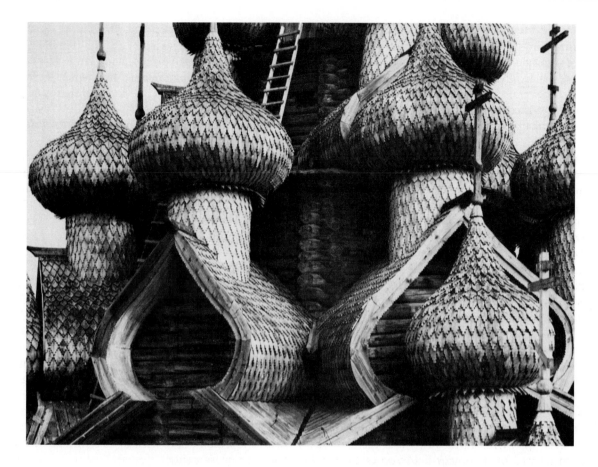

the Oka River in 1480, though no battle was fought because neither side dared cross the river that separated them. When the enemy withdrew, over two centuries of Mongol rule in Russia quietly ended.

Under Ivan's successor Basil III, the principalities of Pskov, Riazan, and Smolensk were added; Moscow, which in 1462 had ruled some 15,000 square miles of territory, by the middle of the sixteenth century ruled 40,000 square miles, and the borders of the principality of Moscow included nearly all the areas settled by the Great Russians. The princes of Moscow now confronted beyond their frontiers not another Russian prince but foreign sovereigns. The reign of Ivan III thus began a new epoch in the relations between Russian and non-Russian peoples.

INSTITUTIONAL AND SOCIAL CHANGE

Ivan III refashioned Russian institutions to suit the newly achieved national unity. The ruler of all the Russians could no longer be considered a

▶ **ONION DOMES AT KIZHI**
Constructed entirely of wood, the remarkable churches of northern Russia, such as this eighteenth-century example from Kizhi, were made into magnificently elaborate structures even though they often served only small settlements. The onion domes were the characteristic symbol of the Russian Orthodox Church, and they were multiplied across the roofs of Russian churches.

mere feudal prince, so Ivan adopted the title *tsar*, the Slavic equivalent of the Latin term *Caesar*, the traditional title of Roman and Byzantine emperors. Ivan also sought to depict himself as the successor of the Byzantine emperors. He adopted the Greek title *autokrator* ("autocrat") and introduced at his court the elaborate pomp and etiquette that had been characteristic of Byzantium. The Byzantine double-headed eagle became the seal and symbol of the new Russian Empire. Ivan also made his capital more splendid in appearance. Under the influence of his wife, Sophia Paleologus, who was the niece of the last Byzantine emperor and had been educated in Italy, he invited Italian artists to Moscow to help rebuild the Kremlin, the ancient citadel of the city. The Italians exerted considerable influence on Russian artistic style, especially Aristotele Fioravanti, who designed some of the Kremlin's most graceful churches and palaces.

Law Ivan was the first prince since the Kievan period to legislate for the whole of Russia. In 1497 he promulgated a new code of laws known as the *Sudebnik*, which was the first national legal code since the *Russkaia Pravda*, compiled by the Kievan Prince Iaroslav the Wise in the eleventh century. The new strength and splendor of the tsar inspired several monastic scholars to propose the idea that Moscow was the third Rome. The first Rome, they said, had fallen into heresy, and the second, Constantinople, had been taken by the infidel. Moscow alone, the capital of the one Orthodox ruler, preserved the true religion.

The Boyars In administering their state, the princes of Moscow had traditionally relied on the boyars, the hereditary nobles who were obliged to serve the prince in the army and the civil administration. Many boyars held vast estates, and their economic independence sometimes made them unreliable servants. Without directly attacking the boyars, Ivan created a new class of serving nobles who depended on the tsar's favor for their social position. He inaugurated a land grant called a *pomest'e*, which, like the Western fief, was made on condition of faithful service. The *pomeshchik*, as the holder of the grant was called, retained the property only so long as he fulfilled his obligations, and in the system's early days the land could not be inherited. This new class of officials acted as a counterpoise to the power of the boyars and as a major support of the tsar's authority.

Although Ivan's reforms were not completed until the reign of his grandson, Ivan IV, known as the Terrible—a tsar who brutally destroyed the old nobility of boyars and imposed on all landowners the status of servant to the tsar—Ivan III can be seen as the founder of the Russian state. He created a class of serving nobles; he finished the task of gathering the Russian land and unifying its people; he brought a united Russia to face the outside world; and he declared himself to be tsar, autocrat of Russia. Ivan III bequeathed to his successors one of the most characteristic institutions of modern Russia: its centralized, autocratic government.

Although Western Europe was spared the nomadic invasions that always threatened and frequently struck the Eastern peoples, it, too, sustained in the 1300s and 1400s a series of disastrous blows—famines, plagues, economic depression, and wars. These catastrophes caused profound dislocations in the society of the medieval West. The following two chapters examine this crisis, which transformed the medieval world and helped create the civilization of modern Western Europe.

Recommended Reading

▼

Sources

The Chronicle of Novgorod. Robert Mitchell and Neville Forbes (trs.). 1914. Portrays social and political life of the principal commercial town of medieval Russia.

*De Villehardouin, Geoffrey, and Jean De Joinville. *Chronicles of the Crusades.* Margaret R. Shaw (tr.). 1963.

*Available in paperback.

Howes, Robert Craig (ed. and tr.). *The Testaments of the Grand Princes of Moscow.* 1967.

William of Tyre. *A History of Deeds Done beyond the Sea.* Emily A. Babcock and A. C. Krey (trs.). 1943. One of the most important of the crusader chronicles.

Studies

Ashtor, Eliyahu. *Levant Trade in the Later Middle Ages.* 1982.

Atiya, Azia S. *Crusade, Commerce and Culture.* 1962. An evaluation of the results of the crusades in European history.

Bartlett, Robert. *The Making of Europe: Conquest, Colonization and Cultural Change 950–1350.* 1993. An analysis of the effect on Europe of the outward movement of its peoples in the Late Middle Ages.

Billington, James H. *The Icon and the Axe: An Interpretive History of Russian Culture.* 1966.

Erdmann, Carl. *The Origin of the Idea of the Crusade.* Marshall W. Baldwin and Walter Goffart (trs.). 1977. Perceptive study by a German scholar of the idea that war could be holy.

Fennell, J. L. *Ivan the Great of Moscow.* 1963. A political biography.

*Halperin, Charles J. *Russia and the Golden Horde: The Mongol Impact on Medieval Russian History.* 1985.

Holt, P. M. *The Age of the Crusades. The Near East from the Eleventh Century to 1517.* 1986.

Housely, Norman. *The Later Crusades: From Lyons to Alcazar 1274–1580.* 1992.

Kedar, Benjamin Z. *Crusade and Mission. European Approaches toward the Muslims.* 1984. The shift in aims from conquest to conversion.

Mayer, Hans Eberhard. *The Crusades* (2d ed.). 1988. A standard account.

Merriman, Roger B. *Suleiman the Magnificent. 1520–1566.* 1966.

Meyendorff, John. *Byzantium and the Rise of Russia: A Study of Byzantine-Russian Relations in the Fourteenth Century.* 1981. Byzantine contributions to the rise of Muscovy.

Morgan, David. *The Mongols.* 1986. Emphasizes the impact of the Mongol conquests and empire on Eastern Europe.

Mylonas, George E. *The Balkan States: An Introduction to Their History.* 1947.

Riley-Smith, Jonathan. *The Crusades: A Short History.* 1987. Follows history of crusader states in some detail.

Runciman, Steven. *A History of the Crusades* (3 vols.). 1951–1954.

Setton, Kenneth M. (ed.). *A History of the Crusades.* (6 vols.) (2d ed.). 1969–1989. The most comprehensive history of the crusades.

————. *The Papacy and the Levant (1204–1571).* 1976–1978. The basic survey of papal relations with the East.

Vernadsky, George. *The Mongols and Russia.* 1953.

————. *Russia at the Dawn of the Modern Age.* 1959. Part of the author's monumental *History of Russia.*

Wittek, Paul. *The Rise of the Ottoman Empire.* 1971.

SIEGE OF MORTAIGNE
This manuscript illustration from the Hundred Years' War shows a city under siege by both land and sea. The French defender is using a crossbow; the English besiegers are using cannon as well as their famous longbows.

CHAPTER ELEVEN

THE WEST IN TRANSITION: ECONOMY AND INSTITUTIONS

THE vigorous expansion that marked European history from the eleventh to the thirteenth centuries came to an end in the 1300s. Plague, famine, and recurrent wars decimated populations and snuffed out their former prosperity. At the same time, feudal governments as well as the papacy struggled against mounting institutional chaos. But for all the signs of crisis the fourteenth and fifteenth centuries were not merely an age of breakdown. The failures of the medieval economy and its governments prompted change and drove the Western peoples to repair their institutions. By the late fifteenth century the outlines of a new equilibrium were emerging. In 1500 Europeans remained fewer in number than they had been in 1300, but they also had developed a more productive economy and a more powerful technology than they had possessed 200 years before. These achievements were to equip them for their great expansion throughout the world in the early modern period. Some historians refer to the fourteenth and fifteenth centuries as the "autumn of the Middle Ages," and their somber theme is the decline and death of a formerly great civilization. But the study of any past epoch requires an effort to balance the work of death and renewal. In few periods of history do death and renewal confront each other so dramatically as in the years between 1300 and 1500.

I. Population Disaster and Agricultural Change

▼

The plagues and famines that struck European society in the fourteenth and fifteenth centuries profoundly affected economic life. Initially, they disrupted the established patterns of producing and exchanging goods and led directly to widespread hardship and depression. But the effects of the disruptions were not entirely negative; in reorganizing the economy under greatly changed demographic conditions, Europeans were able to make significant advances in the efficiency of economic production. To understand this paradox, we must see how the disasters affected the population of Europe.

DEMOGRAPHIC CATASTROPHE

A few censuses and other statistical records give us an insight into the size and structure of the European population in the 1300s. Nearly all these records were drawn up for purposes of taxation, and usually they survey only limited geographical areas—a city or a province. They are rarely complete even in limited areas and give us no reliable totals, but they still enable us to perceive with some confidence how the population was changing.

Almost every region of Europe from which we possess such records shows an appalling decline of population between approximately 1300 and 1450. Thus the population of Provence in southern France seems to have shrunk during the century after 1310 from between 350,000 and 400,000 to roughly one-third, or at most one-half, of its earlier size; only after 1470 did it again begin to increase. The city and countryside of Pistoia, near Florence, fell from about 43,000 people in the mid-thirteenth century to 14,000 by the early fifteenth. The nearby city and countryside of San Gimignano has not regained to this day the approximately 13,000 residents it had in 1332.

For the larger kingdoms of Europe the figures are less reliable, but they are similar. England had a population of about 3.7 million in 1347 and 2.2 million by 1377. By 1550 it had no more people than it had had in the thirteenth century. France

by 1328 may have reached 15 million; it, too, was not again to attain this size for 200 years. In Germany, of some 170,000 inhabited localities named in sources before 1300, about 40,000 disappeared during the 1300s and 1400s. Since many of the surviving towns were also shrinking in size, the population loss was only greater.

Certain favored regions of Europe—the fertile lands surrounding Paris and the Po valley—did continue to attract settlers and maintain fairly stable populations, but they owed their good fortune more to immigration than to high birthrates or immunity from disease. It can safely be estimated that all of Europe in 1450 had no more than one-half, and probably only one-third, of the population it had had around 1300.

PESTILENCE

The great plague of the fourteenth century, known as the Black Death, provides a dramatic, but not a complete, explanation for these huge human losses. In 1347 a merchant ship sailing from Caffa in the Crimea to Messina in Sicily seems to have carried infected rats. A plague broke out at Messina, and from there it spread throughout Europe (see Map 11.1).

The Persistence of Plague The Black Death was not so much an epidemic as a pandemic, striking an entire continent. Yet it was not the first pandemic in European history. An earlier one had struck in 542, during the reign of Justinian (see Chapter 7). But this was the first in 800 years, and it erupted repeatedly during the century. A city was lucky if more than 10 years went by without an onslaught; the plague was raging in some part of Europe in almost every year (*see box*, p. 316). Barcelona and its province of Catalonia, for example, lived through this record of misery in the fourteenth century: famine, 1333; plague, 1347 and 1351; famine, 1358 and 1359; plague, 1362, 1363, 1371, and 1397.

Some of the horror of the plague can be glimpsed in this account by an anonymous cleric who visited the French city of Avignon in 1348:

> To put the matter shortly, one-half, or more than a half, of the people at Avignon are already dead. Within the walls of the city there are now more than

Map 11.1 THE BLACK DEATH
For all the impression that the plague spread almost instantly, this reconstruction of its progress reveals that, because it depended on Europe's poor travel conditions and died down each winter, it took three years to move from Sicily to Sweden.

7,000 houses shut up; in these no one is living, and all who have inhabited them are departed.... On account of this great mortality there is such a fear of death that people do not dare even to speak with anyone whose relative has died, because it is frequently remarked that in a family where one dies nearly all the relations follow him....[1]

Nature of the Disease Most historians identify the Black Death as the bubonic plague, but this makes it difficult to explain how the disease

could have spread so rapidly and killed so many, since bubonic plague is more a disease of rats and small mammals than human beings. If bubonic plague is to spread to a human, a flea must bite an infected rat, pick up the infection, and carry it to a human host through a bite. The infection causes the lymphatic glands to swell, but recovery is not uncommon. Only if the infection travels

---

[1]*Breve Chronicon clerici anonymi*, quoted in Francis Aidan Gasquet, *The Black Death of 1348 and 1349*, 1908, p. 46.

Boccaccio on the Black Death

*The following eyewitness description of the ravages of the Black Death
in Florence was written by one of its most famous citizens, the writer Giovanni
Boccaccio. This passage comes from his masterpiece,* **The Decameron,** *written
during the three years following the plague.*

"In the year of our Lord 1348, there happened at Florence a most terrible plague, which had broken out some years before in the Levant, and after making incredible havoc all the way, had now reached the west. There, in spite of all the means that art and human foresight could suggest, such as keeping the city clear from filth and the publication of copious instructions for preservation of health, it began to show itself in the spring. Unlike what had been seen in the east, where bleeding from the nose is the fatal prognostic, here there appeared certain tumors in the groin or under the arm-pits, some as big as a small apple, others as an egg, and afterwards purple spots in most parts of the body—messengers of death. To the cure of this malady neither medical knowledge nor the power of drugs was of any effect; whether because the disease was in its own nature mortal, or that the physicians (the number of whom, taking quacks and women pretenders into account, was grown very great) could form no just idea of the cause. Whichever was the reason, few escaped; but nearly all died the third day from the first appearance of the symptoms, some sooner, some later, without any fever or other symptoms. What gave the more virulence to this plague was that it spread daily, like fire when it comes in contact with combustibles. Nor was it caught only by coming near the sick, but even by touching their clothes. One instance of this kind I took particular notice of: the rags of a poor man just dead had been thrown into the street. Two hogs came up, and after rooting amongst the rags, in less than an hour they both turned around and died on the spot."

From Warren Hollister et al., *Medieval Europe: A Short Sourcebook* (2d ed.), McGraw-Hill, 1992, pp. 248–249.

through the bloodstream to the lungs, causing pneumonia, can the disease be spread directly from person to person. The real killer in the 1300s seems to have been pneumonic plague, which infects the lungs directly; it probably was spread through coughing and was almost always fatal.

In spite of the virulence of pneumonic plague, it is hard to believe that medical factors alone can explain the awesome mortalities. After all, Europeans had maintained close contact with the East, where the plague had been endemic, since the eleventh century, but not until 1347 and 1348 did it make serious inroads in Europe. In addition, pneumonic plague is a disease of the winter months, but the plagues of the 1300s characteristically raged during the summer and declined in the cooler weather of autumn. Some scholars think the weather of the age—it seems to have been unusually cool and humid—somehow favored the disease. Others argue that it was acute, widespread malnutrition that caused starvation and lower resistance to infections.

HUNGER

The second cause of the dramatic fall in population, hunger, was all too common. Even if famines were less lethal than the plague in their initial onslaught, they were likely to persist for several years. In 1315, 1316, and 1317 a severe famine swept the north of Europe; in 1339 and 1340 another struck the south. The starving people ate not only their reserves of grain but also most of the seed they had set aside for planting.

Only a remarkably good harvest could compensate for the loss of grain by providing both immediate food and sufficient seeds for future planting.

Why was hunger so widespread in the early fourteenth century? Some historians see the root of trouble in the sheer number of people the lands had to support by 1300. The medieval population had been growing rapidly since about 1000, and by 1300 Europe, so this analysis suggests, was becoming the victim of its own success. Parts of the continent were crowded, even glutted, with people. Some areas of Normandy, for example, had a population in the early fourteenth century not much below what they supported 600 years later. Thousands, millions even, had to be fed without chemical fertilizers, power tools, and fast transport. Masses of people had come to depend for their livelihood on unrewarding soils, and even in good years they were surviving on the margins of existence. A slightly reduced harvest during any one year took on the dimensions of a major famine.

Even though malnutrition does not directly worsen mortality from plague, it does raise the death rate from respiratory infections and intestinal ailments, which also reached epidemic proportions in the fourteenth century. Furthermore, illness is itself a major cause of malnutrition. Thus hunger, disease, and plague combined to create a grim balance between the numbers of people and the resources that supported them.

▶ **THE TRIUMPH OF DEATH**
The great social disaster of the Black Death left few traces in the visual arts; perhaps people did not wish to be reminded of its horrors. One exception was the *Triumph of Death*, a mural painted shortly after 1348 in the Camposanto (cemetery) of Pisa in Italy. In this detail of the mural, an elegant party of hunters happens upon corpses prepared for burial. Note the rider who holds a handkerchief—scented, undoubtedly—to his nose, to ward off the foul odors.

ECONOMIC EFFECTS

What effects did the fall in population have on the economy of Europe? At first, the losses disrupted production. According to contemporaries, survivors of the plague often gave up toiling in the fields or looking after their shops; presumably, they saw no point in working for the future when it was so uncertain. But in the long run the results were not altogether negative. In agriculture, for example, the contraction of the population enabled the survivors to concentrate their efforts on better soils. Moreover, in both agriculture and industry the shortage of laborers was a challenge to landlords and entrepreneurs to save costs either by adopting productive measures that were less labor intensive or by increasing investment in labor-saving devices. Thus the decline in population eventually encouraged Europeans to find better techniques for making the most of available resources.

AGRICULTURE

Perhaps the best indication of the changes in the European economy comes from the history of prices. This evidence is scattered and rarely precise, but it does reveal roughly similar patterns in prices all over Europe. The cost of most agricultural products—cereals, wine, beer, oil, and meat—shot up immediately after the Black Death and stayed high until approximately 1375 in the north and 1395 in Italy. High food prices in a time of declining population suggest that production was falling even more rapidly than the number of consumers.

The beginnings of an agricultural recovery are apparent in the early fifteenth century. With fewer Europeans to be fed, the demand for cereals (which had long dominated agriculture) lessened perceptibly and their prices declined; with fewer available workers, the cost of labor pushed steadily upward. Landlords had to compete with one another to attract scarce tenants to their lands and did so by offering lower rents and favorable terms of tenancy. The upward movement of wages and the downward price of cereals led to a concentration on commodities that would command a better price in the market or were less expensive to produce. Better wages in both town

▶ **COLLECTING SILKWORMS AND PREPARING SILK**
One of the new industries that appeared in Europe in the fourteenth century was the raising of silkworms. Since the spinning of silk was a craft usually associated with women, this scene, from a fifteenth-century manuscript, shows a woman gathering silkworms from the mulberry bushes on which the worms lived, and from whose cocoons the silk threads were unwound.

and country also enabled the population to consume a more varied and expensive diet. While the price of wheat fell, wine, beer, oil, butter, cheese, meat, fruit, and other foods remained relatively expensive, which indicates a strong market demand.

Enclosure One branch of agriculture that enjoyed a remarkable period of growth in the fifteenth century was sheep raising. Labor costs were low, since a few shepherds could guard thousands of sheep; and the prices for wool, skins, mutton, and cheese remained high. In England, landlords sought to take advantage of this situation by fencing large fields and converting them from plowland into sheep pastures and expelling the peasants or small herders who had formerly lived there; this process, called *enclosure*, continued for centuries and played an important role in English economic and social history.

By the middle of the fifteenth century, agricultural prices tended to stabilize, and this suggests that production had become more dependable. Farms enjoyed the advantages of larger size, better location on more profitable soil, and increased capital investments in tools and animals. Agriculture was now more diversified, which benefited the soil, lowered the risk of famine from the failure of a single staple crop, and provided more nourishment for the people. Europeans were consuming a healthier diet by the middle of the fifteenth century than their ancestors had 200 years before.

II. Depression and Recovery in Trade and Industry

Although agriculture was the main occupation of the age and also the area of economic activity most directly connected with plague and hunger, there were also profound consequences of the disasters of the 1300s for trade and industry. And here, as in agriculture, there was to be a recovery in the late 1400s that was to have a long-term effect on European history.

PROTECTIONISM

The movement of prices created serious problems for employers in cities. As the labor force contracted, wages in most towns surged to levels as much as four times higher than they had been before 1348. Although the prices of manufactured goods also increased, they did not rise as much as wages, and this worked to reduce profit margins. To offset these unfavorable tendencies, the

employers sought government intervention. Between 1349 and 1351, England, France, Aragon, Castile, and other governments tried to fix prices and wages at levels favorable to employers. In enacting the Statute of Laborers, the English Parliament followed a policy typical of the age, forbidding employers to pay more than customary wages and requiring laborers to accept jobs at those wages. Such early experiments in a controlled economy failed. Price and wage ceilings set by law seem to have had little influence on actual prices.

A related problem for businesses was that competition grew as population fell and markets contracted. Traders tried to protect themselves by creating restricted markets and establishing monopolies. Guilds limited their membership, and some admitted only the sons of established masters. Cities, too, imposed heavy restrictions on the importation of foreign manufactures.

The Hanseatic League   Probably the best example of this monopolizing trend is the association of northern European trading cities, the Hanseatic League. The league was a defensive association formed in the fourteenth century by the cities that dominated the commerce of the Baltic and North seas, with the aim of excluding foreigners from the Baltic trade. The cities initially sought this protection because the emperor was too weak to defend their interests. At its height, the Hanseatic League included about 70 or 80 cities, stretching from Bruges to Novgorod and led by Bremen, Cologne, Hamburg, and especially Lübeck. Maintaining its own treasury and fleet, the league supervised commercial exchange, policed the waters of the Baltic Sea, and negotiated with foreign princes. By the late fifteenth century, however, it began to decline and was unable to meet growing competition from the Dutch in northern commerce. Although never formally abolished, the Hanseatic League continued to meet—at lengthening intervals—only until 1669.

THE FORCES OF RECOVERY

Attempts to raise the efficiency of workers proved to be far more effective than wage and trade regulation in laying the basis for recovery. Employers were able to counteract high wages by

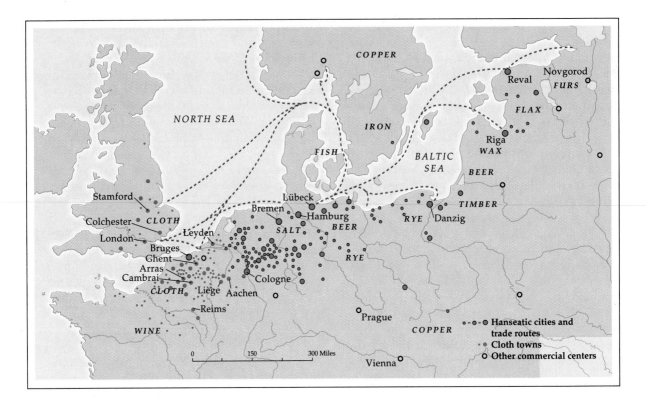

Map 11.2 The Hanseatic League and the Goods it Traded in the Fourteenth Century Even in the age of the Black Death, international trade remained vigorous in northern Europe. Its leaders were the cities of the Hanseatic League, which shipped a variety of commodities across the continent, though the most sought-after commodity was the cloth produced in England, the Netherlands, and northern France.

adopting more rational methods of production and substituting capital for labor—that is, providing workers with better tools. Though largely inspired by hard times and labor shortages, most of the technical advances of the 1300s and 1400s—both in different industries and in business practices—led workers to practice trade more efficiently, and eventually this helped make Europe a richer community.

METALLURGY

Mining and metallurgy benefited from a series of inventions after 1460 that lowered the cost of metals and extended their use. Better techniques of digging, shoring, ventilating, and draining allowed mine shafts to be sunk several hundred feet into the earth, permitting the large-scale exploitation of the deep, rich mineral deposits of Central Europe. Some historians estimate that the output from the mines of Hungary, the Tyrol, Bohemia, and Saxony grew as much as five times between 1460 and 1530. During this period miners in Saxony discovered a method for extracting pure silver from the lead alloy in which it was often found—an invention that was of major importance for the later massive development of silver mines in America. Larger furnaces came into use, and huge bellows and trip-hammers, driven by waterpower, aided the smelting and working of metals. Simultaneously, the masters of the trade were acquiring a new precision in the difficult art of casting.

By the late fifteenth century, European mines were providing an abundance of silver bullion for coinage. Money became more plentiful, and this stimulated the economy. Exploitation also began in the rich coal deposits of northern Europe. Expanding iron production meant more and stronger pumps, gears and machine parts,

ouutıs foditur querente in
argentum es electrum. Alii
gemmas et pretii diguoroqp

▶ **MINING, 1389**
**One does not normally associate miners with
elegant decoration, but in this fourteenth-century
manuscript, a miner provides the subject for the
ornamentation of the capital M that starts the word
metalla (metals). That the artist even considered
such a subject is an indication of the growing
importance of the industry in this period.**

tools, and ironwares; such products found wide
application in construction work and shipbuilding. And skill in metalworking contributed to
two other inventions: firearms and movable
metal type.

FIREARMS

Europeans were constantly trying to improve the
arts of war in the Middle Ages, and one weapon
they sought was a device to hurl projectiles with
great force and accuracy. We do not know how
they first learned that certain mixtures of carbon,
sulfur, and saltpeter burn with explosive force

and can be used to hurl boulders at an enemy.
Firearms are first mentioned in 1328, and cannons were used in the early battles of the Hundred Years' War. At first, their effect was chiefly
psychological: the thunderous roar, merely by
frightening the enemy's horses, did far more
damage than the usually inaccurate shots. Still, a
breakthrough had been made, and cannons
gained in military importance. Their development depended primarily on stronger, more precise casting and on proper granulation of the
powder to ensure that the charge burned at the
right speed and put its full force behind the pro-
jectile. With firearms, fewer soldiers could fight
more effectively; capital, in the form of an efficient though expensive tool, was being substi-
tuted for labor.

PRINTING

The extension of literacy among laypeople and
the greater reliance of governments and businesses on records created a demand for a cheap
method of reproducing the written word. The introduction of paper from the East was a major
step in reducing costs, for paper is far cheaper
than parchment to produce. A substitute for the
time-consuming labor of writing by hand was
also necessary: Scribes and copiers were skilled
artisans who commanded high salaries. To cut
costs, printing was first tried by pressing woodcuts—inked blocks with letters or designs carved
on them—onto paper or parchment. But these
"block books" represented only a small advance
over handwriting, for a separate woodcut had to
be carved for each page. And the woodcuts were
not durable; they tended to split after being
pressed a number of times.

Gutenberg By the middle of the fifteenth century several masters were on the verge of per-
fecting the technique of printing with movable
metal type. The first to prove this practicable was
Johannes Gutenberg of Mainz, a former jeweler
and stonecutter. Gutenberg devised an alloy of
lead, tin, and antimony that would melt at a low
temperature, cast well in the die, and be durable
in the press; this alloy is still the basis of the printer's art. His Bible, printed in 1455, is the first major work reproduced through printing.

[Image of a page from Gutenberg's Bible in Latin blackletter text, two columns]

▶ **GUTENBERG'S BIBLE**
A page from Johannes Gutenberg's Bible marks one of the most significant technical and cultural advances of the fifteenth century: printing with movable type, a process that made possible a wider dissemination of literature and thought.

Aldus In spite of Gutenberg's efforts to keep the technique a secret, it spread rapidly. By 1500 some 250 European cities had presses (see Map 12.1). German masters held an early leadership, but Italians soon challenged their preeminence. The Venetian printer Aldus Manutius, in particular, published works that are minor masterpieces of scholarship and grace. Aldus and his fellow Italians rejected the elaborate Gothic typeface used in the north and developed their own *italic* type, modeled on the clear script they found in old manuscripts. They believed this was the style of writing used in ancient Rome, but in fact they were imitating the Carolingian minuscule script.

The immediate effect of the printing press was to multiply the output and cut the costs of books. It made information available to a much broader segment of the population, and libraries could store larger quantities of information at lower cost. Printing also helped disseminate and preserve knowledge in standardized form—a major contribution to the advance of technology and scholarship. Printing produced a revolution in what we would call *information technology*, and indeed it resembles in many ways the profound changes that computers are making in our own lives. Finally, printing could spread new ideas with unprecedented speed—a fact that was not fully appreciated, however, until the 1500s, when print became essential to the propaganda of religious reformers in the Protestant Reformation (see Chapter 13).

NAVIGATION

Ships People as well as ideas began to travel more easily in the fourteenth and fifteenth centuries. Before about 1325 there was still no regular sea traffic between northern and southern Europe by way of the Atlantic, but it grew rapidly thereafter. In navigation, the substitution of capital for labor meant the introduction of bigger ships, which carried more cargo with relatively smaller crews. Large ships were safer at sea; they could sail in uncertain weather, when smaller vessels had to stay in port; they could remain at sea longer; and they did not have to sail close to the coastline in order to replenish their supplies. Their voyages between ports could be more direct and therefore speedier.

The larger vessels required more sophisticated means of steering and navigation. Before 1300, ships were turned by trailing an oar over the side. This provided poor control, especially in sailing ships, which needed efficient steering to take advantage of shifting winds. Some time during the fourteenth century the stern rudder was developed, which enabled a captain to tack effectively against the wind and control his ship closely when entering or leaving ports. Voyages became quicker and safer, and the costs of maritime transport declined.

Instruments   Ocean navigation also required a reliable means for estimating course and position, and here notable progress had been made in the late thirteenth century. Scholars at the court of King Alfonso X of Castile compiled the Alfonsine Tables, which showed with unprecedented accuracy the position and movements of the heavenly bodies. Using such tables, captains could take the elevation of the sun or stars with an astrolabe and calculate a ship's latitude, or position on a north-south coordinate. (They could not tell their longitude, or position on an east-west coordinate, until they could carry accurate clocks that could compare their time with that of a basic reference meridian, such as Greenwich in England. Until the 1700s, when the first accurate clocks immune to a ship's swaying were developed, navigators who sailed across the Atlantic could not tell how far they had traveled.)

The origin of the compass is unclear, but it was common on Mediterranean ships by the thirteenth century. By 1300, too, Mediterranean navigators sailed with maps of remarkable accuracy and used *portolani*, or port descriptions, which minutely described harbors, coastlines, and hazards. All these technical developments gave European mariners a mastery of Atlantic coastal waters and helped prepare the way for the voyages of discovery in the fifteenth century.

BUSINESS INSTITUTIONS

Banks   The bad times of the fourteenth century also stimulated the development of more efficient business procedures. Merchant houses in the late fourteenth and fifteenth centuries were considerably smaller than those of the thirteenth century, but more flexible. The Medici bank of Florence, which functioned from 1397 until 1498, for example, was not a single monolithic structure; rather, it rested on separate partnerships, which established its various branches at Florence, Venice, Rome, Avignon, Bruges, and London. Central control and unified management were ensured by having the senior partners—members of the Medici family—in all the contracts; but the

branches had autonomy, and most important, the collapse of one did not threaten others. This system of interlocked partnerships resembled a modern holding company.

Banking operations also grew more sophisticated. By the late 1300s "book transfers" had become commonplace; that is, a depositor could pay a debt without using coin by ordering the bank to transfer credit from his own account to his creditor's. At first the depositor had to give the order orally, but by 1400 it was commonly written, making it an immediate ancestor of the modern check.

Financial Practices   Accounting methods also improved. The most notable development was the adoption of double-entry bookkeeping, which makes errors in arithmetic immediately evident and gives a clear picture of the financial position of a commercial enterprise. Although known in the ancient world, double-entry bookkeeping was not widely practiced in the West until the 1300s. In this, as in other business practices, Italy led the way, but these accounting techniques eventually spread to the rest of Europe.

Another financial innovation was the development of a system of maritime insurance, without which investors would have been reluctant to risk their money on expensive vessels. There

▸ **EARLY BANKERS**
This illustration from a printed Italian handbook, which gives instructions to merchants and is dated circa 1496, shows the interior of a bank or accounting house.

are references to the practice of insuring ships in the major Italian ports as early as 1318. In these first insurance contracts the broker bought the ship and cargo at the port of embarkation and agreed to sell them back at a higher price once the ship reached its destination. If the ship sank, it was legally the broker's and he assumed the loss. In the 1300s the leading companies of Florence abandoned the clumsy device of conditional sales and wrote explicit insurance contracts. By 1400 maritime insurance had become a regular item of the shipping business, and it was to play a major role in the opening of the Atlantic.

Insurance for land transport developed in the 1400s but was never common. The first life insurance contracts appeared in fifteenth-century Italy and were limited to particular periods (the duration of a voyage) or particular persons (a wife during pregnancy). But without actuarial tables, life insurance of this sort was far more of a gamble than a business.

THE ECONOMY IN THE LATE FIFTEENTH CENTURY

In the last half of the fifteenth century Europe had recovered fairly well from the economic blows of a hundred years before, and the revived economy differed greatly from what it had been. Increased diversification, capitalization, and rationalization aided production and enterprise in both countryside and city. Europe in 1500 was certainly a much smaller community than it had been in 1300. Possibly, too, the gross product of its economy may not have equaled the output of the best years of the thirteenth century. But in the end the population had fallen more drastically than production. After a century of difficult readjustment Europe emerged more productive and richer than it had been at any time in its history.

III. Popular Unrest

▼

The demographic collapse and economic troubles of the fourteenth century deeply disturbed the social peace of Europe. European society had been remarkably stable and mostly peaceful from the Early Middle Ages until around 1300, and

▶ **VIEW OF PANISSIÈRES, FROM A FIFTEENTH-CENTURY ARMORIAL**
As the population of Europe began to recover from the Black Death, one can see signs of expansion and prosperity in its most fertile regions. This fifteenth-century view of the town of Panissières, in the rich Loire valley in France, indicates that houses were again springing up and fields were being cultivated outside the walls of the fortified heart of the town.

there is little evidence of uprisings or social warfare. The 1300s and 1400, however, witnessed numerous revolts of peasants and artisans against what they believed to be the oppression of the propertied classes.

RURAL REVOLTS

One of the most spectacular fourteenth-century rural uprisings was the English Peasants' War of 1381. This revolt originated in popular resentment against both the policies of the royal government and the practices of the great landlords. The royal government through the Statute of Laborers (1351) had sought to freeze wages and keep the workers bound to their jobs. Although this policy had little practical success, the mere effort to implement it aggravated social tensions, especially in the countryside, where it would have imposed a kind of serfdom on the peasants. Concurrent attempts to collect poll taxes (flat charges on each member of the population), which by their nature demanded less from the prosperous than the humble, crystallized resentment against the government. Rich landlords did nothing to help the situation by trying to revive many half-forgotten feudal dues, which had been allowed to lapse when rents were high in the thirteenth century.

Under leaders of uncertain background—Wat Tyler, Jack Straw, and a priest named John Ball—peasant bands, enraged by the latest poll tax, marched on London in 1381. They called for the abolition of serfdom, labor services, tithes, and other feudal dues, and demanded an end to the poll taxes. The workers of London, St. Albans, York, and other cities, who had similar grievances, rose in support of the peasants. After mobs burned the houses of prominent lawyers and royal officials, King Richard II, then aged 15, bravely met with the peasants in person and was able to placate them by promising to accept their demands. But as the peasants dispersed, the great landlords reorganized their forces and violently suppressed the last vestiges of unrest in the countryside; the young king also reneged on his promises.

The peasant uprising in England was only one of many rural disturbances between 1350 and 1450, including revolts near Paris and in Languedoc, Catalonia, and Sweden. There were also such disturbances in Germany in the fifteenth century and a major peasant revolt in 1524, which was to feed into the tensions of the early days of the Protestant Reformation.

URBAN REVOLTS

The causes of social unrest within the cities were similar to those in the countryside. Governments controlled by the propertied classes tried to prevent wages from rising and workers from moving and also sought to impose a heavier share of the tax burden on the poorer segments of society. In the 1300s and early 1400s, Strassburg, Metz, Ghent, Liège, and Paris were all scenes of riots. Though not entirely typical, one of the most interesting of these urban revolts was the Ciompi uprising at Florence in 1378.

The Ciompi Florence was one of the wool-manufacturing centers of Europe; the industry employed probably one-third of the working population of the city, which shortly before the Black Death may have risen to 120,000 people.

▶ FEBRUARY, *LES TRÈS RICHES HEURES*, 1413–1416
The different labors of the 12 months of the year are depicted in this fifteenth-century book of hours commissioned by the French Duke of Berry.
Despite the snowy, barren season, the rural laborers still have to work. They gather sticks and wood and then carry them to the distant village.

The wool industry, like most, entered bad times immediately after the plague. To protect themselves, employers cut production, thereby spreading unemployment. Since many of the employers were also members of the ruling oligarchy, they had laws passed limiting wages and manipulating taxation and monetary policy to benefit the rich. The poorest workers were denied their own guild and had no collective voice that could influence the government. In all disputes they were subject to the bosses' judges and the bosses' law.

▶ CLOTH MARKET IN BOLOGNA
The manufacture and marketing of textiles was one of the main sources of wealth for the cities of northern Italy. This scene, from a manuscript dated 1411, gives us a sense of what the cloth market in Bologna must have been like as merchants examined, bought, and sold various fabrics. But ordinary cloth workers like the Ciompi rarely shared in the wealth.

The poorest workers—mainly the wool carders, known as Ciompi—rose in revolt. They demanded, and for a short time got, several reforms. The employers would produce at least enough cloth to ensure work, they would refrain from monetary manipulations considered harmful to the workers, and they would allow the workers their own guild and representation in communal government. This was hardly power for the workers, but it was nevertheless intoler-

able to the ruling oligarchy. Because the Ciompi did not have the leaders to maintain a steady influence on government policy, the great families regained full authority in the city by 1382 and quickly ended the democratic concessions. Although the Ciompi revolt was short-lived and ultimately unsuccessful, the incident is one of the first signs of the urban class tensions that would be a regular disturbance in future centuries.

THE SEEDS OF DISCONTENT

Each of the social disturbances of the 1300s and 1400s was shaped by circumstances that were local and unique. Yet there were similarities in these social movements: for example, the fact that misery does not seem to have been the main cause of unrest. Indeed, the evidence suggests that the conditions of the working classes in both countryside and city were improving after the Black Death. The prosperity of the thirteenth century, which was chiefly a prosperity of landlords and employers, had been founded in part upon the poor negotiating position, and even exploitation, of the workers. The depopulation of the fourteenth century radically altered this situation. The workers, now reduced in number, were better able to bargain for lower rents, higher wages, and a fairer distribution of social benefits.

With the possible exception of the Ciompi, the people who revolted were rarely the desperately poor. In England, for example, the centers of the peasant uprising of 1381 were in the lower Thames valley—a region that was more fertile, more prosperous, less oppressed and with less serfdom than other parts of the kingdom. Also, the immediate provocation for the revolt was the imposition of a poll tax, and poll taxes (or any taxes) obviously do not alarm the truly destitute, whereas they do alarm people who have recently made financial gains and are anxious to hold on to them.

Causes of Revolt The principal goad to revolt in both town and country seems to have been the effort of the propertied classes to retain their old advantages and deny the workers their new ones. In the first decades after the Black Death, governments failed in their efforts to increase taxes and to peg rents, wages, and prices at levels favorable to landlords and employers; meanwhile, they spread hostility among the workers, who felt that their improving social and economic status was being threatened.

The impulse to revolt also drew strength from the psychological tensions of this age of devastating plagues, famines, and wars. The nervous temper of the times predisposed people to take action against real or imagined enemies. When needed, justifications for revolt could be found in Christian belief, for the Christian fathers had taught that neither the concept of private property nor social inequality had been intended by God. In a high-strung world many of these uprisings involved an emotional effort to attain the millennium, to reach that age of justice and equality that Christian belief saw in the past, expected in the future, and put off for the present.

A New Stability In the end, as labor became scarce, the rich had to offer favorable terms if they wanted tillers for their lands and workers for their shops. Thus, by about 1450, after a century of instability, a new equilibrium was emerging in European society, even if slowly and never completely. The humblest classes improved their lot and were fairly secure in their gains. Serfdom all but disappeared in the West; wages remained high and bread cheap. Life, of course, was still very hard for most workers, but it was better than it had been two centuries before. Perhaps reflective of better social conditions for the masses, the population once more began to grow, equipping Europe for its great expansion in the sixteenth century.

IV. *The Governments of Europe*

War was a frequent occurrence throughout the Middle Ages but was never so widespread or long-lasting as in the conflicts of the 1300s and 1400s. The Hundred Years' War between England and France is the most famous of these struggles, but there was fighting in every corner of Europe. The inbred violence of the age indicated a partial breakdown in governmental systems, which failed to maintain stability at home and peace with foreign powers.

THE FEUDAL EQUILIBRIUM

The governmental systems of Europe were founded on multiple partnerships that exercised power under feudal constitutions. The king enjoyed supreme dignity and even a recognized sacred character, but he was far from being an absolute ruler. In return for loyalty and service, he conceded a large share of the responsibility for government to a wide range of privileged persons and institutions: the great secular and ecclesiastical princes, the nobles, religious congregations, powerful military orders such as the Templars, free cities or communes, and even favored guilds such as the universities.

The growth of the feudal constitution in the eleventh and twelfth centuries had been a major step toward a more ordered political life, but it rested on a delicate equilibrium. To keep internal peace, which often meant international peace because of the confused borders of most feudal states, all members of the feudal partnership had to remain faithful to their obligations. This governmental system worked well until the early 1300s, but it could not sustain the blows it suffered during the period of social crisis. Governments had to be slowly rebuilt, though still along feudal lines and still based on shared authority. Nevertheless, many of the new governments that came to dominate the European political scene in the late 1400s conceded far more power to the senior partner in the feudal relationship, the king or prince.

DYNASTIC INSTABILITY

The forces that upset the equilibrium of feudal governments were many. One of the most obvious, itself rooted in the demographic instability of the age, was the failure of dynasties to perpetuate themselves. The Hundred Years' War, or at least the excuse for it, arose from the inability of the Capetian kings of France, for the first time since the tenth century, to produce a male heir in direct line. The English War of the Roses resulted from the uncertain succession to the crown of

▶ *Ambrogio Lorenzetti*
The Peaceful City (detail from Good Government), 1338–1341
The effects of good government, seen in this idealized representation of the *Peaceful City*, by Ambrogio Lorenzetti, include flourishing commerce, dancing maidens, and lavish residences, as opposed to the protective towers of feudal warfare. This fresco in the city hall of Siena was a constant reminder to the citizens of the advantages of living in their city.

England and the claims of the two rival houses of Lancaster and York. In Portugal, Castile, France, England, Naples, Hungary, Poland, and the Scandinavian countries, the reigning monarchs of 1450 were not the direct, male, legitimate descendants of those reigning in 1300. Most of the founders of new lines had to fight for their positions.

FISCAL PRESSURES

War The same powerful economic forces that were creating new patterns of agriculture and trade were also reshaping the fiscal policies and financial machinery of feudal governments. War was growing more expensive, as well as more frequent. Better-trained armies were needed to fight for longer periods of time and with more complex weaponry. Above all, the increasing use of firearms was adding to the costs of war. To replace the traditional, undisciplined, unpaid, and poorly equipped feudal armies, governments came more and more to rely on mercenaries, who were better trained and better armed than the vassals who fought to fulfill their feudal obligations. Many mercenaries were organized into associations known as companies of adventure, whose leaders were both good commanders and businesssmen. They took their enterprise where the market was most favorable, sold their services to the highest bidder, and turned substantial profits. To hire mercenaries, and win battles, was increasingly a question of money.

Taxes While war went up in price, the traditional revenues upon which governments depended sank. Until the fourteenth century, the king or prince was expected to meet the expenses of government from ordinary revenues, chiefly rents from his properties; but his rents, like everyone else's, were falling in the Late Middle Ages. Governments of all types—monarchies, the papacy, cities—desperately sought to develop new sources of revenue. For example, the papacy, because it could not rely on the meager receipts from its lands, built a huge financial apparatus that sold ecclesiastical appointments, favors, and dispensations from normal canonical requirements; imposed tithes on ecclesiastical revenues; and sold remissions of sin known as *indulgences*. In France the monarchy established a monopoly over the sale of salt. In England the king at various times imposed direct taxes on hearths, individuals (the poll tax), and plow teams, plus a host of smaller levies. The Italian cities taxed a whole range of items from windows to prostitutes. Under acute fiscal pressures, governments scrutinized the necessities, pleasures, and sins of society to find sources of revenue; and surviving fiscal records indicate that, in spite of the disturbed times, they managed to increase their incomes hugely through these taxes. For example, the English monarchy never collected or spent more than £30,000 per year before 1336; thereafter, the budget rarely sank below £100,000 and at times reached £250,000 in the late fourteenth century.

This new reliance on extraordinary taxes had important political consequences. The most lucrative taxes were not limited to the ruler's own lands but extended over all the realm. Since he had no established right to these demands, he had to seek the consent of his subjects, and he therefore had to summon territorial or national assemblies of estates, such as Parliament in England or the Estates General in France, to grant new taxes. But these assemblies, in turn, often balked at the demands or offered taxes only in return for political concessions. Even in the Church many reformers maintained that a general council should have ultimate control over papal finances. The extraordinary expansion of governmental revenues thus raised profound constitutional questions in both secular and ecclesiastical governments.

FACTIONAL CONFLICTS

The nobility that had developed nearly everywhere in Europe also entered a period of instability in the Late Middle Ages. Birth was the main means of access to this class, and membership offered legal and social privileges—exemption from most taxes, immunity from certain juridical procedures (such as torture), and so forth. The nobles saw themselves as the chief counselors of the king and his principal partners in the conduct of government.

By the 1300s, however, the nobles had long since lost whatever economic homogeneity they might once have possessed. Their wealth was

chiefly in land, and they, like all landlords, faced the problem of declining rents. They often lacked the funds needed for the new systems of agriculture, and they were further plagued by the continuing problem of finding income and careers for their younger sons. In short, the nobles were not immune from the acute economic dislocations of the times, and their class included men who lived on the brink of poverty as well as holders of enormous estates.

Factions To maintain their position, some of the nobles joined the companies of adventure to fight as mercenaries. Others hoped to buttress their sinking fortunes through marriage or by winning offices, lands, pensions, or other favors from governments. But as the social uncertainties intensified, the nobles tended to coalesce into factions, which disputed with one another over the control of government and the distribution of its favors. From England to Italy, factional warfare constantly disturbed the peace. A divided and grasping nobility added to the tensions of the age and to its violence.

Characteristically, a faction was led by a great noble house and included people of varying social station—great nobles in alliance with the leading house, poor knights, retainers, servants, sometimes even artisans and peasants. Some of the factions encompassed scores of families and hundreds of men and could almost be considered little states within a state, with their own small armies, loyalties, and symbols of allegiance in the colors or distinctive costumes (livery) worn by their members.

ENGLAND, FRANCE, AND THE HUNDRED YEARS' WAR

All the factors that upset the equilibrium of feudal governments—dynastic instability, fiscal pressures, and factional rivalries—helped to provoke the greatest struggle of the epoch, the Hundred Years' War.

Causes The issue over which the Hundred Years' War was supposedly fought was a dispute over the French royal succession. After more than 300 years of extraordinary good luck, the last three Capetian kings (the brothers Louis X, Philip

V, and Charles IV) failed to produce male heirs. With Charles's death in 1328, the nearest surviving male relative was his nephew King Edward III of England, son of his sister Isabella. But the Parlement of Paris—the supreme court of France—declared that women could not transmit a claim to the crown. In place of Edward, the French Estates chose Philip of Valois, a first cousin of the previous kings. Edward did not at first dispute this decision, and as holder of the French fiefs of Aquitaine and Ponthieu, he did homage to Philip.

More important than the dynastic issue was in fact the clash of French and English interests in Flanders, an area whose cloth-making industry relied on England for wool. In 1302 the Flemings had rebelled against their count, a vassal of the French king, and had remained virtually independent until 1328, when Philip defeated their troops and restored the count. At Philip's insistence, the count ordered the arrest of all English merchants in Flanders; Edward retaliated by cutting off the export of wool, which spread unemployment in the Flemish towns. The Flemings revolted once more and drove out the count. To give legal sanction to their revolt, they persuaded Edward to assert his claim to the French crown, which held suzerainty over Flanders.

The most serious point of friction, however, was the status of Aquitaine and Ponthieu. Edward had willingly performed ordinary homage for them, but Philip then insisted on liege homage, which would have obligated Edward to support Philip against all enemies. Edward did not believe that, as a king, he could undertake the obligations of liege homage to any man, and refused. Philip began harassing the frontiers of Aquitaine and declared Edward's fiefs forfeit in 1337. The attack on Aquitaine pushed Edward into supporting the Flemish revolt and was thus the main provocation for the Hundred Years' War.

Philip, a new king eager for glory, had clearly embarked on a dangerous adventure by harassing Aquitaine; and Edward, in supporting the Flemings, reacted perhaps too strongly. Their minimal concern for traditional obligations suggests that the war was mainly the result of a breakdown of the feudal constitution of medieval France in both its institutions and its spirit.

THE TIDES OF BATTLE

The French seemed to have a decisive superiority over the English at the outset of the war. The population of France was perhaps 15 million; England had between 4 and 7 million. But the war was hardly ever a national confrontation, because French subjects (Flemings, Gascons, Burgundians) fought alongside the English against other French subjects. The confused struggle may, however, be divided into three periods: initial English victories from 1338 to 1360; French resurgence, then stalemate, from 1367 to 1415; and a wild denouement with tides rapidly shifting from 1415 to 1453.

First Period The English never fully exploited their early victories, nor did the French ever manage to undo them. An English naval victory at Sluys in 1340 ensured English communications across the Channel and determined that France would be the scene of the fighting. Six years later Edward landed in France on what was more a marauding expedition than a campaign of conquest. Philip pursued the English and finally overtook them at Crécy, where the French knights attacked before their own forces could be fully marshaled and organized. The disciplined English, making effective use of the longbow, cut the confused French army to pieces. The victory also ensured the English possession of Calais, which they took in 1347. The scenario was repeated in 1356 at Poitiers when John II, who had succeeded Philip, attacked an English army led by Edward's son, the Black Prince, and suffered an even more crushing defeat. English victories, the Black Death, and mutual exhaustion led to the Peace of Brétigny in 1360. The English were granted Calais and an enlarged Aquitaine, and Edward, in turn, renounced his claim to the French crown.

Second Period But the French were not willing to allow so large a part of their kingdom to remain in English hands. In 1369, under John's successor, Charles V, they opened a second phase of the war. Their strategy was to avoid full-scale battles and wear down the English forces, and they succeeded. By 1380 they had pushed the English nearly into the sea, confining them to Ca-

CHRONOLOGY OF THE HUNDRED YEARS' WAR

1351 Charles IV, last Capetian king in direct line, dies; Philip of Valois elected king of France as Philip VI; Philip defeats Flemings at Cassel; unrest continues in Flemish towns.

1329 Edward III of England does simple homage to Philip for continental possessions but refuses liege homage.

1336 Edward embargoes wool exports to Flanders.

1338 Philip's troops harass English Guienne; Edward, urged on by the Flemings, claims French crown; war begins.

1346 Major English victory at Crécy.

1347–1351 Black Death ravages Europe.

1356 Black Prince defeats French at Poitiers.

1358 Peasants' uprising near Paris.

1360 Peace of Brétigny; English gain major territorial concessions but abandon claim to French crown.

1369 Fighting renewed in France.

1370 Bertrand du Guesclin, constable of France, leads French resurgence.

1381 Peasants' Revolt in England.

1392 Charles VI of France suffers first attack of insanity; Burgundians and Armagnacs contend for power over king; fighting wanes as both sides exhausted.

1399 Henry IV of Lancaster takes English throne.

1415 Henry V wins major victory at Agincourt.

1420 Treaty of Troyes; Charles VI recognizes Henry V as legitimate heir to French crown; high-water mark of English fortunes.

1429 Joan of Arc relieves Orléans from English siege; Dauphin crowned king at Reims as Charles VII.

1431 Joan burned at the stake at Rouen.

1435 Peace of Arras; Burgundy abandons English side.

1436 Charles retakes Paris.

1453 Bordeaux falls to French; English retain only Calais on Continent; effective end of war, though no treaty is signed.

lais and a narrow strip of the Atlantic coast from Bordeaux to Bayonne. Fighting was sporadic from 1380 until 1415, with both sides content with a stalemate.

Third Period The last period of the war, from 1415 to 1453, was one of high drama and rapidly shifting fortunes. Henvy V of England invaded France and shattered the French army at Agincourt in 1415. His success was confirmed by the Treaty of Troyes in 1420, an almost total French capitulation. King Charles VI of France declared his son the Dauphin (the future Charles VII) illegitimate, named Henry his successor and re-

gent of France, and gave him direct rule over all French lands as far south as the Loire River (see Map 11.3). Charles also gave Henry his daughter Catherine in marriage.

The Dauphin could not accept this forced abdication, and from his capital at Bourges he led an expedition across the Loire River. The English drove his forces back and systematically took the towns and fortresses north of the river that were loyal to him. In 1428 they finally laid siege to Orléans, a city whose fall would have given them a commanding position in the Loire valley and would have made the Dauphin's cause desperate.

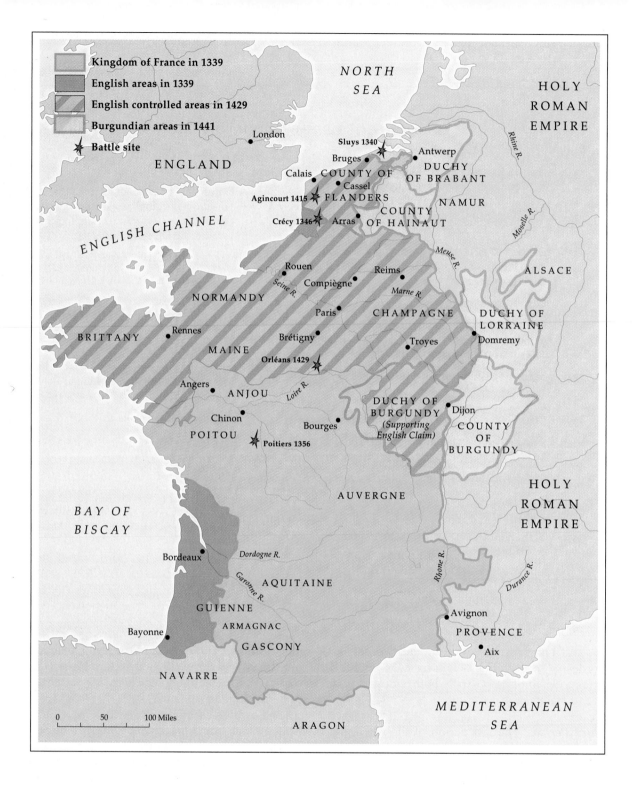

Map 11.3 THE HUNDRED YEARS' WAR

Because of their closeness to the continent and their naval power, the English were able to dominate northern France, the area which traditionally had been that kingdom's heartland. As a result, Joan of Arc's decisive victory came not in Paris but in Orléans on the Loire River—which proved to be a crucial boundary between the two sides.

JOAN OF ARC

The intervention of a young peasant girl, Joan of Arc, saved the Valois dynasty. Convinced that heavenly voices were ordering her to rescue France, Joan persuaded several royal officials, and finally the Dauphin himself, of the authenticity of her mission and was given command of an army. In 1429 she marched to Orléans and forced the English to raise the siege. She then escorted the Dauphin to Reims, the historic coronation city of France, where his crowning confirmed his legitimacy and won him broad support as the embodiment of French royalist sentiment. The tide had turned.

Joan passed from history as quickly and as dramatically as she had arrived. The Burgundians, allies of the English, captured her in 1430 and sold her to the English, who put her on trial for witchcraft and heresy (*see box*, p. 334). She was burned at the stake at Rouen in 1431. Yet Joan's commitment was one sign of an increasingly powerful feeling among the people. They had grown impatient with continuing destruction and had come to identify their own security with the expulsion of the English and the establishment of a strong Valois monarchy. This growing loyalty to the king finally saved France from its long agony. A series of French successes followed Joan's death, and by 1453 only Calais was left in English hands. No formal treaty ended the war, but both sides accepted the outcome: England was no longer a continental power.

THE EFFECTS OF THE HUNDRED YEARS' WAR

Like all the disasters of the era, the Hundred Years' War accelerated change. It stimulated the development of firearms and the technologies needed to manufacture them, and it helped establish the infantry—armed with longbow, pike, or gun—as superior in battle to mounted knights.

Parliament The war also had a major effect on government institutions in England and France. The expense of fighting forced the kings on each side to look for new sources of revenue through taxation. In England the king willingly gave Parliament a larger political role in return for grants

▶ JOAN OF ARC, 1484
Surrounded by the clerics who had condemned her, Joan of Arc is bound to the stake in this scene from a manuscript that was prepared half a century after she was executed in 1431. Despite Joan's own preference for short hair and manly costume, she is here shown as a conventionally idealized female figure.

of new taxes. The tradition became firmly established that Parliament had the right to grant or refuse new taxes, to agree to legislation, to channel appeals to the king, and to offer advice on important decisions such as peace and war. The House of Commons gained the right to introduce all tax legislation, since the Commons, unlike the Lords, were representatives of shires and boroughs. Parliament also named a committee to audit tax records and supervise payments. Equally important, the Commons could impeach high royal officials, a crucial step in establishing the principle that a king's ministers were responsible to Parliament as well as to their royal master. By the end of the Hundred Years' War, Parliament had been notably strengthened at the expense of royal power.

French Government The need for new taxes had a rather different outcome in France, where it enhanced the power of the monarchs while weakening the Estates General, the national representative assembly. In 1343 Philip VI established a monopoly over the sale of salt, laying down in many areas of France how much it cost and how much each family had to consume. The tax on salt, called the *gabelle*, was to be essential to

The Trial of Joan of Arc

The records of the trial of Joan of Arc in Rouen in 1431 give us a rare opportunity to hear her directly, or at least the words a secretary heard. Whether recorded accurately or not, her testimony does give us a glimpse of her extraordinary spirit and determination.

"When she had taken the oath the said Jeanne was questioned by us about her name and her surname. To which she replied that in her own country she was called Jeannette. She was questioned about the district from which she came.

"She said she was born in the village of Domrémy. Asked if in her youth she had learned any craft, she saw yes, to sew and spin; and in sewing and spinning she feared no woman in Rouen.

"Afterwards she declared that at the age of 13 she had a voice from God to help her and guide her. And the first time she was much afraid. And this voice came towards noon, in summer, in her father's garden. Asked what instruction this voice gave her for the salvation of her soul, she said it taught her to be good and to go to church often; and the voice told her that she should raise the siege of the city of Orléans.

"Asked whether, when she saw the voice coming to her, there was a light, she answered that there was a great deal of light on all sides. She added to the examiner that not all the light came to him alone!

"Asked whether she thought she had committed a sin when she left her father and mother, she answered that since God commanded, it was right to do so. She added that since God commanded, if she had had a hundred parents, she would have gone nevertheless.

"Jeanne was admonished to speak the truth. Many of the points were read and explained to her, and she was told that if she did not confess them truthfully she would be put to the torture, the instruments of which were shown to her.

"To which Jeanne answered in this manner: 'Truly if you were to tear me limb from limb and separate my soul from my body, I would not tell you anything more; and if I did say anything, I should afterwards declare that you had compelled me to say it by force.'"

From *The Trial of Jeanne d'Arc*, as cited in Leonard Bernard and Theodore B. Hodges (eds.), *Readings in European History* (New York: Macmillan, 1958), pp. 181–182.

French royal finance until 1789. In gaining support for this and other taxes, Philip and his successors sought the agreement of regional assemblies of estates as well as the national Estates General. The kings' reliance on the local estates hindered the rise of a centralized assembly that could speak for the entire kingdom. By the reign of Charles VII, during the last stages of the war, the monarchy obtained the right to impose national taxes (notably the *taille*, a direct tax from which nobles and clerics were exempt) without the consent of the Estates General. By then, too, the royal government was served by a standing professional army—the first in any European country since the fall of the Roman Empire.

The War of the Roses Both England and France experienced internal dissension during the Hundred Years' War. After the death of Edward III in 1377, England faced over a century of turmoil, with nobles striving to maintain their economic fortunes through factional conflicts—that is, by preying on one another. In time, these conflicts led to a struggle between two factions, the Lancastrians and the Yorkists, over the throne itself, with all English nobles aligning themselves on one side or the other. The civil war that followed is known to historians as the War of the Roses (the Lancastrians' emblem was a red rose, the Yorkists' a white rose). It lasted some 35 years, ending in 1485, when Henry Tudor defeated the

Yorkists at Bosworth Field and came to the throne as Henry VII. By this time, prosperity had relieved the pressures on the English nobles, and the people in general, weary of war, welcomed the strong and orderly regime that Henry established.

Burgundy   In France, too, the power of the monarchy was threatened by rival factions of nobles, the Armagnacs and the Burgundians. The Armagnacs wanted the war with England vigorously pursued, while the Burgundians favored accommodation. The territorial ambitions of the Burgundians also posed a threat to the French monarchy. King John the Good of France had granted the huge Duchy of Burgundy to his younger son, Philip the Bold, in 1363. Philip and his successors greatly enlarged their possessions in eastern France, the Rhône and Rhine valleys, and the Low Countries (see Map 11.3). They were generous patrons of literature and the arts, and they made their court at Dijon the most brilliant in Europe. The dukes seem to have sought to establish a Burgundian "middle kingdom" between France and the Holy Roman Empire; such a state would have affected the political geography of Europe permanently and undermined the position of the French monarch. But the threat vanished in 1477 when the last duke, Charles the Bold, was killed in battle with the Swiss at Nancy. His daughter and heir, Mary of Burgundy, could not hold her scattered inheritance together, and a large part of it came under French control.

The English and French States   With the loss of most of its continental possessions, England emerged from the war geographically more consolidated. It was also homogeneous in its language (English now replaced French as the language of the law courts and administration) and more conscious of its cultural distinctiveness and national identity. Freed from its continental entanglements, England was ready for its expansion beyond the seas and for a surge in national pride and self-consciousness.

France never achieved quite the territorial consolidation of England, but with the expulsion of the English from his lands and the sudden disintegration of the Duchy of Burgundy, the French king was without a major rival among his feudal

princes. The monarchy emerged from the war with a permanent army, a rich tax system, and no clear constitutional restrictions on its exercise of power. Most significantly, the war gave the French king high prestige and confirmed him as the chief protector and patron of the people.

In both France and England, government at the end of the Middle Ages was still decentralized and "feudal," if we mean by that term that certain privileged persons and institutions (nobles, the Church, towns, and the like) continued to hold and to exercise some form of private jurisdiction. They retained, for example, their own courts. But the king had unmistakably emerged as the dominant partner in the feudal relationship. Moreover, he was prepared to press his advantages in the sixteenth century.

▶ **CHRISTINE DE PISAN PRESENTS POEMS TO ISABEAU OF BAVARIA**
Christine de Pisan (1364–1430) was the author of several important historical and literary works, including a biography of King Charles V of France and *The Book of the Three Virtues*, a manual for the education of women. She is here depicted presenting a volume of her poems to the queen of France, who is surrounded by ladies in waiting and the symbol of the French royal family, the fleur-de-lis. It is significant that there were such scenes of elegance and intellectual life even amidst the chaos and destruction of the Hundred Years' War.

THE HOLY ROMAN EMPIRE

With the death of Emperor Frederick II of Hohenstaufen (1250), the Holy Roman Empire ceased to function as a major power in European affairs. The empire continued to link Germany and Italy, but real authority fell to the princes in Germany and the city republics in Italy. In 1273, after a tumultuous period known as the Interregnum, during which several rivals contended for the title, the princes chose as emperor Rudolf of Habsburg, the first of that long-enduring family to hold the office. Instead of rebuilding the imperial authority, Rudolf sought to advance the interests of his own dynasty and its ancestral possessions. His successors also tended to use the office of emperor for their own narrow dynastic advantage.

The most significant event of the fourteenth century was the issuance in 1356 of the Golden Bull, which essentially defined the constitution of the empire until 1806. Although issued by the pope, the bull reflected the interests of the leading German princes. The right of naming the emperor was given to seven electors—the archbishops of Mainz, Trier, and Cologne; the count palatine of the Rhine; the duke of Saxony; the margrave of Brandenburg; and the king of Bohemia. As the bull assigned the papacy no role in naming or crowning the emperor, it was a victory for imperial autonomy.

The Swiss An indication of the growing autonomy of regions within the empire was the emergence of the Swiss Confederation of cantons (districts), which won virtual independence in the Late Middle Ages. In the early 1200s Emperor Frederick II of Hohenstaufen had recognized the autonomy of two cantons, Uri and Schwyz, and had given them the responsibility of guarding the Saint Gotthard Pass through the Alps, the shortest route from Germany to Italy. The lands of the cantons were technically part of the ancient Duchy of Swabia, and in the late thirteenth century the Habsburg princes, seeking to consolidate their possessions in the duchy, attempted to subjugate the Swiss lands as well. To resist the Habsburg threat, the cantons of Uri, Schwyz, and Unterwalden joined in a Perpetual Compact in 1291. They formed the nucleus of what was eventually to become the 22 cantons of present-day Switzerland.

The Swiss had to fight for their autonomy, and they acquired a reputation as the best fighters in Europe. At the same time, their confederated system of government, which allowed each canton to run its own affairs, was a notable exception to the tendency, evident elsewhere in Europe, for central governments to grow stronger in the 1300s and 1400s.

THE STATES OF ITALY

Free cities, or communes, dominated the political life of central and northern Italy in the early fourteenth century. The Holy Roman Empire claimed a loose sovereignty over much of the peninsula north of Rome, and the papacy governed the area around Rome; but in fact most of the principal cities, and many small ones too, had gained the status of self-governing city-states.

However, the new economic and social conditions of the 1300s worked against the survival of the smaller communes. The economic contraction made it increasingly difficult for industries and merchant houses in the smaller cities to compete with their rivals in the larger ones. And the rising costs of war made it hard for small communes to defend their independence. In addition, all of Italian society, in both large and small towns, was deeply disturbed by factional strife that often made political order impossible.

In response to these pressures, two major tendencies became evident. Much stronger governments, amounting at times to despotisms, tended to replace the weak governments of free communes. And regional states, dominated politically and economically by a single metropolis, replaced the numerous, free, and highly competitive communes.

Milan Perhaps the most effective Italian despot was the ruler of Milan, Gian Galeazzo Visconti (1378–1402), who set about enlarging the Visconti inheritance of 21 cities in the Po valley. Through shrewd negotiations and opportune attacks, he secured the submission of cities to his east, which gave him an outlet to the Adriatic Sea. He then seized Bologna, purchased Pisa, and through a variety of methods was accepted as ruler of Siena, Perugia, Spoleto, Nocera, and Assisi. In the course of this advance deep into central Italy,

▶ FAMILY TOWERS AT LUCCA
This fourteenth-century view of the Italian city of Lucca testifies to the violence of factional conflict within these cities. Each major family and its leading supporters built a defensible structure, topped by an identifiable tower. Here, in a large building that surrounded a central courtyard and had its own chapel, they could find refuge from rival families and factions.

Gian Galeazzo kept his chief enemies, the Florentines and the Venetians, divided, and he seemed ready to create a united Italian kingdom.

To establish a legal basis for his power, Gian Galeazzo secured from the emperor an appointment as imperial vicar in 1380 and then as hereditary duke in 1395. This made him the only duke in all Italy, and it seemed a step toward a royal title. He revised the laws of Milan, but the chief administrative foundation of his success was his ability to wring enormous tax revenues from his subjects. Gian Galeazzo was also a generous patron of the new learning of his day; and with his conquests, wealth, and brilliance, he seemed to be awaiting only the submission of the Florentines before adopting the title of king. But he died unexpectedly in 1402, leaving two minor sons, who were incapable of defending their inheritance.

Venice   Even those states that escaped the despotism of a Gian Galeazzo moved toward stronger governments and the formation of territorial or regional states. In Venice the government came to be run by a small and closed oligarchy—a group of families that dominated the Council of Ten, the body that controlled the Venetian state. Its policies were geared to preserving oligarchic rule and suppressing opposition to the government.

Whereas Venice had long devoted its main energies to maritime commerce and overseas possessions, it could not now ignore the growth of territorial states on the mainland, which might threaten its agricultural imports or jeopardize its inland trade routes. From the early fifteenth century onward, Venice, too, initiated a policy of territorial expansion on the mainland. By 1405, Padua, Verona, and Vicenza had become Venetian dependencies.

Florence   While retaining the trappings of republican government, Florence also came under stronger central control. In 1434 a successful banker named Cosimo de Medici established a form of boss rule over the city. His tax policies favored the lower and middle classes, and he also gained the support of the middle classes by appointments to office and other forms of political patronage. He made peace in Italy his supreme goal and started his family's brilliant tradition of patronage of learning and the arts.

▶ **INVESTITURE OF GIAN GALEAZZO VISCONTI, CA. 1395**
This contemporary depiction of the investiture of Gian Galeazzo Visconti as duke of Milan is from a manuscript he commissioned to commemorate the occasion. The picture on top shows Visconti in a white cape seated next to the emperor's representative, who in the picture below places the diadem on the kneeling Visconti's head. The spectators come from all walks of life, including bishops and soldiers carrying cannon, but the ceremony itself takes place in front of an altar. The margins contain such Visconti family symbols as the eagle, the cheetah, and various fruit trees; and the entire manuscript leaf is a rich and colorful glorification of a central event in Visconti's life.

This tradition was enhanced by Cosimo's grandson, Lorenzo the Magnificent (1469–1492), who beat back the plots of other powerful Florentine families and strengthened centralized control over the city. Lorenzo's Florence came to set the style for Italy, and eventually for Europe, in the splendor of its festivals, the elegance of its social life, the beauty of its buildings, and the lavish support it extended to scholars and artists.

THE PAPAL STATES AND THE KINGDOM OF NAPLES

The popes were as concerned as the leaders of city-states to consolidate their rule over their possessions in central Italy, but they faced formidable obstacles because the papacy was now located in Avignon in southern France. The difficult terrain of the Italian Papal States—dotted with castles and fortified towns—enabled communes, petty lords, and plain brigands to defy papal authority. Continuing disorders discouraged the popes from returning to Rome, and their efforts to pacify their tumultuous lands were a major drain on papal finances. Even after its return to Rome in 1378 the papacy had difficulty maintaining authority. Not until the pontificate of Martin V (1417–1431) was a stable administration established, and Martin's successors still faced frequent revolts throughout the fifteenth century.

The political situation was equally confused in the Kingdom of Naples and Sicily. With papal support, Charles of Anjou, younger brother of St. Louis of France, had established a dynasty of Angevin rulers over the area. But in 1282 the people of Sicily revolted against the Angevins and appealed for help to the king of Aragon. For the next 150 years the Aragonese and the Angevins battled for dominion over Sicily and Naples. Then in 1435 the king of Aragon, Alfonso V, the Magnanimous, reunited Sicily and southern Italy and made the kingdom the center of an Aragonese empire in the Mediterranean. Alfonso sought to suppress the factions of lawless nobles and to reform taxes and strengthen administration. His efforts were not completely successful, for southern Italy and Sicily were rugged, poor lands and difficult to subdue; but he was at least able to overcome the chaos that had prevailed earlier. Alfonso thus extended to the Mediterra-

Christendom was at least technically excommunicated.

THE CONCILIAR MOVEMENT

Theologians and jurists had long speculated on who should rule the Church if the pope were to become heretical or incompetent; some concluded that it should be the College of Cardinals or a general council of Church officials. Since the College of Cardinals had split into two factions, each backing one of the rival popes, many prominent thinkers supported the theory that a general council should rule the Church. These conciliarists, as they were called, went further. They wanted the Church to have a new constitution to confirm the supremacy of a general council. Such a step would have reduced the pope's role to that of a limited monarch, but the need to correct numerous abuses, particularly in the fiscal support and morality of the clergy, lent strength to the idea that a general council should rule and reform the Church.

Pisa and Constance The first test of the conciliarists' position was the Council of Pisa (1409), convened by cardinals of both Rome and Avignon. This council asserted its supremacy within the Church by deposing the two popes and electing another. But this act merely compounded the confusion, for it left Christendom with three rivals claiming to be the lawful pope.

A few years later another council finally resolved the situation. Some 400 ecclesiastics assembled at the Council of Constance (1414–1418), the greatest international gathering of the Middle Ages. The council was organized in a new way, with the delegates voting as nations to offset the power of the Italians, who constituted nearly half the attendance. This procedure reflected the new importance of national and territorial churches. It enabled the assembled delegates immediately to depose both the Pisan pope and the pope at Avignon and to persuade the Roman pope to resign. In his stead they elected a Roman cardinal, who took the name Martin V. Thus the Great Schism was ended, and the Western Church was once again united under a single pope.

As the meetings continued, the views of the conciliarists prevailed. The delegates formally declared that a general council was supreme within the Church. To ensure continuity in Church government, the delegates further directed that new councils be summoned periodically.

The Revival of the Papacy In spite of this assertion of supremacy, the council made little headway in reforming the Church. The delegates, mostly great prelates, were the chief beneficiaries of the fiscal system and were reluctant to touch their own privileges and advantages. The real victims of the fiscal abuses, the lower clergy, were poorly represented. As a result, the council could not agree on a general program of reform—a failure that illustrated the fatal flaw in the vision of conciliar rule over the Church. The council was too large, too cumbersome, and too divided to maintain an effective ecclesiastical government. The restored papacy quickly reclaimed its position as supreme head of the Western Church (*see box*, p. 344).

The practical weaknesses of the conciliar movement were amply revealed at the Council of Basel (1431–1449). Because disputes broke out almost at once with the pope, the council deposed him and elected another, Felix V, to replace him. The conciliar movement, designed to heal the schism, now seemed responsible for renewing it. Recognizing the futility of its actions, the council at the death of Felix tried to rescue its dignity by endorsing the election of a new pope, Nicholas V, in 1449 and then disbanding. This action ended efforts to reform the Church by giving supreme authority to councils. But the idea of government by representation that they advanced was to have an important influence on later political developments in Europe.

Territorial Independence Although the popes remained suspicious of councils, they had much more serious rivals to their authority in the powerful lay princes, who were exerting ever tighter control over territorial churches. Both England and France issued decrees that limited papal powers within their kingdoms, and this policy was soon imitated in Spain and the stronger principalities of the Holy Roman Empire. Although such decrees did not establish national or territorial churches, they do document the decline of papal control over the international Christian community.

The Papacy Condemns Conciliarism

By 1460, the papacy was firmly back in command of the Church, and in that year, Pope Pius II issued a decree forbidding all further appeals above his head to a council. Decrees are known by their first Latin words, and it is appropriate that this angry denunciation of conciliarism should have been called "Execrabilis"—that is "execrable."

"The execrable and hitherto unknown abuse has grown up in our day, that certain persons, imbued with the spirit of rebellion, and not from a desire to secure a better judgment, but to escape the punishment of some offence which they have committed, presume to appeal from the pope to a future council, in spite of the fact that the pope is the vicar of Jesus Christ and to him, in the person of St. Peter, the following was said: 'Feed my sheep' [John 21:16] and 'Whatsoever thou shalt bound on earth shall be bound in heaven' [Matthew 16:18]. Wishing therefore to expel this pestiferous poison from the church of Christ and to care for the salvation of the flock entrusted to us, and to remove every cause of offence from the fold of our Savior, with the advice and consent of our brothers, the cardinals of the holy Roman church, and of all the prelates, and of those who have been trained in the canon and civil law, who are at our court, and with our own sure knowledge, we condemn all such appeals and prohibit them as erroneous and detestable."

From Warren Hollister et al., *Medieval Europe: A Short Sourcebook* (2d ed.), McGraw-Hill, 1992, p. 245.

THE REVIVAL OF ROME

When Martin V returned to Rome in 1417, the popes faced the monumental task of rebuilding their office and their prestige as both political and cultural leaders of Europe. They wanted Rome to be a major capital, a worthy home for the papacy, and not dependent on French rulers or culture as they had been for the past century. To this end, they adopted enthusiastically the new literary and artistic ideas of the Renaissance that were beginning to come out of Florence in the 1400s (see Chapter 12). The result was a huge rebuilding program that symbolized the restored authority of the popes. They sought, as one contemporary put it, "by the construction of grand and lasting buildings to increase the honor of the Roman Church and the glory of the Apostolic see, and widen and strengthen the devotion of all Christian people." One of the popes even proclaimed that if any city "ought to shine by its cleanliness and beauty, it is above all that which bears the title of capital of the universe." The building of a new St. Peter's Church in the 1400s was but the climax of this campaign of beautification, designed to assert a cultural supremacy that went along with the supremacy of the Pope's authority. At the same time, vigorous military campaigns in the Papal States subdued that difficult territory and established the papacy as a major Italian power.

It could be argued, however, that in identifying itself so closely with Rome and with Italian politics, the papacy became less universal. For all its splendor and its renewed control over the institution of the Church, it was failing to retain the spiritual allegiance of Europe, especially in the north. The popes may have succeeded in reshaping the Church into a powerful and centralized body, and in making Rome once again a cultural capital of the Western world, but the new cultural and intellectual forces that were at work in the 1400s were ultimately to undermine the centrality of the papacy to the life of Europe.

Recommended Reading

Sources

Council of Constance. Louise R. Loomis (tr.). 1961.

*Froissart, Jean. *The Chronicles of England, France, Spain and Other Places Adjoining.* 1961.

*Vespasiano da Bisticci. *Renaissance Princes, Popes and Prelates.* 1963.

Studies

Allmand, Christopher. *The Hundred Years War: England and France at War, c. 1300–1450.* 1988.

———. *Florentine Politics and Society, 1373–1378.* 1962.

Brucker, Gene A. *The Civic World of Early Renaissance Florence.* 1977. Important studies of Florentine politics and society from about 1300 to 1430.

Burne, Alfred H. *The Agincourt War: A Military History of the Latter Part of the Hundred Years War, from 1369 to 1453.* 1991.

De Roover, Raymond. *The Rise and Decline of the Medici Bank.* 1963.

Eisenstein, Elizabeth L. *The Printing Press as an Agent of Change in Early-Modern Europe* (2 vols.). 1979. Provocative interpretation of the place of printing in European history.

Gillingham, John. *The Wars of the Roses: Peace and Conflict in Fifteenth-Century England.* 1981. Readable political and military history.

Gottfried, Robert S. *The Black Death: Natural and Human Disaster in Medieval Europe.* 1983. With particular emphasis on the medical consequences.

Harvey, L. P. *Islamic Spain 1250–1500.* 1990. A survey of the one non-Christian territory in Western Europe and its steady decline.

Hatcher, John. *Plague, Population and the English Economy.* 1977. Economic effects of the great mortality in England.

*Hilton, Rodney. *Bond Men Made Free.* 1979. A study of peasant unrest in the Late Middle Ages.

*Hilton, Rodney, and T. H. Aston (eds.). *The English Rising of 1381.* 1987. Collected essays.

Kaeuper, Richard W. *War Justice and Public Order: England and France in the Late Middle Ages.* 1988.

Mallett, M. E., and J. R. Hale. *The Military Organization of a Renaissance State: Venice c. 1400 to 1617.* 1984.

*Mattingly, Garrett. *Renaissance Diplomacy.* 1964.

Miskimin, Harry A. *The Economy of Early Renaissance Europe, 1300–1460.* 1969.

———. *The Economy of Later Renaissance Europe, 1460–1600.* 1977.

Monahan, Arthur P. *Consent, Coercion and Limit: The Medieval Origins of Parliamentary Democracy.* 1987.

Oakley, Francis. *The Western Church in the Later Middle Ages.* 1979.

*Perroy, Edouard. *The Hundred Years' War.* 1965. An excellent survey.

Russell, J. C. *British Medieval Population.* 1948.

Seward, Desmond. *The Hundred Years War.* 1978. Short and readable.

Unger, Richard W. *The Ship in the Medieval Economy.* 1980. The evolution of medieval ship design.

Vaughan, Richard. *John the Fearless: The Growth of Burgundian Power.* 1979.

———. *Philip the Bold: The Formation of the Burgundian State.* 1979.

*Available in paperback.

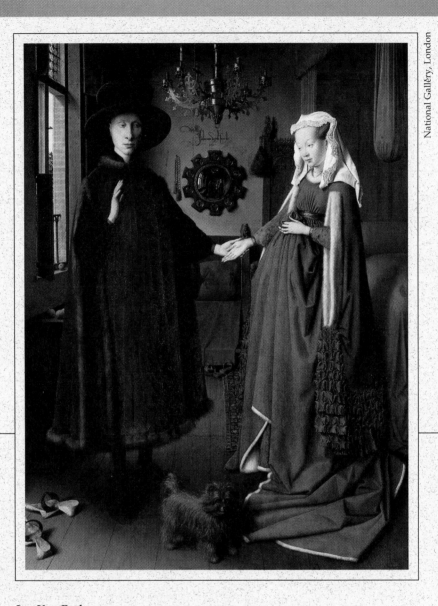

Jan Van Eyck
PORTRAIT OF GIOVANNI ARNOLFINI AND HIS WIFE, 1434
The symbolism that permeates this depiction of a husband and wife has led
to the suggestion that it is a wedding picture. The bed and seeming
pregnancy are symbols of marriage, and the husband blesses his wife as he
bestows the sacrament of marriage (for which the Church did not yet
require a priest). On the back wall, the mirror reflects the witnesses
attending the wedding. Van Eyck's use of the new medium of oil paint
allowed him to reproduce vividly the texture of the fur-edged robe and the
glimmer of the mirror's glass.

CHAPTER TWELVE

THE WEST IN TRANSITION: SOCIETY AND CULTURE

B Y 1300 the civilization of Europe appeared to have settled into stable and self-assured patterns. The division of society into the vast majority who labored, the knights and nobles who fought, and the clergy who prayed for the salvation of all seemed accepted and secure. If this was primarily a rural pattern, into which city dwellers did not easily fit, they were no more than a minor exception. The whole society shared assumptions about religious beliefs, about the appropriate way to integrate the heritage of the ancient world with faith, about the purposes of scholarship, and about the forms of literature and art; and this has led historians to describe the outlook of the age as "the medieval synthesis." But such moments of stability or apparent stability rarely last long. Within a few generations, major changes had overtaken European society, and profound doubts had arisen on such fundamental questions as the nature of religious faith, the authority of the Church, the aims of scholarship, the source of moral ideals, and the standards of beauty in the arts. As challenges to old ideas arose in each of these areas, there was an outpouring of creativity that has dazzled us ever since. Because those who sought new answers tended to look for guidance to what they considered a better past—the ancient world, or the early days of Christianity—and sought to revive those long-lost values, their efforts, and the times in which they lived, have been called an age of rebirth, or Renaissance.

I. Italian Society

In the fourteenth and fifteenth centuries the ideas that we associate with the Renaissance flourished mainly in Italy. Before looking at those ideas, therefore, we need to understand the elements that made Italy distinctive. What possibilities arose when, in the 1300s, the two major international powers that had dominated the peninsula for centuries—the pope and the emperor—turned their attention elsewhere and gave the Italians the opportunity to shape their own destinies?

CITIES

One basic social characteristic clearly distinguished Italy from most European areas: the number and size of its cities, particularly in the northern regions of Tuscany and the Lombard plain. In 1377, for example, only 10 percent of the people in England lived in urban centers with a population greater than 3200—a percentage fairly typical for most of northern Europe—whereas in Tuscany about 26 percent lived in urban centers. The cities were large. Venice, for instance, probably had 120,000 inhabitants in 1338, and despite the plagues of the next two centuries, the city had grown to 169,000 by 1563—a figure it was not to reach again until the twentieth century.

This remarkable urban concentration affected Italian culture. The large nonagrarian population depended for its support on a vigorous commerce and active urban industries. All levels of society participated in commerce, including the great landlords, nobles, and knights—classes that in northern Europe remained mainly on their rural estates. Moreover, success in urban occupations required a level of training higher than that needed in agriculture; therefore, many Italian cities supported public schools to assure themselves of an educated citizenry. Frequently even girls were given an elementary education, since literacy was a nearly essential skill for the wives of shopkeepers and merchants. Finally, many towns were politically independent and offered their affluent citizens the opportunity to participate in

governmental decisions. To many great families, such participation was essential to the protection of their interests and required a mastery of the arts of communicating with their fellow citizens. In sum, Italian urban society in the fourteenth and fifteenth centuries was remarkably well educated and committed to active participation in the affairs of business and of government.

FAMILIES

The cities were populous, but the households within them tended to be small and unstable. The average household size in Florence in 1427 was only 3.8 persons, and in some other cities it was even smaller. The low numbers reflected the numerous deaths in a time of plagues, but marital customs also had an effect. For urban males tended to be much older than their brides when they married. In fifteenth-century Florence, men tended to postpone marriage until they were 30, and some did not marry at all. Economic factors—the lengthy apprenticeships men served in urban trades, their extended absences from home on commercial ventures, and their need to accumulate capital before starting a family—delayed and sometimes prevented marriage. Florentine women, on the other hand, were, on the average, less than 18 years old when they married for the first time; the modal (most common) age of first marriage for these women in 1427 was 15 years.

Gender Roles   The result of this distinctive marriage pattern, when combined with high mortality, was that the pool of prospective grooms (men approximately 30 years old) was distinctly smaller than the pool of eligible young women (in their middle and late teens). A girl faced acute competition in the search for a husband; young women, in consequence, often entered marriage under unfavorable terms. Their families had to pay substantial dowries, and families with many daughters faced financial ruin. This was one reason why girls were married so young; their fathers or families were eager to settle their uncertain futures as soon as possible. Those who could not be married before the age of 20 had no honorable alternative but to enter a convent—which many did reluctantly. A contemporary saint, Bernardino of Siena, called the unwilling nuns "the scum and vomit of the world."

Given the wide age difference separating the spouses, urban marriages were not likely to last long before the death of the husband. Often, too, the young widow did not remarry. Florentine husbands typically tried to discourage their spouses from remarrying because widows, once remarried, might neglect the offspring of earlier unions. Thus the wills of Florentine husbands often gave their widows special concessions that would be lost on remarriage: use of the family home, the right to serve as guardians over their children, sometimes a pension. In general, after the death of a husband a woman tended to find herself suddenly in control of significant assets. The dowry that her family had paid at her marriage became her own property as a widow, and for the first time in her life she was freed from the male tutelage of a father, brother, or husband. Many widowed women relished this newfound freedom. At Florence in 1427, more than one-half of the female population, age 40 or over, were widowed. Thus the city teemed with mature women, many of them widows and some wealthy enough to influence urban culture.

Even while her husband lived, the Florentine woman was of great importance within the household. Men were likely to be occupied by affairs of business or politics, and the wife was responsible for running the household and bringing up the children. She was also usually destined for longer contact with her children. The average baby in Florence in 1427 was born to a mother of 26 and a father of 40. To many Florentines of the fourteenth and fifteenth centuries, the father was a distant figure, routinely praised but rarely intimately known; the mother dominated the formative years of the children. A friar named Giovanni Dominici, writing in the 1410s, complained that Florentine mothers were spoiling their children. They dressed them in elegant clothes and taught them music and dancing, but not rough games or sports. The result, Dominici implied, was an effeminization of Florentine culture because women, as crucial intermediaries between the generations, shaped the values and attitudes of the young. Thus the elegance and refinement that were essential attributes of Renais-sance culture seem to have been nurtured within the bosom of the urban family.

Migration The short duration of urban marriage, the reluctance of many widows to remarry, and the commitment of many girls to the convent limited the number of pregnancies. In the countryside, men characteristically married in their middle twenties and took as brides women nearer in age to themselves. Rural marriages lasted longer, and couples had more children. The city thus ran a demographic deficit in relation to the countryside. This, too, had important social consequences. The city was forced to replenish its numbers by encouraging immigration from the countryside and small towns, and this promoted both physical and social mobility, because the city often attracted and rewarded skilled and energetic immigrants. Many of the leaders of the Renaissance—Boccaccio and Leonardo da Vinci, to name but two—came from rural or small-town origins to the city to meet its constant need for immigrants. The Renaissance city was highly successful in identifying the talented and in using its human capital to best effect.

Theories of Family Life The unstable character of the urban household and of human relations within it prompted much reflection on the family. Earlier, social thinkers had viewed the family in the abstract, in terms of humanity's ultimate destiny; they said it accorded with nature and was a training ground for faith and morality, but they did not examine how it functioned in the real world. In contrast, writers of the fifteenth century in Italy were concerned about the welfare, even the survival, of families. Foremost among them was the Florentine scholar, artist, and architect Leon Battista Alberti, who in the 1430s wrote a tract entitled *Four Books on the Family*. He suggested how children should be reared, wives chosen, domestic affairs managed, and friends cultivated—all to ensure the survival of threatened lineages. There were also many books on the education of children and attempts to reform schools, all of which showed a new awareness of the special psychology of children. And the artists of the period presented young people, even the infant Christ, not as miniature adults but authentically as children, looking and acting as children do. The playful baby angels known as *putti* appear in even the most solemn religious paintings. The very fragility of the Italian urban family thus seems to have inspired a deeper appreciation for the values of family life and the contributions that are made by every one of its members, even the youngest.

LIFE EXPECTANCY

A major reason for the instability of the urban family was the high mortality in Europe during the fourteenth and fifteenth centuries. The family memoirs of Florentine merchants, which record births and deaths, suggest that life expectancy from birth for these relatively affluent persons was 40 years in about 1300, dropping to only 18 years in the generation of the Black Death, and rising to 30 years in the fifteenth century as the plagues declined in virulence. (Today in the United States a newborn may be expected to survive for over 70 years.) To be sure, the high death rates attributable to plague were strongly "age specific"; that is, they varied considerably by age. The principal victims were the very young. In many periods, between a half and a third of the babies born never reached 15. Society swarmed with little children, but their deaths were common occurrences in almost every family.

The plague took a greater toll among young adults than among the aged. In effect, a person who survived one or more major epidemics had a good chance of living through the next onslaught. Thus a favored few did reach extreme old age, despite horrendous mortalities. But young adults always faced high risks of dying. Friars who entered the convent of Sta. Maria Novella at Florence in the last half of the fourteenth century, for example, lived an average of only 20 years after entering their order (which they usually did in their late teens). Although there are exceptions, the normal adult career was short.

Leadership of the Young For this reason, in every activity of life, the leaders of the 1300s and 1400s were often very young and were subject to rapid replacement. The young were not frustrated by the survival of their immediate elders, who in other times would have clung to the available jobs. There was far less of the generational tensions and conflicts that have disturbed modern societies. Indeed, the leaders of the age show psychological qualities that may be attributed, in part at least, to their youth: impatience and imagination; a tendency to turn quickly to violence; a love of extravagant gesture and display; and a rather small measure of prudence, restraint, and self-control. High mortality and a rapid turnover of leaders contributed to making this an age of opportunity, especially within cities. Early death created room at the top for the energetic and the gifted, especially in business and the arts, where birth mattered little and skill counted for much.

The power given to the young, the rapid replacement of leaders, the openings for talent, and the thin ranks of an older generation that might counsel restraint intensified the pace of cultural change. To be sure, poor communications hampered the spread of ideas. The quickest a person or a letter could travel on land was between 20 and 30 miles per day: To get to Bruges by sea from Genoa took 30 days; from Venice, 40 days. The expense and scarcity of manuscripts before the age of printing further restricted intellectual dialogue. Nevertheless, new generations pressed upon the old at a much more rapid rate than in our own society, and they brought with them new preferences and ideas—or at least a willingness to experiment—because the individual had his or her main chance early in life and passed early from the scene.

FLORENCE AND VENICE

The two chief sources of the new ideas and art of the Italian Renaissance were its richest cities, Florence and Venice. Both were governed by oligarchies of leading families, but it was their wealth rather than their political system that set them apart, because in one city the families were in constant competition, while in the other they ruled cooperatively.

Florence Florence by the mid-1300s was the principal banking center in Europe and one of the most important producers of luxury goods. Its silks, textiles, fine leather, and silver and gold ob-

Map 12.1 **THE SPREAD OF PRINTING BEFORE 1500**
After its invention in the Rhineland, printing first spread along the rivers that were Europe's main highways. By 1500 it was concentrated mainly in southern Germany, the Netherlands, and northern Italy.

jects were much prized, and the training its guilds offered in design and craftsmanship was a major reason for the high skills of its artists. The florin, the city's gold coin, had international standing as one of the most reliable currencies of the time, and the broad contacts of its merchants gave Florence a cosmopolitan air. The citizens took special pride in the fame of two of their sons, Dante and Giotto, who during the first decades of the fourteenth century had become, respectively, the most famous poet and the most famous artist in Italy.

It was ironic that the Florentines should have taken credit for Dante, because he had been ex-iled from the city as a result of its vicious factional divisions. By the 1300s Florence had been a self-governing commune for two centuries, but it had rarely enjoyed political stability. It was ruled by a series of councils, whose members were drawn from the leading families. From time to time, however, as movements for wider representation

▶ *Giotto*

LAMENTATION

The Florentine Giotto di Bondone (1266?–1337) was the most celebrated painter of his age. He painted fresco cycles in a number of Italian cities, and this segment from one of them indicates the qualities that made him famous: the solid bodies, the expression of human emotion, and the suggestion of landscape, all of which created an impact that was without precedent in medieval art.

arose, such as the Ciompi revolt of 1378, places on the councils were opened to a broader segment of the citizenry—at times, as many as 20 percent of adult males may have been eligible for office. The volatile fortunes of the different groups did not give way to a more stable regime until the rich Medici banking family gained control of the city's government in 1434 and made sure that only people they favored were defined as eligible for government positions. Even amidst the disputes, however (and partly *because* of their competitive instincts), Florence's wealthy families eagerly provided the patronage that enabled this city of some 60,000 people to become one of Europe's most influential cultural centers in the fifteenth century.

Venice   The city of Venice reached its greatest power and influence at the same time. Already independent for over 500 years, by 1400 it controlled a far-flung empire in northern Italy and the eastern Mediterranean and kept a large army and navy. Venice's wealth came from its dominance of the import of goods from Asia, notably spices like pepper and cloves, which were probably the most expensive commodities, per ounce, sold in Europe. Its wealthiest citizens also controlled its government; unlike Florence, Venice was ruled by a cohesive, rather than faction-ridden, group of some 150 families, who inherited this dominance from generation to generation. From among their number they elected the *doge*, the head of the government, who held that position for life. (To increase turnover, older men were usually elected.)

Venice enjoyed remarkable political stability. There were occasional outbursts of discontent, but usually the patricians—who stayed united, relied on informers, made decisions in secret, and were ready to punish troublemakers severely— were able to maintain an image of orderliness and justice in goverment. They were also careful to show a concern for public welfare. The chief

▶ *Antonio Natale*

VENICE ARSENAL

This eighteenth-century depiction of the huge complex that made up the Arsenal in Venice indicates some of the specialized buildings that formed the production line around the pools where the ships were built. At the back, hulls are being laid, and in the foreground, a ship is being scuttled. At the very front are the two towers that flanked the entrance gate to the Arsenal.

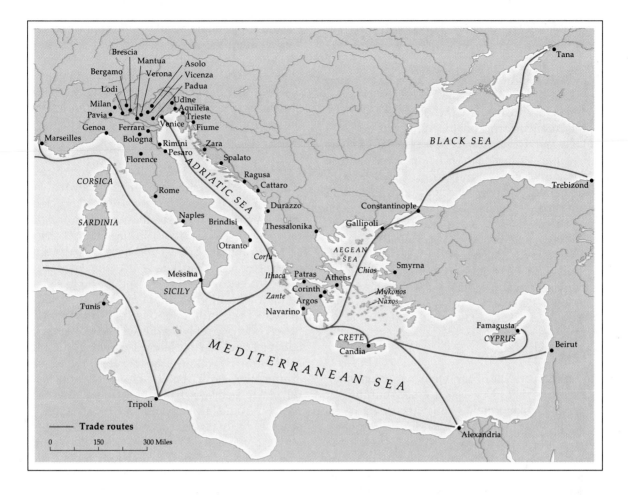

Map 12.2 THE VENETIAN EMPIRE IN THE 1400s
Thanks to its trade, Venice became a major power, controlling dozens of cities in northern Italy and the eastern Mediterranean.

support of the navy, for instance—an essential asset for a city that, though containing over 100,000 people, was built on a collection of islands in a lagoon—was a unique ship-building and arms manufacturing facility, the Arsenal. This gigantic complex, which employed over 5 percent of the city's adult population, was not only the largest industrial enterprise in Europe but also a crucial source of employment. The Arsenal could build a fully equipped warship, starting from scratch, in just one day, and the skills it required helped maintain Venice's reputation as a haven for the finest artisans of the day. Not only men but entire families came to work there; one visitor described a "hall where about 50 women were making sails for ships" and another where 100 women were "spinning and making ropes and doing other work related to ropes."

An institution like the Arsenal promoted economic and social stability by offering so many jobs and also helped improve the craftsmanship

and skills of the city's artisans. In addition, because of its location and its easy openness to all who wished to trade, Venice was a meeting ground for Slavs, Turks, Germans, Jews, Muslims, Greeks, and other Italians. It was a favorite tourist spot for travelers and for pilgrims on the way to the Holy Land; it was a major center of the new international art of printing (see Map. 12.1); and it was famous for its shops and entertainments. By the mid-1400s, its coin, the ducat, was replacing the florin as a standard for all Europe; and its patrons, often interested in more earthy themes than the Florentines, were promoting a flowering of literature, learning, and the arts that made Venice a focus of Renaissance culture.

II. The New Learning

Although traditional forms of learning retained considerable vitality in the fourteenth and fifteenth centuries, medieval Scholasticism, with its highly refined forms of reasoning, did not adequately serve the literate lay population. The curriculum remained largely designed for the training of teachers and theologians, whereas increasingly the demand was for practical training in the arts of persuasion and communication: good speaking and good writing. Moreover, many laypeople believed that Scholastics failed to offer moral guidance. As Petrarch was to note, education should train people in the art of leading a wise, pious, and happy life. A central concern of the Renaissance was to develop a system of education that would do exactly that.

HUMANISM

One minor branch of the medieval educational curriculum, rhetoric, was concerned with the art of good speaking and writing. Increasingly, its practitioners in Italy began to turn to the Latin classics for models of good writing. This interest in the Classical authors was helped by the close relationship between the Italian language and Latin, by the availability of manuscripts, and by the presence in Italy of countless Classical monuments. It was rhetoricians who first began to argue, in the late thirteenth century, that education should be reformed to give more attention to the classics and to help people lead more moral lives.

These rhetoricians were to found an intellectual movement known as Humanism. The term *Humanism* was not coined until the nineteenth century. In fifteenth-century Italy, *humanista* signified a professor of humane studies or a Classical scholar, but eventually Humanism came to mean Classical scholarship—the ability to read, understand, and appreciate the writings of the ancient world. The aim of a humanist education was to train individuals in the classics, which offered models both of the wisdom a person needed to follow the right path in any situation and of the eloquence necessary to persuade others to that path. The modern use of the word *Hu-*

manism to denote a secular philosophy that denies an afterlife has no basis in the Renaissance. Most Renaissance humanists read the Church fathers as avidly as they read pagan authors and believed that the highest virtues included piety. Humanism was far more an effort to enrich traditional religious attitudes than a revolt against them.

Petrarch   The most influential early advocate of Humanism was Francesco Petrarca, known as Petrarch (1304–1374). He was a lawyer and cleric who practiced neither of those professions but rather devoted his life to writing poetry, scholarly and moral treatises, and letters. He became famous for his Italian verse—his sonnets inspired poets for centuries—but he sought above all to emulate Virgil by writing a Latin epic poem. A master of self-promotion, he used that work as the occasion for reviving the ancient title of "poet laureate" and having himself crowned in Rome in 1341. But he was also capable of profound self-examination. In a remarkable work, which he called *My Secret*—a dialogue with one of his heroes, St. Augustine—he laid bare his struggles to achieve spiritual peace despite the earthly temptations of fame and love. Increasingly, he became concerned that nowhere in the world around him could he find a model of virtuous behavior that he could respect. The leaders of the Church he considered poor examples, for they seemed worldly and materialistic. Convinced that no guide from his own times or the immediate past would serve, Petrarch concluded that he had to turn to the Church fathers and the ancient Romans to find worthy examples of the moral life (*see box*, p. 355).

How, then, could one be a good person? By imitating such figures from antiquity as Cicero and Augustine, who knew what proper values were and pursued them in their own lives, despite temptations and the distractions of public affairs. The period between their time and his own—which Petrarch regarded as the "middle" ages—he considered contemptible. His own world, he felt, would improve only if it tried to emulate the ancients, and in fact a central purpose of education ought to be to teach what they did and said. In particular, like the good rheto-

Petrarch on Ancient Rome

Petrarch was so determined to relive the experience of antiquity that he wrote letters to famous Roman authors as if they were acquaintances. In one letter, he even described Cicero coming to visit him. While he was passing through Padua in February 1350 he recalled that the city was the birthplace of the Roman historian Livy, and he promptly wrote to him.

"I only wish, either that I had been born in your time or you in ours. If the latter, our age would have benefited; if the former, I myself would have been the better for it. I would surely have visited you. As it is, I can merely see you reflected in your works. It is over those works that I labor whenever I want to forget the places, times, and customs around me. I am often filled with anger at today's morals, when people value only gold and silver, and want nothing but physical pleasures.

"I have to thank you for many things, but especially because you have so often helped me forget the evils of today, and have transported me to happier times. As I read you, I seem to be living with Scipio, Brutus, Cato, and many others. It is with them that I live, and not with the ruffians of today, among whom an evil star had me born. Oh, the great names that comfort me in my wretchedness, and make me forget this wicked age! Please greet for me those older historians like Polybius, and those younger than you like Pliny.

"Farewell forever, you unequalled historian!

"Written in the land of the living, in that part of Italy where you were born and buried, in sight of your own tombstone, on the 22nd of February in the 1350th year after the birth of Him whom you would have seen had you lived longer."

Petrarch, *Epistolae Familiares*, XXIV, 8. Passages selected and translated by Theodore K. Rabb.

rician he was, he believed that only by restoring the mastery of the written and spoken word that had distinguished the great Romans—an imitation of their style, of the way they had conveyed their ideas—could his contemporaries learn to behave like the ancients.

Boccaccio The program Petrarch laid out soon caught fire in Florence, the city from which his family had come and where he found influential friends and disciples. The most important was the poet and writer Giovanni Boccaccio (1313–1375). He became famous in Florence for a collection of short stories known as *The Decameron*, written between 1348 and 1351. It recounts how a group of young Florentines—seven women and three men—fled during the Black Death of 1348 to a secluded villa, where for 10 days each told a story. The first prose masterpiece in Italian, *The Decameron*'s frank treatment of sex and its

vivid creation of ordinary characters make it one of the first major works in Western letters intended to divert and amuse rather than edify. But in his later years Boccaccio grew increasingly concerned with the teaching of moral values, and he became a powerful supporter of Petrarch's ideas.

THE CIVIC HUMANISTS

In the generation after Petrarch and Boccaccio, Humanism became a rallying cry for the intellectual leaders of Florence. They argued that, by associating their city with the revival of antiquity, Florentines would be identified with a distinctive vision that would become the envy of their rivals among the cities and states of Italy. And that was indeed what happened. The campaign for a return to the classics started a revolution in education that soon began to take hold throughout

Italy; the writing and speaking skills the humanists emphasized came to be in demand at every princely court (including that of the papacy); and the crusade to study and imitate the ancients transformed art, literature, and even political and social values.

Led by the chancellor of Florence, Coluccio Salutati (whose position, as the official who prepared the city's official communications, required training in rhetoric), a group of humanists began to collect ancient manuscripts and form libraries, so as to make accessible to scholars virtually all the surviving writings of Classical Latin authors. These Florentines also sought to reestablish in Italy a command of the Greek language, and in 1396 they invited the Byzantine scholar Manuel Chrysoloras to lecture at the University of Florence. In the following decades—troubled years for the Byzantine Empire—other Eastern scholars joined the exodus to the West, and they and Western visitors returning from the East brought with them hundreds of Greek manuscripts. By the middle of the fifteenth century Western scholars had both the philological skill and the manuscripts to establish direct contact with the most original minds of the Classical world and were making numerous Latin and Italian translations of Greek works. Histories, tragedies, lyric poetry, the dialogues of Plato, many mathematical treatises, and the most important works of the Greek fathers of the Church fully entered Western culture for the first time.

Salutati and his contemporaries and successors in Florence are often called *civic humanists*, because they stressed that participation in public affairs is essential for full human development. Petrarch had wondered whether individuals should cut themselves off from the larger world, with its corruptions and compromises, and focus only on what he called (using its Latin name) the *vita contemplativa*—the contemplative life—or try to improve that world through the *vita activa*—the active life. Petrarch's models had offered no clear answer. Cicero had suggested the need for both lives, but Augustine had been fearful of outside temptations. In the generations following Petrarch, however, the doubts declined, and the humanists argued that only by participating in public life, seeking higher ends for one's society

as well as oneself, could an individual be truly virtuous. Republican government was the best form, they argued, because unless educated citizens made use of their wisdom for the benefit of all, their moral understanding would remain socially barren. These were lessons exemplified by the ancient classics, and thus in one connected argument the civic humanists defended the necessity of studying the ancients, the superiority of the active life, and the value of Florentine republican institutions.

HUMANISM IN THE FIFTEENTH CENTURY

As the humanist movement gained in prestige, it spread from Florence to other cities of Italy. Pope Nicholas V (1447–1455), for example, founded a library in the Vatican that was to become the greatest repository of ancient manuscripts in Italy. And princely courts, such as those of the Gonzaga at Mantua and the Montefeltro at Urbino, gained fame because of their patronage of humanists. Moreover, the influence of antiquity was coming to be felt in all areas of learning and writing. Literature was profoundly influenced by the ancients, as a new interest in Classical models reshaped the form and content of both poetry and drama, from the epic to the bawdy comedy. Purely secular themes, without religious purpose, became more common. And works of history grew increasingly analytic, openly acknowledging such ancients as Thucydides, Livy, and Tacitus as their inspiration.

Education Perhaps the most direct effect was on education itself. Two scholars from the north of Italy, Guarino da Verona and Vittorino da Feltre, succeeded in turning the diffuse educational ideas of the humanists into a practical curriculum. Guarino argued for a reform of traditional methods of education, and Vittorino brought the new methods to their fullest development in the various schools he founded, especially his Casa Giocosa ("Happy House") at Mantua. The pupils included boys and girls, both rich and poor (the latter on scholarships). All the students learned Latin and Greek, mathematics, music, and philosophy; in addition—because Vittorino believed that education should aid physical, moral, and social development—they were taught social graces, such as dancing and courteous manners, and received instruction in physical exercises like riding and fencing. Vittorino's school attracted pupils from all over Italy, and his methods were widely imitated.

Ultimately, a humanist education was to give the elite throughout Europe a new way of measuring social distinction. It soon became apparent that the ability to quote Virgil or some other ancient writer was not so much a sign of moral seriousness as a badge of superiority. What differentiated people was whether they could use or recognize the quotations, and that was why the new curriculum was so popular—even though it seemed to consist, more and more, of endless memorizations and repetitions of Latin texts.

New Standards of Behavior The growing admiration for the humanists and their teachings also gave an important boost to the patronage of arts and letters. In the age of gunpowder, it was no longer easy to claim that physical bravery was the supreme quality of noblemen. Instead, nobles began to set themselves apart not just by seeking a humanist education but by winning fame through the patronage of artists and writers whose praise made their benefactors famous. Thus a new image of gentlemanly behavior, which included the qualities that Guarino fostered—a commitment to refinement, taste, and elegance as well as to courage—became widely accepted. This new life style was to be summarized and promoted in a book, *The Courtier*, written in 1516 by Baldassare Castiglione, that became a manual of proper behavior for gentlemen and ladies for centuries. Castiglione's patron, duke Federigo Montefeltro of Urbino, even had his portrait painted sitting in his study reading a book, but dressed in armor.

By the mid-1400s Humanism was a dominant intellectual force throughout Italy, and by the end of the century it was sweeping all of Europe, transmitted not only by its devoted adherents but also by a recent invention, printing, which made the texts of both humanists and ancients far more easily available. Dozens of new schools and universities were founded, and no court of any significance was without its roster of artists and

▶ *Raphael*
Baldassare Castiglione
Raphael painted this portrait of his friend, the count Baldassare Castiglione, around 1514. Castiglione's solemn pose and thoughtful expression exude the dignity and cultivation that were described as essential attributes of the courtier in Castiglione's famous book on courtly behavior.

writers familiar with the latest ideas. Even legal systems were affected, as the principles of Roman law (which tended to endorse the power of the ruler) were adopted in many countries. But in the late fifteenth century the revival of antiquity took a direction that qualified the commitment to the *vita activa* that had been the mark of the civic humanists. A new movement, Neoplatonism, brought to the fore the interest in spiritual values that was the heart of the *vita contemplativa*.

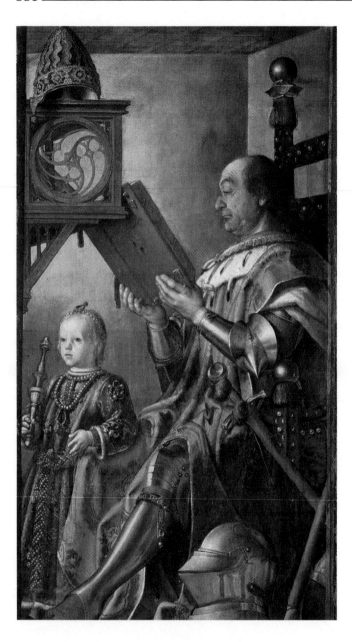

▶ *Joos van Wassenhove and Pedro Berruguete*
FEDERIGO DA MONTEFELTRO
This remarkable painting embodies the new ideal of the gentleman that emerged in the Renaissance. Federigo da Montefeltro was both one of the most notable warriors and one of the most distinguished patrons of learning of the age, and this portrait captures both sides of his princely image. Sitting in his study with his richly clothed son, Guidobaldo, Duke Federigo is reading a book but is also dressed in armor.

THE FLORENTINE NEOPLATONISTS

The turn away from the practical concerns of the civic humanists toward a renewed exploration of grand ideals of truth and perfection was a result of the growing interest in Greek as well as Roman antiquity—especially the works of Plato. A group of Florentine philosophers, active in the last decades of the fifteenth century and equally at home in Greek and Latin, led the way.

Ficino The most gifted of these Neoplatonists, as they are called—"new" followers of Plato—was the physician Marsilio Ficino. His career is a tribute to the cultural patronage of the Medici family, which spotted his talents as a child and gave him the use of a villa and library near Florence. In this lovely setting a group of scholars and statesmen met frequently to discuss philosophical questions. Drawn to the idealism of Plato, Ficino and his colleagues argued that Platonic ideas demonstrated the dignity and immortality of the human soul. To spread these views among a larger audience, Ficino translated into Latin all Plato's dialogues and the writings of Plato's chief followers. In his *Theologica Platonica* (1469), he made an ambitious effort to reconcile Platonic philosophy and the Christian religion.

Pico Another member of the group was Count Giovanni Pico della Mirandola, who thought he could reconcile all philosophies in order to show that there was a single truth that lay behind every quest for the ideal. In 1486 Pico sought to defend publicly, in Rome, some 900 theses that would show the essential unity of all philosophies. The pope, fearful that the theses contained several heretical propositions, forbade the disputation, but Pico's introductory "Oration on the Dignity of Man" remains one of the supreme examples of the humanists' optimism about the potential of the individual.

The message of both Ficino and Pico was founded on two essential assumptions. First, the entire universe is arranged in a hierarchy of excellence, with God at the summit. Second, each being in the universe, with the exception only of God, is impelled by "natural appetite" to seek perfection; it is impelled, in other words, to achieve—or at least to contemplate—the beauti-

Map 12.3 THE SPREAD OF UNIVERSITIES IN THE RENAISSANCE
A significant indication of the rising status accorded to learning, and the growing importance of education in general during the Renaissance, is the opening of major new universities. Even where earlier universities existed, as at Oxford, many new colleges were founded, and the number of graduates increased rapidly in the fifteenth and sixteenth centuries.

ful. As Pico expressed it, man is unique in that he is placed in the middle of the universe, linked with both the spiritual world above and the material one below. His free will enables him to seek perfection in either direction; he is free to become all things. A clear ethic emerges from this scheme: The good life should be an effort to achieve personal perfection, and the highest human value is the contemplation of the beautiful.

These writers believed that Plato had been divinely illumined and therefore that Platonic philosophy and Christian belief were two wholly reconcilable faces of a single truth. Because of this synthesis, and also its passionate idealism, Neoplatonic philosophy was to be a major influence on artists and thinkers for the next two centuries.

THE HERITAGE OF HUMANISM

Although its scholarship was often arid and difficult, fifteenth-century Italian Humanism left a deep imprint on European thought and education. The humanists greatly improved the command of Latin; they restored a large part of the Greek cultural inheritance to Western civilization; their investigations led to a mastery of other languages associated with great cultural traditions, most notably Hebrew; and they laid the basis of modern textual criticism. They also developed new ways of examining the ancient world—through archaeology, numismatics (the study of coins), and epigraphy (the study of inscriptions on buildings, statues, and the like), as well as through the study of literary texts. As for the study of history, while medieval chroniclers had looked to the past for evidence of God's providence, the humanists used the past to illustrate human behavior and provide moral examples. They also helped standardize spelling and grammar in vernacular languages; and the Classical ideals of simplicity, restraint, and elegance of style that they promoted helped reshape Western literature.

No less important was the role of the humanists as educational reformers. The curriculum they devised spread throughout Europe in the sixteenth century, and until our own century it continued to define the standards by which the lay leaders of Western society were trained. In the thirteenth century, learning was largely a monopoly of monks and Scholastics; during the Renaissance, the humanists introduced a narrow but still important segment of lay society to the intellectual treasury of the European past, both ancient and medieval. Simultaneously, they reinterpreted that heritage and enlarged the function of education and scholarship to serve human beings in their present lives by teaching them, as Petrarch recommended, the art of living wisely and well. Moreover, the fact that, regardless of

religious and other divisions, men and women throughout Europe were steeped in the same classics meant that they thought and communicated in similar fashion. In spite of the continent's bitter conflicts, this common humanistic education helped preserve the fundamental cultural unity of the West.

III. Art and Artists in the Italian Renaissance

The most visible effect of Humanism and its admiration for the ancients was on the arts. Since the movement first took hold in Florence, it is not too surprising that its first artistic disciples appeared among the Florentines. They had other advantages. First, the city was already famous throughout Italy for its art, because the greatest painters of the late 1200s and 1300s, Cimabue (1240–1302) and his pupil Giotto (1276–1336), were identified with Florence. Giotto, in particular, had decorated buildings from Padua to Naples and thus gained a wide audience for the sense of realism and powerful emotion that he created; he became celebrated for an immediacy that had never been seen in the formal and restrained styles of earlier artists. Second, Florence was full of wealthy citizens who were ready to patronize art; and third, the city had a long tradition of excellence in the design of luxury goods such as silks and gold objects. Many leading artists of the 1400s and 1500s started their careers as apprentices to goldsmiths, in whose workshops they mastered creative techniques as well as aesthetic principles that informed their work when they turned to painting, sculpture, or architecture.

THREE FRIENDS

The revolution in these three disciplines was started by three friends, who were united by a determination to apply the humanists' lessons to art. They wanted to break with the styles of the immediate past and create paintings, statues, and buildings that would not merely imitate the glories of Rome but actually bring them back to life. All three went to Rome in the 1420s, hoping by direct observation and study of ancient master-

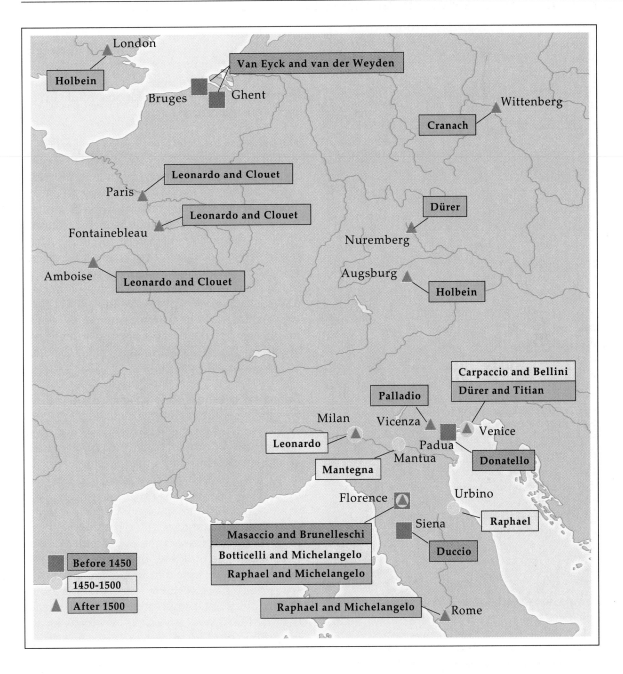

Map 12.4 MAJOR CENTERS OF RENAISSANCE ART
From its beginnings in Florence, Renaissance art
spread throughout Italy, while in northern Europe,
after the pioneering work of Van Eyck, the Italian
influence took hold mainly in Germany and France.

pieces to re-create their qualities and thus fulfill the humanists' goal of reviving the spirit of Classical times. The locals regarded the three as rather strange, for they went around measuring, taking notes, and calculating sizes and proportions. But the lessons they learned enabled them to transform the styles and purposes of art.

Masaccio The painter among the three, Masaccio (1401–1428), used the inspiration of the an-

cients to put a new emphasis on nature, on three-dimensional human bodies, and on perspective. In showing Adam and Eve, he not only depicted the first nudes since antiquity but showed them coming through a rounded arch that was the

▶ *Masaccio*

THE EXPULSION OF ADAM AND EVE, CA. 1425
Masaccio shows Adam and Eve expelled from
paradise through a rounded archway that recalls
ancient architecture. Also indicative of the influence
of Roman art is the attempt to create what we
would consider realistic (rather than stylized)
human beings and to portray them nude, displaying
powerful, recognizable emotions. This was one of
the paintings that made the Brancacci Chapel an
inspiration to generations of artists.

pointed arch of the Middle Ages. The chapel he decorated in a Florentine church, the Carmine, became a place of pilgrimage for painters for centuries, for here the values of ancient art—especially its emphasis on the individual human figure—were reborn.

Donatello Masaccio's friend Donatello (1386–1466) was primarily a sculptor, and the figures he created in three dimensions had the same qualities as Masaccio's had in two. Once again the focus was on the beauty of the body itself, because that had been a notable and distinctive concern of the ancients. The interest in the nude, accurately displayed, transformed the very purpose of art, for it led to an idealized representation of the human form that had not been seen in centuries. Donatello's depiction of the biblical hero David shows him in contemplation after his triumph over Goliath. Because his story symbolized vigor and youth, the Florentines made David a favorite subject.

Brunelleschi The most spectacular of these three pioneers was the architect Brunelleschi (1377?–1446). For decades, his fellow citizens had been building a new cathedral, which, as a sign of their artistic superiority, was going to be the largest in Italy. Seen from above, it was shaped—as was traditional—like a cross. The basic structure was in place, but the huge space where the horizontal and vertical met, the crossing, had not yet been covered. In response to a competition for a design to complete the building, Brunelleschi, inspired by what he had learned in Rome, proposed covering the crossing with the largest dome built in Europe since antiquity. Although the first reaction was that it was impossible, eventually he got the commission. In an extraordinary feat of engineering, which required that he build the dome in rings, without using scaffolding, he erected a structure that became not only a fitting climax to the cathedral but also the hallmark of Renaissance Florence and an inspiration for all architects. And the symmetrical simplicity of his other buildings shaped a new aesthetic of harmony and balance that matched what Masaccio and Donatello accomplished in painting and sculpture. In all three, the imitation of ancient Rome inspired subjects and styles that broke decisively with their immediate medieval past.

During the remaining years of the 1400s, a succession of artists, not just in Florence but increasingly in other parts of Italy as well, built on the achievements of the pioneer generation. They experimented with perspective and the modeling of bodies and drapery, so as to recapture the an-

▶ *Donatello*
DAVID, CA. 1430–1432
Like Masaccio, Donatello imitated the Romans by creating idealized nude bodies. His *David* has just killed and decapitated Goliath, whose head lies at his feet. Goliath's helmet recalls those worn by Florence's enemies, which makes this sculpture a work of patriotism as well as art. It happens also to have been the first life-size bronze figure cast since antiquity.

▶ *Brunelleschi*
DOME OF FLORENCE CATHEDRAL, 1420–1436
Brunelleschi's famous dome—the first built in Italy since the fall of the Roman Empire—embodied the revival of Classical forms in architecture. The contrast with the bell tower designed a century earlier by Giotto, with its suggestion of pointed Gothic arches, is unmistakable. The dome was a feat of engineering as well as design: Its 135-feet diameter was spanned without scaffolding, and Brunelleschi himself invented the machines that made the construction possible.

cients' mastery of depth, and they made close observations of nature. The sculptors created monumental figures, some on horseback, in imitation of Roman models. And the architects perfected the use of the rounded arches and symmetrical forms they saw in antique buildings. Subject matter also changed, as artists produced increasing numbers of portraits of their contemporaries and depicted stories out of Roman and Greek myths as well as traditional religious scenes. By the end of the 1400s, the leading Florentine painter of the day, Botticelli (1444?–1510), was presenting ancient subjects like the Birth of Venus, goddess of love, in exactly the way a Roman might have fashioned them.

THE HIGH RENAISSANCE

The artists at work in the early years of the 1500s are often referred to as the generation of the High Renaissance. Four, in particular—Leo-

▶ *Sandro Botticelli*
BIRTH OF VENUS, CA. 1480
Sandro Botticelli was a member of the intellectual
circle of Lorenzo de Medici, and this painting is
evidence of the growing interest in Neoplatonism at
the Medici court. The wistful, ethereal look on
Venus' face reflects the otherworldliness that was
emphasized by the Neoplatonists; moreover, their
belief in the analogies that link all ideas suggests
that Botticelli may have been implying that Venus
resembled the Virgin Mary as a source of divine
love. In depicting an ancient myth as ancient
painters would have shown it, Botticelli represents
the triumph of Renaissance ambitions, and the
idealized beauty of his work helped shape an
aesthetic standard that has been admired ever since.

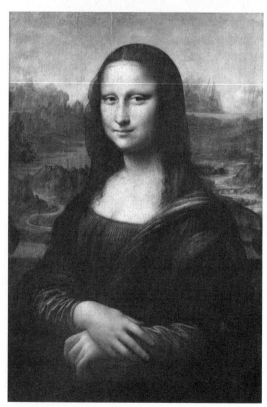

▶ *Leonardo da Vinci*
MONA LISA, CA. 1503–1505
This is probably the most celebrated image in
Renaissance art. The famous hint of a smile and the
calm and solid pose are so familiar that we all too
easily forget how striking it seemed at the time and
how often it inspired later portraits. As in his *Last
Supper*, however, Leonardo was experimenting with
his materials, and the picture has therefore faded
over the years.

nardo, Raphael, Michelangelo, and Titian—are thought of as bringing the new movement that had begun a hundred years before to a climax.

Leonardo   The oldest, Leonardo (1452–1519), was the epitome of the experimental tradition. Always seeking new ways of doing things, whether in observing anatomy or designing fortifications, he was unable to resist the challenge of solving practical problems, even in his paintings. They are marvels of technical virtuosity, which make difficult angles, tricks of perspective, and bizarre geological formations look easy. His portrait of the *Mona Lisa*, for example, is famous not only for her mysterious smile but for the incredible rocky landscape in the background. Unfortunately, Leonardo also experimented with methods of painting; as a result, one of his masterpieces, the *Last Supper*, has almost completely disintegrated.

Raphael   By contrast, Raphael (1483–1520) used the mastery of perspective and ancient styles that had been achieved in the 1400s to produce works of perfect harmony, beauty, and serenity. His paintings give an impression of utter relaxation, of an artist in complete command of his materials and therefore able to create sunny scenes that are

▶ *Raphael*
SCHOOL OF ATHENS
Painted in 1510 and 1511, this fresco celebrating the glories of Greek philosophy represents the triumph of the Renaissance campaign to revive antiquity. That the Classical setting and theme could have been accepted as appropriate for a wall of the Vatican suggests how completely Humanism had captured intellectual life. A number of the figures are portraits of artists whom Raphael knew: Plato, pointing to heaven at the back, has the face of Leonardo, and the notoriously moody Michelangelo broods, with his head on his arm, at the front.

▶ *Michelangelo*
THE CREATION OF MAN
Michelangelo worked on the ceiling of the Sistine Chapel in the Vatican from 1508 to 1512 and painted hundreds of figures. None has come to symbolize the rebirth associated with the Renaissance and the power of creative genius so forcefully as the portrayal of God extending a finger to bring the vigorous body of Adam to life. Tucked under God's other arm is the figure of Eve, ready to join Adam in giving birth to mankind.

balanced and at peace. His tribute to the ancient world, *The School of Athens*, places in a Classical architectural setting the great philosophers of Greece, many of whom are portraits of the artists of the day: Aristotle, for instance, has Leonardo's face. If the philosophers were the chief glory of Athens, Raphael seems to be saying, then the artists are the crowning glory of the Renaissance.

Michelangelo For Michelangelo (1475–1564), painting was but one means of expression. Equally at home in poetry, architecture, and sculpture, he often seems the ultimate embodiment of the achievements of his age. Yet there are few of Raphael's relaxed qualities in his work. He once said that no two of the thousands of figures he depicted were the same, and one might add that just about every one of them conveys the sense of latent strength, of striving, that was

Michelangelo's signature. Although Adam, shown at the moment of his creation, has not yet received the gift of life from God, he already displays the vigor that Michelangelo gave to every human body. The same is true of his version of David, seemingly tranquil but showing his potential power in his massive, oversized hand. The sculptor relishes his ability to show the human being in full majesty, as an independent and potent individual.

Titian In Venice, the developments in art took a slightly different form. This was also a rich trading city, sophisticated, with broad international connections. But here Humanism was not so central, and the art—as befitted this most down-to-earth and cosmopolitan of Europe's cities—was more sensuous. The most famous Venetian painter, Titian (1482?–1576), depicted rich velvets, lush nudes, stormy skies, and dogs with wagging tails with a directness and immediacy that enable the viewer almost to feel them. His friend Aretino said of one of his pictures: "I can say nothing of the crimson of the garment nor of its lynx lining, for in comparison real crimson and real lynx seem painted, and these seem real." Titian was Europe's most sought-after portraitist, and to this day we can recognize the leading figures of his time, and sense their character, because of the mastery of his depictions.

STATUS AND PERCEPTION

The Artist as Craftsman To the generation of Masaccio, a painter was merely one of the many craftsmen in a city, not inherently more admired than a skilled leather finisher or mason. Like them, he was a member of a guild, he had to pass a carefully regulated apprenticeship, and he was subject to the rules that controlled his trade. Both Donatello and Brunelleschi were trained as goldsmiths, and the latter was even briefly imprisoned by his guild for not paying his dues while he was working—as an independent person, so he thought, and thus outside the guild structure—on the cathedral dome.

Given the Florentines' interest in gaining fame by beautifying their city, it was not surprising that the work of these artists should have at-

▶ ***Titian***
BACCHANAL, CA. 1518
The earthy realism of Venice contrasted sharply with the idealization common in Florentine art. The setting and even the sky seem more tangible, and Titian's lush nude in the foreground (who was to be much copied) is the essence of sensuality. It has been suggested that the painting represents the different stages of life, from the incontinent child through the vigorous youths and adults to the old man who has collapsed in the back.

tracted considerable attention. But it rarely occurred to anyone in the early 1400s—as Brunelleschi discovered from his guild—that they might deserve special respect or be considered anything more elevated than middle-class tradesmen. It was true that some of them were becoming famous throughout Italy, but would that lead to a change in their social status?

Humanism and the Change in Status The answer was that it did, and again the impetus came from the humanist movement. Three consequences of the revival of antiquity, in particular, began a reevaluation of the position of the artist. First was the recognition that the most vivid and convincing re-creations of the achievements of the ancient world were being produced in the visual arts. No letter written like Cicero's could compare with a painting, a statue, or a building as a means of bringing Rome back to life for all to see—as an open and public display of the virtues of Classical times.

A second influence was the humanists' new interest in personal fame. This had been an acceptable aspiration in antiquity, but during the Middle Ages spiritual concerns encouraged a disdain for worldly matters, and so it was a problem for Petrarch to admit that, like the ancients he admired, he wanted to be famous. In the book he called *My Secret* he struggled to justify his ambition, but he could never shake free of the guilt it aroused in him. For later humanists, the doubts receded, and the princes who valued their ideas eagerly accepted the notion that they should devote their lives to attaining fame. That was what nobles had won as warriors, but now there was a more reliable way to ensure that one's name lived forever.

The New Patrons That way was provided by the third of the humanists' lessons: that the truly moral person had to combine the contemplative with the active life. A prince, therefore, ought to cultivate the fine as well as the martial arts. No aristocratic court could be complete without its poets and painters, who sang their patron's praises while fashioning the masterpieces that not only brought prestige but also endured far longer than a brief human life. As a result, if a duke or a count wanted to be remembered, it was

no longer enough to be a famous warrior; increasingly, it became essential to build a splendid new palace or have his portrait done by a famous painter. To be most like the virtuous heroes of Rome who were the society's ideal, he had to be a patron of culture as well as a vigorous leader. And this outlook was not confined to the males who now tried to unite artistic and military glory. Noble women, whose chief role had long been to offer an idealized object of chivalric devotion and who continued to struggle to gain access to education, occasionally won that struggle, and the result was a refined patronage that could be crucial in fashioning a princely image. Without Isabella d'Este, for example, the court in Mantua would not have achieved all the fame it won as a center of painting, architecture, and music. That both Leonardo and Titian did her portrait was a reflection not of her husband's importance but of her own independent contribution to the arts. Her rooms, surrounding a lovely garden, remain one of the wonders of the palace at Mantua and a worthy testimony to the fame she achieved as a patroness (*see box*, p. 369).

The effect of this new attitude was to transform the status of artists. They became highly prized at the courts of aristocrats, who saw them as extraordinarily effective image makers. Perhaps the most famous family of patrons in Italy, the Medici of Florence, were envied throughout Europe mainly because, for generations, they seemed always to be surrounded by the finest painters, sculptors, and architects of the age. Two of the Medici became popes, and they brought Raphael and Michelangelo to Rome, just as their ancestors had patronized Brunelleschi, Donatello, and Botticelli in Florence. The Church as an institution had been the main sponsor of art in the Middle Ages, but now it was the papacy in particular that promoted and inspired artistic production. In their determination to rebuild and beautify Rome as a worthy capital of Christendom, the popes gave such artists as Raphael and Michelangelo their most famous commissions—notably Michelangelo's Sistine Chapel within the Vatican. It was thus as a result of shifting patterns in the commissioning and buying of art that, as honored members of papal as well as princely courts, Renaissance artists created both a new aesthetic and a new social identity.

Isabella d'Este's Quest for Art

As the passion for art took hold, the great patrons of the Renaissance became relentless in their search for new works. None was more avid than Isabella d'Este (1474–1539), who became the wife of the Gonzaga prince of Mantua at the age of 16 and made her private suite of rooms (which she called her **studio***) a gathering place for artists, musicians, and poets for nearly 50 years. Her passion for art shines through her letters; in these extracts, she is pursuing both the Venetian painter Bellini and Leonardo da Vinci.*

"*To an agent, 1502*: 'You may remember that many months ago we gave Giovanni Bellini a commission to paint a picture for the decoration of our studio, and when it ought to have been finished we found it was not yet begun. We told him to abandon the work, and give you back the 25 ducats, but now he begs us to leave him the work and promises to finish it soon. As till now he has given us nothing but words, tell him that we no longer care to have the picture, but if instead he would paint a Nativity, we should be well content, as long as he does not keep us waiting any longer.'

"*Two months later:* 'As Bellini is resolved on doing a picture of the Madonna and Child and St. John the Baptist in place of the Nativity scene, I should be glad if he would also include a St. Jerome; and about the price of 50 ducats we are content, but above all urge him to serve us quickly and well.'

"*Three years later, to Bellini himself:* 'You will remember very well how great our desire was for a picture painted by your hand, to put in our studio. We appealed to you for this in the past, but you could not do it on account of your many other commitments. [We recently heard you might be free,] but we have been ill with fever and unable to attend to such things. Now that we are feeling better it has occurred to us to write begging you to consent to painting a picture, and we will leave the poetic invention for you to make up if you do

not want us to give it to you. As well as the proper payment, we shall be under an eternal obligation to you. When we hear of your agreement, we will send you the measurements of the canvas and an initial payment.'

"*In the meantime, in May 1504, she wrote to Leonardo da Vinci*: 'Hearing that you are staying in Florence, we have conceived the hope that something we have long desired might come true: to have something by your hand. When you were here and drew our portrait in charcoal, you promised one day to do it in color. Since it would be inconvenient for you to move here, we beg you to keep your good faith with us by substituting for our portrait a youthful Christ of about twelve years old, executed with that sweetness and soft ethereal charm which is the peculiar excellence of your art.'

"*Five months later she wrote again:* 'Some months ago we wrote to you that we wanted to have a young Christ, about twelve years old, by your hand. You replied that you would do this gladly, but owing to the many commissioned works you have on your hands, we doubt whether you remembered ours. Wherefore it has occurred to us to send you these few lines, begging you that you will turn to doing this little figure for us by way of recreation, which will be doing us a very gracious service and of benefit to yourself.'"

From D. S. Chambers (ed.), *Patrons and Artists in the Italian Renaissance* (London: Macmillan, 1970), pp. 128–130 and 147–148.

Vasari   In the mid-1500s, a leading protégé of the Medici, an architect and painter named Giorgio Vasari (1511–1574), decided to try and figure out how and why it was that artists like him were

being showered with privileges. He himself had been given the responsibility to design, build, and decorate a large new building in the center of the city for the government's offices—or, in

▶ *Benvenuto Cellini*
SALT CELLAR FOR FRANCIS I
Benvenuto Cellini, a Florentine goldsmith who challenged Giorgio Vasari's distinction between artisan and artist in his lively *Autobiography* (1562), executed this work for the French king Francis I in 1543. Juxtaposing allegorical images of the Earth and the Sea, which he presented as opposing forces, Cellini created figures as elegant as any sculpture and set them on a fantastic base of gold and enamel. His extraordinary skills indicate why so many Renaissance artists began their careers in goldsmiths' workshops.

Italian, Uffizi (now the main museum of Renaissance art in Florence). He had been knighted for his services, and he was a significant figure at the court ruled over by the Medici, who in 1530 had been named Grand Dukes of Tuscany. To understand his own good fortune, he looked to the past and wrote the first major work of what became, in his hands, a new field of study: the history of art.

Vasari put forward the idea that certain artists were filled with a special spirit, which he called genius, that set them apart from—and above—other people. The status artists had achieved was, in Vasari's account, richly deserved. They were appropriate courtiers, and even minor aristocrats, because of their genius and their fame. He wrote of them as if it were impossible to remember that, just a century before, they had been considered mere craftsman. Titian, for example, lived like a member of one of the finest families in Venice. He had a splendid house and was wel-

comed at the grandest occasions. Although he was in huge demand throughout Europe, he chose not to leave his native city. He might visit a king or an emperor, but he did not need to be attached to their court—as Botticelli was, for instance, to the Medici—in order to maintain his high standing. The acceptance of artists into the uppermost levels of society was one of the most remarkable transformations produced by the Italian Renaissance.

IV. The Culture of the North

North of the Alps the transformations of the 1300s and 1400s were not as dramatic as those that took place in Italy, but they were to have consequences after 1500 that were no less dramatic than the effects of Humanism, Neoplatonism, and the social changes of the south. This area of Europe did not have the many large cities and the high percentages of urban dwellers that were crucial to the humanist movement in Italy. Nor did the physical monuments and languages of northern Europe offer ready reminders of the Classical heritage. Humanism and the revival of Classical learning—with its literate, trained laity—did not come to the north until the last decade of the fifteenth century. But here, where the princely court rather than the city, and the knight rather than the merchant, dominated cultural life, there were other vital shifts in outlook.

CHIVALRY

In 1919 a Dutch historian, Johan Huizinga, described northern European culture in the 1400s and 1500s not as a renaissance but as the decline of medieval civilization. The stimulating book in which he made that argument, *The Waning of the Middle Ages*, focused primarily on the court of the dukes of Burgundy, who were among the wealthiest and most powerful princes of the north. Huizinga found tension and frequent violence in this society, with little of the serenity that had marked the thirteenth century. Instead, writers and artists seemed to have little grasp on reality and displayed deep emotional instability. Although many now consider Huizinga's interpretation exaggerated, his analysis clearly contains much that is accurate.

The poor grasp of reality that Huizinga noted is evident in the extravagant cultivation of the notion of chivalry. Militarily, the knight was becoming less important than the foot soldier armed with longbow, pike, or firearms. But the noble classes of the north continued to pretend that knightly virtues governed all questions of state and society; they discounted such lowly considerations as money, arms, number of forces, supplies, and the total resources of countries in deciding the outcome of wars. For example, before the Battle of Agincourt, one knight told the French King Charles that he should not use contingents from the Parisian townsfolk because that would give his army an unfair numerical advantage; the battle should be decided strictly on the basis of chivalrous valor.

Bravery and Display   This was the age of the perfect knight and the "grand gesture." King John of Bohemia insisted that his soldiers lead him to the front rank of battle, so that he could strike at the enemy even though he was blind. The feats of renowned knights won the admiration of chroniclers but affected the outcome of battle hardly at all. And the reason for the foundation of new orders of chivalry—notably the Knights of the Garter in England and the Burgundian Knights of the Golden Fleece—was that these orders would reform the world by cultivating knightly virtues.

Princes rivaled one another in the sheer glitter of their arms and the splendor of their tournaments. They waged wars of dazzlement, seeking to confound rivals and confirm friends with spectacular displays of gold, silks, and tapestries. Court ceremony was marked by excess, as were the chivalric arts of love. A special order was founded for the defense of women, and knights frequently took lunatic oaths to honor their ladies, such as keeping one eye closed for weeks. Obviously people rarely made love or war in this artificial way. But they still drew satisfaction in dreaming about the possibilities for love and war if this sad world were only a perfect place.

THE CULT OF DECAY

Huizinga called the extravagant life style of the northern courts the "cult of the sublime," or the impossibly beautiful. But he also noted that both knights and commoners showed a morbid fascination with death and its ravages. Reminders of the ultimate victory of death and treatments of decay are frequent in both literature and art. One popular artistic motif was the *danse macabre*, or dance of death, depicting people from all walks of life—rich and poor, clergy and laity, good and bad—dancing with a skeleton. Another melancholy theme favored by artists across Europe was the Pietà—the Virgin weeping over her dead son.

This morbid interest in death and decay in an age of plague was not the result of lofty religious sentiment. The obsession with the fleetingness of material beauty in fact indicated how attached people were to earthly pleasures; it was a kind of inverse materialism. Above all, the gloom reflected a growing religious dissatisfaction. In the 1200s Francis of Assisi addressed death as a sister; in the fourteenth and fifteenth centuries people apparently regarded it as a ravaging, indomitable fiend. Clearly (as Petrarch, too, had noted) the Church was failing to provide consolation to many of its members, and a religion that fails to console is a religion in crisis.

The Devil   Still another sign of the unsettled religious spirit of the age was a fascination with the devil, demonology, and witchcraft. The most enlightened scholars of the day argued at length about whether witches could ride through the air on sticks and about their relations with the devil. One of the more notable witch trials of Western history was held at Arras in 1460, when scores of people were accused of participating in a witches' sabbath, giving homage to the devil, and having sexual intercourse with him. In 1486 two inquisitors who had been authorized by the pope to prosecute witches published the *Malleus Maleficarum* (hammer of witches), which defined witchcraft as heresy and became the standard handbook for prosecutors. This fear of the devil and interest in occult arts among all levels of society were departures from the serene, confident religion of the thirteenth century.

Relics At the same time, there was a growing fascination with concrete religious images. The need to have immediate, physical contact with the objects of religious devotion added to the popularity of pilgrimages and stimulated the obsession with the relics of saints. These were usually fake, but they became a major commodity in international trade. Some princes accumulated collections of relics numbering in the tens of thousands.

Huizinga saw these aspects of northern culture as signaling the disintegration of the cultural synthesis of the Middle Ages. Without a disciplined and unified view of the world, attitudes toward war, love, and religion lost balance, and disordered behavior followed. This culture was not young and vigorous but old and dying. However, this concept of decadence must be used with caution. Certainly this was a psychologically disturbed world that had lost the self-confidence of the thirteenth century; but these supposedly decadent people, though dissatisfied, were also passionately anxious to find solutions to the tensions that unsettled them. We need to recall that passion when trying to understand the appeal and the power behind other cultural movements—lay piety, northern Humanism, and efforts for religious reform.

CONTEMPORARY VIEWS OF NORTHERN SOCIETY

Froissart Huizinga wrote about chivalric society from the perspective of the twentieth century. One of the best contemporary historians of that society was Jean Froissart (1333?–1400?) of Flanders, who traveled widely across England and the continent, noting carefully the exploits of valiant men. His chronicles, which survey the years 1325 to 1400, give the richest account of the first half of the Hundred Years' War, and he has no equal among medieval chroniclers for colorful, dramatic narration. Nonetheless, Froissart seems overly preoccupied with chivalric society; his narrative treats peasants and townspeople with contempt, or simply ignores them. Yet these emphases suited his purpose, which was, as he put it, to record the wars of his day, lest "the deeds of present champions should fade into oblivion."

Langland The works of two contemporary English writers give a broader picture of northern society in the fourteenth century. One of them, a poet known as William Langland, offered the viewpoint of the humbler classes. His *Vision of Piers Plowman*, probably written about 1360, is one of the most remarkable works of the age. The poem gives a loosely connected account of 11 visions, each of which is crowded with allegorical figures and is filled with spirited comment about the various classes of people, the impact of plague and war on society, and the failings of the Church.

Chaucer Geoffrey Chaucer (1340?–1400) came from a middle-class background; his father was a London vintner, and he himself was a soldier, diplomat, and government official. His *Canterbury Tales*, written in the 1390s, is the greatest work of imaginative literature of the late fourteenth century. It recounts the pilgrimage of some 30 persons to the tomb of St. Thomas Becket at Canterbury. For entertainment on the road, each pilgrim agrees to tell two stories. Chaucer's lively portraits provide a rich tapestry of English society, especially in its middle ranges. The stories also sum up the moral and social ills of the day. His robust monk, for example, ignores the Benedictine rule; his friar is more interested in donations than in the cure of souls; his pardoner knowingly hawks fraudulent relics; and the wife of Bath complains of prejudice against women. But Chaucer's picture remains balanced and good-humored; he praises the student of Oxford, who would gladly learn and gladly teach, and the rural parson, who cares for his flock while others search out benefices to the neglect of the faithful. Apart from the grace of his poetry, Chaucer had the ability to delineate character and spin a lively narrative. The *Canterbury Tales* is a masterly portrayal of human personalities and human behavior that can delight readers in any age.

THE FINE ARTS

The leaders of the transformation in both the style and the status of artists in the 1400s were mainly Italians. But there were also major advances in northern Europe. Indeed, oil painting—

on wood or canvas—was invented in the Netherlands, and its first great exponent, Jan Van Eyck, a contemporary of Donatello, revealed both the similarities and the differences between north and south. Van Eyck was less interested in idealization than the Florentines and more fascinated with the details of the physical world. One sees almost every thread in a carpet. But his portrait of an Italian couple, the Arnolfinis, is shot through with religious symbolism as well as a sly sense of humor about sex and marriage. The dog is a sign of fidelity, and the carving on the bedpost is of St. Margaret, the patron saint of childbirth; but the single candle is what newlyweds are supposed to keep burning on their wedding night, and the grinning carved figures behind their clasped hands are a wry comment on their marriage. The picture displays a combination of earthiness and piety that places it in a tradition unlike any that one finds in Italy (see p. 346).

Dürer The leading northern artist of the period of the High Renaissance was a German, Albrecht Dürer, who deliberately sought to blend southern and northern styles. He made two trips to Venice, and the results were clear in a self-portrait that shows him as a fine gentleman, painted in the Italian style. But he continued, especially in the engravings that made him famous, to emphasize the detailed depiction of nature and the religious purposes that were characteristic of northern art.

Dürer refused to break completely with the craft origins of his vocation. He knew, from his visits to Venice, that Italian painters could live like lords, and he was invited by the Holy Roman Emperor to join his court. But he preferred to remain in his home city of Nuremberg, earning his living more through the sale of his prints than from the stipends he was offered by patrons. Indeed, he became a highly successful entrepreneur, creating different kinds of prints for different markets—the elite liked elegant and expensive copper engravings, while others preferred cruder but cheaper woodcuts—and producing a best-seller in a book of illustrations of the Apocalypse. Working with his wife, who was a highly effective seller of his prints, he seemed as much engaged in business as in art.

▶ *Albrecht Dürer*
THE FOUR HORSEMEN
OF THE APOCALYPSE
The best-seller Dürer published in 1498, *The Apocalypse*, **has the text of the biblical account of the apocalypse on one side and full-page woodcuts on the other. The four horsemen who will wreak vengeance on the damned during the final Day of Judgment are Conquest holding a bow, War holding a sword, Famine or Justice holding scales, and Death or Plague riding a pale horse and trampling a bishop.**

MUSIC

Interestingly, the process that was at work in the visual arts had similar effects in music, which again had been created primarily for liturgical purposes in the Middle Ages. In the Renaissance, musicians became as prized as artists at princely courts, and their growing professionalism was demonstrated by the organists and choir singers hired by churches, the trumpeters employed by cities for official occasions, and the composers and performers who joined the households of the wealthy. Musical notation became standardized, and instruments became more diverse as old ones were improved and new ones—such as the viol, the oboe, and the clavichord—were invented.

Unlike the visual arts, the chief musical center of Europe around 1500 was in the Low Countries, not Italy. The choirmasters of cathedral towns like Bruges employed professional singers who brought the traditional choral form of four-part polyphony (that is, four different lines playing against one another) to new levels. This complex vocal harmony had no need of instrumental accompaniment; as a result, freed from their usual subservience to the voice, instruments could be developed in new ways. The greatest masters of the time, Guillaume Dufay and Josquin des Prez, excelled in secular as well as religious music, and theirs was one field of creativity in which new techniques and ideas flowed mainly from the north to Italy, not the other way around.

V. Scholastic Philosophy, Religious Thought, and Piety

In theology, Scholasticism retained its hold even as Humanism swept the literary world. But it was not the Scholasticism of the thirteenth century, of Thomas Aquinas, which asserted that human reason could construct a universal philosophy that did justice to all truths and reconciled all apparent conflicts among them. Nor did the traditional acceptance of ecclesiastical law continue, with its definition of Christian obligations and the Christian life in terms of precise rules of behavior rather than interior spirit. This style of thinking changed as the Scholastics of the 1400s and 1500s were drawn to analysis (breaking apart) rather than synthesis (putting together) in

their examinations of philosophical and theological statements. Many of them no longer shared Aquinas' confidence in human reason, and they hoped to repair his synthesis or to replace it with new systems that, though less comprehensive, could at least be more easily defended in an age growing increasingly doubtful about reason. Piety changed too, as more and more Christian leaders sought ways of deepening interior, mystical experience.

THE "MODERN WAY"

The followers of Aquinas remained active in the schools, but the most original of the Scholastics in the fourteenth century took a different approach to their studies. They were known as *nominalists*, because they focused on the way we describe the world—the names (in Latin *nomina*) that we give to things—rather than on its reality. The nominalists denied the existence, or at least the knowability, of universal forms—"manness," "dogness," and the like. The greatest among them was the English Franciscan William of Ockham (1300?–1349?), and the fundamental principle of his logical analysis later came to be called *Ockham's razor*. It can be stated in various ways, but essentially it affirms that between alternative explanations for the same phenomenon, the simpler is always to be preferred.

Ockham On the basis of this "principle of parsimony," Ockham attacked the traditional focus of philosophy on ideal forms, which required Aquinas to argue that all individual beings had to be understood as reflections of their universal forms. The simplest way to explain the existence of any specific object, Ockham said, is just to affirm that it exists. The mind can detect resemblances among objects and form general concepts about them; these concepts can then be examined in coherent and logical ways. But they offer no certainty that Aquinas' ideal forms—the grand principles of unity like "manness" that all individual beings and objects reflect—actually exist.

The area of reality in which the mind functions is thus severly limited. The universe, as far as human reason can detect, is a collection of separate individual beings, not a hierarchy of ideal forms. The proper way to deal with this universe is by direct experience, not by speculating about ideal or abstract natures. This theology, based on observation and reason, was obviously rather limited. Ockham believed that one could still prove the existence of some necessary principles in the universe, but he thought human beings could know very little about the ultimate necessary principle, God.

Nominalist Theology   Ockham and many of his contemporaries insisted on the total power of God and emphasized humanity's absolute dependence on him. God's freedom allowed him, if he chose, to reward vice or punish virtue. But if God was free to act in erratic ways, how could there be a stable system of dogma, a fixed theology or ethics? To escape this dilemma, the nominalists made a crucial distinction between the absolute and the ordained power of God. With his absolute power, God could act in any way he chose. But through a covenant, or agreement, God assures people that he will act in consistent and predictable ways. Given these assumptions, theology becomes the study not of metaphysics but of God's will and covenant regarding the human race.

Nominalists thus rejected Aquinas' high assessment of human powers and his confident belief in the ordered and knowable structure of the natural world. Living in a disturbed, pessimistic age, they reflected the crisis of confidence in natural reason and human capability that is a major feature of the cultural history of the north in these years.

Nominalists enjoyed wide popularity in the universities, and Ockhamite philosophy, in particular, came to be known as the *via moderna* ("modern way"). Although nominalists and humanists were frequently at odds, they did share a dissatisfaction with aspects of the medieval intellectual tradition, especially the speculative abstractions of medieval thought; and both advocated approaches to reality that concentrated on the concrete and the present and demanded a strict awareness of method.

SOCIAL AND SCIENTIFIC THOUGHT

Marsilius   The belief of the nominalists that reality was to be found not in abstract forms but in concrete objects had important implications for social thought. Among social thinkers influenced by nominalism, the most remarkable was Marsilius of Padua, an Italian lawyer who served at the French royal court. In 1324 he wrote a book, *Defender of Peace*, which attacked papal authority and supported lay sovereignty within the Church. His purpose was obviously to endorse the independent authority of his patron, the king of France, who was engaged in a running battle with the pope. But his work had wider implications. Using nominalist principles, Marsilius argued that the reality of the Christian community, like the reality of the universe, consists of the aggregate of all its parts. The sovereignty of the Church thus belongs to its membership, which alone can define the collective will of the community.

Marsilius is sometimes described as one of the first theorists of the modern concept of sovereignty, and he certainly endorsed secular authority. He maintained that only regulations supported by force are true law, and that therefore the enactments of the Church do not bind because they are not supported by coercive force. The Church has no right to power or to property and is entirely subject to the sovereign will of the state, which is indivisible, absolute, and unlimited. *Defender of Peace* is noteworthy not only for its radical ideas but also for its reflection of the deep dissatisfactions in medieval society. Marsilius and others revealed a hostile impatience with the papal and clerical domination of Western political life. They wanted the guidance of the Church and the Christian community to rest with laypeople. In this respect at least, the book was a prophecy of things to come.

Nature   In studies of nature, a few nominalists at Paris and Oxford in the fourteenth century took the first hesitant steps toward a criticism of the Aristotelian world system that had dominated European studies of physics since antiquity. At the University of Paris, for example, Jean Buridan proposed an important revision in Aristotle's theory of motion. If, as Aristotle had said, all objects are at rest in their natural state, what keeps an arrow flying after it leaves the bow? Aristotle had reasoned rather lamely that the arrow disturbs the air through which it passes and that it is this disturbance that keeps pushing the arrow forward.

But this explanation did not satisfy the nominalists. Buridan suggested that the movement of the bow lends the arrow a special quality of motion, an "impetus," which stays with it permanently unless removed by the resistance of the air. In addition, Buridan and other fourteenth-century nominalists theorized about the acceleration of falling objects and made some attempt to describe this phenomenon in mathematical terms. Although they were often inadequate or inaccurate, these attempts at new explanations started the shift away from an unquestioned acceptance of ancient systems (such as Aristotle's) that was to climax, 300 years later, in the scientific revolution.

The humanists also helped to prepare the way for scientific advance. Not only did they rediscover important ancient writers whose works had been forgotten, but their skills in textual and literary criticism taught people to look with greater precision at works inherited from the past. As more of the classics became available, it became apparent that ancient authors did not always speak in unison. Could they, therefore, always be correct? Furthermore, the idealism of Plato and the number mysticism of Pythagoras suggested that unifying forms and harmonies lay behind the disparate data of experience and observation. Once this assumption took hold, it was soon being argued that perhaps the cosmic harmonies might be described in mathematical terms.

STYLES OF PIETY

The natural world was never a central object of study in the fourteenth and fifteenth centuries, because theology remained the queen of the sciences. Within the world of faith, however, important changes began to take place as new forms of piety and religious practice appeared in order to meet the needs of laypeople. Where once praying for the salvation of the community had been considered the province of the clergy, it was now increasingly felt that each individual ought to take responsibility for seeking the favor of God.

Lay Mysticism and Piety One consequence was that mysticism—an interior sense of the direct presence and love of God—which previously had been characteristic only of monastic religious life, began to move out of the monasteries in the thirteenth century. The prime mission of the Franciscans and the Dominicans was preaching to the laity, and increasingly they were communicating some of the satisfactions of mystical religion. Laypeople wishing to remain in the outside world could join special branches of the Franciscans or Dominicans known as third orders. Confraternities, which were religious guilds founded largely for laypeople, grew up in the cities and, through common religious services and programs of charitable activities, tried to deepen the spiritual lives of their members. Humanism had strong overtones of a movement for lay piety. And hundreds of devotional and mystical works were written for laypeople to teach them how to feel repentance, not just how to define it. Translations of the Scriptures into vernacular languages also appeared, though the Church disapproved of such efforts and the high cost of manuscripts before the age of printing severely limited their circulation.

This growth of lay piety was, in essence, an effort to put at the disposal of all what hitherto had been restricted to a spiritual elite. Frightened by the disasters of the age, people hungered for emotional reassurance, for evidence of God's love and redeeming grace within them. Moreover, the spread of education among the laity, at least in the cities, made people discontented with empty forms of religious ritual.

FEMALE PIETY

The commitment to personal piety among the laity was particularly apparent among women. It is significant that, whereas male saints outnumbered females in the years between 1000 and 1150 by 12 to 1, in the years 1348 to 1500 the ratio dropped to 2.74 to 1. Moreover, the typical female saints of the later Middle Ages were no longer queens, princesses, and abbesses. They were mystics and visionaries, ordinary yet charismatic people who gained the attention of the Church and the world by the power of their message and the force of their own personalities. Catherine of Siena (1347–1380), for example, was the youngest of the 25 children of a humble Italian dyer. Her reputation for holiness attracted a company of followers from as far off as England, and she wrote (or dictated, for she probably couldn't write) devotional tracts that are monuments of Italian literature. Similar charismatic qualities made a simple Englishwoman, Margery Kempe, famous for her visions and her piety.

Women who out of poverty or preference lived a religious life outside convents became numerous, especially in towns. Some lived with their families, and others eked out a living on the margins of society. Still others lived in spontaneously organized religious houses—called Beguines in northern Europe—where they shared all tasks and property. The Church was suspicious of these women professing a religious life outside convents, without an approved rule. But the movement was too large for the Church to suppress or control. And many of them came to be particularly identified with one of the most powerful forms of lay piety in this period, mysticism.

THE MYSTICS

It was appropriate that one of the most active centers of the new lay piety should have been the Rhine valley, a region that was especially noted for its remarkable mystics. The most famous was the Dominican Meister Eckhart (1260?–1327?), a spellbinding preacher and a devoted student of Aquinas, who sought to bring his largely lay listeners into a mystical confrontation with God. Believers, he maintained, should cultivate the "divine spark" that is in every soul. To achieve this, they had to banish all thought from their minds and seek to attain a state of pure passivity. If they succeeded, God would come and dwell within them. Eckhart stressed the futility of dogma and, implicitly, traditional acts of piety. God is too great for such categories and cannot be moved by conventional piety.

Brethren of the Common Life Just as the nominalists argued for philosophical reasons that God is unknowable, so the mystics dismissed the value of formal knowledge and stressed the need

▶ *Pisan Artist of XIV Century*
THE MYSTIC MARRIAGE OF CATHERINE OF SIENA
Catherine of Siena was a nun who was known for her efforts to return the papacy to Rome. Part of the reason for her sainthood was that, like Joan of Arc, she experienced visions from an early age. She is shown here with her symbol, the lily, in a scene from one of her visions. About to enter into a mystic marriage with Christ, she is accepting the wedding ring directly from him. Note that in the Renaissance, wedding rings were often placed on the third finger.

for love and an emotional commitment to God and his attributes. Perhaps the most influential of them was Gerhard Groote of Holland. Groote wrote sparingly, exerting his influence over his followers largely through his personality. After his death in 1384 his disciples formed a religious congregation known as the Brethren of the Common Life. Taking education as their principal task, they founded schools in Germany and the Low Countries that imparted a style of lay piety known as the *devotio moderna* (modern devotion). Later reformers, such as Erasmus of Rotterdam and Martin Luther, were to be among their pupils.

Thomas à Kempis   The richest statement of the *devotio moderna* appeared about 1425 in *The Imitation of Christ*, a small devotional manual attributed to Thomas à Kempis, a member of the Brethren of the Common Life. *The Imitation of Christ* says almost nothing about fasting, pilgrimages, or other traditional acts of private piety. Instead, it emphasizes interior experience as essential to religious life. The believer, it argued, needed only to emulate the life of Jesus. The book's ethical and social consciousness is also unusual. Powerful interior faith leads not to extreme acts of personal expiation but to highly ethical behavior: "First, keep yourself in peace, and then you shall be able to bring peace to others."

Features of Lay Piety   The new lay piety was by no means a revolutionary break with the medieval Church, but it implicitly discounted the importance of many traditional institutions and practices. In this personal approach to God there was no special value in the monastic vocation. As Erasmus would later argue, what was good in monasticism should be practiced by every Christian. Stressing simplicity and humility, the new lay piety was reacting against the pomp and splendor that had come to surround popes and prelates and to mark religious ceremonies. Likewise, the detailed rules for fasts, abstinences, and devotional exercises; the cult of the saints and their relics; and the traffic in indulgences and pardons all seemed peripheral to true religious needs. Without the proper state of soul, these traditional acts of piety were meaningless; with the proper state, every act was worship.

This new lay piety, emerging as it did out of medieval religious traditions, was clearly a preparation for the reformations of faith that took place in the sixteenth century among both Protestants and Catholics. It helped produce a more penetrating faith at a time when the formal beliefs of the Middle Ages, for all their grandeur and logical intricacies, no longer fully satisfied the religious spirit and were leaving hollows in the human heart.

Although the *devotio moderna* was a religious movement and had little regard for humanist learning, it shared Humanism's distaste for the abstractions and intellectual arrogance of the Scholastics and the humanists' belief that a wise and good person will cultivate humility and maintain toward the profound questions of religion a "learned ignorance." Moreover, both movements addressed their message primarily to laypeople, in order to help them lead a higher moral life. The humanists, of course, drew their chief inspiration from the works of pagan and Christian antiquity, whereas the advocates of the new lay piety looked almost exclusively to Scripture. But the resemblances were close enough for scholars like Erasmus and Thomas More, writing in the early 1500s, to combine elements from both in the movement known as Christian Humanism.

MOVEMENTS OF DOCTRINAL REFORM

The effort to reform the traditions of medieval Christianity also led to open attacks on the religious establishment—fueled, of course, by antagonism toward the papacy and corruption in the Church and by the larger tensions of this troubled epoch. Above all, these attacks gained support because the Church remained reluctant to adapt its organization and teachings to the demands of a changing world.

Wycliffe   The most prominent of the assaults of the 1300s was launched by an Englishman, John Wycliffe (1320?–1384), a clergyman who taught at Oxford University. He argued that the Church had become too remote from the people, and he wanted its doctrines simplified. To this end, he sought a more direct reliance on the Bible itself (which he suggested having translated into English so as to make it easier to understand) and less power for priests. Beyond his unease over the Church's remoteness from ordinary believers, he may have had political reasons (and thus support) for his stand. He was close to members of the royal court, who were increasingly resistant to papal demands and who were troubled that, in the midst of England's war with France, the papacy should have come under French influence when it moved from Rome to Avignon. In 1365 Wycliffe denounced the payment of Peter's pence, the annual tax given by English people to the papacy, and shortly thereafter he publicly denounced the papal Curia, monks, and friars for their vices.

Wycliffe argued that the Scriptures alone declared the will of God and that neither the pope and the cardinals nor the Scholastic theologians could tell Christians what they should believe. In particular, he questioned one of the central dogmas of the Church that emphasized the special power of the priest: *transubstantiation*, which asserts that priests at the Mass work a miracle when they change the substance of bread and wine into the substance of Christ's body and blood. Besides attacking the exalted position and privileges of the priesthood in such rites as transubstantiation, Wycliffe denied the authority of the pope and the hierarchy to exercise jurisdiction or to hold property. He claimed that the true Church was that of the predestined—that is, those whom God would save and were thus in a state of grace. Only these elect could rule the elect; therefore, popes and bishops who had no grace could have their properties removed and had no right to rule. Responsibility for ecclesiastical reform rested with the prince, and the pope could exercise only as much authority as the prince allowed.

The Lollards   Many of Wycliffe's views were branded heretical, but even though he was forced to leave Oxford when he offended his protectors at the royal court, they did keep him unharmed until he died. His followers, mostly ordinary people who were known as Lollards—a name apparently derived from "lollar" (idler)—were not so lucky. They managed to survive as an underground movement in the countryside until the Protestant Reformation exploded more than a century later, but they were constantly hounded, and in 1428 the Church had Wycliffe's remains dug up, burned, and thrown into a river.

Hus   An even harsher fate awaited Wycliffe's most famous admirer, a Bohemian priest named Jan Hus (1369–1415), who started a broad and even more defiant movement in his homeland. Hus was a distinguished churchman and scholar. He served as rector (the equivalent of president) of the Charles University in Prague, one of Europe's best-known institutions, and he was the main preacher at a fashionable chapel in Prague. Like Wycliffe, he argued that priests were not a holy and privileged group, set apart from laymen, but that the Church was made up of all the

Hus at Constance

A few weeks before he was executed, Jan Hus wrote to his Czech followers to tell them how he had responded to his accusers at the Council of Constance:

"Master Jan Hus, in hope a servant of God, to all faithful Czechs who love God: I call to your attention that the proud and avaricious Council, full of all abomination, condemned my Czech books having neither heard nor seen them; even if it had heard them, it would not have understood them. O, had you seen that Council which calls itself the most holy, and that cannot err, you would have seen the greatest abomination! I have heard it commonly said that Constance would not for thirty years rid itself of the sins which that Council has committed. That Council has done more harm than good.

"Therefore, faithful Christians, do not allow yourselves to be terrified by their decrees, which will profit them nothing. They will fly away like butterflies, and their decrees will turn into a spiderweb. They wanted to frighten me, but could not overcome God's power in me. They did not dare to oppose me with Scripture.

"I am writing this to you that you may know that they did not defeat me by any Scripture or any proof, but that they sought to seduce me by deceits and threats to recant and abjure. But the merciful Lord God, whose law I have extolled, has been and is with me, and I hope that He will be with me to the end and will preserve me in His grace until death.

"This letter was written in chains, in the expectation of death."

From Matthew Spinka (ed.), *The Letters of John Hus* (Manchester University Press, 1972), pp. 195–197.

faithful. To emphasize this equality, he rejected the custom of allowing the congregation at a Mass to eat the wafer that symbolized Christ's body but allowing only the priest to drink the wine that symbolized his blood. In a dramatic gesture, Hus shared the cup of wine with all worshipers, thus reducing the distinctiveness of the priest. His followers adopted a chalice, or cup, as the symbol of their movement.

Hus was not hesitant about defying the leadership of the Church. Denounced for the positions he had taken, he replied by questioning the authority of the pope himself:

> If a Pope is wicked, then like Judas he is a devil and a son of perdition and not the head of the Church militant. If he lives in a manner contrary to Christ he has entered the papacy by another way than through Christ.

In 1415 Hus was summoned to defend his views before the Church Council at Constance. Although he had been guaranteed safe passage if he came to answer accusations of heresy,

the promise was broken. He was condemned, handed over to the secular authorities, and executed (*see box*, p. 379). But his followers, unlike the Lollards who stayed out of sight in England, refused to retreat in the face of persecution.

The Hussites   A new leader, Jan Žižka, known as John of the Chalice, raised an army and led a successful campaign against the emperor, who was also king of Bohemia and the head of the crusade that was now mounted against the Hussites. The resistance lasted 20 years, outliving Žižka, but sustained by Bohemian nobles, and eventually the Hussites were allowed to establish a special church, the Utraquist Church, in which both cup and wafer were shared by all worshipers at Mass. But Hus's other demands, such as the surrender of all personal possessions by the clergy (an echo of St. Francis), were rejected. Those who tried to fight on for these causes were defeated in battle, and after a long struggle the resistance came to an end, having made only a minor dent in the unity of the Church.

The popular appeal of Wycliffe and Hus reflected the widespread dissatisfaction with official teachings in the late 1300s and 1400s—a dissatisfaction that Petrarch, too, had shown, although in his case there was no question of challenging traditional doctrine. Instead of trying to change the Church itself, he merely sought moral guidance elsewhere. And yet, when Wycliffe and Hus chose to risk an open confrontation, they demonstrated that reform ideas, advanced by charismatic leaders, could find a following among those who resented the authoritarian and materialistic outlook of the Church. At the same time, however, it became clear that such dissent could not survive without support from nobles, princes, or other leaders of society. Even with such help, the Hussites had to limit their demands; without it, they would have gained nothing. It was 100 years after Hus's death before a new reformer arose who had learned these lessons, and he was to transform Western Christianity beyond recognition.

Recommended Reading

▼

Sources

*Brucker, Gene A. (ed.). *The Society of Renaissance Florence: A Documentary Study.* 1971.

---

*Available in paperback.

*Cassirer, Ernst, P. O. Kristeller, and J. H. Randall, Jr. (eds.). *The Renaissance Philosophy of Man.* 1953. Selections from Petrarch, Ficino, Pico, and others.

*Chambers, David, and Brian Pullan (eds.). *Venice: A Documentary History. 1450–1630.* 1992.

Eckhart. *Meister Eckhart, a Modern Translation.* R. B. Blakney (tr.). 1956.

Kempe, Margery. *The Book of Margery Kempe (1436)*. B. A. Windeatt (tr.). The autobiography of an extraordinary woman. 1985.

*Kohl, Benjamin G., and Ronald G. Witt (eds.). *The Earthly Republic: Italian Humanists on Government and Society*. 1978.

*Marsilius of Padua. *Defender of Peace*. Alan Gerwith (tr.). 1986.

Studies

*Baron, Hans. *The Crisis of the Early Italian Renaissance: Civic Humanism and Republican Liberty in the Age of Classicism and Tyranny*. 1966. Fundamental analysis of Florentine "civic humanism."

Becker, M. B. *Civility and Society in Western Europe. 1300–1600*. 1988.

*Berenson, Bernard. *The Italian Painters of the Renaissance*. 1968. Classic essays on the history of art.

Bergin, Thomas G. *Boccaccio*. 1981. Learned and readable.

Brucker, Gene A. *Renaissance Florence*. 1983. The standard introduction.

*Burckhardt, Jacob. *The Civilization of the Renaissance in Italy*. 1958. One of the pioneering works of European history, first published in 1860.

Clark, J. M. *The Great German Mystics: Eckhart, Tauler and Suso*. 1949.

Cole, Bruce. *The Renaissance Artist at Work: From Pisano to Titian*. 1983.

Crombie, Alistair C. *Medieval and Early Modern Science*. 1961.

Funkenstein, Amos. *Theology and the Scientific Imagination from the Middle Ages to the Seventeenth Century*. 1986.

*Goldthwaite, Richard A. *The Building of Renaissance Florence: An Economic and Social History*. 1980. Imaginative examination of the relations between society and architecture.

Grendler, Paul F. *Schooling in Renaissance Italy: Literacy and Learning. 1300–1600*. 1989. A recent survey.

Hanning, Robert W., and David Rosand (eds.). *Castiglione: The Ideal and the Real in Renaissance Culture*. 1983.

*Herlihy, David, and Christiane Klapisch-Zuber. *Tuscans and Their Families*. 1985. A study of a Florentine census of 1427.

Holmes, George. *Florence, Rome and the Origins of the Renaissance*. 1986.

*Huizinga, Johann. *The Waning of the Middle Ages*. 1954.

Hutchison, Jane C. *Albrecht Dürer: A Biography*. 1990.

*Keen, Maurice. *Chivalry*. 1984. Sympathetic survey of knightly culture.

Kent, F. W., and Patricia Simons (eds.). *Patronage, Art and Society in Renaissance Italy*. 1987. A collection of interesting essays.

Klapisch-Zuber, Christiane. *Women, Family and Ritual in Renaissance Italy*. 1985. Collected essays.

*Kristeller, Paul O. *Renaissance Thought and Its Sources*. 1979. By a leading historian of Renaissance thought.

Leff, Gordon. *William of Ockham*. 1975. Authoritative examination of a difficult philosopher.

Martines, Lauro. *The Social World of the Florentine Humanists*. 1963. The humanists examined in the light of their social background.

Rosand, David (ed.). *Titian, His World and His Legacy*. 1981.

Tobin, Frank. *Meister Eckhart: Thought and Language*. 1986.

Wilkins, Ernest Hatch. *Life of Petrarch*. 1961.

Lucas Cranach the Elder
LUTHER IN THE VINEYARD
This work of propaganda uses the biblical image
of Christians toiling in the vineyard of the Lord
to contrast the seriousness and fruitfulness of
the Protestants on the left with the greed and
destructiveness of the Catholics on the right. Luther
himself rakes in the center, while Melanchthon at
the far left goes to the source (the Bible) and draws
from the well; meanwhile, on the right, bishops and
monks ruin the crops, burn the wood, and fill the
well with stones.

CHAPTER THIRTEEN

REFORMATIONS IN RELIGION

ALTHOUGH it may have seemed monolithic and all-powerful, the Roman Church in the fifteenth century was neither a unified nor an unchallenged institution. It had long permitted considerable variety in individual beliefs, from the analytic investigations of canon lawyers to the emotional outpourings of mystics. There were local saints, some of whom were recognized as holy only by a few villages; and for many Europeans the papacy remained a distant and barely comprehensible authority. To assume that its theological pronouncements were understood by the average illiterate Christian is to misrepresent the loose, fragmentary nature of the medieval Church. Moreover, doubts had been raised, by the political disputes and reform movements of the fourteenth and fifteenth centuries, about the central structure and doctrines of the Church. That the papacy had weathered these storms by 1500 indicated both how flexible and how powerful it was. What was to be remarkable in the years that followed was the sudden revelation of the Church's fragility, as a protest by a single monk snowballed into a movement that shattered the thousand-year unity of Western Christendom.

I. Piety and Dissent

DOCTRINE

The fundamental question all Christians face is: How can sinful human beings gain salvation? In 1500, the standard official answer was that the Church was an essential intermediary. Only through participation in its rituals, and particularly through the seven sacraments its priests administered—baptism, confirmation, matrimony, the eucharist, ordination, penance, and extreme unction—did the believer have access to the grace that God offered as an antidote to sin. But there was another answer, identified with distinguished Church fathers such as St. Augustine: People can be saved by their faith in God and love of him. This view emphasized inward and personal belief and focused on God as the source of grace.

The two traditions were not incompatible; for centuries they had coexisted without difficulty. Yet the absence of precise definition in many areas of Christian doctrine was a major problem for theologians, because it was often difficult to tell where orthodoxy ended and heresy began. The position taken by the papacy, however, had grown less inclusive and adaptable over the years; by 1500 it was stressing the outward and institutional far. more than the inward and personal route to salvation. The aim of reformers for over a century had been to reverse this trend, and it remained unclear whether the change would be accomplished by reform from within or by a revolution and split in the Church.

FORMS OF PIETY

The root of the demand for change was the need of many laypeople for a more personal way of expressing their piety than official practices offered. Church rituals meant little, they felt, unless believers could cultivate an interior sense of the love and presence of God. They looked for nourishment, therefore, to those who emphasized religious individualism. Rejecting the theological subtleties of Scholasticism, they sought divine guidance in the Bible and the writings of the early Church fathers, especially St. Augustine. Lay religious fraternities dedicated to private forms of worship and charitable works proliferated in the cities, especially in Germany and Italy. The most widespread of them in Germany, the Brotherhood of the Eleven Thousand Virgins, consisted of laypeople who gathered together, usually in a church, to sing hymns. In the mid-fifteenth century, more than 100 such groups had been established in Hamburg, a city of slightly more than 10,000 inhabitants. Church leaders, unhappy about a development over which they had no control, had tried to suppress them but to no avail.

Savonarola The most spectacular outburst of popular piety around 1500 occurred in seemingly materialist Florence, which embraced Girolamo Savonarola, a zealous friar who wanted to banish the irreligion and materialism he saw everywhere about him. The climax of his influence came in 1496, when he arranged a tremendous bonfire in which the Florentines burned cosmetics, light literature, dice, and other such frivolities. Savonarola embodied the desire for personal renewal that had long been a part of Western Christianity but seemed to be gaining intensity in the 1400s. His attempts at reform eventually brought him into conflict with the papacy, which rightly saw him as a threat to its authority. The Church therefore denounced him and gave its support to those who resented his power in Florence. His opponents had the friar arrested in 1498 and then executed on a trumped-up charge of treason.

The widespread search for a more intense devotional life was a sign of spiritual vitality. But Church leaders in the age of Savonarola gave little encouragement to ecclesiastical reform and the evangelization of the laity. Only in Spain was there a deliberate attempt to eradicate abuses and encourage religious fervor, and there the leadership in the effort came not from Rome but from the head of the Spanish Church, Cardinal Francisco Ximenes. Elsewhere, the hierarchy reacted harshly when such movements threatened its authority.

THE LEGACY OF WYCLIFFE AND HUS

Such threats had arisen from time to time, notably at universities, where the basic method of instruction, the disputation, encouraged the discussion of unorthodox ideas. At disputations, students learned by listening to arguments for and against standard views. It was not impossible for someone taking the "wrong" side in such a debate to be carried away and cross the line between a theoretical discussion and open dissent.

That is what had happened with the Englishman John Wycliffe, who taught at Oxford University in the late 1300s, and with the Bohemian Jan Hus, a professor at the University of Prague a few years later. They had demanded a simplification of doctrines, more reliance on the Bible, and less power for priests. Both had been condemned by the Church, and Hus had been burned at the stake in 1415. But their disciples had kept their ideas alive. Known in England as "Lollards," Wycliffe's followers managed to survive as an underground movement in the coun-

▶ *Anonymous*
THE MARTYRDOM OF SAVONAROLA, CA. 1500
This painting still hangs in the monastery of San Marco where Savonarola lived during his years of power. It shows the city's central square—a setting that remains recognizable to anyone who visits Florence today—where the bonfire of the "vanities" had been held in 1496, and where Savonarola was executed in 1498. The execution is depicted here as an event that the ordinary citizens of Florence virtually ignore as they go about their daily routines.

tryside. In Bohemia the Hussites had raised an army and won acceptance for their own church, which allowed worshipers greater participation in the Mass than did the Roman Church.

These protests revealed the extent of the dissatisfaction with official teachings. Charismatic leaders could find a following for unorthodox ideas if they could tap popular piety and resentment toward the Church. It was not easy for dissent to survive without support from nobles or princes; aristocrats had protected Wycliffe, and they had formed and led the Hussite army. Even without such patronage, however, the concerns persisted.

CAUSES OF DISCONTENT

By 1500 the spiritual authority of the papacy had been declining for more than two centuries. During the 70 years of the Babylonian captivity, when the pontiffs had lived in Avignon, they had seemed to be captives of the French monarchy rather than symbols of the universal Church. Far more demoralizing, the Great Schism that followed had threatened to undermine the unity of Western Christendom, as two and then three pretenders each claimed to be the true pope. The Council of Constance had closed this breach by 1418 but had also encouraged the conciliar movement. This attempt to subordinate papal power to the authority of Church councils ultimately failed, but it was yet another direct challenge to the pope's supremacy.

Secular Interests   The papacy had also lost spiritual influence because of its secular interests. Increasingly, popes conducted themselves like princes. With skillful diplomacy and even military action, they had consolidated their control over the papal lands in the Italian peninsula. They had surrounded themselves with an elaborate court, had become patrons of the arts, and for a time had taken over the cultural leadership of Europe. This concern with political power and grandeur had eclipsed religious duties to the point that some popes used their spiritual powers to raise funds for their secular activities. The fiscal measures developed at Avignon, which furnished the papacy with income from appointments to Church offices and from various fees, had enlarged revenues but led to widespread abuses. High ecclesiastical offices could be bought and sold, and men (usually sons of nobles) were attracted to these positions by the opportunities they provided for wealth and power, not by a religious vocation.

Abuses were widespread at lower levels in the Church as well. Some prelates held several offices

at a time and could not give adequate attention to any of them. The ignorance and moral laxity of the parish and monastic clergy also aroused antagonism. Even more damaging was the widespread impression that the Church was failing to meet individual spiritual needs because of its remoteness from the day-to-day needs of the average believer, its elaborate and incomprehensible system of canon law and theology, and its formal ceremonials. Above all, there was a general perception that priests and monks were profiting from their positions, exploiting the people, and giving minimal moral leadership or religious guidance in return.

Anticlericalism   These concerns provoked anticlericalism (hostility to the clergy) and calls for reform which, except in the Spain of Cardinal Ximenes, went unheeded. For increasing numbers of deeply pious people, the growing emphasis on ritual and standardized practices seemed irrelevant to their personal quest for salvation. And their reaction was symptomatic of the broad commitment to genuine piety that was apparent, not only in the followers of Wycliffe, Hus, and Savonarola but in many segments of European society in the early 1500s.

POPULAR RELIGION

It was not only the educated elite and the city dwellers (a minority of Europe's inhabitants) who sought to express their faith in personal terms. The yearning for religious devotion among ordinary villagers, the majority of the population, was apparent even when the local priest—who was often hardly better educated than his parishioners—did little to inspire spiritual commitments. People would listen avidly to news of distant places brought by travelers who stopped at taverns and inns (a major source of information and ideas), and increasingly the tales they told were of religious upheaval. In addition, itinerant preachers roamed some regions, notably Central Europe, in considerable numbers, and they drew crowds when they started speaking—on street corners in towns or out in the fields—and described the power of faith. They usually urged direct communication between believers and God, free from ritual and complex doctrine. To the vast crowds they often drew, many of them seemed to echo the words of St. Augustine: "God and the soul I want to recognize, nothing else."

Equally important as a means of learning about and discussing the latest religious issues were the gatherings that regularly brought villagers together. Throughout the year, they would assemble to celebrate holidays—not only the landmarks of the Christian calendar like Christmas and Easter but also local festivals. Religion was always essential to these occasions. When, for example, the planting season arrived, the local priest would lead a procession into the countryside to bless the fields and pray for good crops. Family events, too, from birth to death, had important religious elements.

The Veillée The most common occasion when the community's traditional beliefs and assumptions were discussed, however, was the evening gathering—generally referred to by its French name, *veillée*, which means staying up in the evening. Between spring and autumn, when the weather was not too cold, a good part of the village came together at a central location after each day's work was done. There was little point in staying in one's own home after dark, because making a light with candles or oil was too expensive. Instead, sitting around a communal fire, people could sew clothes, repair tools, feed babies, resolve (or start) disputes, and discuss news. It was one of the few times when women were of no lesser status than men; the views they expressed were as important as any in shaping the common outlook of the villagers.

A favorite occupation at the *veillée* was listening to stories. Every village had its storytellers, who recounted wondrous tales of local history, of magical adventures, or of moral dilemmas, as the mood required. Biblical tales and the exploits

▶ *Hans Sebald Beham*
CHURCH FESTIVAL, WOODCUT, 1535
The celebration of the anniversary of a church's consecration was one of the most important holidays in a village. Not everyone, however, used this opportunity for spiritual ends, like the couple getting married in front of the church. Some overindulged at the tavern (lower right); some had a tooth extracted (center left); and some, as the chickens in the center and various couples in the scene suggest, used the occasion for pleasure alone. (Hans Sebald Beham, *Large Peasant Holiday*, 1535, Art Institute of Chicago.)

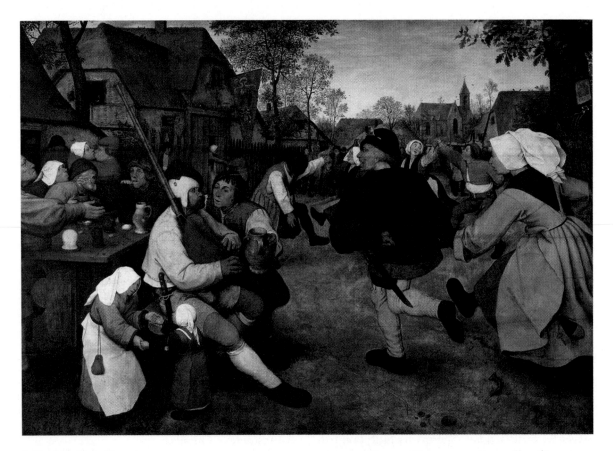

▶ *Peter Brueghel*
THE PEASANT DANCE, CA. 1567
The most vivid images of life in the village during the sixteenth century were created by the Flemish artist Peter Brueghel. The different human types, and the earthiness of country life, are captured in scenes that show the villagers both at work and, as here, at ease and relaxed.

of Christian heroes like the Crusaders had always drawn an attentive audience. Now, however, in addition to entertainment and general moral uplift, peddlers and travelers who attended the *veillée* brought news of challenges to religious traditions. They told of attacks on the pope and Church practices, and of arguments for a simpler and more easily understood faith. This was how the ideas of religious reformers spread and how those with unorthodox views like the Lollards kept their faith alive. In some cases, the beliefs that were described made converts of those who heard them, and traveling preachers came to regard the gatherings at the *veillées* as ready-made congregations. They were usually far more knowledgeable, better trained, and more effective than local priests.

The response of the traditional Church to this challenge, after decades of indifference, was to insist that the local priest be better educated and more aware of what was at stake in the religious struggles of the day. As long as he had the support of the local authorities, he could make sure that his views dominated the *veillée* and that contrary beliefs were not expressed. Whichever way the discussions at these communal gatherings went, however, they demonstrated the power of popular piety in the tens of thousands of villages that dotted the European countryside.

THE IMPACT OF PRINTING

The expression of this piety received unexpected assistance from technology: the invention of a printing press with moveable type in the mid-1400s. At least a hundred years earlier, Europeans had known that by carving words and pictures into a wood block, inking them, and pressing the block onto paper, they could make an image that could be repeated on many sheets of paper. We do not know exactly when they discovered that they could speed up this cumbersome process and therefore change the text from page to page, if they used individual letters and put them together within a frame. We do know, however, that a printer named Johannes Gutenberg, who lived in the city of Mainz on the Rhine, was producing books this way by the 1450s. The technique spread rapidly (see table below) and made reading material available to a much broader segment of the population.

As a result, new ideas could travel with unprecedented speed. Perhaps a third of the trading and upper classes—townspeople, the educated, and the nobility—could read, but books could reach a much wider audience, because peddlers began to sell printed materials throughout Europe. They were bought everywhere and became favorite material for reading out loud at *veillées*. Thus people who had had little contact with written literature in the days of manuscripts now gained access to the latest ideas of the time.

Printing and Religion Printers were not slow to take advantage of the popular interest in books

Der Buchdrücker.

▶ *Jost Amman*
"THE PRINTER" FROM DAS STÄNDEBUCH
(THE BOOK OF TRADES), 1568
This is the first detailed depiction of a printer's shop, showing assistants taking type from large wooden holders in the back, the press on the right, the pages being prepared and inked in the foreground, and finally the sheets of paper before and after they are printed. The caption notes that printing had been invented in the German city of Mainz.

THE SPREAD OF PRINTING THROUGH 1500
Number of towns in which a printing press was established for the first time, by period and country

Period	German-Speaking Areas	Italian-Speaking Areas	French-Speaking Areas	Spain	England*	Netherlands	Other	Total
Before 1471	8	4	1	1	—	—	—	14
1471–1480	22	36	9	6	3	12	5	93
1481–1490	17	13	21	12	—	5	4	72
1491–1500	9	5	11	6	—	2	8	41
Total by 1500	56	58	42	25	3	19	17	220

*In order to try to control the printers, the English government ordered that they work only in London and at Oxford and Cambridge universities.

Adapted from Lucien Febvre and Henri-Jean Martin, *The Coming of the Book: The Impact of Printing 1450–1800*, translated by David Gerard, London, NLB, 1976, pp. 178–179 and 184–185.

by publishing almanacs filled with home-spun advice about the weather and nature that were written specifically for simple rural folk. Even the almanacs, however, carried religious advice; and, more importantly, translations of the Bible made it available to ordinary people in a language that, for the first time, they could understand. Books thus became powerful weapons in the religious conflicts of the day. Devotional tracts, lives of the saints, and the Bible were the most popular titles—often running to editions of around 1000 copies. They became means of spreading new ideas, and the ready markets they found reflected the general interest of the age in spiritual matters.

Printing clearly lessened laypeople's dependence on the clergy; whereas traditionally the priest had read and interpreted the Scriptures for his congregation, now people could consult their own copies. By 1522, 18 translations of the Bible had been published. Some 14,000 copies had been printed in German alone, enough to make it easy to buy in most German-speaking regions. The Church frowned on these efforts, and governments tried to regulate the numbers and locations of presses; but in the end it proved impossible to control the effects of printing.

PIETY AND PROTEST IN LITERATURE AND ART

The printing press broke the Church's monopoly over the public discussion of religious teachings. Authorities might be dismayed by, but could not totally prevent, the publication of writings that criticized doctrines or practices. Thus the most gifted satirist of the sixteenth century, the French humanist François Rabelais, openly ridiculed the clergy and the morality of his day. Rabelais was a monk (as well as a doctor), and he was deeply unhappy that traditional religious practices had diverged so far from the ideals of Jesus. He was most famous for his earthy bawdiness, but again and again he returned to clerical targets, as in this passage from his *Gargantua* (1533):

> "Don't monks pray to God for us?" "They do nothing of the kind," said Gargantua. "All they do is keep the whole neighborhood awake by jangling their bells.... They mumble over a lot of legends and psalms, which they don't in the least under-

stand; and they say a great many paternosters ... without thinking or caring about what they are saying. And all that I call a mockery of God, not prayer."

Scurrilous broadsides no less stinging in tone became very popular during the religious disputes of the 1500s. These single sheets often contained vicious attacks on religious opponents and were usually illustrated by cartoons with obscene imagery. The broadsides were examples of par-

▶ *Hans Baldung Grien*
THE THREE AGES OF WOMAN AND DEATH, CA. 1510
The preoccupation with the transitoriness of life and the vanity of earthly things took many forms in the sixteenth century. Here the point is hammered home unmistakably, as the central figure—a young woman at the height of her beauty between infancy and old age—is reminded of the passage of time (the hourglass) and the omnipresence of death even as she admires herself in a convex mirror.

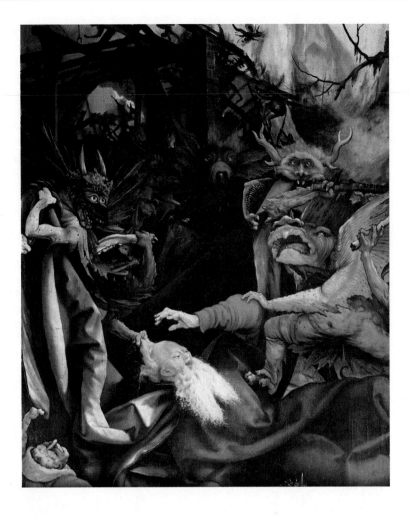

tisan hostility, but their broader significance should not be ignored. Even the most lowly of hack writers could share with a serious author like Rabelais a sense of outrage at indifference in high places and a dismay with the lack of spiritual leadership of the time.

Art This emphasis on the importance of religious belief, so evident in European literature, also permeated the work of northern artists in the late fifteenth and early sixteenth centuries (see plates on p. 390 and above). The gruesome paintings of Hieronymus Bosch, for example, depicted the fears of devils and of hell that his contemporaries felt endangered them at all times. He put on canvas the demons, the temptations, the terrible punishments for sin that people considered as real as their tangible surroundings. Bosch's younger contemporary Matthias Grünewald con-

▷ *Matthias Grünewald*
THE TEMPTATION OF ST. ANTHONY, CA. 1510
This detail from a series of scenes Grünewald painted for the Isenheim Altar suggests the power the devil held over the imagination of sixteenth-century Europeans. The gentle, bearded St. Anthony is not seated in contemplation, as in Dürer's portrayal (see plate on p. 392). Instead, he is surrounded by the monsters the devil has sent to frighten him out of his faith. This was a favorite subject of the period, and provided artists like Bosch and Grünewald the opportunity to make vivid and terrifying the ordinary Christian's fear of sin.

veyed the same mixture of terror and devotion. Like Bosch, he painted a frightening *Temptation of St. Anthony*, showing the travails of the saint who steadfastly resisted horrible attacks by the devil. These artists explored the darker side of faith, taking their inspiration from the fear of damnation and the hope for salvation—the first seen in the demons, the second in the redeeming Christ.

Dürer

The most famous northern artist of this period was Albrecht Dürer, and it is significant that his fame began when he produced an illustrated edition of a biblical book, *The Apocalypse*, which describes God's punishment of sinners on the final Day of Judgment. The book became a best-seller and made Dürer a rich man. He was sought after throughout Europe, and he became known at all levels of society because he was a master of the art of the woodcut. Dürer enjoyed this medium more than painting because, as he noted, many copies could be sold quite cheaply, and his fame and his finances profited accordingly. His wife Agnes was a shrewd businesswoman who accompanied her husband on his travels and set up a stall to sell his works whenever she found a convenient marketplace. Dürer's subjects were largely religious—the life of Christ, portraits of saints, and scenes with the Virgin Mary—which ensured that they had the widest possible appeal.

The depth of piety conveyed by artists like Dürer reflected the temper of Europe. In art and literature, as in lay organizations and the continuing popularity of itinerant preachers, people showed their concern for individual spiritual values and their dissatisfaction with a Church that was not meeting their needs.

▶ *Albrecht Dürer*
ST. ANTHONY, ENGRAVING, 1519
The ease and mastery Dürer brought to the art of engraving made it as powerful and flexible a form as painting. Here the massive figure of the saint, deep in study, is placed in front of a marvelously observed city. The buildings display Dürer's virtuosity—their shapes echo the bulk and solidity of the figure—and they may have symbolized the temptations of city life for a saint who was revered for his solitary piety in the desert.

CHRISTIAN HUMANISM

No segment of society expressed the strivings and yearnings of the age more eloquently than the northern humanists. The salient features of the humanist movement in Italy—its theory of education, its emphasis on eloquence, its reverence for the ancients, and its endorsement of active participation in affairs of state—began to win wide acceptance north of the Alps in the late 1400s. But the northerners added a significant religious dimension to the movement by devoting considerable attention to early Christian literature: the Bible and the writings of the Church fathers. As a result, they have been called *Christian humanists*.

The first major center of humanism in the north was at the University of Heidelberg; but by the end of the fifteenth century the movement's influence, carried by the printing press, was European-wide. The northern humanists were particularly determined to probe early Christianity for the light it could throw on the origins and accuracy of current religious teachings. Indeed, northern humanism's broad examination of religious issues in the early 1500s helped create an atmosphere in which much more serious criticism of the Church could flourish.

The Christian humanists did not abandon the interest in classical authors or the methods for analyzing ancient texts, language, and style that had been developed by Italian humanism. But they put these methods to a new use: analysis of the Bible in order to explain more clearly the message of Jesus and his apostles, and thus to provide a better guide to true piety and morality. This deeply religious undertaking dominated the writings of the two most famous Christian humanists, one English and one Dutch.

MORE AND ERASMUS

More   Sir Thomas More (1478–1535), a lawyer and statesman, was the central figure of English humanism. His reputation as a writer rests primarily on a short work, *Utopia*, published in Latin in 1516, which describes an ideal society on an imaginary island. In it, More condemned war, poverty, intolerance, and other evils of his day and defined the general principles of morality that he felt should underlie human society.

The first book of *Utopia* returns to the conflict between the *vita contemplativa* and the *vita activa* that Petrarch had emphasized, and asks whether a learned person should withdraw from the world to avoid the corruptions of politics or actively participate in affairs of state so as to guide policy. In his own career, More chose the latter path, with fatal results. The second, more famous book of *Utopia* leaves such practical issues aside and describes what an ideal commonwealth might be like. In political and social organization, Utopia is a carefully regulated, almost monastic community that has succeeded in abolishing private property, greed, and pride—and thus has freed its inhabitants from some of the worst sins of More's day. The Utopians have accomplished all this without Christianity, and More implies that a society based on Christian principles can attain even greater good. Well-designed institutions, education, and discipline are his answer to the fall of Adam and Eve: Weak human nature can be led to virtuousness only if severely curbed.

Deeply devout and firmly attached to the traditional Church, More entered public life as a member of Parliament in 1504. He rose high in government service, but eventually he gave his life for remaining loyal to the pope and refusing to recognize the decision of his king, Henry VIII, to reject papal authority and become head of the English Church. When Henry determined to break with Rome, he found it intolerable that this prominent political figure rejected his actions and would not compromise; and so, to discourage any further disobedience, Henry had him beheaded. More's last words revealed his unflinching adherence to the Christian principles he pursued throughout his life: "I die the King's good servant, but God's first."

Erasmus   The supreme representative of Christian humanism was the Dutchman Desiderius Erasmus (1466?–1536). Erasmus early acquired a taste for ancient writers, and he determined to devote himself to classical studies. For the greater part of his life, he wandered through Europe, writing, visiting friends, and occasionally working for important patrons. He always retained his independence, however, for unlike More, he answered the question of whether a scholar should best-sellers created by the printing press. Some of it is gay, lighthearted banter that pokes fun at the author himself, his friends, and the follies of everyday life, and suggests that a little folly is essential to human existence. The book also points out that Christianity itself is a kind of folly, a belief in "things not seen." In many passages, though, Erasmus launches sharply satirical attacks against monks, the pope, meaningless ceremonies, and the many lapses from what he perceived to be the true Christian spirit.

The Philosophy of Christ At the heart of Erasmus' work was the message that he called the "philosophy of Christ." He believed that the life of Jesus and, especially, his teachings in the Sermon on the Mount should be models for Christian piety and morality. For the Church's ceremonies and for rigid discipline he had only censure: Too often, he said, they served as substitutes for genuine spiritual concerns. People lit thousands of candles for Mary but cared little about the humility she is supposed to inspire. They forgot that what counts is the spirit of religious devotion, not the form. By simply following the precepts of Jesus, he argued, a Christian could lead a life guided by sincere faith. Because of his insistence on ethical behavior, Erasmus could admire a truly moral man even if he was a pagan. "I could almost say, 'Pray for me, St. Socrates!' " he once wrote.

Erasmus believed that the Church had lost sight of its original mission. In the course of 15 centuries, traditions and practices had developed that obscured the intentions of its founder, and purity could be restored only by studying the Scriptures and the writings of the early Church fathers. Here the literary and analytic tools of the humanists became vitally important, because they enabled scholars to understand the meaning and intention of ancient manuscripts. Practicing what he preached, Erasmus spent 10 years preparing a new edition of the Greek text of the New Testament so as to correct errors in the Latin Vulgate, which was the standard version, and he revised it repeatedly for another 20 years.

But the calm, scholarly, and tolerant moderation Erasmus prized was soon left behind by events. The rising intensity of religious reformers and their opponents destroyed the effort he had

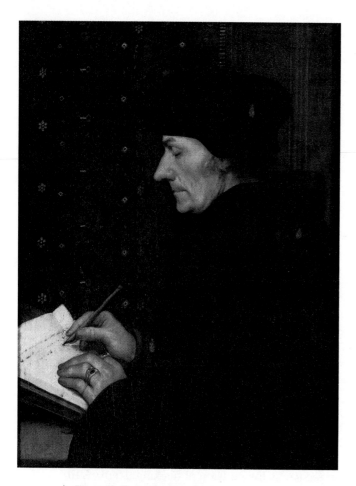

▶ *Hans Holbein the Younger*
Portrait of Erasmus, 1523
The leading portraitist of the age, Hans Holbein, painted his friend Erasmus a number of times. Here he shows the great scholar at work, possibly writing one of the many elegantly constructed letters that he sent to colleagues throughout Europe. The richness of the scene bears noting—the gold ring, the fine coat with a fur collar, and the splendid tapestry hanging over the paneled wall.

enter public life by avoiding the compromises that would be necessary in the service of a ruler.

Erasmus was so famous for his learning and his literary skills that he dominated the world of letters of his time. Constantly consulted by scholars and admirers, he wrote magnificently composed letters that reflected every aspect of the culture of his age. He became known throughout Europe, however, as a result of a little book, *The Praise of Folly* (1509), which was one of the first led to cure the ills of the Church quietly, from within. Erasmus wanted a revival of purer faith, but he would never have dreamed of rejecting the traditional authority of the Church. As Europe entered an age of confrontation, he found it impossible to preserve a middle course between the two sides. Unable to choose, Erasmus was swept aside by revolutionary forces that he himself had helped build but that Martin Luther was to unleash.

II. The Lutheran Reformation

THE CONDITIONS FOR CHANGE

That a major religious conflict should have erupted in the Holy Roman Empire is not surprising. In this territory of fragmented government, with hundreds of independent local princes, popular piety was noticeably strong. Yet anyone who was unhappy with Church leadership had all the more reason to resent the power of bishops, because in the empire they were often also princes—such as the aristocratic bishop who ruled the important city of Cologne on the Rhine. There were few strong secular princes who could protect the people from the fiscal demands of the Church, and the popes therefore regarded the empire as their surest source of revenue.

This situation was made more volatile by the ambitions of the secular princes. Their ostensible overlord, the emperor, had no real power over them, and they worked tirelessly to strengthen their control over their subjects and to assert their independence from all outside authority. A number of them were in fact to see the religious upheavals of the 1500s as a means of advancing their own political purposes. Their ambitions help explain why a determined reformer, Martin Luther, won such swift and widespread support.

MARTIN LUTHER

Martin Luther (1483–1546) was born into a miner's family in Saxony in central Germany. The household was dominated by the father, whose powerful presence some modern commentators have seen reflected in his son's vision of an omnipotent God. The boy received a good education and decided to become a lawyer, a profession that would have given him many opportunities for advancement. But in his early twenties, shortly after starting his legal studies, he had an experience that changed his life. Crossing a field during a thunderstorm, he was thrown to the ground by a bolt of lightning, and in his terror he cried out to St. Anne that he would enter a monastery.

Luther as a Monk   Although the decision may well have been that sudden, it is clear that there was more to Luther's complete change of direction than this one incident, however traumatic. A highly sensitive, energetic, and troubled young man, he had become obsessed with his own sinfulness, and he joined a monastery in the hope that a penitential life would help him overcome his sense of guilt. Once he became a monk, he pursued every possible opportunity to earn worthiness in the sight of God. He overlooked no means of discipline or act of contrition or self-denial, and for added merit he endured austerities, such as self-flagellation, that went far beyond normal requirements. But it was all to no avail: When called upon to officiate at his first Mass after his ordination in 1507, he was so terrified at the prospect of a sinner like himself administering the sacrament—that is, transforming the wafer and wine of the Mass into the body and blood of Christ—that he almost failed to complete the ritual.

Fortunately for Luther, his superiors took more notice of his intellectual gifts than of his self-doubts and in 1508 assigned him to the faculty of a new university in Wittenberg, the capital of Saxony. It was from his scholarship, which was excellent, and especially from his study of the Bible that he was able at last to draw comfort and spiritual peace.

This second crucial turning point in Luther's life, as important as the lightning bolt, occurred while he was preparing his university lectures. Until this point, which is known as "the experience in the tower," he could see no way that he, a despicable mortal, could receive anything but the fiercest punishments from a God of absolute

Map 13.1 THE EMPIRE IN THE AGE OF LUTHER
The fragmentation that divided the empire into dozens of distinct principalities, independent cities, and autonomous territories enabled Luther to find the political support that kept his religious reform alive.

justice. Now, however, he had an insight that led him to understand that he needed only to rely on God's mercy, a quality as great as divine justice (*see box*, below). The many advances in Luther's thinking thereafter came from this insight: that justification—which removes sin and bestows righteousness through a gift of grace—is achieved by faith alone.

THE INDULGENCE CONTROVERSY

In 1517 an event occurred that was ultimately to lead Luther to an irrevocable break with the Church. In the spring, a friar, Johann Tetzel, began to peddle indulgences a few miles from Wittenberg as part of a huge fund-raising effort to pay for the new Church of St. Peter in Rome. Originally, an indulgence had been granted to anyone going on a crusade. It was then extended to those who, though unable to join a crusade, gave enough money for a poor crusader to be able to reach the Holy Land. Indulgences released sinners from a certain period of punishment in purgatory before they went on to heaven and were justified doctrinally as a sort of credit that could be drawn from the treasury of merit built up by Jesus and the saints. But neither the doctrine nor the connection with money had been fully defined, and clerics had taken advantage of this vagueness simply to sell indulgences. Tetzel, an expert peddler, was offering complete releases from purgatory without bothering to mention the repentance that, according to Church teachings, was essential if a sinner was to be forgiven or absolved.

The 95 Theses The people of Wittenberg were soon flocking to Tetzel to buy this easy guarantee

Luther's "Experience in the Tower"

The following passage was written by Luther in 1545, at least 25 years after the experience it described. As a result, scholars have been unable to decide (a) whether the breakthrough was in fact as sudden as Luther suggests; (b) when it took place—possibly as early as 1512, five years before the indulgence dispute, or as late as 1519, when Luther was already under attack for his views; or (c) how it should be interpreted—as a scholar's insight, as a revelation from God, or as Luther's later crystallization into a single event of a process that had taken many years.

I wanted very much to understand Paul's Epistle to the Romans, but despite my determination to do so I kept being stopped by the one word, "the *righteousness* of God." I hated that word, because I had been taught to understand it as the active righteousness by which a just God punishes unjust sinners. The trouble was that, although I may have been an impeccable monk, I felt myself to be a sinner before God. As a result, not only was I unable to love, but I actually hated this just God, who punishes all sinners. And so I raged, yet I still longed to understand St. Paul.

At last, as I grappled with the words day and night, God had mercy on me, and I saw the connection between the words "the righteousness of God" and "The righteous shall live by faith" (Romans 1:17). I understood that the righteousness of God refers to the gift by which God enables the just to live—that is, by faith. A merciful God justifies us by faith, as it is written: "The righteous shall live by faith." At that point, I felt as if I had been reborn and had passed through open doors into paradise. The whole of Scripture took on new meaning. As I had previously hated the phrase, "the righteousness of God," so now I lovingly praised it.

Translation from the Latin by Theodore K. Rabb of Luther's Preface to the 1545 edition of his writings, in Otto Scheel (ed.), *Dokumente zu Luthers Entwicklung* (Tübingen: Mohr, 1929), pp. 191–192.

▶ *Jörg Breu*
ENGRAVING DEPICTING THE SALE OF
INDULGENCES, CA. 1530
**This would have been a familiar scene in Europe
until Luther's attacks brought it to an end. The
clerics on their fine horses on the right bring a cross
and the papal bull, which is authenticated by the
elaborate seals and ribbons that hang from it. The
faithful put money in the barrel in the middle or
hand it to the dispenser of certificates on the left,
who sits near the large locked chest that will hold
the revenues from the sales.**

a general pardon was damnable; and that every
true believer shared in the treasury of merit left
by Jesus and the saints, whether or not he or she
obtained an indulgence. Within a few weeks the
story was all over the empire that a monk had
challenged the sale of indulgences. The proceeds
of Tetzel's mission began to drop off; and other
members of his order, the Dominicans, rallied to
their brother by attacking his presumptuous
critic, Luther, who happened to belong to a rival
order, the Augustinians.

of salvation. For Luther, a man groping toward
an evangelical solution of his own doubts, it was
unforgivable that people should be deprived of
their hard-earned money for spurious, worthless
promises. On October 31, 1517, he published in
Wittenberg 95 theses, or statements, on indulgences that he offered to debate with experts in
Christian doctrine.

This was no revolutionary document. It
merely described what Luther believed to be correct teachings on indulgences: that the pope
could remit only the penalties that he himself or
canon law imposed; that therefore the promise of

Luther Elaborates The controversy soon drew
attention in Rome. At first, Pope Leo X regarded
the affair as merely a monks' quarrel. But, in
time, Luther's responses to the Dominicans' attacks began to deviate radically from Church
doctrine, and by 1520 he had gone so far as to
challenge the authority of the papacy itself
in three pamphlets outlining his fundamental
position.

In *An Address to the Christian Nobility of the
German Nation,* Luther made a frankly patriotic
appeal to his fellow Germans to reject the foreign
pope's authority. The Church, he said, consisted

of all Christians, including the laity; hence the nobles were as much its governors as the clergy, and they had a responsibility to remedy its defects. Indeed, Emperor Charles V had an obligation to call a council to end abuses. In *The Babylonian Captivity*, the most radical of the three works, Luther attacked the system of seven sacraments, the basis of the Church's authority, on the ground that only two are mentioned in the Bible. In *The Liberty of the Christian Man*, a less polemical work, he explained his doctrine of faith and justification by stressing that, although he did not reject good works, only the faith of the individual believer could bring salvation from an all-powerful, just, and merciful God. These three pamphlets had an overwhelming impact on Luther's fellow Germans. His emotional appeal to their resentment of Church power and their wish for a more personal faith made him, almost overnight, the embodiment of a widespread yearning for religious reform.

THE DIET OF WORMS

There could no longer be any doubt that Luther was breaking with the Church, and in 1520 Pope Leo X issued a bull excommunicating him. Luther publicly tossed the document into a bonfire, defending his action by calling the pope an Antichrist. In 1521 Emperor Charles V, who was officially the papacy's secular representative, summoned the celebrated monk to offer his defense against the papal decree at a Diet of the Empire (a meeting of princes, city leaders, and churchmen) at Worms, a city on the Rhine.

The journey across Germany was a triumphant progress for Luther, who now seemed a heroic figure. Appearing before the magnificent assembly dressed in his simple monk's robe, he offered a striking contrast to the display of imperial and princely grandeur. First in German and then in Latin, he made the famous declaration that closed the last door behind him: "I cannot and will not recant anything, since it is unsafe and wrong to go against my conscience. Here I stand. I cannot do otherwise. God help me. Amen." On the following day the emperor gave his reply: "A single friar who goes counter to all Christianity for a thousand years must be wrong."

Luther Protected Charles added legality to the papal bull by issuing an imperial edict calling for Luther's arrest and the burning of his works. At this point, however, the independent power of the German princes and their resentment of for-

▶ *Lucas Cranach the Elder*
PORTRAIT OF MARTIN LUTHER, 1525
One of the first faces made familiar by portraits, but not belonging to a nobleman, was Luther's. Cranach painted the reformer a number of times, so we can see what he looked like at various periods of his life. Luther here is in his early forties, a determined figure who four years earlier had made his stand at the Diet at Worms.

eign ecclesiastical interference came to the reformer's aid. The Elector Frederick III of Saxony, who had never met Luther and who was never to break with the traditional Church, nonetheless determined to protect the rebel who lived in his territory. He had him taken to the Wartburg castle, one of his strongholds, and here Luther remained for almost a year, safe from his enemies.

LUTHERAN DOCTRINE AND PRACTICE

While at the Wartburg, Luther, together with his friend Philipp Melanchthon, developed his ideas and shaped them into a formal set of beliefs that influenced most of the subsequent variations of Protestant Christianity. Codified in 1530 in a document known as the Augsburg Confession, these doctrines have remained the basis of Lutheranism ever since.

Luther's Debt to Nominalism It is important to realize that some of Luther's positions had roots in nominalism, the most influential philosophical and theological movement of the fourteenth and fifteenth centuries, which had flourished at his old monastery. Two nominalist teachings in particular left a lasting impression on Luther and later reformers. First, in opposition to Thomas Aquinas and the thirteenth-century attempts to unite reason and faith, the nominalists stressed the primacy of faith, the inadequacy of reason, and the unknowableness of God. Second, as a natural corollary to God's mystery, they emphasized his overwhelming power and majesty. Both of these beliefs were to reappear frequently in the reformers' writings.

Faith and the Bible The influence of nominalism is apparent in the two fundamental assertions of Luther's teachings. First, faith alone—not good works or the receiving of the sacraments—justifies the believer in the eyes of God and wins redemption. People themselves are helpless and unworthy sinners who can do nothing to cooperate in their own salvation; God bestows faith on those he chooses to save. Second, the Bible is the sole source of religious authority. It alone carries the word of God, and Christians must reject all other supposed channels of divine inspiration:

Church tradition, commentaries on the Bible, or the pronouncements of popes and Church councils.

These two doctrines had far-reaching implications. According to Luther, all people are equally capable of understanding God's word as expressed in the Bible and can gain salvation without the help of intermediaries; they do not need a priest endowed with special powers or an interceding church. Luther thus saw God's faithful as a "priesthood of all believers," a concept totally foreign to the traditional Church, which insisted on the distinction between clergy and laity. The distinction disappeared in Luther's doctrines, because all the faithful shared the responsibilities formerly reserved for priests.

Sacraments and the Mass True to his reliance on biblical authority, Luther denied the efficacy of five of the sacraments. Only baptism and the eucharist are mentioned in Scripture; therefore they alone are the means by which God distributes grace. Moreover, the ceremony of the eucharist, or Lord's Supper, was now called *communion* (literally, "sharing") to emphasize that all worshipers, including the officiating clergy, were equal. Luther also reduced the distinctiveness of priests by abolishing the sacrament of confession and by giving them the right to marry.

Luther's teachings on the sacraments transformed the Mass, the ceremony that surrounds the eucharist, which had caused him such trouble when he first became a monk. According to traditional dogma, when the priest raises the wafer, the host, during the Mass and recites the words *Hoc est corpus meum* ("This is my body"), the sacrifice of Jesus on the cross is reenacted. The wafer and the wine retain their outward appearance, their "accidents," but their substance is transformed into the body and blood of Christ—in other words, transubstantiation takes place.

Luther asserted that the wafer and wine retain their substance as well as their accidents and undergo *con*substantiation at the moment the priest says "This is my body." The real presence of Christ and the natural substance *coexist* within the wafer and wine. Nothing suddenly happens; there is no miraculous moment. Instead, the believer is simply made aware of the real presence of God, who is everywhere at all times. Again, it is the faith of the individual, not the ceremony itself, that counts.

Luther further reduced the mystery of the Lord's Supper by allowing the congregation to drink the wine, which was reserved for the priest in the traditional ceremony. This change, which undermined the position of the priest, had been demanded by Hus. But Luther went further. He simplified services radically and gave ordinary people a greater role in worship by abolishing the use of Latin, processions, incense, and votive candles.

Translation of the Bible   With the priest reduced in stature, it was vital to make God's word more readily available to the faithful, so that they could read or hear the Bible for themselves. To this end, Luther began the long task of translating the Bible. He was to complete the work in 1534, creating a text that is a milestone in the history of the German language. Families were encouraged to read Scripture on their own, and the reformed faith stimulated rising literacy among women as well as men. This was Luther's last major contribution to the religious changes of the sixteenth century. Although he was to live until 1546, henceforth the progress of the revolution he had launched would rely on outside forces: its popular appeal and the actions of political leaders.

THE SPREAD OF LUTHERANISM

It is usually said that Lutheranism spread from above, advancing only when princes and rulers helped it along. Although this view has some merit, it does not adequately explain the growth of the movement. The response to Luther's stand was immediate and widespread. Even before the Diet of Worms, preachers critical of the Church were drawing audiences in many parts of the Holy Roman Empire, and in 1521 there were waves of image smashing, reports of priests marrying, and efforts to reform and simplify the sacraments.

Soon there were congregations following Luther's teachings throughout the empire and neighboring countries. Broadsides and pamphlets fresh from the printing presses dissemi-

nated the reformer's message with breathtaking speed, and they stimulated an immediate response from thousands who welcomed the opportunity to renew their faith.

Radical Preachers   As long as his own doctrines remained unaltered, Luther was naturally delighted to see his teachings spread. But from the start, people drew inferences that he could not tolerate. Early in 1522, for example, three men from the nearby town of Zwickau appeared in Wittenberg claiming to be prophets who enjoyed direct communication with God. Their ideas were both radical and, in Luther's eyes, damnable. When he returned from the Wartburg, therefore, he preached eight sermons to expose their errors—a futile effort, because the movement to reform the Church was now too dispersed to control. Capitalizing on mass discontent, radical preachers incited disturbances in the name of faith, and soon social as well as religious protest exploded, posing a new challenge for Luther as he struggled to keep his protest alive and under control.

DISORDER AND REVOLT

The first trouble arose in the summer of 1522, started by the weakest independent group in the empire, the imperial knights. The knights occupied a precarious position in the social hierarchy because their holdings rarely consisted of more than a single castle. They accepted no authority but the emperor himself, and they resented the growing power of cities and princes (rulers of large territories) in the empire.

Calling themselves true representatives of the imperial system—that is, loyal supporters of the emperor's authority, in contrast to the cities and princes who wanted to be more independent—and using Lutheranism as further justification, the knights launched an attack on one of the leading ecclesiastical rulers, the archbishop of Trier. The onslaught was crushed within a year, but the Lutherans' opponents could now suggest that the new religious teachings undermined law and order.

Peasant Revolt   The banner of the new faith rose

over popular revolts as well. A peasant uprising began in Swabia in 1524 and quickly engulfed the southern and central parts of the empire. Citing Luther's inspiration, and especially his teaching that faith was all the individual needed, the peasants published a list of 12 demands in 1525. Admittedly, 10 of their grievances concerned social, not religious, injustices: They wanted an end to serfdom, tithes, and the restrictions and burdens imposed by their overlords, including prohibitions on hunting and fishing, excessive rents and services, and unlawful punishments. But they also had two religious aims: They wanted the right to choose their own pastors, and they refused to accept any authority other than Scripture to determine if their demands were justified.

Luther sympathized with the last two claims, and at first he considered the peasants' demands reasonable. But when it became apparent that they were challenging all authority, he ignored the oppressions they had suffered and wrote a vicious pamphlet, *Against the Rapacious and Murdering Peasants*, calling on the nobility to cut them down without mercy so as to restore peace. A few months later the rebels were defeated in battle, and thereafter Luther threw his support unreservedly on the side of the princes and the established political and social order. He also grew more virulent in his attacks on Catholics and Jews, and became as insistent as the Roman Church he was defying that his doctrines were not to be questioned.

LUTHERANISM ESTABLISHED

The advance of Lutheranism thus far had depended largely on its appeal to the ordinary believer, and it continued to enjoy wide support. But when Luther was forced to choose between the demands of his humblest followers and the authority of the princes who had protected him, he opted for the princes. It was a decision that enabled his movement to survive and may well have saved him from the fate of Hus—burned at the stake a century before because he defied po-

► **CARTOON FROM LUTHERAN WOODCUT BROADSIDE**
Vicious cartoons were a favorite device of religious propaganda during the Age of Religious Reformation. They were especially popular for an illiterate audience, which had to get the message from pictures. The more vivid the image, the easier it was to understand. Here the Protestants show the enemies of Luther as vicious animals. One theologian is a cat eating a mouse; another is a dog holding a bone.

litical as well as religious leaders. Had Luther not condemned the disorders, he would doubtless have been abandoned by the princes, and without their backing he and his followers could not have stood up to the traditional Church or been safe from the power of Charles V.

Luther's Conservatism One of the reasons the new set of beliefs could attract these princes was its conservatism. Any person who accepted the basic doctrines of justification by faith alone and Scripture as the sole authority could be accepted as a Lutheran. Consequently, the new congregations could retain much from the old religion: most of the liturgy, the sacred music, and, particularly important, a structured church that, though less hierarchical than before, was still organized to provide order and authority.

The Lutheran Princes Some rulers were swept up by the same emotions that moved their subjects, but others were moved by more material interests. Since the Church lost all its property when reform was introduced, princes could confiscate the rich and extensive ecclesiastical holdings in their domains. Furthermore, they now had added reason for flaunting their independence from Emperor Charles V, an unwavering upholder of orthodoxy. It was risky to adopt this policy, for Charles could strip a prince of his title. On the other side, if a prince promised to remain loyal to the Church, he could blackmail the pope into offering him almost as many riches as he could win by confiscation. Nevertheless, the appeal of the new faith eventually tipped the balance for enough princes to create a formidable party capable of resisting Charles's power. While they were attending an imperial Diet at Speyer in 1529, they signed a declaration "protesting" the Diet's decree that no religious innovations were to be introduced in the empire. Thereafter all who accepted religious reform, including the Lutherans, were known as Protestants; and adherents of the traditional Church, which was led from Rome and continued to claim that it was universal (or catholic), came to be known as Roman Catholics.

The following year, at another imperial Diet, the Lutheran princes announced their support of the Augsburg Confession, the official statement of Lutheran doctrines that had been prepared by

Melanchthon and Luther. Charles V now threatened to use military force to crush the heresy, and in the face of this danger, the Lutherans formed a defensive league in 1531 at the small Saxon town of Schmalkalden. Throughout the 1530s this alliance consolidated Protestant gains, brought new princes into the cause, and, in general, amassed sufficient strength to deter Charles from immediate military action.

War over Religion The reform party became so solidly established that it negotiated with the pope on equal terms about the possibility of reconciliation in 1541, but the talks collapsed, and the chances for a reunification of Christendom evaporated. Not until 1546, the year of Luther's death, however, did open war begin. Then, after a brief campaign, Charles won a crushing victory over the Lutherans in 1547. But matters had advanced too far for their movement to collapse merely because of a single defeat on the battlefield. The new faith had won the devotion of a large part of the German people, particularly in the north and the east, farthest away from the center of imperial power. Some of the great cities of the south, such as Nuremberg, which had been centers of humanism, had also come over to the Lutheran side. By the 1550s Lutheranism had captured about half the population of the Empire.

The Catholic princes also played a part in ensuring the survival of the new faith. Fearful of Charles V's new power, they refused to cooperate in his attempt to establish his authority throughout the empire, and he had to rely on Spanish troops, who further alienated him from his subjects. The Lutherans regrouped after their 1547 defeat, and in 1555 the imperial Diet at Augsburg drew up a compromise settlement that exposed the decline of the emperor's power. Henceforth each prince was allowed to determine the religion of his own territory, Lutheran or Catholic. Religious uniformity was at an end, and the future of Lutheranism was secure.

The Heritage of Lutheranism The influence that this first Protestant Church was to exert on all of European life was immense. The idea that all believers were equal in the eyes of God inspired revolutionary changes in thought and society. It justified antimonarchical constitutional theories,

▶ ENGRAVING OF THE DIET OF AUGSBURG, 1530
At the Diet—the meeting of the princes and cities
of the Holy Roman Empire—in Augsburg in 1530,
the Lutherans presented to the emperor, Charles V,
a statement, or "confession," of their faith. This
"Confession of Augsburg" became the founding
doctrine of the Lutheran church. It was rejected as
heretical by Charles, but he could not suppress it.
One of the Lutheran princes told him in 1530 that
he would rather have his head cut off than attend
a Catholic mass. And Charles was unable to crush
such defiance.

it allowed people to feel that all occupations were
equally worthy and that there was nothing
wrong with the life of the merchant or even the
moneylender, and it undermined the hierarchic
view of the universe. One can easily overstate the
notion that Lutheranism made people more self-
reliant, because independent and pioneering behavior was far from new. Nevertheless, there is
no question that, by condemning the traditional
reliance on priests and the Church and by mak-

ing individuals responsible for their own salvation, Luther did encourage his followers to act on
their own. Yet the new faith had its most immediate effect on religious life itself: Before the century was out, the dissent started by Luther inspired a multitude of sects and a ferment of ideas
without precedent in the history of Europe.

III. The Growth of Protestantism

ZWINGLIANISM

Hardly had Luther made his protest in 1517
when religious dissent in many different forms
suddenly appeared. It was as if no more was
needed than one opening shot before a volley of
discontent broke out—testimony to the deep and
widespread desire for individual piety of the

times. The most influential of these new initiatives began in the Swiss city of Zurich.

Zwingli This new reformer, Ulrich Zwingli (1484–1531), was a priest, a learned humanist, and a disciple of Erasmus. The doctrines he began to develop between 1519 and 1522 were similar to Luther's. Like the Saxon reformer, Zwingli based his ideas entirely on Scripture and emphasized faith alone. He rejected the Church's role as the channel of God's grace to believers, the idea that the clergy should be celibate, and the belief in purgatory after death. Suspicious of any reliance on Church rituals, Zwingli, even more than Luther, wanted to simplify religious belief and practice. In his view, none of the sacraments bestowed grace; they were merely signs of grace already given. Thus, baptism is symbolic, not a ceremony that regenerates the recipient; and communion is no more than a memorial and thanksgiving for the grace given by God, who is present only symbolically—not in actuality, as Luther believed.

Despite his obvious debt to Luther, Zwingli's divergences were significant. When the two reformers met in 1529, hoping to iron out differences in order to present a united front, their inability to agree on a doctrine of communion kept them apart. Zwingli had founded a new form of Protestantism, more thoroughly dependent on the individual believer and more devoid of mystery and ritual than anything Luther could accept.

Zwingli held that people need constant correction to lead godly lives. Since he recognized no distinction between secular and religious authority, he established a tribunal of clergy and secular officials to enforce discipline among the faithful. They supervised all moral issues, from compulsory church attendance to the public behavior of amorous couples. The court could excommunicate flagrant transgressors, and it maintained constant surveillance—through a network of informers—to keep the faithful moral and godly.

Because Zwingli considered it vital for discipline that the faithful receive a continuing education, he founded a theological school and authorized a new translation of the Bible. He also insisted on lengthy sermons at each service. Worship was stripped bare, as were the churches, and preaching began to assume tremendous importance as a means of instructing believers and strengthening their faith. Zwingli also revived the ancient Christian practice of public confession of sin—yet another reinforcement of discipline.

Zwingli's Church Zwingli's ideas spread rapidly in the Swiss Confederation, helped by the virtual autonomy of each canton, or region. By 1529 a number of cantons had accepted Zwinglianism. As a result, two camps formed in the country, and a war broke out in 1531 in which Zwingli himself was killed. Thereafter the Swiss Confederation remained split between Catholics and reformers. Zwinglianism never grew into a major religion, but it had a considerable effect on later forms of Protestantism, particularly Calvinism.

THE RADICALS

Both Luther and Zwingli wanted to retain church authority, and both therefore insisted that infant baptism was the moment of entry into the church, even though this belief had no scriptural sanction. Some radical reformers, however, insisted on taking the Bible literally and argued that, as in biblical times, baptism should be administered only to mature adults who could make a conscious choice to receive grace, not to infants who could not understand what was happening. Soon these reformers were being called *Anabaptists* ("rebaptizers") by their enemies. The term is often applied to all radicals, though in fact it described only one conspicuous group.

Sects Diversity was inevitable among the radical reformers, most of whom refused to recognize church organization, rejected priests, and gave individual belief free rein, sometimes to the point of recognizing only personal communication with God and disregarding Scripture. Many groups of like-minded radicals formed small sects—voluntary associations which rarely included more than 100 or so adults—in an effort to achieve complete separation from the world and avoid compromising their ideals. They wanted to set an example for others by adhering fervently to the truth as they saw it, regardless of the consequences.

Some sects established little utopian communities, holding everything in common, including property and spouses. Others disdained all worldly things and lived only for the supreme ecstasy of a trance in which they made direct contact with God himself. Many, believing in the imminent coming of the Messiah, prepared themselves for the end of the world and the Day of Judgment.

PERSECUTION

Such variety in the name of a personal search for God was intolerable to major reformers like Luther and Zwingli, who believed that their own doctrines were the only means of salvation. Once these branches of Protestantism were firmly entrenched, they, like the Catholic Church, became deeply committed to the status quo and to their own hierarchies and traditions. The established reformers thus regarded the radicals' refusal to conform as an unmistakable sign of damnation; Heinrich Bullinger, Zwingli's successor, put it bluntly when he wrote that individual interpretation of the Bible allowed each man to carve his own path to hell. Indeed, Lutherans were just as ready as Catholics to persecute those who rejected their particular brand of salvation.

Münster   The assault on the radicals began in the mid-1520s and soon spread through most of Europe. The imperial Diet in 1529 called for the death penalty against all Anabaptists, and indeed, most members of a group of more than 30 Anabaptist leaders who met to discuss their ideas in 1533 eventually met a violent death. Finally, in the northwest German city of Münster, a particularly fiery sect, inspired by a "prophet" named Melchior and known as Melchiorites, provoked a reaction that signaled doom even for less radical dissenters.

The Melchiorites had managed to gain considerable influence over the ordinary workers of Münster and over the craft guilds to which many belonged. They gained political control of the city early in 1534 and began to establish their "heavenly Jerusalem" on earth. They burned all books except the Bible, abolished private property, introduced polygamy, and, in an atmosphere of abandon and chaos, dug in to await the coming of the Messiah.

Here was a threat to society sufficient to force Protestants and Catholics into an alliance, and they captured the city and brutally massacred the Melchiorites. Thereafter the radicals were savagely persecuted throughout the empire. To survive, many fled first to Poland, then to the Low Countries and England, and eventually to the New World.

JOHN CALVIN

During the 1530s, Protestantism began to fragment. Neither Lutherans nor Zwinglians expanded much beyond the areas where their reforms had begun, radicals multiplied but gained few followers, and it might have seemed that the original energy had left the movement. In the early 1540s, however, a new dynamism and also a more elaborate and systematic body of doctrine were brought to Protestantism by a second-generation reformer, John Calvin (1509–1564). Born in Noyon, a small town in northern France, Calvin studied both law and the humanities at the University of Paris. In his early twenties he apparently had a shattering spiritual experience that he later called his "sudden conversion," an event about which he would say almost nothing else. Yet from that moment on, all his energy was devoted to religious reform.

In November 1533 Calvin was indicted by French Church authorities for holding heretical views, and after more than a year in hiding, he took refuge in the Swiss city of Basel. There in 1536 he published a little treatise, *Institutes of the Christian Religion*, outlining the principles of a new system of belief. He would revise and expand the *Institutes* for the remainder of his life, and it was to become the basis of Calvinism, the most vigorous branch of Protestantism in the sixteenth century.

Geneva   Later in 1536 Calvin settled in Geneva, where, except for a brief period, he was to remain until his death and where he was to create a new church in the 1540s. The citizens of this prosperous market center had just overthrown their prince, a Catholic bishop. In achieving their independence, they had allied with other Swiss cities, notably Bern, a recent convert to Zwinglianism. Rebels who, with the help of Protestants, had just freed themselves from an ecclesiastical overlord were understandably receptive to new religious teachings, and they welcomed the beliefs that Calvin proclaimed.

CALVINISM

Outwardly, Calvinism seemed to have much in common with Lutheranism. Both emphasized people's sinfulness, lack of free will, and helplessness; both rejected good works as a means of salvation; both accepted only two sacraments, baptism and communion; both regarded all occupations as equally worthy in the sight of God; both strongly upheld established political and social authority; and both leaned heavily on St. Paul and St. Augustine in their views of faith, people's weaknesses, and God's omnipotence. But the emphases in Calvinism were very different.

Predestination In arguing for justification by faith alone, Luther assumed that God can predestine a person to be saved but rejected the idea that damnation can also be preordained. Calvin's faith was much sterner. He recognized no such

▶ **An Engraving of the Army from Bern Invading a Neighboring Province in 1536, from Johannes Stumpf's Chronicle, 1548** These are the soldiers who helped Geneva win its independence from the bishop who was the city's ruler. The Bernese also encouraged the acceptance of Protestantism, which John Calvin was soon to help establish in Geneva.

distinction: If people are damned, they should praise God's justice, because their sins certainly merit such a judgment; if people are saved, they should praise God's mercy, because their salvation is not a result of their own good deeds. Either way, the outcome is predestined, and nothing can be done to affect an individual's fate. It is up to God to save a person; he then perseveres in his mercy despite the person's sins; and finally, he alone decides whether to receive the sinner into the small band of saints, or elect, whom he brings into heaven. Calvin's was a grim but powerful answer to the age-old Christian question: How can sinful human beings gain salvation?

Calvin believed that our behavior here on

earth, whether good or bad, is no indication of our fate. He did suggest that someone who is to be saved by God is likely to be upright and moral, but such conduct is not necessarily a sign of salvation. However, because we should try to please God at all times, and because our communities ought to be fitting places for the elect to live, we must make every effort to lead lives worthy of one of the elect.

Morality and Discipline   Calvin therefore developed a strict moral code for the true believer that banned frivolous activities, like dancing, in favor of constant self-examination, austerity, and sober study of the Bible. To help the faithful observe such regulation, he reestablished public confessions, as Zwingli had, and required daily preaching. He made services starkly simple: Stripped of ornaments, worship concentrated on uplifting sermons and the celebration of communion. His doctrine of communion occupied a middle ground between Luther's and Zwingli's. He rejected Zwingli's interpretation, saying instead that Christ's body and blood were actually and not just symbolically present. But unlike Luther, he held that they were present only in spirit and were consumed only spiritually, by faith.

To supervise the morals of the faithful and ensure that the community was worthy of the elect, Calvin gave his church a strict hierarchical structure. It was controlled by church officials called deacons and by lay elders, who were able to function even in the hostile territories where many Calvinists found themselves. A body of lay elders called the *consistory* served as the chief ecclesiastical authority. They enforced discipline and had the power of excommunication, though they always worked with local officials, who imposed the actual punishments for failures in religious duties.

Church Organization   Calvin's system produced a cohesiveness and organization achieved by no other Protestant church. The *Institutes* spelled out every point of faith and practice in detail—an enormous advantage for Calvin's followers at a time when new religious doctrines were still fluid. The believer's duties and obligations were absolutely clear, as was his or her position in the very carefully organized hierarchy

of the church. In France, for example, there was a small community (or cell) in each town, a governing synod (or council) in each local area, a provincial synod in each province, and a national synod at the top of the pyramid. Tight discipline controlled the entire system, with the result that Calvinists felt themselves to be setting a moral and religious example that all the world would eventually have to follow. They were part of a very privileged community from whom the elect would be drawn. Thus they could be oppressive when they had power, yet holy rebels when they were a minority. After all, since they were freed of responsibility for their own salvation, they were acting selflessly at all times. Like the children of Israel, they had a mission to live for God, and this sense of destiny was to be one of Calvinism's greatest strengths.

Preachers from Geneva traveled through Europe to win adherents and organize the faithful wherever they could. In 1559 the city opened a university for the purpose of training preachers, because Calvin regarded education as an essential means of instilling faith. From Geneva flowed a stream of pamphlets and books, which strengthened the faith of all believers and made sure that none who wished to learn would lack the opportunity. A special target was Calvin's homeland, France, where his preachers had their first successes, especially in the cities. Calvinism also won important support in the nobility, notably among women aristocrats who often influenced their families to adopt the new beliefs.

By 1564, when Calvin died, his church was well established: more than a million adherents in France, where they were called Huguenots; the Palatinate converted; Scotland won; and considerable groups of followers in England, the Low Countries, and Hungary. Despite its severity, Calvin's coherent and comprehensive body of doctrine proved to have wide appeal in an age of piety that yearned for clear religious answers. To whom, however, did it appeal?

The Appeal of Calvinism   When those who adopted the new faith explained their conversion, they usually did so in terms of a slow or sudden revelation—God had finally shown them the truth. But historians have noted that there were certain groups who seemed especially open to Protestant, and particularly Calvinist, teachings. All the reformed faiths did particularly well in cities, and it has been suggested that the long history of independence among townspeople made them more inclined to challenge traditional authorities. In addition, they tended to be more literate, and thus were drawn to beliefs that emphasized reading the Bible for oneself. And Calvinism put an emphasis on sobriety, discipline, and communal responsibility that would have appealed strongly to the increasingly self-confident merchants and artisans of the cities. That the Calvinists were also successful in the areas of southern France farthest away from central authority in Paris only reinforces the connection with an inclination toward independence and self-reliance.

Geneva itself became a determinedly independent place—the only city in Europe that successfully resisted becoming part of a territorial state and remained an autonomous political force during the two centuries following Calvin's death. Because of the dominance of Calvinism, morals were strictly supervised, and there was an aura of public discipline that all visitors noted. At the same time, artisans and merchants made Geneva an important economic center, and the university achieved an international reputation. Gradually in the seventeenth century the atmosphere of austerity softened, but the city continued to be seen as a model community for all Calvinists.

Women and Reform Cities were not the only centers of religious reform. In some parts of Europe, such as Scotland, new beliefs flourished outside towns because they won political support. But in all areas, the importance of women to the spread of Protestantism was unmistakable. Calvin's earliest significant converts were aristocratic women, whose patronage helped his faith take root at the highest levels of society. Like the literate women of the cities, they saw in its message an opportunity to express themselves and to work for others in ways that had not been possible before. They were often the main readers of the Bible in family gatherings; they took the lead in demanding broader access to education, especially for girls; and they were regularly prominent in radical movements.

One theologian who despaired at the results of Luther's translation of the New Testament reserved his most bitter complaints for the women who were studying the Bible for themselves. And the results were apparent not only among the literate. The records of the Inquisition, the Catholic tribunal charged with rooting out heresy, are full of the trials and executions of women who were martyrs for their beliefs and who died defending doctrines they had learned from preachers or other women. Again and again, they rejected the authority of priests and asserted their right to individual faith. It was determination like this that enabled the Reformation to establish itself and to spread until it posed a major challenge to the traditional Church (*see box,* p. 410).

IV. The Catholic Revival

REFORM AND COUNTER REFORM

Those with Protestant sympathies usually refer to the Catholic revival that started in the 1530s as the Counter Reformation, implying that the Roman Church acted only as a result of criticisms by Luther and others. Catholic historians call it the Catholic Reformation, implying that the movement began within the Church and was not merely a reaction to Protestantism. There is justification for both views. Certainly the papacy was aware of its loss of control over millions of Christians, but a great deal of the effort to put the Catholic Church's house in order was a result of deep faith and a determination to purify the in-

Although a major effort was certainly needed, and serious problems had to be addressed, one must not forget that there was a vast reserve of loyalty and affection that the Church could draw on. Many more Europeans remained Catholic in the long run than converted to Protestantism. They took comfort from tradition and from priests who, rather than demanding that believers achieve salvation on their own, offered the Church's mediation, beautiful ceremonies, and rituals to help people overcome their sins. Catholicism had a long history of charity for the

The Trial of Elizabeth Dirks

In radical groups, women often occupied central roles they never achieved in the larger churches. Since the most important attributes of a believer in these groups were faith, commitment, and the presence of the holy spirit, there was frequently an egalitarianism not found elsewhere in sixteenth-century society. Thus it was that the radical "teacher" (or leader) whom the Inquisition in the Netherlands interrogated in January 1549 was a woman named Elizabeth Dirks. Her replies give us a vivid sense of the beliefs the Reformation was stimulating among ordinary people—though in this case they were put forward with a clarity and a conviction that would lead to Elizabeth's execution two months later.

Examiner: We understand you are a teacher and have led many astray. Who are your friends?

Elizabeth: Do not press me on this point. Ask me about my faith and I will answer you gladly.

Examiner: Do you not consider our Church to be the house of the Lord?

Elizabeth: I do not. For it is written that God said "I will dwell with you."

Examiner: What do you think of our mass?

Elizabeth: I have no faith in your mass, but only in the word of God.

Examiner: What do you believe about the Holy Sacrament of the Eucharist?

Elizabeth: I never in my life read in Scripture about a Holy Sacrament, but only of the Supper of the Lord.

Examiner: You speak with a haughty tongue.

Elizabeth: No. I speak with a free tongue.

Examiner: Do you not believe that you are saved by baptism?

Elizabeth: No: all the water in the sea cannot save me. My salvation is in Christ, who commanded me to love my God and my neighbor as myself.

Examiner: Do priests have the power to forgive sins?

Elizabeth: How should I believe that? Christ is the only priest through whom sins are forgiven.

As torture was applied:

Examiner: You can recant everything you have said.

Elizabeth: No, I will not, but I will seal it with my blood.

Adapted from Thieleman von Bracht, *The Bloody Theater or Martyr's Mirror*, Daniel Rupp (trans.) (Lancaster, Pa.: David Miller, 1837), pp. 409–410.

poor, and this was strengthened during the sixteenth century. For ordinary Christians, the familiarity, support, and grandeur they found in the Church were often more than enough reason to resist the appeals of reformers.

CRISIS AND CHANGE IN THE CHURCH

Yet there was no doubt that the first half of the sixteenth century was the lowest point in the history of the Catholic Church and that few would have expected the recovery that followed. By 1550 many areas of Europe had been lost to the Protestants, and even in regions that were still loyal, the papacy was able to exercise little control. The French Church, for example, had a well-established tradition of autonomy, exemplified by the right France's kings had had since 1516 to make ecclesiastical appointments. In Spain, too, the monarchy retained its independence and even had its own Inquisition. In the Holy Roman Empire, those states that had rejected Protestantism gave the pope no more than token allegiance.

Moreover, there was still no comprehensive

definition of Catholic doctrine on justification, salvation, and the sacraments. Worse yet, the Church's leadership was far from effective. Although one pope, Leo X, had attempted to correct notorious abuses such as simony, the sale of church offices, in the early sixteenth century, Rome simply did not have the spiritual authority to make reform a vital force in the Catholic Church.

Paul III The situation changed with the pope elected in 1534: Paul III, a man not renowned for saintliness but a genius at making the right decisions for the Church. By the end of his reign, in 1549, the Catholic revival was under way. The heart of Paul's strategy was his determination to assert papal responsibility throughout the Church. Realizing that uncertainties in Catholic doctrine could be resolved only by a reexamination of traditional theology, he decided within a few months of taking office to call a Church council for that purpose, despite the danger of rekindling the conciliar movement. It took 10 years to overcome resistance to the idea, but in the meantime Paul attacked abuses throughout the

▶ *Titian*
POPE PAUL III AND HIS NEPHEWS, ALESSANDRO
AND OTTAVIO FARNESE, 1546
The psychological tension Titian created in this family portrait is extraordinary. The shrewd 77-year-old pope who had launched the Church's vigorous response to Protestantism looks benignly on Ottavio, whose seemingly calculated gesture of deference hints at the aggressiveness that was soon to cause a major family quarrel over land and money. And Cardinal Alessandro, standing apart, was already a famous patron of art with little concern for Church affairs. Perhaps because of its revelation of character, the painting was never finished.

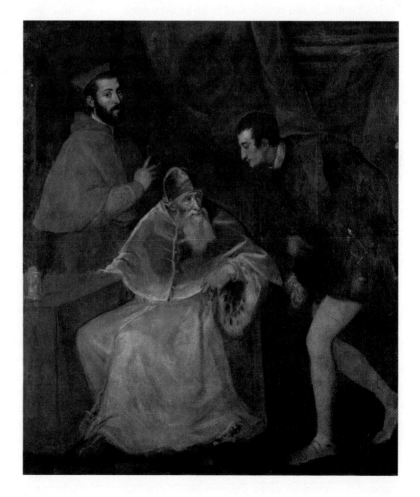

Church, disregarding both vested interests and tradition. He aimed his campaign at all levels of the hierarchy, undeterred by powerful bishops and cardinals long used to a lax and corrupt regime. In addition, he founded a Roman Inquisition, a decision that reflected the era's growing reliance on persecution as a means of destroying dissent.

Paul realized that, in the long run, the revival of Catholicism would depend on whether his successors maintained his efforts. During his 15-year reign, therefore, he made a series of superb appointments to the College of Cardinals (the body that elects the popes); the result was the creation of possibly the most illustrious College in history. Many of its members were famous for their piety, others for their learning. They came from all over Europe, united by their devotion to the Church and their resolve to see it once again command admiration and reverence. The result of Paul's farsighted policy was to be a succession of popes through the early seventeenth century who would fully restore the atmosphere of spirituality and morality that had long been missing from the papacy.

THE COUNCIL OF TRENT

The ecumenical, or general, council of Church leaders called by Paul finally assembled at Trent, a northern Italian city, in 1545, and met irregularly until the delegates managed to complete their work in 1563. The council's history was one of stormy battles between various national factions. The non-Italians pressed for decentralization of religious authority; the Italians, closely tied to the papacy, advocated a consolidation of power. For both sides, the divisions were political as well as ecclesiastical, because at issue was the independence not only of bishops but also of local princes and kings. A large majority of the delegates were Italians, however, and their conclusions almost always reinforced the dominance of the pope. The threat of a revival of conciliarism never materialized.

Doctrine In keeping with Paul's instructions, the Council of Trent gave more of its time to the basic issue of Church doctrine than to the problem of reform. Nearly all its decisions were intended to establish clear definitions of practice and belief, and to bring to an end long-standing theological uncertainties or differences of opinion. The main sources for these decisions were the interpretations put forward by Thomas Aquinas, who now became the central theologian of the Catholic Church. At the same time, Trent's decrees were designed to affirm precisely those teachings that the Protestants had rejected. Catholicism from then on would be committed primarily to the outward, sacramental heritage of Christianity. In this view, the Bible is not the exclusive authority for the believer: Church tradition holds an equal place in establishing religious truth. Human will is free, good works as well as faith are a means of salvation, all seven sacraments are channels of grace, and Christ's sacrifice is reenacted in every Mass. The Council of Trent endorsed the special position of the priest and insisted that God be worshiped with appropriately elaborate ceremonies and rites.

These were the principal decisions at Trent, but hundreds of minor matters were also settled: For the first time, the priest's presence was declared to be essential at the sacrament of marriage, a further reinforcement of his importance; the Vulgate, the Latin translation of the Bible prepared chiefly by St. Jerome, was decreed to be a holy text, a decision which rebutted humanists and other scholars who had found mistranslations of Greek and Hebrew in Jerome's work; and in direct contrast to the Protestants, gorgeous ritual was heavily stressed, which encouraged artists to beautify church buildings and ceremonies.

Restoring the Church The achievement of the council was to adjust the Church to the world. Many ordinary people, troubled by the stern self-denial and predestination taught by most Protestant churches and sects, preferred the traditional comfort and support Catholicism had long offered. They were ready to champion their old faith as soon as its leadership restored its sense of purpose by removing abuses and defining doctrines. And the new discipline of the Church was apparent in the council's effort to deal with morality as thoroughly as with belief. When it gave its approval to the Inquisition and to the "Index of Forbidden Books," which informed all Catholics of the heretical works they were not allowed to read, the council signaled the determination of the Church to recover the ground it had lost.

THE AFTERMATH OF TRENT

The new atmosphere of dedication swept through the Catholic Church, inspiring thinkers and artists throughout Europe to lend their talents to the cause. In many ways, Baroque art was to be the genre of the Counter Reformation: Painters, architects, and musicians caught up by the new moral fervor in Catholicism expressed their faith in brilliant and dramatic portrayals of religious subjects and in churches that were designed to dazzle the observer in a way that most Protestants could not allow.

This artistic outpouring was, of course, far more than a reflection of the decisions of a few hundred prelates assembled in a council. It was also one of many indicators of the new vigor of Catholicism. In France the new generation of Church leaders who appeared in the late sixteenth century was distinguished for its austerity, learning, and observance of duties. The inheritors of the traditional Scholastic philosophy multiplied, and in the late sixteenth and early seventeenth centuries they were to become influential throughout Europe.

▶ *Titian*
THE COUNCIL OF TRENT, CA. 1564
The splendor of the gathering of representatives of the Catholic Church from all of Europe is conveyed by this scene, attributed to Titian. The ranks of bishops in their miters, listening to one of their number address the assembly from the pulpit on the right, visibly embodied a Church putting itself in order as it faced the challenge of Protestantism.

Women in the Church Moreover, the crucial contribution to Protestantism of its women adherents was echoed in the revival of Catholicism. There was a remarkable flowering of new religious orders for women in the sixteenth and seventeenth centuries, many of which became identified with charitable works. Since one of the most important ways the Church set about winning back the faithful was by expanding its philanthropic activities—through new hospitals and expanded assistance to the poor, to orphans, and to other unfortunates—its female orders played an essential role in the Counter Reformation. And nowhere was their devout spirituality more apparent than in Spain, the most fiercely Catholic of all European countries.

The Spaniards expressed their religious passion in many ways—by insisting on converting the native peoples they conquered overseas, by giving great power to the Inquisition that guarded orthodoxy from large Muslim and Jewish communities at home, by encouraging lay as well as clerical piety, and by founding the most famous new order of the age, the Jesuits (see below). But no indication of their devotion was as distinctive as the great flowering of mysticism, which was most famously represented by St. Teresa (1515–1582).

St. Teresa   The mystic seeks to worship God directly and immediately, in an encounter that usually takes place in a trance and without the intervention of a priest. Because this is an entirely personal religious experience, which does not require the mediation of the Church, it has always been looked on with suspicion by the authorities. St. Teresa was no exception. As a rich and spoiled young girl, she had led a rather loose life, and her concerned father had sent her to a convent to instill some discipline. Perhaps because the family had only recently converted from Judaism, considerable attention was also given to Teresa's religious education. She later recalled a time when, after reading the lives of saints, she decided to become a martyr for Christ. She set out with her brother for North Africa, where she was determined to die fighting Muslims but was caught by an uncle. Of more lasting effect were the visions of God she began to have, which gradually convinced her that she had a special religious mission (*see box*, p. 415).

Church authorities became worried when, after becoming a nun, Teresa began to attract a following as a spiritual adviser to a number of women in her native city of Avila. Some churchmen suggested that her visions were the work of the devil, not God. After many examinations, however—and finally an interview with the king of Spain himself, who was deeply impressed by her holiness—the doubts evaporated. Teresa founded a strict new order of nuns and traveled all over Spain establishing convents. She soon became a legendary figure and was made a saint only 40 years after her death. To Spaniards she has remained a heroine, the subject of many affectionate stories. Once, when her carriage got stuck in the mud, she apparently looked heavenward and said: "If this is the way you treat your friends, God, no wonder you have so few of them." Above all, she came to embody the deep religious devotion of Counter Reformation Spain.

The Papacy   The most conspicuous embodiments of the new energy of the Church, however, were the popes themselves. Paul III's successors used their personal authority and pontifical resources not to adorn their palaces but to continue the enormous cleansing operation within the Church and to lead the counterattack against Protestantism. If a king or prince refused to help, the popes would try to persuade one of his leading subjects (for example, the Guise family in France and the dukes of Bavaria in the empire) to organize the struggle. Their diplomats and agents were everywhere, ceaselessly urging Catholics to stamp out Protestantism wherever it was found. And the pontiffs insisted on strict morality so as to restore their reputation for piety and to set a proper example to the faithful: One pope even ordered clothes painted on the nudes in Michelangelo's *Last Judgment* in the Sistine Chapel.

With the leaders of the Church thus bent on reform, the restoration of the faith and the reconquest of lost souls could proceed with maximum effect. And the popes had at their disposal a religious order established by Ignatius Loyola in 1540 specifically for these purposes: the Society of Jesus.

IGNATIUS LOYOLA

The third of the great religious innovators of the sixteenth century, after Luther and Calvin, was Ignatius Loyola (1491–1556); unlike his predecessors, however, he sought to reform the Catholic Church from within.

Loyola was the son of a Basque nobleman, raised in the chivalric and intensely religious atmosphere of Spain, and he was often at the court of Ferdinand of Aragon. In his teens he entered the army, but when he was 30, a leg wound ended his military career. While convalescing, he was deeply impressed by a number of popular

St. Teresa's Visions

These two are among the most famous passages from the autobiography St. Teresa began writing in 1562, when she was 47 years old. The book is essentially the story of a spiritual journey, as a restless young woman gains purpose and strength through mystical visions and unwavering faith. Her account of a mystical transport in the second passage quoted here was the inspiration for a famous sculpture by Gian Lorenzo Bernini, **The Ecstasy of St. Teresa,** *in the seventeenth century.*

I: One day, when I was at prayer, the Lord was pleased to reveal to me nothing but His hands, whose beauty was so great as to be indescribable. This made me very fearful. A few days later I also saw the Divine face. On St. Paul's Day, I saw a complete representation of his sacred Humanity. If there were nothing else in Heaven to delight the eyes but the extreme beauty of the glorified bodies there, that alone would be the greatest bliss. If I were to spend years and years imagining how to invent anything so beautiful, I could not do it. In its whiteness and radiance, it exceeds all we can imagine. It is a soft whiteness which, without wearying the eyes, causes them the greatest delight. By comparison with it, the brightness of our sun seems quite dim.

II: It pleased the Lord that I sometimes saw beside me an angel in bodily form. He was not tall, but short, and very beautiful, his face aflame. In his hands I saw a long golden spear, and at the end of the iron tip I seemed to see a point of fire. With this he seemed to pierce my heart several times. When he drew it out, he left me completely afire with a great love for God. During the days when this continued, I went about as if in a stupor.

From E. Allison Peers, *The Life of Teresa of Jesus* (London: Sheed & Ward, 1944; reprinted New York: Doubleday, 1960), pp. 258–260 and 273–274.

lives of the saints he read, and soon his religious interests began to take shape in chivalric and military terms. He visualized Mary as his lady, the inspiration of a Christian quest in which the forces of God and the devil fight in mighty battle. This was a faith seen from the perspective of the knight, and though the direct parallel lessened as Loyola's thought developed, it left an unmistakable stamp on his future work.

In 1522 Loyola gave up his knightly garb and swore to go on a pilgrimage to Jerusalem. He retired to a monastery for 10 months to absolve himself of the guilt of a sinful life and to prepare spiritually for the journey to the Holy Land. At the monastery he had a momentous experience that, like Luther's and Calvin's, dominated the rest of his life. According to tradition, he had a vision lasting eight days, during which he saw in detail the outline of a book, the *Spiritual Exercises,* and a new religious order, the Society of Jesus.

The **Spiritual Exercises** The first version of the *Spiritual Exercises* certainly dated from this period, but like Calvin's *Institutes,* it was to be thoroughly revised many times. The book deals not with doctrines or theology but with the discipline and training necessary for a God-fearing life. Believers must undertake four weeks of contemplation and self-examination that culminate in a feeling of union with God, in which they surrender their minds and wills to Christ. If successful, they are then ready to submit completely to the call of God and to pursue the Church's commands without question.

The manual was the heart of the organization of the Society of Jesus, and it gave those who followed its precepts (known as Jesuits) a dedication and determination that made them seem the Church's answer to the Calvinists. But while the end might be similar to Luther's and Calvin's— the personal attainment of grace—the method,

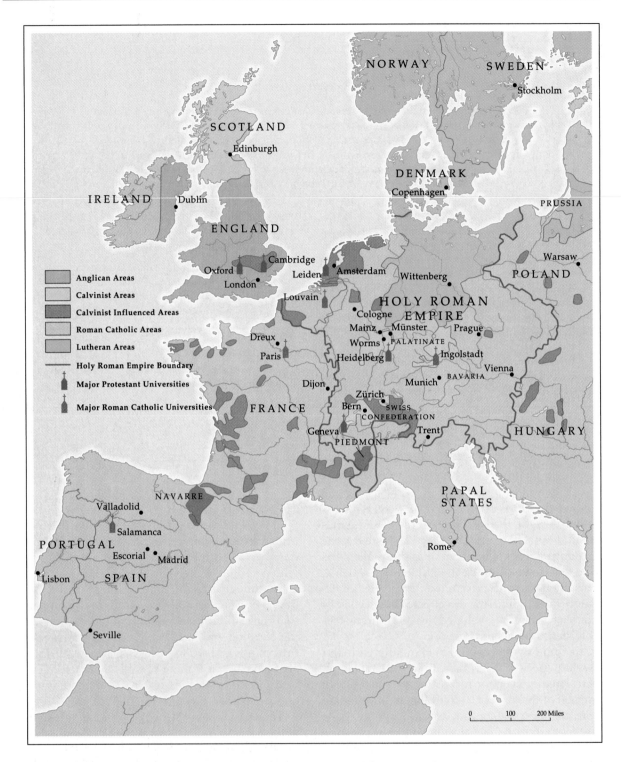

Map 13.2 RELIGIOUS DIVISIONS IN EUROPE AT THE END OF THE SIXTEENTH CENTURY
By the late sixteenth century, the division of Europe into distinct areas, each committed primarily to one church, was virtually complete. Now that they were solidly established, the major faiths became associated with universities that elaborated and promoted their beliefs.

with its emphasis on individual effort and concentration, could not have been more different. For the *Spiritual Exercises* emphasize that believers can *act* for themselves; they do not have to depend on faith alone to gain salvation, as Protestants assert. One can prepare for grace through a tremendous act of will and not depend solely on a gift from God. Loyola makes immense demands precisely because he insists that the will is free and that good works are efficacious.

Loyola's Followers During the 16 years after he left the monastery, Ignatius led a life of poverty and study. Though lame, he traveled to Jerusalem and back barefoot in 1523–1524, and two years later he found his way to the University of Alcalá, where he attracted his first disciples, three fellow students. Suspected by the Inquisition of being rather too independent in their beliefs, the little band walked to Paris, where they were joined by six more disciples. Ignatius now decided to return to the Holy Land, but the companions found themselves unable to travel beyond Venice because of war. Instead, they preached in the streets, visited the poor and the sick, urged all who would listen to rededicate themselves to piety and faith, and in 1537 achieved ordination as priests. Their activities were beginning to take definite shape, and so they decided to seek the pope's blessing for their work. They saw Paul III in 1538, and two years later, despite opposition from those who saw it as a threat to the authority of local bishops, the pope approved a plan Ignatius submitted for a new religious order that would owe allegiance only to the papacy.

THE JESUITS

The Society, or Company, of Jesus had four principal functions: preaching, hearing confessions, teaching, and founding and maintaining missions. The first two were the Jesuits' means of strengthening the beliefs of individual Catholics or converting Protestants. The third became one of their most effective weapons. Loyola, much influenced by the Christian humanists he had encountered, was convinced of the tremendous power of education. The Jesuits therefore set about organizing the best schools in Europe and

were so successful that some Protestants sent their children to the Society's schools despite the certainty that the pupils would become committed Catholics. The instructors followed humanist principles and taught the latest ideas, including the most recent advances in science. The Jesuits' final activity, missionary work, brought them their most spectacular successes among both non-Christians and Protestants.

▶ *Peter Paul Rubens*
THE MIRACLE OF ST. IGNATIUS, 1619
Loyola quickly became one of the major heroes of the Catholic revival. Within less than 60 years of his death (1556), he was to become a saint of the Church. He became one of the heroes of Baroque art, as is apparent in this painting by Peter Paul Rubens, which creates a powerful image that represents Loyola at the moment when he cures a man and a woman who have been possessed by the devil.

A number of qualities combined to make the Jesuits extraordinarily effective in winning converts and turning Catholics into militant activists. First, the order demanded very high intellectual abilities. It selected recruits carefully (turning many applicants away) and gave them a superb

---

CHRONOLOGY OF THE REFORMATION AND COUNTER REFORMATION

1517	Luther's protest begins: the 95 Theses on indulgences.
1521	Diet of Worms: Luther condemned by Emperor Charles V.
1524–1525	Peasants' Revolt in Germany. Zürich adopts Zwingli's Reformation.
1531	Protestant League of Schmalkalden formed in Germany. Death of Zwingli. King Henry VIII proclaims himself head of the Church of England.
1534	Paul III becomes pope. Anabaptists take over the city of Münster in Germany.
1535	Thomas More executed for not accepting Henry VIII as head of the Church of England.
1536	Calvin comes to Geneva; first edition of his *Institutes*. Death of Erasmus.
1540	Pope Paul III approves the Jesuit Order.
1541	Calvin settles in Geneva permanently.
1545	Council of Trent begins.
1546	Death of Luther.
1556	Death of Loyola.
1559	First "Index of Forbidden Books" published. Execution of Protestants after Inquisition trials in Spain.
1564	Publication of the Decrees of the Council of Trent. Death of Calvin.

---

education. Jesuits were famous for their knowledge of Scripture and traditional teachings and their ability to out-argue opponents. In addition, they were trained to be highly effective preachers and excellent educators. And their discipline, determination, and awareness of the contemporary world soon won them a fearsome reputation. They had no equal in the forcefulness with which they advanced the aims of the Council of Trent and the papacy.

There is every reason to regard the Jesuits as the striking arm of the Counter Reformation; indeed, their organization was to some extent modeled on the medieval military orders. A Jesuit at a royal court was often the chief inspiration for a ruler's militant support of the faith, and in many areas the Society was the main conqueror of rival beliefs—for example, in Poland, where Jesuits in the late sixteenth century led a campaign that eradicated widespread Protestantism and created a devotedly Catholic country. Yet it must be noted that in an age that took persecution for granted, the Jesuits always opposed execution for heresy; they far preferred to win a convert than to kill a heretic. Their presence was soon felt all over the world: As early as the 1540s, one of Loyola's first disciples, Francis Xavier, was conducting a mission to Japan. Despite the many enmities they aroused by their single-mindedness and their self-assurance, their unswerving devotion was a major reason for the revival of the Roman Church.

RELIGION AND POLITICS

As a revived Catholic Church confronted the Protestants, religious warfare of unprecedented ferocity erupted throughout Europe (see Chapter 15). More people seemed to feel more passionately about faith than at any other time in Western history. But the conflict would not have continued as long as it did without the armies and resources provided by princes and monarchs. Both sides drew crucial support from rulers who were determined either to suppress any sign of heresy (that is, any faith other than their own) in their territories or to overthrow heretical regimes in neighboring lands. The struggle over religion was, for these rulers, a means of establishing their authority in their own realms and a justification for aggression abroad.

The strong connection between politics and belief, and its dire consequences, was the result of a transformation that was almost as far-reaching as the Reformation itself. Just as Western Christianity was changed forever in the sixteenth century, so too were the power and the ambition of the territorial state. At the same time as a handful of reformers, building on powerful social and intellectual forces, reshaped religious structures and practices, a handful of political leaders—building on no less powerful military, social, and economic forces—created armies, systems of taxation, and bureaucratic organizations that reshaped the structures and practices of central governments throughout Europe.

Recommended Reading

▼

Sources

*Calvin, John. *On God and Political Duty.* J. T. McNeill (ed.). 1950.

*Erasmus, Desiderius. *Essential Works of Erasmus.* W. T. H. Jackson (ed.). 1965.

Loyola, Ignatius. *The Spiritual Exercises of St. Ignatius.* R. W. Gleason (ed.). 1964.

*Luther, Martin. *Martin Luther: Selections from His Writings.* John Dillenberger (ed.). 1961.

Studies

*Bainton, Roland H. *Here I Stand: A Life of Martin Luther.* 1955. A classic biography in English, with many quotations from Luther's writings.

Bangert, William. *A History of the Society of Jesus.* 1972. The best basic history in English of the work of Loyola and the Jesuits.

*Bossy, John. *Christianity in the West. 1400–1700.* 1985. An overview of the religious history of Europe by one of the leading historians of Catholic thought and practice.

*Bouwsma, William J. *John Calvin: A Sixteenth-Century Portrait.* 1988. The standard biography.

*Davis, Natalie Zemon. *Society and Culture in Early Modern France.* 1975. A collection of essays about popular beliefs and attitudes, particularly on religious matters, during the sixteenth century.

Delumeau, Jean. *Catholicism between Luther and Voltaire: A New View of the Counter-Reformation.* 1977. The standard introduction.

Hillerbrand, Hans J. (ed.). *Radical Tendencies in the Reformation: Divergent Perspectives.* 1986. Important essays on the emergence of radical ideas and sects in the Reformation.

*Huizinga, Johan. *Erasmus and the Age of Reformation.* 1957. A warm and sympathetic biography, beautifully written.

*Kenny, Anthony. *Thomas More.* 1983. An excellent brief introduction to the life and work of the humanist-statesman.

Kittelson, James M. *Luther the Reformer: The Story of the Man and His Career.* 1986. The best introduction to Luther's life and thought.

Moeller, Bernd. *Imperial Cities and the Reformation.* H. C. E. Midelfort and M. U. Edwards (trs.). 1972. Three stimulating essays about the special role of cities in establishing the Reformation in Germany.

Po-chia Hsia, R. (ed.). *The People and the German Reformation: Approaches in the Social History of Religion.* 1988. A set of essays that reflects recent trends in the social interpretation of the Reformation.

Scribner, Robert. *For the Sake of Simple Folk: Popular Propaganda for the German Reformation.* 1981. A path-breaking analysis of how the Reformation was spread.

Scribner, Robert, and Gerhard Benecke (eds.). *The German Peasant War of 1525: New Viewpoints.* 1979. A stimulating set of essays about the social upheaval that accompanied the Reformation.

*Weber, Max. *The Protestant Ethic and the Spirit of Capitalism.* Talcott Parsons (tr.). 1958. Originally published in 1904 and 1905, this study of the way in which the Reformation helped create the modern world has influenced much of the historical thinking about the Reformation.

Williams, George H. *The Radical Reformation.* 1962. The most comprehensive account of the sects and their founders.

*Available in paperback.

Hans Holbein the Younger
THE AMBASSADORS, 1533
Hans Holbein the Younger's *The Ambassadors*
shows the worldliness that was expected of
diplomats (many of whom were also soldiers) in the
sixteenth century. The two men are surrounded by
symbols of the skills, knowledge, and refinement
their job required—geography, mathematics,
literature, and music. But despite this emphasis on
material concerns, Holbein reminds us (in the
optically distorted skull across the bottom of the
painting) that death and spiritual needs cannot be
forgotten.

CHAPTER FOURTEEN

ECONOMIC EXPANSION AND A NEW POLITICS

EUROPE in 1400 was a poor, technologically backward, and politically disorganized area compared to the realms of the Indian moguls or Chinese emperors. And yet within little more than a century, Europeans were expanding aggressively into Asia and the Americas. Their numbers were growing, their economy was booming, their technological advances were making possible the creation of new markets and new empires, and their political leaders were developing structures of government and authority more elaborate than any that had been seen since the fall of the Roman Empire. The emergence of this new world power was one of the most astonishing transformations in Western history, and historians have long debated its causes. Their suggestions have ranged from the personal (the initiatives of specific kings, entrepreneurs, or explorers) to the abstract (such forces as demographic change or a gradual warming of the climate). Like the fall of the Roman Empire, however, this was so profound a reshaping of Europe that one cannot suggest a single comprehensive explanation. Indeed, it is only by looking at the individual changes in some detail that one can understand how far-reaching was the reordering that had taken place by the late sixteenth century.

I. Expansion at Home

POPULATION INCREASE

It was during the last third of the fifteenth century that signs of change appeared in the demographic, economic, and political history of Europe. Some have argued that the root cause lay in politics: Because assertive regimes restored order and authority in a number of states, confidence rose, trade quickened, and populations grew. Others regard either economic or demographic advance as the source of change. In fact, it is clear that all three were connected and that all three reinforced one another. Thus, although we are not certain why the number of Europeans began to increase after more than 100 years of decline, we can see the effects of the increase in many areas of life.

Exact measurements are not possible, but it seems likely that the loss of population that began with the Black Death in the 1340s had run its course by the 1460s. Plagues, though recurrent, began to take less of a toll (perhaps because immunities developed); bad harvests became less frequent (perhaps because of a warming climate); and families were thus able to produce more surviving children. As a result, Europe's population rose by some 50 percent between 1470 and 1620. And cities expanded even faster: London had fewer than 50,000 inhabitants in the early sixteenth century but over 200,000 a hundred years later. There was also extensive reoccupation of marginal farmland, which had been abandoned in the fourteenth and fifteenth centuries because a shrinking population had provided no market for its produce. Now there were more mouths to feed, and the extra acres again became profitable.

Consequences of the Increase The rise in population was followed by a staggering jump in food prices. By the early 1600s wheat cost approximately five times more than in the late 1400s, an increase that far outpaced the movement of prices in general. It is not surprising, therefore, that this period witnessed the first wave of enclosures in England: Major landowners put up fences around common tilling or grazing ground, traditionally open to all the animals of the locality, and reserved it for their own crops or their sheep, whose wool was also in increasing demand. By 1600 about one-eighth of England's arable land had been enclosed. The only answer, when changes like these made a village incapable of supporting its growing population, was for people to move to towns and cities.

ECONOMIC GROWTH

As markets began to grow in response to population pressures, the volume of trade also shot upward; commercial profits thus kept pace with those of agriculture. Customs receipts rose steadily, as did the yield of tolls from ships entering the Baltic Sea, one of the main routes of European trade. In many areas, too, shipbuilding boomed. This was the heyday of the English cloth trade and the great Spanish sheep farms, of the central German linen industry and the northern Italian silk industry. Printing became a widespread occupation, and gun making and glassmaking also expanded rapidly. Glassmaking had a major effect on European society because the increasing use of windows allowed builders to divide houses into small rooms, thus giving many people a little privacy for the first time.

Leading financiers who invested in the growing volume of trade accumulated large fortunes. For centuries the Italians had been in the vanguard of economic advance, but in the sixteenth century firms of other nations were achieving international prominence. The most successful of the new enterprises was run by a family descended from a fourteenth-century weaver, Johannes Fugger of Augsburg. The sixteenth-century Fuggers financed the Spanish King Charles I's quest for the throne of the Holy Roman Empire and his later wars after he became the Emperor Charles V. Great bankers were thus often closely allied with monarchs, and like all merchants, they gained from the mounting power of central governments. Rulers encouraged commerce in the hope of larger revenues from customs duties and taxes, and they gave leading entrepreneurs valuable privileges. Such alliances were eventually the undoing of some firms, which were ruined when kings went bankrupt, but until the late sixteenth century, Italian and German bankers controlled Europe's finances.

Almost every level of commercial activity offered opportunities for advancement. The guild system expanded in the sixteenth century to incorporate many new trades, and the structure of merchant enterprises became more elaborate. The idea took hold that a business firm was an impersonal entity—larger than the person who owned it—with an identity, legal status, permanence, and even profits that were not the same as those of its members. Here was yet another indication of the changes taking place in economic affairs.

INFLATION AND SILVER

The surest sign of growth, however, was the slow inflation of prices, which began around 1500 after some 150 years of either stagnant or falling prices. By modern standards, the increase was tiny—1 or 2 percent a year, totaling 75 percent in Spain by 1600 and slightly less elsewhere in Europe—but it prompted bitter protests from those who thought a loaf of bread had a "just" price and that any increase was mere exploitation by the baker. In general, however, the modest inflation was an indication that demand was rising, and it not only boosted profits but also reduced people's debts (because the amount that had been borrowed was worth less each year).

Silver Imports A major reason for the inflation was the growth of the population, but it was also propelled by the huge quantities of silver the

IMPORTS OF TREASURE TO SPAIN FROM THE NEW WORLD, 1511–1600	
Decade	*Total Value**
1511–1520	2,626,000
1521–1530	1,407,000
1531–1540	6,706,000
1541–1550	12,555,000
1551–1560	21,437,000
1561–1570	30,418,000
1571–1580	34,990,000
1581–1590	63,849,000
1591–1600	85,536,000

*In ducats.

Source: Adapted from J. H. Elliott, *Imperial Spain, 1469–1716* (New York, 1964), p. 175.

▶ *Anonymous French Miniature*
MERCHANTS CLEARING ACCOUNTS
This sixteenth-century depiction of a group of people in a fine house calculating accounts gives a sense of the increasingly complicated exchanges that became necessary as commerce expanded. Books had to be checked and moneys counted, and it is noteworthy that the transactions involve the monk on the left and the woman holding her purse on the right.

Spaniards imported from the New World, which made money more readily available (see accompanying table). Most of the silver passed from Spain to the Italian and German merchants who financed Spanish wars and controlled the American trade, and it thus affected all of Europe. Other sources of supply, notably silver mines in Austria, were appearing at this time; but the flow of New World silver was the main reason for the end of the crippling shortage of precious metals and, hence, of coins that had plagued Europe for centuries. By the middle of the seventeenth century, the continent's holdings in gold had increased by one-fifth and, more important, its stock of silver had tripled.

With money circulating more freely and markets growing, the profits of traders and financiers improved dramatically. They could invest more widely (for example, in overseas ventures), and they could achieve new levels of wealth.

THE COMMERCIAL REVOLUTION

As the volume of trade rose, new mechanisms for organizing large-scale economic activity were put in place—a process that has been called Europe's *commercial revolution*. Bookkeepers devised new, standardized principles for keeping track of a firm's accounts, bankers created elaborate systems of agents and letters of credit to transfer funds across large distances, merchants developed more effective means of forming broad partnerships that were capable of major investments and of ensuring against losses, and governments gave increased support to new ventures and to the financial community in general. Essential to these activities was an attitude and a way of conducting business that is known as *capitalism*.

Capitalism Capitalism was both a product of economic change and a stimulus to further change. It is often thought of as a system, but it refers primarily to the distinct outlook and kinds of behavior displayed by certain people as they make, buy, and sell goods. At its root capitalism means the accumulation of capital—that is, tangible wealth—for its own sake. In practice, this requires taking risks and also reinvesting whatever one earns so as to enlarge one's profits. Those who undertook long-distance trade had many capitalist traits: They took great risks, and they were prepared to wait months and even years in order to make as large a financial gain as possible. Similarly, bankers were prepared to lend their capital, despite the danger that the loan might not be repaid, in the hope of profit; and if

▶ *Jost Amman*
ALLEGORY OF TRADE, WOODCUT
This late-sixteenth-century celebration of the world of the merchant shows, around the sides, the shipping of goods, the keeping of accounts, and the exchange of money that were transforming economic life. In the center, the virtues of the merchant are symbolized: integrity (a man looking over his shoulder), taciturnity (two men on his right), and a knowledge of languages (two men in turbans) in front of judiciousness on a throne and a book representing invention.

▶ *Petrus Christus*

ST. ELIGIUS AS A GOLDSMITH, 1449
Goldsmiths played a vital financial role in the early days of capitalism. Because of the value of the merchandise they made and sold, their shops—like the one here, with customers looking in the window, as one can see in the convex mirror on the right—were sources of capital as well as goods. In addition to providing such items as the ring he is handing to the young woman, the goldsmith might well have provided investments for the traders in his city.

they succeeded, they continually plowed their earnings back into their businesses to make them ever larger. The fortunes that these capitalists accumulated, and the desire for worldly riches that they displayed, became an essential stimulus to economic growth. Far from the rural world where food was grown primarily for survival, not for profit, they were forging a new way of thinking about money and wealth. Although their outlook had existed before, only in the sixteenth century did it come to dominate Europe's economy. As a result, traditional religious prohibitions on the charging of interest began to weaken, and materialist ambitions became more open and accepted.

Unease over this new outlook did not disappear. Shakespeare's play *The Merchant of Venice*, written in the 1590s, attacked the values that capitalism was coming to represent. He contrasted unfavorably the quest for profit with more tra-

ditional commitments, such as charity and mercy. And his choice of Venice as a setting was appropriate because the large empire this city built in the eastern Mediterranean was mainly the result of a single-minded pursuit of trade. But criticism had no effect. The spread of capitalism was now irresistible.

SOCIAL CHANGE: THE COUNTRYSIDE

Not everyone shared in the new prosperity of the sixteenth century. Landowners, food producers, artisans, and merchants benefited most from the rising population and could amass fortunes. Tenants who were able to harvest a surplus beyond their own needs did well, because for a while rents did not keep pace with food prices. But the wages of ordinary laborers lagged miserably. By the early seventeenth century, a laborer's annual income had about half the purchasing power it had had at the end of the fifteenth century, a decline that had its most drastic impact in Eastern Europe, where serfdom reappeared.

In the West, the large numbers of peasants who were forced off the land as the population rose turned to begging and wandering across country, often ending up in towns, where crime became a serious problem. Peasant uprisings directed at tax collectors, nobles, or food suppliers were almost annual affairs in one region or another of France after the mid-sixteenth century, and in England the unending stream of vagrants gave rise to a belief that the country was overpopulated. The extreme poverty was universally deplored, particularly as it promoted crime and disorder.

Relief of Distress Nobody could understand, much less control, the forces that were transforming society. Some governments tried to relieve the economic distress, but their efforts were not always consistent. English legislation in the sixteenth century, for example, treated beggars sometimes as shirkers who should be punished and at other times as unfortunates who needed to be helped. Not until the enactment of the English Poor Law of 1601, which provided work for the poor, did the more compassionate view begin to prevail. In the years that followed, governments in a number of countries began to create institutions that offered basic welfare benefits.

The traditional source of food for the hungry and care for the ill, the monastery, had lost its importance because of the Reformation and because governments were now considered responsible for the needy. Among the remedies they offered were the workhouses established by the English Poor Law where, although conditions

▶ *Hieronymus Bosch*
THE PRODIGAL SON, CA. 1516
Usually known for his horrific paintings of devils and monsters, Bosch here creates a realistic scene of his time to illustrate the biblical story of the prodigal son. He shows the son as one of the many poor peddlers, in torn clothes and ill-matching shoes, who roamed the European countryside. The house he is leaving is hardly in better condition, with holes in the roof and a broken shutter; and the residents show in various ways their indifference to his departure.

could be horrible, the destitute could at least find work, food, and shelter. Other governments founded hospitals, often staffed by nuns, which were especially important as places that looked after abandoned women or children. But these institutions were few and far between, and it was exceptional for a poor person to find such relief. The conditions were especially harsh for women forced off the land, because few trades were open to them even if they got to a town; their choice might be either continued vagrancy or prostitution.

SOCIAL CHANGE: THE TOWN

Vagrancy was only one of the signs that Europeans were witnessing the beginnings of modern urbanization with all its dislocations. Major differences also developed between life in the country and life in the town. Rural workers may have led a strenuous existence, but they escaped the worst hazards of their urban counterparts. Whole sections of most large cities were controlled by the sixteenth-century equivalent of the underworld, which offered sanctuary to criminals and danger to most citizens. Plagues were much more serious in towns—the upper classes soon learned to flee to the country at the first sign of disease—and famines more devastating because of the far poorer sanitation in urban areas and their remoteness from food supplies.

New Opportunities Nevertheless, it was in towns and cities that the economic advances of the age were most visible. As cities grew, they stimulated construction, not only of houses but also of public buildings and city walls. Anyone skilled in bricklaying, in carpentry, or even in carrying heavy loads found ready employment.

Townsfolk needed endless services, from sign painting to the transportation of books, which created jobs at all levels. Given the demand for skills, guilds increasingly allowed the widows of members to take over their husbands' trades, and women shopkeepers were not uncommon. Nobody would have been taken aback, for example, to see an artisan's daughter or wife (like Agnes Dürer, the wife of the famous German artist) take charge of a market stall or a shop. In some trades, such as oil making and baking, women were often essential to production as well as sales, and

▶ *Pieter Brueghel the Elder*
Carnival and Lent, 1559
This detail from a huge scene shows one of the customary practices during the season of Lent: giving alms to the poor. Beggars were a common subject for Brueghel, who used them to convey a vivid sense of the appearance and behavior of the unfortunate as well as the more comfortable members of his society.

there is also evidence of their growing importance as the keepers of the paperwork and the accounts in family businesses. The expansion of opportunity in the cities, in other words, had social as well as economic consequences.

At the top levels of society—at princely courts and in royal administrations, in the law, among the leaders of the burgeoning cities, and in growing empires overseas—the economic expansion enabled ambitious families to win fortunes and titles and to found new aristocratic dynasties. The means of advancement varied. Once a family had become rich through commerce, it could buy the lands that, in Protestant countries, rulers had confiscated from the Church, or the offices that many governments sold to raise revenue and build bureaucracies. In addition, the New World offered the possibility of acquiring vast estates. Since the possession of land or high office was the key to noble status, the newly rich were soon able to enter the ranks of the nobility. The long boom in commerce thus encouraged a broad spectrum of social change. By the 1620s, when the upward trend of the economy came to an end, a new aristocracy had been born that was destined to dominate Europe for centuries.

II. Expansion Overseas

THE PORTUGUESE

Long before Europe's demographic and economic recovery began in the late fifteenth century, pioneer explorers had taken the first steps that were to lead to the creation of huge empires overseas. Taking farther the voyages beyond Europe of the crusaders and such travelers as Marco Polo, sailors had been inching around Africa seeking a route to the Far East. The riches in goods and lands they eventually found would help fuel the boom of the sixteenth century. But there was little expectation of world-shattering consequences among the Portuguese who began these voyages in the 1410s.

Henry the Navigator The Portuguese lived in an inhospitable land whose seafarers had always been essential to the country's economy. The need for better agricultural opportunities had long turned their eyes toward Atlantic islands like the Canaries and the territories held by the Muslims (Moors) in North Africa. But this ambition had to be organized into a sustained effort if it was to achieve results, and in the early fifteenth century Prince Henry the Navigator, a younger son of the king, undertook that task.

Henry participated in the capture of the North African port of Ceuta from the Muslims in 1415, a crusading expedition that only whetted his appetite for more such victories. At Ceuta he probably heard stories about lost Christians and mines of gold somewhere in the interior of Africa. A mixture of motives—profit, religion, and curiosity—spurred him on; and in 1419 he began patronizing sailors, mapmakers, astronomers (because their contributions to celestial navigation were vital), shipbuilders, and instrument makers who were interested in discovery. They were mainly Italians, and their aim was not merely to make contact with Africans but to find an alternative route to India and the Far East around Africa (in order to avoid the Ottoman Empire, which was coming to dominate the eastern Mediterranean). The early adventurers did not succeed, but during their gradual advance down the West African coast, they opened a rich new trade in ivory, gold, and slaves.

To India and Beyond Then, in 1488, a Portuguese captain, Bartholomeu Dias, returned to Lisbon after making a landfall on the east coast of Africa, beyond the Cape of Good Hope, which previously no one had been able to pass. The way to India now seemed open, but before the Portuguese could send out their first expedition, the news arrived that a sailor employed by the Spaniards, one Christopher Columbus, had apparently reached India by sailing west. To avoid conflicting claims which might interfere with their trade, Portugal and Spain signed the Treaty of Tordesillas in 1494. This gave Portugal possession of all the lands to the east of an imaginary line about 300 miles west of the Azores, and Spain a monopoly of everything to the west. Portugal thus kept the only practical route to India (as well as the rights to Brazil, which one of her sailors may already have discovered). Three years later Vasco da Gama took the first Portuguese fleet across the Indian Ocean.

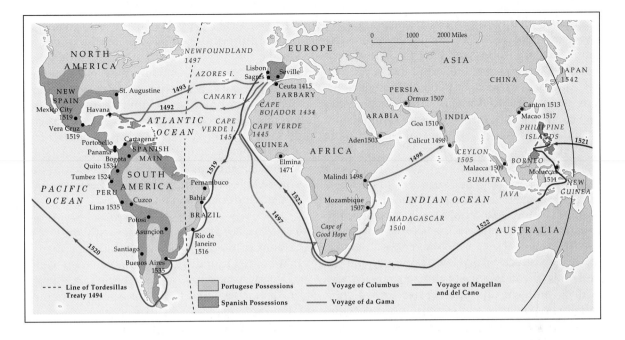

Map 14.1 EXPLORATION AND CONQUEST IN THE FIFTEENTH AND SIXTEENTH CENTURIES
The division of the world between the Portuguese and the Spaniards led to distinct areas of exploration and settlement, demarcated by the line that both sides accepted at the Treaty of Tordesillas.

At first, he found it hard to trade, because the Arabs, who had controlled these waters for centuries, tried to keep out all rivals. Within 14 years, however, the Portuguese merchants had established themselves. The key to their success was naval power, for their ship designers had learned to combine their old square sails, which provided speed, with the Arabs' lateen sails, which increased maneuverability. The Portuguese were also the first to give their fleets effective fire power, realizing that cannon, not soldiers, won battles at sea. In addition, they deployed their ships in squadrons rather than individually, a tactic that further increased their superiority. The result was overwhelming military success. A series of victories reduced Arab naval strength, and bombardments quieted stubborn cities. By 1513 Portugal's trading posts extended beyond India to the rich Spice Islands, the Moluccas.

The Portuguese Empire The empire Portugal created remained dependent on sea power, not overseas colonies. Except in Brazil, which was virtually unpopulated and where the settlers were able to establish huge estates worked by slave labor, the Portuguese relied on a chain of small trading bases that stretched from West Africa to China. They supplied and defended these bases, which usually consisted of little more than a few warehouses and a fort, by sea; and they

tended to keep contacts with the local people to a minimum, so as to maintain friendly relations and missionary and trading rights. The one exception to the isolation was a result of the small numbers of women who traveled to the settlements from Portugal: In these early years there were more marriages with local women than there were in other European empires. But even though their effort remained relatively small-scale, the Portuguese soon began to profit from their explorations—between 1442 and 1446 almost 1000 slaves were brought home from Africa—and in the sixteenth century their wealth grew as they became major importers of luxuries from the East, such as spices, which were in great demand as medicines, preservatives, and tasty delicacies.

By dominating commerce with the Oriental civilizations, which were not only richer but also more sophisticated than their own, Portugal's merchants controlled Europe's most valuable trade. But their dominance was to last less than a century, for their success spurred a competition for empire that was to stimulate new waves of overseas expansion. First Spain determined to emulate her neighbor; and later the Dutch, English, and French sought to outdo their predecessors and one another. This competition gave the Europeans the crucial stimulus that other peoples lacked, and it projected them into a dominance over the rest of the globe that would last for more than 450 years.

THE SPANIARDS

Inspired by the same centuries-old crusading ambitions as the Portuguese, the Spaniards rode the second wave of expansion overseas. Because Spain was much larger than Portugal, and directed its attention toward a more sparsely populated continent, the Spaniards founded their empire on conquest and colonization, not trade. But they got their start from a stroke of luck.

Columbus Christopher Columbus—an experienced Genoese sailor who was widely read, well versed in Atlantic sailing, and familiar with the leading geographers of his day—seems to have believed (we do not know for certain because he was a secretive man) that Asia lay only 3500 miles beyond the Canary Islands. Thus convinced that sailing west across the Atlantic to the Far East was perfectly feasible, Columbus took his proposal in 1484 to the Portuguese government, which refused to underwrite the venture. With a mystic belief in his own destiny, he persisted, gained the financial backing and blessing of Ferdinand V and Isabella I of Spain, and set sail in 1492. He was an excellent navigator (one of his discoveries on the voyage was the difference between true and magnetic north), and he kept his men going despite their horror of being so long at sea without sight of land. After 33 days he reached the Bahamas. He was disappointed that he found no Chinese or Japanese as he investigated Cuba and the west coast of Hispaniola (today's Haiti), but he was certain that he had reached Asia, even though the few natives he saw did not resemble those whom travelers such as Marco Polo had described.

Columbus crossed the Atlantic Ocean three more times, but he made no other significant discoveries. Yet he did also start the tradition of vi-

olence against local people that was to characterize the European conquest of the New World. During his first stay in the Caribbean, his men killed some of the natives they encountered. From the very beginning, therefore, it became clear that the building of empires in the Americas would be a process of destruction as well as creation, of cruelty as well as achievement (*see box*, p. 431). For the victims, the legacy of the brutality, soon intensified by the devastating diseases that accompanied the Europeans, was the eradication of their ancient civilizations.

The Limits of Westward Voyages By the end of Columbus' life in 1506, it was becoming apparent that he had found islands close by a new continent, not Asia. When, in 1513, the Spaniard Vasco de Balboa saw the Pacific Ocean from Central America, some thought that an easy westward passage to the riches of East Asia might still be found. But the last hope of a quick journey was dashed in 1522, when the one surviving ship from a fleet of five that had set out under Ferdinand Magellan three years before returned to Spain after the ordeal of having sailed around the world.

▶ **WOODCUT OF COLUMBUS**
This picture, by a contemporary, shows King Ferdinand, back in Spain, pointing to Columbus' three ships and the natives greeting the explorer in the New World.

Two Views of Columbus

The following two passages suggest the enormous differences that have arisen in interpretations of the career of Christopher Columbus. The first, by Samuel Eliot Morison, a historian and a noted sailor, represents the traditional view of the explorer's achievements that held sway until recent years. The second, by Kirkpatrick Sale, a writer and environmentalist, indicates how radically the understanding of the effects of exploration has changed in recent years.

1. "Columbus had a Hellenic sense of wonder at the new and strange, combined with an artist's appreciation of natural beauty. Moreover, Columbus had a deep conviction of the sovereignty and the infinite wisdom of God, which enhanced all his triumphs. One only wishes that the Admiral might have been afforded the sense of fulfillment that would have come from foreseeing all that flowed from his discoveries.

   The whole history of the Americas stems from the Four Voyages of Columbus, and as the Greek city-states looked back to the deathless gods as their founders, so today a score of independent nations unite in homage to Christopher the stout-hearted son of Genoa, who carried Christian civilization across the Ocean Sea."

   From S. E. Morison, *Admiral of the Ocean Sea: A Life of Christopher Columbus* (Boston: Little, Brown, 1942), pp. 670–671.

2. "For all his navigational skill, about which the salty types make such a fuss, and all his fortuitous headings, Admiral Colón [Christopher Columbus] could be a wretched mariner. The four voyages, properly seen, quite apart from bravery, are replete with lubberly mistakes, misconceived sailing plans, foolish disregard of elementary maintenance and stubborn neglect of basic safety—all characterized by the assertion of human superiority over the natural realm. Almost every time Colón went wrong it was because he had refused to bend to the inevitabilities of tide and wind and reef or, more arrogantly still, had not bothered to learn about them.

   "Many of those who know well the cultures that once existed in the New World have reason to be less than enthusiastic about [the 1992 celebrations of] the event that led to the destruction of much of that heritage and the greater part of the people who produced it; others are planning to protest the entire goings-on as a wrongful commemoration of an act steeped in bloodshed, slavery and genocide."

   Kirkpatrick Sale, *The Conquest of Paradise: Christopher Columbus and the Columbian Legacy* (New York: Knopf, 1990), pp. 209–210 and 362.

Magellan's 98-day crossing of the Pacific was the supreme accomplishment of seamanship in the age of discovery. But the voyage persuaded the Spaniards that Portugal had the fastest route to the East, and in 1529 they renounced all attempts to trade with the Spice Islands. Spain could now concentrate on the Americas, those unexpected continents that were to become not an obstacle on the way to the Spice Islands but possessions of unbelievable richness.

The Conquistador Volunteers for empire building were amply available. When the last Muslim kingdom in southern Spain was conquered by the Castilians in 1492, soldiers with long experience of military service found themselves at loose ends. Many were the younger sons of noble families, who were often kept from inheriting land because Spanish law usually allowed only the eldest son to inherit. The prospect of unlimited land and military adventure across the Atlantic appealed to them, as it did to ambitious members of Castile's lower classes, and thus the conquistador, or conqueror, was born. There were not many of them—fewer than 1000—but they overran much of the Americas in search of wealth and glory.

The first and most dramatic of these leaders was Hernando Cortés, who in 1519 landed on the Mexican coast and set out to overcome the rich Aztec civilization in the high plateau of central Mexico. His army consisted of only 600 troops, but in two years, with a few reinforcements, he had won a complete victory. Guns alone made no important difference because Cortés had only 13 muskets and some unwieldy cannon. More effective were his horses, his manipulation of the Aztecs' beliefs (especially after he murdered their ruler) to make them regard him as more powerful than he was, and the unshakable determination of his followers. The conquest of the Mexican Mayas also began under Cortés, while the Incas of Peru fell to Francisco Pizarro. Other conquistadors repeated these successes throughout Central and South America. By 1550 the conquest was over, and the military leaders gave way to administrators who began organizing the huge empire they had won.

THE FIRST COLONIAL EMPIRE

The Spanish government established in the New World the same pattern of political administration that it was setting up in its European territories. Representatives of the throne, viceroys, were sent to administer each territory and to impose centralized control. They were advised by the local *audiencia*, a kind of miniature council that also acted as a court of law, but the ultimate authority remained in Spain.

Real growth did not begin, however, until women pioneers came out to the settlements. In this empire, unlike Portugal's, intermarriage was strongly discouraged. Indeed, the indigenous peoples were treated with a brutality and disdain that set a dismal model for overseas empires. Not only was their labor cruelly exploited (both on farms and especially in silver mines that the Spaniards discovered, where working conditions were dreadful) and not only were families split apart so that men could be put to work, but local beliefs and traditions were actively suppressed

(though many survived despite the oppression). Over the years, there was to be increased intermarriage between Europeans and natives, and the creation of a more united society, but this took centuries to achieve. In the early days, only a few humane voices were raised, mainly by Spanish clergymen, to denounce the oppression. That they were ignored was only one indication of the indifference shown by Europe's colonizers to the well-being of other peoples as the empires were built.

For Spain's neighbors, the colonies were an object of envy because of their mineral wealth. In 1545 a major vein of silver was discovered at Potosí, in Bolivia, and from those mines came the treasure that made fortunes for the colonists, sustained Spain's many wars, and ultimately enriched much of Europe. For the balance of the sixteenth century, however, despite the efforts of other countries, Portugal and Spain remained the only conspicuous participants in Europe's overseas expansion.

THE LIFE OF THE SETTLERS

It took a great deal of determination to board one of the ships that set off across the oceans from Europe. Life at sea offered discomfort and peril: horrible overcrowding, inadequate and often rotting food, disease, dangerous storms, poor navigation, and threats from enemy ships. One cannot determine numbers precisely, but it has been estimated that in some decades of the sixteenth and seventeenth centuries, fewer than two-thirds of those who embarked reached their destination. And their troubles did not end when they came off the ships. Unfamiliar countries, famine, illness, and attacks by natives and European rivals made life precarious at best. Although 5000 people sailed for Virginia between 1619 and 1624, for instance, disease and massacre kept the colony the same size at the end of that period—about 1000 inhabitants—as it had been at the beginning. And yet, despite the difficulties and dangers, people found reasons to keep coming.

The Aims of the Colonists For a few leaders, like the Spanish minor nobles known as *hidalgos* who commanded most of Spain's first missions, the attraction was partly adventure, partly the chance to command a military expedition of con-

Map 14.2 EMPIRE AND SETTLEMENT IN THE AMERICAS, 1493–1610
The leadership of the Spaniards in expanding into the New World during the century following
the voyages of Columbus is apparent from the territories they dominated. The much smaller area
controlled by the Portuguese, the tentative activities of the English in Virginia, and the occasional
settlements of fishermen in Newfoundland, paled by comparison with the Spanish empire.

quest, and partly the hope of making a fortune which seemed unlikely at home. For another fairly small group, the clergy, the aim was to bring the word of God to people who had never encountered Christianity before. As for government officials and traders, they were usually just following orders, bringing overseas the activities and skills that had earned them their living in their native country. For these middle and upper levels of society, moreover, survival was rarely an issue: They might die in battle or from illness, and life may not have been as comfortable as it would have been at home, but the opportunities to exercise power or to make a fortune were far greater. The outlook was very different for the vast majority of those who populated the new settlements.

For most of the settlers, leaving Europe was a fairly desperate act, an indication that almost any alternative seemed preferable to the bleak prospects in their homeland. If it had not been for the growth of population in the sixteenth century—and the many thousands it made homeless, unable to remain in their villages or make a living in towns—it is unlikely that enough emigrants would have been found to do the work in ports and on the land that was crucial to the building of empires in Asia and America. It is significant that fewer people moved from a rich country like France than from the less prosperous Spain and Portugal. Despite the pressures that persuaded thousands of people to leave their homelands, therefore, additional means had to be found to populate the empires.

Long before the English colonized Australia with convicts in the eighteenth century, for example, they were taking people out of prison to send them overseas to places desperate for settlers. Another tactic was to offer land to anyone who was willing to work for others for seven years. The English, and to a lesser extent the French, permitted religious minorities who feared persecution at home to start a new and more independent existence in America. In general, powerful inducements like poverty or persecution were needed to drive Europeans to accept the hazards of the journey and the subsequent struggles of the pioneer. Some settlers, such as the religious refugees, set out as families, but usually many more men than

women made the voyage. In a society suspicious of single females, women had far more to risk by emigrating, and the chronic imbalance between genders became yet another hardship of life overseas.

Exploitation When even distress at home provided too few volunteers, the colonizers relied on force to obtain the workers they needed. Just as captains often kidnapped men for a ship's crew, so, too, did the suppliers of settlers. Many woke up at sea surprised to find where they were. And once in the colonies, wage earners could expect their employment to be harsh. Indigenous populations, however, faced the most ruthless treatment: In South America millions died (estimates vary between 25 and 90 percent of the native peoples) as a result mainly of the diseases that accompanied the Europeans, though the susceptibility may have been made worse by the terrible conditions of forced labor and oppression. Even exploitation, however, was not enough to feed the insatiable need for miners, laborers, servants, and farmhands.

Slaves The solution the colonizers found was slavery, familiar since ancient times but virtually nonexistent among Europeans by 1500. To find the slaves, ships began visiting the west coast of Africa, where the local inhabitants were either captured or purchased from local rulers and then transported to the New World under the most ghastly conditions. They were thrown together in cramped, filthy quarters, often bound, barely fed, and beaten at the slightest provocation. Nor was there much improvement for those—often less than half—who survived the crossing. The slaves sustained the empires and made it possible for their white masters to profit from the silver, tobacco, cotton, and other goods they produced; but the grim conditions of their lives, and their high rates of mortality, would have wiped them out if there had not been a constant stream of slaves from Africa to replenish their numbers.

For those settlers who reaped rewards from the mines and the agricultural products of America, or from the trade with Europe that enriched all the colonies, the hardships did not last long. They created flourishing cities and universities, and made huge fortunes. Their commercial net-

▶ **Slave Ship**
This picture, made aboard a slave ship, shows the dangerously crowded conditions in which Africans were brought to the New World. It is small wonder that so many of them died of disease even before the end of this miserable voyage.

works began to link the entire world together for the first time in history. But for the many who struggled to expand these empires, life on the frontier, despite the promise of new opportunities, remained hard and dangerous for centuries. And for the slaves, there was not the slightest improvement in conditions or even hope of improvement, until revolts and civil wars finally abolished slavery in the nineteenth century.

III. The Centralization of Political Power

THE "NEW MONARCHS"

The economic and social transformations that began around 1500 gained important support from the actions of central governments. Especially in England, France, and Spain, rulers gave vital en-

couragement to the growth of trade, overseas expansion, and attempts to relieve social distress. At the same time, the growing prosperity of the age enhanced the tax revenues that were essential to their power. Both of these mutually reinforcing developments had long-term effects, but it could be argued that the creation of well-organized states, built around strong central governments, was even more decisive than the economic boom in shaping the future of Western Europe.

The rulers of England, France, and Spain in the late fifteenth and early sixteenth centuries were especially successful in accumulating and centralizing power, and historians have therefore called them "new monarchs." The reigns of

Henry VII, Louis XI, and Ferdinand and Isabella, in particular, have come to be regarded as marking the end of more than a century of political fragmentation. They set in motion a revival of royal authority that eventually weakened all rivals to the crown and created the bureaucracies characteristic of the modern state.

TUDOR ENGLAND

The English monarchs had relied for centuries on local cooperation to run their kingdom. Unlike other European countries, England contained only 50 or 60 families who were legally nobles out of a population of perhaps 2.5 million. But many other families, though not technically members of the nobility, had large estates and were dominant figures at the parish, county, and even national levels. They were known as *gentry*, and it was from their ranks that the crown appointed the local officers who administered the realm—notably the justices of the peace (usually referred to as JPs). These voluntary unpaid officials served as the principal public servants in the more than 40 counties of the land.

For reasons of status as well as out of a feeling of responsibility, the gentry had always sought such appointments. From the crown's point of view, the great advantage of the system was its efficiency: Enforcement was in the hands of those who could enforce. As a "great man" in his neighborhood, the justice of the peace rarely had trouble exerting his authority. Thus, the king had at his disposal an administrative structure without rival in Europe because, unlike other rulers, he could count on the cooperation of the leaders of each locality. Since the gentry had been given so much responsibility, they had developed a strong sense of duty over the centuries, and the king had increasingly sought their advice.

Parliament and Common Law In the sixteenth century an institution that had developed from this relationship, Parliament, began to take on a general importance as the chief representative of the country's wishes; it was increasingly considered to be the only body that could give a ruler's actions a wider sanction than he could draw from his prerogatives alone. Although Parliament remained subordinate to the crown for a long time, England's kings already realized that they could not take such measures as raising extraordinary taxes without its consent.

Just as Parliament served to unify the country, so too did another ancient institution: the common law. This was a system of justice based on precedent and tradition that was the same, or "common," throughout England. In contrast to the Roman law that prevailed on the continent, common law grew out of the interpretations of precedent made by individual judges and the decisions of juries. A court could be dominated by local leaders, but in general this was a system of justice, administered by judges who traveled from area to area, that helped bind England together. Like Parliament, the common law would eventually be regarded by opponents of royal power as an independent source of authority with which the crown could not interfere. In the late 1400s, however, it was an important help to a king who was trying to overcome England's political fragmentation and forge a more unified realm.

HENRY VII

Henry VII (1485–1509), who founded the Tudor dynasty, came to the throne as a usurper in the aftermath of more than 30 years of civil conflict, the Wars of the Roses. England's nobles had caused chaos in these wars, and they had consistently ignored the wishes of the monarchy. The situation hardly looked promising for a reassertion of royal power. Yet Henry both extended the authority of the crown and restored order with extraordinary speed.

Finance His first concern was finance, because he knew that unless he had sufficient funds to run his government, his ability to control the nobles would remain uncertain. At the same time, he was aware that extra taxes were the surest way to alienate subjects who expected a king to "live of his own," that is, from the income his lands provided, from customs duties, and from the contributions he received at special times, such as the marriage of his daughter. It is a testimony to the care with which Henry nurtured his revenues that by the end of his reign he had paid off the crown's debts and accumulated a substantial reserve. His success came, first, from increases in the profits of justice—fees and fines—which also cowed unruly subjects. In addition, he improved his returns by putting collection and supervision of revenue in the hands of a small, efficient group of officials in his own household. Above all, it was by careful management, and avoidance of foreign entanglements, that he was able to "live of his own."

Restoring Order Where domestic order was concerned, the revival of royal authority was largely due to the energy of the king and his chief servants. Henry increased the powers of the justices of the peace, thus striking severely at the independence attained by leading nobles during the previous two centuries. Under his leadership, too, the royal Council became a far more active and influential body. Leading officials not only exercised executive powers but also resumed hearing legal appeals—a policy that further undermined the independence of gentry and nobles, who could dominate proceedings in local common law courts. When the royal councillors sat as a court (known as Star Chamber from the decorations on the ceiling of the room where they met), there was no jury, local lords had no influence, and decisions were quick and fair. Eventually, Star Chamber and other so-called royal courts (which derived their jurisdiction from the authority of the king himself) came to be seen as threats to England's traditional common law. Under the Tudors, however, they were accepted as highly effective means of restoring order and asserting the power of the central government.

HENRY VIII AND HIS SUCCESSORS

The first Tudor was a conservative, building up his authority and finances by applying vigorously the traditional methods and institutions that were available to a king. The young man who followed him on the throne, Henry VIII (1509–1547), was an arrogant, dazzling figure, a strong contrast to his careful father. In 1513 he removed a long-standing threat from England's north by inflicting a shattering defeat on an invading Scots army at Flodden. With his prestige thus enhanced, he spent the next 15 years taking little part in European affairs and consolidating royal power at home with the capable assistance of his chief minister, Cardinal Thomas Wolsey.

The Divorce This successful continuation of Henry VII's policies ended in 1529 when Wolsey fell from power, ruined by the king's wish for a divorce from his wife, who had failed to produce a male heir to continue the dynasty. Henry had married his brother's widow, Catherine of Aragon, under a special papal dispensation from the biblical law that normally prohibited a union between such close relatives. Obsessed with dynastic continuity—and infatuated with a young lady at court, Anne Boleyn—Henry urged Wolsey to ask the pope to declare the previous dispensation invalid. Under ordinary circumstances there would have been no trouble, but at this moment the pope was in the power of Charles V, the Holy Roman Emperor, who was also Catherine's nephew. When Wolsey's efforts to get papal approval for the divorce failed, Henry dismissed him and accused him of treason.

For three years thereafter the king kept trying to get the Church to grant him the divorce. He called Parliament and gave it free rein to express bitter anticlerical sentiments, he sought opinions in European universities in favor of the divorce, he attacked his own clergy for having bowed to Wolsey's authority, and he even extracted a vague recognition from the clergy of his position as "supreme lord" of the Church. Finally, he placed his confidence in Thomas Cromwell, a former servant of Wolsey's and, like Wolsey, a talented man from a humble background who had risen rapidly in royal service. Cromwell suggested a radical but simple solution: that Henry break with the pope, declare himself supreme head of the Church, and divorce Catherine on his own authority. The king agreed, thus unleashing a revolution that dramatically increased the powers of the royal government. At the same time, although he himself had written a book attacking Martin Luther, Henry established the Reformation in England. By identifying his kingdom with Europe's Protestants, in opposition to the Catholics, Henry gave his subjects an emotional cause that eventually stimulated a sense of national pride.

The Reformation Parliament The instrument chosen to accomplish the break with Rome was Parliament, the only body capable of giving the move legal sanction and an aura of national approval. Henry called the assembly in 1529 and did not dissolve it until 1536. During its sessions it acted on more matters of importance than a Parliament had ever considered before. It forbade litigants from making ecclesiastical appeals to Rome, thus allowing Henry to obtain his divorce and remarry, and in 1534 it took the decisive step: It declared the king supreme head of the Church in England, thus bringing to an end over 1000 years of papal supremacy (*see box,* below). Royal power gained enormously from these acts, but so, too, did the stature of Parliament, thanks to its new responsibilities and the length of its sessions.

Previously, election to Parliament had been considered a chore by the townsmen and landed gentry in the House of Commons, who found the expense of unpaid attendance and the time it took more irksome than did the wealthy nobles in the House of Lords (so named during Henry VIII's reign). But this attitude began to change in the 1530s as members of the Commons, returning to successive sessions, came to know one another

and to regard themselves as guardians of Parliament's traditions and privileges. Eventually, they were to make the Commons the dominant house in Parliament.

Royal Power Following his successful suggestion for solving Henry's conflict with Rome, Thomas Cromwell became the king's chief minister. He was a tireless bureaucrat, who reorganized the administration of the country into six departments, each with specific functions, and took the chief executive position, the secretaryship. At the same time, a Privy Council, consisting of the king's principal advisers, was created to coordinate and direct royal administration.

The principal beneficiary of the events of the 1530s was the crown. Royal income rose markedly when Henry became head of the English Church and took over the ecclesiastical fees that previously had gone to the pope. He gained an even larger windfall when he dissolved all Eng-

Henry VIII Claims Independence from the Pope

One of the crucial acts of Parliament through which Henry VIII made the Church of England independent of Rome was the so-called Act in Restraint of Appeals, which became law in 1533. This law forbade Englishmen from appealing court decisions to Rome, which they had been allowed to do when the pope was accepted as the supreme authority. To justify this action, the preamble of the act made a claim for the independence of England and the authority of the king that was typical of the new monarchs of the age.

"Where by divers sundry old authentic histories and chronicles it is manifestly declared that this realm of England is an empire, governed by one supreme head and king, having the dignity and royal estate of the imperial crown of the same, unto whom a body politic be bound and owe next to God a natural and humble obedience; he being also furnished by the goodness of Almighty God with whole and entire power, preeminence, authority, prerogative and jurisdiction to render justice and final determination in all causes, debates and contentions, without restraint to any foreign princes, [and] without the intermeddling of any exterior person, to declare and determine all such doubts. In consideration whereof the King's Highness, his Nobles and Commons, enact, establish and ordain that all causes, already commenced or hereafter coming into contention within this realm or within any of the King's dominions, whether they concern the King our sovereign lord or any other subject, shall be from henceforth heard, examined, discussed, finally and definitely adjudged and determined within the King's jurisdiction and authority and not elsewhere."

From 24 Henry VIII, c. 12, as printed in *Statutes of the Realm,* 11 vols. (London, 1810–1828), vol. III, pp. 427–429.

lish monasteries and confiscated their immensely valuable lands, which were sold over the next few decades. The result was that fortunes were made by speculators, and new families rose to prominence as major landowners.

For all the stimulus he gave to parliamentary power, Henry now had a much larger, wealthier, and more sophisticated administration at his disposal; and he left no doubt where ultimate authority lay. He did not establish a standing army, as some of the continental kings did, because he had no need for one. He was fully capable of intimidating ambitious nobles or crushing such uprisings as a 1536 revolt against the Reformation.

The English Church Where doctrine and the structure of the Church were concerned, Henry was a conservative; he allowed few changes in dogma or liturgy and seems to have hoped that he could simply continue the old ways, changing only the person at the head of the institution. He tried to restrain the spread of Reformation beliefs, which travelers and books brought into

► *Unknown Artist*
EDWARD VI AND THE POPE
The anti-Catholic feelings that began to grow in England during the reign of Edward VI are expressed in this painting. The young king sits on his throne. His father, Henry VIII, who started the Reformation in England, points to him as the victor over Catholicism. The crushing of the old faith is symbolized by Christ's conquering of the pope and monks (below) and the destruction of Roman churches and images (through the window).

England from the continent, and he persecuted heresy. But it proved impossible to do no more than expel the papacy. Although many English men and women clung to tradition, others were drawn to the new religious ideas, and they pressured Henry to accept Protestant doctrines. Followers of the fourteenth-century reformer John Wycliffe, known as Lollards, had kept his ideas alive, and they now joined forces with Protestants inspired by continental reformers to demand services in English and easier access to Scripture. New translations of the Bible appeared in the 1530s, as did echoes of the opposition to clerical privilege that had swept Protestant areas on the continent. Perhaps realizing that the pressure would only grow, Henry had his son, Edward, tutored by a committed reformer.

Edward VI and Mary I During the reign of that son, Edward VI (1547–1553), who died while still a minor, the nobility attempted to regain control of the government. There was a relaxation of central authority, and the Reformation advanced rapidly. But Edward's half-sister, Mary I, reestablished Roman Catholicism as England's official religion when she became queen in 1553, forcing many of her subjects into exile and provoking two major revolts during her five-year reign. Royal power, however, was now strong enough to survive both the nobles' ambitions and the revolts. The revival of the nobles was short-lived, and Mary's death, in 1558, brought an end to the reversal of religions. She was succeeded by Henry VIII's last surviving child, Elizabeth, who demonstrated that the growth of the monarchy's authority had been but briefly interrupted under Edward and Mary.

VALOIS FRANCE

The rulers of France in the fifteenth century, unlike their English counterparts, lacked a well-formed organization for local government. Aristocrats dominated many regions, particularly those farthest from Paris, and great nobles had become virtually independent rulers. They had their own administrations and often their own courts and taxation, leaving the crown little say in their affairs. The size of the kingdom also placed restraints on royal power; it took more than a week to travel from Paris to the remoter parts of the realm—almost double the time for the equivalent English journey. Delays of this nature inevitably hampered central authority.

The monarchy had tried to resolve the problem of ruling distant provinces by granting to close relatives large blocs of territory that the crown seized or inherited. Theoretically, these relatives would devote full attention to their lands and execute royal wishes more effectively than the king could from Paris. In practice, however, an ambitious family member often became

just as difficult to handle as any powerful noble. After 1469 the crown kept control over such acquisitions—an indication that it now had the resources to exercise authority even in areas far from the capital.

Royal Government The administrative center of the government in Paris was the royal council and its chief departments: the Chancery, which had charge of all formal documents, and the Treasury. The greatest court of law in the land was the Parlement of Paris, which had remained a judicial body, unlike the English Parliament, and whose members were appointed by the crown. As the central administration grew in the fifteenth and early sixteenth centuries, various provinces received their own parlements, a recognition of the continuing strength of the demand for local autonomy. But there was a countervailing force: the dominance of Roman law, which (unlike England's common law) was based on royal decree and which allowed the monarch to govern by issuing ordinances and edicts. These had to be registered by the parlements in order to take effect, but usually that was a formality.

Representative assemblies, known as Estates, also challenged the power of the throne. A number of provinces had such Estates, and they had to approve the level of taxation and other royal policies. But France's chief representative body, the Estates General—consisting of clergy, nobles, and townsmen from every region—never attained the prestige of the English Parliament and was never able to bind the country together or function as an essential organ of government.

For all the threats from nobles and assemblies, therefore, French kings had a degree of independence that English monarchs did not achieve, most notably in one critical area: finances. For centuries they had supplemented their main sources of income, from lands and customs duties, with special levies in the form of a sales tax (*aide*), a hearth tax (*taille*), and a salt tax (*gabelle*). Consequently the average French family that was subject to taxation (all nobles and many towns were exempt) usually bore a heavier burden than its English counterpart. In earlier days the consent of the localities had been required before such levies could be raised, but after 1451 the taxes could be collected on the king's authority alone, although he still had to negotiate the exact rate with provincial Estates and be careful not to go beyond what would seem reasonable to his subjects.

The Army The most decisive source of power available to the French king (unlike the English king) was his standing army. The upkeep of the troops accounted for more than half the royal expenditures in Louis XI's reign, mainly because their numbers grew as revenues increased. In the 1480s a force probably larger than 15,000 men, chiefly professional mercenaries and military-minded nobles, was held in permanent readiness every campaigning season from spring to fall. Because of the rising costs that were associated with the development of gunpowder weapons, only the central government could afford to maintain such an army. And the troops had to be billeted in various provinces, with support from the local Estates. As a result, the entire French population eventually bore the indirect burden of heavier taxation, while many regions of France had direct contact with royal soldiers. Although frequently short of pay, the troops were firmly under royal control and hence a vital device—rarely used, but always a threat—in the strengthening of royal authority.

LOUIS XI AND CHARLES VIII

When Louis XI (1461–1483) began his reign, he faced a situation as unpromising as that of Henry VII at his succession, for the country had just emerged from the Hundred Years' War and royal authority was generally ignored. English troops, which had been in France for most of the war, had finally departed in the 1450s; but a new and equally dangerous menace had arisen in the east: the conglomeration of territories assembled by successive dukes of Burgundy.

Burgundy By the 1460s this duke, though a vassal of the French crown in his southern holdings, was among the most powerful lords in Western Europe. He ruled a loosely organized dominion that stretched from the Low Countries to the Swiss Confederation, and his Burgundian capital, Dijon, had become a major cultural and political center. In 1474 Louis XI put together a coalition against Duke Charles the Bold, who had been at war with him for some seven years, and in 1477 Charles was killed in battle with the French king's Swiss allies. Louis then reannexed the duchy of Burgundy itself; but Mary, the duke's daughter, retained the Low Countries, which would later form part of the inheritance of her grandson, the Holy Roman Emperor Charles V.

Diplomacy The Burgundian lands added considerably to Louis' sphere of authority. His masterly maneuvering in the tortuous diplomacy of his day soon won him other territories; he was appropriately nicknamed "the Spider" because the prizes he caught in his web were the result of waiting or shrewd negotiation rather than victories on the battlefield. Such was the case at the beginning of his reign when, by a typical combination of force and fraud, he pried two provinces on his southern border away from Spain. Simple luck enlarged his realm as well: In 1481 he inherited the three large provinces of Anjou, Maine, and Provence. The result was that by the end of his reign, though government procedures had not noticeably changed, royal power had penetrated into massive areas where previously it had been unknown.

The Invasion of Italy Louis XI's son and successor, Charles VIII (1483–1498), was equally dedicated to increasing the territories under the Valois dynasty's command. In 1494, he led an army into Italy at the request of the duke of Milan, who was afraid of being attacked by Florence and Naples. After some initial successes the French settled into a prolonged struggle with the Habsburgs for control of the rich Italian peninsula. The conflicts lasted for 65 years, ending in defeat for the French. Although the Italian wars failed to satisfy the territorial ambitions of Charles and his successors, they provided an outlet and distraction for the restless French nobility and gave the monarchs, as commanders in time of war, an opportunity to consolidate royal power at home.

THE GROWTH OF GOVERNMENT POWER

After Charles VIII's reign, France's financial and administrative machinery grew in both size and

**Map 14.3 FRANCE IN THE FIFTEENTH
AND SIXTEENTH CENTURIES**
This map shows in detail the successive stages whereby the
monarchy extended its control throughout France.

effectiveness, largely because of the demands of the Italian wars. There was rarely enough money to support the adventure; the kings therefore relied heavily on loans from bankers, who sometimes shaped France's financial policies. At the same time, the crown made a determined effort to increase traditional royal revenues.

Taxes France was a rich country of 15 million people with the most fertile land in Europe; yet the financial needs of the monarch always outstripped his subjects' ability to pay. Nobles, many towns, royal officeholders, and the clergy were exempt from the *taille* and the *gabelle*. Thus the bulk of the taxes had to be raised from the very classes that had the least to give. Other means of raising revenue were therefore needed to supplement royal income. One solution was the sale of offices. Positions were sold in the administration, the parlements, and every branch of the bureaucracy to purchasers eager to obtain both the tax exemption and the considerable status (sometimes a title of nobility) that the offices bestowed. From modest and uncertain beginnings under Louis XII (1498–1515), the system widened steadily; by the end of the sixteenth century, the sale of offices provided the crown with one-twelfth of its revenues.

Many other rulers were adopting this device, and everywhere it had similar effects: It stimulated social mobility, creating dynasties of noble officeholders and a new administrative class; it caused a dramatic expansion of bureaucracies; and it encouraged corruption. The system spread most rapidly, and the effects were most noticeable in France, where the reign of Francis I (1515–1547) witnessed a major increase in the government's power as its servants multiplied. Francis tried hard to continue the expansion of royal control by launching expeditions into Italy, but in fact, he contributed more to the development of the crown's authority by his actions at home.

The Church One of the most remarkable of Francis' accomplishments was the power he gained over his formidable rival, the Church. He was highly successful in his Italian campaigns early in his reign, and he used the power he attained in Italy to persuade the pope in 1516 to give the crown the right to appoint all of France's bishops

and abbots. According to this agreement, the income a bishop earned during his first year in office still went to the Vatican, but in effect, Francis now controlled the French Church. Its enormous patronage was at his disposal, and he could use it to reward servants or raise money. Since he had reached an agreement with the pope, he did not need to break with Rome in order to obtain the authority over the clergy that Henry VIII was soon to achieve in England.

▶ *Anonymous Miniature*
FRANCIS I AND HIS COURT, FROM THE MANUSCRIPT OF ANTOINE MACAULT'S TRANSLATION OF DIODORUS SICULUS, CA. 1532
The splendor and the patronage of learning for which the "new monarchs" were known are evoked by this tiny painting of the French king. He sits at a table with his three sons, surrounded by his courtiers and listening to the author reading the very manuscript (a translation of an ancient Greek historian) that this picture illustrates.

The Advance of Centralization   In the 1520s Francis also began a major reorganization of the government. He legalized the sale of offices, and the purchasers gradually replaced local nobles as the administrators of the various regions of France. He also formed an inner council, more manageable than the large royal council, to act as the chief executive body of the realm. As part of this streamlining, in 1523 all tax-gathering and accounting responsibilities were centralized in one agency. Against the parlements, meanwhile, the king invoked the *lit de justice*, a prerogative that allowed him to appear in person before an assembly that was delaying the registration of any of his edicts or ordinances and declare them registered and therefore law. The Estates General was no threat because it did not meet between 1484 and 1560.

By the end of Francis' reign, royal power was stronger than ever before; but signs of disunity had begun to appear that would intensify in the years to come. The Reformation was making gains in the Holy Roman Empire, and one of its movements, Calvinism, was soon to cause religious divisions and social unrest in France. As the reign of Francis' son Henry II (1547–1559) came to a close, the Italian wars finally ended in a French defeat, badly damaging royal prestige. The civil wars that followed came perilously close to destroying all that France's kings had achieved during the previous 100 years.

UNITED SPAIN

The Iberian peninsula in the mid-fifteenth century was divided into three very different kingdoms. Portugal, with some 1.5 million inhabitants, was in the midst of its overseas expansion. Castile, in the center, with a population of more than 8 million, was the largest and richest area. Sheep farming was the basis of its prosperity, and its countryside was dominated by powerful nobles. Castile was the last kingdom still fighting Muslims on its southern frontier, and in this ceaseless crusade the nobles played a leading part. They had built up both a great chivalric tradition and considerable political strength as a result of their exploits, and their status was enhanced by the religious fervor that the long struggle had inspired. The third kingdom, Aragon, approximately the same size as Portugal, consisted of three areas: Catalonia, the heart of the kingdom and a great commercial region centered on the city of Barcelona; Aragon itself, which was little more than a barren hinterland to Catalonia; and Valencia, a farming and fishing region south of Catalonia along the Mediterranean coast.

In October 1469, Isabella, future queen of Castile, married Ferdinand, future king of Sicily and heir to the throne of Aragon. Realizing that the marriage would strengthen the crown, the Castilian nobles opposed the union, precipitating a 10-year civil war. But the two monarchs emerged victorious, and they created a new political entity: the Kingdom of Spain. They and their successors were to be as effective as the kings of England and France in centralizing power and establishing royal control over their realms.

FERDINAND AND ISABELLA

When Ferdinand and Isabella jointly assumed the thrones of Castile in 1474 and Aragon five years later, they made no attempt to create a monolithic state. Aragon remained a federation of territories, administered by viceroys who were appointed by the king but who allowed local customs to remain virtually intact. The traditions of governing by consent and preserving the subjects' rights were particularly strong in this kingdom, where each province had its own representative assembly, known as the Cortes. Ferdinand left the system untouched, but he did make the viceroys a permanent feature of the government and created a special council for Aragonese affairs, through which he controlled the kingdom. In Castile, however, the two monarchs were determined to assert their superiority over all possible rivals to their authority. Their immediate aims were to restore the order in the countryside that had been destroyed by civil war, much as it had been in England and France, and to reduce the power of the nobility.

The first objective was accomplished with the help of the Cortes of Castile, an assembly dominated by urban representatives who shared the wish for order because peace benefited trade. The Cortes established special tribunals to pursue and try criminals, and by the 1490s it had succeeded in ending the widespread lawlessness in the kingdom.

The Centralization of Power To reinforce their authority, Ferdinand and Isabella sharply reduced the number of great nobles in the royal council and overhauled the entire administration, particularly the financial agencies, applying the principle that ability, rather than social status, should determine appointments. As the bureaucracy spread, the *hidalgo*, a lesser aristocrat who was heavily dependent on royal favor, became increasingly important in government. Unlike the great nobles, whose enormous wealth was little affected by reforms that reduced their political role, the *hidalgos* were hurt when they lost their tax exemptions. The new livelihood they found was in the service of the crown, and they became essential figures in the centralization of power in Castile as well as in the overseas territories.

The monarchs achieved greater leverage over their nobles in the 1480s and 1490s, when they gained control of the aristocracy's rich and powerful military orders. These organizations, which served almost as independent armies, run by Castile's most important aristocratic families, gave allegiance primarily to their own elected leaders. To take over their leadership required assertiveness and determination, especially by Isabella, Castile's inherited ruler. At one point she rode on horseback for three straight days in order to get to one of the order's elections and control the outcome. The great nobles could not be subdued completely; nor did the king and queen wish to destroy their power, because they were essential servants of the crown, especially in the army and in the higher levels of government. But like the kings of England and France, Ferdinand and Isabella wanted to reduce the nobles' autonomy to a level that did not threaten central authority, and for that reason it was crucial that they overcame the independence of the military orders by 1500.

The Church The rulers also succeeded in weakening Spain's bishops and abbots, who were as strong and wealthy as leading nobles. When Ferdinand and Isabella finally destroyed the power of the Muslims in southern Castile in 1492, the pope granted the monarchy the right to make major ecclesiastical appointments in the newly won territory, and this right was extended to the New World shortly thereafter. During the reign of Ferdinand and Isabella's successor, Charles I, the monarchy gained complete control over Church appointments, making Spain more independent of Rome than any other Catholic state.

Royal Administration Mastery over the towns and the Cortes of Castile proved easy to achieve. Where local rule was concerned, a minor royal officials, the *corregidor*, was given new powers and a position of responsibility within the administrative hierarchy. He was usually a *hidalgo*, and he became the chief executive and judicial officer in his region, rather like the justice of the peace in England; he also supervised town affairs. No major local decisions, such as the number of soldiers to be sent to the army, could be made without his (and hence royal) approval. The Cortes did not seriously restrict the crown because Spanish taxes, like French, could be raised without consent. The Castilian assembly met frequently and even provided additional funds for foreign wars, but it never challenged royal supremacy during this reign.

The king and queen supervised the system of justice directly, hearing cases personally once a week. As was true of most Roman law systems, all law was considered to come from the throne, and the monarchs had full power to overrule the decisions of local courts, often run by nobles. Centralized judicial machinery began to appear, and in a few decades Castilian law was organized into a uniform code—always a landmark in the stabilization of a state. The code remained in effect for centuries and was a tribute to the determination and effectiveness with which the crown had centralized its dominions.

Revenues Considering the anarchy at the start of their reign and the absence of central institutions, Ferdinand and Isabella performed greater wonders in establishing royal power than did any of the other new monarchs. A good index of the effectiveness of their growing bureaucracy is the increase in their revenues. As soon as the main administrative reforms were completed in the 1490s, the yield of the sales tax (the *alcabala*), which was the mainstay of royal income, began to rise dramatically. Total annual revenue is estimated to have soared from 80,000 ducats in 1474 to 2.3 million by 1504, the year Isabella died.

Religion   Religious affairs, too, helped in the consolidation of royal authority. After the civil wars in Castile ended in 1479, the two monarchs sought to drive the Muslims from southern Castile. The reasons for the aggressive policy were clear: First, it complemented the drive for centralized power; second, war was a traditional interest for ambitious rulers, and it helped keep restless nobles occupied; and finally, the crusade stimulated the country's religious fervor, which in turn promoted enthusiasm for its rulers.

The religious zeal aroused by the fight with the Muslims intensified Spaniards' loyalty toward their rulers, and it is not surprising that the monarchy sought religious uniformity as a means of strengthening political uniformity. Nor did the campaign come to an end when the last Muslim stronghold in the south, Granada, capitulated in 1492. Later that year, all Jews were expelled from Spain. Some 150,000 of the country's most enterprising people—including prominent doctors, government officials, and other leaders of economic and cultural life—departed overnight. For rulers who sought all means to win their subjects' loyalty, there was much to be gained by targeting a visible and often persecuted minority; it was a popular move, and it stimulated the religious passion that helped sustain the crown's authority. The campaign against the Jews thus went hand in hand with the other efforts to extend royal power.

The Inquisition   The same drive to consolidate their strength had prompted Ferdinand and Isabella to obtain permission from the pope in 1478 to establish their own Inquisition. Since 1483 this body had been run by a royal council and given a mandate to root out Marranos and Moriscos—Jews and Muslims who, usually under coercion, had pretended to accept Christianity but, in fact, retained their original beliefs. After the fall of Granada, the Spanish Church attempted to convert the conquered Muslims, and in 1502 those who had not accepted Christianity were expelled from the country. Nonetheless suspected Moriscos and Marranos kept the Inquisition busy. The persecution welded the country into a religious

unity that paralleled and supported the political centralization achieved by the monarchy. Religious policy was thus as much an instrument of political power as it was of ideological conformity.

FOREIGN AFFAIRS

The fall of Granada extended Spain's dominion southward, but there were also lands to be captured to the north and east. This undertaking was Ferdinand's responsibility, because men took command in war, and he focused on foreign affairs during the 12 years he ruled on his own after Isabella's death in 1504. His first success had come in 1493, when he regained the two provinces on the French border that Louis XI had taken 30 years before. Two years later, fearful that France's Italian invasion might threaten his Kingdom of Sicily, Ferdinand entered the war in Italy.

His achievements in the next two decades were due to a combination of military and diplomatic skills unusual even among the highly capable rulers of the age. A reorganization of Spain's standing army made it the most effective in Europe, and it soon achieved a commanding presence in Italy: By 1504 it had conquered Naples, and Spain had become a major power in the peninsula. Ferdinand also founded the finest diplomatic service of the sixteenth century, centered on five permanent embassies: at Rome, Venice, London, Brussels, and the Habsburg court. The ambassadors' reports and activities made him the best-informed and most effective maneuverer in the international politics of his reign.

Thus by the time of his death in 1516, the united Spain that he and Isabella created had gained both territory and authority at home and international power abroad. The successor to the throne inherited a monarchy fully as dynamic and as triumphant over its rivals as those of England and France.

CHARLES V, HOLY ROMAN EMPEROR

To bolster their dynasty, Ferdinand and Isabella had married their children to members of the leading families of Europe. Their daughter Joanna became the wife of the Habsburg Archduke Philip of Austria, and her son Charles became in turn heir to both the royal throne of Spain and the Habsburg dukedom.

The Revolt of the Communes Early in his reign as King of Spain, however, Charles (1516–1556) had to withstand a major onslaught on the crown's position. Educated in Flanders, he spoke no Castilian, and when he arrived in Spain late in 1517, he soon aroused the resentment of the local nobility, particularly when members of the large Flemish entourage he brought with him were given positions in the government. The young king stayed for two and a half years, during which time he was elected emperor of the Holy Roman Empire (1519). This enhanced his prestige, but it also intensified his subjects' fears that he would become an absentee ruler with little interest in their affairs. The Cortes, in particular, showed open hostility when Charles requested additional tax funds so that he could leave the country with Spanish troops to pursue his Europe-wide ambitions. As soon as he left in 1520, revolts began to break out in Spain's towns, and the risings of these communes racked the country for two years. The troubles Charles now endured were among the first of many major clashes during the next 150 years between the traditional dynastic aims of the leading European monarchs and the jealous sense of distinctiveness felt by their subjects.

Fortunately for the crown, the communes lacked clear aims; their resentments and hopes were deep but vague. They wanted to reverse the growth of royal power and to restore their traditional autonomy—a grievance that central governments were bound to encounter as they extended their authority. To this end, the communes asked for the removal of Flemish royal officials and a reduction in taxation, and at first they had the strong sympathy of the Spanish nobles, who particularly disliked the foreign ruler. But the movement soon revealed other aims, with social overtones: The communes launched attacks on the privileged orders of society, especially the nobility, and this lost the revolt its only chance for success. For the nobles now turned against the communes and defeated them in battle even before Charles returned to Spain.

Imperial Ambitions The king took warning from the uprisings and made sure that his administration was now kept entirely in Spanish hands. As calm returned, his subjects could channel their energies into imperial missions overseas, where the conquest of Mexico was under way, and against the Ottoman Turks in the Mediterranean. As in France, foreign excursions brought a monarch peace at home.

The one notable extension of royal power during Charles's reign was the large empire Spaniards were establishing in Central and South America. Closer to home, however, there was little that gave him or his Spanish subjects cause for pleasure. As Holy Roman Emperor, Charles was the official ruler of almost all of continental Europe west of Poland and the Balkans, with the major exception of France; and although his real power in the Empire was limited, he was almost ceaselessly at war defending his territories. In the Spaniards' view, most of the wars helped Charles's ambitions as emperor and were thus irrelevant to Spain. As far as they were concerned, aside from the widening acquisitions in the New World, Charles did little to further the expansion started by Ferdinand and Isabella.

Royal Government The recurrent crises and wars outside of Spain kept Charles away from his kingdom for more than two-thirds of his 40-year reign. He relied, during these absences, on a highly talented administrator, Francisco de los Cobos, who shaped and clarified the government's policies. De los Cobos confirmed the supremacy of the crown by enlarging the bureaucracy and elaborating the system of councils that Ferdinand and Isabella had begun. In the 1520s this structure, which was to survive for centuries, received its final form.

There were two types of council. One was responsible for each of the departments of the government: finance, war, the Inquisition, and so on. The other supervised each of the territories ruled by the crown: Aragon, Castile, Italy, the Indies, and (later in the century) the Low Countries. At the head of this system was the Council of State, the principal advisory group, consisting of leading officials from the lower councils. All these councils reported to the king or to his chief ministers, but since each one controlled its own bureaucracy, they were perfectly capable of running the empire in the monarch's absence.

Map 14.4 THE EMPIRE OF CHARLES V
This map indicates both the vastness of Charles's empire and the extent of the fighting in which he became involved. Almost every battle his troops fought—against Spanish communes, German Protestants, the Turks, and the French—is included so as to show the full measure of the emperor's never-ending ordeal.

What emerged was a vast federation, with Castile at its heart but with the parts, though directed from the center, allowed considerable autonomy. A viceroy in every major area (there were nine altogether from Naples to Peru) ran the administration under the supervision of the *audiencia*—the territorial council—and while on the whole these officials were left to do as they wished, they had to report to Castile in minute detail at regular intervals and refer major decisions to the central government.

The Bureaucracy Although corruption was widespread and slow communications (it took over eight months to send a message from Castile to Peru) made the system unwieldy, the centralization gave the monarch the power he wanted. The huge bureaucracy was carefully staffed with *hidalgos* and townsmen, while great nobles were given viceroyalties or high army posts. Some local initiative was allowed, but through the hierarchy of loyal servants the crown could exercise full control. As a result, Spain's administrative machine was one of the most remarkably detailed (if not always efficient) structures ever devised for ruling so vast an empire.

THE FINANCIAL TOLL OF WAR

The only serious strain on Charles's monarchy was financial, the result of the Habsburgs' constant wars. A large portion of the money for the fighting came from Italy and the Low Countries, but Spain had to pay a growing share of the costs. During the sixteenth century, the Spaniards increasingly resented the siphoning away of their funds into foreign wars. It was the tragedy of their century of glory that so much of the fantastic wealth they discovered in South America was exported for hostilities that brought them little benefit.

The burden was by no means equally distributed. The more independent Cortes of Aragon was able to prevent substantial increases in taxation, which meant that Castile had to assume the brunt of the payments. To some extent this was balanced by a monopoly of trade with the New World that was granted to the inhabitants of Castile, but in the next century the basic inequality among different Spanish regions would lead to civil war.

New World Trade Charles's finances were saved from disaster only by the influx of treasure—mainly silver—from America. Approximately 40 percent of the bullion went into the royal coffers, while the rest was taken by merchants (mainly Genoese) in the Castilian port of Seville, which was the only city where ships carrying goods to and from America were permitted to load and unload. Charles was receiving some 800,000 ducats' worth of treasure each year by the end of his reign. Unfortunately, it was always mortgaged in advance to the Italian and German bankers whose loans sustained his armies.

The country and the monarchy faced increasing difficulties as the wars continued for more than a century and a half. Seville's monopoly on shipping prevented the rest of the nation from gaining a share of the new wealth, and foreigners—notably the Italian and German financiers—came to dominate its economy and its commerce.

Spain was squeezed dry by the king's financial demands, yet he only just kept his head above water. In 1557, early in the reign of Charles's successor, Philip II, the monarchy had to declare itself bankrupt, a self-defeating evasion of its mammoth debts that it had to repeat seven times in the next 125 years. There has never been a better example of the way that ceaseless war can sap the strength of even the most formidable nation.

IV. The Splintered States

THE HOLY ROMAN EMPIRE

If in England, France, and Spain the authority of kings had begun to replace that of the local lord, to the east of these three kingdoms such centralization advanced fitfully and only within small states. Especially in the largest of these territories, the Holy Roman Empire, weak institutions prevented the emergence of a strong central government. Members of the leading family of Central Europe, the Habsburgs, had been elected to the imperial throne since the thirteenth century, but they lacked the authority and machinery to halt the fragmentation of this large territory; indeed, except for their own personal domain in the southeast of the empire, they ruled most areas and princes in name only. In addition to about 2000 imperial knights, some of whom owned no more than four or five acres, there were 50 ecclesiastical and 30 secular princes, more than 100 counts, some 70 prelates, and 66 cities, all virtually independent politically though officially subordinate to the emperor.

Local Independence The princes, whose territories comprised most of the area of the Holy Roman Empire, rarely had any trouble resisting the emperor's claims; their main concern was to increase their own power at the expense of their subjects, other princes, and the cities. The cities themselves also refused to remain subordinate to a central government. In 1500, 50 of them contained more than 2000 inhabitants—a sizable number for this time—and 20 had over 10,000. Their wealth was substantial because many were situated along a densely traveled trade artery, the

▶ *Hartmann Schedel*
The Nuremberg Chronicle, 1493
This lavishly illustrated book, a history of the world since the creation, is one of the earliest masterpieces of the printer's art. It took about four years to produce and contains dozens of elaborate woodcuts, most of which are recognizable views of European cities. This one depicts the proud and independent German city where the book was printed, Nuremberg, a major center of art and craftsmanship.

Rhine River, and many were also political powers. But their fierce independence meant that the emperor could rarely tap their wealth or the services of their inhabitants.

The only central institution alongside the emperor was the Diet, which consisted of three assemblies: representatives of the cities, the princes, and the electors (the seven princes, including three archbishops, who elected each new emperor). Given this makeup, the Diet became in effect the instrument of the princes; with its legislation they secured their position against the cities and the lesser nobility within their own domains.

By the end of the fifteenth century, most of the princes had achieved considerable control over their own territories. Their success paralleled the accomplishments of monarchs in England, France, and Spain except that the units were much smaller. Although the Habsburgs tried to develop strong central authority, they exercised significant control only over their personal domain, which in 1500 consisted of Austria, the Low Countries, and Franche-Comté. To the rulers of other states of the empire, they were feudal overlords in theory but powerless in practice.

Attempts at Centralization Nevertheless, the need for effective central institutions was recognized in the late fifteenth century, especially in the west and southwest of the Holy Roman Empire. In 1495 the emperor created a tribunal to settle disputes between local powers. Controlled and financed by the princes, the chief beneficiaries of its work, it made considerable headway toward ending the lawlessness that had marked the fifteenth century—an achievement similar to the restoration of order in France, Spain, and England at the same time. The tribunal's use of Roman law had a wide influence on legislation and justice throughout the empire, but again only to the advantage of the princes, who interpreted its endorsement of a leader's authority as referring only to themselves.

Other attempts at administrative reform had little effect, as ecclesiastical and secular princes tightened their hold on the multitude of territories that constituted the empire. The religious dissensions of the Reformation worsened the rivalries, dividing the empire and making Charles V no more than the leader of one party, incapable of asserting his authority over his opponents. The sheer number of Charles's commitments repeatedly diverted him, but even when he won decisive military victories, he could not break the empire's long tradition of local independence. His dream had been to revive the sweeping imperial grandeur of an Augustus or a Charlemagne, and his failure brought to an end the thousand-year ambition to restore in Europe the power of ancient Rome.

▶ *Titian*
Charles V at the Battle of Mühlberg, 1548
Because a statue of an ancient Roman emperor showed him in this pose, it was thought in the sixteenth century that a ruler appeared at his most magnificent on a horse and in full armor. Equestrian sculptures appeared in the fifteenth century, but this portrait is the first such painting. Titian created a heroic Charles V, even though the emperor had not been present at the military victory of the previous year that the picture celebrates.

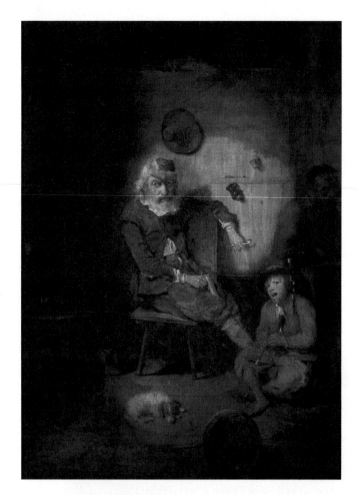

▷ *Christoph Paudiss*
PEASANTS IN A HUT
**The sadness in the eyes of these two figures, even
in a relaxed moment—the old man smoking a pipe,
the boy playing the bagpipes—reflects the
hardships of the peasants who were at the lowest
level of European society and in eastern Europe
were bound to the land as serfs.**

EASTERN EUROPE

Hungary   In the late fifteenth century, the dominant force in Eastern and Central Europe was the Kingdom of Hungary, ruled by Matthias Corvinus (1458–1490). He was in the mold of the other new monarchs of the day: He restrained the great nobles, expanded and centralized his administration, dramatically increased the yield of taxation, and established a standing army. The king's power thus grew spectacularly both at home and abroad. He gained Bohemia and some German and Austrian lands, and he made Vienna his capital in 1485.

Immediately after Matthias' death, however, royal authority collapsed. To gain Habsburg recognition of his right to the throne, his successor Ladislas II (1490–1516) gave up the conquests of Austrian and German territories and married his children to Habsburgs. This retreat provided the nobles of Hungary with an issue over which to reassert their position. First, by refusing the king essential financial support, they forced him to dissolve the standing army. Then, following a major peasant revolt against increasing repression by landowners, the nobles imposed serfdom on all peasants in 1514 at a meeting of the Hungarian Diet, the governing body, which was controlled by the aristocracy. Finally, they became the major beneficiaries of the conquest of Hungary by the Ottoman Empire over the next 30 years. That empire always supported any local leader who promised allegiance to Constantinople; by affirming loyalty to their new masters, the nobles were able to strengthen their power at the expense of both the old monarchy and the peasantry. By the middle of the sixteenth century, a revival of central authority had become impossible.

The Fragmentation of Poland   Royal power in Poland began to decline in the 1490s, when the king was forced to rely on the lesser nobles to help him against the greater nobility. In return, he issued a statute in 1496 that strengthened the lower aristocrats against those below them, the townsmen and the peasants. The latter became virtual serfs, forbidden to buy land and deprived of freedom of movement. Once that was accomplished, the nobles united against the king. In 1505 the national Diet, consisting only of nobles, was made the supreme body of the land, and shortly thereafter it established serfdom officially. Since no law could now be passed without the Diet's consent, the crown's central authority was severely limited.

Royal and noble patronage produced a great cultural flowering around 1500 in Poland, which became an active center of Renaissance humanism and scholarship, most famously represented by the astronomer Nicolaus Copernicus. Yet the monarchy was losing influence steadily, as was revealed by the failure of its attempts to found a standing army. At the end of Sigismund II's reign (1548–1572), his kingdom was the largest in Europe; but his death ended the Jagellon dynasty, which had ruled the country for centuries. The Diet immediately made sure that succession to the crown, which technically had always been elective and in the hands of the nobles, would now depend entirely on their approval. Thus the aristocracy confirmed both its own dominance and the ineffectiveness of royal authority.

The Aristocracy   The political and social processes at work in Eastern and Central Europe thus contrasted starkly with developments in England, France, and Spain in this period. Nevertheless, although the trend was toward fragmentation in the East, one class, the aristocracy, did share the vigor and organizational ability that in the West was displayed by kings and queens. To that extent, therefore, the sense of renewed vitality in Europe during these years, spurred by economic and demographic growth, was also visible outside the borders of the new monarchies. But where nobles dominated, countries lost ground in the fierce competition of international affairs.

The Ottomans   Only in one state in Eastern Europe was strong central authority maintained in the sixteenth century: the Ottoman Empire. From his capital in Constantinople the sultan exercised unparalleled powers throughout the eastern Mediterranean and North Africa. He had a crack army of more than 25,000 men, who stood ready to serve him at all times, and within his domains his supremacy was unquestioned. He was both spiritual and temporal head of his empire, completely free to appoint all officers, issue laws, and raise taxes. But these powers, geared to military conquest and extending over enormous territories, never became a focus of cohesion among the disparate races of the Balkans, the Middle East, and North Africa, because the sultan left authority in the hands of local nobles and princes as long as his ultimate sovereignty was recognized. Whenever questions of loyalty arose (as they did sporadically in the Balkans), they revealed that the authority of the central government rested on its military might. That was more than enough,

though, to prevent any serious challenges to the power of the Ottomans until they began to lose ground to the Habsburgs in the eighteenth century.

The first signs of weakening at the center began to appear after the death in 1566 of the sultan whose conquests brought the empire to its largest size, Suleiman the Great. Suleiman had gained control of the Balkans with a victory at Mohacs in 1526, and he had even briefly laid siege to Vienna in 1529. Under his successors, the determined exercise of authority that had marked his rule began to decline; and harem intrigues, corruption at court, and the loosening of military discipline became increasingly serious. Yet the Ottomans remained an object of fear and hostility throughout the West—a constant threat to Central Europe from the Balkans and, despite naval setbacks, a formidable force in the eastern Mediterranean.

ITALY

Italy, the cultural and economic leader of Europe, had developed a unique political structure during the Renaissance. In the fifteenth century the five major states—Naples, the Papal States, Milan, Florence, and Venice—established a balance among themselves that was preserved without serious disruption from the 1450s to the 1490s. This long period of peace was finally broken in 1494, when Milan, abandoning a long tradition of the Italians settling problems among themselves, asked Charles VIII of France to help protect it against Florence and Naples. Thus began the Italian wars, which soon revealed that these relatively small territories were totally incapable of resisting the force that newly assertive monarchies could bring to bear.

Venice and Florence had long been regarded by Europeans as model republics—reincarnations of Classical city-states and centers of freedom governed with the consent of their citizens. In truth, Venice was controlled by a small merchant oligarchy and Florence by the Medici family, but the image of republican virtue was still widely accepted. Indeed, the political stability Venice had maintained for centuries was the envy of Europe. Tourists came not only to enjoy its many relaxations and entertainments but also

**Map 14.5 THE GROWTH OF THE OTTOMAN EMPIRE UNDER
SULEIMAN THE GREAT, 1520–1566**
The remarkable conquests of the Ottomans in North Africa,
the Middle East, and the Balkans terrified the rulers of Central
and Eastern Europe. Only the failure of the siege of
Vienna in 1529 halted the advance into Europe.

National Gallery, London

to marvel at the institutions that kept the city calm, powerful, and rich. Venice's leaders, elegant patricians who patronized some of the most sought-after artists of the sixteenth century, such as Titian, were thought of as the heirs of Roman senators. Throughout Europe, the Italians were regarded as masters not only of politics but also of culture and manners.

The Italian Wars It was a considerable shock, therefore, when the Italian states crumbled before the onslaught of French and then Spanish and Habsburg armies. Charles VIII's invasion led to the expulsion of the Medici from Florence in 1494 and the establishment of a new Florentine republic, but in 1512 the family engineered a return to power with the help of Ferdinand of Aragon, and eventually the Habsburgs set up the Medici as hereditary dukes of Tuscany. Ferdinand annexed Naples in 1504, and Emperor Charles V ultimately took over Milan. When the fighting ended in 1559, the Habsburgs controlled Italy and

▶ *Titian*
THE VENDRAMIN FAMILY, 1547
The magnificence of the patrician families who ruled Venice is celebrated in this group portrait. Ostensibly, they are worshiping a relic of the true cross, but in fact they are displaying the hierarchy that rules their lives. Only men appear, dominated by the head of the family and his aged father, followed by his eldest son and heir, all of whom convey an image of wealth and power.

would do so for the next century. Only Venice, Tuscany under the Medici, and the Papal States remained relatively independent—though Venice was no longer a force in European affairs after a series of defeats. The one major local beneficiary of the Italian wars was the papacy, as Julius II (1503–1513), known as the Warrior Pope, carved out a new papal territory in central and eastern Italy by force of arms.

The critical lesson of these disastrous events was that small political units could not survive in an age when governments were consolidating their authority in large kingdoms. No matter how brilliant and sophisticated, a compact city-state could not withstand such superior force. Italy's cultural and economic prominence faded only slowly, but by the mid-sixteenth century, except for the papacy, the international standing of its states was fading.

V. The New Statecraft

INTERNATIONAL RELATIONS

The Italian states of the fifteenth century, in their intensive political struggles and competition with one another, developed various new ways of pursuing foreign policy. During the Italian wars these techniques spread throughout Europe and caused a revolution in diplomacy. Any state hoping to play a prominent role in international affairs worked under a serious disadvantage if it did not conform. The Italians' essential innovation was the resident ambassador. Previously rulers had dispatched ambassadors to other states only for specific missions, such as to arrange an alliance, declare war, or deliver a message; but from the sixteenth century on, important states maintained representatives in every major capital or court at all times. The permanent ambassador could keep the home government informed of the latest local and international developments and could also move without delay to protect his country's interests. The Venetians, in particular, were masters of the new diplomacy. Leading patricians served as ambassadors, and they sent home brilliant political analyses that have remained crucial sources for historians ever since.

The New Diplomacy As states established embassies, procedures and organization became more sophisticated: A primitive system of diplomatic immunities (including freedom from prosecution for ambassadors and their households) evolved, formal protocol developed, and embassy officials were assigned different levels of responsibility and importance. Many advances were still to come, but by 1550 the outlines of the new diplomacy were already visible—yet an-

other reflection of the growing powers and ambitions of central governments.

The great dividing line between older arrangements and the new diplomacy was the Italian wars, a Europe-wide crisis that involved rulers as distant as the English King Henry VIII and the Ottoman Sultan Suleiman II. Gradually all states recognized that it was in everybody's interest not to allow one power to dominate the rest. In later years this prevention of excessive aggression was to be known as the balance of power, but by the mid-sixteenth century the idea was already affecting alliances and peace treaties.

MACHIAVELLI AND GUICCIARDINI

As the Italian wars unfolded, political commentators began to seek theoretical explanations for the new authority and aggressiveness of rulers and the collapse of the Italian city-states. Turning from arguments based on divine will or contractual law, they treated effective government as an end in itself. The first full expression of these views came from the Italians, the pioneers of the methods and attitudes that were revolutionizing politics. When their small states proved unable to resist the superior forces of France and Spain, just as the ancient Greek city-states had succumbed to Macedonia and then to Rome, the Italians naturally wanted to find out why. The most disturbing answer was given by an experienced diplomat, Niccolò Machiavelli, who was exiled when the Medici took control of Florence in 1512. Barred from politics and bitter over the collapse of Italy, he set about analyzing exactly how power is won, exercised, and lost.

Machiavelli The result, *The Prince*, is one of the few radically original books in history. To move from his predecessors to Machiavelli is to see legal and moral thought transformed. Machiavelli swept away conventions as he sought, in an age of collapsing regimes, to understand how states function and how they affect their subjects. If he came out of any tradition, it was the Renaissance fascination with method that had produced manuals on cooking, dancing, fencing, and manners. But he wrote about method in an area that had never previously been analyzed in this way: power.

IL PRINCIPE DI NICCHOLO MACHIA
VELLO AL MAGNIFICO LOREN-
ZO DI PIERO DE MEDICI.

LA VITA DI CASTRVCCIO CASTRA-
CANI DA LVCCA A ZANOBI BVON
DELMONTI ET A LVIGI ALEMAN-
NI DESCRITTA PER IL
MEDESIMO.

IL MODO CHE TENNE IL DVCA VA-
LENTINO PER AMMAZAR VITEL
LOZO, OLIVEROTTO DA FER-
MO IL.S.PAOLO ET IL DV
CA DI GRAVINA ORSI
NI IN SENIGAGLIA,
DESCRITTA PER
IL MEDESIMO.

Con Gratie, & Priuilegi di. N.S. Clemente
VII. & altri Principi, che intra il termino di. X.
Anni non si stampino, ne stampi si uendino:
sotto le pene, che in essi si contengono.
M. D. XXXII.

▶ TITLE PAGE OF THE FIRST EDITION OF NICCOLÒ MACHIAVELLI'S THE PRINCE, 1532
This deceptively simple and elegant title page begins the brief but revolutionary book by
which Machiavelli is usually remembered. It remained unpublished for nearly 20 years after
it was written (and for 5 years after its author's death), probably because of concern over the
stir it would cause. And indeed, within 25 years of appearing in print, *The Prince* was
deemed sufficiently ungodly to be added to the index of books that Catholics were
forbidden to read.

Machiavelli showed not why power does or should exist but how it works. In the form of advice to a prince and without reference to divine, legal, or natural justification, the book explains what a ruler needs to do to win and maintain complete control over his subjects. Machiavelli did not deny the force of religion or law; what concerned him was how they ought to be *used* in the tactics of governing—religion for molding unity and contentment, and devotion to law for building the ruler's reputation as a fair-minded person. *The Prince* outlines the methods to be used by conquerors or legitimate heirs, as well as the proper ways to deal with insurrection and the many other problems that rulers encounter. Fear and respect are the bases of their authority, and they must exercise care at all times not to relax their control over potential troublemakers or over their image among the people.

Very few contemporaries of Machiavelli dared openly to accept so harsh a view of politics, but he did not hesitate to expand his analysis in his other masterpiece, the *Discourses*. This book developed a cyclical theory of every government moving inexorably from tyranny to democracy and back again. His conclusion, drawn particularly from a study of Roman history, is that healthy government can be preserved only by the active participation of all citizens in the life of the state. And the state in turn, he suggested, is the force that keeps people civilized. As he put it in the *Discourses*, "Men act rightly only when compelled. The law makes men good." But there were better and worse states. Machiavelli took the Roman Republic as his ideal, and it was this model, together with his Italian patriotism (rather than his cynicism), that was largely responsible for his long-lasting influence on European political thought.

Guicciardini The *History of Italy*, written in the 1530s by another Florentine, Francesco Guicciardini, was the first major work of history to rely heavily on original documents rather than secondhand accounts. If the conclusions he reached seem dauntingly cynical—he attributed even less to underlying historical forces than did Machiavelli, and like Thucydides, he argued dispassionately that fate determines everything—the reasons for his pessimism are not far to seek. The actions of rulers during his generation hardly gave much room for optimism, and shrewd observers like Machiavelli and Guicciardini must therefore have found it difficult to avoid pessimism about public events.

It was appropriate that the political theorists of the sixteenth century should have emphasized the obsession with power that dominated the age in which they lived. The relentless pragmatism and ambition of kings and princes as they extended their authority both at home and abroad reshaped institutions and governments throughout Europe. Given the assertiveness of these rulers and the rising fanaticism generated by religious dispute, it is not surprising that there should have begun in the mid-sixteenth century a series of wars of a ferocity and destructiveness that Europe had never before seen.

Recommended Reading

▼

Sources

*Guicciardini, Francesco. *The History of Italy and Other Selected Writings*. Cecil Grayson (tr.). 1964.

*Machiavelli, Niccolò. *The Prince* and the *Discourses*. Luigi Ricci (tr.). 1950.

*Parry, J. H. (ed.). *The European Reconnaissance: Selected Documents*. 1968.

Studies

Bonney, Richard. *The European Dynastic States 1494–1660*. 1991. An excellent overview.

Cipolla, Carlo M. *Guns, Sails, and Empires: Technological Innovation and the Early Phases of European Expansion 1400–1700*. 1965. This is a lively study of the reasons the expansion succeeded, with particular emphasis on weaponry.

*Crosby, Alfred W. *The Columbian Exchange: Biological and Cultural Consequences of 1492*. 1972. A fascinating study of plants, diseases, and other exchanges between the Old World and the New World.

*Elliott, J. H. *The Old World and the New 1492–1650*. 1970. A survey of the impact on Europe of the overseas discoveries.

Gilbert, Felix. *Machiavelli and Guicciardini: Politics and History in Sixteenth-Century Florence*. 1965. The standard account of the birth of new ideas in political theory and history.

*Jeannin, Pierre. *Merchants of the 16th Century*. Paul Fittingoff (tr.). 1972. A lucid introduction to sixteenth-century economic life.

*Kamen, Henry. *Spain 1469–1714: A Society of Conflict*. 1983. A clear and compact survey that gives a comprehensive account of Spanish history.

*Available in paperback.

*Knecht, R. J. *French Renaissance Monarchy: Francis I & Henry II*. 1984. A lively introduction, with illustrative documents, to the development of governmental powers in France in the sixteenth century.

———, *Renaissance Warrior and Patron: The Reign of Francis I*. 1994.

*Mattingly, Garrett. *Renaissance Diplomacy*. 1971. An elegant account of the changes that began in international relations during the fifteenth century.

*Rady, Martin. *The Emperor Charles V*. 1988. An excellent overview, with illustrative documents, of the reign of the most powerful ruler in Europe.

*Rice, Eugene F., Jr. *The Foundations of Early Modern Europe, 1460–1559*. 1970. One of the best short surveys of the period, with three pages of suggested readings.

Scammell, G. V. *The First Imperial Age: European Overseas Expansion c. 1400–1715*. 1989. The best recent survey.

Scarisbrick, J. J. *Henry VIII*. 1968. A detailed but vivid biography of one of the most forceful of the new monarchs.

*Skinner, Quentin. *Machiavelli*. 1981. An excellent brief introduction to the man and his thought.

Strauss, Gerald. *Law, Resistance and the State*. 1986. A suggestive exploration of the development of legal and political thought.

Wilford, John Noble. *The Mysterious History of Columbus: An Exploration of the Man, the Myth, the Legacy*. 1991. A judicious account, both of Columbus' career and of the ways it has been interpreted.

*Williams, Penry. *The Tudor Regime*. 1981. The most recent comprehensive assessment of the workings of England's government.

*Wrigley, E. A. *Population and History*. 1969. An introduction to the methods and findings of historical demography by one of the pioneers of the field.

Francois Dubois
THE MASSACRE OF ST. BARTHOLOMEW'S DAY
Although it makes no attempt to depict the
massacre realistically, this painting by a Protestant
does convey the horrors of religious war. As the
victims are hanged, disemboweled, decapitated,
tossed from windows, bludgeoned, shot, or
drowned, their bodies and homes are looted.
Dubois may have intended the figure dressed in
widow's black, and pointing at a pile of corpses
near the river at the back, to be a portrait of
Catherine de Medici, who many thought inspired
the massacre.

CHAPTER FIFTEEN

WAR AND CRISIS

I N the wake of the rapid and bewildering changes of the early sixteenth century—the Reformation, the rises in population and prices, the overseas discoveries, and the dislocations caused by the activities of the new monarchs—Europe entered a period of fierce upheaval. Such radical alterations were taking place in so many elements of society that conflict became inevitable. Many people, often led by nobles who saw their power dwindling, revolted against their monarchs. The poor launched hopeless rebellions against their social superiors. And the two religious camps struggled relentlessly to destroy each other. From Scotland to Russia, the century following the Reformation, from about 1560 to 1660, was dominated by warfare; and the constant military activity had widespread effects on politics, economics, society, and thought. The fighting was, in fact, a crucial element in the long and painful process whereby Europeans came to terms with the revolutions that had begun about 1500. Almost imperceptibly, fundamental economic, political, social, and religious changes took root; and troubled Europeans found ways to accept their altered circumstances.

I. Wars of Religion in the Age of Philip II

Although many other issues were involved in the wars that plagued Europe from the 1560s to the 1650s, religion was the burning motivation, the one that inspired fanatical devotion and the most vicious hatred. A deep conviction that heresy was dangerous to society and hateful to God made Protestants and Catholics treat one another brutally. Even the dead were not spared: Corpses were sometimes mutilated to emphasize how dreadful their sins had been. These emotions gave the fighting a brutality and a relentlessness that was unprecedented in European history.

THE CRUSADES OF PHILIP II

During the second half of the sixteenth century, international warfare was ignited by the leader of the Catholics, Philip II of Spain (1556–1598), the most powerful monarch in Europe. He ruled the Iberian peninsula, much of Italy, the Netherlands, and a huge overseas empire; but his main obsessions were the two enemies of his church, the Muslims and the Protestants. Against the Muslims in the Mediterranean area, Philip's campaigns seemed to justify the financial strains they caused. In particular, his naval victory at Lepanto, off the Greek coast, in 1571 made him a Christian hero at the same time as it reduced Muslim power. But elsewhere he fared less well.

Philip tried to prevent a Protestant, Henry IV, from succeeding to the French crown, and after he failed, he continued to back the losing side in France's civil wars even though Henry converted to Catholicism. Spain's policy toward England was similarly ineffective. After the Protestant Queen Elizabeth I came to the throne in 1558, Philip remained uneasily cordial toward her for about 10 years. But relations deteriorated as England's sailors and explorers threatened Philip's wealthy New World possessions. Worse, in 1585 Elizabeth began to help the Protestant Dutch who were rebelling against Spanish rule.

The Armada Philip decided to end all these troubles with one mighty blow: In 1588 he sent a mammoth fleet—the Armada—to the Low Countries to pick up a Spanish army, invade England, and crush his Protestant enemies. By this time, however, English mariners were among the

National Gallery, London

▶ *El Greco*
THE DREAM OF PHILIP II, 1578
Characteristic of the mystical vision of El Greco is this portrayal of the devout, black-clad figure of Philip II. Kneeling alongside the doge of Venice and the pope, his allies in the victory of Lepanto over the Turks, Philip adores the blazing name of Jesus that is surrounded by angels in heaven, and he turns his back on the gaping mouth to hell.

▶ *Anonymous*
THE ARMADA
This depiction suggests the sheer splendor of the scene as Philip II's fleet sailed through the channel on its way to invading England. The opposing ships were never this close, but the colorful flags (red cross English, yellow cross Spanish) and the elaborate coats of arms must have been dazzling. The firing cannon and the sinking ship remind us that, amidst the display, there was also death and destruction.

best in the world; and their ships, which had greater maneuverability and fire power than the Spaniards', made up in tactical superiority what they lacked in size. After several skirmishes, the English set fire to a few of their own vessels with loaded cannons aboard and sent them drifting toward the Spanish ships, anchored off Calais. The Spaniards had to raise anchor in a hurry, and some of the fleet were lost. The next day the remaining Spanish ships retreated up the North Sea. The only way home was around Ireland; and wind, storms, and the pursuing English ensured that less than half the fleet reached Spain safely. This shattering reversal was comparable in scale and unexpectedness only to Xerxes' disaster at Salamis over 2000 years earlier.

THE DUTCH REVOLT

Philip's most serious reversal was the revolt of the provinces he inherited from his father, the Emperor Charles V, in the Netherlands. Here his single-mindedness provoked a fierce reaction that grew into a successful struggle for independ-

ence—the first major victory in Western Europe by subjects resisting their monarch's assertions of authority.

Causes of Revolt The original focus of opposition was Philip's reorganization of the ecclesiastical structure so as to gain control over the country's Catholic Church, a change that deprived the aristocracy of important patronage. At the same time, the billeting of troops aroused the resentment of ordinary citizens. In this situation, the local nobles, led by William of Orange, warned of mass disorder, but Philip kept up the pressure:

HAERLEM.

Nachdem sich Harlem ergeben hatt / Da hangen vnd köpfen nam kein ende / Vom hispanischen gesind dermassen / Gefangen seind mit grosser vnzucht / fil angericht ein gross bluit batt / Die Weiber auch wurden geschendt / Dass sie gar nackend auf den strassen / Wider alle eher, vnd Gottes frucht.
Anno Dñi. M. D. LXXIII. ...

He put the Inquisition to work against the Calvinists, who had begun to appear in the Netherlands, and also summoned the Jesuits to combat the heretics. These moves were disastrous because they further undermined local autonomy and made the Protestants bitter enemies of the king.

Philip's aggressiveness provoked violence in 1566: Although the Protestants were still a tiny minority, they formed mobs in a number of cities, assaulted Catholics, and sacked churches. In response, Philip tightened the pressure, appointing as governor the ruthless duke of Alba, whose Spanish troops were now used to suppress heresy and treason. Protestants were hanged in public, rebel groups were hunted down, and two nobles who had been guilty of nothing worse than demanding that Philip change his policy were executed.

Organized revolt broke out in 1572, when a small group of Dutch sailors flying the flag of William of Orange seized the fishing village of Brill, on the North Sea. The success of these "sea beggars," as the Spaniards called them, stimu-

▶ *Anonymous*
Engraving of the Spaniards in Haarlem
This engraving was published to arouse horror at Spanish atrocities during the Dutch revolt. As the caption indicates, after the Spanish troops (on the right) captured the city of Haarlem, there was a great bloodbath (*ein gross bliut batt*). Blessed by priests, the Haarlemites were decapitated or hung, and then tossed in a river so that the city would be cleansed of them. The caption states that even women and children were not spared.

lated uprisings in towns throughout the Low Countries. The banner of William of Orange became the symbol of resistance, and under his leadership full-scale rebellion erupted. By 1576, when Philip's troops mutinied and rioted in Antwerp, 16 out of the 17 provinces in the Netherlands had united behind William. The next year, however, Philip offered a compromise to the Catholic nobles, and the 10 southern provinces returned to Spanish rule.

The United Provinces In 1579 the remaining seven provinces formed the independent United

Provinces. Despite the assassination of William in 1584, they managed to resist Spain's army for decades, mainly because they could open dikes, flood their country, and thus drive the invaders back. Moreover, Philip was often diverted by other wars and, in any case, never placed total confidence in his commanders. The heart of the resistance was the Calvinists, who (though still a minority) had the most to lose: They sought freedom for their religion as well as for their country. William never showed strong religious commit-

ments, but his son, Maurice of Nassau, a brilliant military commander who won a series of victories in the 1590s, embraced Calvinism and helped make it the country's official religion. Unable to make any progress, the Spaniards agreed to a 12-year truce in 1609, but they did not recognize the independence of the United Provinces until the Peace of Westphalia in 1648. The new state demonstrated that warfare could have positive effects in this period: It could unite a people and give them the means to achieve dignity and full autonomy.

▶ *Pieter Brueghel the Elder*
THE MASSACRE OF THE INNOCENTS, CA. 1560
Probably to avoid trouble, Brueghel hid his critique of the Spanish rulers of the Netherlands in this supposed portrayal of a biblical event. It would have been clear to anyone who saw it, however, that this was a scene of Spanish cruelty toward the local inhabitants in the harsh days of winter, as soldiers tear babies from their mothers and kill them.

CIVIL WAR IN FRANCE

The warfare that religion inspired had no such redeeming effects in France. By the 1550s Calvinism was widespread among the peasants and in the towns of the south and southwest, and its leaders had virtually created a small semi-independent state. To meet this threat, a great noble

Map 15.1 THE NETHERLANDS, 1579–1609
The 17 provinces making up the Netherlands, or the Low Countries, were detached from the Holy Roman Empire when Charles V abdicated in 1556. As the map indicates, their subsequent division into two states was determined not by the linguistic difference between French-speaking people of the south and Dutch-speaking people of the north but rather by geography. The great river systems at the mouth of the Rhine eventually proved to be the barriers beyond which the Spaniards could not penetrate.

family, the Guises, assumed the leadership of the Catholics; and in response the Bourbons, another noble family, championed the Calvinists, about a twelfth of the population. Their struggle split the country apart.

It was ominous that in 1559—the year that Henry II, France's last strong king for a generation, died—the Calvinists (known in France as Huguenots) organized their first national synod, an indication of impressive strength. During the next 30 years, the throne was occupied by Henry's three ineffectual sons. The power behind the crown was Henry's widow, Catherine de Medici (see the genealogical table below), who tried desperately to preserve royal authority. But she was often helpless because the religious conflict intensified the factional struggle for power between the Guises and the Bourbons, both of whom were closely related to the monarchy and hoped one day to inherit the throne.

The Wars Fighting started in 1562 and lasted for 36 years, interrupted only by short-lived peace agreements. Catherine switched sides whenever one party became too powerful; and she may have approved the notorious massacre of St. Bartholomew's Day—August 24, 1572—which started in Paris, spread through France, and destroyed the Huguenots' leadership. Henry of Navarre, a Bourbon, was the only major figure who escaped. When Catherine switched sides again and made peace with the Huguenots in 1576, the Guises formed the Catholic League,

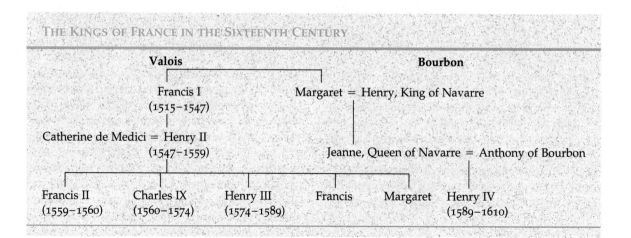

THE KINGS OF FRANCE IN THE SIXTEENTH CENTURY

Valois				Bourbon	
Francis I (1515–1547)			Margaret = Henry, King of Navarre		
Catherine de Medici = Henry II (1547–1559)				Jeanne, Queen of Navarre = Anthony of Bourbon	
Francis II (1559–1560)	Charles IX (1560–1574)	Henry III (1574–1589)	Francis	Margaret	Henry IV (1589–1610)

which for several years dominated the eastern half of the country. In 1584 the league allied with Spain's Philip II to attack heresy in France and deny the Bourbon Henry's legal right to inherit the throne.

The defeat of the Armada in 1588 proved to be the turning point in the French civil wars, for the duke of Guise lost his principal support, Spain, and was soon assassinated. Within a few months Henry of Navarre inherited the throne as Henry IV (1589–1610), though he had few advantages as he began to reassert royal authority. The Huguenots and Catholics ran almost independent governments in large sections of France. The Catholic League was in command of the east, including the capital, Paris; the Huguenots dominated the south and southwest, remote from the central government. In addition, the royal administration was in a sorry state because the crown's oldest rivals, the great nobles, could now resist all outside interference in their domains.

Peace Restored Yet largely because of the assassination of the duke of Guise, Henry IV was able to restore order. The duke had been a forceful leader, a serious contender for the throne. His replacement was a Spanish candidate for the crown who had little chance of success. The distaste for a possible foreign ruler, combined with war weariness, destroyed much of the support for the Catholic League, which finally collapsed as a result of revolts against it in eastern France in the 1590s. These uprisings, founded on a demand for peace, increased in frequency and intensity after Henry IV renounced Protestantism in 1593 in order to win acceptance by his Catholic subjects. The following year Henry had himself officially crowned, and all of France rallied to the king as he beat back a Spanish invasion—Spain's final, rather weak, attempt to put its own candidate on the throne.

When Spain finally withdrew and signed a peace treaty in 1598, the fighting came to an end. To complete the reconciliation, Henry issued (also in 1598) the Edict of Nantes, which granted limited toleration to the Huguenots. Although it did not create complete religious liberty, the edict made Calvinist worship legal, protected the rights of the minority, and opened public office to Huguenots.

Map 15.2 CATHOLIC AND PROTESTANT POWERS IN THE LATE SIXTEENTH CENTURY
The heart of the Catholic cause in the wars of religion was the Spain of Philip II. Spanish territories surrounded France and provided the route to the Netherlands where the Protestant Dutch had rebelled against the Spaniards. The Armada was launched to help that cause by crushing the ally of the Dutch, Protestant England. In the meantime, the surrounded French had problems of their own with the Huguenots, who protected their Protestantism in a network of fortified towns.

Political Thought But the effects of decades of strife could not be brushed aside. A basic change in political thought, for example, was an inevitable response to the civil wars. The Huguenots had found ways to justify resistance to a monarch, and the Catholics used a similar justification when they were fighting the king. Even when order was restored, however, the advocates of peace and national unity, known as *politiques*, still had to argue forcefully for stability and a more powerful central government.

Their most famous representative, Jean Bodin, made his case by examining the basic structure of the state, and his analysis influenced political theorists for centuries. His principal work is *The Six Books of the Republic* (1576), in which he defines the nature and limits of the sovereignty exercised by governments. By seeking a balance between power and restraint, Bodin hoped to find a principle for restoring order in an age of shattering upheaval. But in the process, he also exposed the dilemma that has been the primary focus of political theory ever since: control versus freedom, the need for authority and yet the equal need for subjects' rights.

II. War and International Crisis

THE THIRTY YEARS' WAR

In the Holy Roman Empire, religious hatreds were especially disruptive because the empire lacked a central authority and unifying institutions. Small-scale fighting broke out repeatedly after the 1550s, always inspired by religion. And though in most of Western Europe the first two decades of the seventeenth century were a time of relative peace, which seemed to signal a decline of conflict over faith, in the empire the stage was being set for the bloodiest of all the wars fired by religion.

Known as the Thirty Years' War, this ferocious struggle began in the Kingdom of Bohemia in 1618 and continued until 1648. The principal battleground, the empire, was ravaged by the fighting, which eventually involved every major ruler in Europe. At first it was a renewed struggle between Protestants and Catholics, but eventually it became a fight among political rivals who were eager to take advantage of the fragmentation of

▶ "THE HANGING TREE," ENGRAVING FROM JACQUES CALLOT'S MISERIES OF WAR, 1633
An indication of the growing dismay over the brutality of the Thirty Years' War was the collection of 16 prints produced by the French engraver Callot, depicting the life of the soldier and the effects of armies on civilian populations. His soldiers destroy, loot, and rape, and only a few of them receive the punishments they deserve, like this mass hanging.

Ifrael ex. Cum Priuil. Reg.

A la fin ces Voleurs infames et perdus ,
Comme fruits malheureux a cet arbre pendus

Monftrent bien que le crime (horrible et noire engeance)
Eft luy mefme inftrument de honte et de vengeance ,

Et que ceft le Deftin des hommes vicieux
Defprouuer toft ou tard la iuftice des Cieux . 1}

the empire to advance their own ambitions. As the devastation spread, international relations seemed to be sinking into total chaos; but the chief victims were the Germans, who, like the Italians in the sixteenth century, found themselves at the mercy of well-organized states that used another country as the arena for settling their quarrels.

The First Phase, 1618–1621 The immediate problem was typical of the situation in the empire. In 1609 Emperor Rudolf II promised toleration for Protestants in Bohemia, one of his own domains. When his cousin Ferdinand, a pious Catholic, succeeded to the Bohemian throne in 1617, he refused to honor Rudolf's promise, and the Bohemians rebelled in 1618. Since the crown was elective, they declared Ferdinand deposed, replacing him with the leading Calvinist of the empire, Frederick II of the Palatinate. Frederick accepted the crown, an act of defiance whose only possible outcome was war.

The first decade or so of the war was a time of victories for the Catholics, and in particular the Habsburgs. Ferdinand became emperor (1619–1637), and the powerful Catholic Maximilian of Bavaria put an army at his disposal. Within a year the imperial troops won a stunning victory over the Bohemians at the Battle of the White Mountain. Leading rebels were executed or exiled, and Ferdinand II confiscated all of Frederick's lands. Maximilian received half as a reward for his army, and the remainder went to the Spaniards, who occupied it as a valuable base for their struggle with the Dutch. In this first round, the Catholic and imperial cause had triumphed.

The Second Phase, 1621–1630 When the truce between the Spaniards and the Dutch expired in 1621, and warfare resumed in Germany as well as in the Netherlands, the Protestants made no progress for 10 years. A new imperial army was raised by Albrecht von Wallenstein, a minor Bohemian nobleman and remarkable opportunist who had become one of the richest men in the empire. In 1624 Wallenstein, realizing that the emperor remained weak because he lacked his own army, offered to raise a force if he could billet it and raise its supplies wherever it happened

Die ficht man die 12. Köpff auff den Prager Bruckenthurn aufgesteckt.

▶ "HEADS OF THE BOHEMIAN REBELS," ENGRAVING FROM MATHÄUS MERIAN, THEATRUM EUROPAEUM, CA. 1630
Since the scene had not changed when the engraving was made, this illustration is probably a fairly accurate representation of the punishment in 1621 of the leaders of the Bohemian rebellion. Twenty-four rebels were executed, and the heads of twelve of them were displayed on long poles at the top of the tower (still standing today) on the bridge over Prague's river. The heads were kept there for 10 years.

to be stationed. Ferdinand agreed, and by 1627 Wallenstein's army had begun to conquer the northern region of the empire, the last major center of Protestant strength. To emphasize his supremacy, Ferdinand issued the Edict of Restitution in 1629, ordering the restoration to Catholics of all the territories they had lost to Protestants since 1552.

But these Habsburg successes were more apparent than real, because it was only the extreme disorganization of the empire that permitted a mercenary captain like Wallenstein to achieve such immense military power. Once the princes realized the danger he posed to their independence, they united (Catholic as well as Protestant) against the Habsburgs, and in 1630 they made Ferdinand dismiss Wallenstein by threatening to keep his son from the imperial succession. The emperor's submission proved fatal to his cause, for Sweden and France were preparing to unleash new aggressions against the Habsburgs, and Wallenstein was the one military leader who might have been able to beat back the onslaught.

The Third Phase, 1630–1632 The year 1630 marked the beginning of a change in fortune for the Protestants and also a drift toward the purely political aim (of resisting the Habsburgs) that was coming to dominate the war. Although France's king was a Catholic, he was ready to join with Protestants against other Catholics so as to undermine Habsburg power. Early in 1630 the French attacked the duke of Savoy, a Habsburg ally, and occupied his lands. Then, in 1631, they allied with Gustavus Adolphus of Sweden, who, dismayed by Ferdinand's treatment of Protestants and fearing a Habsburg threat to Swedish lands around the Baltic Sea, had invaded the empire in 1630. The following year Gustavus destroyed an imperial army at Breitenfeld in one of the few decisive battles of the war. The tide had turned against the Habsburgs.

Ferdinand hastily recalled Wallenstein, whose troops met the Swedes in battle at Lützen in 1632. Although Gustavus' soldiers won the day, he himself was killed, and his death saved the Habsburg dynasty from being destroyed by Sweden. Nothing, however, could restore Ferdinand's former position. The emperor was forced by the princes to turn against Wallenstein once more; A few months later he had him assassinated. The removal of the great general marked the end of an era, for he was the last leader in more than two centuries who was capable of establishing unified authority in what is now Germany.

The Fourth Phase, 1632–1648 Gustavus' success opened the final phase of the war, as political ambitions—the quest of the empire's princes for independence, and the struggle between the Habsburgs and their enemies—almost completely replaced religious aims. The Protestant princes began to raise new armies, and by 1635 Ferdinand had to make peace with them. In return for their promise of assistance in driving out the Swedes, Ferdinand agreed to suspend the Edict of Restitution and to grant amnesty to all but Frederick of the Palatinate and a few Bohemian rebels. Ferdinand was renouncing most of his ambitions, and it seemed that peace might return at last.

But the French could not let matters rest. In 1635 they finally declared war on Ferdinand. For the next 13 years, the French and Swedes rained unmitigated disaster on Germany. Peace negotiations began in 1641, but not until 1648 did the combatants agree to lay down arms and sign the treaties of Westphalia. Even thereafter the war between France and Spain, pursued mainly in the Spanish Netherlands, continued for another 11 years; and hostilities around the Baltic among Sweden, Denmark, Poland, and Russia, which had started in 1611, did not end until 1661.

The Effect of War The wars and their effects (such as the diseases spread by armies) killed off over a third of Germany's population. The conflict caused serious economic dislocation because a number of princes—already in serious financial straits—sharply debased their coinage. This worsened the continentwide trade depression that had begun around 1620 and had brought the great sixteenth-century boom to an end, causing the first drop in prices since 1500. Few contemporaries perceived the connection between war and economic trouble, but nobody could ignore the drain on men and resources or the destructive effects of the conflict.

THE PEACE OF WESTPHALIA

By the 1630s it was becoming apparent that the fighting was getting out of hand and that it would not be easy to bring the conflicts to an end. There had never been such widespread or devastating warfare, and many diplomats felt that the settlement had to be of far greater scope than any negotiated before. And they were right. When at last the treaties were signed in 1648, after seven years of negotiation in the German province of Westphalia, a landmark in international relations was passed—remarkable not

▶ *Jan Asselyn*
THE BATTLE OF LÜTZEN
Although it is not an accurate rendition of the scene, this painting of Gustavus Adolphus (the horseman in a brown coat with sword raised) shot by a gunman in red does give the flavor of seventeenth-century battle. Because of the chaos, the smoke, and the poor visibility that often obscured what was happening, Gustavus' escort did not notice when he was in fact hit by a musket shot that shattered his left arm and caused his horse to bolt. Further shots killed him, and not until hours after the battle was his seminaked body found, stripped of its finery.

only because it brought an anarchic situation under control but because it created a new system for dealing with wars.

The most important innovation was the gathering at the peace conference of all the participants in the Thirty Years' War, rather than the usual practice of bringing only two or three belligerents together. The presence of ambassadors from Bavaria, Brandenburg, Denmark, France, the Holy Roman Empire, Saxony, Spain, Sweden, Switzerland, and the United Provinces made possible, for the first time in European history, a series of all-embracing treaties that dealt with nearly every major international issue at one stroke. Visible at the meetings was the emergence of a state system. These independent states recognized that they were creating a mechanism for controlling their relations with one another. Although some fighting continued, the Peace of Westphalia in 1648 became the first comprehensive rearrangement of the map of Europe in modern times.

The Peace Terms The principal beneficiaries were France and Sweden, the chief aggressors during the last decade of the war. France gained the provinces of Alsace and Lorraine, and Swe-

National Gallery, London

▶ *Gerard Terborch*
THE PEACE OF WESTPHALIA, 1648
The artist was an eyewitness to this scene, the formal signing of peace between the United Provinces and Spain in Münster on May 15, 1648. The two leaders of the Spanish delegation on the right put their hands on a Bible as they swear to uphold the terms of the treaty, and the Dutch on the left all raise their hands as they declare "So help me God." Terborch himself, dressed in brown, is looking out at the viewer on the far left.

den obtained extensive territories in the Holy Roman Empire. The main loser was the House of Habsburg, since both the United Provinces and the Swiss Confederation were recognized as independent states, and the German princes, who agreed not to join an alliance against the emperor, were otherwise given almost complete independence.

The princes' autonomy was formally established in 1657, when they elected as emperor Leopold I, the head of the House of Habsburg, in return for two promises. First, Leopold would give no help to his cousins, the rulers of Spain; and second, the empire would be a state of princes, in which each ruler would be free from imperial interference. This freedom permitted the rise of Brandenburg-Prussia and the growth of absolutism—the belief that the political authority of the ruler was unlimited—within the major principalities. Moreover, the Habsburgs' capitulation prepared the way for their reorientation toward the east along the Danube River—the beginnings of the Austro-Hungarian Empire.

The Effects of Westphalia For more than a century, the settlement reached at Westphalia was regarded as the basis for all international negotiations. Even major new accords, such as the one that ended yet another series of wars in 1713, were seen mainly as adjustments of the decisions of 1648. In practice, of course, multinational conferences were no more effective than brief, limited negotiations in reducing tensions among states. Wars continued to break out, and armies grew in size and skill. But diplomats did believe that international affairs were under better control and that the chaos of the Thirty Years' War had been replaced by something more stable and more clearly defined.

This confidence was reinforced as it became clear after 1648 that armies were trying to improve discipline and avoid the excesses of the previous 30 years. As religious passions waned, combat became less vicious and the treatment of civilians became more orderly. On battlefields, better discipline reduced the casualty rate from 1 death per 3 soldiers in the 1630s to 1 death in 7, or even 1 in 20, during the early 1700s. And the aims of war also changed significantly.

Changed International Relations The most obvious differences after the Peace of Westphalia were that France replaced Spain as the continent's dominant power and that northern countries—especially England and the Netherlands,

Map 15.3 TERRITORIAL CHANGES. 1648–1661
This map shows the territorial changes that took place after the Thirty Years' War. The treaties of Westphalia (1648) and the Pyrenees (1659) arranged the principal transfers, but the settlements in the Baltic were not confirmed until the treaties of Copenhagen, Oliva (both 1660), and Kardis (1661).

where growth in population and in commerce resumed more quickly than elsewhere—took over Europe's economic leadership. But behind this outward shift a more fundamental transformation was taking place. What had become apparent in the later stages of the Thirty Years' War was that Europe's states were prepared to fight only for economic, territorial, or political advantages. Dynastic aims were still important, but supranational goals like religious causes could no longer determine a state's foreign policy.

The Thirty Years' War was the last major international conflict in Europe in which two religious camps organized their forces as blocs. After 1648 such connections gave way to more purely national interests. This shift marked the decisive stage of a process that had been under way since the Late Middle Ages: the emergence of the state as the basic unit and object of loyalty in Western civilization. That it had taken a major crisis, a descent into international anarchy, to bring about so momentous a change is an indication of how profoundly the upheavals of the mid-seventeenth century affected European history. Indeed, the reshaping of the relations among Europe's states for centuries to come that was achieved at Westphalia is but one example of the multiple military and political consequences of this age of crisis.

III. The Military Revolution

WEAPONS AND TACTICS

The constant warfare of the sixteenth and seventeenth centuries brought about dramatic changes in the ways battles were fought and armies were organized. Gunpowder, which had been used occasionally and to little effect since the 1330s, now came to occupy a central place in warfare. The result was not only the creation of a new type of industry, cannon and gun manufacture, but also a transformation of tactics. Individual castles could no longer be defended against explosives; even towns had to build heavy and elaborate fortifications if they were to resist the new fire power. Sieges became compli-

cated, expensive operations, whose purpose was to bring explosives right up to a town wall so that it could be blown up. This required an intricate system of trenches, because walls were built in star shapes so as to multiply angles of fire and make any approach dangerous. Although they became increasingly costly, sieges remained essential to the strategy of warfare until the eighteenth century.

Tactics In open battles, the effects of gunpowder were equally expensive. The new tactics that appeared around 1500, perfected by the Spaniards, relied on massed ranks of infantry, organized in huge squares, that made the traditional cavalry charge obsolete. Interspersed with the gunners were soldiers carrying pikes. They fended off horses or opposing infantry while the men with guns tried to mow the enemy down. The squares with the best discipline usually won, and for over a century after the reign of Ferdinand of Aragon, the Spaniards had the best army in Europe. Each square had about 3000 troops, and to maintain enough squares at full strength to fight all of Spain's battles required an army numbering approximately 40,000. The cost of keeping that many men clothed, fed, and housed, let alone equipped and paid, was enormous. But worse was to come: New tactics emerged in the early seventeenth century that required even more soldiers.

Since nobody could outdo the Spaniards at their own methods, a different approach was developed by their rivals. The first advance was made by Maurice of Nassau, who led the Dutch revolt against Spain from the 1580s. He relied not on sheer weight and power but on flexibility and mobility. Then Sweden's Gustavus Adolphus, one of the geniuses of the history of warfare, found a way to achieve mobility on the field without losing power. His main invention was the salvo: Instead of having his musketeers fire one row at a time, like the Spaniards, he had them all fire at once. What he lost in continuity of shot he gained in a fearsome blast that, if properly timed, could shatter enemy ranks. Huge, slow-moving squares were simply no match for smaller, faster units that riddled them with well-coordinated salvos.

THE ORGANIZATION AND SUPPORT OF ARMIES

These tactical changes brought about steady increases in the size of armies, because the more units there were, the better they could be placed on the battlefield. Although the Spanish army hardly grew between 1560 and 1640, remaining at 40,000 to 60,000 men, the Swedes had 150,000 by 1632; and at the end of the century, Louis XIV considered a force of 400,000 essential to maintain his dominant position in Europe.

This growth had far-reaching consequences. One was the need for conscription, which Gustavus introduced in the late 1620s. At least half his army consisted of his own subjects, who were easier to control than foreign mercenaries. Because it also made sense not to disband such huge forces each autumn, when the campaigning season ended, most armies were kept permanently ready. The need to maintain so many soldiers the year round caused a rapid expansion of support-

ing administrative personnel. Taxation mushroomed. All levels of society felt the impact but especially the lower classes, who paid the bulk of the taxes and provided most of the recruits. To encourage enlistment, rulers made military service as attractive as possible—a task made easier by the problems many people faced in finding regular meals, clothing, housing, and wages. Social distinctions were reduced; an able young man could rise high in the officer corps, though the top ranks were still reserved for nobles. Even the lower echelons were given important responsibilities because the new system of small, flexible units gave considerable initiative to the junior officers who led them.

New Ranks Other changes followed. Maneuverability on the field demanded tighter discipline, which was achieved by the introduction of drilling and combat training. The order of command was clarified, and many ranks familiar today—major, colonel, and the various levels of general—appeared in the seventeenth century. The distinctions were reinforced by uniforms, which became standard equipment. These developments created a sense of corporate spirit among military officers, an international phenomenon that was to occupy an important place in European society for three centuries.

THE LIFE OF THE SOLDIER

For the average soldier, who was now a common sight in Europe, life in the army began with recruitment. Some genuinely wanted to join up. They had heard stories of adventure, booty, and comradeship, and they were tempted by free

▶ *Anonymous Engraving after Jacques de Gheyn*
WAFFENHANDLUNG
The expansion of armies and the professionalization of war in the seventeenth century were reflected in the founding of military academies and the growing acceptance of the notion that warfare was a science. There was now a market for published manuals, especially if they had illustrations like this one, which shows how a pikeman was supposed to crouch and hold his weapons (stabilizing his pike against his foot) when facing a cavalry charge.

Map 15.4 AREAS OF FIGHTING, 1618–1660
The endemic fighting of this age of crisis engulfed most of Central Europe
and involved soldiers from every country.

food and clothing. But in many cases the "volunteers" did not want to go, for they had also heard of the hardship and danger. Unfortunately for them, recruiting officers had quotas, and villages had to provide the numbers demanded of them. Community pressure, bribery, enlistment of drunken men, and even outright kidnapping helped fill the ranks.

Joining an army did not necessarily mean cutting oneself off from friends or family. Men from a particular area enlisted together, and in some cases, wives came along. There were dozens of jobs to do aside from fighting, because soldiers needed cooks, laundresses, peddlers, and other tradespeople. It has been estimated that an army in the field might need five people for every soldier. The large majority of the troops, though, were on their own. For companionship, they looked to camp followers or the women of the town they were occupying. Few barracks had been built, and therefore, unless they were on the march or out in the open on a battlefield, they were housed (or billeted) with ordinary citizens. Since soldiers almost never received their wages on time—delays could be as long as a year or more—they rarely could pay for their food and housing. Local civilians therefore had to supply their needs, or risk the thievery that was universal. It was no wonder that the approach of an army was a terrifying event.

Military Justice Officially, there were severe penalties for misbehavior—imprisonment, flogging, or, for crimes like desertion, execution. Yet discipline, though harsh, was only occasionally

▶ *Sebastian Vrancx*
A MILITARY CAMP
Vrancx was himself a soldier, and the many military scenes he painted during the Thirty Years' War give us a sense of the life of the soldier during the many months when there were no campaigns or battles. Conditions could be grim, but there were many hours when one could simply nap, chat, or play dice.

enforced, because men were needed for combat and it was easy to slip away from an army. Troops had their own law and courts, but the main goal of their officers was to maintain an effective fighting force. And disputes with civilians rarely ended in a judgment against a soldier. Punishments were rare even for corruption at an army's upper levels (for instance, when officers who were paid to raise troops listed phantom recruits and kept their wages).

Discomforts   The relatively light legal restrictions did not mean that military life was easy. Soldiers suffered constant discomfort. A garrison might be able to settle into a town in reasonable conditions for a long stretch; but if it was besieged, it became hungry, fearful, and vulnerable. Days spent on the march could be grim, exhausting, and uncertain; and even in camps soldiers were often filthy and wet. Real danger was not common, though it was intense during battles and occasionally during sieges. Even a simple wound could be fatal, because medical care was generally appalling. Yet the most persistent discomfort for the soldier was boredom. Sieges dragged, and even the hard labor of digging trenches or dragging cannons must have been a relief from the tedious waiting. Despite traditional recreations—drink, gambling, and the brawls common among soldiers—the attractions were limited; and most military men had few regrets when they returned to civilian life.

IV. Revolution in England

In the 1640s and 1650s the growing burdens of war and taxation, and the mounting assertiveness of governments, sparked upheavals throughout Europe that were the equivalent in domestic politics of the crisis in international relations. In country after country, people rose up in vain attempts to restore the individual and regional autonomies that were being eroded by powerful central governments. Only in England, however, did the revolt become a revolution—an attempt to overturn the social and political system and create a new structure for society.

ELIZABETH I

Before 1630, no such eruption could have been foreseen. With few wars, and those largely at sea, England was less affected than other countries by the fighting of the age. In addition, the people were united by such common bonds as the institution of Parliament and a commitment to the international Protestant cause that was carefully promoted by Queen Elizabeth I (1558–1603).

Elizabeth is an appealing figure because she combined shrewd hardheadedness and a sense of the possible with a disarming appearance of frailty. Her qualities were many: her dedication to the task of government; her astute choice of advisers; her civilizing influence at court, where she encouraged elegant manners and the arts; her tolerance of religious dissent as long as it posed no political threat; and her ability to feel the mood of her people, to catch their spirit, to inspire their enthusiasm. Although social, legal, and economic practices usually subordinated women to men in this age, inheritance was respected; thus a determined woman with a recognized claim to authority could win complete acceptance. Elizabeth was the most widely admired and most successful queen of her time, but she was by no means alone: Female rulers also shaped the histories of France, Sweden, and the southern Netherlands in the sixteenth and seventeenth centuries.

Royal Policy   Elizabeth could be indecisive, notably where the succession was concerned. Her refusal to marry caused serious uncertainties, and it was only the shrewd planning of her chief minister, Robert Cecil, that enabled the king of Scotland, James Stuart, to succeed her without incident in 1603. Similar dangers arose from her indecisive treatment of England's remaining Catholics. They hoped that Mary Queen of Scots, a Catholic, would inherit the throne; and since she was next in line, they were not above plotting against Elizabeth's life. Eventually, in 1587, Elizabeth had Mary executed and the plots died away. But her reluctance to take firm positions was also apparent in her choice of advisers. Some advocated caution, inaction, and discretion in international affairs; whereas others favored an aggressive foreign policy. Yet Elizabeth showed

Queen Elizabeth's Armada Speech

Elizabeth's ability to move her subjects was exemplified by the speech she gave to her troops as they awaited the fight with the Spanish Armada. She understood that they might have doubts about a woman leading them in war, but she turned that issue to her own advantage in a stirring cry to battle that enhanced her popularity at the time and her legendary image thereafter.

"My loving People: We have been persuaded by some that are careful of our safety, to take heed how we commit ourselves to armed multitudes, for fear of treachery; but I assure you, I do not desire to live to distrust my faithful and loving people.

"Let tyrants fear; I have always so behaved myself, that, under God, I have placed my chiefest strength and safeguard in the loyal hearts and good will of my subjects, and therefore I am come amongst you, as you see, at this time, not for my recreation . . . but being resolved in the midst and heat of the battle, to live or die amongst you all, to lay down for my God, and for my kingdoms, and for my people, my honour and my blood, even in the dust.

"I know I have the body of a weak and feeble woman; but I have the heart and stomach of a king, and of a king of England too; and think foul scorn that . . . Spain, or any prince of Europe should dare to invade the borders of my realm; to which rather than any dishonour shall grow by me, I myself will take up arms, I myself will be your general, judge, and rewarder of every one of your virtues in the field. . . . By your concord in the camp, and your valour in the field, we shall shortly have a famous victory over those enemies of my God, of my kingdoms, and of my people."

From Walter Scott (ed.), *A Collection of Scarce and Valuable Tracts, on the Most Interesting and Entertaining Subjects: but Chiefly Such as Relate to the History and Constitution of these Kingdoms,* vol. I (London, 1809), pp. 429–430.

great skill in balancing the contrasting viewpoints, and her adroit maneuvering assured her of her ministers' loyalty at all times.

She also inspired the devotion of her subjects by traveling throughout England to make public appearances: by brilliant speeches (*see box,* above); and by shaping her own image, even regulating how she was to be depicted in portraits. She thus retained her subjects' allegiance despite the profound social changes that were eroding traditional patterns of deference and order. England's nobility, for instance, no longer dominated the military and the government; nearly all Elizabeth's ministers were new in national life, and the House of Commons was beginning to exert more political influence within Parliament than the House of Lords. The nobles, less directly involved in commerce, did not benefit as much as other sections of society from England's rising prosperity; and in general they were losing their hold over the power, wealth, and goverment of the country.

The Gentry The gentry, the new group that joined the nobles at the head of society, ranged from people considered great in a parish or other small locality to courtiers considered great throughout the land. There were never more than 60 nobles during Elizabeth's reign, but the gentry may have numbered close to 20,000 by the time she died. Most of these gentry were doing well economically, profiting from their agricultural holdings as well as from crown offices. A number also became involved in industrial activity, and hundreds invested in new overseas trading and colonial ventures. The gentry's participation in commerce made them unique among the landed classes of Europe, whose members were tradi-

▶ *William Segar* (attrib.)
PORTRAIT OF ELIZABETH I, 1585
Elizabeth I was strongly aware of the power of propaganda, and she used it to foster a dazzling public image. Legends about her arose in literature. And in art she had herself portrayed in the most elaborate finery imaginable. Here, she is every inch the queen, with her magnificent dress, the trappings of monarchy, and the symbol of virginity, the ermine.

tionally contemptuous of business affairs, and it testified to the enterprise and vigor of England's social leaders. Long important in local administration, they flocked to the House of Commons to express their views of public matters. Their ambitions eventually posed a serious threat to the monarchy, especially when linked with the effects of rapid economic change.

Economic Advance   In Elizabeth's reign, thanks to a general boom in trade, England's merchants, helped by leading courtiers, began to transform the country's economy. They opened commercial links throughout Europe and parts of Asia and began English expansion overseas. At home, there was significant industrial development. Mining and manufacture developed rapidly, and shipbuilding became a major industry. The production of coal increased 14-fold between 1540 and 1680, creating fortunes and an expertise in industrial techniques that took England far ahead of its neighbors.

The economic vigor and growth that ensued gave the classes that benefited most—gentry and merchants—a cohesion and a sense of purpose that made it dangerous to oppose them when they felt their rights infringed. They increasingly regarded themselves as the leaders of the nation, second only to the nobility. They wanted respect for their wishes, and they bitterly resented the economic interference and political high-handedness of Elizabeth's successors.

The Puritans   Heightening this unease was the sympathy many of the gentry felt toward a small but vociferous group of religious reformers, the Puritans. Puritans believed that the Protestant Anglican Church established by Elizabeth was still too close to Roman Catholicism, and they wanted further reductions in ritual and hierarchy. Elizabeth refused, and although she tried to avoid a confrontation, in the last years of her reign she had to silence the most outspoken of her critics. As a result, the Puritans became a disgruntled minority. By the 1630s, when the government tried to repress such religious dissent more vigorously, there were many in England, non-Puritan as well as Puritan, who felt that the monarchy was leading the country astray and was ignoring the wishes of its subjects. Leading parliamentarians in particular soon came to believe that major changes were needed to restore good government in England.

PARLIAMENT AND THE LAW

The place where the gentry made their views known was Parliament, the nation's supreme legislative body. Three-quarters of the House of Commons consisted of gentry. They were better educated than ever before, and nearly half of them had legal training. Since the Commons had to approve all taxation, the gentry had the leverage to pursue their grievances.

The monarchy was still the dominant force in

the country when Elizabeth died in 1603, but Parliament's demand to be heard was gathering momentum. Although the queen had been careful with money, in the last 20 years of her reign her resources had been overtaxed by war with Spain and an economic depression. Thus she bequeathed to her successor, Scotland's James Stuart, a huge debt—£400,000, the equal of a year's royal revenue—and the struggle to pay it off gave the Commons the means to seek changes in royal policy.

James I Trouble began in the reign of James I (1603–1625), who had a far more exalted view of his own powers than Elizabeth had had and who did not hesitate to tell his subjects, in the most tactless way, that he considered his authority almost unlimited. As a result, gentry opposed to royal policies dominated parliamentary proceedings, and they engaged in a running battle with the king. They blocked the union of England with Scotland that James sought. They drew up an "Apology" explaining his mistakes and his ignorance, as a Scotsman, of English traditions. They forced two of his ministers to resign in disgrace. And they wrung repeated concessions from him, including the unprecedented right for Parliament to discuss foreign policy.

Law The Commons used the law to justify their resistance to royal power. The basic legal system of the country was the common law—justice administered on the basis of precedents and parliamentary statutes, and relying on the opinions of juries. This system stood in contrast to Roman law, prevalent on the continent, where royal edicts could make law and decisions were reached by judges without juries. Such practices existed in England only in a few royal courts of law, such as Star Chamber, which, because it was directly under the crown, came to be seen as an instrument of repression.

The common lawyers, whose leaders were also prominent in the Commons, resented the growing business of the royal courts and attacked them in Parliament. Both James and his successor were accused of pressuring judges, particularly after they won a series of famous cases involving a subject's right to criticize the monarch. Thus the crown could be portrayed as disregarding not only the desires of the people but the law itself.

The king still had broad powers, but when he exercised them contrary to Parliament's wishes, his actions seemed to many to be taking on the appearance of tyranny.

RISING ANTAGONISMS

The confrontation between Parliament and king grew worse during the 1620s, especially in the reign of James's son, Charles I (1625–1649). At the Parliament of 1628–1629, the open challenge to the crown reached a climax in the Petition of Right, which has become a landmark in constitutional history. The petition demanded an end to imprisonment without cause shown, to taxation without the consent of Parliament, to martial law in peacetime, and to the billeting of troops among civilians. Charles agreed, in the hope of gaining much-needed subsidies, but then broke his word. To many, this betrayal seemed to threaten Parliament's essential role in government alongside the king. Seeking to end discussion of these issues in the Commons, Charles ordered Parliament dissolved, but with great daring, two members denied the king even this hallowed right by holding the speaker of the House in his chair while they passed a final angry resolution denouncing Charles's actions.

Resentful subjects were clearly on the brink of openly defying their king. Puritans, common lawyers, and disenchanted country gentry had taken over the House of Commons; and Charles avoided further trouble only by refusing to call another session of Parliament. This he managed to do for 11 years, all the while increasing the repression of Puritanism and using extraordinary measures (such as reviving crown rights to special taxes that had not been demanded for a long time) to raise revenues that did not require parliamentary consent. But in 1639, the Calvinist Scots took up arms rather than accept the Anglican prayer book, and the parliamentarians had their chance. To raise funds for an army to fight the Scots, Charles had to turn to Parliament, which demanded that he first redress its grievances. When he resisted, civil war followed.

CIVIL WAR

The Parliament that met in 1640 began with a two-hour speech by John Pym, a prominent critic of the monarch, who outlined long-standing grievances against both church and government. Charles refused to change his policies, the Commons refused to grant a subsidy, and the king angrily dissolved the session. But there was no way to pay for an army without taxes. By the summer of 1640, the Scots occupied most of northern England, and Charles had to summon a new Parliament. This one sat for 13 years, earning the appropriate name of the Long Parliament.

In its first year, the House of Commons abolished the royal courts, such as Star Chamber, and made mandatory the writ of habeas corpus (which prevented imprisonment without cause shown); it declared taxation without parliamentary consent illegal; and it ruled that Parliament had to meet at least once every three years. Meanwhile, the Puritans in the Commons prepared to reform the church. Oliver Cromwell, one of their leaders, demanded abolition of the Anglican Book of Common Prayer and strongly attacked the institution of episcopacy. The climactic vote came the next year when the Commons passed a Grand Remonstrance, which outlined for the king all the legislation they had passed and asked that bishops be deprived of votes in the House of Lords.

The Two Sides This was the prelude to a more revolutionary Puritan assault on the stucture of the Church, but in fact the Grand Remonstrance passed by only 11 votes. A moderate group was detaching itself from the Puritans, and it was to become the nucleus of a royalist party. The nation's chief grievances had been redressed, and there was no longer a uniform desire for change. Still Charles misjudged the situation and tried to arrest five leaders of the Commons, supposedly for plotting treason with the Scots. But Parliament resisted, and the citizens of London, openly hostile to Charles, sheltered the five. England now began gradually to split in two. By late 1642 both the royalists and the antiroyalists had assembled armies, and the Civil War was under way.

What made so many people overcome their habitual loyalty to the monarchy? We know that the royalists in Parliament were considerably younger than their opponents, which suggests that it was long experience with the Stuarts and

nostalgia for Elizabeth that created revolutionaries. Another clear divide was regional. The south and east of England were primarily antiroyalist, while the north and west were mostly royalist. This indicated that the more cosmopolitan areas, closer to the continent and also centers of Puritanism, were largely on Parliament's side. The decision was often a personal matter: A prominent family and its locality chose one side because its rival, a nearby family, had chosen the other. The Puritans were certainly antiroyalist, but they were a minority in the country and influential in the House of Commons only because they were so vociferous and determined. Like all revolutions, this one was animated by a small group of radicals (in this case, Puritans) who alone kept the momentum going.

Independents and Presbyterians As the fighting began, a group among the Puritans known as Independents urged that the Anglican Church be replaced by a congregational system, in which each local congregation, free of all central authority, would decide its own form of worship. The most important leader of the Independents in Parliament was Oliver Cromwell. Opposed to them, but also considered Puritans, were the Presbyterians, who wanted to establish a strictly organized Calvinist system, like the one in Scotland, where local congregations were subject to centralized authority, though laypeople did participate in church government. Since both the Scots, whose alliance was vital in the war, and a majority of the Puritans in the Commons were Presbyterians, Cromwell agreed to give way, but only for the moment. There was also a quarrel over the goals of the war because the antiroyalists were unsure whether they ought to defeat Charles completely. This dispute crossed religious lines, though the Independents were in general more determined to force Charles into total submission, and eventually they had their way.

As the fighting continued, Cromwell persuaded the Commons to allow him to reorganize the antiroyalist troops. His New Model Army— whipped to fervor by sermons, prayers, and the singing of psalms—became unbeatable. At Naseby in 1645, it won a major victory, and a year later Charles surrendered. The next two years were chaotic. The Presbyterians and Independ-

▶ *Anonymous*
ENGRAVING OF THE EXECUTION OF CHARLES I
This contemporary Dutch engraving of the
execution of Charles I shows the scaffold in front of
the Banqueting House in Whitehall—a building
that still can be seen in London. On the far right of
the scaffold, the executioner displays the severed
head for the crowd.

ents quarreled over what to do with the king, and
finally Civil War resumed. This time the Presbyterians and Scots backed Charles against the
Independents. But even with this alliance the royalists were no match for the New Model Army;
Cromwell soon defeated his opponents and captured the king.

The King's Fate   At the same time, in 1647, the
Independents abolished the House of Lords and
removed all Presbyterians from the House of
Commons. This "Rump" Parliament tried to negotiate with Charles but discovered that he continued to plot a return to power. With Cromwell's approval, the Commons decided that their
monarch, untrustworthy and a troublemaker,
would have to die. A trial of dubious legality was
held, and though many of the participants refused to sign the death warrant, the "holy,
anointed" king was executed by his subjects in
January 1649, to the horror of all Europe and
most of England.

ENGLAND UNDER CROMWELL

Oliver Cromwell was now master of England.
The republic established after Charles's execution
was officially ruled by the Rump Parliament, but
a Council of State led by Cromwell controlled
policy with the backing of the army. And they
had to contend with a ferment of political and
social ideas. One group, known as the Levellers,

demanded the vote for nearly all adult males and
parliamentary elections every other year. The
men of property among the Puritans, notably
Cromwell himself, were disturbed by the egalitarianism of these proposals and insisted that
only men with an "interest" in England—that is,
land—should be qualified to vote.

Radical Ideas   Even more radical were the Dig-
gers, a communistic sect that sought to implement the spirit of primitive Christianity by abolishing personal property; the Society of Friends,
which stressed personal inspiration as the source
of faith and all action; and the Fifth Monarchists,
a messianic group who believed that the
"saints"—themselves—should rule because the
Day of Judgment was at hand. People of great
ability, such as the famous poet John Milton, contributed to the fantastic flood of pamphlets and
suggestions for reform that poured forth in these
years, and their ideas inspired future revolutionaries. But at the time, they merely put Cromwell

on the defensive, forcing him to maintain control at all costs.

Cromwell's Aims Cromwell himself fought for two overriding causes: religious freedom (except for the Anglican and Catholic churches) and constitutional government. But he achieved neither, and he grew increasingly unhappy at the Rump Parliament's refusal to enact reforms. When the assembly tried to prolong its own existence, he dissolved it in 1653 (the final end of the Long Parliament), and during the remaining five years of his life he tried desperately to lay down a new constitutional structure for his government. Cromwell always hoped that Parliament itself would establish the perfect political system for England, but he refused to influence its proceedings. The result was that he ignored the realities of politics and could never put his ideals into practice.

Cromwell was driven by noble aspirations, but in the end he had to rule by military dicta-torship. From 1653 on he was called lord protector and ruled through 11 major generals, each responsible for a different district of England and supported by a tax on the estates of royalists. To quell dissent, he banned newspapers, and to prevent disorder, he took such measures as enlisting innkeepers as government spies.

Cromwell was always a reluctant revolutionary; he hated power and sought only limited ends. Some revolutionaries, like Lenin, have a good idea of where they would like to be carried by events; others, like Cromwell, move painfully, hesitantly, and uncertainly to the extremes they finally reach. It was because he sought England's benefit so urgently and because he considered the nation too precious to abandon to irreligion or tyranny that Cromwell remained determinedly in command to the end of his life.

The End of the Revolution Gradually, more traditional political forms reappeared. The Parliament of 1656 offered Cromwell the crown, and

Oliver Cromwell's Aims

When Parliament in late 1656 offered to make Oliver Cromwell the king of England as a way of restoring political stability, he hesitated before replying. He soon came to realize, however, that this was a solution that went against his deepest principles. When he finally came to Parliament with his reply on April 13, 1657, he turned down the offer of a crown and explained in a long speech—from which a passage follows—why he felt it would be wrong to reestablish a monarchy in England.

"I do think you ought to attend to the settling of the peace and liberties of this Nation. Otherwise the Nation will fall in pieces. And in that, so far as I can, I am ready to serve not as a King, but as a Constable. For truly I have, before God, often thought that I could not tell what my business was, save comparing myself to a good Constable set to keep the peace of the parish. And truly this hath been my content and satisfaction in the troubles I have undergone.... I was a person who, from my first employment, was suddenly lifted up from lesser trusts to greater.... The Providence of God hath laid aside this Title of King; and that not by sudden humor, but by issue of ten or twelve years Civil War, wherein much blood hath been shed. I will not dispute the justice of it when it was done. But God in His severity hath eradicated a whole Family, and thrust them out of the land. And God hath seemed providential not only in striking at the family but at the Name [of king]. It is blotted out. God blasted the very Title. I will not seek to set up that which Providence hath destroyed, and laid in the dust: I would not build Jericho again."

From Thomas Carlyle (ed.), *Oliver Cromwell's Letters and Speeches* (London, 1908), vol. III, pp. 230, 231, and 235.

though he refused, he took the title of "His Highness" and ensured that the succession would go to his son. Cromwell was monarch in all but name, yet only his presence ensured stability (*see box*, p. 484). After he died, his quiet, retiring son Richard proved no match for the scheming generals of the army, who created political turmoil. To bring an end to the uncertainty, General George Monck, the commander of a well-disciplined force in Scotland, marched south in 1660, assumed control, and invited the son of Charles I, Charles II, to return from exile and restore the monarchy.

Only the actions taken during the first months of the Long Parliament—the abolition of royal courts, the prohibition of taxation without parliamentary consent, and the establishment of the writ of habeas corpus—persisted beyond the revolution. Otherwise, everything seemed much the same as before: Bishops and lords were reinstated, religious dissent was again repressed, and Parliament was called and dissolved by the monarch. But the tone and balance of political relations had changed for good.

Henceforth the gentry could no longer be denied a decisive voice in politics. In essence, this had been their revolution, and they had succeeded. When in the 1680s a king again tried to impose his wishes on the country without reference to Parliament, there was no need for another major upheaval. A quiet bloodless coup reaffirmed the new role of the gentry and Parliament. Thus a new settlement was reached after a long period of growing unease and open conflict. The crisis had been resolved, and the English settled into a system of rule that with only gradual modification remained in force for some two centuries.

V. Revolts in France and Spain

▼

THE FRANCE OF HENRY IV

In the 1590s Henry IV resumed the strengthening of royal power that had been interrupted by the civil wars that had begun in the 1560s. He mol-

lified the traditional landed aristocracy, known as the nobility of the sword, with places on his Council of Affairs and large financial settlements. The principal bureaucrats, known as the nobility of the robe, controlled the country's administration, and Henry made sure to turn their interests to his benefit. Since all crown offices had to be bought, he used the system both to raise revenues and to guarantee the loyalty of the bureaucrats. He not only accelerated the sales of offices but also invented a new device, an annual fee known as the *paulette*, which ensured that an officeholder's job would remain in his family when he died. This increased royal profits (by the end of Henry's reign in 1610, receipts from the sales accounted for one-twelfth of crown revenues), and also reduced the flow of newcomers and thus strengthened the commitment of existing officeholders to the crown.

By 1610 Henry had imposed his will throughout France, and he was secure enough to plan an invasion of the Holy Roman Empire. Although he was assassinated as he was about to join his army, his heritage, especially in economic affairs, long outlived him. France's rich agriculture may have had one unfortunate effect—successful merchants abandoned commerce as soon as they could afford to move to the country and buy a title of nobility (and thus gain exemption from taxes)—but it did ensure a solid basis for the French economy. Indeed, agriculture suffered little during the civil wars, though the violence and the rising taxes did cause uprisings of peasants (the main victims of the tax system) almost every year from the 1590s to the 1670s.

Mercantilism   By restoring political stability Henry ended the worst economic disruptions, but his main legacy was the notion that his increasingly powerful government was responsible for the health of the country's economy. This view was justified by a theory developed mainly in France: mercantilism, which became an essential ingredient of absolutism. Mercantilism was more a set of attitudes than a systematic economic theory. Its basic premise—an erroneous one—was that the world contained a fixed amount of wealth and that each nation could enrich itself only at the expense of others. To some thinkers, this meant hoarding bullion (gold and

▶ *Anonymous*
THE SEINE FROM THE PONT NEUF, CA. 1635
Henry IV of France, celebrated in the equestrian statue overlooking the Seine that stands in Paris to this day, saw the physical reshaping of his capital as part of the effort to restore order after decades of civil war. He laid out the first squares in any European city, and under the shadow of his palace, the Louvre, he built the Pont Neuf (on the right)—the first open bridge (without houses on it) across the Seine.

silver); to others, it required a favorable balance of trade—more exports than imports. All mercantilists, however, agreed that state regulation of economic affairs was necessary for the welfare of a country. Only a strong, centralized government could encourage native industries, control production, set quality standards, allocate resources, establish tariffs, and take other measures to promote prosperity and improve trade. Thus mercantilism was as much about politics as economics and fitted in perfectly with Henry's restoration of royal power. In line with their advocacy of activist policies, the mercantilists also approved of war. Even economic advance was linked to warfare in this violent age.

LOUIS XIII

Unrest reappeared when Henry's death left the throne to his nine-year-old son, Louis XIII (1610–1643). The widowed queen, Marie de Medicis, served as regent and soon faced revolts by Calvinists and disgruntled nobles. In the face of these troubles, Marie summoned the Estates General in 1614. This was their last meeting for 175 years, until the eve of the French Revolution; and the weakness they displayed, as various groups within the Estates fought one another over plans for political reform, demonstrated that the monarchy was the only institution that could unite the nation. The session revealed the impotence of those who opposed royal policies, and Marie brought criticism to an end by declaring her son to be of age and the regency dissolved. In this absolutist state, further protest could be defined as treason.

Richelieu   For a decade, the monarchy lacked energetic direction; but in 1624, one of Marie's favorites, Armand du Plessis de Richelieu, a churchman who rose to be a cardinal through her favor, became chief minister and took control of the government. Over the next 18 years, this ambitious and determined leader resumed Henry IV's assertion of royal authority (*see box*, p. 487).

The monarchy had to manage a number of vested interests as it concentrated its power, and Richelieu's achievement was that he kept them under control. The strongest was the bureaucracy, whose ranks had been swollen by the sale of office. Richelieu always paid close attention to the views of the bureaucrats, and one reason he had such influence over the king was that he acted as the head and representative of this army of royal servants. He also reduced the independence of traditional nobles by giving them positions in the regime as diplomats, soldiers, and officials without significant administrative responsibility. Finally, he took on the Huguenots in a military campaign that led to the capture of their chief bastion, the port of La Rochelle, in 1628. Following the victory he abolished most of the guarantees in the Edict of Nantes and ended the Huguenots' political independence.

Royal Administration   Under Richelieu the sale of office broke all bounds: By 1633 it accounted for approximately one-half of royal revenues. Ten years later more than three-quarters of the crown's direct taxation was needed to pay the salaries of the officeholders. It was a vicious circle, and the only solution was to increase the taxes on the lower classes. As this financial burden grew, Richelieu had to improve the government's control over the realm to obtain the revenue he needed. He increased the power of the *intendants*, the government's chief agents in the localities, and established them (instead of the nobles) as the principal representatives of the monarchy in each province of France. Unlike the nobles, the *intendants* depended entirely on royal favor for their position; and so it was with enthusiasm that they recruited for the army, arranged billeting, supervised the raising of taxes, and enforced the king's decrees. They soon came to be hated figures, both because of the rising taxes and because they threatened the power of the nobles. The result was a succession of peasant uprisings, often led by local notables who resented the rise of the *intendants* and of royal power.

POLITICAL CRISIS

France's foreign wars made the discontent worse, and it was clear that eventually the opponents of the central government would reassert themselves. But the amassing of centralized power by the crown had been so successful that when trou-

Richelieu on Diplomacy

The following passages are taken from a collection of the writings of Cardinal Richelieu that was put together after his death and published in 1688 under the title Political Testament. *The book is presented as a work of advice to the king and summarizes what Richelieu learned of politics and diplomacy as one of Europe's leading statesmen during the Thirty Years' War.*

"One cannot imagine how many advantages States gain from continued negotiations, if conducted wisely, unless one has experienced it oneself. I admit I did not realize this truth for five or six years after first being employed in the management of policy. But I am now so sure of it that I dare say boldly that to negotiate everywhere without cease, openly and secretly, even though one makes no immediate gains and future gains seem unlikely, is absolutely necessary for the good of the State. . . . He who negotiates all the time will find at last the right moment to achieve his aims, and even if he does not find it, at least it is true that he can lose nothing, and that through his negotiations he knows what is happening in the world, which is of no small consequence for the good of the State. . . . Important negotiations must not be interrupted for a moment. . . . One must not be disheartened by an unfortunate turn of events, because sometimes it happens that what is undertaken with good reason is achieved with little good fortune. . . . It is difficult to fight often and always win. . . . It is often because negotiations are so innocent that one can gain great advantages from them without ever faring badly. . . . In matters of State one must find an advantage in everything; that which can be useful must never be neglected."

From Louis André (ed.), *Testament Politique* (Paris, 1947), pp. 347–348 and 352. Translated by T. K. Rabb.

ble erupted, in a series of revolts known as the Fronde (or "tempest"), there was no serious effort to reshape the social order or the political system. The principal actors in the Fronde came from the upper levels of society: nobles, townsmen, and members of the regional courts and legislatures known as parlements. Only occasionally were these groups joined by peasants, and there was little foretaste of the revolution that was to overtake France in 1789.

Mazarin   The death of Louis XIII, in 1643, followed by a regency because Louis XIV was only five years old, offered an opportunity to those who wanted to reverse the rise of absolutism. Louis XIII's widow, Anne of Austria, took over the government and placed all the power in the hands of an Italian, Cardinal Giulio Mazarin. He used his position to amass a huge fortune, and he was therefore a perfect target for the anger caused by the encroachment of central government on local authority

Early in 1648 Mazarin sought to gain a respite from the monarch's perennial financial trouble by withholding payment of the salaries of some royal officials for four years. In response, the members of various institutions in Paris, including the Parlement, drew up a charter of demands. They wanted the office of *intendant* abolished, no new offices created, power to approve taxes, and enactment of a habeas corpus law. The last two demands reflected what the English Parliament was seeking at this very time, but the first two were long-standing French grievances.

THE FRONDE

Mazarin reacted by arresting the Paris Parlement's leaders, thus sparking a popular rebellion in the city that forced him and the royal family to flee from the capital—an experience the young Louis XIV never forgot. In 1649, Mazarin promised to redress the parlementaires' grievances, and he was allowed to return to Paris. But the trouble was far from over; during that summer uprisings spread throughout France, particularly among peasants and in the old Huguenot stronghold, the southwest.

For the next three years there was political chaos, mainly as a result of intrigues and shifting alliances among the nobility. As it became clear

that the perpetual unrest was producing no results, Mazarin was able to take advantage of the disillusionment among the nobles and the parlementaires to reassert the position of the monarchy. He used military force and threats of force to subdue Paris and most of the rebels in the countryside, and he brought the regency to an end by declaring the 14-year-old Louis of age in 1652. Although peasants continued their occasional regional uprisings for many years to come, the Fronde was over and the crown was established as the basis for order in the realm. As surely as England, France had surmounted its crisis and found a stable solution for long-standing conflicts.

SOURCES OF DISCONTENT IN SPAIN

For Spain the crisis that swept much of Europe in the mid-seventeenth century—with revolt in England and France, and war in the empire—meant the end of the country's international power. Yet the difficulties the monarchy faced had their roots in the sixteenth century. Philip II (1556–1598) had already found it difficult to hold his sprawling empire together, despite his elaborate bureaucracy. Obsessively suspicious, he maintained close control over all administrative decisions, and government action was therefore agonizingly slow. Moreover, the bureaucracy was run by Castilian nobles, who were resented as outsiders in other regions of the empire. And the standing army, though essential to royal power, was a terrible financial drain.

Philip did gain wide admiration in Spain for his devoutness. He persecuted heresy, encouraged the Inquisition, and for a while was even suspicious of the great flowering of Spanish mysticism, led by St. Teresa. Philip's commitment to religion undoubtedly promoted political cohesion, but the economic strains caused by relentless religious warfare eventually undermined Spanish power.

Economic Difficulties   Spain was a rich country in Philip's reign, but the most profitable activities were monopolized by limited groups. Because royal policy valued convenience above social benefit, the city of Seville (dominated by foreign bankers) received a monopoly over shipping to and from the New World; and other lucrative

INQVISITION

▶ *Anonymous Engraving*
THE SPANISH INQUISITION, 1560
The burning of heretics was a major public event in sixteenth-century Spain. Aimed mainly at people who practiced Judaism or Islam secretly, and in a few cases at Protestants, the Inquisition's investigations usually led to imprisonment or lesser punishments. The occasional executions of those who determinedly refused to accept Catholic teachings, even after torture, were carried out by secular authorities, and they attracted huge crowds.

pursuits, such as wool and wine production, were also controlled by a small coterie of insiders. The only important economic activities that involved large numbers of Spaniards were shipping and the prosperous Mediterranean trade, centered in Barcelona, which brought wealth to much of Catalonia.

Thus the influx of silver into Spain was not profitably invested within the country. Drastically overextended in foreign commitments, Philip had to declare himself bankrupt three times. For a while it seemed that the problems might ease because there was peace during the reign of Philip's son, Philip III (1598–1621). But,

in fact, Philip III's government was incompetent and corrupt, capable neither of dealing with the serious consequences of the spending on war nor of broadening the country's exports beyond wool and wine. And when the flow of treasure from the New World began to dwindle after 1600, the crown was deprived of a major source of income that it was unable to replace (see table below).

IMPORTS OF TREASURE TO SPAIN FROM THE NEW WORLD, 1591–1660

Decade	Total Value*
1591–1600	85,536,000
1601–1610	66,970,000
1611–1620	65,568,000
1621–1630	62,358,000
1631–1640	40,110,000
1641–1650	30,651,000
1651–1660	12,785,000

*In ducats.

Adapted from J. H. Elliott, *Imperial Spain 1469–1716*, New York, 1964, p. 175.

The decline was caused partly by a growing use of precious metals in the New World colonies but also by the depletion of the mines.

In the meantime, tax returns at home were shrinking. The most significant cause of this decrease was a drop in the population of Castile and Aragon as a result of severe plagues—from 10 million in 1600 to 6 million in 1700. No other country in Europe suffered a demographic reversal of this proportion during the seventeenth century. In addition, sheep farming took over huge tracts of arable land, and Spain had to rely increasingly on the importation of expensive foodstuffs to feed its people.

When Spain resumed large-scale fighting against the Dutch and French under Philip IV (1621–1665), the burdens became too much to bear. The effort to maintain the commitment to war despite totally inadequate finances was to bring the greatest state in Europe to its knees.

REVOLT AND SECESSION

The final crisis was brought about by the policies of Philip IV's chief minister, the count of Olivares. His aim was to unite the realm so that all the territories shared equally the burden of maintaining Spanish power. Although Castile would no longer dominate the government, it would also not have to provide the bulk of the taxes and army. Olivares' program was called the Union of Arms, and while it seemed eminently reasonable, it caused a series of revolts in the 1640s that split Spain apart.

The reason was that Castile's dominance had made the other provinces feel that local independence was being undermined by a centralized regime. They saw the Union of Arms, imposed by Olivares, as the last straw. Moreover, the plan appeared at a time when Spain's military and economic fortunes were in decline. France had declared war on the Habsburgs in 1635, the funds to support an army were becoming harder to raise, and in desperation Olivares pressed more vigorously for the Union of Arms. But all he accomplished was to provoke revolts against the Castilians in the 1640s by Catalonia, Portugal, Naples, and Sicily. By 1641 both Catalonia and Portugal had declared themselves independent republics and placed themselves under French protection. Plots began to appear against Oli-

vares, and Philip dismissed the one minister who had understood Spain's problems but who, in trying to solve them, had made them worse.

The Revolts   The Catalonian rebellion continued for another 11 years, and it was thwarted in the end only because the peasants and town mobs transformed the resistance to the central government into an attack on the privileged and wealthy classes. When this happened, the Catalan nobility abandoned the cause and joined the government side. About the same time, the Fronde forced the withdrawal of French troops from Catalonia. When the last major holdout, Barcelona, fell to a royal army in 1652, the Catalan nobles could regain their rights and powers, and the revolt was over.

The Portuguese had no social upheaval; as a result, though not officially granted independence from Spain until 1668, they defended their autonomy easily and even invaded Castile in the 1640s. But the revolts that the people of Sicily and Naples directed at their Castilian rulers in 1647 took on social overtones. In Naples the unrest developed into a tremendous mob uprising, led by a local fisherman. The poor turned against all the representatives of government and wealth they could find, and chaos ensued until the leader of the revolt was killed. The violence in Sicily, the result of soaring taxes, was aimed primarily at government officials. In both Naples and Sicily, however, a forceful response enabled the government to regain control within a few months.

The effect of all this unrest was finally to end the Spanish government's international ambitions and thus the worst of its economic difficulties. Like England and France, Spain found a new way of life after its crisis, as a stable second-level state, heavily agricultural, run by its nobility.

VI. Political Change in an Age of Crisis

THE UNITED PROVINCES

The Dutch did not escape the struggles against the power of centralized governments that created an atmosphere of crisis in much of Europe during the middle decades of the seventeenth century. Despite the remarkable fluidity of their society, the Dutch, too, became embroiled in a confrontation between a ruling family seeking to extend its authority and citizens defending the autonomy of their local regions. The outcome determined the structure of their government for over a century.

The United Provinces were unique in a number of ways. Other republics existed in Europe, but they were controlled by small oligarchies; the Dutch, who had a long tradition of a strong representative assembly, the Estates General, had created a nation in which many citizens participated in government through elected delegates. Although powerful merchants and a few aristocrats close to the House of Orange did create a small elite, the social differentiation was less than elsewhere in Europe. The resulting openness and homogeneity underlay the economic mastery and cultural brilliance of the United Provinces.

▶ *Anonymous*
ENGRAVING OF A DUTCH SHIPYARD
The Dutch became the best shipbuilders in Europe in the seventeenth century; the efficiency of their ships, which could be manned by fewer sailors than those of other countries, was a major reason for their successes in trade and commerce.

Commerce and Tolerance   The most striking accomplishment of the Dutch was their rise to supremacy in the world of commerce. Amsterdam displaced Antwerp as the continent's financial capital and gained control of the trade of the world's richest markets. In addition, the Dutch rapidly emerged as the cheapest international shippers. As a result, by the middle of the seventeenth century they had become the chief carriers of European commerce.

The openness of Dutch society permitted the freest exchange of ideas of the time. The new state gave refuge to believers of all kinds, whether extreme Protestant radicals or Catholics who wore their faith lightly, and Amsterdam became the center of a brilliant Jewish community. This freedom attracted some of the greatest minds in Europe and fostered remarkable artistic creativity. The energy that produced this outpouring reflected the pride of a tiny nation that was winning its independence from Spain.

Two Political Parties Yet there was a basic split within the United Provinces. The two most urbanized and commercial provinces, Holland and Zeeland, dominated the Estates General because they supplied a majority of its taxes. Their representatives formed a mercantile party, which advocated peace abroad so that their trade could flourish unhampered, government by the Estates General so that they could make their influence felt, and religious toleration so that their cities could attract enterprising people of all faiths. In opposition to this mercantile interest was the House of Orange: the descendants of William of Orange, who sought to establish their family's leadership of the Dutch. They were supported by the more rural provinces and stood for war because their authority and popularity derived from their command of the army, for centralized power to enhance the position of the family, and for the strict Calvinism that was upheld in the rural provinces.

The differences between the two factions led Maurice of Nassau to use religion as a pretext for executing his chief opponent, Jan van Oldenbarneveldt, the main representative of the province of Holland, in 1618. Oldenbarneveldt opposed war with Spain, and his removal left the House of Orange in full control of the country. Maurice resumed the war in 1621, and for more than 20 years, his family remained in command, unassailable because it led the army in wartime. Not until 1648—when a new leader, William II, tried to prolong the fighting—could the mercantile party reassert itself by insisting on peace. As a result, the Dutch signed the Treaty of Westphalia, which officially recognized the independence of the United Provinces. It now seemed that Holland and Zeeland had gained the upper hand. But their struggle with the House of Orange continued (there was even a threat by Orange troops

to besiege Amsterdam) until William II suddenly died in 1650, leaving as his successor a baby son, William III.

Jan De Witt The mercantile interest now assumed full power, and Jan De Witt, the representative of the province of Holland, took over the government in 1653. De Witt's aims were to leave as much authority as possible in the hands of the provinces, particularly Holland; to weaken the executive and prevent a revival of the House of Orange; to pursue trading advantage; and to maintain peace so that the economic supremacy of the Dutch would not be endangered. For nearly 20 years, he guided the country in its golden age. But in 1672 French armies overran the southern provinces, and De Witt lacked the military instinct to fight a dangerous enemy. The Dutch at once turned to the family that had led them to independence; a mob murdered De Witt; and the House of Orange, under William III, resumed the centralization that henceforth was to characterize the political structure of the United Provinces. The country had not experienced a midcentury upheaval as severe as those of its neighbors, but it had nevertheless been forced to endure unrest and violence before the form of its government was securely established.

SWEDEN

The Swedes, too, settled their political system in the mid-seventeenth century. In 1600 Sweden, a Lutheran country of a million people, was one of the backwaters of Europe. A feudal nobility dominated the countryside, a barter economy made money almost unknown, and both trade and towns were virtually nonexistent. Moreover, the country lacked a capital, central institutions, and government machinery. The royal administration consisted of the king and a few courtiers; other officials were appointed only to deal with specific problems as they arose.

Gustavus Adolphus (1611–1632) transformed this situation. He won over the nobles by giving them dominant positions in a newly expanded bureaucracy, and he reorganized his army. Thus equipped both to govern and to fight, Gustavus embarked on a remarkable series of conquests abroad. By 1629 he had made Sweden the most powerful state in the Baltic area. He then entered the Thirty Years' War, advancing victoriously through the Holy Roman Empire until his death, in 1632, during the showdown battle with Wallenstein. Although without their general the Swedes could do little more than hang on to the gains they had made, they were now a force to be reckoned with in international affairs.

Government and Economy The system of government that Gustavus and his chief adviser, Axel Oxenstierna, established was to be the envy of other countries until the twentieth century. At the heart of the system were five administrative departments, each led by a nobleman, with the most important—the Chancellery, for diplomacy and internal affairs—run by Oxenstierna. An administrative center emerged in Stockholm, and the new bureaucracy proved that it could run the nation, supply the army, and implement policy even during the last 12 years of Gustavus' reign, when the king himself was almost always abroad.

A major cause of Sweden's amazing rise was the development of the domestic economy, stimulated by the opening up of copper mines and the development of a major iron industry. The country's traditional tar and timber exports were also stepped up, and a fleet was built. By 1700 Stockholm had become an important trading and financial center, growing in the course of the century from fewer than 5000 to more than 50,000 inhabitants.

The Nobles The one source of tension amidst this remarkable progress was the position of the nobles. After Gustavus died, they openly challenged the monarchy for control of government and society. Between 1611 and 1652 they more than doubled the proportion of land they owned in Sweden, and much of this growth was at the expense of the crown, which granted away or sold lands to help the war effort abroad. Both peasants and townspeople viewed these developments with alarm, because the nobility usually pursued its own rather than public interests. The concern intensified when, in 1648, the nobles in neighboring Denmark took advantage of the

death of a strong king to gain control of the government. Two years later the showdown came in Sweden.

Political Confrontation The monarch now was Gustavus' daughter Christina, an able but erratic young queen who usually allowed Oxenstierna

CHRONOLOGY OF AN AGE OF CRISIS, 1618–1660

1618	Revolt in Bohemia, beginning of Thirty Years' War.
1621	Resumption of war between Spanish and Dutch.
1629	Edict of Restitution—high point of Habsburg power.
1630	Sweden enters war against Habsburgs.
1635	France declares war on Habsburgs.
1639	Scots invade England.
1640	Revolts in Catalonia and Portugal against Spanish government.
1642	Civil War in England.
1647	Revolts in Sicily and Naples against Spanish government.
1648	Peace of Westphalia ending Thirty Years' War. Outbreak of Fronde in France. Coup by nobles in Denmark. Revolt of Ukraine against Poland. Riots in Russian cities.
1650	Constitutional crisis in Sweden. Confrontation between William of Orange and Amsterdam in Netherlands.
1652	End of Catalan revolt.
1653	End of Fronde.
1655	War in Baltic region.
1659	Peace of the Pyrenees between France and Spain.
1660	End of English revolution. Treaties ending war in Baltic.

to run the government. For some time, she had hoped to abdicate her throne, become a Catholic, and leave Sweden—an ambition she fulfilled in 1654. She wanted her cousin Charles recognized as her successor, but the nobles threatened to create a republic if she abdicated. The queen therefore summoned the Riksdag, Sweden's usually weak representative assembly, in 1650; she encouraged the townspeople and peasants to raise their grievances and allowed them to attack the aristocracy. Very soon these groups were demanding the return of nobles' lands to the crown, freedom of speech, and real power; and under this pressure the nobility gave way and recognized Charles X as successor to the throne.

The political upheaval of 1650 was short-lived. Once Christina had her way, she turned her back on the Riksdag and rejected the demands of the lower estates. Only gradually did power shift away from the great nobles toward a broader elite of lesser nobles and bureaucrats, but the turning point in Sweden, as elsewhere, was during the crisis years of the mid-seventeenth century.

EASTERN EUROPE AND THE "CRISIS"

In Eastern Europe, too, long-term patterns became clear in this period. The limits of Ottoman rule were reconfirmed when an attack on Vienna failed in 1683. Poland's weak central government lost all claim to real authority when it proved unable to stop a group of nobles in the rich province of the Ukraine, who rebelled in 1648, from switching allegiance from the king of Poland to the tsar in Moscow. And in Russia, following a period of disorder known as the Time of Troubles (1584–1613), the new Romanov dynasty began consolidating its power. The nobility was won over, the last possibilities for escaping serfdom were closed, the legal system was codified, the church came under the tsar's control, and the revolts that erupted against these changes between 1648 and 1672 were brutally suppressed. As elsewhere in Europe, long-standing conflicts between centralizing regimes and their opponents were resolved, and a new political system, supported by the government's military power, was established for centuries to come.

Because these struggles were so widespread, historians have called the midcentury period an age of "general crisis." In country after country, people tried to resist the growing ambitions of central governments. These confrontations reached crisis proportions in almost all cases during the 1640s and 1650s, and then subsided, at the very time that the anarchy of warfare and international relations seemed to be getting out of hand, only to be resolved by the Peace of Westphalia. As a result, the sense of settlement after 1660 contrasted sharply with the turmoil of the preceding decades. Moreover, the progression in politics from turbulence to calm had its analogies in the cultural and social developments of the sixteenth and seventeenth centuries.

Recommended Reading

Sources

Bodin, Jean. *On Sovereignty.* Julian H. Franklin (ed. and tr.). 1992. An abridgment of Bodin's *Six Books of the Republic.*

*Franklin, Julian H. (ed. and tr.). *Constitutionalism and Resistance in the Sixteenth Century: Three Treatises by Hotman, Beza, & Mornay.* 1969. Three of the most radical tracts of the period, each justifying rebellion.

*Available in paperback.

Kossmann, E. H., and A. E. Mellink. *Texts Concerning the Revolt of the Netherlands.* 1974. A collection of Spanish and Dutch documents which reveal the different political and religious goals of the two sides.

Studies

*Aston, Trevor (ed.). *Crisis in Europe 1560–1660: Essays from Past and Present.* 1965. This is a collection of the essays in which the "general crisis" interpretation was initially put forward and discussed.

Brummett, Palmira. *Ottoman Seapower and Levantine Diplomacy in the Age of Discovery.* 1993.

*DeVries, Jan. *The Economy of Europe in an Age of Crisis, 1600–1750.* 1976. The standard introduction to the economic history of the period.

*Elliott, J. H. *Richelieu and Olivares.* 1984. A comparative study of the two statesmen who dominated Europe in the 1620s and 1630s, this book also analyzes the changing nature of political authority.

*Forster, Robert, and Jack P. Green (eds.). *Preconditions of Revolution in Early Modern Europe.* 1972. An excellent series of essays on resistance to central governments, and its causes, in a number of European countries.

*Hale, J. R. *War and Society in Renaissance Europe 1450–1620.* 1985. A vivid account of what it meant to be a soldier.

Hellie, Richard. *Enserfment and Military Change in Muscovy.* 1971. This study shows the links between military affairs and social change in Russia during the early modern period.

Hirst, Derek. *Authority and Conflict: England, 1603–1658.* 1986. The most recent survey of the revolution and its origins.

Lupinin, N. B. *Religious Revolt in the Seventeenth Century: The Schism of the Russian Church.* 1984. A thorough account of a major feature of Russia's crisis in this period.

Maczak, Antoni, Henryk Samsonowitz, and Peter Burke (eds.). *East-Central Europe in Transition: From the 14th to the 17th Century.* 1985. Essays on the history of Eastern Europe in this period.

*Mattingly, Garrett. *The Armada.* 1959. This beautifully written book, which was a best-seller when it first appeared, is a gripping account of a major international crisis.

Moote, A. Lloyd. *The Revolt of the Judges: The Parlement of Paris and the Fronde 1643–1652.* 1971. This is the most detailed account of the causes of the Fronde and its failures.

*Palliser, D. M. *The Age of Elizabeth: England under the Later Tudors 1547–1603.* 1983. A comprehensive history of English society and government.

Parker, Geoffrey. *The Dutch Revolt.* 1977. This brief book gives a good introduction to the revolt of the Netherlands and the nature of Dutch society in the seventeenth century.

———. *The Military Revolution: Military Innovation and the Rise of the West, 1500–1800.* 1988. The most recent history of the transformation of warfare in this period.

———. *The Thirty Years' War.* 1984. The most up-to-date history of the war.

Pierson, Peter. *Philip II of Spain.* 1975. A clear and lively biography of the dominant figure of the second half of the sixteenth century.

*Rabb, Theodore K. *The Struggle for Stability in Early Modern Europe.* 1975. An assessment of the "crisis" interpretation, including extensive bibliographic references.

Roberts, Michael. *Gustavus Adolphus and the Rise of Sweden.* 1973. This is the best biography of the Swedish king, emphasizing especially his military and administrative achievements.

Salmon, J. H. M. *Society in Crisis: France in the Sixteenth Century.* 1975. A clearly written overview, focusing mainly on the religious wars and Henry IV.

*Skinner, Quentin. *The Foundations of Modern Political Thought.* 1978. The standard account of the political theories of the fifteenth and sixteenth centuries.

Stone, Lawrence. *The Causes of the English Revolution, 1529–1642.* 1972. A short but comprehensive assessment of the reasons for the outbreak of the seventeenth century's most far-reaching revolution.

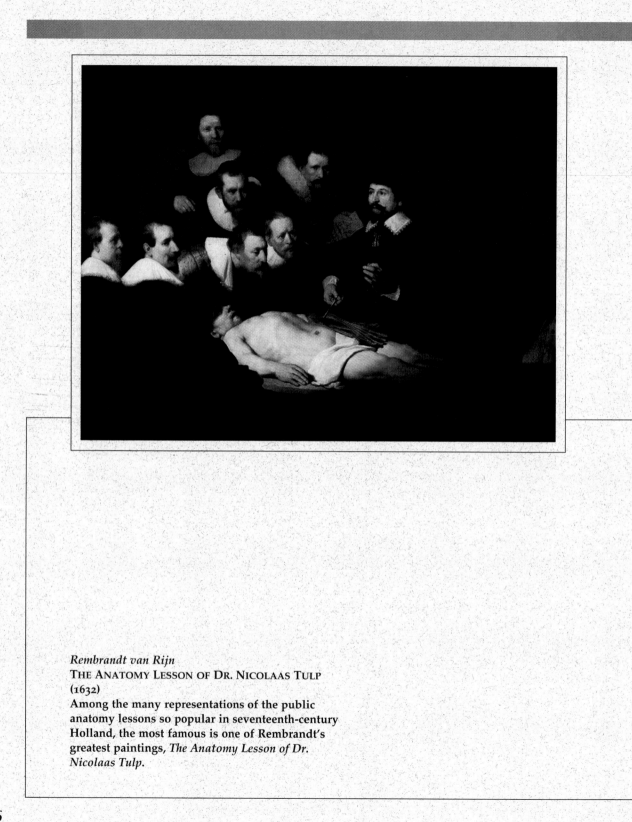

Rembrandt van Rijn
THE ANATOMY LESSON OF DR. NICOLAAS TULP
(1632)
Among the many representations of the public
anatomy lessons so popular in seventeenth-century
Holland, the most famous is one of Rembrandt's
greatest paintings, *The Anatomy Lesson of Dr.
Nicolaas Tulp.*

CHAPTER SIXTEEN

CULTURE AND SOCIETY IN THE AGE OF THE SCIENTIFIC REVOLUTION

O F all the many changes of the sixteenth and seventeenth centuries, none had a more far-reaching impact than the scientific revolution. By creating a new way of understanding how nature worked—and by solving long-standing problems in physics, astronomy, and anatomy—the theorists and experimenters of this period convinced their contemporaries that they had discovered new knowledge. They were not merely adapting the ideas of the revered figures of Greece and Rome; they had gone further than the ancients. Although their revolution began with disturbing questions but few clear answers about traditional ideas, they ended up by offering a promise of certain knowledge and truth that was eagerly embraced by a society that had been racked by decades of religious and political turmoil and the horrors of war. Indeed, it is remarkable how closely intellectual and cultural patterns paralleled the progression from struggle and uncertainty to stable resolution that marked the political developments of these years. In international and domestic politics a series of clashes grew ever more intense until, following a major crisis in the mid-seventeenth century, Europe's states were able to create more settled conditions. Similarly, in the realms of philosophy and the study of nature, a long period of searching, anxiety, and dispute (epitomized by the confrontation of one scientist, Galileo Galilei, with traditional authority) was resolved in the mid-seventeenth century by scientists whose discoveries and self-assurance helped restore a sense of order in intellectual life. And in literature, the arts, and social relations, a time of insecurity and doubt gave way to an atmosphere of confidence and calm.

I. The Scientific Revolution

ORIGINS OF THE SCIENTIFIC REVOLUTION

The Importance of Antiquity Until the sixteenth century, the study of nature in Europe was inspired by the ancient Greeks. Their work shaped subsequent research in three main fields: Aristotle in physics, Ptolemy in astronomy, and Galen in medicine. The most dramatic advances during the scientific revolution came in these fields, to some extent because it was becoming evident that the ancient theories could not account for new observations without highly complicated adjustments.

For instance, Aristotle's belief that all objects in their natural state are at rest created a number of problems, such as explaining why an arrow kept on flying after it left a bow. Similarly, Ptolemy's picture of the heavens, in which all motion was circular around a central earth, did not readily explain the peculiar motion that observers no-

ticed in some planets, which at times seemed to be moving backward. And Galen's anatomical theories were often shown by dissections to be wrong.

Still, it is not likely that scientists (who in the sixteenth and seventeenth centuries were still known as "natural philosophers," or seekers of wisdom about nature) would have abandoned their cherished theories—they far preferred making adjustments to accepted theories than beginning anew—if it had not been for other influences at work in this period. One such stimulus to rethinking was the humanists' rediscovery of a number of previously unknown ancient scientists, who had not always agreed with the theories of Aristotle or Ptolemy. A particularly important rediscovery was the work of Archimedes, whose writings on dynamics helped inspire new ideas in physics.

"Magic" Another influence was a growing interest in what we now dismiss as "magic," but which at the time was regarded as a serious intellectual enterprise. There were various sides to magical inquiry. Alchemy was the belief that matter could be understood and transformed by mixing substances and using secret formulas. A famous sixteenth-century alchemist, Paracelsus, suggested that metals as well as plants might have medicinal properties, and he helped demonstrate that mercury (if carefully used) could cure syphilis. Another favorite study was astrology, which suggested that natural phenomena could be predicted if planetary movements were properly interpreted.

What linked these "magical" beliefs was the conviction that the world could be understood through simple, comprehensive keys to nature. The theories of Neoplatonism—an influential school of thought during the Renaissance, based

▶ *Peter Brueghel*
THE ALCHEMIST, ENGRAVING
This down-to-earth portrayal, typical of Brueghel's art, shows the alchemist as an undisciplined figure. He is surrounded by a chaos of instruments and half-finished experiments, and his helpers resemble witches. Like Brueghel, most people thought it unlikely that this disorganized figure would make a major contribution to the understanding of nature.

on Plato's belief that truth lay in essential but hidden "forms"—supported this conviction, as did some of the mystical ideas that attracted attention at the same time. One of the latter, derived from a system of Jewish thought known as *cabala*, suggested that the universe might be built around magical arrangements of numbers. The ancient Greek mathematician Pythagoras had also suggested that numerical patterns might connect all of nature, and his ideas now gained new attention. For all its irrational elements, it was precisely this interest in new and simple solutions for long-standing problems that made natural philosophers capable, for the first time, of discarding the honored theories they had inherited from antiquity, trying different ones, paying greater attention to mathematics, and eventually creating an intellectual revolution.

Observations, Experiments, and Instruments Two other influences deserve mention. The first was Europe's fascination with technological invention. The architects, navigators, engineers, and weapons experts of the Renaissance were important pioneers of a new reliance on measurement and observation that affected not only how domes were built or heavy cannon were moved but also how problems in physics were addressed. A second, and related, influence was the growing interest in experiment among anatomists. In particular, the medical school at the university of Padua became famous for its dissections and direct observations of nature; many leading figures in the scientific revolution were trained there.

It was not too surprising, therefore, that important new instruments were invented in the sixteenth and seventeenth centuries which helped make scientific discovery possible: the telescope, the vacuum pump, the thermometer, the barometer, and the microscope. These instruments encouraged the development of a scientific approach that was entirely new in the seventeenth century: It did not go back to the ancients, to the practitioners of magic, or to the engineers. It was to be pioneered by the Englishman Francis Bacon (1561–1626—see p. 505) and consisted of the belief that in order to make nature reveal its secrets, it had to be made to do things it did not do normally: In Bacon's phrase, one had to "twist

the lion's tail." What this meant was that one did not simply observe phenomena that occurred normally in nature—for instance, the way a stick seems to bend when it is placed in a glass of water—but created conditions that were *not* normal. With the telescope, one saw secrets hidden to the naked eye; with the vacuum pump, one could understand the properties of air.

THE BREAKTHROUGHS

The earliest scientific advances came in anatomy and astronomy, and by coincidence they were announced in two books published in 1543, which was also the year when the earliest printed edition of Archimedes appeared. The first book, *The Structure of the Human Body* by Andreas Vesalius (1514–1564), a member of the Padua faculty, pointed out errors in the work of Galen, the chief authority in medical practice for over a thousand years. Using dissections, Vesalius produced anatomical descriptions that opened a new era of careful observation and experimentation in studies of the body.

Copernicus The second book, *On the Revolutions of the Heavenly Spheres* by Nicolaus Copernicus (1473–1543), a Polish cleric who had studied at Padua, had far greater consequences. A first-rate mathematician, he felt that the calculations of planetary movements under Ptolemy's system had grown too complex. In Ptolemaic astronomy, the planets and the sun, attached to transparent, crystalline spheres, revolved around the earth. All motion was circular, and irregularities were accounted for by epicycles—movement around small revolving spheres that were attached to the larger spheres. Influenced by Neoplatonic ideas, Copernicus believed that a simpler picture would reflect more accurately the true structure of the universe. In good Neoplatonic fashion, he argued that the sun, as the most splendid of celestial bodies, ought rightfully to be at the center of an orderly and harmonious universe. The earth, no longer immobile, would thus circle the sun.

Copernicus' system was, in fact, scarcely simpler than Ptolemy's—the spheres and epicycles were just as complex—and he had no way of demonstrating the superiority of his theory. But he was such a fine mathematician that his suc-

▶ *Titian* (attrib.)
**ENGRAVING ILLUSTRATING ANDREAS VESALIUS,
THE STRUCTURE OF THE HUMAN BODY (1543)**
**Almost as remarkable as the findings themselves
were these illustrations of the results of Vesalius'
dissections. Traditionally, professors of anatomy
read from textbooks to their students while lowly
barber-surgeons cut up a cadaver and displayed the
parts being discussed. Vesalius did his dissections
himself, and thus could observe directly such
structures as the musculature. Here his illustrator
displays the muscles on a gesturing figure and
places it in a stretch of countryside near Padua,
where Vesalius taught.**

cessors found his calculations of planetary motions indispensable. His ideas thus became part
of intellectual discussion, drawn on when Pope
Gregory XIII decided to reform the calendar in
1582. The Julian calendar, in use since Roman

times, counted century years as leap years, thus
adding extra days that caused Easter—whose
date is determined by the position of the sun—to
drift farther and farther away from its normal occurrence in late March. The reform produced the
Gregorian calendar, which we still use. Ten days
were simply dropped: October 5, 1582, became
October 15; and since then only one out of every
four century years has been counted as a leap
year (1900 had no February 29, but 2000 will have
one). The need for calendar reform had been one
of the motives for Copernicus' studies, which
thus proved useful even though his theories remained controversial.

Theories in Conflict The effect of *Revolutions* for
more than half a century was to cause growing
uncertainty, as the scholarly community argued
over the validity of the new ideas and the need
to abandon the old ones. The leading astronomer
of the period, the Dane Tycho Brahe (1546–1601),
produced the most remarkable observations of
the heavens before the invention of the telescope
by plotting the paths of the moon and planets
every night for decades. But the only theory he
could come up with was an uneasy compromise
between the Ptolemaic and Copernican systems.
There was similar indecision among anatomists,
who admired Vesalius but were not ready to dis-
card Galen. As late as 1600 or so, it seemed that
scientists were creating more problems than answers. But then two brilliant discoverers—Johannes Kepler (1571–1630), a German disciple of
Brahe, and Galileo Galilei, an Italian professor of
mathematics—made major advances on the work
of Copernicus and helped resolve the uncertainties that had arisen in the field of astronomy.

KEPLER AND GALILEO

Kepler Like Copernicus, Kepler believed that
only the language of mathematics could describe
the movements of the heavens. He was a famous
astrologer and an advocate of magical theories,
but he was also convinced that Copernicus was
right. He threw himself into the task of confirming the sun-centered (heliocentric) theory, and by
studying Brahe's observations, he discovered
three laws of planetary motion (published in 1609
and 1619) that opened a new era in astronomy.

Kepler was able to prove that the orbits of the planets are ellipses and that there is a regularity, based on their distance from the sun, that determines the movements of all planets. So revolutionary were these laws that few astronomers accepted them until Isaac Newton used them 50 years later as the basis for a new system of the heavens.

Galileo A contemporary of Kepler's, the Italian Galileo Galilei (1564–1642) took these advances a stage further when he became the first to perceive the connection between planetary motion and motion on earth. His studies revealed the importance to astronomy not only of observation and mathematics but also of physics. Moreover, he was the first to bring the new understanding of the universe to the attention of a reading public beyond the scholarly world. Galileo's self-consciousness about technique, argument, and evidence marks him as one of the first investigators of nature to approach his work in essentially the same way as a modern scientist.

Physics The study of motion inspired Galileo's most fundamental scientific contributions. When he began his investigations, the Aristotelian view that a body is naturally at rest and needs to be pushed constantly to keep moving dominated the study of dynamics. Galileo broke with this tradition, developing instead a new type of physical explanation that was perfected by Isaac Newton half a century later. Much of Galileo's work was based on observation. From watching how workers at the Arsenal in Venice used pulleys and other devices to lift huge weights, he gained insights into physics; adapting a Dutch lens maker's invention, he built himself a primitive telescope that was essential to his studies of the heavens; and his seemingly mundane experiments, such as swinging a pendulum or rolling balls down inclined planes, were crucial means of testing his theories. Indeed, it was by moving from observations to abstraction that Galileo arrived at the first wholly new way of understanding motion since Aristotle: the principle of inertia.

This breakthrough could not have been made by observation alone. For the discovery of inertia depended on mathematical abstraction, the ability to imagine a situation that cannot be created experimentally: the motion of a perfectly smooth ball across a perfectly smooth plane, free of any outside forces, such as friction. Galileo's conclusion was that "any velocity once imparted to a moving body will be rigidly maintained as long as external causes of acceleration and retardation are removed. . . . If the velocity is uniform, it will not be diminished or slackened, much less destroyed." This insight overturned the Aristotelian view. Galileo had demonstrated that only mathematical language could describe the underlying principles of nature.

Astronomy Galileo's most celebrated work was in astronomy. He first became famous in 1610, when he published his discoveries with the telescope that Jupiter has satellites and the moon has mountains. Both these revelations were further blows to traditional beliefs, which held that the earth is changing and imperfect while the heav-

▶ *Galileo Galilei*
THE MOON, 1610
This sketch of the moon's surface appeared in Galileo's *Starry Messenger* (1610). It shows what he had observed through the telescope and had interpreted as proof that the moon had a rugged surface because the lighted area within the dark section had to be mountains. These caught the light of the setting sun longer than surrounding lower terrain and revealed, for example, a large cavity in the lower center of the sketch.

ens are immutable and unblemished. Now, however, it seemed that other planets had satellites, just like the earth, and that these satellites might have the same rough surface as the earth.

This was startling enough, but Galileo also argued that the principles of terrestrial physics could be used to explain phenomena in the heavens. He calculated the height of the mountains on the moon by using the geometric techniques of surveyors, and he described the moon's secondary light—seen while it is a crescent—as a reflection of sunlight from the earth. Galileo was treating his own planet simply as one part of a uniform universe. Every physical law, he was saying, is equally applicable on earth and in the heavens, including the laws of motion. As early as 1597 Galileo had admitted (in a letter to Kepler) that some of his discoveries in physics could be explained only if the earth were moving, and during the next 30 years he became the most famous advocate of Copernicanism in Europe (*see box*, below).

Galileo made a powerful case. Why, he asked, was it necessary to say that the entire universe revolved around the earth when all celestial motions could be explained by the rotation of a single planet, the earth? When academic and religious critics pointed out that we would feel the earth moving, or that the Bible said Joshua made the sun stand still, he reacted with scorn. In response to religious objections, he asserted that "in discussions of physical problems we ought to begin not from the authority of scriptural passages, but from sense experience and necessary demonstrations."

Conflict with the Church For all the brilliance of his arguments, Galileo was now on dangerous ground. Although traditionally the Catholic Church had not concerned itself with investigations of nature, in the early seventeenth century the situation was changing. The Church was deep in the struggle with Protestantism, and it responded to the challenge to its authority by try-

---

Galileo and Kepler on Copernicus

In 1597 Kepler sent Galileo a copy of his New Astronomy, *which argued for the Copernican theory of the heavens and asked the Italian for his opinion. The exchange of letters that followed, with Galileo cautious and Kepler urging him on, reflects an age when the new ideas were not yet proved and also gives a hint, in Kepler's last comments, of the troubles that lay ahead.*

Galileo to Kepler: "Like you, I accepted the Copernican position several years ago. I have written up many reasons on the subject, but have not dared until now to bring them into the open. I would dare publish my thoughts if there were many like you; but, since there are not, I shall forbear."

Kepler's Reply: "I could only have wished that you, who have so profound an insight, would choose another way. You advise us to retreat before the general ignorance and not to expose ourselves to the violent attacks of the mob of scholars. But after a tremendous task has been begun in our time, first by Copernicus and then by many very

learned mathematicians, and when the assertion that the Earth moves can no longer be considered something new, would it not be much better to pull the wagon to its goal by our joint efforts, now that we have got it under way, and gradually, with powerful voices, to shout down the common herd? Be of good cheer, Galileo, and come out publicly! If I judge correctly, there are only a few of the distinguished mathematicians of Europe who would part company with us, so great is the power of truth. If Italy seems a less favorable place for your publication, perhaps Germany will allow us this freedom."

From Giorgio de Santillana, *The Crime of Galileo* (Chicago: University of Chicago Press, 1955), pp. 11 and 14–15.

ing to control potentially questionable views. And Galileo's biting sarcasm toward other scientists antagonized Jesuit and Dominican astronomers. These two orders were the chief upholders of orthodoxy in the Church. They referred Galileo's views to the Inquisition and then guided the attack on Copernicanism by seeking to condemn the brilliant advocate who had made the theory famous throughout Europe.

In 1616 the Inquisition forbade Galileo, within certain limits, to teach the heretical doctrine that the earth moves. When one of his friends was elected pope in 1623, however, Galileo thought he would be safe in writing a major work on astronomy, as long as he remained within the limits set in 1616. The result was Galileo's masterpiece, the *Dialogue on the Two Great World Systems*, published in 1632 (with the approval, probably accidental, of the Church). A marvelously witty, elegant book, the *Dialogue* is one of the few monuments in the history of science that the layperson can read with pleasure. And so it was intended. Galileo wrote it in Italian, not the Latin that had always been used for scholarly works, because he wanted it to reach the widest possible audience.

In April 1633 he was brought before the Inquisition for having defied the order not to teach Copernicanism. To establish their case, his accusers used a forged document that suggested the 1616 limits were stricter than they were. In a trial that has caused controversy ever since, the aged astronomer, under threat of torture, abjured the "errors and heresies" of believing that the earth moved. But he did not remain docile for the remainder of his life, though he was kept under house arrest and progressively lost his eyesight. He had his principal work on physics, the *Two New Sciences*, published in tolerant Holland in 1638, while many of his letters ridiculed his opponents.

Galileo's Legacy Galileo's condemnation discouraged further scientific activity by his compatriots. Italy had been a leader of the new investigations, but now major further advances were to be made by the English, Dutch, and French. Yet this shift showed merely that the rise of science, once begun, could not be halted for long. By the late 1630s no self-respecting astron-

omer could deny the correctness of the Copernican theory.

The new studies of nature may have started out by causing tremendous bewilderment, as scientists struggled with the ideas of pioneers like Copernicus and Vesalius. But in the end these investigations created a renewed sense of certainty about the physical world that was to have a far-reaching influence. And this was true not only in physics and astronomy but also in anatomy, where, in 1628, another genius of the scientific revolution, the English doctor William Harvey, revolutionized the understanding of the human body when he identified the function of the heart and proved that the blood circulates.

ISAAC NEWTON

The culmination of the scientific revolution was the work of Isaac Newton (1642–1727), who made decisive contributions to mathematics, physics, astronomy, and optics and brought to a climax the changes that had begun with Copernicus. He united physics and astronomy in a single system to explain all motion, he helped transform mathematics by the development of the calculus, and he established some of the basic laws of modern physics.

Part of the explanation of his versatility lies in the workings of the scientific community at the time. Newton was a retiring man who nevertheless got into fierce arguments with such prominent contemporaries as the learned German scholar and scientist Wilhelm von Leibniz, who was working on the calculus. If not for his active participation in meetings of scientists at the recently founded Royal Society of London (see p. 509) and the effort he had to make to demonstrate his views to his colleagues, Newton might never have pursued his researches to their conclusion. He disliked the give-and-take of these discussions, but he felt forced in self-justification to prepare some of his most important papers for the Royal Society. Such institutions were now being established throughout Europe to promote the advance of science, and their creation indicates how far the scientific community had come since the days of Copernicus, who had worked largely in isolation.

The Principia Newton's masterpiece, *The Mathematical Principles of Natural Philosophy* (1687)—usually referred to by the first word of its Latin title, the *Principia*—was the last widely influential book to be written in Latin, the traditional language of scholarship. Latin was still useful to Newton, who wanted as many experts as possible to read the book because he was seeking to refute the approach to science associated with the widely admired French philosopher and mathematician René Descartes (see p. 506). In contrast to Descartes, who emphasized the powers of the mind and pure reason in investigating nature, Newton felt that mere hypotheses, constructions of logic and words, were not the tools of a true scientist. As he put it in a celebrated phrase, *"Hypotheses non fingo"* ("I do not posit hypotheses"), because everything he said was proved by experiment or by mathematics.

The most dramatic of Newton's findings was the solution to the ancient problem of motion. Building on Galileo's advances and overturning Aristotle's theories once and for all, Newton defined his system in three laws: first, in the absence of force, motion continues in a straight line; second, the rate of change of the motion is determined by the forces acting on it (such as friction); and third, action and reaction between two bodies are equal and opposite. To arrive at these laws, he defined the concepts of mass, inertia, and force in relation to velocity and acceleration as we know them today.

Newton extended these principles to the entire universe by demonstrating that his laws govern the motions of the moon and planets too. Using the concept of gravity, he provided the explanation of the movement of objects in space that is the foundation for current space travel. There is a balance, he said, between the earth's pull on the moon and the forward motion of the satellite, which would continue in a straight line were it not for the earth's gravity. Consequently the moon moves in an elliptical orbit in which neither gravity nor inertia gains control. The same pattern is followed by the planets around the sun (as Kepler had shown).

The Influence of Newton It was largely on the basis of the uniformity and the systematic impersonal forces Newton described that the view of the universe as a vast machine gained ground. According to this theory, all motion is a result of precise, unvarying, and demonstrable forces. There is a celestial mechanics just like the mechanics that operates on earth. It was not far from this view to the belief that God is a great watchmaker who started the marvelous mechanism going but intervenes only when something goes wrong and needs repair. The general philosophical implication that the world was stable and orderly was as important as the specific discoveries in making Newton one of the idols of his own and the next centuries. The educated applauded Newton's achievements, and he was the first scientist to receive a knighthood in England. Only a few decades after the appearance of the *Principia*, the poet Alexander Pope summed up the public feeling:

> Nature and nature's law lay hid in night;
> God said, "Let Newton be!" and all was light.

So overpowering was Newton's stature that in physics and astronomy the remarkable advances of 150 years slowed down for more than half a century after the publication of the *Principia*. There was a general impression that somehow Newton had done it all, that no important problems remained. There were other reasons for the slowdown—changing patterns in education, an inevitable lessening of momentum—but none was so powerful as the reverence for Newton, who became the intellectual symbol of his own and succeeding ages.

A NEW EPISTEMOLOGY

Galileo had stressed that his discoveries rested on a way of thinking that had an independent value, and he refused to allow traditional considerations, such as common sense or theological teachings, to interfere with his conclusions. Scientists were now moving toward a new epistemology, a new theory of how to obtain and verify knowledge. They stressed experience, reason, and doubt; they rejected all unsubstantiated authority; and they developed a revolutionary way of determining what was a true description of physical reality.

The process the scientists said they followed,

after they had formulated a hypothesis, consisted of three parts: first, observations; second, a generalization induced from the observations; and third, tests of the generalization by experiments whose outcome could be predicted by the generalization. A generalization remained valid only as long as it was not contradicted by the experiments specifically designed to test it. The scientist used no data except the results of strict observation—such as the time it took balls to roll down Galileo's inclined planes, or the path Kepler saw the plants following—and scientific reasoning was confined to the perception of the laws, principles, or patterns that emerged from the observations. Since measurement was the key to the data, the observations had a numerical, not a subjective, value; and the language of science naturally came to be mathematics.

In fact, scientists rarely reach conclusions in the exact way this idealized scheme suggests. Galileo's perfectly smooth balls and planes, for instance, did not exist, but Galileo understood the relevant physical theory so well that he knew what would have happened if one had rolled across the other, and he used this "experiment" to demonstrate the principle of inertia. In other words, experiments as well as hypotheses can occur in the mind; the essence of scientific method still remains a special way of looking at and understanding nature.

THE WIDER INFLUENCE OF SCIENTIFIC THOUGHT

The principles of scientific inquiry received attention throughout the intellectual community only gradually; it took time for the power of the scientists' method to be recognized. For decades, as Galileo found out, even his fellow astronomers continued to use what he would have considered irrelevant criteria, such as the teachings of the Bible, in judging scientific work. If the new methods were to be accepted, then their effectiveness would have to be demonstrated to more than a few specialists. This wider understanding was eventually achieved by midcentury as much through the efforts or ardent propagandizers like Francis Bacon as through the writings of the great innovators themselves. Gradually, they were able to convince a broad, educated public that science,

▶ *Anonymous*
PORTRAIT OF ISAAC NEWTON
The increasingly common portraits of scientists in the seventeenth century—Descartes was even painted by one of the leading artists of his age, Frans Hals—testify to their growing fame. In this case, the intensity of Newton's gaze hints at the power of scientific insight that contemporaries thought he embodied.

after first causing doubts by challenging ancient truths, now offered a promise of certainty that was not to be found anywhere else in an age of general crisis.

BACON AND DESCARTES

Bacon Although he was not an important scientist himself, Francis Bacon was the greatest of science's propagandists, and he inspired a whole generation with his vision of what it could accomplish for humanity. His description of an ideal society in the *New Atlantis*—published in

1627, the year after his death—is a vision of science as the savior of the human race. It predicts a time when those doing research at the highest levels will be regarded as the most important people in the state and will work on a vast government-supported project to gather all known facts about the physical universe. By a process of gradual induction, this information will lead to universal laws that, in turn, will enable people to improve their lot on earth.

Bacon's view of research as a collective enterprise inspired a number of later scientists, particularly the founders of the Royal Society of London. By the mid-seventeenth century, his ideas had entered the mainstream of European thought, an acceptance that testified to the broadening interest in science.

Descartes The Frenchman René Descartes (1596–1650) made the first concentrated attempt to apply the new methods of science to theories of knowledge, and, in so doing, he laid the foundations for modern philosophy. The impulse behind his work was his realization that for all the importance of observation and experiment, people can be deceived by their senses. In order to find some solid truth, therefore, he decided to apply the principle of doubt—the refusal to accept any authority without strict verification—to all knowledge. He began with the assumption that he could know unquestionably only one thing: that he was doubting. This allowed him to proceed to the observation "I think, therefore I am," because the act of doubting proved he was thinking, and thinking, in turn, demonstrated his existence.

The heart of his philosophy was his statement that whatever is clearly and distinctly thought must be true. This was a conclusion drawn from the proof of his own existence, and it enabled him to construct a proof of God's existence. We cannot fail to realize that we are imperfect, he argued, and we must therefore have an idea of perfection against which we may be measured. If we have a clear idea of what perfection is, then it must exist; hence there must be a God.

This proof may have served primarily to show that the principle of doubt did not contradict religious belief, but it also reflected the emphasis on the power of the mind in his great work, *Dis-*

course on the Method of Rightly Conducting the Reason and Seeking Truth in the Sciences (1637). Thought is a pure and unmistakable guide, and only by reliance on its operations can people hope to advance their understanding of the world.

Descartes developed this view into a fundamental proposition about the nature of the world—a proposition that philosophers have been wrestling with ever since. He stated that there is an essential divide between thought and extension (tangible objects) or, put another way, between spirit and matter. Bacon and Galileo had insisted that science, the study of nature, is separate from and unaffected by faith or theology, the study of God. But Descartes turned this distinction into a far-reaching principle, dividing not only science from faith but even the reality of the world from our perception of that reality. There is a difference, in other words, between a chair and how we think of it as a chair.

The Influence of Descartes The emphasis Descartes placed on the operations of the mind gave a new direction to epistemological discussions. A hypothesis gained credibility not so much from external proofs as from the logical tightness of the arguments used to support it. The decisive test was how lucid and irrefutable a statement appeared to be to the thinking mind, not whether it could be demonstrated by experiments. Descartes thus applied what he considered to be the methods of science to all knowledge. Not only the phenomena of nature but all truth had to be investigated according to what he regarded as the strict principles of the scientist.

At the same time, his insistence on strict definitions of cause and effect helped create a general scientific and intellectual theory known as *mechanism*. In its simplest form, mechanism holds that the entire universe, including human beings, can be regarded as a complicated machine and thus subject to strict physical principles. The arm is like a lever, the elbow is like a hinge, and so on. Even an emotion is no more than a simple response to a definable stimulus. This view was to influence philosophers for generations.

Descartes' contributions to the scientific research of his day were theoretical rather than experimental. In physics, he was the first to perceive the distinction between mass and weight; and in mathematics, he was the first to apply algebraic notations and methods to geometry, thus founding analytic geometry. Above all, his emphasis on the principle of doubt undermined forever such traditional assumptions as the belief in the hierarchical organization of the universe. And the admiration he inspired indicated how completely the methods he advocated had captured his contemporaries' imagination.

BLAISE PASCAL

At midcentury only one important voice still protested against the new science and, in particular, against the materialism of Descartes. It belonged to a Frenchman, Blaise Pascal, a brilliant mathematician and experimenter. Before his death at the age of 39 in 1662, Pascal's investigations of probability in games of chance produced the theorem that still bears his name, and his research in conic sections helped lay the foundations for integral calculus. He also helped discover barometric pressure and invented a calculating machine. In his late twenties, however, Pascal became increasingly dissatisfied with scientific research, and he began to wonder whether his life was being properly spent. His doubts were reinforced by frequent visits to his sister, a nun at the Abbey of Port-Royal, where he came into contact with a new spiritual movement within Catholicism known as *Jansenism*.

Jansenism, which insisted that salvation was entirely in the hands of an all-powerful God and that unswerving faith was the only path to salvation, was not a particularly popular movement. But it guided the nuns at Port-Royal; and Pascal was profoundly impressed by their piety, asceticism, and spirituality. Moved by a growing concern with faith, Pascal had a mystical experience in November 1654 that made him resolve to devote his life to the salvation of his soul. He adopted the austere doctrines of Jansenism, and wrote a series of devastating critiques of the more worldly Jesuits, accusing them of irresponsibility and, as he phrased it, of placing cushions under sinners' elbows.

***The* Pensées** During the few remaining years of his life, Pascal put on paper a collection of reflec-

tions—some only a few words long, some many pages—that were gathered together after his death and published as the *Pensées* (or "reflections"). These writings revealed not only the beliefs of a deeply religious man but also the anxieties of a scientist who feared the growing influence of science. He did not wish to put an end to research; he merely wanted people to realize that the truths uncovered by science were limited and not as important as the truths perceived by faith. As he put it in one of his more memorable *Pensées*, "The heart has its reasons that reason cannot know."

Pascal was warning against the replacement of the traditional understanding of humanity and its destiny, gained through religious faith, with the conclusions reached by the methods of the scientists. The separation between the material and the spiritual would be fatal, he believed, because it would destroy the primacy and even the importance of the spiritual. Pascal's protest was unique, but the fact that it was put forward at all indicates how high the status of the scientist and his methods had risen by the 1650s. Just a quarter-century earlier, such a dramatic change in fortune would have been hard to predict. But now the new epistemology, after its initial disturbing assault on ancient views, was offering one of the few promises of certainty in an age of upheaval and general crisis. In intellectual matters as in politics, turmoil was gradually giving way to assurance.

SCIENCE INSTITUTIONALIZED

There were many besides Bacon who realized that scientific work should be a cooperative endeavor and that information should be exchanged among all its practitioners. A scientific society founded in Rome in 1603 made the first major effort to apply this view, and it was soon followed up in France, where in the early seventeenth century a friar named Marin Mersenne became the center of an international network of correspondents interested in scientific work. He also spread news by bringing scientists together for discussions and experiments. Contacts that were developed at these meetings led eventually to a more permanent and systematic organization of scientific activity.

Map 16.1 SPEED OF NEWS TRAVELING TO VENICE IN 1500 AND 1700
Although the dramatic advances in communications lay in the future, by 1700
improved roads and canals and more efficient shipping did bring about
significant advances in the distance news could travel in two or three weeks.

508

The Royal Society In England, the first steps toward such organization were taken at Oxford during the Civil War in the 1640s, when the revolutionaries captured the city and replaced those at the university who taught traditional natural philosophy. A few of the newcomers formed what they called the Invisible College, a group that met to exchange information and discuss one another's work. The group included only one first-class scientist, the chemist Robert Boyle; but in 1660 he and 11 others formed an official organization, the Royal Society of London for Improving Natural Knowledge, with headquarters in the capital. In 1662 it was granted a charter by Charles II—the first sign of a connection with political authority that not only boosted science but also indicated the growing presence of central governments in all areas of society.

The Royal Society's purposes were openly Baconian. Its aim for a few years—until everyone realized it was impossible—was to gather all knowledge about nature, particularly if it had practical uses. For a long time the members offered their services for the public good, helping in one instance to develop the science of social

statistics ("political arithmetic," as it was called) for the government. Soon, however, it became clear that the society's principal function was to serve as a headquarters and clearing center for research. Its secretaries maintained an enormous correspondence to encourage English and foreign scholars to send in news of their discoveries. And in 1665 the society began the regular publication of *Philosophical Transactions*, the first professional scientific journal.

Imitators were soon to follow. In 1666 Louis XIV gave his blessing to the founding of a French Royal Academy of Sciences, and similar organi-

▶ *Charles-Nicolas Cochin*
THE ACADÉMIE ROYALE DES SCIENCES, PARIS, ENGRAVING, 1698
This celebration of the work done by one of the first scientific societies suggests the variety of research that these organizations promoted. In contrast to the students of theology who merely read books (as we see through the arch on the right), the geographers, engineers, astronomers, physicists, and anatomists of the scientific academy examine the real world.

L'ACADEMIE DES SCIENCES ET DES BEAUX ARTS
DEDIÉE
AU ROY

zations were established in Naples and Berlin by 1700. Membership in these societies was limited and highly prized, a sign of the glamour that was beginning to attach itself to the new studies. By the 1660s there could be no doubt that science, secure in royal patronage, had become a model for all thought. Its practitioners were extravagantly admired, and throughout intellectual and high social circles, there was a scramble to apply its methods to almost every conceivable activity.

The Wider Appeal of Science Descartes himself had applied the ideas of science to philosophy in general; Bacon had put them at the service of social thought. But the applications were not only on these high levels. Formal gardens were designed to show the order, harmony, and reason that science had made such prized qualities. And methods of fortification and warfare were affected by the principles of the new investigations, such as the need for accurate measurement.

As the scientists' activities became more popular and fashionable, even aristocrats began to spend time playing at science. Herbariums and small observatories were added to country estates, and parties featured an evening of star gazing. Science also fascinated the general populace. Among the most eagerly anticipated occasions in seventeenth-century Holland was the public anatomy lesson. The body of a criminal would be brought to an enormous hall that was packed with students and a fascinated public. A famous surgeon would dissect the cadaver, announcing and displaying each organ as he removed it.

On the whole, the reverence for science and its methods did not develop from an understanding of its actual accomplishments or its potential consequences. Rather, it was caused by the fame of the spectacular discoveries that had offered new and convincing solutions to centuries-old problems in astronomy, physics, and anatomy. Here was a promise of certainty and order in a world that otherwise was bedeviled by conflict and doubt. As a result, the protests of Pascal could be ignored, and the new discipline could be given unblemished admiration. The entire world was coming to be viewed through the scientist's eyes—a striking achievement for a recently minor member of the intellectual community—and the qualities of regularity and harmony associated with science began to appear in the work of artists and writers.

II. Literature and the Arts

We have seen that the late sixteenth and early seventeenth centuries were a time of political turbulence, culminating in a general crisis in the mid-seventeenth century from which a more settled Europe emerged. Not only did the development of science follow a similar pattern—with decades of uncertainty as old truths were challenged, followed by a new sense of assurance in the mid-seventeenth century—but so too did the concerns of literature and the arts.

MANNERISM

One response that was provoked by the upheavals of the sixteenth century was the attempt to escape reality, an effort that was echoed by some of the painters of the age, known as Mannerists. The Mannerists and their patrons cultivated artificial and esoteric images of the world; they undermined perspective, distorted human figures, and devised unnatural colors and lighting to create startling effects.

El Greco Mannerism was embodied in El Greco (1541–1614), a Greek who was trained in Italy and settled in Spain. His compelling and almost mystic canvases created an otherworldly alternative (reminiscent of St. Teresa's visions) to the troubles of his time. El Greco's elongated and often agonized human beings, cool colors, and eerie lighting make him one of the most distinctive painters in the history of art (see p. 462). Increasingly after 1600, though, painters were to reject the Mannerists' flight from reality; eventually the arts, too, were to reflect the sense of settlement that descended over European civilization in the mid-seventeenth century.

MICHEL DE MONTAIGNE

In the world of literature, the concerns of the age were most vividly expressed by the Frenchman

Michel de Montaigne (1533–1592). Obsessed by the death he saw all around him and determined to overcome his fears, he retired in 1570 to his country home in order to "essay," or test, his innermost feelings by writing short pieces of prose even about subjects he did not fully comprehend. In the process he created a new literary form, the essay, that also helped shape the modern French language. But his chief influence was philosophical: He has inspired the search for self-knowledge ever since.

At first Montaigne's anxieties led him to the radical doubt about the possibility of finding truth that is known as *Skepticism*; this inspired the total uncertainty of his motto *"Que sais-je?"* ("What do I know?"). Eventually, however, Montaigne struggled toward a more confident view, taking as his model the ancient saying "Know thyself." By looking into one's own person, one can find values that hold true at least for oneself, and these will reflect the values of all humanity. Montaigne came close to a morality without theology, because good and self-determination were more important to him than doctrine, and he saw everywhere religious people committing inhuman acts. Trying to be an angel is wrong, he said; being good is enough.

Neostoicism   A more general application of some of these ideas was a theory known as *Neostoicism*, inspired by the ancient Stoics' emphasis on self-knowledge and a calm acceptance of the world. The most influential of the Neostoics, a Dutch writer named Justus Lipsius, argued that public leaders ought to be guided by profound self-examination. Lipsius urged rulers to be restrained and self-disciplined, and he was much admired by the kings and royal ministers of the seventeenth century.

CERVANTES AND SHAKESPEARE

Cervantes   In Spain the disillusionment that accompanied the political and economic decline of Europe's most powerful state was perfectly captured by Miguel de Cervantes (1547–1616). He was heir to a brilliant satirical tradition that had already produced in the sixteenth century the writings of Erasmus and Rabelais. Cervantes saw the wide gap between the hopes and the realities

of his day—in religion, in social institutions, in human behavior—and made the dichotomy the basis of scathing social satire in his novel *Don Quixote*.

At one level, Cervantes was ridiculing the excessive chivalry of the Spanish nobility in his portrayal of a knight who was ready to tilt at windmills, though he obviously admired the sincerity of his well-meaning hero and sympathized with him as a perennial loser. On another level, the author brought to life the Europe of the time—the ordinary people and their hypocrisies and intolerances—with a liveliness rarely matched in literature. His view of that society, however, was far from cheery. "Justice, but not for my house," says Don Quixote. Cervantes avoided politics, but he was clearly directing many of his sharpest barbs at the brutality and disregard for human values that were characteristic of his fanatical times. And in England another towering figure was grappling with similar problems.

Shakespeare   For the English-speaking world, the most brilliant writer of this and all other periods was William Shakespeare (1564–1616), whose characters bring to life almost every conceivable mood: searing grief, airy romance, rousing nationalism, uproarious humor. Despite his modest education his imagery shows a familiarity with subjects ranging from astronomy to seamanship, from alchemy to warfare. It is not surprising, therefore, that some have doubted that one man could have produced this amazing body of work.

Shakespeare started writing in the 1590s, when he was in his late twenties, and continued until his death in 1616. During most of this time, he was also involved with a theatrical company, where he often had to produce plays on short notice. He thus had the best of all possible tests—audience reactions—as he gained mastery of theatrical techniques.

Shakespeare's plays made timeless statements about human behavior: love, hatred, violence, sin. Of particular interest to the historian, however, is what he tells us about attitudes that belong especially to his own era. For example, the conservatism of his characters is quite clear. They believe firmly in the hierarchical structure of society, and throughout the long series of historical plays, events suggest that excessive ambition does not pay. Again and again, legality and stability are shown as fundamental virtues amidst turbulent times. Shakespeare's expressions of patriotism are particularly intense; when in *Richard II* the king's uncle, John of Gaunt, lies dying, he pours out his love for his country in words that have moved the English ever since:

> This royal throne of kings, this scepter'd isle,
> This earth of majesty, this seat of Mars,
> This other Eden, demi-paradise, . . .
> This happy breed of men, this little world,
> This precious stone set in the silver sea, . . .
> This blessed plot, this earth,
>   this realm, this England.
>
> *RICHARD II,* ACT 2, SCENE 1

As in so much of the art and writing of the time, instability is a central concern of Shakespeare's plays. His four most famous tragedies—*Hamlet, King Lear, Macbeth,* and *Othello*—end in disillusionment: The heroes are ruined by irresoluteness, pride, ambition, or jealousy. Shakespeare was exploring a theme that had absorbed playwrights since Euripides—the fatal flaws that destroy the great—and producing dramas of revenge that were popular in his day; but the plays also demonstrate his deep understanding of human nature. Whatever one's hopes, one cannot forget human weakness, the inevitability of decay, and the constant threat of disaster. The contrast appears with compelling clarity in a speech delivered by Hamlet:

> What a piece of work is man! How noble in reason! how infinite in faculties! in form and moving how express and admirable! in action how like an angel! in apprehension how like a god! the beauty of the world, the paragon of animals! And yet to me what is this quintessence of dust? Man delights not me.
>
> *HAMLET,* ACT 2, SCENE 2

Despite such pessimism, despite the deep sense of human inadequacy, the basic impression Shakespeare gives is of immense vigor, of a restlessness and confidence that recall the many achievements of the sixteenth century. Yet a sense of decay is never far absent. Repeatedly, people seem utterly helpless, overtaken by events they cannot control. Nothing remains constant or dependable, and everything that seems solid or reassuring, be it the love of a daughter or the crown of England, is challenged. In this atmosphere of ceaseless change, where landmarks easily disappear, Shakespeare conveys the tensions of his time.

THE BAROQUE: GRANDEUR AND EXCITEMENT

After 1600, the arts began to move toward the assurance and sense of settlement that was descending over other areas of European civilization. A new style, the Baroque, sought to drown the uneasiness of Mannerism in a blaze of grandeur. Passion, drama, mystery, and awe were the qualities of the Baroque: Every art form—from music to literature, from architecture to opera—had to involve, arouse, and uplift its audience.

The Baroque style was closely associated with the Counter Reformation's emphasis on gorgeous display in Catholic ritual. The patronage of leading Church figures made Rome a magnet for the major painters of the period. Elsewhere, the Baroque flourished primarily at the leading Catholic courts of the seventeenth century, most notably the Habsburg courts in Madrid, Prague, and Brussels. Few periods have conveyed so strong a sense of grandeur, theatricality, and ornateness.

Caravaggio The artist who first shaped the new aesthetic, Caravaggio (1571–1610), lived most of his life in Rome. Although he received commissions from high Church figures and spent time in a cardinal's household, he was equally at home among the beggars and petty criminals of Rome's dark back streets. These ordinary people served as Caravaggio's models, which shocked those who felt it inappropriate for such humble characters to represent the holy figures of biblical scenes. Yet the power of Caravaggio's paintings—their depiction of highly emotional moments, and the drama created by their sharp contrasts of light and dark—made his work much prized. He had to flee Rome after he killed someone in a brawl, but he left behind a body of work that influenced an entire generation of painters.

National Gallery, London

▶ *Caravaggio*

The Supper at Emmaus, ca. 1597

By choosing moments of high drama and using sharp contrasts of light, Caravaggio created an immediacy that came to be one of the hallmarks of Baroque painting. This is the moment during the supper at Emmaus when his disciples suddenly recognized the resurrected Christ. The force of their emotions and their almost theatrical gestures convey the intensity of the moment, but many at the time objected to the craggy, tattered appearance of the disciples. These were not idealized figures, as was expected, but ordinary people at a humble table.

Rubens Among those who came to Rome to study Caravaggio's art was Peter Paul Rubens (1577–1640), the principal ornament of the brilliant Habsburg court at Brussels. His major themes typified the grandeur that came to be the hallmark of Baroque style: glorifications of great rulers and also of the ceremony and mystery of Catholicism. Rubens' secular paintings convey enormous strength; his religious works overwhelm the viewer with the majesty of the Church and excite the believer's piety by stressing the power of the faith.

Velázquez Other artists glorified rulers through idealized portraiture. The greatest court painter of the age was Diego Velázquez (1599–1660). His portraits of members of the Spanish court depict rulers and their surroundings in the stately atmosphere appropriate to the theme. Yet occasionally Velázquez hinted at the weakness of an ineffective monarch in his rendering of the face, even though the basic purpose of his work was always to exalt royal power. And his celebration of a notable Habsburg victory, *The Surrender of Breda*, managed to suggest the sadness and emptiness as much as the glory of war.

Bernini GianLorenzo Bernini (1598–1680) brought to sculpture and architecture the qualities that Rubens brought to painting, and like Ru-

▶ *Peter Paul Rubens*
The Descent from the Cross, 1612
This huge altarpiece was one of the first pictures Rubens painted after he returned to his native
Antwerp, after spending most of his twenties developing his art in Italy. The ambitious scale,
the strong emotions, the vivid lighting, and the dramatic action showed the artist's commitment
to the Baroque style that had recently evolved in Italy, and the powerful impact of the altarpiece
helped make him one of the most sought-after painters of the day.

bens he was closely associated with the Counter Reformation. Pope Urban VIII commissioned him in 1629 to complete both the inside and the outer setting of the basilica of St. Peter's in Rome. For the interior Bernini designed a splendid papal throne that seems to float on clouds beneath a burst of sunlight, and for the exterior he created an enormous plaza, surrounded by a double colonnade, that is the largest such plaza in Europe. Similarly, his dramatic religious works reflect the desire of the Counter Reformation popes to electrify the faithful. The sensual and overpowering altarpiece dedicated to the Spanish mystic St. Teresa makes a direct appeal to the emotions of the beholder that reveals the excitement of Baroque at its best.

▶ *Diego Velázquez*
THE SURRENDER OF BREDA, 1635
The contrasting postures of victory and defeat are masterfully captured by Diego Velázquez in *The Surrender of Breda*. **The Dutch soldiers droop their heads and lances, but the victorious Spaniards hardly show triumph, and the gesture of the victorious general, Ambrogio Spinola, is one of consolation and understanding.**

Music The seventeenth century was significant, too, as a decisive time in the history of music. New instruments, notably in the keyboard and string families, enabled composers to create richer effects than had been possible before. Particularly in Italy, which in the sixteenth and seventeenth centuries was the chief center of new ideas in music, musicians began to explore the

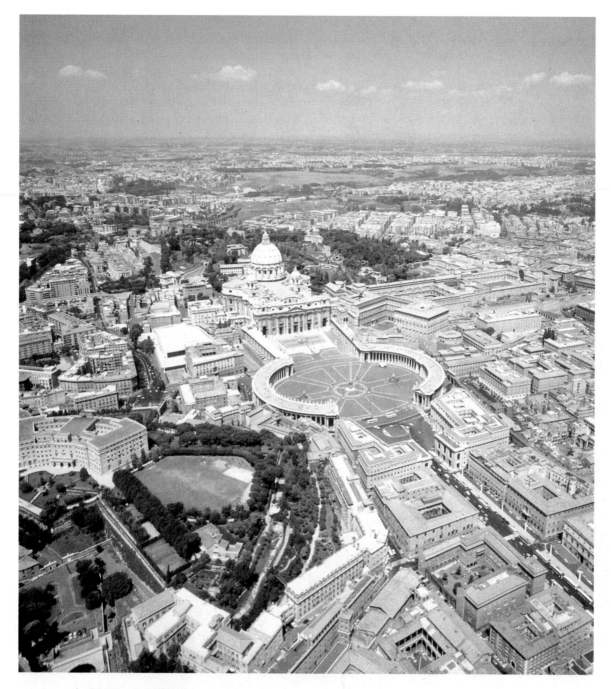

▷ *GianLorenzo Bernini*
ST. PETER'S SQUARE AND CHURCH, ROME
The magnificent circular double colonnade that Bernini created in front of St. Peter's is
one of the triumphs of Baroque architecture. The church itself was already the largest
in Christendom (markers in the floor still indicate how far other famous churches
would reach if placed inside St. Peter's), and it was topped by the huge dome
Michelangelo had designed. The vast enclosed space that Bernini built reinforced the
grandeur of a church that was the pope's own.

▶ *GianLorenzo Bernini*
THE ECSTASY OF ST. TERESA, 1652
Bernini's sculpture is as dramatic an example
of Baroque art as the paintings of Caravaggio.
The moment that St. Teresa described in her
autobiography when she attained mystic ecstasy, as
an angel repeatedly pierced her heart with a dart,
became in Bernini's hands the centerpiece of a
theatrical tableau. He placed the patrons who had
commissioned the work on two walls of the chapel
that houses this altarpiece, sitting in what seem to
be boxes and looking at the stage on which the
drama unfolds.

potential of a form that first emerged in these
years: the opera. Drawing on the resources of the
theater, painting, architecture, music, and the
dance, an operatic production could achieve
splendors that were beyond the reach of any one
of these arts on its own. The form was perfectly
attuned to the courtly culture of the age, to the
love of display among the princes of Europe, and
to the Baroque determination to overwhelm
one's audience.

The dominant figure in seventeenth-century
music was the Italian Claudio Monteverdi
(1567–1643), one of the most innovative composers of all time. He has been called with some justification the creator of both the operatic form
and the orchestra. His masterpiece *Orfeo* (1607)
was a tremendous success, and in the course of
the next century operas gained in richness and
complexity, attracting composers, as well as audiences, in ever increasing numbers.

CLASSICISM: GRANDEUR AND RESTRAINT

Classicism, the other major style of the seventeenth century, attempted to recapture (though
on a much larger scale than Renaissance imitations of antiquity) the aesthetic values and the
strict forms that had been favored in ancient
Greece and Rome. Like the Baroque, Classicism
aimed for grandiose effects, but unlike the
Baroque, it achieved them through restraint and
discipline within a formal structure. The gradual
rise of the Classical style in the seventeenth century echoed the trend toward stabilization that
was taking place in other areas of intellectual life
and in politics.

Poussin The epitome of disciplined expression
and conscious imitation of Classical antiquity is
the work of Nicolas Poussin (1594–1665), a
French artist who spent much of his career in
Rome. Poussin was no less interested than his
contemporaries in momentous and dramatic subjects, but the atmosphere is always more subdued
than in the work of Velázquez or Rubens. The
colors are muted, the figures are restrained, and
the settings are serene. Peaceful landscapes, men
and women in togas, and ruins of Classical buildings are features of his art.

Map 16.2 CENTERS OF MUSIC, 1500–1800
This map indicates the shifting centers of new ideas in music from Flanders and Italy in the sixteenth century; to Italy in the seventeenth; and on to Germany, England, and France in the eighteenth.

The Dutch In the United Provinces different forces were at work, and they led to a style that was much more intimate than the grandiose outpourings of a Rubens or a Velázquez. Two aspects of Dutch society, Protestantism and repub-

licanism, had a particular influence on its painters. The Reformed Church frowned on religious art, which reduced the demand for paintings of biblical scenes. Religious works therefore tended to express personal faith. And the absence of a court meant that the chief patrons of art were sober merchants, who were far more interested in precise, dignified portraits than in ornate displays. The result, notably in the profound and moving works of Rembrandt, was a compelling art whose beauty lies in its calmness and restraint.

Rembrandt   Rembrandt van Rijn (1606–1669) explored an amazing range of themes, but he was particularly fascinated by human character, emo-

▶ *Nicolas Poussin*
THE INSPIRATION OF THE EPIC POET, CA. 1628
Whereas Baroque art emphasized emotion, the Classical style sought to embody reason. Poussin, the leading Classical artist of his time, believed that painting, like poetry, had to elevate the minds of its audience. The poet was thus a particularly apt subject for him—a noble and serious theme that could be presented as a scene from antiquity, with formal figures, muted colors, and ancient symbols like the laurel wreath. Poussin's views became the official doctrine of the academy of art founded in France with royal approval, and they influenced generations of painters.

tion, and self-revelation. Whether children or old people, simple servant girls or rich burghers, his subjects are presented without elaboration or idealization; always the personality speaks for itself. Rembrandt's most remarkable achievement in portraiture—and one of the most moving series of canvases in the history of art—is his depiction of the changes in his own face over his lifetime. The brash youth turns into the confident, successful, middle-aged man, one of the most sought-after painters in Holland. But in his late thirties the sorrows mounted: He lost his beloved wife, and commissions began to fall off. Sadness fills the eyes in these pictures. The last portraits move from despair to a final, quiet resignation as his sight slowly failed. Taken together, these paintings bear comparison with Montaigne's es-

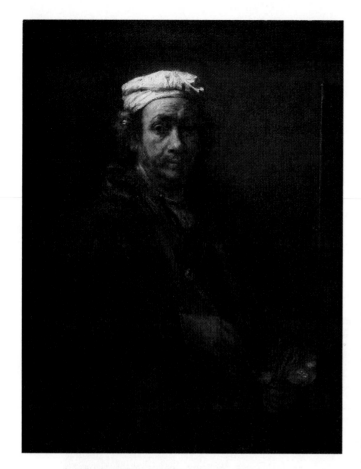

▶ *Rembrandt*
Self-Portrait with Palette, 1660
Over 60 self-portraits by Rembrandt have survived; though all are penetrating explorations of human character, those from his last years are especially moving. We see him here in his mid-fifties with the tools of his trade. Adapting Caravaggio's interest in light, he uses different shades of brown and the illumination of the face to create a somber and reflective mood. The very act of thinking is captured in this canvas, not to mention the full life that is etched in Rembrandt's wrinkles.

says as monuments to the exploration of one's own spirit—a searching appraisal that brings all who see it to a deeper understanding of human nature.

One could argue that Rembrandt cannot be fitted into either of the dominant styles of his time. Except for his powerful use of light, his work is far more introspective than most of the Baroque. Nor did he adopt the forms of antiquity, as did Poussin and other Classical painters. Yet, like the advocates of Classicism, Rembrandt in his restraint seemed to anticipate the art of the next generation. After his death in 1669, serenity, calm, and elegance became the watchwords of European painting. An age of repose and grace was succeeding a time of upheaval as surely in the arts as in other spheres of life.

Drama   By the middle of the seventeenth century, the formalism of the Classical style was also being extended to literature, especially drama. This change was most noticeable in France, but it soon moved through Western Europe, as leading critics insisted that new plays conform to the structure laid down by the ancients. In particular, they wanted the three Classical unities observed: unity of place, which required that all scenes take place without change of location; unity of time, which demanded that the events in the play occur within a 24-hour period; and unity of action, which dictated simplicity and purity of plot.

Corneille   The work of Pierre Corneille (1606–1684), the dominant figure in the French theater during the midcentury years, reflects the rise of Classicism. His early plays were complex and involved, and even after he came into contact with the Classical tradition, he did not accept its rules easily. His masterpiece *Le Cid* (1636), based on the legends of a medieval Spanish hero, technically observed the three unities, but only by compressing an entire tragic love affair, a military campaign, and many other events into one day. The play won immediate popular success, but the critics, urged on by the royal minister Cardinal Richelieu, who admired the regularity and order of Classical style, condemned Corneille for imperfect observance of the three unities. Thereafter he adhered to the Classical forms, though he was never entirely at ease with their restraints.

Passion was not absent from the Classical play; the works of Jean Racine (1639–1699), the model Classical dramatist, generate some of the most intense emotion ever seen on the stage. But the exuberance of earlier drama was disappearing. Nobody summed up the values of Classicism better than Racine in his eulogy of Corneille:

You know in what a condition the stage was when he began to write. . . . All the rules of art, and even those of decency and decorum, broken everywhere. . . . Corneille, after having for some time sought the right path and struggled against the bad taste of his day, inspired by extraordinary genius and helped by the study of the ancients, at last brought reason upon the stage.

Paul Mesnard (ed.), *Oeuvres de J. Racine*, IV (1886), p. 366, translated by T. K. Rabb

This was exactly the progression—from turbulence to calm—that was apparent throughout European culture in this period.

III. Social Patterns and Popular Culture

POPULATION TRENDS

The sixteenth-century rise in Europe's population was succeeded by a period of decline that in most areas lasted long after the political and intellectual upheavals subsided. The rise had been fragile, because throughout these centuries only one child in two reached adulthood. Each couple had to give birth to four children merely to replace themselves, and since they had to wait until they were financially independent to marry—usually in their mid-twenties—they rarely had the chance to produce a big family. Women in this period lost the capacity to bear children in their late thirties, and on the average, therefore, a

woman had some 12 years in which to give birth to four children to maintain the population. Because lactation delayed ovulation, the mean interval between births was almost two and a half years, which meant that most couples were only just capable of raising two adults. As soon as there was outside pressure—such as plague, famine, or war—population growth became impossible.

The worst of these outside pressures in the seventeenth century was the Thirty Years' War, which alone caused the death of more than 5 million people. It also helped plunge Europe into a debilitating economic depression, which, in turn, decreased the means of relieving famine. Disasters of such magnitude could not easily be absorbed. Only when better times returned could population increase resume. Because they led in economic recovery, England and the Netherlands experienced a demographic revival long before their neighbors; indeed, the rise in their numbers, which began in the 1660s, accounted for almost all of the slight population increase the whole of Europe was able to achieve in this difficult century.

SOCIAL STATUS

The determinants of status in modern times— wealth, education, and family background— were viewed rather differently in the seventeenth century. Wealth was significant chiefly to merchants, education was important mainly among professionals, and background was vital primarily to the nobility. But in this period the signifi-

EUROPE'S POPULATION, 1600–1700, BY REGIONS

Region	1600*	1700	Percentage Change
Spain, Portugal, and Italy	23.6	22.7	− 4
France, Switzerland, and Germany	35.0	36.2	+ 3
British Isles, Low Countries, and Scandinavia	12.0	16.1	+34
Total	70.6	75.0	+ 6

*All figures are in millions.

Source: Jan de Vries, *The Economy of Europe in an Age of Crisis, 1600–1750*, Cambridge, 1976, p. 5.

cance of these three social indicators began to shift. Wealth became a more general source of status, as ever-larger numbers of successful merchants bought offices, lands, and titles that allowed them to enter the nobility. Education was also becoming more highly prized; throughout Europe attendance at institutions of higher learning soared after 1550, bringing the sons of artisans as well as nobles to universities. And although background was being scrutinized ever more defensively by old-line nobles, who regarded family lineage as the only criterion for acceptance into their ranks, their resistance to change was futile as the "new" aristocrats multiplied.

In general, it was assumed that everyone occupied a fixed place in the social hierarchy and that it was against the order of nature for someone to move to another level. The growing social importance of wealth and education, however, indicates that mobility was possible. Thanks to the expansion of bureaucracies, it became easier to move to new levels, either by winning favor at court or by buying an office. High status conferred important privileges: Great landowners could demand services and fees from their tenants; those with political rights in cities, nobles, and bureaucrats were often exempt from taxes; and courtiers controlled portions of the vast patronage that the government disbursed. At each level, however, women were always considered subordinate: In many countries, even the widows of aristocrats could not inherit their husbands' estates; an abbess could never become prominent in Church government; and the few women allowed to practice a trade were excluded from the leadership of their guild. Nevertheless, there were businesswomen and female artists, writers, and even scientists among the growing numbers of successful self-made people in this period.

MOBILITY AND CRIME

The Peasant The remarkable economic advances of the sixteenth century helped change attitudes toward wealth, but they brought few benefits to the lower levels of society. Peasants throughout Europe were, in fact, entering a time of increasing difficulty at the end of the sixteenth century. Their taxes were rising rapidly, but the prices they got for the food they grew were stabilizing. Moreover, landowners were starting what has been called the "seigneurial reaction"— making additional demands on their tenants, raising rents, and squeezing as much as they could out of the lands they owned. The effects of famine and war were also more severe at this level of society. The only escapes were to cities or armies, both of which grew rapidly in the seventeenth century. Many of those who fled their villages, however, remained on the road, part of the huge bodies of vagrants and beggars who were a common sight throughout Europe.

A few of those who settled in a town or city improved their lot, but for the large majority, poverty in cities was even more miserable and hungry than poverty on the land. Few could become apprentices, and day laborers were poorly paid and usually out of work. As for military careers, armies were carriers of disease, frequently ill fed, and subject to constant hardship.

Crime For many, therefore, the only alternative to starvation was crime. One area of London in the seventeenth century was totally controlled by the underworld. It offered refuge to fugitives and was never entered by respectable citizens. Robbery and violence—committed equally by desperate men, women, and even children—were common in most cities. As a result, social events like dinners and outings, or visits to the theater, took place during the daytime because the streets were unsafe at night.

If caught, Europe's criminals were treated harshly. In an age before regular police forces, however, catching them was difficult. Crime was usually the responsibility of local authorities, who depended on part-time officials (known in England as *constables*) for law enforcement. Only in response to major outbreaks, such as a gang of robbers preying on travelers, would the authorities recruit a more substantial armed band (rather like a posse in the American West) to pursue criminals. If such efforts succeeded in bringing offenders to justice, the defendants found they had few rights, especially if they were poor, and that punishments were severe. Torture was a common means of extracting confessions; various forms of maiming, such as chopping off a hand or an ear, were considered acceptable

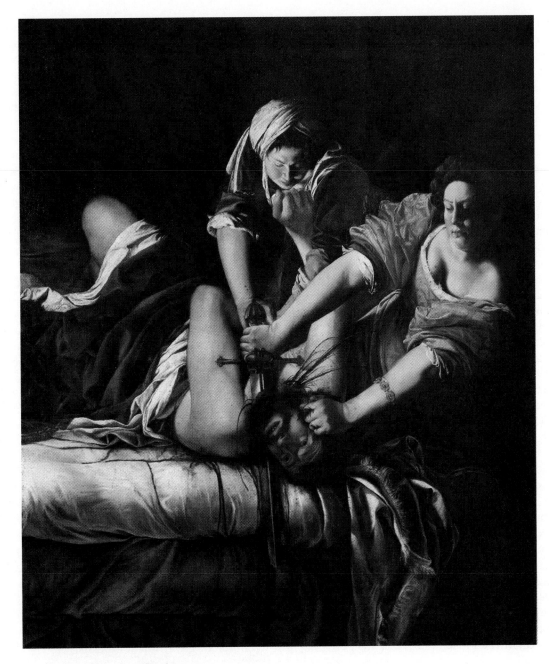

▶ *Artemisia Gentileschi*
JUDITH SLAYING HOLOFERNES, CA. 1620
Women artists are rare in the seventeenth century because they were not allowed to become apprentices. But Artemisia (1593–1652) was the daughter of a painter who happened to be a friend of Caravaggio, and she had the opportunity to become a gifted exponent of Baroque style. Known throughout Europe for her vivid portrayals of dramatic scenes (she painted the murder of Holofernes by the biblical heroine Judith at least five times), she practiced her chosen profession with considerable success, despite the trauma of being raped at 17 by a friend of her father's—an act of violence that may be reflected (and avenged) in this painting.

penalties; and repeated thefts could lead to execution.

Society's hierarchical instincts were apparent even in civil disputes, where nobles were usually immune from prosecution and women often could not start a case. If a woman were raped, for example, she had to find a man to bring suit. In one famous case in Italy, a girl's father sued the rapist because it was *his* honor that had been damaged by the attack.

CHANGE IN THE VILLAGE

Over three-quarters of Europe's population still lived in small village communities, but their structure was not what it once had been. In Eastern Europe, peasants were being reduced to serfdom; in the West—our principal concern—familiar relationships and institutions were changing.

The essence of the traditional village had been its isolation. Cut off from frequent contact with the world beyond its immediate region, it had been self-sufficient and closely knit. Everyone knew everyone else, and mutual help was vital for survival. There might be distinctions among villagers—some more prosperous, others less so—but the sense of cohesiveness was powerful. It extended even to the main "outsiders" in the village, the priest and the local lord. The priest was often indistinguishable from his parishioners: almost as poor and sometimes hardly more literate. He adapted to local customs and beliefs, frequently taking part in semipagan rituals so as to keep his authority with his flock. The lord could be exploitative and demanding; but he considered the village his livelihood, and he therefore kept in close touch with its affairs and did all he could to ensure its safety, orderliness, and well-being.

Forces of Change   The main intrusions onto this scene were economic and demographic. As a result of the boom in agricultural prices during the sixteenth century, followed by the economic difficulties of the seventeenth, differences in the wealth of the villagers became more marked. The richer peasants began to set themselves apart from their poorer neighbors, and the feeling of village unity began to break down. These divi-

sions were exacerbated by the rise in population during the sixteenth century, which strained resources and forced the less fortunate to leave in search of better opportunities in cities, and by the pressures of "seigneurial reaction," plague, and famine during the more difficult times of the seventeenth century.

Another intrusion which undermined the traditional cohesion of the community was the increased presence of royal officials. For centuries, elected councils, drawn from every part of the population, had run village affairs throughout Europe. In the late seventeenth century, however, these councils began to disappear as outside forces—in some cases a nearby lord, but more often government officials—asserted their control over the localities. Tax gatherers and army recruiters were now familiar figures throughout Europe. Although they were often the target of peasant rebellions, they were also welcomed when, for example, they distributed food during a famine. Their long-term influence, however, was the creation of a new layer of outside authority in the village, which was another cause of the division and fragmentation that led many to flee to the city.

As these outside intrusions gathered force, the interests of the local lord, who traditionally had defended the village's autonomy and had offered help in times of need, also changed. Nobles were beginning to look more and more to royal courts and capital cities, rather than to their local holdings, for position and power. The natural corollary was the "seigneurial reaction," with lords treating the villages they dominated as sources of income and increasingly distancing themselves from the inhabitants. Their commitment to charitable works declined, and they tended more and more to leave the welfare of the local population to church or government officials.

CITY LIFE

As village life changed, the inhabitants who felt forced to leave headed for the city—an impersonal place where, instead of joining a cohesive population, they found themselves part of a mingling of peoples that was breaking down the isolation of local areas. The growing cities needed ever wider regions to provide them with food

Map 16.3 THE GROWTH OF CITIES, 1500–1800
In addition to the remarkable rise in the population of Europe's cities, particularly after 1550, this map reveals the northward shift in the distribution of the largest cities: in 1500, three of the four largest were in Italy; in 1700, only one.

and goods, and they attracted the many who could not make ends meet in the countryside. Long-distance communications became more common, especially as localities were linked into national market and trade networks, and in the cities the new immigrants met others from distant villages.

There was no question that a city was far a more chaotic place than a rural community. Even if one of its areas, such as a parish, seemed distinct and even cohesive—some parishes, for example, were associated with a single trade—urban society in general was fragmentary and disorganized. A city's craft guilds gave structure to artisans and shopkeepers, regulating their lives and providing welfare, but less than half the population could join a guild. The rest did odd jobs or turned to crime.

The chief attraction of cities was the wide variety of economic opportunity: for women, in such areas as selling goods and processing food;

for men, in construction, on the docks, and in delivery services. But employment was unpredictable, and citizens did not have community support to fall back on in hard times as they did in the village. Even the forms of recreation and enjoyment were different in the city.

POPULAR CULTURE IN THE CITY

One major difference between country and town was the level of literacy. Only in urban areas were there significant numbers of people who could read: It has been estimated that in cities perhaps a third of adult males were literate by 1700. Not only was reading necessary for commerce but it had been strongly encouraged by the Reformation, with its insistence that the faithful read the Bible for themselves. This stimulus ensured that

literacy also rose among women, who increasingly became pupils at the growing number of schools in Europe (though they were still not admitted to universities). It has been estimated that as many as 20 percent of the adult women in cities were able to read.

These changes had a notable effect on urban life. There was now a readership for newspapers, which became common in the late seventeenth century, as did the coffeehouses in which they were often read. Theater and opera became popular entertainments, with women for the first time taking stage roles and able to obtain performances for plays they had written. When the English royal official Samuel Pepys hired a new servant in the 1660s, he made sure she could play an instrument so that she could take part in the family's musical evenings. Sales of books multiplied, often because they served a popular audience, and they gave wide circulation to traditional favorites like travel stories and lives of saints as well as to the latest ideas of science.

MAGIC AND RITUALS

Although in the countryside cultural patterns looked different—with lower literacy, simpler recreations, and more visible religiosity—there was one area of popular culture in which the outlook of the city and the village was remarkably similar: the belief in magic. The townspeople may have seemed more sophisticated, but the basic assumption they shared with their country cousins was that nature and their own lives were controlled by mysterious forces, and there was little they could do to ensure their own well-being. The world was full of spirits, and all one could do was

▶ *Anonymous Woodcut*
THE NEWSVENDOR
The ancestor of the regularly published newspaper was the occasional single sheet describing the latest news or rumors. Printers would produce a few hundred copies and have them sold by street vendors whenever they had an event of some importance to describe: a battle, the death of a ruler, or some fantastic occurrence like the birth of a baby with two heads. As cities and the potential readership grew, the news sheets expanded; by the seventeenth century they had distinctive names and began to appear every week.

encourage the good, defend oneself against the evil, and hope that the good would win. Nothing that happened—a calf dying, lightning striking a house—was accidental. Everything had a purpose. Any unusual event was an omen, part of a larger plan, or the action of some unseen force.

"Charivari" To strengthen themselves against trouble, people used whatever help they could find. They organized special processions and holidays to celebrate good times such as harvests, to lament misfortunes, to complain about oppression, or to poke fun at scandalous behavior. These occasions, known as "rough music" in England and "charivari" in France, often used the theme of "the world turned upside down" to make their point. In the set pieces in a procession, a fool might be dressed up as a king, a woman might be shown beating her husband, or a tax collector might appear hanging from a tree. Whether ridiculing a dominating wife or lamenting the lack of bread, the community was expressing its solidarity in the face of difficulty or distasteful behavior through these rituals. It was a way of letting off steam and declaring public opinion.

The potential for violence was always present at such gatherings, especially when religious or social differences became entangled with other resentments. The viciousness of ordinary Protestants and Catholics toward one another—it was not uncommon for one side to mutilate the dead bodies of the other—revealed a frustration and aggressiveness that was not far below the surface. When food was scarce or new impositions had been ordered by their rulers, peasants and townspeople needed little excuse to show their anger openly. Women took the lead, not only because they had firsthand experience of the difficulty of feeding a family but also because troops were more reluctant to attack them. This tradition was still alive in 1789, in the early days of the French Revolution, when a band made up primarily of women marched from Paris to the royal court at Versailles to demand bread.

The Belief in Magic Ordinary people also had other outlets for their frustrations. Recognizing their powerlessness in the face of outside forces, they resorted to their version of the magic that

the literate were finding so fashionable at this very time. Where the sophisticated patronized astrologers, paying handsomely for horoscopes and advice about how to live their lives, the peasants and the poor consulted popular almanacs or sought out "cunning men" and wise women for secret spells, potions, and other remedies for their anxieties. Even religious ceremonies were thought of as being related to the rituals of the magical world, in which so-called white witches—the friendly kind—gave assistance when a ring was lost, when a new bride could not become pregnant, or when the butter would not form out of the milk.

WITCHCRAFT

Misfortunes, in other words, were never just plain bad luck; rather, there was intent behind everything that happened. Events were *willed*, and if they turned out badly, they must have been willed by the good witch's opposite, the evil witch. Such beliefs often led to cruel persecutions of innocent victims—usually helpless old women, able to do nothing but mutter curses when taunted by neighbors and easy targets if someone had to be blamed for unfortunate happenings.

This quest for scapegoats naturally focused on the most vulnerable members of society, such as Jews or, in the case of witches, women. Accusations were often directed at a woman who was old and alone, with nobody to defend her. She was feared because she seemed to be an outsider, or not sufficiently deferential to her supposed betters. It was believed that witches read strange books and knew magic spells, an indication of what many regarded as inappropriate and dangerous levels of literacy and learning for a woman.

Witch-hunts In the sixteenth and seventeenth centuries, the hunt for witches intensified to levels never previously reached. This has been called the era of "the great witch craze," and for good reason. There were outbursts in every part of Europe, and tens of thousands of the accused were executed. Dozens of men, most of them clerics, made witch-hunting a full-time profession, and persuaded civic and other government au-

▶ *Hans Baldung Grien*
WITCHES, WOODCUT

This woodcut, by the German artist Grien, shows the popular image of witches in early
modern Europe. One carries a potion while flying on a goat. The others put together
the ingredients for a magic potion in a jar inscribed with mystical symbols. The fact that
witches were thought to be learned women who could understand magic was another
reason they were feared by a Europe that expected women to be uneducated.

thorities to devote their resources to stamping out this threat to social and religious stability. Suspects were almost always tortured, and it is not too surprising that they usually "confessed" and implicated others as servants of the devil. The practices that were uncovered varied—in some areas witches were said to dance with the devil, in others to fly on broomsticks, in others to be possessed by evil spirits who could induce dreadful (and possibly psychosomatic) symptoms—but the punishment was usually the same: burning at the stake. And the hysteria was infectious. One accusation could trigger dozens more until entire regions were swept with fear and hatred.

FORCES OF RESTRAINT

By the middle of the seventeenth century the wave of assaults on witches was beginning to recede (*see box,* below). Social and political leaders came to realize how dangerous to authority campaigns against witches could become, especially when accusations were turned against the rich and privileged classes. Increasingly, therefore, cases were not brought to trial, and when they were, lawyers and doctors (who approached the subject from a different point of view than the clergy) cast doubt on the validity of the testimony. Gradually, excesses were restrained and control was reestablished; by 1700 there was only a trickle of new incidents.

The decline in accusations of witchcraft reflected not only the more general quieting down of conflict and upheaval in the late seventeenth century but also the growing proportion of Europe's population that was living in cities. Here, less reliant on the luck of good weather, people could feel themselves more in control of their own fates. If there were unexpected fires, there were fire brigades; if a house burned down, there might even be insurance—a new protection for

A Witness Analyzes the Witch Craze

Although for most Europeans around 1600 witchcraft was real—a religious problem caused by the devil—there were a few observers who were beginning to think more analytically about the reasons for the rapid spread of accusations. One such observer was a clergyman named Linden, who was attached to the cathedral of the great city of Trier in western Germany. His description of a witch-hunt in the Trier region ignored the standard religious explanations.

"Inasmuch as it was popularly believed that the continued sterility of many years was caused by witches, the whole area rose to exterminate the witches. This movement was promoted by many in office, who hoped to gain wealth from the persecution. And so special accusers, inquisitors, notaries, judges, and constables dragged to trial and torture human beings of both sexes and burned them in great numbers. Scarcely any of those who were accused escaped punishment. So far did the madness of the furious populace and the courts go in this thirst for blood and booty that there was scarcely anybody who was not smirched by some suspicion of this crime. Meanwhile, notaries, copyists and innkeepers grew rich. The executioner rode a fine horse, like a noble of the court, and dressed in gold and silver; his wife competed with noble dames in the richness of her array. A direr pestilence or a more ruthless invader could hardly have ravaged the territory than this inquisition and persecution without bounds. Many were the reasons for doubting that all were really guilty. At last, though the flames were still unsated, the people grew poor, rules were made and enforced restricting the fees and costs of examinations, and suddenly, as when in war funds fail, the zeal of the persecutors died out."

From George L. Burr (ed.), "The Witch Persecutions," *Translations and Reprints from the Original Sources of European History,* III (Philadelphia: University of Pennsylvania, 1902), pp. 13–14.

individuals that was spreading in the late 1600s. A process that has been called the "disenchantment" of the world—growing skepticism about spirits and mysterious forces, and greater self-reliance—was under way.

Religious Discipline The churches played an important part in the suppression of the traditional reliance on magic. In Catholic countries the Counter Reformation produced better-educated priests who were trained to impose official doctrine instead of tolerating unusual local customs. Among Protestants, ministers were similarly well educated and denounced magical practices as idolatrous or superstitious. And both camps treated passion and enthusiasm with suspicion. Habits did not change overnight, but gradually ordinary people were being persuaded to abandon old fears and beliefs.

Even at the level of popular culture, therefore, Europeans had reason to feel, by the late seventeenth century, that a time of upheaval and uncertainty was over. A sense of confidence and orderliness was returning, and in intellectual circles the optimism seemed justified by the achievements of science. In fact, there arose a scholarly dispute around 1700, known as "the battle of the books," in which one side claimed, for the first time, that the "moderns" had outshone the "ancients." Using the scientists as their chief example, the advocates of the "moderns" argued—in a remarkable break with the reverence for the past that had dominated medieval and Renaissance culture—that advances in thought were possible and that one did not always have to accept the superiority of antiquity. Such self-confidence made it clear that, in the world of ideas as surely as in the world of politics, a period of turbulence had given way to an era of renewed assurance and stability.

Recommended Reading

Sources

*Drake, Stillman (tr. and ed.). *Discoveries and Opinions of Galileo*. 1957. The complete texts of some of Galileo's most important works.

*Hall, Marie Boas (ed.). *Nature and Nature's Laws: Documents of the Scientific Revolution*. 1970. A good collection of documents by and about the pioneers of modern science.

Studies

Braudel, Fernand. *Capitalism and Material Life 1400–1800*. Miriam Kochan (tr.). 1973. A classic, pioneering study of the structure of daily life in early modern Europe.

*Burke, Peter. *Popular Culture in Early Modern Europe*. 1978. A lively introduction to the many forms of expression and belief among the ordinary people of Europe.

*Butterfield, Herbert. *The Origins of Modern Science*. 1949. An elegantly written history of the scientific revolution that conveys its excitement.

Drake, Stillman. *Galileo*. 1980. The standard biography of a central figure in the scientific revolution.

Frame, Donald M. *Montaigne: A Biography*. 1965. The best biography of this influential thinker.

*Ginzburg, Carlo. *The Cheese and the Worms: The Cosmos of a Sixteenth-Century Miller*. John and Ann Tedeschi (trs.). 1980. A remarkable account, focusing on the beliefs of a man who lived in a small northern Italian town, which brings to life the extraordinary variety of the popular culture of the time.

*Gutmann, Myron P. *Toward the Modern Economy: Early Industry in Europe 1500–1800*. 1988. A clear survey of recent work on economic development in this period.

*Hibbard, Howard, *Bernini*. 1965. A graceful account of the life and work of the artist who was the epitome of the Baroque.

*Krailsheimer, Alban. *Pascal*. 1980. The best brief biography, with good discussions of the life, the science, and the turn to religion.

*Available in paperback.

*Kuhn, Thomas S. *The Structure of Scientific Revolutions.* 1962. A suggestive interpretation of the reasons the scientific revolution developed and took hold.

*Ladurie, Emmanuel Le Roy. *The Peasants of Languedoc.* John Day (tr.). 1966. A brilliant evocation of peasant life in France in the sixteenth and seventeenth centuries.

*Levack, Brian P. *The Witch-Hunt in Early Modern Europe.* 1987. An excellent survey of the belief in witchcraft and its consequences.

Maland, David. *Culture and Society in Seventeenth-Century France.* 1970. This survey of art, drama, and literature contains a good discussion of the rise of Classicism.

Palisca, Claude. *Baroque Music.* 1968. The best survey of this period in the history of music.

*Popkin, Richard H. *The History of Scepticism from Erasmus to Descartes.* 1964. Taking one strand in European thought as its subject, this lively study places both Montaigne and Descartes in a new perspective.

Rabb, Theodore K. *Renaissance Lives.* 1993. Brief biographies of 15 people, both famous and obscure, who lived just before and during this period.

*Shearman, John. *Mannerism.* 1968. The best short introduction to a difficult artistic style.

Tapié, V. L. *The Age of Grandeur: Baroque Art and Architecture.* A. R. Williamson (tr.). 1960. Although concentrating primarily on France and Austria, this is the most comprehensive survey of this period in art.

*Thirsk, Joan. *Economic Policy and Projects: The Development of a Consumer Society in Early Modern England.* 1978. A fascinating study of changing social and economic patterns.

*Thomas, Keith. *Religion and the Decline of Magic.* 1976. The most thorough account of popular culture yet published, this enormous book, while dealing mainly with England, treats at length such subjects as witchcraft, astrology, and ghosts in a most readable style.

*Westfall, Richard S. *The Construction of Modern Science: Mechanisms and Mechanics.* 1971. A cogent analysis of a central theme in the history of the scientific revolution.

———. *Never at Rest: A Biography of Isaac Newton.* 1980. The best introduction to the life and work of the great scientist.

White, Christopher. *Rembrandt and His World.* 1964. A brief but wide-ranging introduction to the artist's work and life.

———. *Rubens and His World.* 1968. As good on Rubens as the previous title is on Rembrandt.

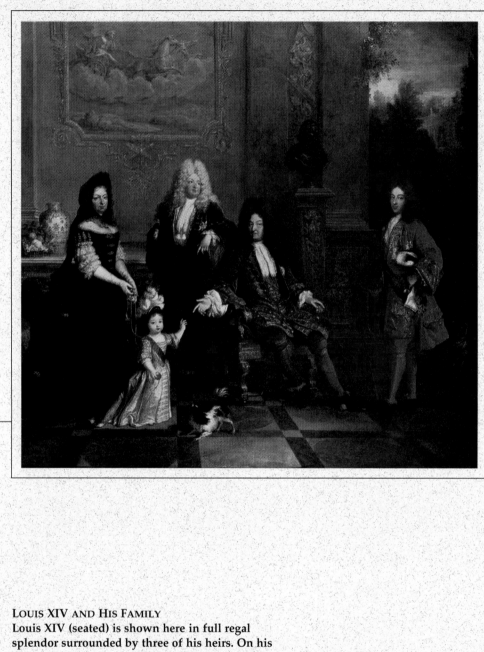

LOUIS XIV AND HIS FAMILY
Louis XIV (seated) is shown here in full regal splendor surrounded by three of his heirs. On his right is his eldest son, on his left is his eldest grandson, and, reaching out his hand, his eldest great-grandson, held by his governess. All three of these heirs died before Louis, and thus they never became kings of France.

CHAPTER SEVENTEEN

THE EMERGENCE OF THE EUROPEAN STATE SYSTEM

THE acceptance of the strong central governments that emerged out of the crisis of the mid-seventeenth century was a victory not merely for kings but for an entire way of organizing political structures. As a result of huge increases both in the demands of warfare and in the availability of resources, bureaucracies had mushroomed, and their presence was felt throughout Europe. Yet no central administration, however powerful, could function without the support of the nobles who ruled the countryside. Regional loyalties had dominated European society for centuries, and only a regime that drew on those loyalties could hope to maintain the support of its subjects. The political structures that were developed during the century following the 1650s were therefore as much the work of a nobility that had long been accustomed to exercising authority, but was now prepared to find new ways of exerting its influence, as they were the product of ambitious princes. There were conflicts between monarchs and their subjects, to be sure, but it was clear to the leaders of society during the century following the crisis of the 1640s and 1650s that state building required a common effort to create political, social, military, financial, and religious structures that would enable governments to function more effectively. The result was the emergence of a set of institutions and practices that have remained essential to the functioning of the modern state ever since.

I. The Creation of Absolutism in France

VERSAILLES

The setting in which a central government operated often told a great deal about its power and its methods. Philip II in the late sixteenth century had created, at the Escorial outside Madrid, the first isolated palace that controlled a large realm. A hundred years later, the French King Louis XIV (1643–1715) created at Versailles, near Paris, a far more elaborate court as the center of an even larger and more intrusive bureaucracy than Philip's. It was as if the isolation of government and the exercise of vast personal power went hand in hand.

The king moved the court out of the capital in the 1680s and eventually, at a cost of half a year's royal income, transformed a small château his fa-

ther had built at Versailles, 12 miles from Paris, into the largest building in Europe. There he could enjoy in peace the splendor and the daily round of ceremonies, centered on himself, which exalted his majesty. His very name, "Sun King" was a means of self-aggrandizement, symbolized by coins that showed the rays of the sun falling first on Louis and then by reflection onto his subjects, who thus owed life and warmth to their monarch.

Louis himself was almost never alone. Every nobleman of any significance in France spent time each year at Versailles, not only to maintain access to royal patronage and governmental af-

▶ **THE PALACE OF VERSAILLES IN 1668**
This painting shows Versailles not long before Louis decided to move there; he was soon to begin an enormous expansion into the gardens at the back which more than doubled the size of the buildings. In this scene, the royal coach, with its entourage, is just about to enter the château.

fairs but also to demonstrate the countrywide support for the system of rule Louis was developing. Historians have called this process the domestication of the aristocracy, in which great lords who had once drawn their status primarily from their lineage or their lands came to regard service to the throne as the best route to power. But the benefits cut both ways. The king gained the services of qualified and influential administrators, and they gained privileges and rewards without the uncertainties that had accompanied their traditional resistance to central control.

Absolutism   The belief that the monarch was absolute—that all power emanated from his unlimited authority—was based on a widely held theory known as the divine right of kings. This theory, which derived from the fact that kings were anointed with holy oil at their coronations, had long asserted that the monarch was God's representative on earth. Taken to an extreme, as it was at Versailles, this view justified absolute power and regarded treason as blasphemy. The leading advocate of the theory, Bishop Bossuet, called Louis God's lieutenant and argued that the Bible itself endorsed absolutism. In reality, the king worked in close partnership with the nobles to maintain order, and he often (though not always) felt obliged to defend their local authority as a reinforcement of his own power. Nevertheless, the very notion that the king not only was supreme but could assert his will with armies and bureaucracies of unprecedented size gave absolutism both an image and a reality that set it apart from previous systems of monarchical rule. This was, at last, a force that could hold together and control the increasingly complex interactions of regions and interest groups that made up a state.

Court Life   The visible symbol of Louis' absolutism was his court at Versailles. Here the leaders of France assembled, and around them swirled the most envied social circles of the time. From the court emanated the policies and directives that increasingly affected the lives of the king's subjects and also determined France's relations with other states.

At Versailles, too, French culture was shaped by the king's patronage of those artists and writ-

ers who appealed to the royal taste. For serious drama and history, Louis turned to the playwright and writer Racine (1639–1699); for comedy, to the theatrical producer and playwright Molière (1622–1673); and for opera and the first performances of what we now call ballet, to the composer Lully (1632–1687). Moreover, all artistic expression, from poetry to painting, was regulated by royal academies that were founded in the seventeenth century; backed by the king's authority, they laid down rules for what was acceptable in such areas as verse forms or architectural style. When the famous Italian sculptor and architect Bernini, for example, came to Paris to design part of a royal palace and fashion a sculpture of the king, both works were rejected as overly ornate. Official taste was all that counted. The dazzling splendor of Versailles had to be achieved in strict conformity to rules of dignity and gravity that were considered the only means of exalting the king. Yet everything was done on a scale and with a magnificence that no other European ruler could match, though many tried.

Paris and Versailles   The one alternative to Versailles as a center of society and culture was Paris, and indeed it has been suggested that the split between the court and the capital was one of the divisions between government and people that was eventually to lead to the French Revolution. A particularly notable difference was in the role of women. Versailles was overwhelmingly a male society. Women achieved prominence only as royal mistresses in Louis' early years, or as the creators of a rigidly pious atmosphere in his last years. They were also essential to the highly elaborate rituals of civility and manners that developed at Versailles. But they were allowed no independent initiative in social or cultural matters. In Paris, by contrast, women established and dominated the salons that promoted easy conversation, a mixture of social backgrounds, and forms of expression—political discussion and ribald humor, for example—that were not acceptable at the staid and sober court. Yet the contrasts were not merely between the formalities of a palace and the relaxation of a salon. Even before the king moved to Versailles, he banned as improper one of Molière's comedies, *Tartuffe*, which mocked excessive religious devoutness. It took

▷ *Antoine Watteau*
FÊTE IN THE PARK, 1718
The luxurious life of the nobility during the eighteenth century is captured in this scene of men and women in fine silks, enjoying a picnic in a lovely park setting.

five years of reworking by Molière before Louis would allow the play to be performed (1669), and it then became a major hit in Paris; significantly, though, it was never to be a favorite at court.

GOVERNMENT

Absolutism was not merely a device to satisfy royal whims, for Louis was a gifted administrator and politician who used his power for state building. In creating or reorganizing government institutions, he strengthened his authority at home and increased his ascendancy over his neighbors. The most durable result of the absolutist regime he commanded was that the French state won control over three crucial activities: the use of armed force, the formulation and execu-

tion of laws, and the collection and expenditure of revenue. These functions, in turn, depended on a centrally controlled bureaucracy responsive to royal orders and efficient enough to carry them out in distant provinces over the objections of local groups.

Although it was impossible to suppress all vested interests and local loyalties, an absolute monarch's bureaucracy was supposed to be insulated from outside pressure by the king's power to remove and transfer appointees. This independence was also promoted by training programs, improved administrative methods, and the use of experts wherever possible—both in the central bureaucracy and in provincial offices. Yet the system could not have functioned without the cooperation of local aristocrats, who were encouraged to use the power and income they derived from official positions to strengthen central authority.

Louis as King   At the head of this structure, Louis XIV carried off successfully a dual function that few monarchs had the talent to sustain: He was both king in council and king in court. Louis the administrator coexisted with Louis the courtier, who hunted, cultivated the arts, and indulged in huge banquets. In his view, the two roles went together, and he held them in balance. Among his numerous imitators, however, the easier side of absolutism, court life, consumed an excessive share of a state's resources and became an end in itself. The effect was to give prestige to the leisure pursuits of the upper classes while sapping the energies of influential figures. Louis was one of the few who avoided sacrificing affairs of state to regal pomp.

Like court life, government policy under Louis XIV was tailored to the aim of state building. As he was to discover, there were limits to his absolutism; the resources and powers at his disposal were not endless. But until the last years of his reign, they served his many purposes extremely well (*see box*, below). Moreover, Louis had superb support at the highest levels of his administration—ministers whose viewpoints differed but whose skills were carefully blended by their ruler.

Colbert and Louvois The king's two leading advisers until the late 1680s were Jean-Baptiste Colbert and the marquis of Louvois. Colbert was a financial wizard who regarded a mercantilist policy as the key to state building. He believed that the government should give priority to increasing France's wealth. As a result, he felt that the chief danger to the country's well-being was the United Provinces, Europe's great trader state, and that royal resources should be poured into the navy, manufacturing, and shipping. By contrast, Louvois, the son of a military administrator, consistently emphasized the army as the foundation of France's power. He believed that the country was threatened primarily by land—by the Holy Roman Empire on its flat, vulnerable northeast frontier—and thus that resources should be allocated to the army and to border fortifications.

Louis XIV on Kingship

From time to time, Louis XIV put on paper brief accounts of his actions: For example, he wrote some brief memoirs in the late 1660s. These reflections about his role as king were intended as a guide for his son and indicate both his high view of kingship and the seriousness with which he approached his duties. The following are extracts from his memoirs and other writings.

"Homage is due to kings, and they do whatever they like. It certainly must be agreed that, however bad a prince may be, it is always a heinous crime for his subjects to rebel against him. He who gave men kings willed that they should be respected as His lieutenants, and reserved to Himself the right to question their conduct. It is His will that everyone who is born a subject should obey without qualification. This law, as clear as it is universal, was not made only for the sake of princes: it is also for the good of the people themselves. It is therefore the duty of kings to sustain by their own example the religion upon which they rely; and they must realize that, if their subjects see them plunged in vice or violence, they can hardly render to their person the respect due to their office, or recognize in them the living image of Him who is all-holy as well as almighty.

"It is a fine thing, a noble and enjoyable thing, to be a king. But it is not without its pains, its fatigues, and its troubles. One must work hard to reign. In working for the state, a king is working for himself. The good of the one is the glory of the other. When the state is prosperous, famous, and powerful, the king who is the cause of it is glorious; and he ought in consequence to have a larger share than others do of all that is most agreeable in life."

From J. M. Thompson, *Lectures on Foreign History, 1494–1789* (Oxford: Blackwell, 1956), pp. 172–174.

FOREIGN POLICY

Louis tried to balance these goals within his overall aims—to expand France's frontiers and to assert his superiority over other European states. Like the magnificence of his court, his power on the international scene served to demonstrate "la gloire" (the glory) of France. But his effort to expand that power prompted his neighbors to form coalitions and alliances of common defense, designed to keep him in check. From this response was to emerge the concept of a state system and the notion of a balance of power among the states of Europe.

In his early years Louis relied heavily on Colbert, who moved gradually toward war with the Dutch when all attempts to undermine their control of French maritime trade failed. But the war (1672–1678) was a failure, and so the pendulum swung toward Louvois. In the early 1680s Louis adopted the marquis' aims and asserted his right to a succession of territories on France's northeast border. No one claim seemed important enough to provoke his neighbors to military action, especially since the Holy Roman Emperor, Leopold I, was distracted by a resumption in 1682 of war with the Turks in the East. The result was that France was able to annex large segments of territory until, in 1686, a league of other European states was formed to restrain Louis' growing power (see Map 17.1).

Map 17.1 THE WARS OF LOUIS XIV
A. Louis XIV's aggressive aims took his troops to many areas of Europe.
B. The main conflict was on France's eastern border, where Louis made small but significant gains.

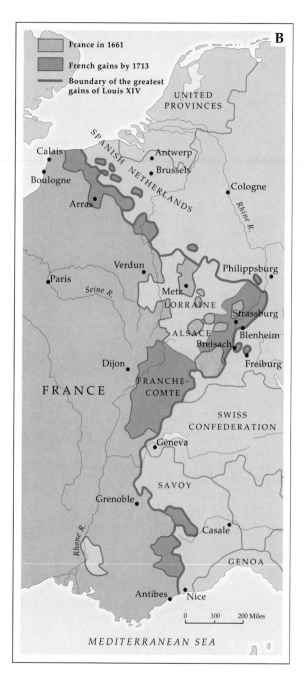

France in 1661

French gains by 1713

Boundary of the greatest gains of Louis XIV

B

UNITED PROVINCES

Calais
Boulogne
Antwerp
Brussels
SPANISH NETHERLANDS
Cologne
Arras
Rhine R.
Verdun
Philippsburg
Paris
Seine R.
Metz
LORRAINE
Strassburg
ALSACE
Blenheim
Breisach
Freiburg
Dijon
FRANCHE-COMTE
FRANCE
SWISS CONFEDERATION
Geneva
SAVOY
Grenoble
Casale
Rhone R.
GENOA
Antibes
Nice

0   100   200 Miles

MEDITERRANEAN SEA

Louis versus Europe The leaders of the league were William III of the United Provinces and Emperor Leopold. Leopold was prepared to join the struggle because, even though his war with the Turks was to continue until 1699, the fighting turned in his favor after 1683, when his troops broke a Turkish siege of Vienna. And six years later William became a far more redoubtable foe when he gained the English throne. The league finally went to war to put an end to French expansion in 1688, and when Louis began to lose the territories he had gained in the 1680s, he decided to seek peace and remove Louvois from power in 1690, though the war did not end until 1697. But the respite did not last long. Four years later France became involved in a bitter war that brought famine, wretched poverty, and humiliation. Louis was now seeking the succession to the Spanish throne for his family, with no regard for the terrible consequences of the fighting. This final, ruinous enterprise revealed both the new power of France and its limits. By launching an all-out attempt to establish his own and his country's supremacy in Europe, Louis showed that he felt capable of taking on the whole of the continent; but by then he no longer had the economic and military base at home or the weak opposition abroad to ensure success.

Economic strains had begun to appear in the 1690s, when shattering famines throughout France reduced tax revenues and the size of the work force, even as enemies began to unite abroad. Louis had the most formidable army in Europe—400,000 men by the end of his reign—but both William and Leopold believed he could be defeated by a combined assault, and they led the attack in the final showdown when the Habsburg king of Spain, Charles II, died without an heir in 1700.

There were various possible claimants to the Spanish throne, and Charles himself had changed his mind a number of times, but at his death his choice was Philip, Louis XIV's grandson (see the genealogical table on p. 540). Had Louis been willing to agree not to unite the thrones of France and Spain and to allow the Spanish empire to be opened (for the first time) to foreign traders, Charles's wish might well have been respected. But Louis refused to compromise, and in 1701 William and Leopold created the so-called Grand Alliance, which declared war on France the following year. The French now found themselves fighting virtually all of Europe in a war over the Spanish succession, not only at home but also overseas, in India, Canada, and the Caribbean.

Led by two brilliant generals—the English-

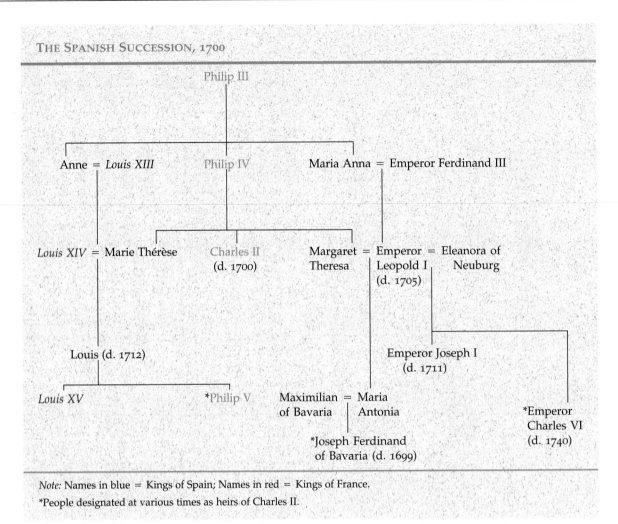

THE SPANISH SUCCESSION, 1700

Note: Names in blue = Kings of Spain; Names in red = Kings of France.
*People designated at various times as heirs of Charles II.

man John Churchill, duke of Marlborough, and the Austrian Prince Eugène—the Grand Alliance won a series of smashing victories. France's hardships were increased by a terrible famine in 1709. Although the criticism of his policies now became fierce, and dangerous rebellions erupted, the Sun King retained his hold over his subjects. Despite military disaster he was able to keep his nation's borders intact and the Spanish throne for his grandson (though he had to give up the possibility of union with France and end the restrictions on trade in the Spanish empire) when peace treaties were signed at Utrecht in 1713 and 1714. When it was all over, Louis' great task of state building, both at home and abroad, had withstood the severest of tests: defeat on the battlefield.

DOMESTIC POLICY

The assertion of royal supremacy at home was almost complete by the time Louis came to power, but he extended centralized control to religion and social institutions. Both the Protestant Huguenots and the Catholic Jansenists interfered with the spiritual and confessional uniformity that Louis considered essential in an absolutist state. As a result, pressures against them mounted steadily. In 1685 Louis revoked the Edict of Nantes, now almost a century old, which had granted Protestants limited toleration, and he forced France's 1 million Huguenots either to leave the country (four-fifths did) or to convert to Catholicism. This was a political rather than a religious step, taken to promote unity despite the economic consequences that followed the departure of a vigorous and productive minority.

Jansenism was more elusive. It had far fewer followers, and it was a movement that emphasized spiritual values within Catholicism. But the very fact that it challenged the official Church emphasis on ritual and was condemned by Rome made it a source of unrest. Even more unsettling was its success in gaining support among the magistrate class—the royal officers in the parlements, who had to register all royal edicts before they became law. The Parlement of Paris was the only governmental institution that offered Louis any real resistance. The issues over which it caused trouble were usually religious, and the link between parlementaire independence and Jansenism gave Louis more than enough reason for displeasure. He razed the Jansenists' headquarters, the Abbey of Port-Royal, and persuaded the pope to issue a bull condemning Jansenism. He was prevented from implementing the bull—over parlementaire opposition—only by his death in 1715.

Control and Reform The drive toward uniformity that prompted these actions was reflected in all of domestic policy. Louis kept in check what little protest arose in the parlements and either forbade or overruled their efforts to block his decrees; major uprisings by peasants in central France in the 1690s and 1700s were ruthlessly suppressed, as were all disturbances; Parisian publishers came under bureaucratic supervision; and the *intendants*, the government's chief provincial officers, were given increased authority, particularly to supply the ever-growing money and recruitment needs of the army.

At the outset of his rule, Louis used his power to improve France's economy. In this, he followed a pattern familiar from earlier monarchs' reigns: an initial burst of reform measures designed to cure the country's economic ills, which were gradually forgotten because foreign policy demanded instant funds. In the early years, under Colbert's ministry, major efforts were made to stimulate manufacturing, agriculture, and home and foreign trade. Some industries, notably those involving luxuries, like the silk production of Lyons, received considerable help and owed their prosperity to royal patronage. Colbert also tried, not entirely effectively, to reduce the crippling effects of France's countless internal tolls. These were usually nobles' perquisites, and they could multiply the cost of goods shipped any distance. The government divided the country into a number of districts, within which shipments were to be toll-free, but the system never removed the worst abuses. Louis also tried to boost foreign trade, at first by financing new overseas trading companies and later by founding new port cities as naval and commercial centers. He achieved notable success only in the West Indies, where sugar plantations became a source of great wealth.

THE CONDITION OF FRANCE

Louis' success in state building was remarkable, and France became the envy of Europe. Yet ever since the Sun King's reign, historians have recalled the ruination caused by famine and war during his last years and have contrasted his glittering court with the misery of most French people. Taxes and rents rose remorselessly, and in many regions the hardships were made worse by significant declines in the population. Particularly after the famines of the 1690s and 1709, many contemporaries remarked on the dreadful condition of France's peasants.

The reign of Louis XIV can thus be regarded as the end of an era in the life of the lower classes. By pushing his need for resources to its limits, he inflicted a level of suffering that was not to recur, because governments increasingly came to realize that state building depended on the welfare and support of their people. In the eighteenth century, though there was still much suffering to come, the terrible subsistence crises, with their cycles of famine and plague, came to an end, largely because of official efforts to distribute food in starving areas and to isolate and suppress outbreaks of plague. Thus, although the hand of the central government was heavier in 1715 than a hundred years before, it was becoming more obviously a beneficent as well as a burdensome force. And the Counter Reformation Church, growing in strength since the Council of Trent, also had a more salutary influence as religious struggles died away, for it brought into local parishes better-educated and more dedicated priests who, as part of their new commitment to service, exerted themselves to calm the outbreaks of witchcraft and irrational fear that had swept the countryside for centuries. Despite the strains Louis had caused, therefore, his absolutist authority was now firmly in place and could ensure a dominant European role for a united and powerful France.

FRANCE AFTER LOUIS XIV

Although the Sun King created a model for absolutism in partnership with his nobility, the traditional ambitions of the nobles reasserted themselves after he died in 1715, leaving a child as his heir. The duke of Orléans, Louis XIV's nephew, who became regent until 1723, was committed to giving authority to the aristocracy. He also restored the parlements to political power and replaced royal bureaucrats with councils composed of leading members of the nobility. The scheme was a failure because the councils were unable to govern effectively. The parlements, however, would never again surrender their power to veto royal legislation. They became a rallying point for those who opposed centralization and wished to limit the king's powers.

Finance was also a serious problem for the government, because of the debts left by Louis XIV's wars. A brilliant Scottish financier, John Law, suggested an answer: a government-sponsored central bank that would issue paper notes,

▷ *P. D. Martin*
PROCESSION AFTER LOUIS XV'S CORONATION AT RHEIMS, 1722
This magnificent scene, in front of the cathedral where French kings traditionally were crowned, gives one a sense of the throngs who came to celebrate the day in 1722 when Louis XV officially came of age and received his crown. Paintings depicting royal virtue were erected around the cathedral, and Louis himself (in red on a white horse just to the right of center) was preceded by a flag covered with his symbol, the fleur-de-lis. The other flags remind us that this was an occasion for international pageantry.

expand credit, and encourage investment in a new trading company for the French colonies. By tying the bank to this company, the Company of the Occident, a venture that promised subscribers vast profits from the Louisiana territory in North America, Law set off an investment boom. But the public's greed soon pushed prices for the company's stock to insanely high levels. A bust was inevitable, and when it came, in 1720, the entire scheme of bank notes and credit collapsed.

Fleury The same political and financial problems were to plague France, in different forms, throughout the eighteenth century, until the leaders of the French Revolution sought radical ways to solve them in the 1790s. Yet the uncertainties of the regency did give way to a long period of stability after 1726, when Louis XV gave almost unlimited authority to his aging tutor and adviser, Cardinal Fleury. Cautious, dedicated to the monarchy, and surrounded by talented subordinates, Fleury made absolutism function quietly and effectively, and enabled France to recover from the setbacks that had marked the end of Louis XIV's reign. Fleury's tenure coincided with abundant harvests, slowly rising population, and increased commercial activity.

Political Problems Fleury was able to contain the ambitions of the governing class. When he died in 1743 at the age of 90, these pressures exploded. War hawks immediately plunged France into the first of several unsuccessful wars with its neighbors that strained French credit to the breaking point. At home royal authority likewise deteriorated. Having no one to replace Fleury as unofficial prime minister, Louis XV put his confidence in a succession of advisers, some capable and some mediocre. But he did not back them when attacks from factions at court became uncomfortable. Uninterested in government, the king avoided confrontations and neglected affairs of state, devoting his energy instead to the pleasures of the hunt and court ceremony.

Although Louis XV provided weak leadership, France's difficulties were not simply personal but rather structural. The main problems—special privileges, political power, and finance—posed almost impossible challenges. Governments that levy new taxes arbitrarily seem despotic, even if the need for them is clear

and the distribution equitable. One of France's soundest taxes was the *vingtième*, or twentieth, which was supposed to tap the income of all parts of French society roughly equally. The nobility and clergy, however, all but evaded the tax. Naturally, aggressive royal ministers wanted to remedy that situation. In the 1750s, for example, an effort was made to put teeth into the *vingtième*'s bite on the clergy's huge wealth. But the effort merely ruined the career of the capable royal official who devised it. The clergy resisted furiously; and the parlements joined the attack against the "despotism" of a crown that would arbitrarily tax its subjects. Thus the privileged groups not only blocked reforms but also made the monarch's position more difficult by taking up opposition and a rhetoric of liberty as they fought to limit royal absolutism.

Despite the demands of these special interests, the eighteenth century was a time of notable advance for Europe's most populous and wealthy state. As we will see, France in this period experienced remarkable expansion in population, in the rural economy, in commerce, and in empire building. No one knew at the time that the failures of reforming royal ministers in the mid-1700s foretold a stalemate that would help bring the old regime crashing down.

II. The Creation of Absolutism outside of France

THE HABSBURGS AT VIENNA

The pattern set at Versailles was repeated at the court of the Habsburg Leopold I, the Holy Roman Emperor (1658–1705). Heir to a reduced inheritance that gave him control over only Bohemia, Austria, and a small part of Hungary, Leopold still maintained a splendid establishment. His plans for a new palace, Schönbrunn, that was to have outshone Versailles were modified only because of a lack of funds. And his promotion of the court as the center of all political and social life turned Vienna into what it had never been before: a city for nobles as well as small-time traders.

Nevertheless, Leopold did not display the pretensions of the Sun King. He was a younger son and had come to the throne only because of the death of his brother. Indecisive, retiring, and deeply religious, he had no fondness for the bravado Louis XIV enjoyed. He was a composer of some talent, and his patronage laid the foundation for the great musical culture that was to be one of Vienna's chief glories. But he did inherit considerable royal authority, which he sought to expand—though unlike Louis XIV he relied on a small group of leading nobles to devise policy and run his government.

Government Policy   The Thirty Years' War that ended in 1648 had revealed that the elected head of the Holy Roman Empire could no longer control the princes who nominally owed him allegiance. In his own dominions, however, he could maintain his control with the cooperation of his nobility. The Privy Council, which in effect ran Leopold's domain, was filled largely with members of aristocratic families, and his chief advisers were always prominent nobles. To make policy, he carefully consulted each of his ministers and then, even when all of them agreed, came to decisions with agonizing slowness.

Unlike the other courts of Europe, Schönbrunn did not favor only native-born aristocrats. The leader of Austria's armies during the Turks' siege of Vienna in 1683 was Charles, duke of Lorraine, whose duchy had been taken over by the French. His predecessor as field marshal had been an Italian, and his successor was to be one of the most brilliant soldiers of the age, Prince Eugène of Savoy. They became members of the Austrian nobility only when Leopold gave them titles within his own dominions, but they all fitted easily into the aristocratic circles that controlled the government and the army.

Eugène   Prince Eugène (1663–1736) was a spectacular symbol of the aristocracy's continuing dominance of politics and society. A member of one of Europe's most distinguished families, he had been raised in France but found himself passed over when Louis XIV awarded army commissions, perhaps because he had been intended for the Church. Yet he was determined to have a military career, and he volunteered to serve the

Austrians in the war with the Turks that, following the siege of Vienna, was to expand Habsburg territory in the Balkans by the time peace was signed in 1699 (see Map 17.2). Eugène's talents quickly became evident: He was field marshal of Austria's troops by the time he was 30. Over the next 40 years, as intermittent war with the Turks continued, he became a decisive influence in Habsburg affairs. Though foreign-born, he was the minister primarily responsible for the transformation of Vienna's policies from defensive to aggressive.

Until the siege of Vienna by the Turks in 1683, Leopold's cautiousness kept Austria simply holding the line, both against Louis XIV and against the Turks. In the 1690s, however, he tried a bolder course at Eugène's urging and in the process laid the foundations for a new Habsburg empire along the Danube River: Austria-Hungary. He helped create the coalition that defeated Louis in the 1700s, intervened in Italy so that his landlocked domains could gain an outlet to the sea, and began the long process of pushing the Turks out of the Balkans. Leopold did not live to see the advance more than started, but by the time of Eugène's death, the Austrians' advances against the Turks had brought them within a hundred miles of the Black Sea.

Yet the local power of the aristocracy tempered the centralization of Leopold's dominions. Louis XIV supported his nobles if they worked for him; Leopold, by contrast, gave them influence in the government without first establishing control over all his lands. The nobility did not cause the Habsburgs as much trouble as they had during the Thirty Years' War, but Leopold had to limit his ambitions outside Austria. Moreover, as Austrians came increasingly to dominate the court, the nobles of Hungary and Bohemia reacted by clinging stubbornly to their local rights. Thus Leopold's was an absolutism under which the nobility retained far more autonomous power—and a far firmer base of local support—than was the case in France, despite the centralization he achieved during his reign.

THE HABSBURGS AT MADRID

In Spain the Habsburgs had little success in state building either at home or abroad. The king,

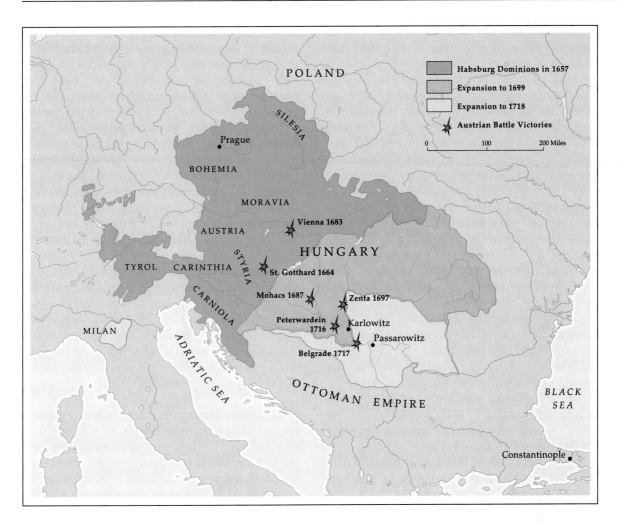

Map 17.2 THE AUSTRIAN EMPIRE, 1657–1718
The steady advance of the Habsburgs into the
Balkans was marked by a succession of victories;
their gains were confirmed by treaties with the
Turks at Karlowitz (1699) and Passarowitz (1718).

Charles II (1665–1700), was a sickly man, incapable of having children; and the War of the Spanish Succession seriously reduced the inheritance he left. Both the southern Netherlands and most of Italy passed to the Austrian Habsburgs, and Spain's overseas possessions often paid little notice to the homeland.

The Spanish nobility was even more successful than the Austrian in turning absolutism to its advantage. In 1650 the crown had been able to recapture Catalonia's loyalty only by granting the province's aristocracy virtual autonomy, and this pattern recurred throughout Spain's territories. Parasitic, unproductive nobles controlled the regime, often for personal gain. The country fell into economic and cultural stagnation, subservient to a group of powerful families, with its former glory visible in the eighteenth century only in its strong navy.

THE HOHENZOLLERNS AT BERLIN

The one new power that emerged to prominence during the age of Louis XIV was Brandenburg-Prussia, and here again state building was made possible by a close alliance between a powerful ruler and his nobles. Frederick William of Hohenzollern (1640–1688), known as the "great elector," ruled scattered territories that stretched 700 miles from Cleves, on the Rhine, to a part of Prussia on the Baltic. That so fragmented and disconnected a set of lands could be shaped into a major European power was a testimony to the political abilities of the Hohenzollerns. The process began when, taking advantage of the uncertainties that followed the Thirty Years' War, Frederick William made his territories the dominant principality in northern Germany and at the same time strengthened his power over his subjects.

Foreign Policy   His first task was in foreign affairs, because when he became elector, the troops of the various states that were fighting the Thirty Years' War swarmed over his possessions at will. Frederick William realized that by determination and intelligent planning, even a small prince could emerge from these disasters in a good position *if* he had an army. With some military force at his disposal, he could become a useful ally for the big powers, who could then help him against his neighbors; while at home he would have the strength to crush his opponents.

By 1648 Frederick William had 8000 troops, and he was backed by both the Dutch and the French as a possible restraint on Sweden in northern Europe during the negotiations leading to the treaty of Westphalia in that year. Without having done much to earn new territory, he did very well in the peace settlement, and he then took brilliant advantage of wars around the Baltic in the 1650s to confirm his gains by switching sides at crucial moments. In the process, his army grew to 22,000 men, and he began to use it to impose his will on his own lands. The fact that the army was essential to all Frederick William's successes—both at home and abroad—was to influence much of Prussia's and thus also Germany's subsequent history.

Domestic Policy   The role of the military in establishing the elector's supremacy was apparent throughout Brandenburg-Prussia's society. In 1653 the Diet of Brandenburg met for the last time, sealing its own fate by giving Frederick William the right to raise taxes without its consent. The War Chest, the office in charge of financing the army, took over the functions of a treasury department and collected government revenue even when the state was at peace. The implementation of policies in the localities was placed in the hands of war commissars—who originally were responsible for military recruitment, billeting, and supply in each district of Brandenburg-Prussia, but who now became the principal agents of all government departments.

Apart from the representative assemblies, Frederick William faced real resistance only from the long-independent cities of his realm. Accustomed to going their own way because authority had been fragmented in the empire for centuries, and especially during the Thirty Years' War, city leaders were dismayed when the elector began to intervene in their affairs. Yet once again sheer intimidation swept opposition aside. The last determined effort to dispute his authority arose in the rich city of Königsberg, which allied with the Estates General of Prussia to refuse to pay taxes. But this resistance was crushed in 1662, when Frederick William marched into the city with a few thousand troops. Similar pressure brought the towns of Cleves into submission after centuries of proud independence.

The Junkers   The nobles were the main supporters and beneficiaries of the elector's state building. It was, in fact, an alliance between the nobility and Frederick William that made it possible for the Diet, the cities, and the representative assemblies to be undermined. The leading families saw their best opportunities for the future in cooperation with the central government, and both in the representative assemblies and in the localities, they worked to establish absolutist power—that is, to remove all restraints on the elector. The most significant indicator of the nobles' success was that by the end of the century, two tax rates had been devised, one for cities and one for the countryside, to the great advantage of the latter.

Not only did the nobles staff the upper levels of the elector's army and bureaucracy, but they also won new prosperity for themselves. Particularly in Prussia, the support of the elector enabled them to reimpose serfdom and consolidate their land holdings into vast, highly profitable estates. This was a major grain-producing area, and they made the most of its economic potential. To maximize profits, they eliminated intermediaries not only by growing but also by distributing their produce themselves. Efficiency became their hallmark, and their wealth was soon famous throughout the Holy Roman Empire. Known as Junkers (from the German for young lord, *jung herr*), these Prussian entrepreneurs were probably the most successful group of European aristocrats in pursuing economic and political power.

Frederick III   Unlike Louis in France, Frederick William had little interest in court life. The Berlin court became the focus of society only under his son, Elector Frederick III, who ruled from 1688. The great elector himself was more interested in organizing his administration, increasing tax returns, building his army, and imposing his authority at home and abroad. He began the development of his capital, Berlin, into a cultural center—he founded what was to become one of the finest libraries in the world, the Prussian State Library—but this was never among his prime concerns. His son, by contrast, had little interest in state building, but he did enjoy princely pomp and he encouraged the arts with enthusiasm.

Frederick III lacked only one attribute of royalty: a crown. When Emperor Leopold I, who still had the right to confer titles in the empire, needed Prussia's troops during the War of the Spanish Succession, he gave Frederick, in return, the right to call himself "king in Prussia," and the title soon became "king of Prussia." At a splendid coronation in 1701, Elector Frederick III of Brandenburg was crowned King Frederick I, and thereafter his court could feel itself the equal of the other monarchical settings of Europe.

Frederick determinedly promoted social and cultural glitter. He made his palace a center of art and polite society to compete, he hoped, with Versailles. A construction program beautified Berlin with new churches and huge public buildings. He also established an Academy of Sciences and persuaded the most famous German scientist and philosopher of the day, Gottfried Wilhelm von Leibniz, to become its first president. All these activities obtained generous support from state revenues, as did the universities of Brandenburg and Prussia. By the end of his reign in 1713, Frederick had given his realm a throne, celebrated artistic and intellectual activity, and an elegant aristocracy at the head of social and political life.

PETER THE GREAT AT ST. PETERSBURG

One of the reasons the new absolutist regimes of the late seventeenth and eighteenth centuries seemed so different from their predecessors was that many of them consciously created new settings for themselves. Versailles, Schönbrunn, and Berlin were all either new or totally transformed sites for royal courts. But only one of the autocrats of the period went so far as to build an entirely new capital: Tsar Peter I (the Great) of Russia (1682–1725), who named the new city St. Petersburg after his patron saint.

The Tsar's Rule   None of the state-building rulers of the period had Peter's terrifying energy or ruthless determination to exercise absolute control. This he made clear when he destroyed ecclesiastical independence in one stunning gesture: He simply did not replace the patriarch of the Russian Church when he died in 1700. The government took over the monasteries, using their enormous income for its own purposes, and appointed a procurator (at first an army officer) to supervise all religious affairs. The church was, in effect, made a branch of government.

In ruling, Peter virtually ignored the Duma, the traditional advisory council, and concentrated instead on his bureaucracy. He carried out change after change until he had created an administrative complex many times larger than the one he had inherited. In this effort he determinedly copied Western models—notably Prussia, where nobles ran the bureaucracy and the army, and Sweden, where a complex system of government departments had been created. Peter organized his administration into similar departments: Each had either a specialized function, such as finance, or responsibility for a geographic area, such as Siberia. The result was an elaborate but unified hierarchy of authority, rising from local agents of the government through provincial officials up to the staffs and governors of 11 large administrative units and finally to the leaders of the regime in the capital. Peter began the saturating bureaucratization that characterized Russia from that time on.

Russian Society   The tsar's policies laid the foundations for a two-class society that persisted until the twentieth century. Previously, a number of ranks had existed within both the nobility and the peasantry, and a group in the middle was seen sometimes as the lowest nobles and sometimes as the highest peasants. Under Peter such mingling disappeared. All peasants were reduced to one level, subject to a new poll tax, military conscription, and forced public work, such as the building of St. Petersburg. Below them were serfs, whose numbers were increased by legislation restricting their movement. Peasants had a few advantages over serfs, such as the freedom to move, but their living conditions were often equally dreadful. Serfdom itself spread throughout all areas of Peter's dominions and became essential to his state building, because on royal lands as well as the estates of the nobles, serfs worked and ran the agricultural enterprise that was Russia's economic base.

At the same time, Peter created a single class of nobles by substituting status within the bureaucracy for status within the traditional hierarchy of titles. In 1722 he issued a table of bureaucratic ranks that gave everyone a place according to the office he held. Differentiations still existed, but they were no longer unbridgeable, as they had been when family was the decisive determinant of status. The result was a more controlled social order and greater uniformity than in France or Brandenburg-Prussia. The Russian aristocracy was the bureaucracy, and the bureaucracy the aristocracy.

▶ PETER THE GREAT AT ST. PETERSBURG
In the eighteenth century Peter the Great of Russia outstripped the grandeur of other monarchs of the period by erecting an entirely new city for his capital. St. Petersburg was built by forced labor of the peasants under Peter's orders; they are shown here laying the foundations for the city.

The Nobility But this was not a voluntary alliance between nobles and government, such as existed in the West; in return for his support and his total subjection of the peasantry, Peter *required* the nobles to provide officials for his bureaucracy and officers for his army. When he began the construction of St. Petersburg, he also demanded that the leading families build splendid mansions in his new capital. In effect, the tsar offered privilege and wealth in exchange for conscription into public service. Thus there was hardly any sense of partnership between nobility and throne: The tsar often had to use coercion to ensure that his wishes were followed.

On the other hand, Peter did a good deal to build up the nobles' fortunes and their ability to control the countryside. It has been estimated that by 1710 he had put under the supervision of great landowners more than 40,000 peasant and serf households that had formerly been under the crown. And he was liberal in conferring new titles—some of them, such as count and baron, copies of German examples.

Western Models In creating an aristocratic society at his court, Peter mixed imitations of what he admired in the West with native developments. He sought to apply Western models because he felt that Russia had much to learn from the advances its neighbors had made. To observe these achievements at firsthand, Peter traveled secretly through France, England, and the Netherlands in 1697 and 1698, paying special attention to economic, administrative, and military practices (such as the functioning of a Dutch shipyard). Many of his initiatives derived from this journey, including his importation of Western court rituals and his founding of an Academy of Sciences in 1725. Italian artists were brought to Russia, along with Scandinavian army officers, German engineers, and Dutch shipbuilders, not only to apply their skills but also to teach them to the Russians. St. Petersburg, the finest example of a city built in eighteenth-century Classical style, is mainly the work of Italians. But gradually, the Russians took over their own institutions—military academies produced native officers, for example—and by the end of Peter's reign the nobles had little need of foreign experts to help run the government. Peter the Great had laid the foundations for the aristocratic society that would rule his people for 200 years.

The purpose of these radical internal changes was to assert the tsar's power both at home and abroad. Peter established a huge standing army, more than 300,000 strong by the 1720s, and imported the latest military techniques from the West. One of Peter's most cherished projects, the creation of a navy, had limited success, but there could be no doubt that he transformed Russia's capacity for war and its position among European states. He extended Russia's frontier to the south and west, beginning the destruction of Sweden's empire at the battle of Poltava in 1709 and following this triumph by more than a decade of advance into Estonia, Livonia, and Poland. The very vastness of his realm justified Peter's drive for absolute control, and by the time of his death he had made Russia the dominant power in the Baltic and a major influence in European affairs.

III. *Alternatives to Absolutism*

THE TRIUMPH OF THE GENTRY IN ENGLAND

The absolutist regimes provided one model of political and social organization, but an alternative model—equally committed to uniformity, order, and state building—was also created in the late seventeenth century: governments dominated by aristocrats or merchants. The contrast between the two was noted by contemporary political theorists, especially opponents of absolutism, who compared France unfavorably with England. And yet the differences were often less sharp than the theorists suggested, mainly because the position of the aristocracy was similar throughout Europe.

England's King Charles II (1660–1685), for example, seemed to have powers similar to those of his father, Charles I. He still summoned and dissolved Parliament, he made all appointments in the bureaucracy, and he signed every law. But he no longer had royal prerogative courts like Star Chamber, he could not arrest a member of

Parliament, and he could not create a new seat in the Commons. Even two ancient prerogatives, the king's right to dispense with an act of Parliament for a specific individual or group and his right to suspend an act completely, proved to be empty when Charles II tried to exercise them. Nor could he raise money without parliamentary assent: Instead, he was given a fixed annual income, financed by a tax on beer.

The Gentry and Parliament The real control of the country's affairs had by this time passed to the group of substantial landowners known as the *gentry.* In a country of some 5 million people, perhaps 15,000 to 20,000 families were considered gentry—leaders of the various localities throughout England, though they had neither titles of nobility nor special privileges. They represented about 2 percent of the population, a proportion that was probably not much different from the percentage of titled and privileged nobles in the populations of other states.

The gentry were distinguished from the nobles of other countries by the right they had won in England's civil war to determine national policy through Parliament. Whereas in France, Austria, Brandenburg-Prussia, and Russia nobles depended on the monarch for power and were subservient to him, the English revolution had made the gentry an independent force. Their authority was now hallowed by custom, upheld by law, and maintained by the House of Commons, a representative assembly that was both the supreme legislature and the body to which the executive government was ultimately responsible.

Not all the gentry took a continuing, active interest in affairs of state, and no more than a few of their number sat in the roughly 500-member House of Commons. Even the Commons did not exercise a constant influence over the govern-

THE ENGLISH SUCCESSION FROM THE STUARTS TO THE HANOVERIANS

Note: Names in blue = Monarchs of England.

ment; nevertheless, the ministers of the king had to be prominent representatives of the gentry, and they had to be able to win the support of a majority of the members of the Commons. Policy was still set by the king and his ministers. But the Commons had to be persuaded that the policies were correct; without parliamentary approval, a minister could not long survive.

The Succession   Despite occasional conflicts, this structure worked relatively smoothly throughout Charles II's reign. But the gentry feared that Charles's brother, James, next in line for the succession and an open Catholic, might try to restore Catholicism in England. To prevent this, they attempted in 1680 to force Charles to exclude James from the throne. But in the end the traditional respect for legitimacy, combined with some shrewd maneuvering by Charles, ensured that there would be no tampering with the succession.

Soon, however, the reign of James II (1685–1688) turned into a disaster. Elated by his acceptance as king, James rashly attempted the very encouragement of Catholicism that the gentry feared. This was a direct challenge to the gentry's newly won power, and in the fall of 1688, seven of their leaders—including members of some of the oldest families in the realm—invited the Protestant ruler of the United Provinces, William III, to invade the country and take over the throne. Although William landed with an army half the size of the king's, James, uncertain of his support, decided not to risk battle and fled to exile in France.

William and Mary   The new king gained what little title he had to the crown through his wife, Mary (see the genealogical table on p. 550), and the couple were proclaimed joint monarchs by Parliament early in 1689. The Dutch ruler had taken the throne primarily to bring England into his relentless struggles against Louis XIV, and he willingly accepted a settlement that confirmed the essential position of Parliament in the government. A Bill of Rights settled the future succession to the throne, defined Parliament's powers, and established basic civil rights; an Act of Toleration put an end to all religious persecution, though members of the official Church of England were still the only people allowed to vote,

The Metropolitan Museum of Art

▶ *Sir Joshua Reynolds*
LADY SMITH AND HER CHILDREN
The quiet serenity and assurance of England's gentry in the eighteenth century is apparent in all their portraits, whether the head of the household is present or, as in this case, only his wife and children.

sit in Parliament, hold a government office, or attend a university; and in 1694 a statute laid down that Parliament had to meet and new elections had to be held at least once every three years.

Despite the restrictions on his authority, William exercised strong leadership following this so-called Glorious Revolution.* He guided England into a new, aggressive foreign policy, picked the ministers favorable to his aims, and

---

*It got its name because it was bloodless and confirmed the supremacy of Parliament once and for all.

never let Parliament sit when he was out of the country to pursue the war or to oversee Dutch affairs. In his reign, too, the central government grew significantly, creating new positions, new powers, and new opportunities for political patronage. But unlike James, William recognized his limits. He tried to have the Bill of Rights reversed and a standing army established, but he gave up when these efforts provoked major opposition. By and large, therefore, the gentry were content to let the king rule as he saw fit. For they had shown by their intervention in 1688 that ultimately they controlled the country.

POLITICS AND PROSPERITY

The political system in England now reflected the social system: A small elite controlled both the country's policy and its institutions. This group was far from united, however, as was apparent when a party system began to appear in Parliament during Charles II's reign. On one side were the Whigs, who opposed royal prerogatives and Catholicism and were largely responsible for the attempt to exclude James II from the throne. Their rivals, the Tories, stood for the independence and authority of the crown and favored a ceremonial and traditional Anglicanism.

Party Conflict Because the Whigs had been the main advocates of the removal of James II, they controlled the government for most of William III's reign. They supported his war against Louis XIV (1689–1697), since France harbored both James and his followers, the romantic but ill-fated Jacobites, who kept trying to restore James's line to the throne. This was a relatively nonpartisan issue, but the Tories and Whigs still competed fiercely for voters. Because the qualification for voting—owning land worth 40 shillings a year in rent—had become less restrictive as a result of inflation (which made 40 shillings a fairly modest sum) and was not to be raised to a higher minimum until the late 1700s, England now had what would be its largest electorate before the 1860s. Almost 5 percent of the population (more than 15 percent of adult males) could vote, and although results were usually determined by powerful local magnates, fierce politicking was common. And in the election of 1700 there was a major upset: The Tories won by opposing a resumption of war against Louis XIV, who seemed to have been contained since the end of the previous war in 1697.

Within two years, however, and despite William's death in 1702, England was again at war with France, this time over the Spanish succession; and soon the Whigs were again in control of the government. The identification of the parties with their attitude toward war continued until 1710, when weariness over the fighting brought the Tories back into power. They persuaded Queen Anne, William's successor, to make peace with France at Utrecht in 1713; and it was only because the Tories made the mistake of negotiating with the rebel Jacobites after Anne died in 1714 without an heir that they lost power. Anne's successor was a German prince, the elector of Hanover, who founded the new Hanoverian dynasty as George I (1714–1727). Since they firmly supported his succession, the Whigs regained control of the government when George came to the throne. They then entrenched themselves, and under the leadership of Robert Walpole, they began almost a century of political ascendancy.

The Sea and the Economy At the same time, England was winning for itself unprecedented prosperity and laying the foundations of its world power. Its navy made it the premier force on the sea, the decisive victor over France during the worldwide struggle of the early eighteenth century. Overseas, new colonies were founded, and the empire expanded steadily. When England and Scotland joined into one kingdom in 1707, the union created a Great Britain ready to exercise a worldwide influence.

The economic advances were equally remarkable. A notable achievement was the establishment of the Bank of England in 1694. The bank was given permission to raise money from the public and then lend it to the government at a favorable 8 percent interest. Within 12 days its founders raised more than a million pounds, demonstrating not only the financial security and stability of England's government but also the commitment of the elite to the country's political structure. London was becoming the financial capital of the world, and British merchants were gaining control over maritime trade from East Asia to North America. Significantly, the benefits of this boom also helped the lower levels of society.

English Society There is little doubt that with the possible exception of the Dutch, ordinary English people were better off than their equivalents elsewhere in Europe. Compared with the sixteenth century, there was little starvation. The system of poor relief may often have been inhumane in forcing the unfortunate to work in horrifying workhouses, but it did provide them with the shelter and food that they had long lacked. It is true that thousands still found themselves unable to make a living in their home villages each year and were forced by poverty to take to the roads. And the many who ended up in London hardly improved their situation. The stream of immigrants was driving the capital's population toward half a million, and the city contained frightful slums and miserable crime-ridden sections. Even a terrible fire in London in 1666 did little to improve the appallingly crowded living conditions because the city was rebuilt much as before, the only notable additions being a series

▶ *William Hogarth*
THE POLLING, 1754
Despite the high reputation of the polling day as the central moment in the system of representative government, Hogarth's depiction of it in this scene suggests how corrupt and disheveled the process of voting was. The sick and the foolish are among the mob of voters; the central figure looks bewildered as he is told what to do; on the right a bloated official cannot decide whether a voter should be allowed to take his oath on the Bible with a wooden hand; and all ignore the distress of Britannia, the symbol of Britain, in her coach on the left.

The Metropolitan Museum of Art

▶ *Samuel Scott*
THE BUILDING OF WESTMINSTER BRIDGE, CA. 1742
The elegance, but not the squalor, of city life in the eighteenth century is suggested by this view of Westminster.

of splendid churches. But the grimness should not be overdrawn.

After more than a century of inflation, the laborer could once again make a decent living, and artisans were enjoying a growing demand for their work. Higher in the social scale, more men had a say in the political process than before, and more found opportunities for advancement in the rising economy—in trade overseas, in the bureaucracy, or in the expanding market for luxury goods. It has been estimated that in 1730 there were about 60,000 adult males in what we would recognize as the professions. England also had better roads than any other European country and a more impartial judicial system.

Yet none of these gains could compare with those that the gentry made. In fact, many of the improvements, such as fair administration of justice, were indirect results of what the upper classes had won for themselves. The fruits of progress clearly belonged primarily to the gentry.

ARISTOCRACY IN THE UNITED PROVINCES, SWEDEN, AND POLAND

In the Dutch republic, the succession of William III to the offfice of Stadholder in 1672 seemed to be a move toward absolutism. As he led the successful resistance to Louis XIV in war (1672–1678), he increasingly concentrated government in his own hands. Soon, however, the power of merchants and provincial leaders in the Estates General reasserted itself. William did not want to sign a peace treaty with Louis when the French invasion failed. He wanted instead to take the war into France and reinforce his own authority by keeping the position of commander in chief. But the Estates General, led by the province of Holland, ended the war.

A decade later it was only with the approval of the Estates General that William was able to seek the English throne, and he had to leave the representative assemblies that governed the two countries separate. When William died without an heir, his policies were continued by his close friend Antonius Heinsius, who held the same position of grand pensionary of Holland that Jan de Witt had once occupied; but the government was in effect controlled by the Estates General.

This representative assembly now had to preside over the decline of a great power. In finance and trade, the Dutch were gradually overtaken by the English, while in the war against Louis XIV, they had to support the crippling burden of maintaining a land force, only to hand command over to England. Within half a century Frederick II of Prussia was to call the republic "a dinghy boat trailing the English man-of-war."

Dutch Society The aristocrats of the United Provinces differed from the usual European pattern. Instead of ancient families and bureaucratic dynasties, they boasted merchants and mayors. The prominent citizens of the leading cities were the backbone of the Dutch upper classes. Moreover, social distinctions were less prominent than in any other country of Europe. The elite was composed of hard-working financiers and traders, richer and more powerful but not essentially more privileged or leisured than those farther down the social ladder. The inequality discussed in much eighteenth-century political writing—the special place nobles had, often including some immunity from the law—was far less noticeable in the United Provinces. There was no glittering court, and although here as elsewhere a small group controlled the country, it did so for largely economic ends and in different style.

Sweden The Swedes created yet another non-absolutist model of state building. Here the nobles emerged from a long struggle with the king as the country's dominant political force. During the reign of Charles XI (1660–1697) the monarchy was able to force the great lords to return to the state the huge tracts of land they had received as rewards for loyalty earlier in the century. Since Charles stayed out of Europe's wars, he was able to conserve his resources and avoid relying on the nobility as he strengthened the smoothly running bureaucracy he had inherited from Gustavus Adolphus.

His successor, Charles XII (1697–1718), however, revived Sweden's tradition of military conquest. He won land from Peter the Great, but then made the fatal decision to invade Russia. Defeated at the battle of Poltava in 1709, Charles had to retreat and watch helplessly as the Swedish empire was dismembered. By the time he was killed in battle nine years later, his neighbors had begun to overrun his lands, and in treaties signed from 1719 to 1721, Sweden reverted to roughly the territory it had had a century before.

Naturally the nobles took advantage of Charles XII's frequent absences to reassert their authority. They ran Sweden's highly efficient government while he was campaigning and forced his successor, Queen Ulrika, to accept a constitution that gave the Riksdag effective control over the country. The new structure was consciously modeled on England's political system, and the nobility came to occupy a position like England's gentry—leaders of society and the shapers of its politics. A splendid court arose, and Stockholm became one of the more elegant and cultured aristocratic centers in Europe.

Warsaw fared less well. In fact, the strongest contrast to the French political and social model in the late seventeenth century was Poland. The sheer chaos and disunity that plagued Poland until it ceased to exist as a state in the late eighteenth century were the direct result of continued dominance by the old landed aristocracy, which blocked all attempts to centralize the government. There were highly capable kings in this period—notably John III, who achieved Europe-wide fame by relieving Vienna from the Turkish siege in 1683. These monarchs could quite easily gather an enthusiastic army to fight, and fight well, against Poland's many foes: Germans, Swedes, Russians, and Turks. But once a battle was over, the ruler could exercise no more than nominal leadership. Each king was elected by the assembly of nobles and had to agree not to interfere with the independence of the great lords, who were growing rich from serf labor on fertile lands. The crown had neither revenue nor bureaucracy to speak of, and so the country continued to resemble a feudal kingdom, where power remained in the localities.

CONTRASTS IN POLITICAL THOUGHT

The intensive development of both absolutist and antiabsolutist forms in the seventeenth century stimulated an outpouring of ideas about the nature and purposes of government. Two Englishmen, in particular, developed theories about the basis of political authority that have been influential ever since.

Map 17.3 CONFLICT IN THE BALTIC AREA, 1660–1721
The fighting around the Baltic eventually destroyed Sweden's power in northern Europe; the new powers were to be Brandenburg-Prussia and Russia.

Hobbes A story has it that Thomas Hobbes, a brilliant scholar from a poor family who earned his livelihood as the tutor to aristocrats' sons, once picked up a copy of Euclid's *Elements* and opened the book in the middle. The theorem on that page seemed totally without foundation, but it rested on a proof in the preceding theorem. Working his way backward, Hobbes discovered himself finally having to accept no more than the proposition that the shortest distance between two points is a straight line. He thereupon resolved to use the same approach to analyze political behavior. The story is probably apocryphal

because as a young man Hobbes was secretary to Francis Bacon, who doubtless gave him a taste for science. Yet it does capture the essence of his masterpiece, *Leviathan* (1651), which began with a few premises about human nature from which Hobbes deduced major conclusions about political forms.

Hobbes's premises, drawn from his observation of the strife-ridden Europe of the 1640s and 1650s, were stark and uncompromising. People, he asserted, are selfish and ambitious; consequently, unless they are restrained, they fight a perpetual war with their fellows. The weak are more cunning and the strong more stupid. Given these unsavory characteristics, the state of nature—which precedes the existence of society—is a state of war, in which life is "solitary, poor, nasty, brutish, and short." Hobbes's conclusion was that the only way to restrain this instinctive aggressiveness is to erect an absolute and sovereign power that will maintain peace. Everyone should submit to the sovereign because the alternative is the anarchy of the state of nature. The moment of submission is the moment of the birth of orderly society.

In a startling innovation, Hobbes suggested that the transition from nature to society is accomplished by a contract that is implicitly accepted by all who wish to end the chaos. The unprecedented feature of the contract is that it is not between ruler and ruled; it is binding only on the ruled. They agree among themselves to submit to the sovereign; the sovereign is thus not a party to the contract and is not limited in any way. A government that is totally free to do whatever it wishes is best equipped to keep the peace, and peace is always better than the previous turmoil.

The power of Hobbes's logic, and the endorsement he seemed to give to absolutism, made his views enormously influential. But his approach also aroused hostility. Although later political theorists were deeply affected by his ideas, many of Hobbes's successors denounced him as godless, immoral, cynical, and unfeeling. It was dislike of his message, not weaknesses in his analysis, that made many people unwilling to accept his views.

Locke John Locke, a quiet Oxford professor who admired Hobbes but sought to soften his conclusions, founded his political analysis in a general theory of knowledge. Locke believed that at birth a person's mind is a *tabula rasa*, a clean slate; nothing, he said, is inborn or preordained. As human beings grow, they observe and experience the world. Once they have gathered enough data through their senses, their minds begin to work on the data. Then, with the help of reason, they perceive patterns, discovering the order and harmony that permeate the universe. Locke was convinced that this underlying order exists and that every person, regardless of individual experi-

---

Locke on the Origins of Government

The heart of John Locke's Second Treatise of Civil Government, *written in the mid-1680s before England's Glorious Revolution but published in 1690, is its optimism about human nature—as opposed to Hobbes's pessimism. In this passage Locke explains why, in his view, people create political systems.*

"If man in the state of nature be so free, if he be absolute lord of his own person and possessions, equal to the greatest, and subject to nobody, why will he part with his freedom, and subject himself to the dominion and control of any other power? To which it is obvious to answer, that though in the state of nature he hath such a right, yet the enjoyment of it is very uncertain, and constantly exposed to the invasions of others. This makes him willing to quit this condition, which, however free, is full of fears and continual dangers; and it is not without reason that he seeks out and is willing to join in society with others, who have a mind to unite, for the mutual preservation of their lives, liberties, and estates, which I call by the general name, property. The great and chief end, therefore, of men's putting themselves under government, is the preservation of their property.

"But though men when they enter into society give up the equality, liberty, and power they had in the state of nature into the hands of society; yet it being only with an intention in every one the better to preserve himself, his liberty, and property, the power of the society can never be supposed to extend further than the common good. And all this to be directed to no other end but the peace, safety, and public good of the people."

From John Locke, *The Second Treatise of Civil Government*, Thomas P. Peardon (ed.) (Indianapolis: Bobbs-Merrill, 1952), Chapter IX, pp. 70–73.

ences, must reach the same conclusions about its nature and structure.

When Locke turned his attention to political thought, he put into systematic form the views of the English gentry and other antiabsolutists throughout Europe. The *Second Treatise of Civil Government*, published in 1690, was deeply influenced by Hobbes. From his great predecessor Locke took the notions that a state of nature is a state of war and that only a contract among the people can end the anarchy that precedes the establishment of civil society. But his conclusions were decidedly different.

Using the principles of his theory of knowledge, Locke asserted that the application of reason to politics demonstrates the inalienability of the three rights of an individual: life, liberty, and property. Like Hobbes, he believed that there must be a sovereign power, but he argued that it has no power over these three natural rights of its subjects without their consent. Moreover, this consent—for levying taxes, for example—must come from a representative assembly of men of property, such as the English Parliament.

The affirmation of property as one of the three natural rights (it was changed to "the pursuit of happiness" in the more egalitarian American Declaration of Independence) is significant. Here Locke revealed himself as the spokesman of the gentry. Only people with a tangible stake in their country have any right to control its destiny, and that stake must be protected as surely as their life and liberty. The concept of liberty remained vague, but it was taken to imply the sorts of freedom, such as freedom from arbitrary arrest, that were outlined in the English Bill of Rights. All Hobbes allowed a person to do was protect his or her life. Locke permitted the overthrow of the sovereign power if it infringed on the subjects' rights—a course the English followed with James II and the Americans with George III.

Locke's prime concern was to defend the individual against the state, a concern that has remained essential to liberal thought ever since (*see* box, p. 557). But it is important to realize that Locke's emphasis on property served the elite better than the mass of society. With Locke to reassure them, the upper classes put their stamp on eighteenth-century European civilization.

IV. The State in the Eighteenth Century

STATE BUILDING

It sometimes seems as if international competition was the main preoccupation of eighteenth-century rulers. But, in fact, competition among states went hand in hand with internal state building. Conflict with rival powers compelled rulers to assert their sovereignty as forcefully as possible within their own borders in order to expand their revenues, armies, and bureaucracies. With the exception of Britain, countries where absolutism failed to develop—such as Sweden and the Netherlands—lost international influence. And Poland was partitioned three times by Russia, Austria, and Prussia, until in 1795 it ceased to exist as a sovereign state. The political consolidation of the eighteenth century, and the state system that was created, put a premium on military and economic power. In the process, the basic map of modern Europe emerged and the centralized character of the major states was confirmed.

The relationship between international rivalry and internal development is well illustrated by Prussia and Austria. In the mid-eighteenth century these two powers were vying to dominate Central Europe, and they instituted reforms so as to wage their struggle more effectively. Each was governed by absolute rulers who built their states by increasing the size of their armies, collecting larger revenues, and developing bureaucracies for their war effort. It did not seem to matter whether the ruler was a modern pragmatist like Frederick II of Prussia or a pious traditionalist like Maria Theresa of Austria. In their own way both understood the demands of the state system.

THE PRUSSIA OF FREDERICK WILLIAM I

Prussia's Frederick William I (1713–1740) was relentless in his pursuit of a strengthened absolutism at home and European-wide influence abroad. Strikingly different from his refined father, this spartan ruler approached affairs of state as all business and little pleasure. He disdained court life, dismissed numerous courtiers, and cut the salaries of those who remained. Uncluttered by royal ceremonies, his days were regulated in timetable fashion as he attempted to supervise everything himself.

Map 17.4 THE EXPANSION OF RUSSIA AND THE PARTITION OF POLAND
All three of the powers in Eastern Europe—Prussia, Russia, and Austria—gained territory from the dismemberment of Poland. At the same time, Russia was expanding to the south and east.

The Emphasis on the Military It has been said that Frederick William I organized his state to serve his military power. During his reign the army grew from 38,000 to 83,000, making it the fourth largest in Europe, behind France, Russia, and Austria. While still relying on foreign mercenaries for one-third of his troops, he also instituted a form of conscription. And all his soldiers had to undergo intensive drilling and wear standardized uniforms. Determined to build an effective cadre of professionals, he forbade his subjects to serve in foreign armies and compelled the sons of nobles to attend cadet schools to learn martial skills and attitudes.

In this military state Frederick William I was the number one soldier. A colorful commander in chief, he maintained a personal regiment of towering grenadiers and always wore a uniform, declaring that he would be buried in it. But he did not intend to die in battle. For all his involvement with military life, he avoided committing his army to battle, and he therefore passed it on intact to his son, Frederick II.

The process of centralization kept pace with the growth of the army. In 1723 a government superagency was created; called the General Directory of Finance, War, and Domains, it united the administration of all functions except justice, education, and religion. Its main task was to coordinate the collection of revenue, expenditures (mostly military), and local administration. The king also put resources into education so as to give the population the basic instruction they needed to serve the state. He made education compulsory for all children where schools existed, and where there were none, he instructed local communities and parents to set them up, though he made no attempt to enforce these decrees. The educational policy was thus more theoretical than practical and had few social consequences. Teachers, for example, were often clergy who held their jobs as sidelines. Uninterested in intellectual pursuits for their own sake, the king allowed the universities to decline; they did not fit his relentless vision of how to build his state.

FREDERICK THE GREAT

Frederick William I's most notable triumph, perhaps, was the grooming of his successor. This was no mean task. Frederick II (1740–1786) seemed opposite in temperament to his father and little inclined to follow in his footsteps. The father was a God-fearing German Protestant. The son disdained German culture and was a deist (see p. 611). Sentimental and artistically inclined, Frederick II was a composer of music who played the flute, wrote poetry, and greatly admired French culture. He even wrote philosophical treatises and corresponded with leading European intellectuals.

Since the Prussian monarchy was mobilizing all its subjects for the tasks of state building, how-

ever, the young prince was not exempted. On the contrary, he was forced to work at all levels of the state apparatus so as to experience them directly, from shoveling hay on a royal farm to marching with the troops. The father trained his son for kingship, reshaping his personality, giving him a sense of duty, and toughening him for leadership. Despite Frederick's prolonged resistance, this hard apprenticeship succeeded. In the end, as a modern psychiatrist would put it, the prince identified with the aggressor.

Frederick's Rule When he assumed the throne in 1740, Frederick II was prepared to lead Prussia in a ruthless struggle for power and territory. While his intellectual turn of mind caused him to agonize over moral issues and the nature of his role, he never flinched from exercising power. He did, however, attempt to justify absolutism at home and aggression abroad. He claimed undivided power for the ruler, not because the dynasty had a divine mission but because only absolute rule could bring results. The monarch, he stated, was the first servant of the state. In the long run, he hoped, an enlightened monarch might lead his people to a more rational and moral existence. Some of these objectives, such as religious toleration and judicial reform, could be reached immediately, and in implementing them Frederick gained a reputation as an "enlightened" absolutist.

But these were minor matters. The paramount issue, security, provided the best justification for absolutism. Success here required Prussia to improve its vulnerable geographic position by acquiring more territory, stronger borders, and the power to face other European states as an equal. Until that was achieved, Frederick would not consider the domestic reforms that might disrupt the flow of taxes or men into the army, or provoke his nobility. The capture of territory was his most singular contribution to the rise of Prussia and what earned him his title of Frederick the Great.

By coincidence, the year 1740, when Frederick II came to the throne, was the year when a suitable task for his army presented itself—an attack on the Habsburg province of Silesia. Prussia had no claim to the province; it was simply a wealthy neighboring domain that would expand Prussia's territory and that the Habsburgs were unable to defend. Yet the conquest of Silesia brought to a new level the state building begun in Prussia by the great elector in 1648; the reaction also shaped state building in the Habsburg empire.

THE HABSBURG EMPIRE UNDER ATTACK

The Habsburg empire in the eighteenth century was like a dynastic holding company uniting diverse territories under one crown: Austria, Bohemia, Hungary, and other possessions like the Austrian Netherlands, Lombardy, and Tuscany. The emperors hoped to integrate Austria, Bohemia, and Hungary into a Catholic, centralized, German-speaking superstate. But the traditional representative assemblies in these provinces resisted such centralization.

International Rivalry and War In the reign of Charles VI (1711–1740), yet another problem complicated the destiny of this multinational empire, for his only heir was his daughter, Maria Theresa. In 1713 Charles drafted a document

▶ *E. F. Cunningham*
THE RETURN OF FREDERICK II
FROM A MANEUVRE, 1787
Were it not for the richly embroidered saddle cover and the fine white horse, it would be hard to spot Frederick the Great among his officers. Nor is there anything to indicate that the two men on the black and brown horses behind him are his son and grandson. This sober evocation of a king as a professional soldier contrasts strikingly with earlier glorifications (see plate on p. 451).

known as the Pragmatic Sanction, declaring that all Habsburg dominions would pass intact to the eldest heir, male or female; and for the next 25 years he sought recognition of the Pragmatic Sanction from the European powers. By making all kinds of concessions and promises, he won this recognition on paper. But when he died in 1740, his daughter found that the commitments were worthless: The succession was challenged by force from several sides. Concentrating on diplomacy alone, Charles had neglected the work of state building, leaving an empty treasury, an inadequately trained army, and an ineffective bureaucracy.

In contrast to Austria, Prussia had a full treasury, a powerful army, and a confident ruler, Frederick II, who seized the Habsburg province of Silesia without qualm. His justification was simply "reasons of state" combined with the Habsburgs' faltering fortunes. And Maria Theresa had her hands more than full, because the French declared war on her to support their ally Bavaria's claim to the Habsburg throne. Meanwhile, Spain hoped to win back control of Austria's Italian possessions. Worse yet, Maria Theresa faced a rebellion by the Czech nobles in Bohemia. Her position would probably have been hopeless if Hungary's Magyar nobles had followed suit. But Maria Theresa promised them autonomy within the Habsburg empire, and they offered her the troops she needed to resist the invaders.

In the War of Austrian Succession (1740–1748) that followed, Maria Theresa learned the elements of state building. With her Hungarian troops and with financial help from her one ally, Britain, she fought her opponents to a stalemate. Frederick's conquest of Silesia proved to be the only significant territorial change produced by this major war. Even for England and France, who fought the war mainly in their overseas colonies, it was a standoff. But Maria Theresa now regarded the recovery of Silesia and the humiliation of Prussia as esential. These aims, in turn, required determined state building within Habsburg domains.

MARIA THERESA

The woman whose authority was established not by her father's negotiations but by force of arms was a marked contrast to her archenemy, Frederick. The Prussian king was practical and irreligious; Maria Theresa was moralistic and pious. While Frederick barely tolerated a loveless marriage, the Habsburg ruler enjoyed a happy domestic life, bearing numerous children and taking great personal interest in their upbringing. Her personality and her ruling style were deceptively traditional, for she was a shrewd innovator in the business of building and reasserting the power of her state.

Unlike Frederick, or for that matter her own son and successor, Joseph II, Maria Theresa had a strong regard for her dynasty. In this respect her being a woman made no difference to the policies or government of the empire. She believed in the divine mission of the Habsburgs and conscientiously attended to the practical needs of her realm. It was because she put the state's interests first that this most pious of Catholic sovereigns—who disdained religious toleration and loathed atheists—felt obliged to reform the Church. Responding to waste and self-interest in her monasteries, she forbade the founding of new establishments. She also abolished the clergy's exemptions from taxes, something the French king found impossible to do.

A new bureaucratic apparatus was constructed on the models of French and Prussian absolutism. In Vienna, reorganized central ministries recruited staffs of experts. In the provinces, new agents were appointed who were largely divorced from feudal and local interests, though some concession did have to be made to the regional traditions of the Habsburg realm. The core domains (excluding Hungary and the Italian possessions) were reorganized into 10 provinces, each subdivided into districts directed by royal officials. With the help of these officials, the central government could wrest new taxes from the local diets. Meanwhile, Maria Theresa brought important nobles from all her domains to Vienna to participate in its social and administrative life. She also reformed the military, improving the training of troops and establishing academies to produce a more professional officer corps. Thus did international needs help shape domestic political reforms.

THE GROWTH OF STABILITY IN GREAT BRITAIN

It was not only absolutists who strengthened their states. Britain, too, expanded its government and its international power in the eighteenth century. This was the work not so much of a monarch as of the "political nation"—the landowners and leading townsmen who made up about 5 percent of the population of Great Britain yet who elected almost all the members of Parliament. Their control of the nation was symbolized

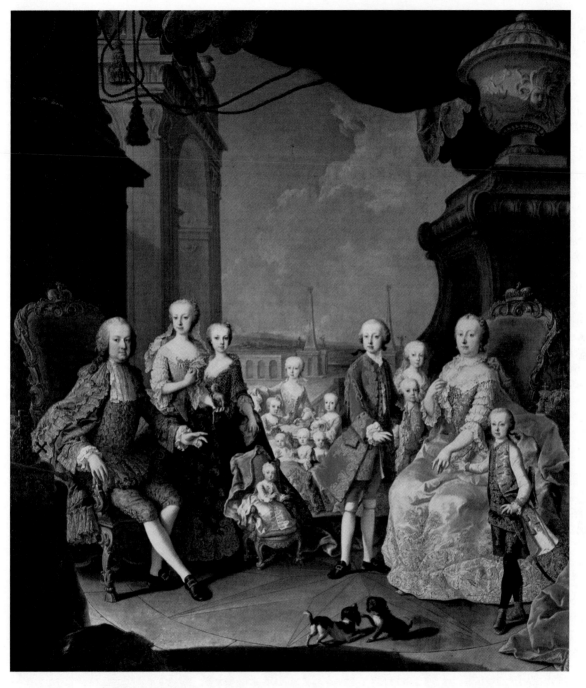

▶ *M. van Meytens*
MARIA THERESA AND HER FAMILY, 1750
Although the setting is just as splendid, the portrayal of Maria Theresa
with her husband and 11 of her 16 children suggests a domesticity that
is absent from Louis XIV's family portrait of half a century before (see
chapter opening plate on p. 532).

by the fact that the distribution of the 558 seats in the House of Commons bore little relation to the size of constituencies. In 1793, for example, 51 English and Welsh boroughs, which contained fewer than 1500 voters, elected 100 members of Parliament, nearly a fifth of the Commons. Many of these districts were safely in the pocket of a prominent local family; and election campaigns elsewhere were often determined by bribery, influence, and intimidation. On a national scale, loose party alignments did exist. The Whigs wanted a strong Parliament and generally preferred commercial to agricultural interests. The Tories usually supported the king and policies that favored large landholders. But the realities of politics were based on small factions within these larger groups, and politics revolved around the control of patronage and office.

As the financial and military needs and capabilities of the government expanded, Parliament now created a thoroughly bureaucratized state. Britain had always prided itself on having a smaller government and lower taxes than its neighbors, largely because, as an island, it had avoided the need for a standing army. All that now came to an end. Starting with the struggle against Louis XIV, wars required constant increases in resources, troops, and administrators. A steadily expanding navy had to be supported, as did an army that reached almost 200,000 men by the 1770s. Before the 1690s, public expenditures rarely amounted to £2 million a year; by the 1770s, they were almost £30 million, and most of that was spent on the military. In this period, as a result, Britain's fiscal bureaucracy more than tripled in size. The recruiting officer became a regular sight, and so too did the treasury men who were imposing increasingly heavy tax burdens.

Unlike their counterparts on the continent, however, the wealthier classes in Britain paid considerable taxes to support this state building, and they maintained more fluid relations with other classes. The landed gentry and the commercial class, in particular, were often linked by

▶ **NEW GALLOWS AT THE OLD BAILEY, ENGRAVING**
It was an indication of the severity of English criminal justice that the gallows erected near the chief court in London, the Old Bailey, in the mid-eighteenth century were specially constructed so that 10 condemned criminals, both men and women, could be executed at once.

marriage and by financial or political associations. Even great aristocrats sometimes had close ties with the business leaders of London. For the lower levels of society, however, the barriers were as high as they had ever been. For all of Britain's prosperity, the lower third of society remained poor and often desperate. As a result, despite the severity of the system of justice and the frequency of capital punishment, crime was endemic in both country and town. The eighteenth century was the heyday of that romantic but violent figure, the highwayman.

The Age of Walpole The first two rulers of the Hanoverian dynasty, George I (1714–1727) and George II (1727–1760), could not speak English fluently. The language barrier and their concern for their German territory of Hanover left them often uninterested in British politics, and this was one reason Parliament grew in authority. Its dominant figure for over 20 years was Sir Robert Walpole, who rose to prominence because of his skillful handling of fiscal policy during the panic following the collapse of an overseas trading company in 1720. This crash, known as the South Sea Bubble, resembled the failure of John Law's

▶ **WILLIAM PITT IN THE COMMONS**
William Pitt the younger is shown here addressing the House of Commons. Like his father during the Seven Years' War, Pitt provided firm leadership against France in the 1790s.

similar scheme in France, but it had less effect on government finances. Thereafter, Walpole controlled British politics until 1742, mainly by dispensing patronage liberally and staying at peace.

Many historians have called Walpole the first prime minister, though the title was not official. He insisted that all ministers inform and consult with the House of Commons as well as with the king, and he himself continued to sit in Parliament in order to recruit support for his decisions. Not until the next century was it accepted that the Commons could force a minister to resign. But Walpole took a first step toward ministerial responsibility and thus shaped the future structure of British government.

In Great Britain as in France, the economic expansion of the eighteenth century increased the wealth and the social and political weight of the commercial and financial middle class. Although Londoners remained around 11 percent of the population, the proportion of the English who lived in other sizable towns doubled in the eighteenth century; and by 1800 some 30 percent of the country's inhabitants were urbanized. Walpole's policy of peace pleased the large landlords but angered this growing body of merchants and businesspeople, who feared the growth of French commerce and colonial settlements. They found their champion in William Pitt, later earl of Chatham, the grandson of a man who had made a fortune in India. Eloquent, self-confident, and infused with a vision of Britain's imperial destiny, Pitt began his parliamentary career in 1738 by attacking the timid policies of the government and demanding that France be driven from the seas. Although Walpole's policies continued even after his resignation in 1742, Pitt's moment finally came in 1758, when Britain became involved in the Seven Years' War (see p. 569). This conflict was to be a testing time throughout Europe for the advances of the previous century in state building and the development of the international system.

V. The International System

While rulers built up their states by enlarging their bureaucracies, strengthening governmental institutions, and expanding their resources, they also had to consider how best to deal with their neighbors. In an age that emphasized reasoned and practical solutions to problems, there was hope that an orderly system could be devised for international relations. If the reality fell short of the ideal, there were nevertheless many who thought they were creating a more impersonal and organized structure for diplomacy and warfare.

DIPLOMACY AND WARFARE

One obstacle to the creation of an impersonal international system was the continuing influence, in eighteenth-century diplomacy, of traditional dynastic interests. Princes and their ministers tried to preserve a family's succession, and they arranged marriages to gain new titles or alliances. Part of the reason that those perennial rivals, Britain and France, remained at peace for nearly 30 years until 1740 was that the rulers in both countries felt insecure on their thrones and thus had personal motives for not wanting to risk aggressive foreign policies.

Gradually, however, dynastic interests gave way to policies based on a more impersonal conception of the state. Men like Frederick II of Prussia and William Pitt of Britain tried to shape their diplomacy to what they considered the needs of their states. "Reasons of state" centered on security, which could be guaranteed only by force. Thus the search for defensible borders and the weakening of rivals became obvious goals. Eighteenth-century statesmen believed that the end (security and prosperity) justified the means (the use of power). Until a country was completely invulnerable, its leaders felt justified in using the crudest tactics in dealing with its neighbors.

The Diplomatic System If there was any broad, commonly agreed principle at work, it was that hegemony, or domination by one state, had to be resisted because it threatened international security. The concern aroused by Louis XIV's ambitions showed the principle at work, when those whom he sought to dominate joined together in order to frustrate his designs. Their aim was to establish equilibrium in Europe by a balance of power, with no single state achieving hegemony. From the War of Spanish Succession until the rise of Napoleon, that balance was maintained, though the means could be unsavory.

The diplomats who were responsible for implementing "reasons of state" and the balance of power knew there were times when they had to deceive. They might fabricate a claim to a province or a princely title, and it was known that ambassadors were spies by vocation. They offered the bribes that were a part of foreign policy and negotiated treaties that they sometimes expected their prince to violate. Yet there was also a more stabilizing side to diplomacy: The eighteenth century marks its growth as a serious profession, parallel to the rationalization of the state itself. Foreign ministries were staffed with experts and clerks, and kept extensive archives, while the heads of the diplomatic machine, the relations. French was now the common language of diplomacy; by 1774 even a treaty between Turks and Russians was drafted in that language. And socially the diplomats were aristocratic and cosmopolitan. Regardless of the ruler they served, all ambassadors saw themselves as members of the same fraternity.

In general, the great powers dominated international agreements, usually at the expense of the smaller states. For example, Prussia, Austria, and Russia satisfied their territorial ambitions by agreeing to partition Poland among themselves. Ignoring the Poles, they declared in 1772 that "whatever the limits of the respective claims, the acquisitions which result must be exactly equal." Resolving disputes by negotiation could be as amoral as war.

ARMIES

Despite the settlement of some conflicts by diplomacy, others led to war. If Britain emphasized its navy, on the continent the focus of bureaucratic innovation and monetary expenditure was the standing army, whose growth was striking. France set the pace. After 1680 the size of its forces never fell below 200,000. In Prussia the army increased in size from 39,000 to 200,000 men between 1713 and 1786. But the cost, technology, and tactics of these armies served to limit the devastation of eighteenth-century warfare. The expenses led rulers to husband their armies carefully. Princes were quick to declare war but slow to deploy their armies at full strength or commit them to battle. And casualties also became less numerous as discipline improved and the ferocity that had been caused by religious passions died away.

Tactics and Discipline The techniques of building and besieging fortifications continued to preoccupy military planners, even though the impregnable fortresses that the French engineer Sebastian Vauban had built to protect France's northeastern border were simply bypassed by the English general Marlborough when he pursued the French army in the War of the Spanish Succession. The decisive encounter was still the battle between armies, where the majority of the troops—the infantry—used their training to

▶ **ENGRAVING FROM THE WESTMINSTER MAGAZINE, 1774**
Political cartoons were standard fare in eighteenth-century newspapers and magazines. This one shows a weeping king of Poland and an angry Turk (who made no gains) after Poland was carved up in 1772 by Frederick the Great, the Austrian emperor, and the Russian empress. Louis XV sits by without helping his ally Poland, and all are urged on by the devil under the table.

ambassadors, were stationed in permanent embassies abroad. This routinized management of foreign relations helped foster a sense of collective identity among Europe's states despite their endless struggles. Linguistically and socially, diplomats gave a sugar coating to international

▶ *L. N. van Blarenberghe*
THE BATTLE OF FONTENOY, 1745
This panorama shows the English and Dutch assaulting the French position in a battle in present-day Belgium. The French lines form a huge semicircle from the distant town to the wood on the left. The main attacking force in the center, surrounded by gunfire, eventually retreated, and news of the victory was brought to Louis XV, in red on the right, by a horseman in blue who is doffing his hat.

maneuver and fire in carefully controlled line formations. The aim of strategy was not to annihilate but to nudge an opposing army into abandoning its position in the face of superior maneuvers. This improved organization also served to reduce brutality. Better supplied by a system of magazines, more tightly disciplined by constant drilling, troops were less likely to desert or plunder than they had been during the Thirty Years' War.

As these military practices took hold, some encounters were fought as if they were taking place on a parade ground, and pitched battles in open fields were increasingly avoided. Even important victories might be nullified if a winning army returned to its home bases for winter camp. And no victor ever demanded unconditional surrender. The same was true of naval battles. Commanders were cautious in combat and rarely pursued a defeated squadron.

The officer corps of the military were generally the preserve of the European nobility, though they also served as channels of upward social mobility for wealthy sons of middle-class families who purchased commissions. In either case, the officer ranks tended to be filled by men who lacked the professional training for effective leadership. Officers were likely to be long on martial spirit but short on technical skills. The branches of service that showed the most progress were the artillery and the engineers, in which competent middle-class officers played an unusually large role.

A final limit on the scale of war in the eighteenth century was the inherent weakness of coalitions, which formed whenever a general war erupted. On paper these alliances looked formidable. On the battlefield, however, they were hampered by primitive communications and lack of mobility even at the peak of cooperation. Moreover, the partnerships rarely lasted very long. The competitiveness of the state system bred distrust among allies as well as enemies. Sudden abandonment of coalitions and the negotiation of separate peace treaties mark the history of almost every major war.

THE SEVEN YEARS' WAR

The pressures created by the competition of states, dynasties, and empires finally exploded in midcentury in a major war, the Seven Years' War (1756–1763). Its roots lay in a realignment of diplomatic alliances that began at Austria's prodding. Previously, the Bourbon-Habsburg rivalry had been the cornerstone of European diplomacy. But by the 1750s two other sets of antagonisms had taken over: French competition with the British in the New World and Austria's ven-

detta against Prussia over Silesia. For Austria, the rivalry with Bourbon France was no longer important. Its position in the Holy Roman Empire depended now on humbling Prussia. France was not yet concerned over Prussia, but French hostility to Austria had lessened. Austria was therefore free to lead a turnabout in alliances—a diplomatic revolution—in order to forge an anti-Prussian coalition with France and Russia. Russia was the key. Aside from her personal loathing of Frederick II, the pious Empress Elizabeth of Russia saw him as an obstacle to Russian ambitions

▶ **ENGRAVING OF A MILITARY ACADEMY, FROM H. F. VON FLEMING, VOLKOMMENE TEUTSCHE SOLDAT, 1726**
This scene, of young men studying fortifications and tactics in a German academy, would have been familiar to the sons of nobles throughout Europe who trained for a military career in the eighteenth century.

in Eastern Europe. Geographical vulnerability also made Prussia an inviting target, and so the stage was set for a diplomatic revolution.

Prussia was active in trying to compensate for that vulnerability. But its countermoves only alienated the other powers. Frederick sought to stay out of the Anglo-French rivalry by coming to terms with both these states. He had been France's ally in the past, and he now sought to negotiate a treaty with England. England—seeking to protect the royal territory of Hanover—willingly signed a neutrality accord, the Convention of Westminster, with Prussia in January 1756. Frederick had no intention of repudiating his friendship with France, but to the French—who had not been informed in advance of these negotiations—the Convention seemed an insult, if not an actual betrayal. The accord with France's

mortal enemy, England, seemed the act of an untrustworthy ally. France overreacted, turned against Prussia, and thus fell into Austria's design (*see box*, p. 571). Russia too considered the Convention of Westminster a betrayal by *its* supposed ally England. English bribes and diplomacy could no longer keep Russia from actively joining Austria to plan Prussia's dismemberment.

Map 17.5 PRUSSIA AND THE AUSTRIAN EMPIRE, 1721–1772
The steady territorial advances of Prussia had created a major power in northern and Eastern Europe, alongside the Austrian Empire, by the time of the first partition of Poland in 1772.

Maria Theresa in Vehement Mood

The animosities and ambitions that shaped international relations in the eighteenth century were exemplified by the Empress Maria Theresa. Her furious reaction to the event that destroyed Europe's old diplomatic system—England's signing of the Convention of Westminster with Maria Theresa's archenemy, Frederick the Great— suggests how deep were the feelings that brought about the midcentury conflagration. After learning the news and deciding (in response) to ally herself with France, she told the British ambassador on May 13, 1756, exactly where she stood.

"I have not abandoned the old system, but Great Britain has abandoned me and the system, by concluding the Prussian treaty, the first intelligence of which struck me like a fit of apoplexy. I and the king of Prussia are incompatible; and no consideration on earth will ever induce me to enter into any engagement to which he is a party. Why should you be surprised if, following your example in concluding a treaty with Prussia, I should now enter into an engagement with France?

"I am far from being French in my disposition, and do not deny that the court of Versailles has been my bitterest enemy; but I have little to fear from France, and I have no other recourse than to form such arrangements as will secure what remains to me. My principal aim is to secure my hereditary possessions. I have truly but two enemies whom I really dread, the king of Prussia and the Turks; and while I and Russia continue on the same good terms as now exist between us, we shall, I trust, be able to convince Europe, that we are in a condition to defend ourselves against those adversaries, however formidable."

From William Coxe, *History of the House of Austria*, vol. III (London: Bohn, 1847), pp. 363–364.

The Course of War Fearing encirclement, Frederick gambled on a preventive war through Saxony in 1756. Although he easily conquered the duchy, his plan backfired, for it activated the coalition that he dreaded. Russia and France met their commitments to Austria, and a combined offensive against Prussia began.

For a time Frederick's genius as a general brought him success. His forces won a spectacular victory at Rossbach in late 1757 over a much larger French-Austrian army. Skillful tactics and daring surprise movements would bring other victories, but strategically the Prussian position was shaky. Frederick had to dash in all directions across his provinces to repel invading armies whose combined strength far exceeded his own. Each successive year of the war, he faced the prospect of Russian attacks on Brandenburg in the north and Austrian thrusts from the south through Silesia and Saxony. Disaster was avoided mainly because the Russian army returned east for winter quarters regardless of its gains, but even so, the Russians occupied Berlin. On the verge of exhaustion, Prussia at best seemed to face a stalemate with a considerable loss of territory; at worst, the war would continue and bring about a total Prussian collapse. But the other powers were also war-weary, and Frederick's enemies were becoming increasingly distrustful of one another.

In the end, Prussia was saved by one of those sudden changes of reign that could cause dramatic reversals of policy in Europe. In January 1762 Empress Elizabeth died and was replaced temporarily by Tsar Peter III, a passionate admirer of Frederick. He quickly pulled Russia out of the war and returned Frederick's conquered eastern domains of Prussia and Pomerania. In Britain, meanwhile, William Pitt was replaced by the more pacific earl of Bute, who brought about a reconciliation with France; both countries then ended their insistence on the punishment of Prussia. Austria's coalition had collapsed.

The terms of the Peace of Hubertusburg (1763), settling the continental phase of the Seven Years' War, were therefore surprisingly favorable to Prussia. Prussia returned Saxony to Austria but paid no compensation for the devastation of the duchy, and the Austrians recognized Silesia as Prussian. In short, the status quo was restored. Frederick could return to Berlin, his dominion preserved partly by his army but mainly by luck and the continuing fragility of international alliances.

If, amidst the state building of the eighteenth century, many of Europe's regimes were able quite easily to sustain a major war even if it brought about few territorial changes, that was not simply because of the expansion of government and the disciplining of armies. It was also the result of remarkable economic advances and the availability of new resources that were flowing into Europe from the development of overseas empires. In politics, this was primarily an age of consolidation; in economics, it was a time of profound transformation.

Recommended Reading

Sources

*Hobbes, Thomas. *Leviathan.* 1651. Any modern edition.

*Locke, John. *Second Treatise of Civil Government.* 1690. Any modern edition.

Luvvas, J. (ed.). *Frederick the Great on the Art of War.* 1966.

Saint-Simon, Louis. *Historical Memoirs.* Lucy Norton (ed. and tr.). 2 vols. 1967 and 1968. Lively memoirs of the court at Versailles.

Studies

*Alexander, John T. *Catherine the Great: Life and Legend.* 1988.

Anderson, M. S. *Historians and Eighteenth-Century Europe, 1715–1789.* 1979. Past and current viewpoints on a number of fundamental issues.

Baxter, S. B. *William III and the Defense of European Liberty 1650–1702.* 1966. A solid and straightforward account of the career of the ruler of both England and the Netherlands.

*Behrens, C. B. A. *Society, Government, and the Enlightenment: The Experience of Eighteenth-Century France and Prussia.* 1985.

Brewer, John. *The Sinews of Power: War, Money and the English State. 1688–1783.* 1989. The work that demonstrated the importance of the military and the growth of bureaucracy in eighteenth-century England.

——— and John Styles (eds.). *An Ungovernable People: The English and Their Law in the Seventeenth and Eighteenth Centuries.* 1980. A rich collection of essays on crime and the administration of justice.

*Carsten, F. L. *The Origins of Prussia.* 1954. The standard account of the background to the reign of the great elector, Frederick William, and the best short history of his accomplishments and the rise of the Junkers.

Corvisier, André. *Armies and Societies in Europe, 1494–1789.* 1979. A comparative study, strongest on the French army.

Duffy, Christopher. *The Army of Frederick the Great.* 1974. A comprehensive account of everything from recruitment to tactics.

*Goubert, Pierre. *Louis XIV and Twenty Million Frenchmen.* Anne Carter (tr.). 1970. This is not so much a history of the king's reign as a study of the nature of French society and politics during Louis' rule.

Hatton, R. N. *Charles XII of Sweden.* 1968. A thorough and well-written biography that does justice to a dramatic life.

*———. *Europe in the Age of Louis XIV.* 1969. A beautifully illustrated and vividly interpretive history of the period that Louis dominated.

---

*Available in paperback.

Hay, D., P. Linebaugh, and E. P. Thompson. *Albion's Fatal Tree: Crime and Society in Eighteenth-Century England.* 1975. A pioneering study.

*Henshall, Nicholas. *The Myth of Absolutism: Change and Continuity in Early Modern European Monarchy.* 1992. A comparison, mainly of England and France, which argues that the term *absolutism*, a later invention, ignores the emphasis on tradition and continuity during the 1660–1789 period.

*Holmes, Geoffrey. *The Making of a Great Power: Late Stuart and Early Georgian Britain, 1660–1722*; and *The Age of Oligarchy: Pre-industrial Britain, 1722–1783.* 1993. The best detailed survey.

Linebaugh, Peter. *The London Hanged: Crime and Civil Society in the Eighteenth Century.* 1991. A detailed study of crime and criminals.

Mettam, Roger. *Power and Faction in Louis XIV's France.* 1988. An analysis of government and power under absolutist rule.

*Plumb, J. H. *The Growth of Political Stability in England, 1675–1725.* 1969. A brief, lucid survey of the developments in English politics that helped create Britain's modern parliamentary democracy.

———. *Sir Robert Walpole* (2 vols). 1956–1961. A masterly biography.

Raeff, Marc. *The Well-Ordered Police State: Social and Institutional Change through Law in the Germanies and Russia, 1600–1800.* 1983.

Rowen, Herbert H. *The King's State: Proprietary Dynasticism in Early Modern France.* 1980. An incisive study of the origins and elaboration of the theory by which Louis XIV ruled France.

Shennan, J. H. *Louis XIV.* 1986. A good introduction to the king and his reign.

Stoye, John. *The Siege of Vienna.* 1964. An exciting account of the last great threat to Christian Europe from the Turkish empire.

*Sumner, B. H. *Peter the Great and the Emergence of Russia.* 1950. This short but comprehensive book is the best introduction to Russian history in this period.

*Tuck, Richard. *Hobbes.* 1989. A clear and compact introduction to Hobbes's thought.

Weigley, R. F. *The Age of Battles: The Quest for Decisive Warfare from Breitenfeld to Waterloo.* 1991. The best military history of the age.

INDEX

CONTEMPORARY EUROPE

0   200   400 Miles

⊛ Capital cities
● Other cities
- - - Commonwealth of Independent
    States boundary

NORWEGIAN SEA

Reykjavik ⊛
ICELAND

SHETLAND
ISLANDS

ORKNEY
ISLANDS

Trondheim

Bergen ⊛   NORWAY   SWEDEN   *Gulf of Bothnia*   FIN

Oslo ⊛   *Dal R.*   Tammer

Stockholm ⊛   Helsi

*ALAND
I.*

Skagerrak   Göteborg

SCOTLAND
Glasgow
Edinburgh

*NORTH
SEA*

Alborg   *Kattegat*

DENMARK ⊛   Copenhagen   *BALTIC SEA*   LATVI

Kaliningrad   LITHU
(Königsberg) ● (RUS.)

NORTHERN
IRELAND
Belfast ⊛

IRELAND

Dublin ⊛

Cork

Liverpool

WALES   Birmingham

ENGLAND

UNITED
KINGDOM

Hamburg   Gdansk
(Danzig)

Elbe R.

NETHERLANDS   Berlin   POLAND   Wars
Amsterdam ⊛

HANOVER   *Vistula R.*

ATLANTIC OCEAN

Brest

English Channel

Rouen

NORMANDY

Antwerp   Dusseldorf   GERMANY   Lodz
Brussels ⊛   Köln   *Rhine R.*   Leipzig   Dresden   *Oder R.*
BELGIUM   Bonn
Luxemburg   Frankfurt   Prague ⊛   Krakow
LUX.   CZECH REP.

London ⊛

Paris ⊛
Orléans   LORRAINE
Seine R.   Strassburg   Munich   SLOVAKIA
*Loire   BADEN   *Danube R.*
R.*   ALSACE   Vienna   Bratislava ⊛
Tours   Vaduz   AUSTRIA   Budapest ⊛
LIECHTENSTEIN   Graz   HUNGARY
Bern ⊛   Ljubljana ⊛
SWITZERLAND   Vaduz   Trieste   Zagreb ⊛   RO
Lyons   Geneva   SLOVENIA   CROATIA
Milan   Belgrade
PIEDMONT   VENEZIA   Venice
LOMBARDY   *Po R.*

Nantes

BRITTANY

FRANCE

*BAY OF
BISCAY*

Bordeaux

GALICIA

Porto

LEON   Bilbao   GASCONY
Basque
Douro R.   COUNTRY   NAVARRE   LANGUEDOC
OLD CASTILE   ANDORRA
Ebro R.   CATALONIA
ARAGON
⊛ Madrid   Barcelona
SPAIN
NEW CASTILE
LA MANCHA   *BALEARIC I.*
(Spain)
Valencia
Palma

PORTUGAL

Lisbon ⊛

Tagus R.

Seville   Cordoba
ANDALUSIA
Málaga
Strait of Gibraltar — Gibraltar
Tangier   Ceuta
Rabat   Melilla   Oran   Algiers
Casablanca

MOROCCO

ALGERIA

Rhône R.   PROVENCE   Genoa
Marseilles   MONACO
Toulon   SAN MARINO
TUSCANY

CORSICA
(France)

Rome ⊛   CAMPANIA
VATICAN CITY

SARDINIA
(Italy)

ITALY   Naples   APULIA

Palermo

SICILY

Pantelleria
(Italy)

Tunis

MALTA
Valetta ⊛

TUNISIA

MEDITERRANEAN SE

Tripoli   LIBYA   *Gulf of Sidra*

BOSNIA-
HERZEGOVINA   Sarajevo ●   SERBIA
MONTE-   YUGO-
NEGRO   SLAVIA   FM
RE
Tiranë ⊛   MA
Skop
ALBANIA

Corfu   GR

Patras